A Probus Guide to World Markets

THE GLOBAL EQUITY MARKETS

State-of-the-Art Research, Analysis and Investment Strategies

JESS LEDERMAN
KEITH K.H. PARK

EDITORS

PROBUS PUBLISHING COMPANY
Chicago, Illinois

Library of Congress Cataloging in Publication Data Available

ISBN 1-55738-152-6

Printed in the United States of America

BB

1 2 3 4 5 6 7 8 9 0

To my pal, Andrew Ballingal
Jess Lederman

To my Onmi and Nicole
Keith Park

Table of Contents

Preface   ix

SECTION I   INTRODUCTION

Chapter 1.   **Reduction of Risk and Enhancement of Return
                 through Global Equity Diversification**   3
                 Keith Park, Global Strategies Group

SECTION II   NORTH AMERICAN EQUITY MARKETS

Chapter 2.   **United States Equity Market**   19
                 Laszlo Birinyi, Jr., Birinyi Associates, Inc.

Chapter 3.   **Foreign Direct Investment in U.S. Real Estate**   27
                 Thomas Sablosky, Tricontinental Group, Inc.
                 Leon G. Shilton, Fordham GBA Real Estate
                 Center

Chapter 4.   **Canadian Equity Market**   45
                 Jim McDonald, Burns Fry Ltd.

SECTION III   AMERICAN DEPOSITORY RECEIPTS

Chapter 5.   **ADRs of Asian Companies as a Financing
                 and Investment Vehicle**   69
                 Steven A. Schoenfeld, Simcha SIMEX Trading
                 (PTE) Ltd.

Chapter 6.   **ADRs**   79
                 Joseph M. Velli, American Depository Receipts
                 Bank of New York

Chapter 7.   **ADRs in the NASDAQ Market**   85
                  Douglas F. Parrillo, N.A.S.D.

SECTION IV   **THE EUROPEAN EQUITY MARKETS**

Chapter 8.   **U.K. Equity Market**   99
                  Carolyn Moses, Shearson Lehman Hutton

Chapter 9.   **German Equity Market**   117
                  O.W. Breycha, KPMG Peat Marwick Treuhand
                  GmbH

Chapter 10.   **French Equity Market**   135
                  Alain Galene, Morgan Stanley

Chapter 11.   **Dutch Equity Market**   145
                  Rob Sweers, Banque Paribas Nederland N.V.

Chapter 12.   **Swiss Equity Market**   161
                  Dr. George Sellerberg, Bank Julius Baer

Chapter 13.   **Italian Equity Market**   211
                  Marco Santi, KPMG Peat Marwick Fides s.n.c.

SECTION V   **THE FAR EAST EQUITY MARKETS**

Chapter 14.   **Japanese Equity Market**   233
                  Andrew Ballingal, Barclays de Zoete Wedd

Chapter 15.   **Australian Equity Market**   259
                  Bruce Rolph and Charles A. Wall,
                  Baring Securities (Australia) Limited

Chapter 16.   **Korean Equity Market**   281
                  Thae S. Kwarg, Baring Brothers & Co. Ltd.

Chapter 17.   **Taiwan Equity Market**   315
                  Sam Chang, Blue Chip Capital Associates
                  Ted Chao, Cathay International

SECTION VI   **COUNTRY FUNDS**

Chapter 18.   **Closed-End Country Funds Review**   339
                  Michael T. Porter, Smith Barney, Harris
                  Upham & Co.

SECTION VII   **GLOBAL EQUITY INVESTMENT STRATEGIES**

Chapter 19.   **Analyzing International Financial Statements**   **403**
Dr. Vinod B. Bavishi, Center for International
Financial Analysis and Research, Inc.

Chapter 20.   **Prospective Equity Returns in a Disinflationary**
Environment   **459**
Richard T. Coghlan, Strategic Investment
Services

Chapter 21.   **European Investment Opportunities**   **473**
Richard T. Coghlan, Strategic Investment
Services

Chapter 22.   **Does the Current State of the Korean Equity**
Market Indicate What Lies Ahead of the Other
Asian Emerging Markets in the 1990s?   **489**
Keith Park, Global Strategies Group

Chapter 23.   **Tactical Asset Allocation**

Chapter 23A.   **Tactical Asset Allocation**   **513**
Jane Buchan, Collins Associates

Chapter 23B.   **Global Tactical Asset Allocation**   **525**
Edgar E. Peters, PanAgora Asset Management
Bruce E. Clarke, Pan Agora Asset Management

Chapter 24.   **Global Equity Indexation**

Chapter 24A.   **Introduction to Global Equity Indexation**   **535**
Keith Park, Global Strategies Group

Chapter 24B.   **Comparison of International Indices**   **541**
Rick Nelson, Bankers Trust Company

Chapter 24C.   **Synthetic Global Index Funds**   **559**
Mark A. Zurack, C.F.A. and William W. Toy,
Goldman, Sachs & Co.

Chapter 25.   **The Cost of Change**   **575**
Francis Enderle, Barclays de Zoete Wedd

Chapter 26.   **Asian-Pacific Financial Futures and Options**
Markets   **593**
Steven Schoenfeld, Simcha SIMEX Trading
(PTE) Ltd.

Chapter 27.   **How to Hedge Currency Risk**   **629**
Lee R. Thomas III, Goldman Sachs
International Ltd.

Appendix   **International Guide to Securities Exchanges**   **655**
Thomas Carrol, Editor
Peat Marwick Main & Co.

Index   **809**

Preface

As the world equity markets become further globalized in the 1990s, we will continue to see the ever-increasing outflow of investment into the foreign equity markets. Many institutional fund managers have expressed in 1989 their interest in increasing the international portion of their portfolios to 20-25% from the current average of 4% in the 1990s. This interest is fueled by excellent investment opportunities in foreign markets. According to modern portfolio theory, global diversification should reduce risk and enhance returns.

In practice, however, few institutions have taken full advantage of the worldwide investment opportunities. It's not difficult to understand why: mastering the global equity markets can be an intimidating task. First, there is the sheer volume of information that must be collected and analyzed. Second, this information must be synthesized and incorporated into a coherent investment strategy.

The Global Equity Markets: State-of-the-Art Research, Analysis and Investment Strategies was written to facilitate this critical process. Within its chapters we have collected detailed information on each of the world's major equity markets, presented by some of the most eminent professionals in the business. We have also included chapters that are strategies, rather than country-specific, including global tactical asset allocation and currency hedging. Thus, the reader has available a wealth of factual information as well as the tools to put this knowledge to work.

Putting *The Global Equity Markets* together was a task that took several years and involved coordination between many people throughout the world. Many thanks must be given to each of the contributing authors for taking time from their hectic schedules, and to Probus Publishing for its assistance.

Jess Lederman
Keith Park

INTRODUCTION

Reduction of Risk and Enhancement of Return through Global Equity Diversification

Keith Park
Global Strategies Group, New York

Research conducted suggests that a globally well-diversified portfolio offers a lower volatility of its return, and at the same time, a superior average return vis-a-vis a well-diversified domestic one. To support this claim, this chapter will explain the modern portfolio theory behind the reduction of dispersion generated by investing in the world equity markets and the empirical evidence for this reduction. Secondly, it will discuss the recent developments in the world equity markets and consequent investment strategies for institutional investors.

Definition of Risk by the Modern Portfolio Theory

According to the modern portfolio theory, risk entailed by an investment can be measured by the variance of its historical returns.[1] The definition of risk by means of variance indicates the upside potential of return as well as the possibility of downside loss. In other words, variance defines risk as the unpredictability, or variability, of returns. For instance, if we assume that the returns from an investment display a bell-shaped, normal distribution, its historical average return of 15% with standard deviation of 7% indicates that the average return of the investment will vary 1) with 68% probability within one standard deviation, which is between 8% and 22%; and 2) with 95% probability within two standard deviations, which is between 1% and 29%.

Risk of a Globally Diversified Portfolio

The modern portfolio theory in the form of the capital asset pricing model (CAPM)[2] claims that the total risk entailed by investment in an individual stock consists of 1) unsystematic or firm-specific risk; and 2) systematic or market risk.[3] According to CAPM, firm-specific risk, not market risk, can be eliminated by diversification. In other words, even if fund managers were able to success-fully diversify their portfolios in a domestic market, their portfolio would still be exposed to the unfavorable movement of the market as a whole. However, if the market movement of an individual country is independent of those of the others, fund managers can reduce the market risk of their portfolios by diversifying their exposure to a number of different equity markets around the globe.

In another case, assume, for example, that the portion invested in two countries is so diversified as to eliminate the firm-specific risk, or unsystematic risk. In this case, fund managers might invest in both countries. Each portion of the portfolio, therefore, would only be susceptible to the market risk, or system-atic risk, of its own market as shown in the following equation:[4]

$$W_1^2 S_1^2 + W_2^2 S_2^2 + 2W_1 W_2 r_{1,2} S_1 S_2$$

W_n = the fraction of the portfolio invested in country n; $W_1 + W_2 = 1$

S_n = the standard deviation of the returns from the portion invested in country n, that is, the market risk of country n

$r_{n,m}$ = the correlation of the returns from the portions invested in country n and m

$r_{n,m} S_n S_m$ = the covariance of the returns from the portions invested in country n and m

This definition of the risk of a portfolio is derived from the statistical defi-nition which states that the variance of a sum is:

$$var (X + Y) = var X + var Y + 2cov (X, Y)$$

In the case of a portfolio that invests in three countries, its variance would be:

$$W_1^2 S_1^2 + W_2^2 S_2^2 + W_3^2 S_3^2 + 2W_1 W_2 r_{1,2} S_1 S_2 +$$
$$2W_2 W_3 r_{2,3} S_2 S_3 + 2W_1 W_3 r_{1,3} S_1 S_3$$

Following this reasoning, we can conclude that a portfolio that invests in n countries with equal weighting will entail the following variance:

$$n (1/n)^2 S_{av}^2 + (n^2 - n) (1/n)^2 r_{av} S_{av}^2$$

$$= (1/n)^2 S_{av}^2 + (1 - 1/n) r_{av} S_{av}^2$$

$$= (1/n) \times \text{average variance} + (1 - 1/n) \times \text{average covariance}$$

S_{av} = the average of the standard deviations of the returns from the portions invested in n countries, that is, the average market risk

r_{av} = the average correlation of the returns from the constituent countries of the portfolio

$r_{av} S_{av}^2$ = the average covariance of the returns from the constituent countries of the portfolio

We can see from this equation that as n increases 1) the first term, $(1/n)S_{av}^2$, will be substantially reduced and could almost become zero[5]; and 2) the second term, $(1 - 1/n) r_{av} S_{av}^2$, will approach $r_{av} S_{av}^2$ In other words, if a portfolio is diversified by making investments in a significant number of countries, the risk of the portfolio will be close to the average covariance of the returns from the portfolio's constituent countries. Consequently, we can conclude that if the average correlation (r_{av}) of the market movements of the portfolio's constituent countries is zero — or completely independent of each other — then the portfolio variance will be reduced almost to zero.[6]

However, the market movement of each country is not completely independent of others. In fact, as the world equity markets become more integrated, each equity market becomes more interdependent on others. Nonetheless, the empirical evidence, which is presented in the next section, shows that the average correlation is still significantly small enough to substantially reduce the variance of a globally diversified portfolio.

Correlations of Major World Equity Markets

The previous equation supports the claim that if fund managers invest in a significant number of countries, and if each country's market movement is independent of others (that is, the low correlation between the market movements), then they will be able to substantially reduce the risk of their portfolios. To ensure this risk reduction, fund managers must monitor the correlations of the world equity markets, which this section will present. To do so however, one must first understand the concept of correlation coefficient, which is used to measure the level of correlation.

Correlation coefficient, which ranges from –1 to 1, measures the strength or degree of linear association between two variables. For example, if the correlation coefficient between the equity market movements of country A and B is 1, then the linear movement of one market is equal to that of the other. If the correlation coefficient is –1, the linear movement of one market is opposite to that of the other. And if the correlation coefficient is zero, then the linear movement of one market has no association with that of the other.

It is essential to note that correlation coefficient does not say anything about the non-linear association between two variables. For instance, even if the correlation coefficient between two variables is zero, the two variables might still have a strong non-linear association. Moreover, correlation coefficient only explains association, not causation. Even if the correlation coefficient between the equity market movements of country A and B is quite strong, perhaps 1 or –1, the equity market of one country is not necessarily causing the other to move in a certain direction.

One statistical measurement, which is conceptually quite different from correlation coefficient but is often referred to in conjunction with correlation coefficient, is the coefficient of determination of bivariate regression — R-squared. R-squared, which ranges from 0 to 1, measures the extent to which the variation in a dependent variable is explained by that of an independent variable. For instance, in the case of a bivariate regression $Y = a + bX$. If R-squared is 0.85, 85% of the variation of Y (dependent variable) can be explained by that of X (independent variable).

This definition of R-squared is quite different from that of correlation coefficient. However, note how R-squared and correlation coefficient are calculated; R-squared is just the square of correlation coefficient.

$$\text{Correlation Coefficient} = \frac{COV_{ab}}{S_a S_b}$$

$$\text{R-squared} = \frac{(COV_{ab})^2}{VAR_a VAR_b}$$

a   =   variable a, b = variable b

COV   =   covariance

VAR   =   variance = S^2

S   =   standard deviation

For example, if the correlation coefficient of U.S. and Japanese equity markets is 0.29, we could say that either U.S. and Japanese markets have 0.29 linear association or that 8.41% of variation of the Japanese market can be explained by that of the U.S. market, or vice versa.

Using the definition and implication of correlation coefficient as a basis, we can now discuss the correlation coefficients of the world equity markets. To provide a sense of continuity and change, the correlation coefficients of different time periods are presented in periodical sequence in Table 1.

Using monthly data, Grubel[7], Solnik[8], Coglan[9] and Roll[10] have estimated the correlation coefficients between the United States and the other world equity markets. Grubel's estimation is for the time period of January 1959 to December 1966; Solnik's is from March 1966 to April 1971; Coglan's is from January 1971 to December 1979; and Roll's is from June 1981 to September 1987. The author measured the post-crash correlation between November 1988 and January 1989. In order to use the statistically significant number of data points, Keith Park, the author, used weekly rather than monthly percentage changes.

As we can see in Table 1, the correlations between the United States and other equity markets have generally been rising steadily since 1959. The average correlation of the world stock markets with the United States has changed from 0.192 in January 1959 to December 1966 to 0.328 in November 1987 to January 1989.

From each equity market's correlation with the United States in Table 1, we can observe the following. One, since 1959 the Canadian equity market has been continuously correlating highly with the United States. Its correlation with the United States was 0.703 in January 1959 to December 1966. It remained relatively high at 0.639 during the period from November 1987 to January 1989. Considering Canada's economic structure and geographic proximity to the United States, these findings are quite understandable. Consequently, the U.S.-based institutional investors have quite often excluded Canada from their internationally invested portfolios. Many investors believe that including Canada does not add any significant value to diversifying U.S. market risk.

Second, the correlation of the United Kingdom with the United States has been increasing steadily from 0.241 in January 1959 to December 1966 to 0.518

Table 1   Correlations of Major World Stock Markets with U.S. Market

Stock Market	Grubel (1/59-12/66)	Solnik (3/66-4/71)	Coglan (1/71-12/79)	Roll (6/81-9/87)	Park (11/87-1/89)
Australia	0.059	—	—	0.328	0.108
Austria	—	—	—	0.138	0.262
Belgium	0.108	0.47	—	0.250	0.136
Canada	0.703	—	—	0.720	0.639
Denmark	—	—	—	0.351	0.171
France	0.194	0.06	0.426	0.390	0.265
Germany	0.301	0.22	0.309	0.209	0.331
Hong Kong	—	—	—	0.114	0.443
Ireland	—	—	—	0.380	—
Italy	0.147	0.07	0.167	0.224	0.212
Japan	0.115	0.19	0.290	0.326	0.290
Malaysia	—	—	—	0.347	—
Mexico	—	—	—	0.063	—
Netherlands	0.211	0.51	—	0.473	0.420
New Zealand	—	—	—	0.083	—
Norway	—	—	—	0.356	0.253
Singapore	—	—	—	0.377	0.355
South Africa	–0.162	—	—	0.218	—
Spain	—	—	—	0.214	0.432
Sweden	—	0.29	—	0.279	0.405
Switzerland	—	0.44	—	0.500	0.334
United Kingdom	0.241	0.20	0.493	0.513	0.518
Average Corr.	0.192	0.27	0.337	0.312	0.328

in November 1987 to January 1989. Germany's correlation with the United States however, has not changed significantly even though it has risen slightly from 0.301 in January 1959 to December 1966 to 0.331 in November 1987 to January 1989.

Third, correlations with the United States and those of Japan, France, and Australia had been rising but declined substantially after the 1987 stock market crash. In contrast, correlations with the United States and those of Spain, Sweden, and Hong Kong, have increased substantially during the post-crash period.

Fourth, even though we have been witnessing the steadily ascending trend in world correlations, correlations are still low enough to diversify a globally invested portfolio's exposure to market risks. The average correlation of 0.328 from November 1987 to January 1989 is still quite low. In this case, R-squared indicates that in average only 10.8% of the movement of the U.S. stock market can be explained by those of the other equity markets, and vice versa.

This phenomenon can be explained: although the world economies have become more interdependent, the idiosyncratic economic characteristics of different countries, due to such factors as the maturity of economic development, tax structure, and political stability, elicit quite independent equity market movements. In other words, a globally invested portfolio can significantly reduce its exposure to market risks, and at the same time enhance its return as we can see in Figure 1.

Figure 1 shows that by investing 50% of its portfolio in the United States by indexing with S&P 500 and the other 50% in the international market and by indexing with the Europe, Australia and Far East (EAFE) index of Morgan Stanley Capital International will generate the lowest volatility, and a return that is far superior to an investment that solely concentrates in the U.S. market.

Note, however, that although the global investment can definitely reduce the risk of an investor's portfolio, the market risk of the global equity market as a whole can never be completely diversified. For instance, during the market crash of October 1987, the low correlations of the major world equity markets were not sustained; together they declined precipitously downward. Table 2 shows the stock market movements during the 1987 world market crash.

Conclusion

As shown in Figure 2, the foreign equity markets have grown more rapidly than the maturing U.S. market. As a result, the U.S. equity market is no longer the largest one in the world.

In 1975, the U.S. market was 58% of the global equity market; at the end of September 1989 the U.S. market was only 31% of the global equity market. Institutional investors can neither ignore 69% of the global equity market, nor the investment opportunities that this 69% offers.

As seen in Table 3, some nine major world equity markets outperformed the U.S. market in U.S. dollar term in the 1980s. In local currency term, thirteen markets had better returns than the U.S. market.[11] Furthermore, according to Table 4 investment in foreign stocks brought about a far superior return than that of any other type of U.S. domestic asset in the 1980's. It seems that global equity diversification, which is an efficient and proper response to the dynamic changes in the world equity markets, will result in an optimal institutional investment.

In closing, since the movements of foreign exchange rates can always be reversed, global investors should be aware that currency movements should not

Figure 1: Efficient Frontier of Global Diversification (from 1981 to 1987)

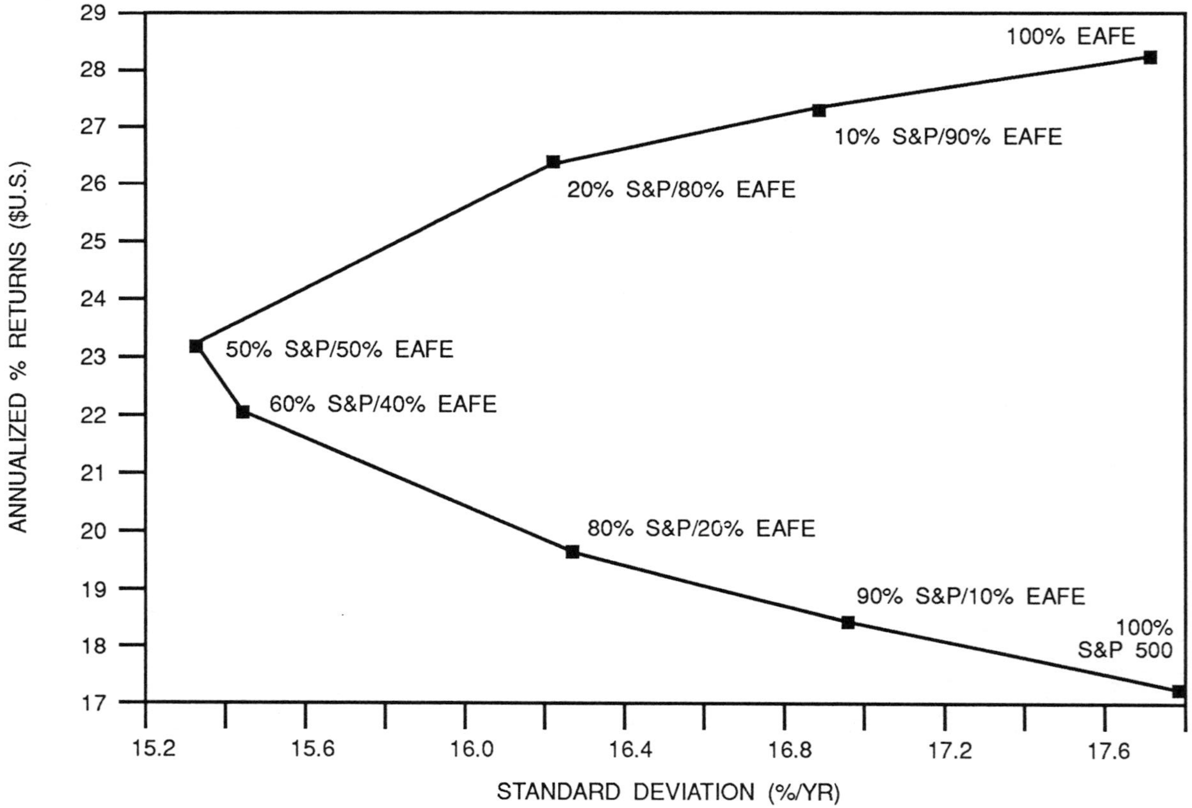

Table 2   Movements of Major World Stock Markets During the Crash of October 1987

Stock Market	October 1987 (in percent)
Australia	–41.8
Austria	–11.4
Belgium	–23.2
Canada	–22.5
Denmark	–12.5
France	–22.9
Germany	–22.3
Hong Kong	–45.8
Ireland	–29.1
Italy	–16.3
Japan	–12.8
Malaysia	–39.8
Mexico	–35.0
Netherlands	–23.3
New Zealand	–29.3
Norway	–30.5
Singapore	–42.2
South Africa	–23.9
Spain	–27.7
Sweden	–21.8
Switzerland	–26.1
United Kingdom	–26.4
United States	–21.6
Average	–26.4

become a determining factor in their decisions. For instance, after its peak in 1985, the U.S. dollar depreciated substantially vis-a-vis other currencies until mid-1988. Consequently, during that period the decline of the U.S. dollar had further enhanced U.S. dollar returns of foreign equity markets. However, since late 1988 the U.S. dollar has reversed its downward trend. According to Table 3, the local currency returns ended the 1980's by exceeding U.S. dollar returns in most countries except Japan, Switzerland, Singapore/Malaysia, and Canada. Finally, the impact of unfavorable movements of foreign exchange rates can be significantly moderated by setting up a disciplined and effective hedging program.

Figure 2   World Equity Market Capitalizations

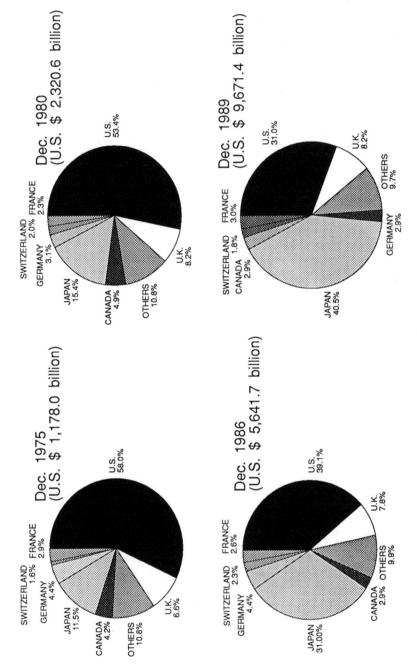

Table 3   Performance of Major World Stock Markets from 12/31/1979 through 12/8/1989

		% change in U.S. Dollar			% change in Local Currency
1.	Japan	1,007.6	1.	Sweden	1,246.8%
2.	Sweden	779.8	2.	Italy	843.9
3.	Italy	481.0	3.	Japan	566.7
4.	Denmark	383.5	4.	Denmark	522.7
5.	Netherlands	278.0	5.	France	393.2
6.	United Kingdom	248.2	6.	United Kingdom	391.2
7.	Belgium	233.3	7.	Spain	388.3
8.	France	227.2	8.	Belgium	328.3
9.	Austria	211.4	9.	Netherlands	297.7
10.	UNITED STATES	207.6	10.	Hong Kong	268.8
11.	West Germany	202.3	11.	Australia	228.4
12.	Spain	182.2	12.	Austria	212.9
13.	Singapore/ Malaysia	163.5	13.	West Germany	211.3
14.	Switzerland	139.1	14.	UNITED STATES	207.6
15.	Australia	132.2	15.	Norway	203.1
16.	Hong Kong	132.1	16.	Switzerland	139.0
17.	Norway	120.4	17.	Singapore/ Malaysia	135.4
18.	Canada	110.0	18.	Canada	108.0

Source: Morgan Stanley Capital International.

Endnotes

[1]   Variance is defined as:

$$\text{Var} = \frac{1}{n-1} \sum_{i=1}^{n} (R_i - \overline{R})^2$$

R_i =   the return in time period i

$\overline{R}$ =   the mean of the returns over n time periods

---

Table 4   Compound Annual Returns From Major Assets Since the End of 1979 through 1989[1]

1.	Foreign Stocks[2]	22.3%
2.	S&P-500 Stocks	17.4
3.	Small-Cap. Stocks	16.1
4.	Stock Mutual Funds	15.3
5.	Corp. & Gov't Bonds	12.2
6.	Commercial Real Estate	10.6
7.	Money Market Funds	9.6
8.	Bank Certificates	9.5
9.	Municipal Bonds[3]	9.3
10.	Residential Real Estate[4]	8.9
	INFLATION	5.1
11.	Gold	–3.1
12.	Silver	–15.7

[1] Figures reflect price change, dividend and interest income. Commercial and residential real estate include rental income as well.
[2] Return for U.S.-based investors.
[3] Federal and same-state tax exemption for interest payment are taken into account.
[4] Through 1988.

Source: *The Wall Street Journal.*

$$\overline{R} = \frac{1}{n} \sum_{i=1}^{n} R_i$$

Standard deviation is the square root of variance

[2]   W.F. Sharpe, "Capital Asset Prices: A Theory of Market Equilibrium Under Conditions of Risk," *Journal of Finance*, 19, (September, 1964), p. 425-442.

J. Lintner, "The Valuation of Risk Assets and the Selection of Risky Investments in Stock Portfolio and Capital Budgets," *Review of Economics and Statistics*, 47, (February, 1965), p. 13–47.

[3]   Portfolio Variance   = Portfolio Market Variance + Portfolio Firm – Specific Variance
Portfolio Market Variance = Portfolio Beta × Market Variance
Portfolio Beta   = the weighted average of the betas of the

constituent stocks of the portfolio.

Market Variance   =   Variance of Benchmark Index

[4] A good example of this type of portfolio is one that is globally indexed to broad market indices. Currently, there are three global equity indices available to achieve this type of diversification: Morgan Stanley Capital International Indices, Financial Times-Actuaries World Indices, and Salomon-Russell Global Equity Indices.

[5] Imagine a fund manager invests in the 15 different markets the average standard deviation of which is 20%. In this case, the first term, $(1/n)S_{av}^2$, will become 0.0027. If she invests in the 20 different markets, the first term will be 0.002. Currently, Morgan Stanley Capital International World Indices consist of 21 countries. In case of Financial Times-Actuaries World Indices and Salomon-Russell Global Equity Indices, the total number of constituent countries is 23.

[6] The author would like to reiterate that here, as we assumed earlier, the portion invested in each country is effectively diversified so that its unsystematic risk is non-existent. As a result, the portfolio is only exposed to the systematic risks (or, market risks) of the equity markets of its constitutent countries. As stated earlier, we can create this kind of equity portfolio through global indexation which broadly replicates local equity markets.

[7] Grubel, Herbert G., "Internationally Diversified Portfolios: Welfare Gains and Capital Flows," *American Economic Review*, 58, no. 5, (December, 1968), p.1299-1314.

[8] Solnik, Bruno H., *European Capital Markets: Towards a General Theory of International Investment*, D.C. Heath and Company, 1973.

[9] Coglan, Richard T., "European Investment Opportunities," *Strategic Investment Services*, June, 1989.

[10] Roll, Richard, "The International Crash of October 1987," U.C.L.A. Graduate School of Management Working Paper, (April, 1988), #9-88.

[11] In Table 3, dividend paid is not included. The annual average dividend yield of the local benchmark indices has usually been in the range of 2% to 5%. However, in the case of Japan and Mexico, the average dividend yield has been less than 1%.

NORTH AMERICAN EQUITY MARKETS

United States Equity Market

Laszlo Birinyi, Jr.
Birinyi Associates, Inc., New York

U.S. stocks are traded in three principal markets: the New York Stock Exchange, the American Stock Exchange and over-the-counter. In addition, there are five regional markets which largely mirror the New York Stock Exchange (NYSE).

The NYSE was not the first market (that distinction being Amsterdam's), and it is no longer the largest market (having been surpassed by Tokyo). In 1989 its volume leadership was also threatened by heavy turnover in Taiwan. Nevertheless, it is still the most closely watched market. A weak opening in New York trading will often result in the still-open European markets trading down even though they had been experiencing higher prices in their trading session up to that point.

The second major exchange in the United States is the American Stock Exchange (ASE) which is also located in New York City. American Stock Exchange issues are not, however, traded on the NYSE. To be listed on the American, corporations need not have the ownership distribution, the historical records and other regulatory requirements required for the New York. Hence, ASE companies tend to be younger and in the emerging stages of development. Since reporting requirements are somewhat less stringent, many foreign companies list there rather than the NYSE.

Wall Street—Past, Present and Future

What is probably the best known street, avenue or road in the world was named in March 1644. The short strip of land known as Wall Street was not then associated with the trading of securities. On May 17, 1792, twenty-four brokers formed the first organized trading post at 68 Wall Street. And, it was not until early 1863 that the name New York Stock Exchange was adopted.

On December 15, 1886, the first million share trading day took place, a momentous occasion given that the facilities were probably limited. The current exchange building was erected in 1903, marking the beginning of the "wild West" period of American finance that lasted until the 1929 crash and the Great Depression. Legendary traders and financiers traded stocks with all sorts of tricks and gimmicks. Daniel Drew, J. P. Morgan, Jesse Livermore and others engaged in schemes and plots that were devious and as chronicled as any mystery or historical tale. Their manipulation (especially of the railroads) were the subject of countless books and articles that are still widely read. The Securities and Exchange Act of 1934, however, put an end to many of their practices.

In recent years many structural changes have affected the NYSE. Members of the exchange have become publicly owned; the fixed commission structure was abolished in May 1975; options, futures and options on futures have altered investment patterns; electronic trading has increased; and, obviously, the 1987 crash all have changed the atmosphere of what was once regarded as an exclusive club. With the increasing interest in the globalization of the equity markets, these changes will probably continue. In years to come the globalization of business and deregulation of capital that has occurred throughout the 1980s are likely to continue. While the NYSE may no longer command its central role as a market place, the focus of interest is likely to continue on the venerable, staid building at Broad and Wall.

Organization and Structure

The NYSE is a corporation owned by its members. The governing body is a board of twenty-four directors, twelve of whom are public or nonindustry members. Membership in the corporation and, therefore, ownership is a function of "seats" at the exchange. In effect, the seat gives the right to trade securities at the exchange as well as the right to do so without paying commissions.

Historically, members fell into two categories, although these are not formal labels: brokers and dealers. Brokers were generally associated with a member firm and represented that firm at the exchange. Thus, if a salesman for a brokerage firm wanted to sell shares on behalf of a customer, it would be the floor broker who actually executed that transaction.

That transaction would be taken to that point on the exchange floor where the stock was traded. In the U.S. system, stock trading is continuous at a specified location. At this location ("post") another NYSE member has been given the responsibility for dealing this security. This member ("specialist") will try to match buyers and sellers by use of a specialist's book or, if need requires, he will deal for his own account in the absence of buyers or sellers. The specialist dealing for his own account makes the NYSE system different than systems used at other major markets. It is most markedly different from the system used in the Japanese market, where the saitori members act only as intermediaries and do not commit their own funds in the absence of buyers or sellers.

A third member of the NYSE is a broker's broker who may work on a contractual or temporary basis for a member firm. Historically, he was paid two dollars for each 100 shares he traded and, thus, was called a "two-dollar broker." A member firm may hire a two-dollar broker to trade in the event it desires special attention toward an order or its own brokers are active elsewhere or even as a substitute in case of vacation.

The New York Stock Exchange Process

In the past, trades came to the NYSE floor from the salespeople who actually talk to the customers. These salespeople were also brokers but were often called registered representatives, account executives, customer men or financial consultants. Their orders were routed to the trading floor and would be handled by the floor brokers. Today this is no longer the case. Larger orders are usually handled over the telephone, but an increasing number of trades are now routed electronically. The electronic system of the NYSE, SuperDOT, gives its members the ability to send orders directly to the trading post to facilitate execution and to do so quickly. In 1987, 92% of all these trades were executed and reported within two minutes.

Market Participants

The active role of buying and selling played by member firms (and especially the specialist members) is a critical component of this system. While floor dealers may exist in other markets (Amsterdam, for example), the dealing done by specialists and other members accounts for well over 10% of the NYSE volume.

The NYSE is also different in that it is a market where the public is becoming less important while institutions are becoming increasingly important. In most European markets, for example, the dealing has traditionally been institutional. Only in recent years has the public become either a direct or indirect participant. Italy, for example, has seen a large unit trust industry develop. In the United States, however, the individual investor who at one time was dominant has gradually decreased in importance. One illustration of this is to show the increase of block trades which are almost always institutional in nature. A block trade is one in which more than 10,000 shares trade at one time (See Exhibit 1).

Most observers believe the institutionalization of the NYSE is likely to continue because the trends that led to the process are also likely to continue:

Exhibit 1   NYSE Block Transactions

	Total Blocks (000)	Shares	% of Volume
1965	2,171	48,262	3.1%
1970	17,217	450,908	15.4
1975	34,420	778,540	16.6
1980	133,597	3,311,132	29.2
1985	539,039	14,222,272	51.7
1988	768,419	22,270,680	54.5

- The ERISA legislation enacted in 1974 greatly expanded the pension plans for individuals in the American work force and remains very much in effect.

- The complexity of financial markets has discouraged investors from making many of their own decisions and giving their funds to unit trusts or professional investors.

- The increasing breakdown and increasing flow of capital across borders is likely to continue.

Although pension plans are the largest pool of investable capital in the market, they are not in most cases the actual investors. Most pension money is given to someone else to actually invest although the pension plan will usually outline strict rules and guidelines as to how the funds should be invested. In the past, commercial banks managed the pension plan assets largely because they had been investing and administering the larger family fortunes and trust accounts.

Other large managers of money include:

- *Professional money management operations*, some of which may be independent, some may be a division of a broker or even, in some cases, a corporation.

- *Mutual funds* often set up separate divisions to manage pension monies.

- Some *pension plans* often set up separate divisions to manage pension monies.

- *Insurance companies*, mostly life insurance companies, also have pension money under their control.

While Americans' pension assets create the largest pool of institutional assets, other large amounts of institutional assets include:

- *Individual money usually in mutual funds.* This continues to grow and by the end of 1990, it may be well in the area of $1 trillion.
- *Corporation investment portfolios.* Corporations do not own large amounts of stock for their own purposes although they may repurchase their own shares. There are, however, certain instances where corporations have investment portfolios. Lowes Corp., for example, owns 80% of CNA Corp., another corporation that trades on the NYSE.

The ownership of U.S. stock is changing as shown below:

	1980	**1988**
Individuals	71.54%	58.71%
Private Pensions	13.99	16.29
Public Pensions	2.77	7.05
Insurance Companies	4.922	5.70
Mutual Funds	2.65	5.94
Foreigners	4.04	6.27
Other	.21	.04

Market Indices

There are a variety of indices used in measuring the U.S. market, several which are summarized below:

Index	**Issues**	**Includes**	**Frequency**	**Method of Calc**
Dow Jones	30	NY issues	Continuous	Avg of Components
S&P Composite	500	All markets	Continuous	Mkt Cap Weighted
NYSE Composite		All NYSE issues	Continuous	Mkt Cap Weighted
Value Line	1600+	All VL issues	Continuous	Geometric Weighted
Wilshire 5000	All markets	All markets	Daily	Mkt Cap Weighted

NYSE Share Types

In recent years, the NYSE has expanded and today trades not only shares but also bonds and futures. However, it is still commonly thought to be the stock exchange; and the usual pictures of the trading floor are of the stock trading areas. (We say "areas" because in actuality stock trading takes place in three closely linked trading rooms which compose the exchange. Bonds and futures are traded elsewhere).

The predominant trading at the NYSE is common stock of companies that have the following characteristics:

- A minimum market value of $9 million
- 1.1 million shares publicly held
- At least 2,000 shareholders
- No nonvoting shares (except for certain quasi-government corporations)

In addition to common stock, preferred shares and warrants may be listed; but, these are relatively small in amount relative to the common shares.

In recent years, American Depositary Receipts (ADRs) have become more popular with American investors. These are certificates representing foreign stock held in deposit by American banks. However, these companies must meet different listing criteria than American companies in that their pre-tax income must be higher ($100 million plus over the total of the last three years) and assets must be $100 million with 5,000 shareholders required.

NYSE Summary

Commissions. Negotiable

Taxation. Capital gains are treated as ordinary income and taxed accordingly. Dividends paid to nonresidents are subject to 30% withholding but tax treaties usually mitigate that number.

Trading hours. 9:30 A.M. to 4:00 P.M., Monday through Friday.

Foreign ownership regulations. Ten percent restrictions on broadcast and certain resource stocks. Settlement in five business days.

1980s Summary

	1980	**1985**	**1988**
Dow Jones Close	963.98	1550.46	2168.56
NYSE Composite:			
PE Ratio	13.1	13.5	12.7
Yield	5.4	3.6	3.6
NYSE Listed Companies	1570	1541	1681
Market Value ($ billion)	1242.8	1950.3	2457.4
Trading Volume ($ billion)	382.4	980.7	1365.8
Trading Volume (million shares)	11561.5	27774.0	41117.7
Average Trade Size (shares)	872	1878	2303
Seat Cost (annual $ high)	275,000	480,000	820,000
Security Industry Personnel	243,700	363,400	458,800

Sources of Information

There are a great many sources of information on the U.S. markets. Among the better known are:

New York Stock Exchange, 11 Wall Street, New York, N.Y. 10005

S&P Stock Guide—Pertinent financial data on more than 5,300 common and preferred stocks. Information includes shares outstanding, price ranges, dividend yields, PE ratios, earnings and industry descriptions.

Standard and Poor's Corporation, 25 Broadway, New York, N.Y. 10004

The Dow Jones Investor's Handbook, Edited by Phyllis S. Pierce, Dow Jones-Irwin, Homewood, Ill. 60430. Historical perspectives on the Dow Jones Industrial Averages, data on NYSE volume, shares, turnover, dividends, mutual funds and major indexes.

Foreign Direct Investment in U.S. Real Estate

Thomas Sablosky
Tricontinental Group, Inc., New York

Leon G. Shilton
Fordham GBA Real Estate Center, New York

Introduction

The continuing and widening foreign investment appetite for U.S. real estate perpetuates the cycle of foreign investment. During the last two centuries the foreign investor has funded the bricks and mortar of the physical development of the United States. The investment wave of the eighties channels toward site-specific commercial real estate, as opposed to the previous regional and national transportation systems of canals, railroads, and regional industrial complexes. It will be interesting to see whether by the year 2000 this current activity will top previous infusions of foreign capital.

Foreign investment follows fairly discernible, almost cyclical patterns.This chapter focuses on the factors behind these patterns.

- the magnitude and trend of investment flows among players,

The authors thank Michael Green for his assistance.

- the forms of investment and the types of players,

- the motivations of the investors,

- financial-economic conditions that provide a clue to past, current, and possibly future levels of investment, and

- the future.

Magnitude of Funds

Conservatively, direct foreign equity first mortgage investment approaches 5% of the value of all U.S. commercial real estate. In 1987 investment totaled over $24 billion according to the Department of Commerce's, Survey of Current Business, *Foreign Direct Investment* (in Real Estate), Exhibit One, Foreign Direct Investment Position, 1980–1987. Various investment house estimates and extrapolations from major lending sources tag the U.S. commercial real estate value at over two trillion dollars.

Total foreign direct investment in all sectors of the American economy has grown from $26.5 billion in 1974 to over the $250 billion in 1986. The biggest annual increases in direct investment were in 1980, with a flow of $35 billion to the United States; in 1981, with a flow of $24 billion; and in 1987, with an increase of $34 billion. Real estate direct investment has not maintained that pace; it has slowly grown from a 6 billion to about a 25 billion dollar industry.

It is more difficult to ascertain the volume of mortgages purchased by foreign investors. There is a distinction between a direct mortgage loan originated by the foreign investor and a mortgage that was originated by a domestic group and then subsequently sold to a foreign investor. The foreign direct investment figure captures only the first case. The volume of these "second round" mortgages has been estimated to be over $50 billion. In contrast, the total volume of first mortgages underwritten by the members of the American Council of Life Insurers from 1980 to 1988 is about $250 billion. These figures do not cover foreign purchase of residential mortgages in the collateralized pools.

While major transactions have garnered media attention, foreign investment in American real estate has lagged behind other foreign investment in the country. The lag in foreign investment in real estate parallels that of the relatively small percentage of American institutional investment in its own real estate. Real estate is generally a longer term investment. Major players interested in the long term investment are the pension funds and the life insurance companies. Proportionately, foreign life insurance companies invest in real estate (direct cad or primary mortgage loan) at the same level that American companies do, about 25%.[1]

Similarly, the pension funds rarely invest more than 10% of their funds in real estate, whether in their own country or overseas. Foreign investment funds were and are restricted in their ability to invest their funds overseas. Consider the case of the Dutch pension fund for government employees. It has an annual cash flow of Dfl 14 billion, and only 6% of its assets are in real estate, all of which is in the Netherlands.

The top twenty United Kingdom pensions funds total over 100 billion pounds. However, from 1980 to 1988, the percentage of funds in domestic and international real estate has varied from a high of 10% to 3% in 1989.

The six countries that dominate the U.S. real estate market are Canada, the United Kingdom, the Netherlands, Germany, Japan, and the Netherlands Antilles. (See Source Countries of R.E. Investment, 1980, 1984, 1987.) These six countries account for over 80% of foreign investment during the 1980s.

Foreign investment in real estate can still be viewed as a largely untapped source of funds. In retrospect, the real estate portion of the direct foreign investment has remained a relatively small portion of all foreign investment in the United States. In 1985 there was over $18 billion of direct real estate investment. In that same year, foreign investors directly poured a total of $182 billion in all U.S. industries.

Direct real estate investing requires a site-specific, property type specific analytical approach. Over the decade, investment patterns have varied by property type and location, and foreign investors have generally preferred office buildings. They annually accrue between 35–62% of the investment. Retail centers were second, varying annually from 14–17% of all acquisitions. There has been a pronounced shift away from direct land purchases. At the start of the decade, raw land was 31% of the annual investment; in 1986 it was 8%.

Only towards the end of the decade was there a tilt towards the big-ticket investment by foreigners. In the early eighties, over 60% of the purchases were less than $10 million each. By 1986, 40% of the purchases were over $40 million each.

Foreigners tend to mirror domestic preferences as to where they spend their money. Following the lure of the Sun Belt, foreigners spent over 60% of their annual real estate dollar in 1981, 50% in Florida, and 10% Texas. As interest in that area declined, California garnered top honors with 30% in 1986, followed by 11% in New York. The state of Washington was a close runner up with 10%. The herd instinct exists among foreign investors. When they decide to drop a place for additional funding, they do it quickly. Florida investment, for example, fell from $9 billion in 1984 to $1.6 billion in 1985. Currently, there are signs that the United Kingdom is also rapidly withdrawing. The British Coal Board Pension Fund plans to dump its American holdings within a year. And a major Canadian group (BCE) will liquidate its billion dollar American account.

Figure 1   Total FDI 1980-1987

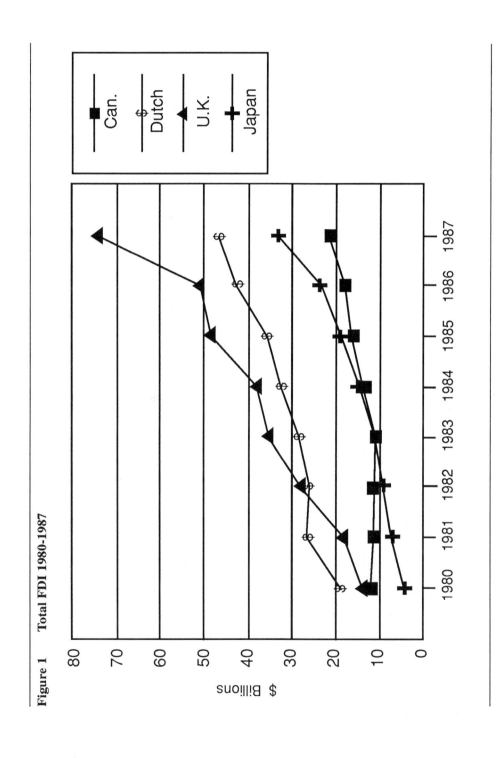

Figure 2   Source Countries of R.E. Investment 1980, 1984, 1987

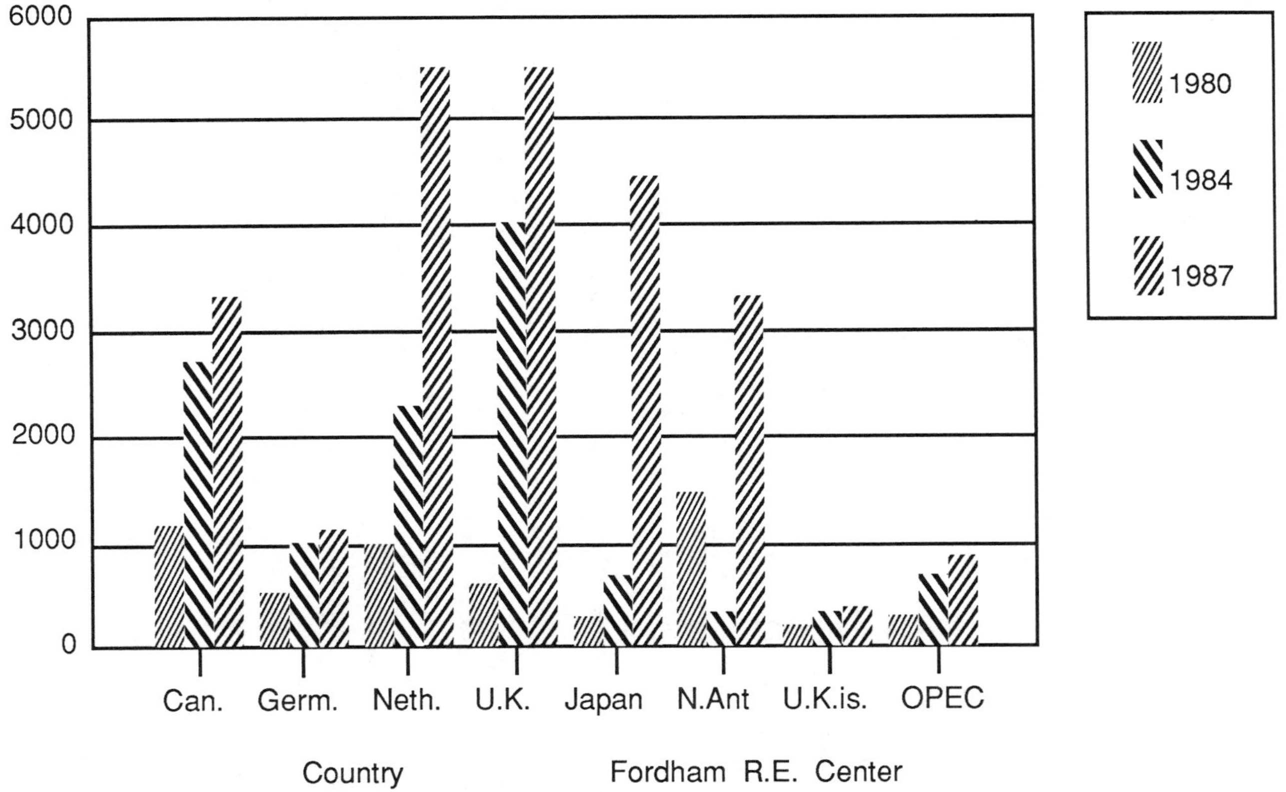

Legend:
- 1980
- 1984
- 1987

Y-axis: 0, 1000, 2000, 3000, 4000, 5000, 6000

X-axis (Country): Can. Germ. Neth. U.K. Japan N.Ant U.K.is. OPEC

Fordham R.E. Center

How and where foreigners view the future for the United States is traced by their acquisitions. For the years 1981 to 1986, the top state for industrial purchases was California; and the top state for plain land purchases was Florida. For shopping center purchases, Florida came in first, followed by California and Texas. Office building leaders were Florida and California, weakly followed by New York and Texas.

Throughout the decade, four countries have rotated as lead players. Canada started the parade, being responsible for over 33% of investment activity in 1981. The industry recognizes several Canadian developers, such as Olympia-York and the then Cadillac Fairview, for this high level of activity. Although Olympia-York's first major incursion into the states was in the mid-1970s with the purchase of a major block of office buildings, they have maintained an aggressive profile. The Netherlands Antilles has also been a major source of funds and is generally viewed as a conduit for a myriad of funding sources. In the early 1980's, the second wave of Mideast oil money sustained the funds from that Caribbean island. In the mid-1980s, the United Kingdom was the major purchaser, although the Dutch were also visible with major purchases. By 1986, having learned the residential and hotel trade in Hawaii in the early 1980s, Japan arose as the major player. Japan was responsible for half — $13 billion — of all new annual foreign investment in the United States. Although the data may be misleading, it appears that Japan and the United Kingdom currently vie for top holders of American real estate.

Each country tends to favor one form of real estate. The Canadians, such as Campeau, like shopping centers and office buildings, while the United Kingdom until recently liked industrial properties. The Japanese favor office buildings, including the largest purchases to date: the Mitsubishi purchase of 51% interest in Rockefeller Center in New York; Mitsui Fudosan purchase of the Exxon Building in New York; and the Shuwa Investment Co. purchase of the ARCO headquarters in Los Angeles. The latter two were purchased for over $600 million each. The Japanese then equally split their yen between industrial and residential hotels. The money shipped from the off shore banks of the Netherlands Antilles prefers plain land.

Investment Strategies

Financial theory states that to reduce risk you should diversify, to spread your wealth among different assets. To achieve a statistically comfortable level of diversifications, the number of assets should be spread over fifteen different types or locations of properties. Consider the plight of the British or Dutch or even Japanese real estate investor who is limited to the assets within his densely populated and spatially confined homeland.

The American real estate investor has plenty of room to roam; the foreign investor does not. The United States offers investment opportunities in over 330 cities. The United States has three of the richest areas in the world: the country as a whole; the state of California; and the Northeast Corridor which includes parts or all of Massachusetts, Connecticut, New York, Pennsylvania, New Jersey, Maryland, and Virginia. A recent study suggests that while foreigners may gain by diversifying in the United States, there may be little improvement for an American's portfolio investing overseas.[2]

In all of the Netherlands, for example, there are 130 million square feet of office space, while New York City alone has 330 million square feet. Americans have the highest rate of consumption in the world. Because of this, the United States has the highest ratio of retail clerks to general population (1–8) of all major countries. These retail clerks must be sheltered. The inventory of American commercial real estate totals over two trillion dollars. Americans are considered the best housed in the world, and their residential debt exceeds $1.7 trillion.

For the foreign real estate developer, lack of land creates price squeezes. Prime land for offices sells for $1500 a square foot in the best spots in Manhattan in New York; $2100 in London; and up to $20,000 in Japan, if land is available. The price squeeze in Japan is reflected in the analysis that the value of real estate in the Tokyo Bay metropolitan area is equal to the value of all American real estate. From how many cities and regions and life-style communities can foreign real estate developers choose? What are the prospects for growth?

The combination of the need to diversify, the chance to grow and develop, and a fortuitous set of economic and financial conditions have pushed foreign investment to the United States. The sequence of ever-increasing involvement and complexity of this investment follows these steps:

Passive arms length financing either through a debt form or silent equity partner. Depending upon the financial conditions and strategy of the foreign investor, this silent form of passive funding may either be competitively priced or, to gain an entry into the American market, may be priced as a "loss leader." All of the major countries participate in this financing. Competitively priced financing is the main forte of the British and the Dutch. The Japanese are motivated by the increase in the value of the yen against the dollar that has occurred within the last several years, and perceive desired returns from a different time horizon. They can both be competitive and undercut. Initially, the Japanese have provided financing at what appears to the American as below-market rates and have acquired buildings at high prices that will generate below-market yields. In retrospect, their strategy is more complex than may at first appear.

Limited Partner. While still passive in nature, the investor becomes more visible and conspicuously appears as either one of the major owners in a limited participation or a major participant in a loan syndicate. At this stage, the investor increases his percentage in the funding and allows himself to be identified. The pricing of the deal can either be competitive or it can appear as below-market. At this stage, the investor comes to the closing, whereas in the first stage an agent or broker settles the papers.

It is advantageous to participate as a limited partner for three reasons. First, it is a more direct way of funding. In addition, for the purely passive foreign investor, the yields are better. Secondly, the real estate activity may compliment other industrial activity. Both the Japanese and the British simultaneously operate their industrial investment and their real estate activity. Thirdly, the limited partner form enables the investor, especially the Japanese, to create new securities at home, which allows him or her to invest in small units in American real estate. Investors then convert the limited partnership interest into small unit partnerships back home.

After completing these two passive stages, the tempo increases.

Joint-Venture Developer.   In this stage, the foreign investor becomes more aggressive. He puts up the money and the American shows him the ropes in putting the deal together. The Canadians and the Japanese have taken advantage of this stage, while other countries have not. The joint venture can occur in two ways, either by developing a physical project or through a brokerage-investment vehicle, such as Eastdil-Nomura.

Independent Developer.   Having gone through the learning process, investors, primarily Canadian, and Japanese, stake out their activity on their own. Again, the Canadians are driven by the real estate, while some of the Japanese have a comprehensive industrial development strategy in which the real estate is just one component.

Development as a complement to other business activity such as manufacturing or services.   Real estate is ancillary to the major role of the foreign entity in the United States. In contrast, this form of real estate participation is the primary form that American firms have used in investing in real estate overseas.

The Organizational Players

The major foreign players that can be divided by organizational type are as follows:

a.   pension funds
b.   life-insurance companies

    c.   trust banks

    d.   trading, holding companies

    e.   real estate development companies

    f.   construction companies

The list is organized according to their degree of active involvement: Pension funds are totally passive, and real estate development/construction companies are active equity owners.

With a few modifications, these organizations are the same as those found in the United States. For example, a small, regional American commercial bank is roughly equivalent to a trust bank. American commercial banks, however, have a time horizon of less than five years for most of their real estate lending activity. They are short-term lenders. The lack of recognizable trading and holding companies in the United States is another noticeable difference. Because of the local nature of real estate development and the anti-trust sentiment in the United States, national scale intertwined industrial-development holding companies are not found in the United States as they are in other countries. Only recently have several American companies begun to develop real estate as a complement to their main activities, such as AT&T and American Express have, with varying degrees of success.

Both the intertwined nature of foreign-based industrial-financing companies and the concentration and limited number of real estate firms have strengthened foreign investors. There are 2000 life insurance companies in the United States; in Japan there are only 23. In 1986 they purchased over 38% of the existing properties sold in Japan. The predominance of large nationally based Japanese banks dwarfs the presence of American banks.

Each of these players has a niche in investing in the United States. The activity varies by the economic conditions within the originating country and in how they perceive American market.

Motivations

Foreign investor motivations range from simple greed to fear of the Soviet Union. They are based on strategic reasons and financial considerations of the particular project or set of projects.

Four strategic reasons include:

    a.   the trite, but true recognition of the political and general economic stability of the United States.

    b.   the size and magnitude of the United States as a fertile investment hunting ground, i.e., the previously mentioned portfolio diversification opportunity.

    c. the lack of federal regulation of real estate, both for the domestic and foreign investor, and the lack of an open door policy for the foreign investor, which exists more through benign neglect than formal governmental policy.

    d. advantageous returns in the American sector.

Economic Stability

While there have been periods when foreign investors have treated American real estate as a speculative commodity, the time horizon for most foreign investors is a minimum of five years; for the Japanese it has been much longer. This raises the question of how the foreign investor reconciles his view of America today with America of the future. The United States maintains economic stability in part because its population is among the youngest of the economically developed countries. In the year 2,000 there will still be a significant number of workers in the economy to man the machines and computers. The same may not necessarily be true for Japan, Britain, and other developed countries. The average population growth for the United States has been 2% a year since 1960. For the first time in its history, the United States Census has predicted the population will begin to decline around the year 2020.

From a real estate perspective, it is not only the absolute growth in population, but the roaming nature of the American that appeals to the investor. The fastest growing, economically developed area today is California. It is fueled by migration both from abroad and from other parts of the United States. It is the favored retail center in the world, and its increase in gross national product is among the highest in the world. It is conceivable that California will become like Japan.

As a proxy for economic conditions, let's examine the automobile industry. Despite the major changes in organization and the thrust of imports, American car makers for 20 years have maintained a domestic production of 8 million cars. Moreover, it appears destined to maintain that level for years to come. This is a stabilizing force behind the gross national product.

Despite an array of problems and national financial upsets, the U.S. population and domestic production will remain stable for the next two holding periods of institutional real estate.

Portfolio Size

The size of American real estate wealth permits ample diversification both for foreign and domestic investors. Residential mortgage debt outstanding is roughly equal to the national debt. It can also be equated to the value of all securities of the New York Stock Exchange, a value of two trillion dollars for each category. More specifically, from 1980 to 1988, the 25 life insurers of the American Council of Life Insurers who underwrite commercial first mortgages wrote over $830 billion worth of loan commitments. It is estimated that major pension funds all have equity positions in another $300 billion worth of commercial real estate.

Empirical verification for measuring the degree of diversification of the American portfolio has been limited to an analysis of the performance of real estate within seven large regional areas. The data of real estate, vacancy rates (from highs of 40% to lows of 9%), project capitalization rates (from 7–10%), rent rates (from $12 to $50 per square foot of office space), and transaction volumes suggest unlimited diversification opportunities for both domestic and foreign investors.

Using the National Council of Real Estate Investment Fiduciaries (NCREIF) data based on the Frank Russell data base, the returns on institutional quality of American real estate has kept pace with and, from 1979 to 1988, has slightly outperformed the American equities market. In comparing American real estate to the domestic real estate of other countries, the results are not clear. Including both rates of return and appreciation, property in the United Kingdom for example, has generated returns equal to those in the United States.

Regulation

Although real estate in the development stage is intensely regulated at the local level and subsequent occupancy may be monitored, the transaction paper of real estate is relatively free of federal regulation and disclosure. There is no central overseer of foreign real estate investment in the United States. Americans are not even sure of the levels of foreign investment in their own country. (The data from the Survey of Current Business, Department of Commerce, used for this report, has been challenged, but it appears to be the one consistent source over time.)

The anonymous nature is valued as the flow of money from the Netherlands Antilles suggests. Whereas it is relatively easy for the foreign investor to participate in the domestic American market, the reverse is not necessarily true.

Advantageous Returns

During most of this decade, American real estate was cited for its high level of annual income returns, compared with the British or the Japanese. It was commonly stated that Americans average 10%, the British average 6%, and the Japanese average 4%. There are two components to the return on real estate: the annual cash flow and reversion, the expected gain upon the sale or refinancing of the project several years in the future.

In terms of average cash flows, Americans still generate a modest cash flow, even though it has declined over the past decade. The overall return (as measured by the capitalization rate) on leveraged properties financed by the participating underwriters of the American Council of Life Insurers has decreased from 10.5% in 1979 to an average of 9.3% in the fourth quarter, in 1988. What is not clear is the magnitude of appreciation for American property compared to other foreign properties.

A comparison of the domestic American returns with those of *Investment Property Database* for the United Kingdom suggests a shadowing of cycles between the two countries. British property, for example, is several years behind in exhibiting the peaks and valleys observed in the United States.

When real estate is treated by the financial community as a commodity instead of a long term investment, it is subject to volatile price fluctuations. The suspected reasons for disenchantment by major overseas investors, such as the Coal Board or Canadian BCE, is because of their entrance timing into the market and the results of a short term horizon. Historically, the boast of sound real estate has been that it outperforms the rate of inflation by 2–3%. That belief still exists.

Financial Ploys

For both the foreign and domestic equity investor, there are three sources of value for real estate held as a medium or long term investment: the periodic cash flow; the sheltering effects of depreciation for the tax-sensitive investor; the expectation of realizing an increase in project value when sold or a new higher loan at refinancing.

Currently the tax field is flat. Prior to the 1986 Tax Reform Act, however, there were additional tax benefits that were realized when the project was sold. The benefit accrued because any gain was a capital gain and thus was subject to the lesser capital gains tax.

The foreign investor looks not only to these sources of value in the real estate project, but also to currency exchange timing. Essentially, real estate is used as a holding account through which the foreign investor can time the flow of funds back to his native country.

The investor is worried about two currency changes. First is the daily day to day changes. These will affect the timing of the return on equity as a result of day to day operations. Through the use of reserve accounts and financing, these returns can either be accelerated or slowed.

The second concern is the preservation of the value of the principal. For example, if a building was purchased when the rate of exchange was one to one, how can the foreign owner protect himself against a drop when the native currency drops to half of its original parity? Hedging is one way that can effectively protect the value of the short-term cash flows that will be converted to the native currency upon the return home. However the preservation of principal is beyond the time horizon of most hedging strategies and possibilities.

Hence, when American property is purchased by foreign investors, they must incorporate one more step than is normally encountered by the domestic investor in his cash flow. This extra step is the currency conversion impact upon returns. The investor can attempt to protect himself in three ways.

First, develop a subsidiary in the United States such that the company is treated as though it is part of a long-term investment strategy and that returns from the real estate investment will be re-invested in the United States. When there are opportune windows, transactions to return funds to the native company will occur during these times.

Second, perform a feasibility analysis in which the expectations of the increases of rents will be offset by adverse currency conversion conditions. The project is torpedoed if the expected increases in rents, and perhaps favorable financing, can not stave off an unfavorable exchange market.

Finally, neutralize the effect of currency exchange risk, creating debt instruments through which the interest and/or the principal are payable in the native currency. In addition to equating the dollar to the native currency at a current exchange rates, the native currency and the dollar can also be adjusted against gold, an adjustment to the London InterBank Offering Rate, and so on. Barter considerations also sometimes occur.

Currency rate risk explains some of the motivations of foreign investors. The Exhibit, and "Currency Rates and FDI," illustrate that when the currency suffered against the dollar, the level of foreign investment in real estate declined, usually by a one to two year lag. As the Canadian dollar slipped in the early eighties, the investment decreased. Similarly, it was only after the yen doubled in value against the dollar that investment significantly rose.

The strength of the currency vis a vis the dollar is a good proxy for the comparative economic strength of one country versus another.

The Future

The "stuff of predictions" as to the future of foreign investment in U.S. real estate comes from three sources: general trends, known regulatory changes, and unknown external surprises.

As to known emerging trends, the musical chairs effect of the Pacific rim are obvious. In sequence we have seen the emergence of Japan and now Korea; looming in the future are Taiwan, the Philippines, and mainland China. The emergence of the Philippines and Korea depends upon the stability of their governments. When growth occurs and stability in government is achieved, then the regulatory restrictions on foreign investments are relaxed increasing the flow of capital for investment. Hong Kong is a viable player in certain American properties, although it is not conspicuously reported by the Department of Commerce.

Figure 3   Japanese F.D.I. in R.E. and Yen/\$ Rate

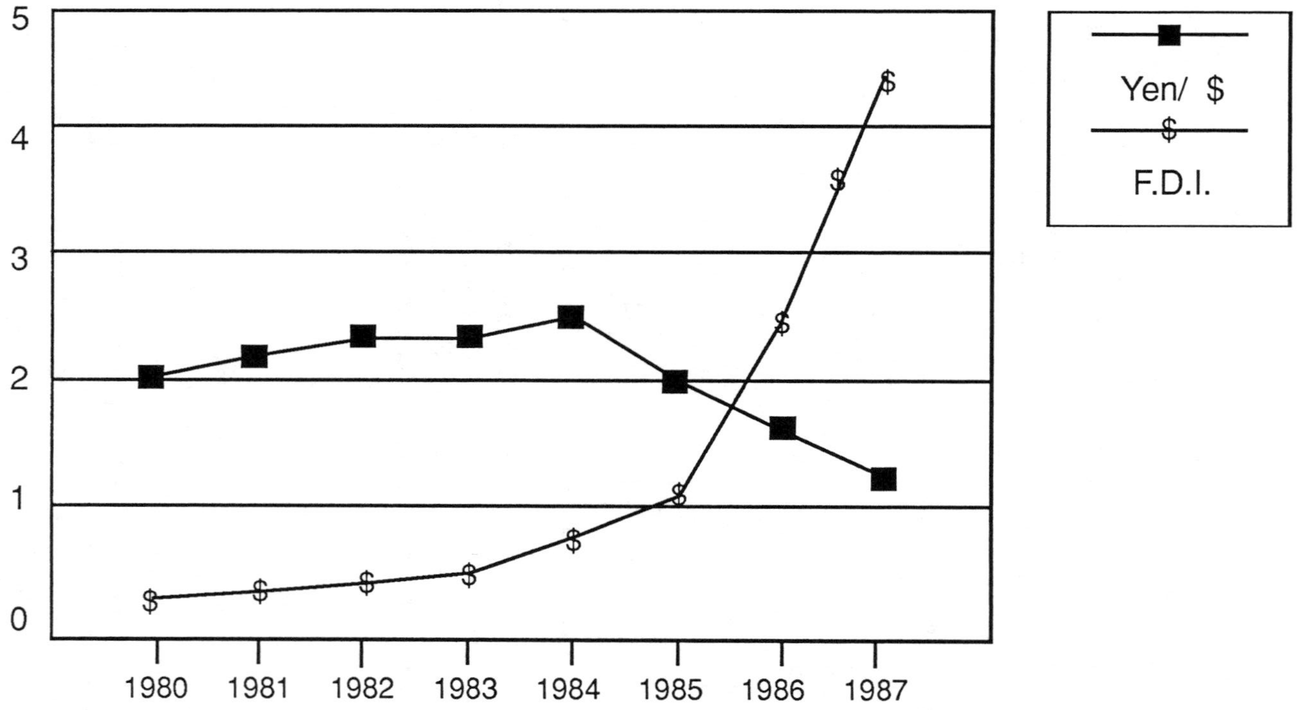

Figure 4   Canadian F.D.I. in R.E. and Canadian $ Rate

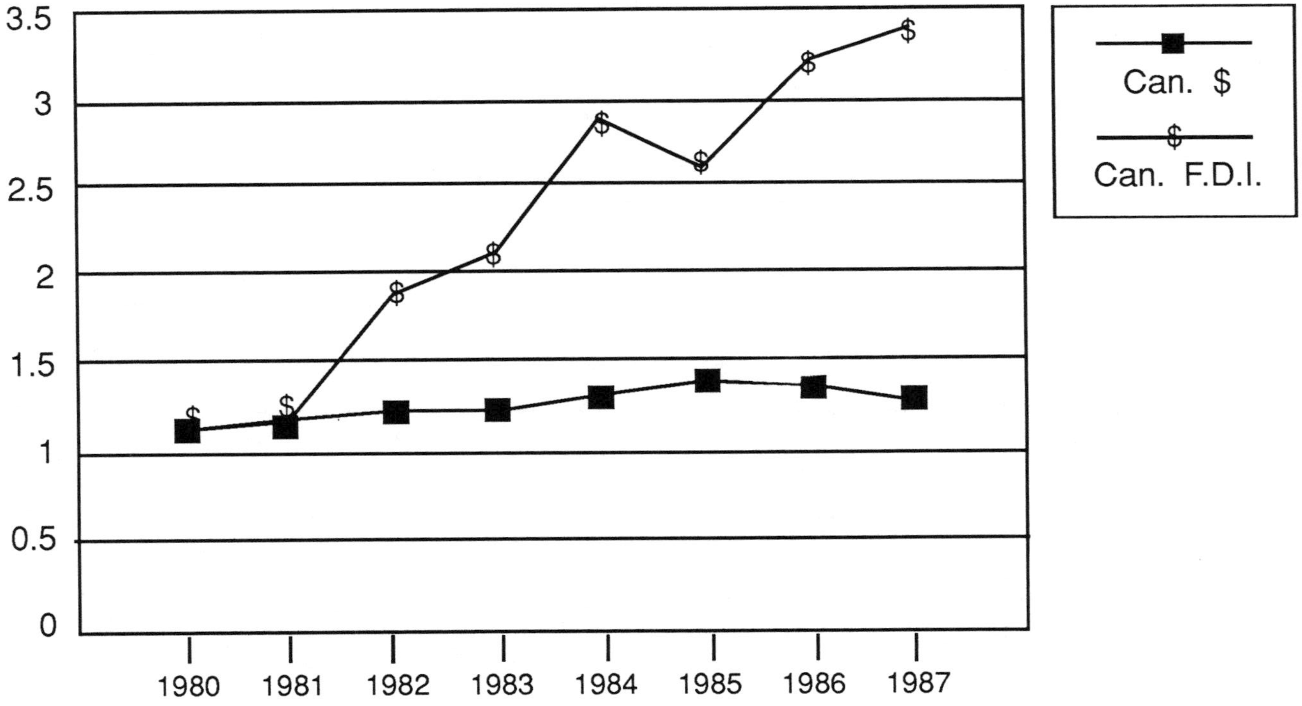

Figure 5   British F.D.I. in R.E. and Pound/$ Rate

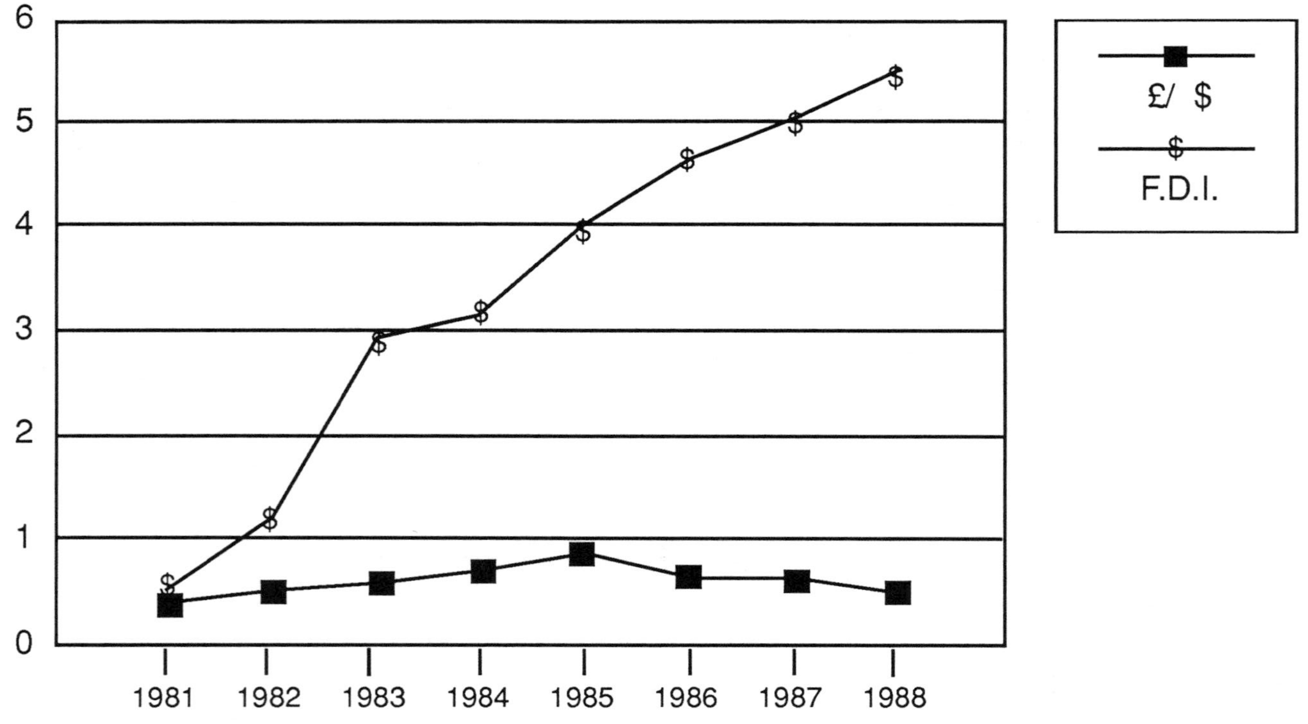

The magnitude of those flows depends upon the nervous factor as the reversion of the protectorate to part of mainland China.

The Netherlands Antilles records the effects of the growth industry of South America, drugs. The question is whether Brazil will restructure itself to capitalize on its energetic population and wealth of natural resources. Investment from Brazil will continue to be selective.

Two themes benchmark Europe. The first is the planned European Economic Union of 1992. In terms of direct investment, this may have a negative effect upon direct investment in the United States. Supposedly, the union will allow for greater ease of transactions among member countries. The wish is that centuries old jealousies will be ameliorated by economic considerations. On the positive side, there are expectations that securitized forms of real estate investment will increase, such as real estate investment trusts that specialize in American properties.

The other event that may throw the spotlight from the United States to Europe is the Olympics in Spain. Real Estate investment like other forms of investment can be determined by trends and the interests of others.

Other forces to be reckoned with include the cyclical nature of oil countries in the Middle East. We suspect that investment in America by these countries is partially a function of the barrel price of oil. We now have endured two peak price cycles with corresponding bumps upward in American real estate purchasing, and it appears that we are entering the third.

Endnotes

[1]   Karen E. Lahey and Frederick W. Schroath, "International Real Estate Investment by Insurance Companies," paper presented at the 1987 American Real Estate Society Meeting.

[2]   James R. Webb and Jack H. Rubens, "Diversification Gains from Including Foreign Real Estate in Mixed-Asset Portfolios," paper presented at the Spring 1989 ARES meeting.

C H A P T E R 4

Canadian Equity Market

Jim McDonald
Burns Fry Ltd., Toronto

Political and Economic Characteristics

Modelled after the British, Canada's government is a parliamentary democracy in which an elected House of Commons holds the reins of power, and an appointed Senate is a forum for "sober second thought." As opposed to the federation of states in the United States, Canada is a confederation of provinces, which have significantly more power than states. As a result, Canada's system of government is more decentralized. In consideration of its two "founding peoples," Canada is officially bilingual in French and English. However, the country is still struggling with the separation of political powers and language rights, as indicated by the current impasse over ratification of the "Meech Lake" constitutional accord. Despite the development of three major political parties, political ideologies are not as polarized in Canada as in most other Western democracies. Power has traditionally swung back and forth between the Liberal and Progressive Conservative parties in a struggle for the political center. While the New Democrats, who have a more clearly defined policy platform that is modestly left of center, steadily attract 20–25% of the voters, the party has never won a federal election. In November 1988, the Conservatives secured another four to five year mandate with a second consecutive majority victory in the Commons.

Canada's population of 26 million people produced a GDP in 1988 of about Cdn$600 billion (US$500 billion). In contrast to the more diversified industrialized economies of the United States, Europe, and Japan, Canada has a relatively large dependence on the extraction and processing of natural resources. Forest products, base and precious metals, oil and gas, and farm and fishery products are the major commodities from which the manufacturing sector draws strength. However, the importance of secondary manufacturing is steadily growing, nourished by the increasingly open trading relationship with the United States. For example, under the Canada-U.S. Auto Pact, Canada's largest exports in 1988 were automobiles and auto parts.

Leverage to the resource sector gives a wider amplitude to cyclical swings in Canadian economic growth. Over the long run, this resource base, as well as strong growth of immigration and population, gives Canada a relatively high potential growth rate within the OECD. While debate rages as to the timing and severity of the next global downturn, Canada is at present well launched on a capital spending-led growth phase. This investment strength is derived primarily from high profits and operating rates in primary industries and a restructuring and rationalization in response to the Canada-U.S. Free Trade Agreement.

Market Valuation and Outlook

The valuation of the Canadian stock market, while strongly influenced by trends in the United States, does exhibit a character of its own. Over the last thirty years the price/earnings (P/E) multiple of the TSE 300 Composite Index, which is adjusted for losses, has averaged half a multiple point lower than that of the Standard & Poor's 500 Composite Index. We attribute this to the modest inflation bias in Canada and to the maintenance of consistently higher interest rates. However, this multiple differential is not stable. Looking at a typical economic cycle reveals that the Canadian multiple can fall two to three multiple points below that of the S&P 500 during economic downturns and the early stages of recoveries. Conversely, in the second half of the cycle investors push TSE valuation to a premium position as they reflect the positive dimension of Canada's greater economic cyclicality. As a general rule, the Canadian market underperforms the U.S. market during the bear market and the initial stages of the bull market. It outperforms the U.S. market toward the end of the bull market.

Prior to the stock market crash of October 1987, the higher multiple reported in Canada was typical of late cycle patterns. The crash affected buying & trading patterns and pushed the TSE multiple two to three points under the S&P 500. As the fear of recession has receded, the valuation differential has shrunk.

Regression tests have shown that both the Canadian and U.S. market multiple are most strongly influenced by inflation, market volatility, the slope of the yield curve, and exchange rate factors. The steady increase in inflation in late 1988 and early 1989 placed downward pressure on P/E's, but this is expected to reverse. The uncertainty created by the tremendous volatility of the crash has also acted to hold down valuations, but this too should weaken with time. Lastly, multiples should receive a further boost from the return of a positive yield curve

Figure 1   TSE 300 P/E - S&P 500 P/E

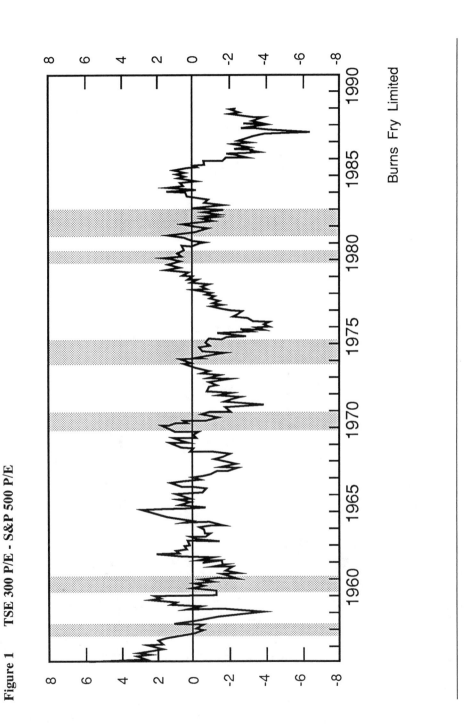

Burns Fry Limited

Figure 2   TSE 300 P/E & S&P 500 P/E

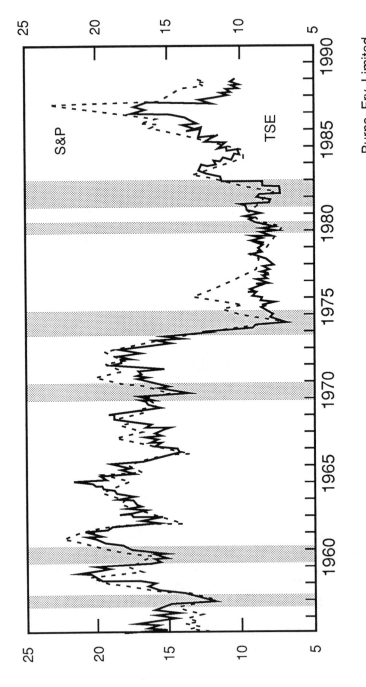

Burns Fry Limited

Figure 3   TSE 300 Composite Index Earnings

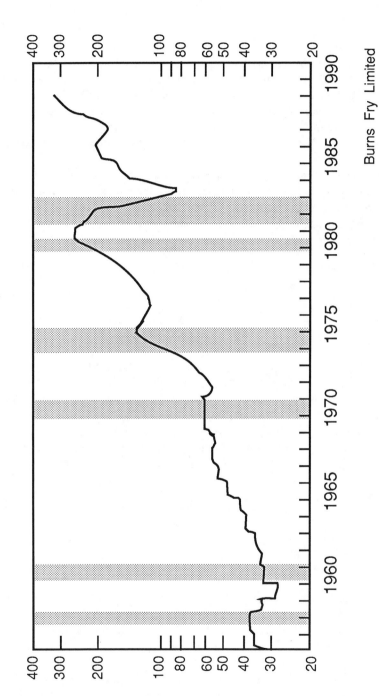

Burns Fry Limited

and lower exchange rates. In sum, the TSE P/E ratio is expected to climb from its current level of 11.25x trailing earnings to approximately 12x to 13x in 1990.

The 1980–1982 recession and the oil price collapse of 1986 crushed earnings in Canada. The subsequent recovery saw earnings for the TSE jump 50% in 1987, with preliminary figures for 1988 suggesting a further increase of 25–30%. The momentum in earnings continues to moderate to more normal levels with 5–10% growth forecast for 1989. This would push trailing earnings to the $350 level.

Performance prospects for the Canadian market are reasonably positive. A gradual recovery in the P/E to a more normal valuation level combined with modest earnings improvement should propel Canada to a median market performance. A first quartile ranking does not appear in prospect as long as world growth is moderating and Canada's greater economic cyclicality appears to be a disadvantage.

The Stock Market

Brief History and Structure[1]

There are five stock exchanges located across Canada in Montreal, Toronto, Winnipeg, Calgary, and Vancouver. The most important exchanges are Toronto, Montreal, and Vancouver, all of which handled 95% of the total share volume and 99.3% of the dollar value in 1987, as seen in the following tables:

In Canada, trading in securities began during the early nineteenth century. Conventional stock exchanges didn't formally appear until 1970 in Toronto and Montreal. A brief history of Canada's four principal stock exchanges follows:

1. **The Montreal Exchange**
    The Stock Exchange Tower
    P.O. Box 61
    800 Victoria Square
    Montreal, Quebec H4Z 1A9

In 1874 the Montreal Stock Exchange was incorporated under the Quebec charter. Prior to this a board of brokers operated under certain rules and membership criteria from 1863 to 1874, with the first formal record of trading dating back to 1817. The Montreal Curb Market was organized in 1926 to provide trading facilities for securities not listed on the MSE. In 1953 the Montreal Curb Market, formally incorporated as the Canadian Stock Exchange and the Montreal and Canadian Stock Exchanges, shared the same permanent executive staff and trading facilities. In 1974 the two exchanges merged into the Montreal Stock

Figure 4   TSE Composite Index

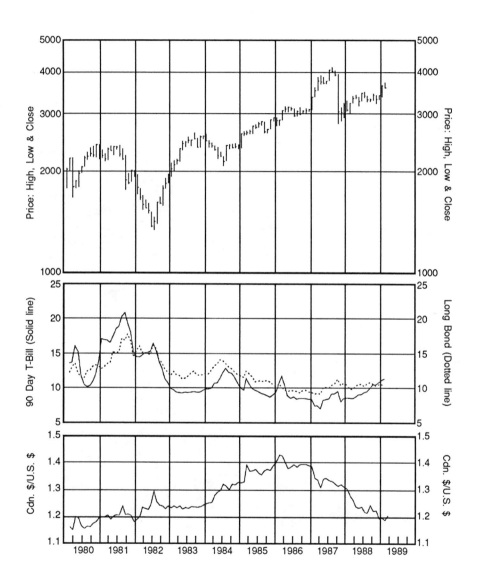

Burns Fry Limited

Figure 5   Average Trading Levels, Canadian Exchanges

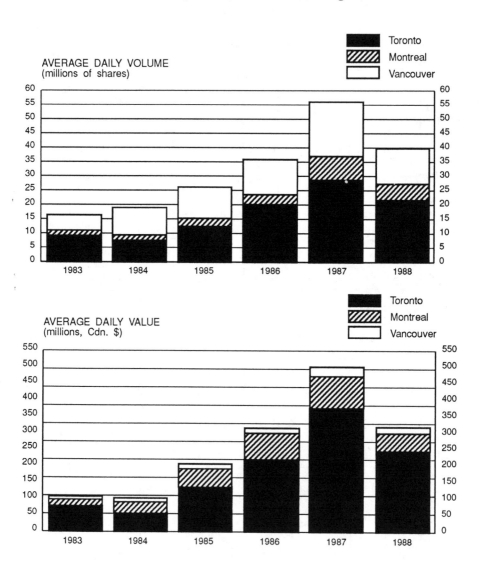

Table 1   Total Share Volume and Dollar Value of Transactions for All Stock Exchanges in Canada in 1987 and 1986

Comparitive Share Volumes (000's)

Exchange	1987	%	1986	%
Toronto	7,393,699	49.4	4,906,702	49.7
Vancouver	4,795,143	32.1	3,493,491	35.4
Montreal	2,022,148	13.5	1,095,878	11.1
Alberta	740,753	5.0	369,244	3.8
Winnepeg	150	—	518	—
Total Shares	14,951,893	100.0	9,965,833	100.0

Comparitive Dollar Values of Transactions (000's)

Exchange	1987	%	1986	%
Toronto	100,224,304	77.3	63,684,095	75.3
Montreal	21,875,597	16.9	15,982,739	18.9
Vancouver	6,650,301	5.1	4,484,518	5.3
Alberta	971,991	0.7	476,110	0.5
Winnepeg	427	—	556	—
Total Value	129,722,620	100.0	84,628,018	100.0

Exchange. This was brought about because although equity trading is still the primary function of the ME, options, futures, and precious metals, certificates have become an integral part of ME business.

2. The Toronto Stock Exchange

The Exchange Tower
2 First Canadian Place
Toronto, Ontario
M5X 1J2

The Toronto Stock Exchange was founded as an association in 1852 by a small group of Toronto businessmen who met to trade securities for half an hour each morning. These founders operated as a partnership until, by an act of the Province of Ontario, the Toronto Stock Exchange was incorporated in 1878.

In 1899, a second stock exchange, the Toronto Stock and Mining Exchange, was organized to trade speculative mining equities. This exchange was succeeded by the Standard Stock and Mining Exchange in 1908, which carried on as a separate exchange until 1934. At that time a merger was complete with the Toronto Stock Exchange so that mining and industrial stock could be traded on one floor. From 1937 to 1983, the TSE was located on Bay Street. In May 1983 the Exchange moved to the Exchange Tower and Trading Pavilion (behind the Exchange Tower) at York and Adelaide Streets.

On the TSE's 30,000 square foot trading floor, five and a half trading posts are used for equity trading, and two trading posts are used for trading equity and non-equity options. In 1984 the TSE established the Toronto Futures Exchange (TFE) as a separate exchange using two trading pits on the TSE's trading floor. The TFE trades bond options and futures, warrants on Canada bonds, silver options, currency futures, TSE 35 index options and futures, and treasury bill futures.

3. **The Alberta Stock Exchange (ASE)**

    300 Fifth Avenue S.W.
    Calgary, Alberta
    T2P 3C4

The history of the Alberta Stock Exchange dates back to the incorporation of the Calgary Stock Exchange in 1913 by an Act of the Alberta government. Trading commenced following the discovery of oil in Turner Valley in 1914. Since then the exchange's trading history has closely paralleled significant oil and gas discoveries in western Canada. In 1974 the name was changed to the Alberta Stock Exchange. In 1983 the ASE was the first exchange in Canada to list corporate bonds with equities.

4. **Vancouver Stock Exchange (VSE)**

    Stock Exchange Tower
    P.O. Box 10333
    609 Granville Street
    Vancouver, B.C.
    V7Y 1H1

Incorporated as the Vancouver Stock Exchange, by the Special Act of the B.C. Legislature in 1907, the VSE has operated continually since its inception. Presently located in the Pacific Center Stock Exchange Tower, the VSE's trading facilities encompass 7,200 square feet and 230 trading booths. The VSE began trading commodity options in gold in 1982, in silver and Canadian currency in 1983 and in platinum in 1987. Trading in listed equity options began in 1984.

Exchange Trading Hours

Exchange	Trading Hours
ME:	EST/EDT (A.M.) (P.M.)
Equities and equity options	9:30 - 4:00
Precious Metal Certificates	9:00 - 4:00
Bond options	9:00 - 4:00
Currency options	
Canadian dollar	8:30 - 2:30
Futures on Bankers' Acceptances	9:00 - 3:00
TSE:	EST/EDT (A.M.) (P.M.)
Equities and equity options	9:30 - 4:00
TFE:	
Govt. of Canada bond and treasury bill futures	9:00 - 3:15
Index futures	10:00 - 4:15
TSE 300 Index	9:30 - 4:15
TSE 35 Index	9:15 - 4:15
Silver options	9:05 - 4:00
U.S. dollar futures	8:30 - 4:00
ASE:	MST/MDT (A.M.) (P.M.)
Equities and bonds	7:30 - 2:30
VSE:	PST/PDT (A.M.) (P.M.)
Equities	6:30 - 1:30
Equity options	6:30 - 1:00
Gold Options and C. $ options	11:30 - 4:00
Silver options	7:30 - 4:00

Market Size

Number of listings and market value

At the end of 1988 there were 1,656 issues listed on the Toronto Stock Exchange issued by 1,208 companies. The total market capitalization was $727.5

Figure 6   World Market Capitalizations (in Billions)

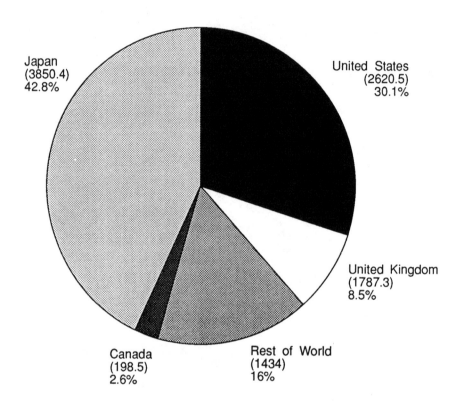

Japan
(3850.4)
42.8%

United States
(2620.5)
30.1%

United Kingdom
(1787.3)
8.5%

Canada
(198.5)
2.6%

Rest of World
(1434)
16%

Source: Morgan Stanley Capital International as at 02/89.

Figure 7 Comparison of Sectors (% of Index)

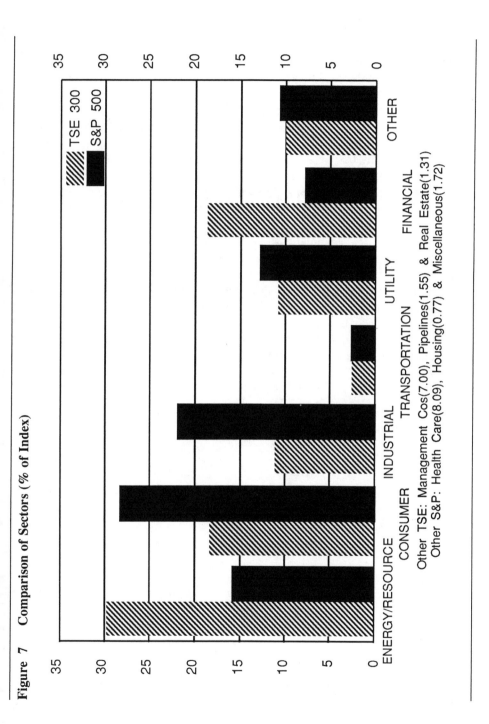

Other TSE: Management Cos(7.00), Pipelines(1.55) & Real Estate(1.31)
Other S&P: Health Care(8.09), Housing(0.77) & Miscellaneous(1.72)

billion, with $288.1 billion of Canadian-based companies. This fact illustrates one of the most unique features of the Canadian market — the effect of interlisted trading. Given Canada's close economic relationship with the United States as its largest trading partner, many leading companies in both countries, (i.e., Alcan, Seagram, Canadian Pacific, IBM, General Motors) have their common shares trading on both Canadian and U.S. exchanges, providing increased visibility and liquidity. At present, there are 140 Canadian companies and 50 U.S. companies listed on both the Toronto Stock Exchange and U.S. Exchanges. In fact, five Canadian companies are presently part of the Standard and Poors 500 Index. The most important sector in the Canadian market is financial services, accounting for 18.3% of total capitalization. The other major sectors are metals and minerals (11.1%) and industrial products (10.85%).

The Canadian market represents approximately 2.6% of the world capitalization.

While many Canadian companies trade in the United States, the makeup of the Canadian market is quite different. As measured by the TSE 300, the Canadian market reflects that over 40% of Canada's exports are resource based raw materials. Hence, there is a heavy representation of resource based companies on the Toronto Exchange relative to the U.S. market.

Table 2   Number of Listed Companies, Listed Issues and Market Value

	1988	1987	1986	1985	1984
Companies Listed	1,208	1,208	1,085	966	933
Issues Listed	1,656	1,695	1,570	1,438	1,389
New Companies Listed	87	180	165	73	100
New Issues Listed	89	190	175	76	102
Delistings	138	126	107	76	67
Total Quoted Market Value (billions)	$727.5	$737.7	$608.9	$585.2	$483.8
Canadian-based Companies (billions)	$288.1	$284.9	$255.7	$220.0	$177.8
Total Outstanding Shares	33.3	30.6	23.4	19.7	17.8
Canadian-based Companies (billions)	22.1	21.5	17.5	14.3	12.4

Source: *TSE Review*, December 1988.

Table 3   Average Trading Levels Canadian Exchanges

New Equity Financing: 1985-1987

Type of Financing	1988	1987	1986	1985
Exchange offering Prospectus (EOP)				
Fixed Price Offerings	5,640	22,547	24,968	9,772
Public Offerings	1,668,098	10,091,832	10,799,747	8,003,047
Private Placements	1,057,182	2,394,977	2,327,796	802,723
Sub-Total	2,730,920	12,486,809	13,127,543	8,805,770
Rights	370,286	196,743	727,440	122,679
Totals	3,101,206	12,706,099	13,879,951	8,938,221

Source: *TSE Review*, December 1988.

Types of Shares

Among the categories, of equity or quasi-equity, that may be traded on Canadian stock exchanges are common shares, preferred shares, convertible securities, and futures and options.

Common shares, which represent ownership in the company, are the most prevalent type of instrument traded on Canadian exchanges. As a common shareholder, you are entitled to receive any common share dividends paid by the company, capital appreciation, and voting rights. Another unusual feature of the Canadian equity market is the issue of voting and non-voting rights with respect to common shares. Many Canadian companies have more than one class of common shares. While the New York Stock Exchange has a one share—one vote rule, the Toronto Stock Exchange allows restricted shares to trade. In fact, of the 1,231 issues listed on the TSE, 176 had different classes of common shares. These restricted shares take the form of non-voting with no voting privileges; subordinate voting where another class of common has greater voting rights; and restricted voting shares that have voting limits.

Preferred shareholders occupy a position between those of the common shareholder and the creditor. Preferred shareholders are usually entitled to a fixed payout out of net earnings, subject to discretion of the board of directors. In many cases, companies issue more than one class of preferred stock. When these various preferred stocks rank equally as to asset and dividend entitlement, the shares are described as ranking pas passu.

Table 4	Top 25 Securities by Value Traded and Volume

		$ Value of Trading	No. of Shares Traded
1.	Inco	4,997,860,226	144,744,415
2.	Alcan Aluminum	3,177,761,035	88,111,590
3.	Falconbridge Ltd.	2,524,368,573	105,455,082
4.	Odn Pac. Ltd.	2,312,299,856	105,194,427
5.	Polysar Energy	2,284,012,732	128,324,961
6.	Laidlaw Cl B. NV	1,890,183,712	108,762,843
7.	Nova Corp. RV	1,825,611,867	153,921,629
8.	Royal Bank	1,518,165,887	47,470,474
9.	BCE Inc.	1,415,434,677	37,500,664
10.	Noranda	1,250,014,010	54,772,677
11.	Toronto Dominion Bk.	1,134,166,882	35,337,993
12.	Odn Imperial Bank	1,096,675,993	47,834,478
13.	Seagram Co.	1,070,526,300	15,618,750
14.	Placer Dome	1,026,350,588	63,968,927
15.	Bk of Nova Scotia	847,332,662	61,831,914
16.	Cominco Ltd.	812,033,140	44,186,150
17.	Imperial Oil CL A	794,511,672	14,509,386
18.	Bank of Montreal	790,766,006	29,041,134
19.	Northern Telecom	781,264,062	35,035,996
20.	Echo Bay	655,653,465	28,362,571
21.	Moore Corp.	651,168,267	22,217,823
22.	American Barrick	576,307,492	24,235,678
23.	Texaco Canada Inc.	571,763,759	15,246,771
24.	MacMillan Bloedel	550,104,502	29,023,509
25.	Dofasco	485,272,403	17,639,942

Source: *TSE Review*, December 1988.

Trading In Canadian Securities

The placement of a purchase or sale order for a Canadian security is a straight forward process, and the procedures are relatively consistent with those practiced in the United States.

Opening an Account

To open an account with a Canadian investment dealer, basic client information must be provided to the licensed registered representative responsible for handling the transactions. Client account information for individual investors would

Table 5   TSE Breakdown by Capitalization (%)

Sector	TSE Weight	1988	Annual Total Return 5 year	20 year
TSE 300	100%	11.1%	9.36%	14.23%
Resource:				
Metals & Minerals	11.11	26.7	8.39	15.33
Gold & Silver	8.20	−27.3	6.36	15.45
Forest Products	3.05	−10.1	14.86	15.45
Energy:				
Oil & Gas	7.42	12.5	2.91	9.02
Industrial:				
Industrial Products	10.85	10.2	3.36	10.13
Transportation	2.25	−0.3	18.92	19.53
Management Cos.	7.00	8.5	15.27	17.99
Consumer Oriented:				
Consumer Products	7.59	10.2	9.55	17.35
Comm. & Media	5.69	35.3	22.61	22.72
Merchandising	5.10	24.2	11.65	16.41
Interest Sensitive:				
Real Estate	1.31	21.8	23.84	21.44
Pipelines	1.56	23.2	13.67	14.70
Utilities	10.59	7.5	9.44	13.93
Financial Services	18.28	25.5	11.11	13.45

include among other information, details pertaining to their employer, net worth, and investment objectives. To satisfy Canadian regulatory requirements, a corporation must provide a corporate resolution for trading authorization.

Type of Accounts

Three different types of accounts can be opened:

- A Cash Account: With a cash account purchase, payment is due on settlement date (normally 5 days after settlement for an equity trade). Similarly, funds are paid on settlement date on the sale of a security position.

Figure 8   Processing a Canadian Equity Trade

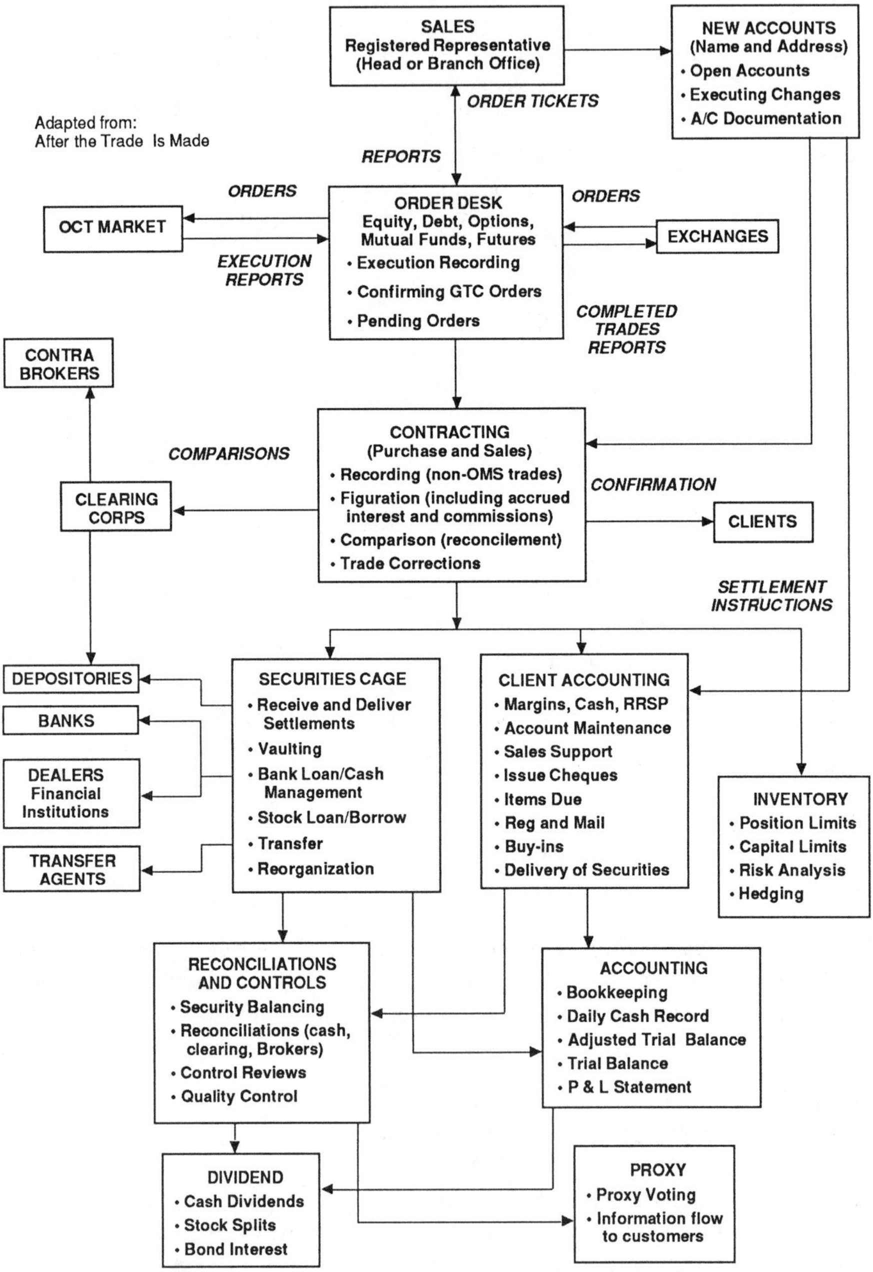

Adapted from:
After the Trade Is Made

- A Margin Account: In the case of margin accounts, the investment dealer loans money to the investor based on regulatory margin rates. Any debits are charged at competitive interest rates and are based upon Canadian lending rates. Canadian regulations require margin accounts to be fully margined at all times.

- A DAP Account: While Delivery Against Payment (DAP) accounts are not common in the United States, they are a familiar account in Canada. With a DAP account, in the case of a purchase, securities are delivered to the investor's settling agent against payment; in the case of a sale, funds are delivered upon receipt of the sold security. DAP transactions are always done on a value for value basis.

Accounts may be opened in either Canadian or U.S. funds. Once an account has been opened, an order may be placed by phoning or writing to the investment dealer.

The client's investment dealer provides a monthly statement to the investor detailing transactions that have taken place during the month, all security positions, and any outstanding credit or debit balance.

Trade Placement and Execution

After an account has been established, a request for the purchase or sale of a security is placed in the same manner as it would be at a U.S. dealer. The investor specifies the securities, quantities, and acceptable price ranges.

Once the trade has been executed by the investment dealer, details of the trade are reported to the investor in the form of a contract or confirmation. The confirmation is normally mailed on the day after the trade has been transacted; this is a requirement of the Canadian stock exchanges and of the Investment Dealers' Association of Canada. The contract specifies the security purchased or sold, the execution price, and the total cost or proceeds of the transaction, including commission charges and accrued interest, where applicable. The registered representative may confirm trade execution to the investor either by phone, telex, or facsimile.

Trade Settlement

Upon settlement date the investor is required either to:

(a) pay the purchase price in full if the purchase has been transacted through a cash account

(b) ensure that sufficient funds and excess margin are available if the security has been acquired in a margin account, or

(c) ensure that settlement instructions have been conveyed to the settlement agent three business days before the settlement date of a DAP trade. In the event of a purchase, the investor must ensure that sufficient funds are at the settling agent to settle the trade.

In the case of cash and margin account trades, funds may be wired through the U.S. bank wire network to ensure that they are received on settlement date.

Canadian equity securities are predominantly settled through the settlement system of the Canadian Depository for Securities (CDS). This is largely a book-based, or non-certificated, settlement system. Participants in the CDS settlement system include major institutions, investment dealers, banks, and trust companies. Ordinarily, all trades are settled on a ledger basis. Settling agents, including Canadian chartered banks and trust companies, provide settlement services on a U.S. investor's behalf. With respect to inter-participant settlements, Canada has its own unique rules that differ minimally from those of the United States. These minor variances have evolved through custom and practices to expedite settlements and have no material impact on any investment decision.

Regulations

Canadian investment dealers are required by Provincial Securities Commissions and the self-regulatory organizations to which they belong to maintain adequate capital in their business; to carry extensive fidelity, theft, and other insurance; and to maintain proper bookkeeping controls and supervision over all employees. Financial positions are examined annually by an independent auditor and are also subject to separate surprise audits by stock exchange or Investment Dealers' Association of Canada examiners.

A National Contingency Fund has been established by the Investment Dealers' Association of Canada and the Toronto, Montreal, and Vancouver Stock Exchanges. This fund is administered by a board of governors who may, at their discretion, authorize payment from the fund to assist clients who suffer loss due to the financial failure of a member.

Taxation Affecting Foreign Investors

Rate of Tax to be Withheld

The statutory rate of tax to be withheld is generally 25%, unless reduced to a lesser rate in accordance with a bilateral tax treaty. Canadian corporations dividend and interest payments to foreign shareholders of treaty countries are also subject to a withholding tax, normally 15%. In the case of a non-resident in-

Table 6   Withholding Tax

Recipient	Rate of Interest	Rate of Dividend
Residents of non-treaty countries	25%	25%
Residents of treaty countries		
Australia	15	15
Austria	15	15
Bangledesh	15	15
Barbados	15	15
Belgium	15	15
Brazil	15/25	15/25
China (People's Republic of)	10	10/15
Cyprus	15	15
Denmark	15	15
Dominican Republic	18	18
Egypt	15	15
Finland	15	15
France	15	15
Germany (West)	15	15
India	15	15/25
Indonesia	15	15
Ireland	15	15
Israel	15	15
Italy	15	15
Ivory Coast	15	15
Jamaica	15	15
Japan	15	15
Korea	15	15
Malaysia	15	15
Morocco	15	15
Netherlands	15/25	15
New Zealand	15	15
Norway	15	15
Pakistan	15	15
Philippines	15	15

Table continues

Table 6   (Continued)

Recipient	Rate of Interest	Rate of Dividend
Rumania	15	15
Singapore	15	15
Spain	15	15
Sri Lanka	15	15
Sweden	15	15
Switzerland	15	15
Thailand	15	15
Trinidad & Tobago	15	15
Tunisia	15	15
UK of Great Britain & Northern Ireland	10	10/15
USSR	15	15
United States	15	10/15

vestor, capital gains from the sale of shares in a Canadian corporation are exempt from Canadian taxation.

Endnote

[1]   The Canadian Securities Course Canadian Securities Institute 1989.

III

AMERICAN DEPOSITORY RECEIPTS

ADRs of Asian Companies as a Financing and Investment Vehicle *

Steven A. Schoenfeld
Simcha SIMEX Trading (PTE) Ltd., Washington

American institutional investors are rapidly becoming more international in outlook and practice. The stellar performance of Far Eastern equity markets in the 1980's has forced fund managers to recognize the region's economic vibrancy and growth potential. U.S. investors still allocate only a small percentage of their assets abroad. A small shift in the ratio—not to mention the doubling that is expected—will result in a large increase in funds available for international investment.

Over $52 billion in U.S. pension assets were invested abroad at the beginning of 1989, and the total is growing at the rate of 15–20% a year. Some experts predict that by the end of the century, one-fifth of the current $1.5 trillion will be in non-U.S. markets.

Asian companies must consider how best to tap this enormous pool of capital and to search for opportunities in the region. Are ADR programs the best way to attract U.S. investors? If so, what are the costs? Companies should be thoroughly informed of their options before they embark on a program. Con-

---

* Parts of this article originally appeared in the November 1989 issue of *Asiamoney* Magazine

cerns of American institutions and fund managers should also be considered and accommodated.

Institutional Concerns

Market access, structure, and liquidity are the most important elements for American institutional investors in Asia. Some of the largest markets—like Taiwan and South Korea—are the most restrictive to foreign participation. Any efficient vehicle for entry in Far Eastern markets is welcome, but institutions have become more selective. Adequate liquidity is also a prerequisite for many institutions. Some Asian markets are very thin, and fund managers are often disappointed by poor execution of orders and inefficient settlement systems.

Differences in Asian corporate disclosure requirements—and an inclination toward minimal reporting—further hampers institutional investment decision-making. Difficulties with settlement and accounting also limit trading in the Far East. The thin float of many shares, physical delivery of script, and long settlement periods create bottlenecks and frustrations. Global custody services alleviate much of the paperwork headache, but come at a high price, usually double that of domestic trust and custody.

Currency issues are no longer a major impediment to foreign investment, and in fact, many fund managers are looking for forex exposure when allocating overseas. However, some American investors are still legally barred from holding securities denominated in foreign currency or outside of the United States. Comfort and familiarity with dollar-priced investments are also factors that discourage direct investment abroad.

In theory, American Depository Receipts (ADR's) solve or ease many problems of overseas investment. An ADR is a bundle or part of a company's shares, bought in its domestic equity market by a U.S. broker and stored as a deposit in a bank. The ownership of the deposit rather than the underlying shares trade on the U.S. market. According to one market professional, ADR's are like coat check slips which represent ownership of the item, but it is the coat checks that are being traded.' Like silver certificates, ADR's are often easier to hold than the underlying asset.

Listed ADR's trade on the New York and American stock exchanges, and the NASDAQ system operated by the National Association of Securities Dealers. Unsponsored ADR's trade on the O-T-C "pink sheet" market. Except for unsponsored ADR's, companies pay the sponsoring depository and an exchange fee and pay for legal and accounting services. What do corporates get in return?

ADR's have been touted as a panacea for many corporate needs. They are an effective way to diversify a company's shareholder base and increase visibility to investors and the business community. Bankers who sponsor firms claim that an ADR program enhances a company's image as a corporate citizen and expresses a commitment to the U.S. market. ADR's also simplify trading by retail investors and are an efficient way to run an employee stock ownership plan (ESOP). Finally, ADR's provide financial flexibility that complement commercial strategy.

Nintendo, the Japanese home video game maker, issued ADR's in June 1989 as part of a long-term strategy to broaden its reputation from a toy company to a consumer electronics firm. The company, whose Nintendo Entertainment System is in over 20% of American homes, is vigorously pursuing alternative uses for its products, particularly information and teletext disemination for stock prices, sports scores, and home shopping. The ADR's are worth one-fourth of the Japanese share price which in late 1989 was about $90, and can be bought in 100 lot units for under $2500. In contrast, the minimum direct investment in Japanese ordinary shares would cost about $90,000. In such cases, ADR's clearly make foreign shares more accessible to U.S. investors.

As a financing vehicle, ADR's help to establish a track record for a company, paving the way for debt or equity offerings, often through ADR issues. In January 1990, about 50% of ADR listings at the NYSE were new issues. In addition, an increasing number of takeovers are partly financed with ADR's.

Large Institutions Not Universally Enthusiastic

While ADR's have significant uses and can play a part in corporate strategy, are they an effective way to attract American institutional investors? By some measures, they are not. There is a resounding lack of enthusiasm for ADR's among fund managers. Most prefer direct investment into the overseas market, and express interest only if there is no other way to participate. Bankers who specialize in listing ADR's estimate that less than 30% of institutions prefer ADR's. However, ADR's do facilitate trading by institutions with restrictions on overseas activity and by smaller institutions that cannot assemble a diversified portfolio because of high minimum investment amounts in certain stocks. In addition, even larger institutions will hold ADR's along with a core holding in ordinary shares, to provide transactional flexibility.

Among active managers, UBS-Phillips and Drew and Batterymarch Financial both have negative stands on ADR investment. UBS-Phillips and Drew, simply prefers to hold ordinary shares because of its straightforward structure; however, investors will use ADR's if they see them as advantageous. UBS-Phillips and Drew has also on occasion been forced to use ADR's when its global custodian could not get a stock that it wanted to purchase.

Batterymarch, on the other hand, takes a principled and almost ideological stance. According to a senior manager at the firm's Boston headquarters, Batterymarch has never used ADR's and never will. He said the firm is "suspicious of the way ADR's are structured" and claims that they tend to be illiquid.

He added that "ADR's inhibit progress toward uniform global accounting standards by allowing foreign companies to attract investment without full disclosure, beyond the basic information in the annual report. For example, if Japanese companies really wanted to have foreigners owning voting shares, they would have to reveal more information, like sales figures." Batterymarch will only invest directly, and in markets that it considers open and fair.

The accelerating trend toward indexation of U.S. international funds should have an impact on ADR investment, but so far, it has been limited. Few of the major indexers, like Wells Fargo and State Street, use ADR's in their funds. Although State Street will occasionally use ADR's at its own discretion to reduce costs in its comingled funds. County NatWest Investment Management, which specializes in customized and tilt products, also avoids ADR's, instead opting for ordinary shares and derivative products to track the indices.

For big institutions, cost, market access, and global custody are not problems. For smaller funds however, it is much easier and cheaper to simulate an index with a portfolio of ADR's. Using stratified sampling with ADR's, money managers can replicate any of the major global indices, like Morgan Stanley Capital International Perspective's EAFE, the Salomon-Russell EPAC, or FT-Actuaries' EurPac.

Some firms specialize in this type of activity, catering to pension funds with statuatory restrictions and institutions that balk at the expense of global custody. They deliver EAFE without the bugs, by eliminating the back-office nightmares of direct overseas investment.

The most prominent of these firms, Axe Core, has developed computer programs to track indices with a minimal amount of issues. For example, although there are over 1010 components in EAFE, there are only about 300 with ADR's, representing about 60% of the capitalization. Yet this firm's longest running account has had only a 1% tracking error against EAFE over five years.

Fund managers can avoid ADR liquidity problems by purchasing ordinary shares in the domestic market and by creating new ADR's. Others are at the mercy of the market, and many investors have complained about how ADR's trade. In particular, the wide bid/ask spread on the less active NASDAQ and "pink sheet" ADR's has prompted a number of active ADR users to shift to direct investment. It can also be difficult to get a quote at times other than the opening or close.

Money managers who have attempted to short ADR's, either as outright bets against a specific stock or as a proxy for an entire equity market, have had painful experiences. Because of thin volume and the dominance of a few market makers, it is relatively easy to squeeze the holders of ADR short positions. The manager of one large, New York-based hedge fund, which was trading heavily in Japanese ADR's last year, has totally abandoned this strategy, opting instead

Table 1   ADR Availability in the MSCI/EAFE Index

	Percent of EAFE	Percent Available as ADR's	Stocks in EAFE	ADR's in EAFE
Australia	2.09	1.60	66	34
Austria	0.15	0.01	14	1
Belgium	0.75	0.02	22	1
Denmark	0.40	0.06	27	2
Finland	0.33	0.03	21	5
France	3.91	1.24	83	9
Germany	4.14	2.29	56	12
Hong Kong	1.31	1.13	32	16
Italy	2.12	0.59	67	10
Japan	66.23	41.71	264	104
Netherlands	2.11	1.73	24	10
New Zealand	0.19	0.10	13	2
Norway	0.37	0.20	17	5
Singapore	0.69	0.36	53	16
Spain	1.51	0.68	31	4
Sweden	1.37	0.39	37	10
Switzerland	2.09	0.02	52	1
United Kingdom	10.25	7.56	36	62
	100.00%	59.73%	1015	304
Building	5.?2	2.32	87	17
Cap Equipment	11.47	7.30	46	49
Consumer Durables	7.88	7.09	43	20
Energy	4.14	2.71	34	12
Finance	28.??	20.48	188	50
Materials	5.5?	2.34	91	28
Metals	5.16	2.39	47	16
Multi-Industry	?.55	1.81	54	20
Nondurables	9.92	4.92	127	39
Services	8.18	5.35	127	36
Transportation	4.66	1.36	42	10
Utilities	6.88	1.67	29	7
	100.00%	59.73%	1015	304

Source: Axe Core Inc.

Table 2   ADR Facility Comparisons

Type	Act	Registration	Disclosure	Cost	Listing	Raise Capital
Unsponsored	1933	F-6	None	0	OTC	No
	1934	12G3-2(b)	None			
Sponsored Level I	1933	F-6	None	$ 5,000	OTC	Not Now
	1934	12G3-2(b)	None			
Sponsored	1933	F-6	None	$ 75,000	Nat'l Exchaneg or NASDAQ	Not Now
Level II	1934	20-F	Detalied			
Sponsored	1933	F-1	Rigorous	$500,000	Nat'l Exchaneg or NASDAQ	Yes
Level III	1934	20-F	Detailed			

Source: The Bank of New York.

for index futures and options. While Asian corporate managers might be pleased that it is difficult to short ADR's, it also highlights inefficiencies in the market.

Many institutions do not see themselves increasing their use of ADR's for developed Asian markets like Japan, Australia, Hong Kong, and Singapore. Most do, however, look forward to ADR's from limited access markets like South Korea and Taiwan. ADR specialists see a number of creative and breakthrough products coming on line that would enable investors to invest in specific Korean and Taiwanese companies, instead of the shotgun approach of closed-end country funds. Furthermore, for less developed markets such as Thailand, the Phillipines, Indonesia, and India, ADR's will greatly ease market access. There is a general desire for greater disclosure by companies, and a subtle preference for sponsored over unsponsored ADR's since the former reveal more corporate information.

Gains for Corporate Issuers

Since it is uncertain whether ADR's significantly increase the level of foreign investment of major institutions, what clear benefits can ADR's provide Asian corporations? The additional exposure that an ADR program creates helps companies in tangible and intangible ways. Even if large institutions prefer direct overseas investment, the existence of ADR's in the U.S. market often makes money managers more aware of the company, particularly if it becomes a popular, heavily researched equity. A shift in corporate strategy can also be advertised better when concurrent with a sales pitch to investors. Increased economic activity in the U.S. market by Asian corporations is often better received when the company shows its commitment by sponsoring an ADR program.

The visibility factor is supplemented by a definite broadening of the shareholder base. ADR's allow companies to better track their American investors, and to communicate with them. For an Asian company intent on becoming global, ADR's are an especially useful tool. ADR's are also an efficient vehicle for the takeover or restructuring of an American company or subsidiary.

Layers of Corporate Decisions

Once a company decides to launch an ADR program, it faces numerous decisions on the type of listing, degree of disclosure, and level of commitment it must make. Much depends on the corporate objectives. There are four general levels of ADR facilities, ranging from unsponsored programs with minimal registration and lack of disclosure to sponsored programs, with rigorous disclosure, high cost, and ability to raise capital (see chart).

Most Asian ADR's in the United States are unsponsored Japanese shares that were created in the 1970s and are "grandfathered," since they predate the 1983 Securities and Exchange Commission mandated increase in ADR reporting requirements. About 120 of the 140 Japanese ADR's are of this type, and few would meet the more stringent standards enforced now. But many are making the move to upgrade their ADR facilities.

The key decision for corporate finance officers is the degree of disclosure and commitment they are willing to make for their ADR program. Until recently many Asian companies shied away from full disclosure, but now they are more willing to foot the expenses and to invest the time for a major commitment.

Many ADR departments at banks advise their clients to start with a small program, usually sponsored level I (see chart), and then build from that base. Although this procedure requires an F-6 and 20-F registration, it usually costs less than $10,000 and necessitates the disclosure of little more information than is released in the domestic market.

Companies that go beyond unsponsored ADR's must also decide on which exchange to list them. While the NYSE remains the ultimate goal for many companies, it often makes little sense to start with a New York listing. A NASDAQ listing costs much less and gives the company flexibility to move to AMEX or NYSE at a later date. AMEX listings may not have the prestige of the NYSE, but a company is likely to be more visible at the smaller exchange than among the giant U.S. corporations at the NYSE. The company should also consider each market's trading system and how it could effect activity in its stock.

If financing is the main objective of the company, there are now alternatives beyond ADR's. Private placement of foreign equity to U.S. institutional investors has been approved by SEC Rule 144A. The rule ascribes to the concept of caveat emptor in limiting private placements to institutions. The major exchanges naturally opposed this proposal, while investment banks and a number of corporations backed it strongly.

Many Promising Areas

Throughout the Asia-Pacific region, ADR activity is vibrant, despite weak market conditions in 1990. Banks and depository companies are optimistic about the prospects for the coming decade. Most practitioners agree that the biggest volume of business will come from Japan, through ADR upgradings and new issues. With the growing involvement of Japanese companies in the fabric of American business, the companies are realizing that ADR's are an effective way to cement relationships with employees and investors. Japanese firms have found that ADR's serve many purposes.

In a notable departure from tradition, Mitsubishi Bank established a fully-sponsored ADR program in September 1989 on the NYSE. Since Mitsubishi went through the substantial expense—and more significantly, the paperwork of rigorous disclosure—it is likely that it is planning a public offering of some type in the United States. This could set a major precedent for the highly-leveraged Japanese city-banks which now have to meet more stringent Bank for International Settlement primary capital ratio requirements. Could ADR issues become a major part of the equity raising process?

The competition is heating up among depository banks to get service contracts for as many of the 120 upgraded unsponsored Japanese ADR's as possible. The Nintendo issue in June 1989 set its own precedent in tying its ADR's to one depository. Thus much competition for revenue will be on the supply side, as opposed to the previous free-for-all in the unsponsored market. Another major activity will be the unbundling of ADR's issued in the 1970s, when Japanese share prices were low. ADR's on Honda and TDK are now high-priced units consisting of many shares. They will likely be divided into much smaller trading units.

Elsewhere in the region, banks see potential in both the developed and emerging Asia-Pacific equity markets. In the summer of 1989, Citibank upgraded the unsponsored pink-sheet ADR's of Singapore's Keppel Shipyards to listed and sponsored. Depository banks are looking only for the top companies to work within Singapore and Malaysia, since the combined market is relatively small. Other potential areas for ADR's are in privatization, and with companies that are at their limit of foreign ownership. For example, Singapore Airlines is constantly mentioned as a prime candidate for an ADR facility.

Hong Kong has a higher market capitalization than Singapore and has much greater ADR activity, although most are unsponsored. Hong Kong Telecom, Swire Pacific, Jardine Matheson, Hong Kong Land, and Cathay Pacific are among the big names with ADR activity. Other major companies, like Hong Kong Bank and China Power and Light, have stated that they have no interest in ADR programs because the colony's capital markets serve their needs.

The Hong Kong stock market's devastating reaction to the crackdown in China in May and June of 1989 gave losses of up to 50% on major shares. Many U.S. investors stepped in on the buy side, and ADR activity surged. Hundreds of thousands of new ADR's were created by depositories at the request of institutional investors. Many U.S. investors were burned by the October 1987 closure of the Hong Kong Stock Exchange, and now prefer to hold the colony's equities in ADR form.

Australia is familiar terrain for ADR promoters. Dunlop, WestPac Bank, and Broken Hill Proprietary have all recently launched ADR programs. London-based investment banks also consider New Zealand a fertile area, although it may have limited potential because of its small size.

South Korea holds great possibilities for ADR issues too, because of its indebted companies' need for capital and its desire to diversify its shareholders, which are primarily individual. Foreign investment activity in Korea will be severely limited until 1992, but banks are still building bridges to the major industrial groupings like Samsung, Lucky-Goldstar, Hyundai, and Daewoo.

Relations are also being cultivated in Taiwan, whose freewheeling capital markets are as restricted as Korea's. Although companies tend to be smaller in Taiwan and many are family-owned, many would like to develop an institutional shareholder base, especially in the United States. Regulations are slated to loosen substantially in 1991, but the 80% drop in the Taipei market during 1990 has dampened institutional investors' appetite for Taiwanese shares.

Companies from less developed markets, like the Philippines and Thailand, could also benefit from ADR programs. Banks are eyeing firms in India and Indonesia as potential ADR issuers, and even China and Vietnam are considered a potential market in the longer term.

Undoubtably, as the world's economic center of gravity shifts toward the Asia-Pacific region, more global investment funds will be searching for opportunities in the area. ADR's will provide the vehicle for many to capitalize on the commercial growth. While not always the ideal financing tool, ADR's will serve an increasingly important role for Asian companies taking their hard-earned place in the international business arena of the 1990s.

6

ADRs

Joseph M. Velli
American Depository Receipts Bank of New York, New York

Origin

In the early 1900s, Americans began developing interest in non-U.S. stocks but were reluctant to trade in such securities due to risks, delays, inconveniences, and the high costs associated with international trade. Differences between American and foreign laws, as well as varying corporate and financial practices, also deterred international trading in securities. American Depositary Receipts (ADR's) were devised in the late 1920s to help Americans invest in overseas securities and to assist non-U.S. companies wanting to have their stock traded in the United States, while reducing or eliminating the prevailing problems associated with international securities trading.

Description

An ADR is a negotiable receipt issued in certificate form that usually represents an existing outstanding class of equity shares of a non-U.S. company. ADR certificates are issued by a U.S. depositary bank after the actual shares are deposited abroad in a custodian bank, usually by a broker who has purchased them on the open market. Once issued, these certificates may be freely traded in the United States on the over-the-counter market or, under certain circumstances, on a national exchange. The ADR investor may also return the ADR for cancellation, in which case the ADR certificate would be cancelled, and the ordinary shares held with the custodian bank are released back into their home market. At any time, the ADR holder can demand delivery of the actual underlying shares, but normally this does not occur.

ADR certificates state the liability of an American depositary bank in terms of its payment of dividends, proxies, charges, and rights offerings.

ADR's are treated in the same manner as American stock certificates for transfer and ownership purposes. Under certain circumstances, they may also be used to raise equity capital or to make acquisitions.

Benefits of ADR's

ADR's offer many benefits to both U.S. investors and non-U.S. companies. From the standpoint of a non-U.S. company, the benefits associated with an ADR program usually lead to greater investor interest in the ordinary shares that are represented by the ADR. This may lead to increased demand and a higher P/E ratio. Many non-U.S. companies also use ADR's to improve their image and/or promote their products in the United States.

Benefits of ADR's to Non-U.S. Companies

ADR's offer numerous advantages to non-U.S. companies that are interested in marketing their products or perhaps one day raising capital in the United States. Some of these advantages include the following:

- ADR's provide the means for establishing a financial and market record in the United States, paving the way for possible future debt or equity offerings.

- They enlarge the market for non-U.S. company securities, which may lead to an increasing or stabilizing effect on the price of the security through broadened exposure and an increase in demand.

- ADR's serve to bring the non-U.S. company's name before financial, commercial, and public communities in the United States.

- ADR's are a publicly traded security in the United States, and may be used to make acquisitions.

- ADR's increase the liquidity of the securities that they represent.

- The lower costs of owning ADR's, compared with owning ordinary shares, help to make non-U.S. company securities competitive in the

American market. Other non-U.S. company securities that do not use ADR facilities are at a disadvantage.

- Since ADR's are becoming more widely used, they can serve to help a non-U.S. company keep pace with its competitors. In addition, most non-U.S. "blue chips" are traded on numerous exchanges worldwide. A listing in the United States is critical to their investor and commercial perception.

- U.S. institutional investors, such as mutual funds, are in some cases required to take physical possession of securities or to invest only in U.S. dollar denominated securities. These requirements may make it impossible for institutional investors to purchase non-U.S. company securities, unless ADR's are available, which are considered U.S. securities. In addition, most U.S. institutions do not maintain custodians, or safekeeping capabilities, outside of the United States and therefore will not invest internationally unless ADR's are available.

- ADR's establish a controlled trading facility where an underlying or ordinary shares market already exists in the United States.

- Some countries will not allow physical delivery of ordinary shares to other countries. ADR's are a means of overcoming this restriction.

Benefits of ADR's to American Investors

The typical investor in an ADR is an American citizen or institution. However, it is important to realize that non-Americans may also invest in ADR's. ADR's offer the following benefits:

- There is a similarity between ADR's and known instruments, such as American stocks.

- ADR's are freely traded in U.S. markets.

- With ADR's no foreign custodian is necessary. As a result, ADR's can save the investor 25 to 50 basis points in carrying costs, compared to director investing.

- Dividends are converted to dollars and disbursed by a U.S. depositary bank to an ADR holder in a short period of time. This is usually done at a higher rate than that obtained by an individual owning ordinary shares.

- Price quotes are readily obtainable in U.S. dollars and are easily transferable.

- As previously stated, in some cases U.S. institutions require ADR's when investing in non-U.S. companies.

- Individual claims relating to U.S. foreign tax treaties are eliminated. If a double taxation treaty exists, a depositary bank may arrange for less foreign tax to be withheld from the dividend payment. An individual holding ordinary shares would have to claim the foreign tax from the foreign authorities for the additional amounts, which can be a lengthy process.

- In contrast to most foreign securities, ADR's are registered certificates, offering several advantages, including records that protect ownership rights and information about a company that can be mailed to the registered owner.

- ADR's avoid the expenses and legal complexities associated with the death of a shareholder. In such cases, ADR holders only have to consider U.S. laws, not foreign regulations.

- American depositary banks, to the extent feasible, pass on information about corporate activities, which is usually written in English and mailed directly to the ADR holder.

- ADR's eliminate delays and costs of transporting foreign certificates to and from home markets, as well as avoiding foreign custodian expenses.

- There is opportunity to buy and sell securities overseas, thereby making ADR's more negotiable and attractive for investment.

Depositary banks also offer special services to brokers such as safekeeping, clearing, and pre-release. In a pre-release, a depositary bank issues the ADR before the ordinary shares are deposited overseas. This service helps to overcome the problem of differing settlement dates throughout the world.

Types of ADR's

An ADR can be established either on an unsponsored or sponsored basis by an American depositary bank. When a depositary bank establishes an unsponsored ADR, it facilitates foreign security trading where a secondary market or U.S. interest already exists. Normally there is no interaction or administrative input from the foreign company with an unsponsored program. All costs of issuing unsponsored ADR's are absorbed by the investor.

Sponsored programs are usually created when a non-U.S. company plans to do an equity offering and/or list on a national exchange, increase the marketability of its ADR, or control and safeguard its future interests in the United States. The company will appoint a single depositary bank to issue its ADR's and will pay the administrative fees associated with the program.

Trading of ADR's

Once created, ADR's may be traded on the over-the-counter market and are quoted on "pink sheets." U.S. market makers or traders use pink sheets to monitor and trade securities. To be listed on the pink sheets, a broker must request that a particular ADR be included.

If certain filings are made with the Securities Exchange Commission, ADR's may also become eligible for trade on the National Association of Securities Dealers Automated Quotation (NASDAQ) and on American and New York stock exchanges. In order to obtain a listing, the non-U.S. corporation must register with the S.E.C. and meet the specific requirements of the exchange. Usually only corporations involved in an ADR offering seek a listing on one of the national exchanges.

Generally, the ADR will trade at a price equivalent to the price of the shares trading in the home market, after allowing for currency transactions. If a discrepancy between the price of the actual shares in the home market and the ADR exceeds a broker's transaction costs, the broker will buy the ordinary shares and create new ADR's. Similarly, if the ordinary shares are selling at a higher price, the broker will repeatedly buy ADR's, cancel them, and sell the corresponding ordinary shares until an equilibrium is achieved. This process, which is commonly referred to as ADR arbitrage, generally accounts for 3–7% of all ADR trading activity.

Regulatory Aspects

In order for ADR's to be traded in the United States, the S.E.C. requires non-U.S. companies to comply with regulations similar to those that a public domestic company must meet. The S.E.C. believes that if a company wants to trade on an exchange, then that company is voluntarily entering the U.S. market and is, therefore, subject to U.S. regulations. However, for those companies that have an ADR program, do not desire to be listed on a national exchange, and are not planning an immediate equity offering in the U.S., the S.E.C. asserts that the company has not voluntarily entered the market. In this case, the ADR is only facilitating trade in a market that already exists. For this situation the S.E.C. has created an exemption from full registration. Generally, in order to obtain an exemption, the S.E.C. must be supplied with all the public information the law requires about the non-U.S. company's home country. This information, which must be supplied to the S.E.C. on an ongoing basis, must include all filings made with the country's stock exchanges and all public announcements.

Exemption from registration is commonly referred to as the "Information Supplying Exemption" or the "ADR Exemption." Once an exemption has been established or registration has been made (usually by completing Form 20-F) with the S.E.C., a depositary bank is eligible to issue the ADR's.

Form 20-F is a consolidated registration and annual report similar in content to the Form 10-K annual report used by U.S. issuers, however, significant disclosure accommodations have been made for non-U.S. issuers using Form 20-F.

With regards to the S.E.C. exemption (Rule 12g3-2[b]), any non-U.S. company with more than 300 U.S. shareholders must register with the S.E.C. or establish the exemption. If a company does have more than 300 U.S. holders and does not register or establish the exemption, the S.E.C. may take action against that company.

If the company wishes to raise capital or be listed on a national exchange through an ADR equity offering in the United States, they must register with the S.E.C. Usually no exemption is available.

The S.E.C. has developed special forms and rules which apply to offerings made in the United States by non-U.S. corporations. These rules and registration forms tend to be less burdensome to non-U.S. companies than the disclosure requirements imposed on U.S. corporations.

Stock Exchange Listings

To list ADR's on a national exchange, or quoted on NASDAQ, the non-U.S. company must apply to the organization of choice and comply with the appropriate exchange's disclosure requirements (regarding content, method, and timing) over and above the requirements of the S.E.C. On the American and New York exchanges, there are alternate listing standards available for those non-U.S. companies that would otherwise qualify but do not have a wide enough distribution of shares in the United States.

ADRs in the NASDAQ Market

Douglas F. Parrillo
N.A.S.D., Washington

The equity securities of many international companies are traded every day by U.S. investors searching for investment opportunities. For the convenience of U.S. investors, many of these securities trade in the form of American Depositary Receipts, or ADR's.

The Advantages of ADR's

An ADR is simply a certificate or receipt, issued by a U.S. bank, that represents title to a specified number of shares deposited by an overseas corporation in its home country. The ADR may be freely traded in the United States, without the delivery of the underlying shares that it represents. This has a number of advantages to the investor: (1) the certificate generally conforms to U.S. standards; (2) settlement and transfer of ADR's take place in the same way as settlement and transfer of any U.S. security; (3) it avoids the double commission fees that often accompany foreign shares purchased or sold directly, as well as other charges that vary from country to country; (4) the issuing U.S. bank ensures timely dividend distributions and timely notification of corporate developments outside the United States; and (5) although ADR investors cannot participate in rights offerings, the issuing bank will try to sell the rights offered and to distribute the funds to ADR holders.

ADR's also have substantial benefits for overseas corporations. They include:

- Ready access to the U.S. capital market, with opportunities for both initial offerings and secondary issues

- Adjustment of the unit price of a security to a level acceptable to U.S. investors

- Support for equity-based compensation plans to attract and keep qualified U.S. personnel

- Heightened visibility, not only for a security, but also for a company and its products

- Greater liquidity through a broader shareholder base

- Often, increased share price and trading volume in the issuer's home country

- Assistance in acquisitions. The acquisition of a U.S. company for stock can be accomplished on a tax-free basis only with SEC-registered securities, which ADR's are.

Preference for NASDAQ

The NASDAQ market is home to more American companies than any other U.S. market. It is also the home-away-from-home for more international companies than all other U.S. markets combined. Many of the world's most dynamic companies, including Jaguar, Fuji, Reuters, Volvo, Cadbury Schweppes, have their ADR's traded in the NASDAQ market.

Why NASDAQ?

There are nine major reasons why overseas companies elect to have their ADR's traded in the NASDAQ market.

1. **NASDAQ is the stock market of tomorrow—today.** It is a screen-based dealer market, spanning the U.S. and the globe. It is a competitive market, where multiple market makers compete openly with one another for order flow in a security. These unique characteristics of NASDAQ have made it an international market model, emulated by the International Stock Exchange in London, the Singapore Stock Exchange, and others.

2. **NASDAQ is a world-class market, the second largest equity market in the U.S. and the third largest in the world.** In the last decade, NASDAQ annual share and dollar volume have grown approximately

Figure 1   ADR Share Volume and Issues NASDAQ, NYSE, and Amex 1988

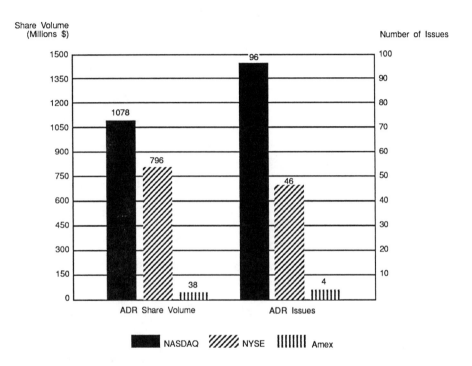

ten times. In terms of share volume, NASDAQ accounts for 42% of the volume of the three principal U.S. securities markets.

3. **U.S. investors look to the NASDAQ market for the securities of major growth companies.** Of the principal U.S. stock markets, NASDAQ has the highest percentage of fast-growing, high-technology, and service companies. Many of the most prominent new-generation companies are listed on NASDAQ—MCI Communications Corporation, Apple Computer, Intel Corporation, Microsoft Corporation, and DSC Communications Corporation, among others. They are consistently among the NASDAQ leaders, by share volume and market value. At the same time, NASDAQ is home to many of the largest U.S. financial service companies, including banks, savings and loans, and insurance companies.

4. **A substantial number of overseas companies identify with the NASDAQ market because of the domestic and foreign companies that are in it.** Since 1983, among the non-U.S. corporations that have listed their ADR's on NASDAQ include:

- Australia: Melcorp Securities, Great Eastern Mines, Pacific Dunlop, and Ramtron.

- England: Cadbury Schweppes, Carlton Communications, English China Clays, Huntingdon International Holdings, Jaguar, Reuters Holdings, and United Newspapers.

- Finland: Instrumentarium Corporation.

- France: Rhone-Poulenc, LVMH Moet Hennessey Louis Vuitton, and Thomson-CSF.

- Ireland: Institute of Clinical Pharmacology, Elan Corporation, and Waterford Glass Group.

- Japan: CSK Corporation.

- The Netherlands: Aegon and Oce-van der Grinten.

- Norway: Norsk Data.

- Sweden: Asea, L.M. Ericsson, Gambro, Svenska Cellulosa, Electrolux, SKF, and Volvo.

5. **NASDAQ's competitive multiple market-maker system offers benefits that are not available from a stock exchange's single specialist system.** Nine hundred U.S. companies on NASDAQ meet the financial requirements for listing on the New York Stock Exchange, and 2,100 could list on the Amex. These U.S. companies make NASDAQ their stock market of choice because they prefer its competitive multiple market-maker system. Superior liquidity, greater financial resources in support of an issuer, security sponsorship through research on companies, and recommendations of securities to a client network are the advantages that distinguish NASDAQ's market-maker system from the single specialist system of the U.S. exchanges.

6. **NASDAQ is a more liquid market.** Scholars at Texas A&M University have prepared three independent academic studies—one of which was published by Georgetown University's *The Journal of Financial Research*—that demonstrate the superior liquidity of the NASDAQ market. They attribute this to NASDAQ's multiple market-maker system. The average non-U.S. security on NASDAQ has more than 10

market makers, which exceeds the average for domestic securities on NASDAQ.

7. **The cost of capital in the NASDAQ market is competitive with that in U.S. exchange markets.** Several academic studies demonstrate that the cost of capital for U.S. companies whose securities are traded in the NASDAQ market is comparable to that of companies traded on U.S. exchanges.

8. **The NASDAQ National Market System (NASDAQ/NMS) uniquely combines the competitive multiple market-maker system with transaction reporting.** This combination provides securities industry professionals and individual and institutional investors with running price and volume information for each NASDAQ/NMS security.

9. The NASDAQ market is a highly visible market. Market data on all NASDAQ securities are available on more than 200,000 quotation terminals located in the United States and 48 other countries. Some 220 U.S. and non-U.S. newspapers, including the *International Herald Tribune*, *USA Today International*, and the European edition of *The Wall Street Journal*, publish major NASDAQ stock tables.

Listing an ADR on NASDAQ

A non-U.S. corporation seeking to have its ADR's traded in the NASDAQ market must satisfy the following requirements:

- Be registered pursuant to Section 12(g) of the Securities Exchange Act of 1934.

- Have total assets of 2 million U.S. dollars.

- Have capital and surplus (net worth) of 1 million U.S. dollars.

- Have two market makers.

The 12(g) registration requirement essentially subjects the overseas corporation to disclosure and reporting standards that are comparable to those for U.S. companies. The document generally used to accomplish 12(g) registration is the SEC's Form 20-F, which is quite similar in form and content to the Form 10-K filed by U.S. issuers. The Form 20-F must either be prepared in accordance with U.S. generally accepted accounting principles (GAAP) or must be accompanied by an explanation of the major differences between GAAP, and the accounting principles followed by the filing non-U.S. corporation.

Table 1   Leading NASDAQ ADR's in 1988

ADR	Dollar Volume ($ mil)	12/31/88 Closing Price	
Reuters	2,370	28	3/8
DeBeers	885	10	3/4
Cadbury Schweppes	629	61	1/8
Beecham Group	411	16	3/4
Jaguar	384	4	23/32
Ericsson Telephone	326	59	1/8
Volvo	309	63	
NEC Corporation	288	78	1/2
Minorco	287	11	3/8
Pharmacia	246	23	
Fuji Photo Film	209	56	7/8
Elan Corporation	183	10	1/8
Electrolux	183	47	1/4
Tokio Marine & Fire	180	91	3/8
Fisons	177	16	1/2
Toyota	176	40	1/2
Vaal Reefs	142	6	11/16
Huntingdon International	125	27	3/4
Telefonos de Mexico	124		9/32
ASEA AB	116	63	1/2
AB/SKF	102	64	7/8

Trading an ADR in NASDAQ/NMS

The nearly 2,900 largest and most active NASDAQ securities traded in NASDAQ/NMS are traded under real-time, last-sale reporting conditions; are automatically eligible for purchase in margin accounts by ruling of the Federal Reserve Board; and are automatically exempt from the registration requirements in many states.

If a non-U.S. corporation wishes to have its ADR's traded in NASDAQ/NMS, it must meet the following requirements shown in Table 2.

NASDAQ/NMS Corporate Governance Standards

In addition to the quantitative criteria, NASDAQ/NMS companies must meet a set of qualitative requirements, generally described as corporate governance

Table 2   Nasdaq National Market System—Quantitative Standards

	Initial Nasdaq/NMS Inclusion		Continued Nasdaq/ NMS
Standard	**Alternative 1**	**Alternative 2**	**Inclusion**
Registration under Section 12(g) of the Securities Exchange Act of 1934 or equivalent	Yes	Yes	Yes
Net Tangible Assets[1]	$4 million	$12 million	$2 million or $4 million[2]
Net Income (in last fiscal year or two of last three fiscal years)	$400,000	—	—
Pretax Income (in last fiscal year or two of last three fiscal years)	$700,000	—	—
Public Float (Shares)[3]	500,000	1 million	200,000
Operating History	—	3 years	—
Market Value of Float	$3 million	$15 million	$1 million
Minimum Bid	$5	—	—
Shareholders	—	400	400[4]
—if between 0.5 and 1 million shares publicly held	800	—	—
—if more than 1 million shares publicly held	400	—	—
—if more than 0.5 million shares publicly held and average daily volume in excess of 2,000 shares	400	—	—
Number of Market Makers	2	2	2

[1]"Net tangible assets" means total assets (excluding good will) minus total liabilities.
[2]Continued Nasdaq/NMS inclusion requires net tangible assets of at least $2 million if the issuer has sustained losses from continuing operations and/or net losses in two of its three most recent fiscal years or $4 million if the issuer has sustained losses from the continuing operations and/or net losses in three of its four most recent fiscal years.
[3]Public float is defined as shares that are not "held directly or indirectly by any officer or director of the issuer and by any person who is the beneficial owner of of more than 10 percent of the total shares outstanding . . ."
[4]Or 300 shareholders of round lots.

standards. *The NASD may exempt foreign issuers from these rules, if compliance would be in contravention of laws or business practice in the issuer's country of domicile.* Where this is not the case, the corporate governance standards require a NASDAQ/NMS company to:

• Maintain a minimum of two independent directors on its board

• Establish an audit committee, a majority of the members of which are independent directors

- Distribute to shareholders an annual report and make available copies of interim reports

- Examine all related-party transactions to review potential conflicts of interest

- Hold an annual meeting of shareholders and provide notice of such meeting to the NASD

- Specify in the company bylaws that, for purposes of shareholder meetings, a quorum is not less than 33.33% of the outstanding shares of the company's common stock

- Obtain prior shareholder approval of certain new-issue distributions

- Solicit proxies and provide proxy statements for all meetings of shareholders, as well as file such proxy solicitations with the NASD

- Comply with SEC Rule 19c-4, which prohibits companies from disenfranchising existing shareholders by taking any action that would nullify, restrict, or disparately reduce the per-share voting rights of its existing stockholders

- Execute a NASDAQ/NMS listing agreement

Required Filings by ADR Issuers

Once an ADR is listed on NASDAQ, its issuer, through its representatives in the United States, must file with NASDAQ on the same date the documents required of it by SEC registration. These include:

- On an annual basis, Form 20-F, containing audited financial statements and various narrative disclosures

- On an interim basis, Form 6-K, to disclose significant corporate events, such as management changes, material payments to directors or principal shareholders, granting of options, and key business transactions.

Required Notifications

The SEC and the NASD also require certain types of notification in a timely manner.

1. **Dividend, Split, or Rights Notification.** Exchange Act Rule 10b-17 requires that notice be sent to the NASD 10 days prior to the record date of:
   - A dividend or other distribution in cash or kind, including a dividend or distribution of a security

   - A stock split or reverse split

   - A rights or other subscription offering

   This advance notice enables the NASD to set the ex-date four days prior to the record date in the case of a cash dividend. The ex-date is the date on which a stock is transferred without the right to the current dividend. In the case of a 25% or greater stock dividend or stock split, the ex-date will be set the first business day following the payable date. The advance notice will also enable the NASD to display the amount and type of dividend paid on the NASDAQ System terminals on the ex-date and to adjust the applicable index values.

   In the case of the issuance of rights and warrants, 10 days' advance notice may not be practicable. In such cases, information concerning the distribution should be provided to the NASD on or before the record date and in no event later than the date the registration statement becomes effective with the SEC or other regulatory agency.

2. *Name and Shares Outstanding Changes.* Exchange Act Rules 13a-17 and 15d-17 require notice to the SEC and the NASD on Form 10-C no later than 10 days after the effective date of a corporate name change and changes in the number of shares outstanding for NASDAQ stock issues of 5% or more than last reported.

   As a result of a name change, it may be necessary to assign a new NASDAQ symbol. A change of 5% or more in the number of shares outstanding requires an adjustment to be made to the base value of the applicable NASDAQ indices.

3. *Material News Notification (Trading Halts).* Schedule D of the NASD By-Laws requires NASDAQ companies to promptly publically disclose any material information that may affect the value of their securities or influence investors' decisions. The NASD Board of Governors requires

that NASDAQ companies notify the NASD of the release of any such information prior to its release to the public.

Upon receipt of the information, the NASD, after consultation with the company, will determine whether a trading halt in the security is appropriate. A trading halt provides the public with an opportunity to evaluate the information and consider it in making investment decisions. It also alerts the marketplace to the fact that news has been released.

Rules for Market Makers

Some 570 firms, spread across the entire United States, make markets in NASDAQ securities. They have 50,000 market-making positions, for an average of 10 market makers per security. Very active securities have upwards of 40 market makers. NASD rules require market makers to make two-sided markets (i.e., both buy and sell a security at their quoted bid and ask prices); to execute transactions at their displayed quotations and for displayed size; and to enter quotations reasonably related to the prevailing market. These quotations should not exceed the parameters for maximum allowable spreads, as set by the NASD.

For market makers in NASDAQ/NMS securities, the NASD imposes affirmative obligations that mandate their participation in the NASD's automated Small Order Execution System. These requirements impose financial commitments on market makers, as well as significant economic penalties for unexcused withdrawal from the system.

Clearance and Settlement

All ADR transactions may be executed by members over the computer, via a NASDAQ terminal, using a variety of automated services that bypass the telephone. They produce what are called locked-in trades. That is, the transactions executed via these services are automatically confirmed, reported to NASDAQ for dissemination to subscribers and vendors over the NASDAQ network, and sent to the clearing corporation for prompt settlement. Another new service allows parties to telephone trades to avail themselves of the same post-execution locked-in features of the other services to speed the confirmation and settlement process. These services make the NASDAQ market one of the most efficient in the world.

Regulation

NASDAQ is a highly regulated market. The NASD carries out this activity through an integrated regulatory plan, involving centralized market surveillance and a nationwide broker-dealer inspection program.

The NASD uses state-of-the-art automated systems for the continuous surveillance of the NASDAQ market. For every NASDAQ issue, including every ADR, parameters for price and volume are built into NASDAQ's on-line and off-line automated systems. Unusual trading patterns are automatically flagged and immediately reviewed by professional analysts. This sophisticated, computer-assisted market surveillance both detects and deters violations of the trading rules.

One objective of NASD's broker-dealer surveillance program is to determine members' compliance with rules relating to sales practices and financial and operational condition. Firms are required to submit monthly, quarterly, and annual financial reports that respond to all NASD requests for information. Firms are also required to register employees who have passed the qualifications examinations so that those employees can sell securities or supervise others. Members must also submit their underwritings, advertising, and sales literature to the NASD for review.

Global Market for ADR's

ADR's on NASDAQ trade in an efficient and vigorously surveilled market offering global exposure to investors. As already indicated, 200,000 securities salesmen's quotation terminals in 49 countries display NASDAQ information. Outside of the United States, the largest concentrations of such terminals are found in the United Kingdom, Canada, Switzerland, West Germany, France, the Netherlands, Japan, Hong Kong, and Luxembourg, making NASDAQ ADR's visible throughout the premier equity markets of the world.

SECTION **IV**

THE EUROPEAN
EQUITY MARKETS

8

U.K. Equity Market

Carolyn Moses
Shearson Lehman Hutton, London

Introduction

Both the historical development and modern existence of the U.K. stock market are focused inside one square mile of territory corresponding to the medieval walled town of London. This small area of today's metropolis between St. Paul's Cathedral and the Tower of London is still properly known and governed as the city of London. Thus, the colloquial terms "the city" or "the square mile" imply in the U.K. financial world everything connoted by Wall Street in the United States.

Historical Development

During the seventeenth century, buying and selling of shares in joint stock enterprises was conducted in and around the coffee houses of London. The market was first centralized as the London Stock Exchange in its own building in 1773, with its first set of rules of conduct adopted in 1802. During the nineteenth century 20 regional exchanges were established to service the needs of local industry and investors, whereas the twentieth century has been a period of consolidation. In 1965 the U.K. stock exchanges formed a federation, followed in 1973 by full unification. Two centuries after its first dedicated building was occupied, the London Stock Exchange moved to modern premises. It has since

cupied, the London Stock Exchange moved to modern premises. It has since changed its name to the International Stock Exchange (ISE), so as to reflect the multinational character of business conducted and listed there.

Many traditional practices, including trading on the floor of the Exchange, were swept away with the reforms of Big Bang on October 27, 1986, which dramatically deregulated, automated, and expanded U.K. stock broking. The number of participants in the market soared, the new screen-based dealing system worked admirably, and business boomed until the market crash one year later. Since then, more straightened market conditions have caused some rationalization in the stock broking industry and modifications to the new practices of Big Bang. There will no doubt be further evolution. The following chapter details the state of the market in July 1989 when U.K. equities had just regained their pre-crash price level.

Scale and Scope of the Market

The U.K. equity market is the third largest by capitalization in the world. While only about one quarter of the size of the Japanese or the U.S. market, it typically accounts for a little less than 10% of total world capitalization. Capitalization of equities listed on the ISE at the end of June 1989 was £1735 bn, growing since June 1980 at an average annual compound growth rate of 40.75%. The total number of companies with a listing on the exchange in mid-1989 was 3047, of which 1962 were U.K. companies, 60 were Irish, and 530 were international companies. There were 432 companies registered on the Unlisted Securities Market, and 63 on the Third Market. Average daily trading volume in July 1989 was £1082.1 mn (customer business only), or 456.8 million shares and 29,258 bargains per day. The value of turnover has grown since 1980 at an average annual compound rate of 27.7%.

Securities traded on the ISE include U.K., Irish, and overseas company shares (ordinary, deferred, preference) and U.K., Irish, and overseas fixed-interest securities (gilts, convertibles, corporate bonds and Eurobonds). Options (on U.K. and overseas shares, the FT-SE index, currencies, and gilts) are still traded by open outcry on the floor of the exchange within the London Traded Options Market. Of relevance to equity investors is also the futures contract on the FT-SE index transacted on the London International Financial Futures Exchange (LIFFE). Regional offices of the ISE are located in Belfast, Birmingham, Bristol, Dublin, Edinburgh, Glasgow, Leeds, Liverpool, Manchester, and Newcastle. Active trading is still carried out on the floors at Birmingham, Dublin, and Glasgow.

The ISE has two junior equity markets. The Unlisted Securities Market (USM), which began in November 1980, provides a formal regulated market for smaller, less mature companies that might be unlikely or unable to comply with

gained access to the financing and dealing opportunities of the stock market—marketability, respectability, and visibility—in exchange for public disclosure of their financial positions and some regulation by the exchange. Several companies have done so well on the USM that they were promoted to full listing status. The Third Market, which started in January 1987, exists for companies that are too small or new to meet the requirements of the USM. Such companies must be sponsored by a stock exchange member firm. Their share price might be shown on dealing screens, but trading is done over the counter. Details of current listing and publicity requirements for the three equity sections of the ISE are in the following table.

The future of the junior markets is under review and likely to be altered. The ISE is examining the impact of EC regulations which will unify listing requirements across Europe and enable mutual recognition of any company listed on any European stock exchange. As a result, the ISE might have to reduce its trading-record requirement for full listing from five years to three, and the USM's to less than three. Other options include merging all three markets into one, but with different listing requirements for different types of companies, or merging the USM and Third Market into a single junior venue.

Restructuring the Market: Big Bang

Prior to the reforms of Big Bang, the London stock market operated more like a closed gentlemen's club, with very tight constraints on membership and outside ownership, single capacity operators, and fixed minimum commissions. These rules were ultimately judged to be anti-competitive and to be restrictive trade practices under U.K. law. As a result, the London Stock Exchange made an agreement with the U.K. government in July 1983 to reform itself rather than be prosecuted. Big Bang was designed over a three year period, with the reforms being introduced together on October 27, 1986, rather than in a piecemeal fashion.

The major changes were as follows. First, fixed minimum commissions, which had prevailed since 1912, were abolished. Average transaction expenses have now fallen by 50%, with net trading (zero stated commission) often possible for bigger investors.

Second, single capacity trading, enforced since 1908 to separate wholesalers (jobbers) from retailers (brokers), gave way to dual capacity. All member firms are now broker/dealers, able to act as broker (agent) for end-investors or as dealer (principal) for the firm's own account. In addition, member firms can choose to be market makers, required to make markets or wholesale in key stocks and stand by the publicly displayed prices at all times. Market makers trade with other broker/dealers and with clients directly.

Table 1   Comparison of ISE Markets

	Official List	USM	Third Market
Minimum market capitalization	£700,000 for equities (but normally sponsors look for companies over £10 million for market liquidity and cost reasons)	No minimum	No minimum
Minimum trading record	5 years	3 years	Usually 1 year
Annual profit before taxation	No minimum but sponsors normally look for over £10 million	No minimum	No minimum
Annual turnover of company	No minimum but sponsors normally look for over £1 million	No minimum but normally over £500,000	No minimum
Minimum percentage of shares which must be held publicly	25%	10%	No minimum
Latest audited results in prospectus	Within six months	Within nine months	Usually within nine months unless a greenfield company
Threshold percentage for circulars to shareholders on acquisitions and disposals after flotation	15% of the assets or profit before taxation or equity being issued	25% of the assets or profit before taxation or equity being issued	No threshold, but recommended at 25%
Publicity Requirements:			
Introductions and Placings	One formal notice in a national daily newspaper and circulation of listing particulars in the Extel Statistical Services	One formal notice in a daily newspaper and circulation of prospectus in the Extel Statistical Services	One formal notice in a daily newspaper and circulation of prospectus in the Extel Statistical Services.
Offers for Sale	Listing particulars to be published in two national daily newspapers and circulated in the Extel Statistical Services	One formal notice in a daily newspaper	One formal notice in a daily newspaper

Third, the limitation on outside ownership in a member firm to less than 30% was removed. This change opened the door for major international securities companies and investment and commercial banks to play a full role in U.K. stockbroking, replacing the poorly capitalized local partnerships of brokers of the past. This opening to global participation and trading was reinforced in November 1986, when the London Stock Exchange agreed to merge with the International Securities Regulatory Organization (representing international banks and securities houses in London) becoming the ISE. Growing numbers of blue-chip multinational companies have listed their shares on the international section of ISE (SEAQ International) to facilitate transactions when their home markets are closed, to take advantage of London's greater liquidity, and to be more accessible to the global investment community centered in London.

Fourth, a computerized screen-based pricing and dealing system was introduced. The Stock Exchange Automated Quotations system (SEAQ) has improved the efficiency, visibility and competitiveness of the market by giving all participants the same universe of share-trading price and volume information at the same time and in the same manner. Market makers are required to show on SEAQ their bid and offer and transaction size quotes for stocks they have agreed to stand by. They must also report every deal to SEAQ within five minutes of its completion. Because SEAQ now delivers all the necessary dealing and market-making information to desks nation-wide and overseas wherever a screen is installed, the floor of the ISE has been deserted by all except options traders. In that sense, although London retains the concentration of U.K. equity business and there is little role for regional exchanges, there is no longer a single physical marketplace where transactions must be conducted. While most trades are executed by telephone calls with client, broker, and market maker, small deals up to 5000 shares in most stocks can be completed at the best SEAQ price through an automatic electronic link from broker to market maker, this transaction is called SAEF—SEAQ Automatic Execution Facility.

The Market Since Big Bang

After some minor teething troubles, the SEAQ system and new rules of operation have worked well throughout a period of unprecedented market fluctuations. The bull market in 1987, with record levels of turnover and issues, was followed by the market crash in October 1987, which sharply raised price volatility and short-term activity. Since the crash, turnover, liquidity, and issuing activity have fallen back to expose overcapacity in the securities industry. Overall, there is now greater competition, liquidity, depth, and transparency to the U.K. equity market with typically more market makers for each actively traded stock than before. Price spreads have narrowed and transaction costs have halved.

There are 28 market makers now operating on narrower margins, with total revenue depressed by the lower volume of transactions since the crash. In response, some withdrawals from market-making have already occurred, and the ISE has amended two operating rules to relieve some of the competitive pressures on market makers. After investigating price volatility, resulting from instant publication on SEAQ of details on large trades in less liquid market conditions, the ISE made the following changes in February 1989. Market makers are no longer obligated to make firm prices to one another; and SEAQ publication of details for trades in excess of £100,000 will be on the following day rather than instantaneously. Further restructuring in the industry and evolution of Big Bang's reforms are likely as experience under differing market conditions grows. The ISE constantly and closely monitors the quality of the market.

How U.K. Equities Are Classified

Equities with the largest turnover, market capitalization, spread of ownership, and market-maker backing are classified as alpha shares. Each alpha stock has a SEAQ page with its price and volume quotes from market makers. Information from reported trades will be immediately displayed on SEAQ, but details of large deals are displayed the next day. (Large deals account for 75% of customer business by value, but only 7% of bargains.) Average total market size of alphas at the end of March 1989 was 781,000 shares.

Beta shares are less actively traded, capitalized, and spread across shareholders and are supported by fewer market makers than alpha stocks. Continuous firm price quotes will be displayed on SEAQ up to a stated deal limit. Hard-copy publication of beta trade details is available on the next day in the ISE's Daily Official List. Average total market size for beta shares at end-March 1989 was 145,000 shares.

The average total market size for gamma shares, the next category down the scale, was 23,800 shares. Indicative two-way price quotes will be provided on screen for gamma stocks, and market makers are required to make firm gamma prices on enquiry. Trade details are also reported the next day in the ISE's Daily Official List. Delta category covers all other equities in which little trade takes place. No prices for deltas are displayed on SEAQ, but the contact names of interested broker/dealers are shown. Market-maker coverage in the first half of 1989 was 14.2 for alphas, 6.3 for betas, 3.3 for gammas, and 1.1 for deltas.

Equity Indices

The oldest U.K. stock market index is the Financial Times Industrial Ordinary Index, first compiled in 1935. Because it comprises the shares of 30 leading companies, it is usually referred to as the FT30 index and can be compared with the Dow Jones Industrial Average index in New York. As such, it is blue-chip but more volatile and less representative than broader market indices. It is calculated as an unweighted geometric mean, every minute throughout the trading day.

A wider market indicator was started on January 3, 1984, by the Stock Exchange (SE) and Financial Times (FT), incorporating the top 100 U.K. companies. Accounting for about 70% of the total market value of all U.K. equities, it shows a very close historical correlation with the most broad index of the market. Called the FT-SE 100 index, or "footsie," it has become the most watched and quoted measure of the market and is calculated continuously throughout the day. There are FT-SE 100 options and futures contracts. Membership of this index is reviewed quarterly, taking into account significant changes in valuation, mergers, acquisitions, and new issues. Constituent companies cannot have residence overseas for tax purposes, subsidiaries of other FT-SE companies, new entrants without dividend prospects, or be subject to large static shareholdings. FT-SE 100 is calculated as a weighted arithmetic index. Base value is 1000 at the opening of business on January 3, 1984. While the news-making stocks are forever changing, the ten most-traded FTSE stocks (by value) during the first half of 1989 were British Steel, Gateway Corporation (now taken over), British Gas, Hanson Trust, GEC, Racal Electronics, ASDA Group, British Telecom, BP, and Rolls Royce.

On a broader scale, the Financial Times and the Faculty and Institute of Actuaries supervise a whole range of daily market indices (the FT-A series). For example, the FT-A Industrial Group Index (486 shares) comprises the industrial sectors like capital goods and electronics. Adding oil and gas companies with the former completes the FT-A 500 Index. Finally, the FT-A All Share Index combines the previous two indexes with the broadest measure of the market. The All Share includes over 700 companies (not all quoted U.K. companies) and is calculated daily as a weighted arithmetic index. Several other proprietorial indices for the U.K. equity market are also available.

The U.K. equity market went through an extremely difficult period in the 1970s. Two OPEC oil shocks, soaring inflation, disruptive periods of labor unrest and strikes, sterling crises, and extremely high taxes all greatly undermined

Figure 1   FT-Actuaries Share Indices

These indices are the joint compilation of the Financial Times,
the Institute of Actuaries and the Faculty of Actuaries

EQUITY GROUPS & SUB-SECTIONS	Monday July 31 1989					Fri Jul 28	Thu Jul 27	Wed Jul 26	Year ago (approx)
Figures in parentheses show number of stocks per section	Index No.	Day's Change %	Est. Earnings Yield% (Max.)	Gross Div. Yield% (Act at 25%)	Est. P/E Ratio (Net)	xd adj. 1989 to date	Index No.	Index No.	Index No.	Index No.
1 CAPITAL GOODS (206)	990.24	-0.5	10.76	4.05	11.43	19.57	995.55	988.39	983.17	812.63
2 Building Materials (29)	1215.05	-0.6	12.14	4.36	10.26	25.92	1222.73	1218.70	1211.50	1026.41
3 Contracting, Construction (37)	1624.16	-0.3	14.59	4.33	8.96	32.70	1628.82	1627.14	1615.16	1604.20
4 Electricals (9)	2941.47	-0.1	7.95	3.91	15.56	50.60	2944.44	2933.92	2929.26	2225.74
5 Electronics (30)	2262.74	-0.9	8.58	3.31	15.22	43.06	2283.36	2264.58	2258.95	1767.29
6 Mechanical Engineering (55)	545.78	-0.6	9.81	3.89	12.50	9.57	549.15	546.13	543.74	424.87
8 Metals and Metal Forming (6)	531.29	+0.3	19.31	5.61	5.68	14.84	529.82	529.05	525.13	501.30
9 Motors (17)	359.51	-0.1	10.29	4.22	11.41	6.83	359.74	345.01	344.43	288.55
10 Other Industrial Materials (23)	1689.03	-0.6	9.17	4.15	13.02	33.56	1698.93	1695.55	1678.46	1341.17
21 CONSUMER GROUP (186)	1325.09	-0.2	8.27	3.22	15.19	20.36	1328.15	1312.95	1299.50	1108.25
22 Brewers and Distillers (22)	1451.71	-0.7	9.20	3.37	13.59	21.93	1462.51	1435.87	1424.39	1121.11
25 Food Manufacturing (20)	1197.52	-0.4	8.43	3.49	14.84	20.55	1202.02	1198.49	1191.14	1016.66
26 Food Retailing (14)	2535.21	....	7.96	2.72	16.61	32.27	2533.86	2519.83	2489.79	2001.18
27 Health and Household (14)	2370.46	+0.2	6.19	1.73	19.03	22.24	2365.86	2346.44	2313.59	1885.93
29 Leisure (33)	1757.13	-0.1	7.17	3.17	17.30	29.39	1759.03	1731.65	1716.15	1354.05
31 Packaging & Paper (15)	601.25	-1.0	9.75	4.12	12.95	9.11	607.07	603.19	601.67	539.17
32 Publishing & Printing (19)	3797.26	+0.1	8.37	4.38	15.40	72.55	3791.66	3755.37	3696.58	3645.24
34 Stores (34)	889.01	-0.3	10.09	4.09	12.94	16.19	891.79	873.26	864.37	810.81
35 Textiles (15)	558.21	-0.9	10.71	5.20	11.18	15.06	563.23	562.63	556.14	612.74
40 OTHER GROUPS (94)	1185.34	-0.7	9.73	4.01	12.51	20.52	1193.70	1188.51	1179.25	988.96
41 Agencies (17)	1479.51	+0.8	7.15	2.28	17.34	18.99	1468.43	1454.87	1410.70	1124.63
42 Chemicals (23)	1311.14	-0.8	11.20	4.73	10.55	28.02	1321.52	1315.42	1311.36	1075.39
43 Conglomerates (13)	1706.05	-0.4	10.03	4.78	11.73	26.22	1712.65	1695.98	1689.77	1230.41
45 Transport (13)	2475.65	-0.3	8.48	3.64	15.32	39.22	2482.11	2495.21	2467.23	1945.09
47 Telephone Networks (2)	1078.34	-0.7	11.37	4.60	11.46	22.38	1085.68	1075.20	1075.73	971.16
48 Miscellaneous (26)	2019.88	-1.7	8.11	2.95	13.98	29.00	2053.95	2058.78	2039.59	1214.98
49 INDUSTRIAL GROUP (486)	1217.84	-0.4	9.35	3.67	13.22	20.83	1223.29	1213.16	1203.20	988.96
51 Oil & Gas (14)	2158.79	-0.4	9.84	5.18	13.52	64.24	2168.22	2159.56	2154.58	1845.63
59 500 SHARE INDEX (500)	1297.94	-0.4	9.41	3.86	13.26	24.38	1303.74	1293.67	1284.04	1061.60
61 FINANCIAL GROUP (124)	788.54	+0.4	–	5.08	–	18.87	785.13	774.19	770.09	710.33
62 Banks (9)	783.25	+0.9	22.06	6.20	5.96	23.46	776.22	749.67	747.21	666.52
65 Insurance (Life) (8)	1177.11	-0.2	–	5.07	–	29.86	1179.12	1175.42	1168.58	1090.17
66 Insurance (Composite) (7)	627.40	+0.6	–	5.74	–	16.75	623.48	619.07	612.11	558.21
67 Insurance (Brokers) (7)	979.90	-0.3	7.70	6.33	17.46	31.63	982.89	976.62	971.90	992.04
68 Merchant Banks (10)	371.13	+0.3	–	4.27	–	7.30	370.16	368.97	363.10	355.88
69 Property (52)	1374.90	+0.1	6.13	2.85	20.75	17.86	1373.58	1373.78	1369.40	1239.96
70 Other Financial (31)	379.78	+0.3	11.19	5.76	11.40	9.63	378.75	376.63	375.71	381.02
71 Investment Trusts (69)	1223.87	+0.3	–	2.70	–	15.47	1220.13	1212.75	1205.73	920.74
81 Mining Finance (2)	690.40	-0.1	8.05	3.72	13.84	10.45	691.20	689.41	681.43	526.50
91 Overseas Traders (8)	1414.11	-1.1	9.85	5.02	11.60	43.33	1429.23	1418.80	1409.05	1149.14
99 ALL-SHARE INDEX (703)	1173.25	-0.3	–	4.02	–	22.73	1176.69	1166.71	1158.37	969.89

Source: *Financial Times*.

Figure 2   U.K. Equities and Politics (FT-A All Share 1971–1989)

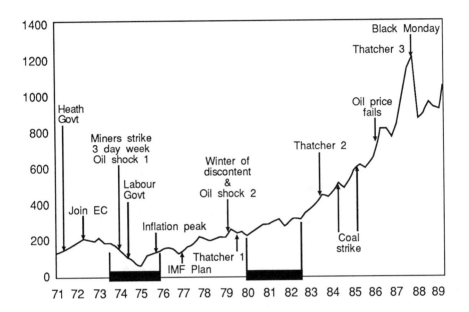

Shaded area = Recession

corporate profitability and the climate for new listings. IMF intervention and the election of a conservative government led by Prime Minister Margaret Thatcher in 1979 were important changes, although the subsequent hard recession in the early 1980s provided little reason for the market to advance. However, the market turned up sharply by 1983. The long bull run to October 1987 was fueled by economic recovery, declining inflation and interest rates, recovery in the corporate sector's profit share of national income, and more favorable tax and investment policies. In addition to these, improved cyclical factors and positive structural forces have boosted equities in the 1980s. They include the government's trend of gilt redemptions and privatizing public-sector companies, both of which boost the relative size of the equity market, as well as the deregulation of Big Bang, which brought so many new participants and additional capital to stockbroking. As a result, during 1987 equity prices and turnover climbed to record levels.

Figure 3   U.K. Equity Market: Prices and Turnover

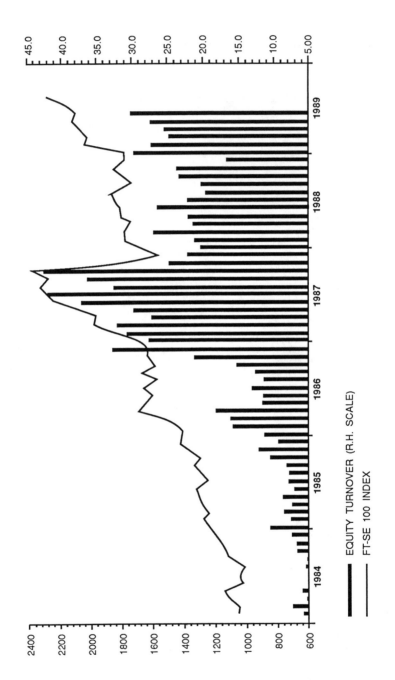

EQUITY TURNOVER (R.H. SCALE)

FT-SE 100 INDEX

In the week of the 1987 crash, FT-SE 100 fell by 22%, compared with a fall of 24% in New York, 18% in Tokyo, and 15% in Frankfurt, Germany. The ISE remained open for business throughout, although fast market conditions were declared at intervals. After the hectic trading period associated with the crash, turnover declined sharply. Prices stagnated and investor confidence hit rock-bottom. During 1988, the market continued to languish, particularly as U.K. monetary policy was progressively tightened from May 1988 onwards to restrain the pace of economic growth and inflation. The year 1989 saw a return to more buoyant conditions. The FT-SE 100 index rose by 21% during the first half of the year. Prices were then further boosted in July by the announcement of the largest take-over bid in U.K. stock market history—£13bn ($21bn) was offered for BAT Industries. By late July 1989, FT-SE had regained all the ground lost in the market crash. The existing all-time high for FT-SE is 2443.4 on 16 July 1987.

Similarly net issuing activity expanded through the 1980's, exploded in 1986 and 1987 after Big Bang's deregulation and internationalization, but then fell back in 1988. Privatizations, which had so boosted new issues in 1986 and 1987, have been absent from the market since the crash. The privatization of British Petroleum in October 1987 unfortunately coincided with the market crash, causing loss to all parties involved. A safety-net scheme for BP was devised in conjunction with the Bank of England, and the government has consequently become very aware that surrounding investment and stock market conditions must be favorable to support big new releases of equity through privatization. The next planned releases from the public sector are to be the Water Authorities (1% of market capitalization) in November 1989 and Electricity Authorities (5% of market capitalization) in 1990, thus creating a utilities sector in the market for the first time.

The two valuation measures illustrated in these graphs, price earnings ratio and yield ratio, show clearly how markedly over-extended the U.K. equity market had become prior to the 1987 crash. Currently, these measures indicate the U.K. market to be fairly valued. By comparison with the U.S. stockmarket, the U.K. price-earnings ratio is of a similar order of magnitude, while the dividend yield tends to be a little higher.

Transactions Information

Transactions on ISE are conducted by 389 member firms (as of March 1989) through the SEAQ dealing system. All the major international firms in the banking and securities industry world-wide are represented or operating in the London market. Through TOPIC terminals, SEAQ provides live prices from 9a.m. to 5 p.m., Monday to Friday, with pre-market trading usually beginning from 7:30 or 8 a.m. Trading is conducted in two-week account periods (three week periods

Figure 4   FTA 500 Price-Earnings & Yield Ratio

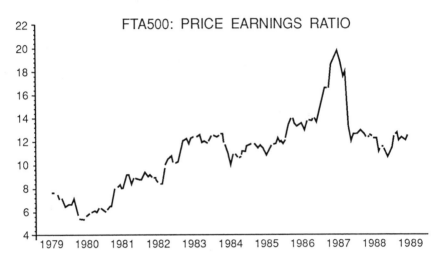

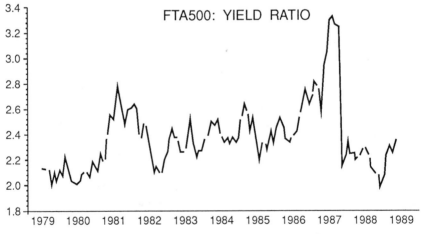

Source: *Datastream.*

if a public holiday occurs), with settlement on account day, which is always a Monday six business days (ten calendar days) after the end of the account. In exceptional circumstances, some stocks will move to cash settlement for a time. This requires payment for the transaction on the second business day after dealing. New time bargains can be undertaken from the second last business day of a previous account period, settling on the regular account day of the subsequent dealing period.

Commissions are fully flexible and negotiable, varying with the size of a transaction. For example, for transactions from £1,000 to £100,000 commission rates might fall from 2% to 0.2%, respectively. Net dealing at zero commission directly with market makers is also possible.

Stamp duty of 1/2% of the consideration (i.e., excluding commission) is payable on purchase of equities or convertibles. Charities can apply for concessionary rates of stamp duty, but the only exemptions from it are for market makers or broker/dealers, acting as principals and reselling the stock within seven calendar days. Value Added Tax (VAT) of 15% of the commission charge is also payable, although this is due to be abolished to comply with an EC directive in the near future. Advance Corporation Tax (ACT) at the basic income tax rate of 25% will be withheld from dividends. Exemptions or reductions from

Figure 5   Domestic Equities: Commission Rates

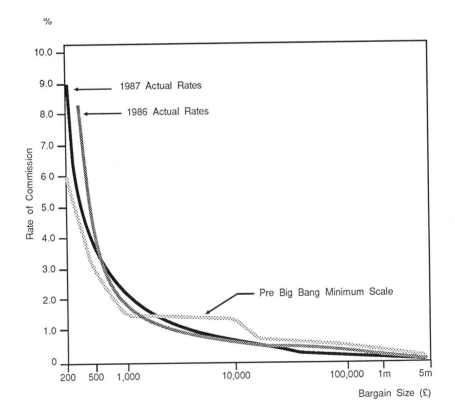

Source: *Quality of Markets Quarterly*, Autumn 1987, ISE, p. 15.

ACT rely on the company obtaining authority under double taxation agreements to pay the full dividend to overseas shareholders so covered. Otherwise, the shareholder receives the dividend net of an ACT with an associated tax credit to offset against other U.K. tax, or is to be repaid if there is no liability. Net capital gain from U.K. investments is treated for tax purposes the same way as income, although individuals currently have a tax-free net capital gain limit of £5,000 while trusts have half this limit.

Settlement and transfer of ownership after equity transactions are currently effected through the ISE's TALISMAN system. TALISMAN settlement can be designated in sterling, U.S. dollars, and Irish punts; and can be settled in Irish, Australian, and South African registered securities. They can also include custody of these overseas securities. Institutional investors use the Institutional Net Settlement System to pay for all bargains in the same account period simultaneously with the Settlements Services Department of the ISE, even if transactions were made with several firms. Development work has been under way since before Big Bang on a Transfer and Automated Registration of Un-certificated Stock, a paperless book-entry transfer system known as TAURUS. A steering committee of ISE is currently consulting with involved parties on how to proceed with the de-materialization of U.K. equity settlement. In the interim, international investors are encouraged to make custodial arrangements with global custodian services, London-based banks, or securities houses. Brokers will often be willing to take custody on behalf of clients.

Overseas investors now rank second only to major U.K. institutional investors in accounting for U.K. equity turnover. Although privatizations, tax incentives for employee share schemes, and Personal Equity Plans have clearly boosted the involvement of individuals, overseas investment has nevertheless overtaken the equity-market activity of individuals since 1987. By number of transactions, individuals are still clearly dominant.

Take-Overs, Regulation and Investor Protection

There are limits on foreign ownership in only two defense-related companies deemed to be of national security interest—Rolls Royce and British Aerospace. The previous limit of 15% has been increased to 29.5% as of August/September 1989.

The Companies Act requires disclosure of significant levels of shareholdings. First, there is a level of notifiable interest. Written notification must be made to the company within five business days of the following transactions: (i) purchase/sale taking the total shareholding above/below 5% and (ii) purchase/sale taking the shareholding up/down to the next percentage point past 5%. Second, if total holdings reach 30% or more, it is deemed the bidder has effective control and rules of the Take-over Code apply. With this size stake, the

Figure 6 U.K. Equities: Distribution of Turnover and Transactions

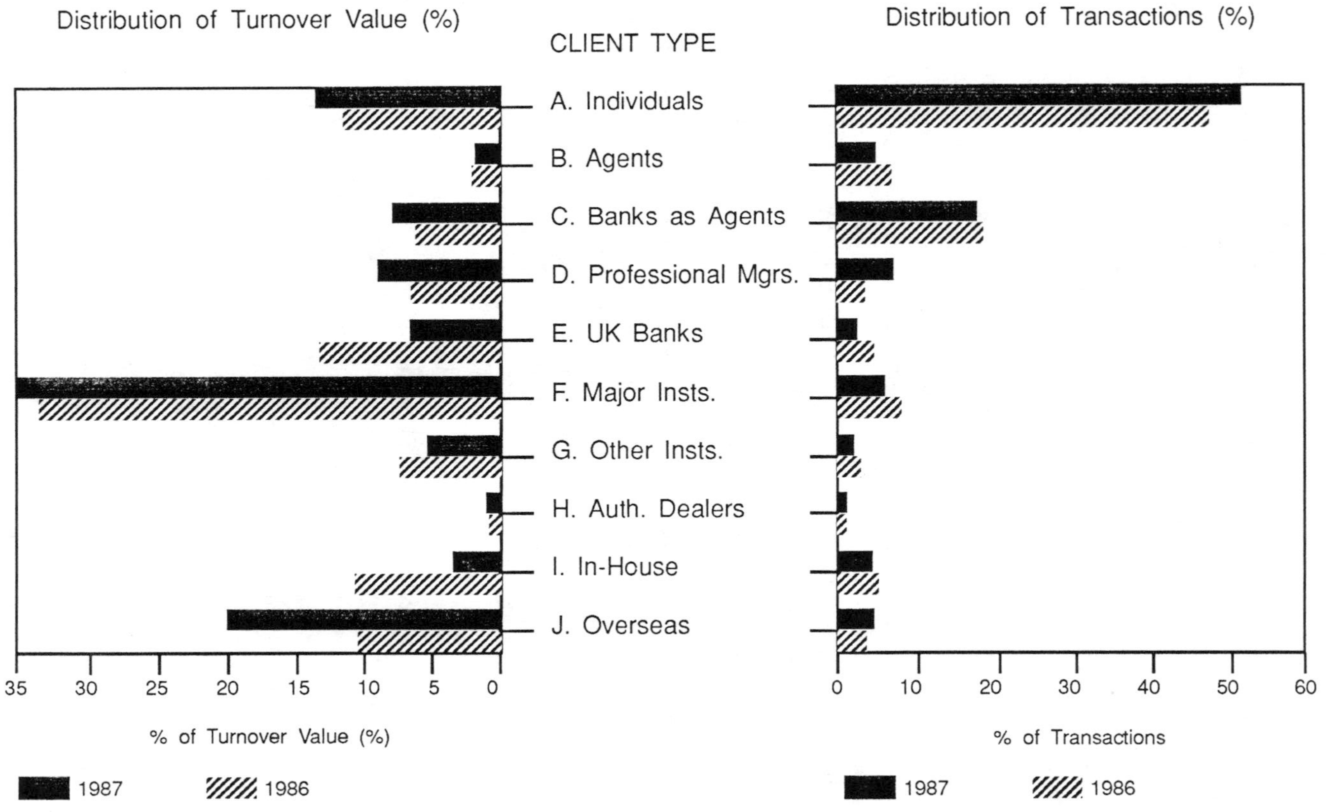

Distribution of Turnover Value (%)
CLIENT TYPE
Distribution of Transactions (%)
A. Individuals
B. Agents
C. Banks as Agents
D. Professional Mgrs.
E. UK Banks
F. Major Insts.
G. Other Insts.
H. Auth. Dealers
I. In-House
J. Overseas
35
30
25
20
15
10
5
0
0
10
20
30
40
50
60
% of Turnover Value (%)
% of Transactions
1987
1986
1987
1986

purchaser is required to make a full bid for the company. The requirement also applies if 30–50% is already held, and more than 2% has been added in any 12 month period. A stake of between 15–30% can be built up over a period of time without the requirement for a full take-over offer being triggered. "Dawn raid" rules were introduced in 1982 to slow down the acquisition of substantial holdings in companies. Under these rules, companies are not permitted to buy 10% or more of the shares from several persons that would exceed a total holding of 15% or more within any seven calendar days.

While there is no statutory control over take-over activity in the U.K., the Panel on Take-overs and Mergers exists to give quick rulings during the course of a take-over. Any party to a bid may refer matters to this panel. If corporate mergers and acquisitions threaten to reduce competition and thus are regarded as being against the public interest, the subject can be referred to the Monopolies and Mergers Commission for a decision.

Investors are protected under the 1986 Financial Services Act of the U.K.. It brings the entire financial services industry under statutory regulation. Since it is expressed as law, any unauthorized or unregulated investment business or activity becomes a criminal offense. Overriding authority for supervision lies with the Secretary of State for Trade and Industry. However, since this department has many other fulltime responsibilities within the economy, the act permits delegation of duty to the Securities Investments Board (SIB) as the jurisdictional authority and regulatory head of investment business in the U.K.. Infringements of the act are reported to and examined by the SIB and, if serious, will be passed on to the Serious Fraud Office or Department of Trade and Industry (i.e., insider trading). SIB can authorize all investment companies and types of investment activity directly.

Beneath SIB, five self-regulatory organizations (SRO's) have been created, offering investor protection equivalent to that afforded by the SIB. SRO's primarily examine the qualifications of financial institutions and professionals to operate under the act and authorize them accordingly. Investors must look for their broker/dealer or investment advisor to be authorized by one of these SRO's. Written complaints first go to the financial firm in question, then, if unresolved, to the authorizing organization. The Securities Association (TSA) is the largest SRO for broker/dealers. TSA, for example, handles investor grievances through a Complaints Bureau and Commissioner and two levels of Arbitration Scheme. Investment advisors usually are under the authorization of the Investment Management Regulatory Organisation (IMRO) or the Financial Intermediaries, Managers and Brokers Regulatory Association (FIMBRA). The Life Assurance and Unit Trust Regulatory Organisation (LAUTRO) and Association of Futures Brokers and Dealers (AFBD) complete the list of SRO's.

ISE does operate a compensation fund to reimburse investors conducting normal business in fully listed or USM stocks for losses arising from the financial failure of a member firm. The SIB also operates a cross-industry compensation scheme funded by all authorized persons to meet claims by investors if any authorized person defaults. The first £30,000 of any claim is fully paid, followed by 90% of the next £20,000, which puts a ceiling of £48,000 on each claim. The fund also limits its per annum total payments to £100,000.

Further Information

The International Stock Exchange of the United Kingdom and the Republic of Ireland, The Stock Exchange, London EC2N 1HP. Tel: 44-1-588-2355.

The ISE Official Yearbook   Stock Exchange Press, published by Macmillan; or Stockton Press for North America.

How To Read The Financial Pages   by Michael Brett, Guild Publishing and Century Hutchinson Ltd, London, 1989.

How The Stock Markets Work   by Colin Chapman Century Hutchinson Ltd, London, 1988 (3rd Edition).

The Square Mile   by John Pender and Paul Wallace, Century Hutchinson Ltd, London, 1986.

Quality Of Markets Quarterly   quarterly market reports and data published by the ISE Publications Unit.

The ISE Fact Sheet   monthly market data, published by the ISE Publications Unit.

The Investors Chronicle and **The Economist**   weekly magazines about U.K. companies, markets, and economics.

Financial Times   daily financial newspaper with wide, professional coverage.

Other daily reading: Business Sections of

The Independent, The Times, The Daily Telegraph, The Guardian

Market and company research available from all securities houses.

9

German Equity Market

O.W. Breycha
KPMG Peat Marwick Treuhand GmbH, Frankfurt

Introduction

Reaching a total capitalization of DM 446.6 billion in 1988, Germany was fifth in the world's stock markets. The strength of Germany's financial markets is founded on four facts. First, Germany's economy has a leading position in Europe and has shown considerable dynamism since 1983, marked by an upswing in economic activity and stability of prices. Second, the German economy has a strong currency supported by the independence of the Federal Bank. Due to its strength the Deutsche Mark has become the backbone of the European Monetary System. Third, strengthening Germany's financial markets is the high level of savings. The amount of capital in existence exceeds DM 2,500 billion, providing a solid base for the financial markets. Finally, Germany has a highly efficient financial system resulting from a universal banking system. Recently, Germany's stock markets have undergone reasonable changes.

In 1988 the market segment was restructured by the creation of the Regulated Market. In 1989 the Stock Exchange Act was reformed, making provisions for actual developments, in particular computer trading and the Futures Exchange. However, the reform of the Stock Exchange Act was not accompanied by the abolition of transfer taxes on securities, thus leaving out an opportunity of making German financial markets even more attractive.

In 1988

Aggregate turnover on Germany's market share in 1988 fell to the amount of DM 716 billion, having reached DM 849 billion in 1987. This decline was due to lower prices, which is illustrated by the fact that the number of shares traded was about 12% above the number traded in 1987. Starting from a low level, resulting from the 1987 October-crash, stock prices declined slightly during January. This period was followed by a steady recovery, only interrupted by technical market reactions, which continued until the end of October. For the rest of the year stock prices remained relatively stable, and by the end of the year the major stock index DAX was about 33% above its level at the beginning of the year. The rise of prices in the course of the year was partly influenced by the return of non-residents as purchasers to the German market, which was due foremost to the exceptionally positive development of overall fundamental factors. This positive development reveals, however, a basic weakness of the German stock market: a relatively strong dependance of foreign investors, which increases the risk of volatility. The German stock exchanges, therefore, endeavor to strengthen the number of domestic shareholders in order to stabilize prices.

Five Year Performance

Table 1 lists the year-end share price index, year-end mean spot rates in DM on the Frankfurt currency market, 1984–1988.

Average Yield

Table 2 lists the average yields of listed public limited companies.

Market Indices and Their Constituents

The German Stock Index (DAX), the major stock index, was introduced on July 1, 1988.

Shares of 30 companies are included in DAX, representing about 80% of aggregate turnover and about 60% of total market value in German shares. The high degree of representation, especially in German "blue chips," is seen as a great advantage of DAX. Another advantage of DAX is that it is being adjusted to take into account price reductions due to dividend payments and changes in capital, which means DAX shows the isolated impact of market forces on share prices. The index is calculated as a weighted index, with the weighting based on listed capital. Once a year the weighting is adjusted. The companies whose shares are part of DAX are those listed in Table 6 (largest quoted companies).

Table 1   Year-end Share Price Index, Year-end Mean Spot Rates in DM on the Frankfurt Currency Market, 1984–1988

Year-end	German Stock Index (DAX)	Exchange Rate DM/US$
1984	820.91	3.1480
1985	1,366.23	2.4613
1986	1,432.25	1.9408
1987	1,000.00[1]	1.5815
1988	1,327.87	1.7803

[1] Year-end 1987 = 1,000, before year-end 1987 the index had not been weighted.

Table 2   Average Yields of Listed Public Limited Companies

Year-end	Yield % Including Tax Credit	Yield % Excluding Tax Credit
1984	3.61	2.31
1985	2.47	1.58
1986	2.74	1.75
1987	4.42	2.83
1988	3.50	2.24

Source: Statistisches Bundesamt.

The Stock Market

Brief History and Structure

The roots of the German stock exchanges go back to the beginning of the nineteenth century when the exchanges started concentrating on securities. In the beginning government bonds dominated, but, in the course of the industrial revolution, shares of private companies were traded increasingly on the stock exchanges. The first companies to enter the stock exchanges in the middle of the nineteenth century were railway companies, followed by industrial and international companies. After World War II the stock exchanges in the soviet sector and in Berlin were closed down. The latter was re-established in West-Berlin in 1950. Today there are eight stock exchanges in Germany.

German stock exchanges are regulated by the Stock Exchange Act of 1896, which was revised in 1975 and in 1986. Actually, the Stock Exchange Act is being revised again in order to make legal provisions for computer trading and for the establishment of a German Futures exchange.

Patrons of the exchanges are either Chambers of Industry and Commerce (Frankfurt and Berlin) or private stock exchange associations. The exchanges are controlled by the appropriate State government.

The board of governors manages the stock exchanges. The board is elected by official and unofficial brokers and by representatives of employees from the firms (in general banks) admitted on the stock exchange. The board's responsibilities are:

- to admit firms and individual persons to the stock exchange,

- to enact trading conditions and to enforce the rules governing the exchange,

- to decide on the opening, suspension, and cancellation of the official trade, and

- to exercise disciplinary powers on the floor.

The admissions board decides on the securities listing on the stock exchange. Half of its members are appointed by the Chambers of Industry and Commerce. These members may not deal professionally on the stock exchange. The other half is appointed by the board of governors for a three-year term.

The board of arbitration handles disputes concerning transactions between admitted members.

The Chamber of Brokers is a public body representing the official brokers. It is responsible for the supervision of the brokers, for the allocation of securities among the brokers, for the control of the settlement and of the prices, and for the publication of the official price list.

Since the restructuring in 1988, there have been three distinct sections on the German stock exchanges: the official market (first segment), the regulated market (second segment), and the free market (third segment).

The first segment comprises the securities listed by the admissions board and is by far the largest one. The second segment comprises mainly newly issued securities and securities issued by small companies, which have only regional importance. In the third segment, securities that are neither listed in the first nor in the second segment are traded. In contrast to the other segments, which are under public law, the third segment is regulated by private law.

German Stock Exchanges

There are eight stock exchanges in Germany, located in Frankfurt/Main, Dusseldorf, Munich, Hamburg, Stuttgart, West-Berlin, Hanover and Bremen. Representing approximately 70% of total turnover, Frankfurt Stock Exchange is the most important one.

Opening Hours, Names and Addresses

Trading hours on all German stock exchanges are from Monday to Friday 11:30 a.m. to 1:30 p.m.

Frankfurt Stock Exchange
Borsenplatz 6
P.O. Box: 10 08 1
D-6000 Frankfurt am Main 1
Telephone Main Switchboard: (069) 2197-0
Information Service: (069) 2197-382

Visitors, Brochures: (069) 2197-383
Telex: 411412
Teletex: 6997242
Telefax: (069) 2197-455
Btx: *67243#

Rhineland-Westphalian Stock Exchange in Dusseldorf
Ernst-Schneider-Platz 1
P.O. Box: 24 02 63
D-4000 Dusseldorf
Tel.: (0211) 13890
Telex: 8582600
Telefax: (0211) 133287
Btx: *20303# *49969#

Bavarian Stock Exchange
Lenbachplatz 2a
D-8000 Munchen 2
Tel.: (089) 5990-0
Telex: 523515
Telefax: (089) 599032

Hanseatic Stock Exchange Hamburg
SchauenburgerstraBe 47/49
P.O. Box: 11 15 09
D-2000 Hamburg 1
Tel.: (040) 361302-0
Telex: 213228
Telefax: (040) 36130223

Baden-Wurttemberg Stock Exchange in Stuttgart
HospitalstraBe 12
P.O. Box: 10 04 41
D-7000 Stuttgart 1
Tel.: (0711) 290183
Telex: 721514
Telefax: (0711) 290185

Berlin Stock Exchange
HardenbergstraBe 16-18
D-1000 Berlin 12
Tel.: (030) 3180-248
Telex: 183663 (indicating: for stock exchange)
Telefax: (030) 3180-278 (indicating: for stock exchange)
Btx: *41800#

Lower Saxony Stock Exchange in Hanover
RathenaustraBe 2
P.O. Box: 44 27
D-3000 Hannover
Tel.: (0511) 327661
Telefax: (0511) 324915

Bremen Stock Exchange
Domshof 12
P.O. Box: 10 07 26
D-2800 Bremen 1
Tel.: (0421) 323037 or 323058
Telex: 246331 bwb d
Telefax: (0421) 323123

Market Size

Number of Listings and Market Value

Table 3 lists the number of public limited companies and market value. Table 4 lists shares issued by residents.

Largest Quoted Companies

At the end of 1988, the largest quoted companies—those included in DAX—accounted for roughly 60% of total market capitalization. Table 5 lists the 30 largest listed companies on the Frankfurt Stock Exchange at year-end 1988.

Table 3   Number of Public Limited Companies and Market Value

Year-end	Number of Public Limited Companies	Share Capital Total	Share Capital of which Listed Ordinary Shares	
			Nominal Value	Market Value
1984	449	51,549	44,330	246,703
1985	451	54,133	47,130	438,810
1986	467	58,233	50,758	480,179
1987	474	60,805	53,721	325,689
1988	465	61,900	54,790	424,739

Source: Statistisches Bundesamt.

Table 4   Shares Issued By Residents

Year-end	Nominal Value DM million	Market Value DM million	Average Issue Price in %
1984	2,992	6,278	209.8
1985	3,769	11,009	292.3
1986	4,560	16,394	359.6
1987	3,082	11,889	386.0
1988	2,712	7,528	277.6

Source: Statistisches Bundesamt.

Table 5   The 30 Largest Listed Companies on The Frankfurt Stock Exchange at Year-end, 1988

Company	Capitalization (DM million)	Capitalization in % of Market Capitalization
Daimler-Benz	31,460.5	7,04
Allianz	28,050.0	6,28
Siemens	25,828.6	5,78
Bayer	20,655.7	4,62
Deutsche Bank	20,080.0	4,50
Hoechst	17,410.7	3,90
BASF	16,155.2	3,62
Volkswagen	10,725.0	2,40
Veba	10,654.2	2,38
RWE	10,026.2	2,25
Dresdner Bank	9,174.5	2,05
BMW	7,822.5	1,75
Thyssen	5,981.4	1,34
Bayer. Hypo-Bank	5,546.9	1,24
Mannesmann	5,424.7	1,21
Commerzbank	5,281.7	1,18
Linde	3,701.3	0,83
Bayer. Vereinsbank	3,594.0	0,81
Lufthansa	3,588.1	0,81
MAN	3,379.7	0,76
Schering	3,223.4	0,72
Kaufhof	2,919.0	0,65
Degussa	2,799.6	0,63
Karstadt	2,764.8	0,62
Viag	2,737.6	0,61
Henkel KGaA	2,376.2	0,53
Continental	2,173.2	0,49
Feldmühle Nobel	1,925.0	0,43
Nixdorf Computer	1,638.6	0,37
Deutsche Babcock	1,095.5	0,25
Total	268,193.7	60.05

Trading Volume

Until 1986 the German share market saw a sharp rise in trading value.

In 1988 trading value declined. A comparison of the years 1987 and 1988 to the former years is not possible. Beginning in 1987, double counting was introduced and the definition of share trading was extended to include transactions among banks and brokers. Table 6 lists share trading value 1984–1988.

Table 6   Share Trading Value 1984–1988 (in DM million)

Year	Domestic Shares	Foreign Shares	Warrants	Total
1984[1]	84,705	16,828	not available	101,533
1985[1]	210,708	26,186	not available	236,894
1986[1]	294,673	33,032	not available	327,705
1987[2]	671,157	57,811	119,860	848,825
1988[2]	615,014	38,782	62,429	716,225

[1] single counting.
[2] double counting and extended definition.

Source: Statistisches Bundesamt.

Table 7   Domestic shares with Highest Turnover, 1988

Ranking	Company	Trading Value in DM billion
1	Siemens	56,911.8
2	Deutsche Bank	42,294.2
3	Bayer	39,894.6
4	Volkswagen	39,662.4
5	Daimler-Benz	34,137.6
6	Hoechst	32,464.4
7	BASF	31,772.8
8	Thyssen	21,957.2
9	VEBA	19,631.6
10	Dresdner Bank	18,697.7
11	BMW	16,146.8
12	Mannesmann	15,733.9
13	Allianz Holding	15,590.4
14	Commerzbank	15,428.7
15	RWE	11,711.7
16	Continental	11,644.4
17	Nixdorf Computer	9,925.2
18	Hoesch	8,740.4
19	VIAG	8,272.7
20	AEG	7,894.7
21	Schering	7,632.0
22	Mercedes-Automobil-Holding	7,187.5
23	MAN	6,521.0
24	Feldmühle Nobel	5,874.7
25	Karstadt	5,540.0

Types of Share

The following types of equity or quasi-equity can be traded on German stock exchanges: common shares, preferred shares, registered shares, subscription rights, warrants, and profit participation certificates.

Compared to common shares, preferred shares take a preferred position in respect to distribution of dividends or surplus assets on liquidation. Usually this preferred position is combined with limited participation rights, especially voting rights. Preferred shares may even have no voting rights at all. Preferred shares without voting rights are frequently issued by family-owned companies when going public.

Registered shares are registered to the bearer. Transactions in registered shares have to be recorded in the share register, and in some cases transactions are not possible without the consent of the issuing company (vinkulierte Namensaktien). By law not fully paid in shares must be in registered form. Registered shares may be either common or preferred shares.

Subscription rights give shareholders the right to subscribe for new shares in case of a capital increase. They can be traded separately for a certain period.

Warrants are issued together with warrant bonds but can be traded separately from the latter. They give the right to subscribe for new shares at specific conditions.

Profit participation certificates usually give the right to a fixed portion of the net profit but to no other rights of participation, e.g., voting rights.

Investors

Table 8 lists share ownership by investor type end of 1988.

Operations

Trading System

Securities can only be traded by representatives of firms who are professionally engaged in trading securities, in general banks, by official brokers, and by unofficial brokers.

Representatives of banks place orders for their clients and orders for their own account.

Official brokers are arranging transactions between the dealers and establishing official quotations in securities assigned to them. They may not deal in their own name or for their own account, unless necessary for the execution of their duties.

Table 8   Share Ownership by Investor Type End of 1988

	Domestic Shares	Foreign Shares	Total
Private households	29.50%	55.46%	31.62%
Public households	5.71%	.00%	5.24%
Non-financial corporations	30.50%	8..20%	28.70%
Institutional investors of which:	12.20%	25.96%	13.32%
insurance companies	5.32%	1.91%	5.07%
investment funds	6.88%	24.04%	8.26%
Non-residents	22.09%	10.38%	21.12%
	100.00%	100.00%	100.00%

Source: Statistisches Bundesamt.

Unofficial brokers are trading for their own account and arranging transactions in securities traded in the regulated market and in the free market.

Transactions can either be carried out in the market with single prices or in the market with variable prices (continuous trading).

Single prices are fixed some time after the opening of the session. They apply for the execution of customers' orders below the minimum volume of 50 shares that are required for transactions in the market with variable prices. Furthermore, they enable banks and unofficial brokers to give orders after having observed the market trend. The single price for a particular security is fixed by the broker as the price that permits him to execute the largest possible number of orders in that security. If no balance can be achieved, the broker enters himself into trading in order to execute all orders compatible with the single price. Each broker may, however, trade up only to a certain limit.

Variable prices are obtained for securities with a broad market during the session by way of "calling out." Orders received before trading starts are balanced in the same manner as the single price. Variable prices apply only for transactions in minimum volume standards or a multiple thereof, the minimum usually being 50 shares.

Settlement and Transfer

Payment and delivery of securities normally is effected on the second day following the day of trading.

Settlement of securities transactions including payment is effected by a central depository bank located at all the stock exchanges except Bremen, which is connected to the Central Depository Bank of Hamburg.

Participants of central depository banks can only be banks in Germany. Each bank has a collective safe deposit of which an investor, who is a client of the bank, becomes a co-owner for the category of securities concerned.

Money accounts of the banks are settled daily at the local branch of the German Central Bank.

Settlement between two banks, which are members of different German stock exchanges, is also possible in this way.

Transaction Costs

Transaction costs consist of brokerage fees, banking fees, and transfer taxes.

Brokerage fees are 0.08% of the transaction value.

Clients of banks have to pay banking fees, which usually are about 1% of the transaction value. For clients trading large volumes fees may be reduced considerably (down to 0.025%).

A transfer tax (Borsenumsatzsteuer) is due on nearly all transactions of securities, whether executed on a stock exchange or not.

The tax rate is: 0.25% for shares, domestic corporate bonds and foreign bonds,

0.2% for investment certificates and

0.1% for domestic bonds of certain issuers (Federal Republic, States, municipalities, mortgage banks, etc).

In principle, transactions between a non-resident and a resident are taxed only at half the rate. Domestic bonds issued in the form of book accounts are no securities according to tax law, and consequently their trading is not subject to the transfer tax. Transactions among banks and brokers and the transfer of newly issued securities to the first acquirer are tax-free. Transactions in newly issued securities representing a participation (e.g., shares) are, however, subject to capital transfer tax. The tax rate is 1%, and it has to be paid by the issuing company.

Taxation and Regulations Affecting Foreign Investors

Dividends and Interest

Distributed profits are subject to a corporation tax at a rate of 36%, payable by the distributing company. The remaining profit distributed (64%) is subject to a withholding tax at a rate of 25%. As a consequence, the net amount paid to shareholders is 48% of distributed profits before corporation tax. While German residents may claim tax credit on both the corporation tax and the withholding tax, non-residents may only claim a partial refund of the withholding tax if their country has concluded a double taxation agreement with Germany. The extent to which the withholding tax may be refunded depends on the maximum tax rate determined in the double taxation agreement. In general, non-residents may claim a refund of the difference between the German withholding tax and the lower maximum tax specified in the double taxation agreement.

Interest payments from bonds are, in general, not subject to withholding tax. The exceptions are convertible bonds and profit-sharing certificates. Interest payments from the latter are subject to the above mentioned 25% withholding tax. Residents from countries who have concluded a double taxation agreement with Germany may claim a full or partial refund.

Table 9 lists countries that have concluded a double taxation agreement with Germany.

As a result of the Tax Reform Act 1990 (decrease of corporation tax rate for retained earnings from 56% to 50%), the maximum withholding tax rate on dividends for participations of at least 10% will decrease for some countries, e.g., United Kingdom and the Netherlands.

Capital Gains

Capital gains resulting from business assets are subject to normal taxation. In case of non-business (i.e., private) assets a "speculation tax" at the personal income tax rate on short-term trading profits, i.e., in cases where the period between purchase and sale of securities other than German fixed interest securities is less than 6 months, is only to be paid by residents. In cases where the period between purchase and sale is longer than 6 months, trading gains are not taxed unless the seller was held more than 25% of the capital any time during the preceding five years. In this case, capital gains are subject to income tax, albeit a reduced rate equal to half the average income tax rate. (From 1990 this reduced rate will be limited to a certain amount of profit.) For non-residents the taxation of capital gains depends on respective double taxation agreements.

Exchange Controls

In general, there are no investment restrictions for non-residents. However, the Federal Administration may, under certain conditions, invoke restrictions on the purchase by non-residents of domestic securities. Currencies are freely transferable but, under certain conditions, may also be subject to restrictions in the form of the deposit of a certain percentage with the federal bank. Transactions by

Table 9   Countries that Have Concluded a Double Taxation Agreement with Germany

| | Maximum Withholding Tax Rate | |
| | Dividends | |
Country	Participation < 10%	Participation ≥ 10%
Argentina	15	15
Australia	15	25,75
Austria	no limit	no limit
Belgium	15	25
Brazil	15	25,75
Canada	15	15
China	15	15
Cyprus	15	27
Czechoslovakia	15	25
Denmark	15	25
Ecuador	15	15
Egypt	15	15
Finland	15	15
France	15	25
Greece	25	25
Hungary	15	15
Iceland	15	27,5
India	15	15
Indonesia	15	25
Iran	20	25
Ireland	15	20
Israel	25	25
Italy	no limit	no limit
Ivory Coast	15	15
Jamaica	15	27
Japan	15	15
Kenya	15	25
Korea (Republic)	15	25
Liberia	15	25,75
Luxemburg	15	25,75
Malaysia	15	27
Malta	15	27
Mauritius	15	25
Morocco	15	25,75
Netherlands	15	25
New Zealand	15	15
Norway	15	25
Pakistan	no limit	15
Philippines	15	15
Poland	15	15
Portugal	15	15
Romania	15	25,75
Singapore	15	27
South Africa	15	25,75

Table continues

Table 9   (Continued)

	Maximum Withholding Tax Rate	
	Dividends	
Country	Participation < 10%	Participation ≥ 10%
Spain	15	25
Sri Lanka	15	15
Sweden	15	15
Switzerland	15	15
Thailand	20	25
Trinidad and Tobago	20	25,75
Tunisia	15	27
United Kingdom	15	20
USA	15	15
USSR	15	15
Zambia	15	27

Source: December 5th, 1988. Regulation of the Federal Ministry of Finance of December 5, 1988, published in *Federal Tax Gazette* (Bundessteuerblatt) 1988 part I, page 491, 499.

non-residents, both in securities and in currencies, are subject to extensive reporting requirements. There are no legal restrictions existing for non-residents opening bank accounts in Germany.

Reporting, Research, Other Information

Reporting Requirements for Listed Companies

Principally all corporations have to publish their annual accounts, and all listed corporations are required to be audited. The auditors have to issue an opinion confirming that "based on an audit performed in accordance with our professional duties, the accounting records and the financial statements comply with the legal regulations. The financial statements present, in compliance with required accounting principles, a true and fair view of the net worth, financial position and results of the company. The management report is in agreement with the financial statements."

In terms of stock exchange and securities, company-publicity as layed down in the Code of Commerce (Handelsgesetzbuch) and stock exchange publicity as layed down in the Stock Exchange Admission Regulation (Borsenzulassungsverordnung) have to be followed.

The stock exchange-publicity is intended to inform the investors about factors relevant for their investment decisions. The company publicity and the stock exchange publicity must address the entire public because German share holders hold predominantly bearer shares.

The primary reporting requirements for admission to the official market (segment 1) are as follows: The issuer has to inform the public about his status in form of a prospectus, which has to be approved in advance by the admission board, for official listing; the issuer is further obliged to provide the public periodically with equivalent information, particularly by publication of the annual and interim (usually half year) reports; after admission, the prospectus has to be published both in the official gazette "Bundesanzeiger" and in a newspaper admitted by the commission.

The reporting requirements for admission to segment 2 (regulated market) differ from those regarding segment 1 in essential points:

1) the company is not obliged to submit a complete prospectus, a short form report is sufficient; 2) interim reports are non obligatory; and 3) publicity instructions are limited to the duty to make records available on call at the place of payment. In this segment no reporting is required.

Shareholder Protection Codes

Insider rules are not codified by law. The German industry associations restrict insider trading by requiring directors and employees to sign contractual agreements. Insider rules are written down in three agreements. According to the general rules for all insiders (Insiderhandels-Richtlinien), insider transactions are prohibited.

The rules define insiders as:

- legal representatives and members of the Supervisory Board of corporations and of their affiliates;

- domestic shareholders, holding participations of more than 25% in a corporation, including their legal representatives and members of their Supervisory Board;

- employees of the said companies who have access to insider information; and

- banks, the members of their supervisory board, their board of managing directors, and their employees.

In case of abuses of insider information, profits have to be transferred to the company with which the insider has agreed to follow the rules. The company may execute further penalties.

Specific rules for securities dealers (Handler-und Beraterregeln) are addressed to banks and investment advisers. They are intended to prevent the above mentioned groups from giving advice to clients that is not in the interest of the latter.

According to the rules of procedure (Verfahrensordnung), a commission of inquiry is formed by all associations involved in insider rules. The duty of this commission is to investigate violations of insider rules.

The actual system of insider rules may undergo considerable changes by the EC. The changes will probably not be installed before July 1st, 1992, the deadline for becoming national law.

Research and Information

Research on German financial markets is provided by the leading banks, including Deutsche Bank, Dresdner Bank, and Commerzbank.

Statistical information:

Annual report of the Federation of the German Stock Exchanges
Monthly report of the Federal Bank
Statistical Exhibits (Beihefte) to the monthly report of the Federal Bank
Annual report of the Federal Office for Statistics

Newspapers, magazines:

Amtliches Kursblatt (daily)
Börsenzeitung (daily)
Handelsblatt (daily)
Bundesanzeiger (weekly)

Brochures:

Federation of German Stock Exchanges
KPMG (Investment in Germany, Corporate Tax Procedures, Tax Treatment of Exchange Gains and Losses)

Literature:

Obst/Hintner, Geld-, Bank- und Borsenwesen, 38th edition, Stuttgart 1988

C H A P T E R **10**

French Equity Market

Alain Galene
Morgan Stanley, Paris

Introduction

After 10 years of stagnation, the French stock market began to move up in 1983 and has done extremely well since then. Among the reasons for its excellent performance are: (1) an end to "Eurosclerosis" and the resultant strong earnings of French firms; (2) the rising tide of global "yuppieism," which has been of particular benefit to many French companies whose businesses are almost a pure play on this trend, including champagne, perfumes, luxury goods, leisure pursuits, and other consumer items; and (3) the positive impact of a strong mergers and acquisitions activity in France since 1986, related to 1992 especially.

There are reasons to think that the Bourse can continue to rise. We expect the French economy to expand further in 1989, and disinflation should continue. We also estimate that corporate earnings will rise about 16%, benefiting not only from the strength in GNP but also from an improvement in corporate margins. In addition, the French government's fiscal and social policies in regard to business have become much more positive. The French market is selling at a price/earnings multiple of 11.8, versus 17.4 for the Morgan Stanley Capital International (MSCI) world index and 12.4 for the MSCI Europe Index. Because of the relatively conservative accounting practices (particularly for depreciation) of French companies, its price/cash-earnings ratio is only 5.1 compared with 7.8 for the world index. This puts the Bourse's valuation below the U.S. cash-flow multiples of 6.9; the United Kingdom's of 7.6; and Switzerland's of 8.5; and only slightly higher than Germany's ratio of 5.0.

How Big Is the French Stock Market?

According to the Morgan Stanley Capital International database, France ranks fifth in stock-market capitalization and accounts for 2.8% of the worldwide total (Table 1). A more meaningful comparison is the relationship of market value to the gross national product of the respective countries. Among the OECD nations, France has the fourth-largest GNP, behind the United States, Japan, and Germany but before the United Kingdom. Yet, as shown in Table 2, the capitalization of the French market represents only 27.6% of GNP, far below the ratios of the other major countries. We see three key reasons for this discrepancy:

1. Historically, a number of companies have chosen to remain private in order to keep their financial information confidential.
2. Until the early 1980s, securities had provided disappointing returns, and many French investors preferred other kinds of investments, such as real estate. Between 1970 and 1983, the average rise in the MSCI France index was only 0.5% a year (in French francs) versus 15.5% for the prices of new buildings in Paris.

Figure 1

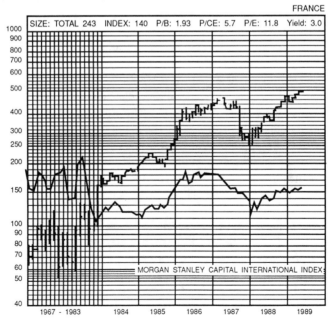

**Table 1   Global Stock Market Capitalization Rankings in 1989
(Expressed in U.S.$ billions)**

Rank	Country	Market Capitalization[*]	% of Worldwide Market Capitalization
1	Japan	3,457.6	39.8
2	United States	2,772.7	31.9
3	United Kingdom	714.9	8.2
4	Germany	247.4	2.9
5	France	242.8	2.8
6	Canada	236.7	2.7
7	Switzerland	156.9	1.8
8	Italy	139.2	1.6
9	Australia	122.1	1.4
10	Sweden	103.2	1.2
11	Netherlands	93.1	1.1
12	Spain	98.6	1.1
13	Hong Kong	62.5	0.7
14	Belgium	59.5	0.7
15	Singapore-Malaysia	53.9	0.7
16	Denmark	34.1	0.4
17	Norway	20.5	0.2
18	Austria	12.2	0.1
	Other Countries	52.3	0.7
	MSCI World Market Value	$8,680.2	100.0%

[*]   As of 06/30/89

Source: *Morgan Stanley Capital International Perspective*, 06/30/89.

3. Even after the privatizations between 1986 and 1988, France still has a great number of large state owned companies such as Renault, Pechiney, Rhone-Poulenc, and Thomson (SA).

At the end of 1988, 646 companies were listed on the "French Bourse," including around 280 on the "second market." Since 1983, almost all new listings have been on the latter. The second market mandates only 10% of a company's total equity be traded, versus 20% on the main exchange. Also, less financial information is required.

Table 2   Global Stock Market Capitalizations as a Percentage of GNP's in 1989 (Expressed in U.S.$ billions)

Country	Market Capitalization*	% of 1987 GNP
Japan	3,457.6	145.5
United Kingdom	714.9	106.7
Switzerland	156.9	91.7
Sweden	103.2	65.1
Australia	122.1	63.0
United States	2,772.7	62.0
Canada	236.7	57.6
Netherlands	93.1	43.7
Belgium	59.5	42.8
Spain	98.6	34.1
Denmark	34.1	33.7
France	242.8	27.6
Germany	247.4	22.1
Italy	139.2	18.4

* As of 06/30/89

Source: *Morgan Stanley Capital International Perspective.*

In Table 3, we show the 15 biggest-capitalization issues, which represent about one third of the total value of the French market. We estimate that, on average, around 40% of the shares of all listed French companies is freely tradeable.

Volume of transactions has increased markedly over the last few years, reaching FFr1.5- to FFr2-billion daily on the major (settlement) market now, versus only FFr550-million at the beginning of 1985. Today, volumes of each of the most active stocks are between FFr30- and FFr100-million a day.

Another feature of the French Bourse is the high weighting relative to that on other exchanges of the services sector, which includes mainly retailing and housing. In turn, the percentage of the energy and materials industries are low in comparison with their proportions in other major markets (Table 4). Note that the privatization of companies, such as CGE, and Saint-Gobain, have increased the weightings of the capital equipment group to a percentage (16%) similar to other markets.

**Table 3   15 Largest-Capitalization Issues on the French Market
(FFr billions)**

Rank	Company	Market Capitalization[*]	Industry
1	Elf-Aquitaine	58.6	Oil and Gas; Chemicals
2	LVMH	49.2	Champagne; Cognac; Perfumes; Luggage
3	Peugeot	42.7	Automobiles
4	Saint-Gobain	36.0	Glass; Building Materials
5	Suez	35.4	Financial Holding
6	BSN	34.3	Foods and Beverages
7	Eaux (Genereie des)	34.1	Public Services
8	Midi (Cie)	32.7	Holding Company
9	CGE	31.3	Capital Equipment
10	Societe Generale	29.2	Banking
11	Paribas	28.9	Financial Holding
12	Air Liquide	27.0	Industrial Gases
13	Rhone-Poulenc	26.8	Chemicals; Drugs
14	Thomson-CSF	23.7	Defense/Aerospace
	Total	513.9	

[*]   As of 06/30/89

Source: *Morgan Stanley Capital International Perspective.*

**Table 4   Breakdown of French Stock Market Capitalization by Industry[*]
(FFr billions)**

Market Capitalization		% of Total
Energy	90.3	6.9
Materials	201.3	15.4
Capital Equipment	209.9	16.0
Consumer Goods	247.0	18.8
Subtotal	748.5	57.1
Services	231.2	17.6
Finances	244.3	18.7
Multi-Industry	86.6	6.6
	1,310.6[*]	100.%

[*]   This figure only covers stocks included in MSCI.

Source: *Morgan Stanley Capital International Perspective,* 06/30/89.

How Well Did the French Stock Market Do?

As shown in Table 5, the MSCI France index, expressed in French francs, has acted extremely well during each of the last five years, except in 1987, the year of the crash. Moreover, in U.S. dollar terms, it has been multiplied by 3.7 since the beginning of 1985.

To appreciate the long-term evolution of the market, however, we must look at its performance on a constant-French francs basis. As can be seen in Table 6, after a decade of disappointment, the decline of inflation and interest rates in France combined with strong earnings turned the market around.

Is the Bourse Fairly Valued?

In Table 7, we show comparative valuations of Morgan Stanley Capital International global stock market indexes. The France index has a price/earnings ratio of 11.8, just below that of the United States (12.3), and midway between those of the United Kingdom (10.9) and Germany (15.1). Moreover, its price/cash-flow multiple is actually less than those of the first two and only slightly above the German ratio. The French market does not, therefore, appear overvalued on the basis of its price/earnings and cash-flow multiples. The gap between the price/cash-flow ratios of the French market relative to those of others can be partly explained by the use of accelerated depreciation in French financial statements rather than the linear method employed by U.S. and British companies.

Table 5   Performance of the French Market 1984–1989
(Morgan Stanley Capital International France Index)

Expressed in FFr	1984	1985	1986	1987	1988	First Half 1989
Increase in Index	20.5%	39.8%	50.0%	−29.3%	53.4%	11.6%
Gross Dividend Yield	3.0%	2.6%	1.8%	3.9%	2.8%	1.5%
Total Return	23.5%	42.4%	51.8%	−25.4%	56.2%	13.1%
Expressed in U.S. Dollars						
Increse in Index	2.0%	78.4%	76.0%	−15.0%	35.5%	2.1%
Gross Dividend Yield	2.6%	2.2%	1.8%	3.9%	2.8%	1.5%
Total Return	4.6%	80.6%	77.8%	−11.1%	38.3%	3.6%

Source: *Morgan Stanley Capital International Perspective*, 06/30/89.

**Table 6   French Stock Market
                Performance in Constant vs. Current French Francs 1970–1988**

	% Change	
Years	**Current FFr**	**Constant FFr**
1970	−7.1	−12.3
1971	−7.8	−13.3
1972	+17.1	+10.9
1973	−2.8	−10.1
1974	−30.8	−44.5
1975	+30.7	+18.9
1976	−17.0	−26.6
1977	−6.3	−15.7
1978	+46.5	+37.4
1979	+17.0	+6.2
1980	+9.0	−4.6
1981	−17.6	−31.0
1982	+0.2	−11.6
1983	+56.4	+46.8
1984	+16.4	+9.0
1985	+45.7	+39.9
1986	+50.0	+47.7
1987	−29.3	−33.4
1988	+35.5	+31.3

Source: L'annee Boursiere (CAC Index); OECD.

We also believe the following factors justify the current French market multiple.

- The earnings outlook remains strong. We expect aggregate profits of companies listed on the Bourse to advance 16% year to year in 1989, following a gain of 21% in 1988, and an 18.5% per annum compound growth rate between 1983 and 1987. For the last three years, the French Government has become more and more favorable to business in both its fiscal and social policies. For example, the corporate tax rate is 39% now for the reinvested earnings (42% on the net incomes share for dividends) against 50% up until 1985. This has helped profitability. We estimate the average net profit margin, which reached a low of around 1.8% in 1981–1982, will be around

Table 7   Global Market valuation[*]

	Price/ Earnings Ratio	Price/ Cash Earnings Ratio	Price/ Book Value Ratio	Yield
France	11.8	5.7	1.93	3.0
World Index	17.4	7.8	2.44	2.4
United States	12.3	6.9	1.96	3.5
Japan	47.3	17.1	4.76	0.5
United Kingdom	10.9	7.6	1.8	4.6
Germany	15.1	5.0	2.11	3.4
Canada	11.5	6.9	1.64	3.2
Italy	13.8	3.7	1.77	2.6
Switzerland	16.2	8.5	1.75	2.2
Australia	9.6	6.7	1.47	5.1
Netherlands	10.2	5.1	1.35	4.5
Sweden	15.7	8.8	2.58	2.0
Hong Kong	8.5	7.7	1.1	5.9
Spain	15.9	5.2	1.35	3.7
Singapore-Malaysia	21.3	12.7	2.17	1.4
Belgium	12.6	5.8	1.84	4.2
Denmark	14.6	9.8	1.89	1.6
Norway	17.4	5.9	2.72	1.6
Austria	37.1	6.5	1.84	1.9
Finland	12.8	6.3	1.44	2.2

[*]   As of 06/30/89

Source: *Morgan Stanley Capital International Perspective*, 06/30/89.

4% this year. For the medium term, we forecast that earnings will grow 8% per year on average.

- Earnings visibility is reasonably good. As a consequence of a relatively stable economic environment, the projected growth of GNP, disinflation, and modest rises in salaries—as well as an improvement in the quality of information provided to analysts—we have greater confidence in our estimates.

- Foreign investors are increasing their weightings. Since overseas investors are mainly interested in high-quality big-cap stocks, the multiples of some such issues have expanded substantially.

- Hopes of takeovers are on the rise. Following the hectic activity in the United States and the United Kingdom, mergers (or expectations thereof) are becoming more frequent in the Paris market, initiated not only by French companies but also by international groups. The P/E's of certain French stocks are explained only by the possibility of takeovers.

Appendix I

Table 8	French Market Data (FFr billions)						
		1983	1984	1985	1986	1987	1988
Trading							
equities		100	97	147	397	595	461
bonds		221	426	740	1,718	2,415	3,495
Total		321	523	887	2,718	3,010	3,956
New Issues							
equities1		11	10	17	63	165	158
bonds		199	255	316	350	290	345
Total		210	265	333	413	455	503
Capital Flow							
equities		11	12	13	14	18	25
bonds		198	250	317	351	295	332
Total		209	262	330	365	313	357

[1] Including privatizations.

Source: Societe des Bourses Francaises.

Appendix II

Dividend Taxation

Dividends of French companies include the "avoir fiscal" which is applicable to residents of Australia, Austria, Belgium, Finland, France, Germany, Japan, Luxembourg, the Netherlands, New Zealand, Norway, Singapore, Spain, Sweden, Switzerland, the United Kingdom, and the United States. In the case of German shareholders, the "avoir fiscal" may be credited against German income tax. If a French company distributes a dividend to an Australian, Austrian, Belgian, Dutch, Finnish, Japanese, Luxembourg, New Zealand, Norwegian, Singapore, Spanish, Swedish, Swiss, United Kingdom, or United States resident, the "avoir fiscal" is paid directly by the French Government. Source: MSCI Perspective.

Appendix III

Societe des Bourses Francaises
4 place de la Bourse
75002 Paris
Tel: 1-40-41-10-00

Chairman: Mr. Regis Rousselle

Public information contact: Mr. Bruno Montier

Trading hours: 10.00am – 5.00pm

Main Indexes: CAC Index

CAC 40

Indicateurs du RM.

Dutch Equity Market

Rob Sweers
Banque Paribas Nederland N.V., Amsterdam

Introduction

Although the Dutch Stock Exchange cannot be considered the most important one in the world, it is the oldest, its roots going back to 1876 when the "Vereenigning voor den Effectenhandel" (Amsterdam Stock Exchange) was founded. In fact, trading in shares had already taken place long before that. History claims that the first company of which shares were traded was the "Oost-Indishe Compagnie" back in 1606.

Today (i.e., as per the end of March, 1990), the Dutch markets' total capitalization is Dfl 287.2 billion ($151.2 billion). Despite this relatively small size the Amsterdam Stock Exchange attracts a great deal of foreign interest. Many stocks are actively traded on other European Stock Exchanges, the New York Stock Exchange or NASDAQ. As the Dutch economy is open and very liberalized and as companies have expanded their activities geographically, quite a few Dutch companies are among to the largest in their sector.

Over the past few years the Dutch financial markets implemented a number of changes in an effort to regain market share from other exchanges, especially London. In the early 1990s further steps will be taken in this respect: the stamp duty will be abolished and commissions will become negotiable.

Five-Year Performance

The results over the past five years are listed in Table 1.

Table 1   Year-end CBS General Index, US Dollar, Sterling, DM Exchange Rate

	1985	1986	1987	1988	1989
CBS general (base 1983)	155.4	162.9	128.7	165.8	202.8
US$	2.776	2.207	1.798	2.016	1.917
£	3.997	3.238	3.338	3.613	3.079
DM	112.710	113.010	112.510	112.925	112.970

Average Yield, Price Earnings Ratios Compared to Government Bond Yields

The average yield on the Amsterdam Stock Exchange is relatively high compared to other markets. However, many companies give the shareholder the option of choosing a stock dividend instead of the cash dividend. (No tax is paid on stock dividends), as they are paid out of the shareholders premium reserve

P/E ratios are relatively low in the Netherlands. An important reason for this is the large number of protective measures which companies have put in pace in order to avoid hostile takeovers. Furthermore, it has to be noted that, as most companies use conservative accounting principles, the net worth of Dutch companies is understated in comparison to companies in other countries.

Market Indices and Their Constituents

The ANP-CBS general index is calculated daily as an average of each individual sub index, giving each sector a fixed weighting (base 1983). As this index is not adjusted for market weighting, new indices have been introduced. The first new index is the total return index which adjusts for share issues and dividends. The second new index is the unweighted tendency index which is calculated 7 times a day. This index is adjusted ever year and can be used as a reliable indicator for short term trends. However, most investors tend to use the EOE stock index which is continuously calculated and uses the shares which are listed on the European Stock Exchange in Amsterdam, including VNU and Fokker. These companies comprise 80% of the market capitalization of the Amsterdam Stock Exchange.

The Stock Market

There is one stock exchange in the Netherlands. It was founded in 1876 and is located in Amsterdam. In the early years, trading also took place in Rotterdam

Table 2   P/E Ratios, Dividend Yield and Government Bond Yield

	P/E Ratio	Dividend Yield	Bond Yield
1984	7.4	4.8	7.4
1985	10.2	4.5	6.8
1986	10.8	4.2	6.5
1987	10.1	5.0	6.2
1988	11.3	3.9	6.3
1989	11.7	3.9	8.0

and in local offices in the country. In 1978 the European Options Exchange was founded. It too is located in Amsterdam. Options are traded on the 24 largest companies, on government bonds, gold and currencies. Over the past few years new products have been introduced such as index options and futures.

After World War II the market faced a very difficult time. The reconstruction of the country and its financial structure caused a lot of pain, especially as Germany was temporarily lost as our most important trading partner. In 1952 and 1953 a turn around took place. Foreign investors showed an increasing interest in Dutch securities, while domestic institutional investors, traditionally concentrated on fixed income investments, started to buy equities. Lower corporate taxes and a steep decline in interest rates boosted activity and stimulated prices. Turnover increased from Dfl 318 million in 1952 to Dfl 474 mil lion in 1953. The ANP-CBS index went up from 136.78 to 167.88 by the end of 1953. In 1954 turnover in equities wend up to Dfl 855 million and the index closed the year at 227.06. The economy continued its expansion well into the sixties supported by strong growth in the industrial sector and later on also by the service industry. The economic survival of Germany enabled Dutch industry to boost their export activities again. International trade was furthermore boosted by the integration and cooperation within the EEC. During this period of prosperity the requirements for financial institutions became increasingly higher leading to a number of mergers in the financial sector in the early sixties. In the late sixties and early seventies the market was faced with a marked slowdown due to rising wages, higher interest rates and higher inflation. However, the seventies can be characterized as a period where Dutch companies expanded internationally and diversified their activities. The oil crisis' in 1974 and 1978 put enormous pressure on the Dutch economy. Interest rates went up to double digit figures and the more leveraged companies were faced with a high financial burden. Especially in the late seventies and the early eighties the number of bankruptcies went up dramatically. The budget deficit of the Government went up significantly and Dutch companies faced with share prices under intrinsic value were not in a position to raise equity capital. Profitability came down also as a result of the slowdown of the world economy.

In 1982 and 1983 things changed for the better. The economy started to show growth again, especially lead by export oriented companies benefiting from the higher dollar exchange rate. Interest rates started to come down from levels as high as 13%. Consumer spending started to pick up and unemployment fell significantly. The market which had become undervalued was discovered again by foreign institutional investors. Particularly American investors showed their interest for the leading Dutch companies boosting share prices to higher levels and turnovers started to pick up again. In the early stage of the markets recovery the market was mainly dominated by foreign investors and private individuals, including investment funds. Domestic institutional investors largely concentrated on fixed income investments.

There are three distinct sections on the Amsterdam Stock Exchange. The first section comprises the larger listed companies which are most actively traded. The second section is what is considered to be the "local market" and lists all other officially quoted companies. The choice for first or second section is made by the Amsterdam Stock Exchange committee for quotation and is made on the back of the average turnover over three periods of six months. The third section is the parallel market, or over the counter market. These are mainly smaller companies or new listings. The parallel market is divided into an official sector and an unofficial sector. The exchange is ruled by the Amsterdam Stock Exchange Board, which has installed various committees to provide an adequate and sophisticated trading system. The Amsterdam Stock Exchange is subject to report to the Ministry of Finance. Members of the Amsterdam Stock Exchange are companies which conduct business in securities and can be banks, stockbrokers and jobbers. Jobbers fulfill a specialist function and can only make markets in a restricted list of securities which are exclusively assigned to them. They act as intermediaries to the other members. The business of the regular members is the buying and selling of securities both for their customers and for their own account. All members have trading posts on the floor of the exchange, although banks and stockbrokers more and more trade from their offices.

In addition to effecting transactions on the exchange, members are allowed to participate in committees of the Amsterdam Stock Exchange. They are also obliged to share in the foundation fund of the exchange, to deposit membership admission fees and to bear expenses.

The general meeting of members is the supreme decision making body of the exchange. Special or informative meetings can be held at any time.

Opening Hours, Names and Addresses

Trading hours on the Amsterdam Stock Exchange:

Government bonds: 9.00-17.00

All other securities: 10.00-16.30

Overnight trade is taking place in the five internationals Royal Dutch, Unilver, Philips, KLM and Akzo. Trade takes place by telephone up to the official close of Wall Street (normally 22.00 local time).

From July 5, 1990 onwards this overnight trade will be extended to all companies traded on the European Options Exchange.

Amsterdam Stock Exchange
Beursplein 5
1012 JW Amsterdam
tel.: (020) 5234567
telex: 12302

European Options Exchange
Rokin 65
1012 KK Amsterdam
tel.: (020)5504510
telex: 14596

Opening hours European Options Exchange: 10.00-16.30 Equities
 9.00-17.00 FTO
10.30-16.30 Stock index
10.10-16.30 Dutch Top 5 index
12.00-16.30 XMI
 9.30-17.00 Bonds
10.30-16.30 Prec. Metal Options
10.00-16.30 Currency
 9.45-16.30 Jumbo $ options

Market Size

At the end of 1989 there were 252 domestic and 271 foreign issues listed, of these, respectively 478 and 2, are Parallel Market stocks.

The total market capitalization of all domestic, officially quoted companies at the end of the year was Dfl 295.9 billion, a 42.8% increase over the prior year, including new placements. The largest sector is the internationals, which includes the second largest company in the world, Royal Dutch.

Largest Quoted Companies

The 25 largest quoted companies represent 75.9% of total market capitalization.

Trading Volume

In 1989 total equity trading value amounted to Dfl 184.9 bln up 54.6% from 1988. The most actively traded shares were Royal Dutch, Philips and Unilever. These three companies accounted for 24.1% of total trading value.

Types of Shares

The following categories of equity or quasi-equity are traded on the Amsterdam Stock Exchange: shares, certificates, preferred shares, profit sharing shares, warrants and falcons.

Certificates are issued by an administration office which holds the shares in custody and acts as voting shareholder. This implies that certificates have no voting rights and can be seen as a protective measure of companies against a hostile takeover. Preferred shares and profit sharing shares take a preferred position in respect to distribution of profits. Convertible shares can be converted into

Table 3   Number of Listed Companies and Market Value 1986–1989

	1986	1987	1988	1989
Official market	225	223	209	205
Parallel market	42	46	48	47
Foreign listings	275	268	268	271
Market value				
Official market	194.0	162.9	216.1	295.9

Source: Amsterdam Stock Exchange.

Table 4   Market Value by Sector, December 1989 (Dfl bln)

Sector	Market Value
Internationals	125.034
Local companies	103.439
financials	37.307
non financials	66.132
Total	228.473
Total excl. Royal Dutch	150.045
Investment trusts	39.387
Insurance trusts	4.985
Real estate companies	15.263
Holding companies	7.772
Total of all quoted companies	295.879

Source: Central Bureau of Statistics.

Table 5   The 25 Largest Listed Companies on the ASE, End 1989

Ranking	Company	Market Value (Dfl mln)
1	Royal Dutch	74,428
2	Unilever	25,703
3	Philips	13,092
4	Robeco	12,572
5	Nationale Nederlanden	10,597
6	Rodamco	10,052
7	Rolinco	6,771
8	Rorento	6,431
9	Akzo	5,931
10	PolyGram	5,721
11	ABN	5,197
12	Elsevier	5,137
13	Aegon	4,598
14	NMB Postbank	4,592
15	Amro Bank	4,513
16	Heineken	4,078
17	DSM	3,948
18	Amev	3,521
19	Dordtsche Petroleum	2,948
20	Ahold	2,945
21	Amro All In Fund	2,697
22	KLM	2,502
23	Wereldhave	2,320
24	Berendaal	2,255
25	KNP	2,174

Source: Amsterdam Stock Exchange.

ordinary shares or certificates. Their issue is rare. Convertible bonds usually have a lower coupon and can be converted into shares or certificates at fixed conditions. For the most part, the conversion price is adjusted for rights issues and stock dividends.

Warrants are issued attached to a bond issue and are separated from the debenture on first quotation. At times war rants are introduced by institutional investors and covered by the underlying shares in their portfolio. Falcons can be considered the equivalent of covered warrants.

Investors

There is no statistical information on stock market transactions done by institutional investors, private individuals and member firms, although information is provided on a daily basis on block trades with a value over Dfl 1 million in equity and over 2.5 million in bonds.

The Dutch Insurance Chamber, the supervisory body of insurance companies and pension funds provided year end figures on total holdings of pension funds and insurance companies by year end.

Traditionally Dutch Institutional Investors concentrate on fixed income investments, however, in the last few years they have shown an increasing willingness to invest more in equities.

Operations

Trading System

All securities must be traded through an authorized securities dealer, i.e., a bank or a stockbroker, all of which are members of the Amsterdam Stock Exchange. The "hoekman" or specialist acts as an intermediary between the members. The specialist acts as a market maker and may also deal for his own account.

In each security a market is maintained by a minimum of two specialists, exclusively assigned by the Amsterdam Stock Exchange. Trading takes place under the "best price system," which means that a price can be improved if the other specialist has a better bid or offer than actually was dealt on with the first specialist. Since 1988 an improved computer system has been installed by the Amsterdam Stock Exchange. (H.O.S., Trading Support System). At the beginning of the trading session, prices are established based on orders which have reached the floor before the opening of business. Other investors then enter the market with further buy orders or sell orders which are matched through the market or can be balanced by the market making book of the bank or broker which is used by the investor. Market orders or limit orders can be executed at

Table 6   Domestic Share Trading Value, 1985–1989 (Dfl mln)

Year	Value
1985	113,000
1986	148,000
1987	159,000
1988	121,000
1989	185,000

Source: Amsterdam Stock Exchange.

Table 7   The 25 Most Actively Traded Shares on the ASE, 1989

Ranking	Company	Trading Value (Dfl mln)
1	Royal Dutch	21,500.7
2	Philips	11,961.7
3	Unilever	11,064.5
4	Hoogovens	9,120.3
5	Akzo	7,159.9
6	Nationale Nederlanden	6,696.4
7	Nedlloyd	5,893.4
8	DSM	5,726.5
9	Rodamco	4,190.0
10	KLM	3,752.2
11	Amro Bank	3,732.2
12	NMB Postbank	3,541.2
13	Aegon	3,305.5
14	Ahold	3,254.1
15	Heineken Bier	3,042.2
16	Elsevier	3,025.5
17	ABN	2,841.8
18	Robeco	2,669.9
19	KNP	2,472.1
20	Fokker	2,395.1
21	Amev	2,315.6
22	Buhrmann Tetterode	2,286.0
23	Rorento	2,205.7
24	Amro All In Fund	2,198.6
25	VNU	2,137.0

Source: Amsterdam Stock Exchange.

Table 8   Holdings of Pension Funds and the Largest 7 Insurance Companies by Sector

Percentage breakdown	1986	1988	1989
Equities	8.7%	10.3%	12.7%
Bonds	13.6%	15.6%	15.1%
Private loans	57.2%	52.9%	50.5%
Mortgages	9.9%	9.6%	9.7%
Short term	1.2%	0.5%	0.8%
Real estate & others	9.4%	11.1%	11.2%
Total funds (Dfl bln)	395.1	485.5	518.8

better prices take precedence over orders which are limited at the same price as is dealt on. The latter orders can be partially executed.

Since all members are corporations, they are represented by their respective employees. The management of each member represent their company on the Stock Exchange. Employees can be authorized dealers or clerks. Clerks are not allowed to execute orders. Orders are conveyed from the office of the members to the trading floor through the Trade Support System or by telephone. All transactions are inputted into the Trade Support System and instantly transferred to the information circuit.

List of Largest Bank and Brokers

A list of the largest bank and brokers is displayed in Table 9.

Settlement and Transfer

Since February 1990, the ASE has used a seven days settlement system, whereby settlement takes place on the seventh day after the transaction date. If this date is a bank holiday, settlements take place on the first business day thereafter.

Amsterdam operates through a clearing system. All Stock Exchange members have their account with this clearing system (NECIGEF). At the end of the business day all transaction of each individual member are balanced, and this balance is settled on the settlement day by delivery versus payment, i.e, by simple entry into the account of the member with NECIGEF. No actual movement of securities takes place.

Securities transactions done for the account of clients take place in the same way. Each private individual or institutional investor has his custody ac-

Table 9   List of Largest Banks and Brokers

Amro Bank	14.4%
NMB Postbank	8.4%
Rabo Bank	7.6%
ABN	7.4%
Kempen & Co.	4.6%
Strating	4.4%
Pierson Heldering & Pierson	4.0%
Bank Mees & Hope	3.5%
CLN Oyens & Van Eeghen	2.7%
Swiss Bank Corporation	2.6%
Banque Paribas	2.6%

count with a bank or licensed broker. According to the client's instructions settlement takes place by delivery versus payment from one custodian bank's account into the other using the NECIGEF clearing system.

Commission

After allowing fixed discounts on large transactions and latter allowing negotiated commission rates on transactions in shares over a value of Dfl 1 million and over Dfl 2.5 million in bonds, rates will be come fully negotiable as per July 1, 1990.

Taxation and Regulations Affecting Foreign Investors

Dividends

All cash dividends paid by Dutch corporations are subject to a withholding tax of 25% of their gross amount. Most companies offer a non-taxable stock option paid out of the share premium reserve. Foreign investors accepting a cash dividend may obtain a reduced rate if the country of their residence has a tax treaty with the Netherlands. These investors can reclaim 10%, thus being charged only a 15% withholding tax.

No tax is paid if an individual shareholder, private or non private, owns 5% or more in the issued capital of a corporation. On received interest their is no withholding tax in the Netherlands.

Capital Gains

There is no capital gain tax in the Netherlands. Only companies which use excess funds to invest in the market are changed normal corporate tax on their trading profits.

Exchange Controls

There are no limitations to foreign investors with regard to investing in the Netherlands. However, takeovers must be approved by the SER, the supervisory board on takeover and mergers.

Reporting

Reporting Requirements for Listed Companies

The basic listing requirements are governed by ASE authorities. A company wishing to have equity listed on the ASE is required to file an application for listing with the ASE. A prospectus must be issued prior to the listing, containing relevant information on the company, including a brief history of the company, a five year historic record, balance sheet and profit and loss account and a summary of the articles of association.

Having obtained approval the company is required to enter into a listing agreement with the Amsterdam Stock Exchange, whereby the company agrees that it shall abide by the ASE rules and regulations. As per the end of 1989 new

---

Table 10   List of Most Important Countries which the Netherlands Has a Tax Treaty

Austria
Belgium
France
Germany
Italy
Japan
Luxembourg
Spain Sweden
Switzerland
United Kingdom
U.S.A.

---

listed companies are allowed to adopt only two protective measures against hostile takeovers. Companies which have a listing on the ASE must issue an annual report prior to the annual meeting of shareholders, which must be held within six months of the end of the fiscal year. Furthermore, companies must provide a semi annual statement and relevant information on acquisitions, disinvestments and any other developments having a material impact on its business. Notice must also be given of various corporate decisions or resolutions such as dividends, the issuance of new shares, stock splits and any other matter of importance with regard to rights or privileges attached to its securities.

**Figure 1   CBS—All Share General—Price Index
From 25/6/80 to 27/6/90 Weekly**

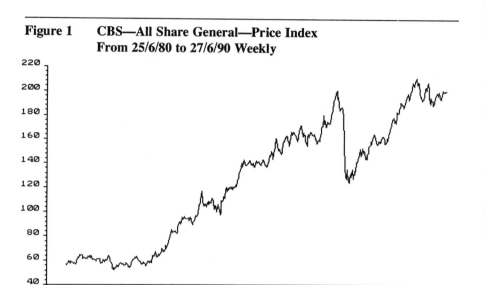

HIGH 210.100 13/ 9/89 LOW 52.400 30/ 9/81 LAST 198.700
Source : Datastream

Figure 2   From 26/6/85 to 27/6/90 Weekly

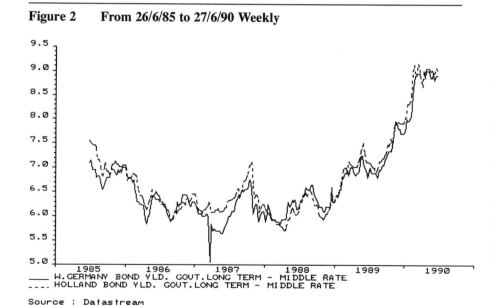

—— W.GERMANY BOND YLD. GOVT.LONG TERM - MIDDLE RATE
---. HOLLAND BOND YLD. GOVT.LONG TERM - MIDDLE RATE

Source : Datastream

Figure 3   From 26/6/85 to 27/6/90 Weekly

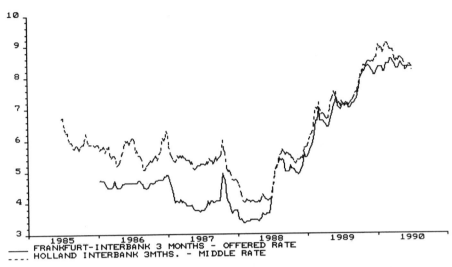

____ FRANKFURT-INTERBANK 3 MONTHS - OFFERED RATE
---- HOLLAND INTERBANK 3MTHS. - MIDDLE RATE

Source : Datastream

Figure 4   From 26/6/85 to 27/6/90 Weekly

____ DUTCH GUILDERS TO STERLING - EXCHANGE RATE
---- DUTCH GUILDERS TO UTD.STATES $ - EXCHANGE RATE

Source : Datastream

Swiss Equity Market

Dr. George Sellerberg
Bank Julius Baer, Zürich

Brief History and Structure

There are seven stock exchanges in Switzerland, the largest of which is Zürich, followed by Basle and Geneva. The Geneva Stock Exchange is the oldest and was formally organized in 1850. The stock exchange in Basle followed in 1876, and the Zürich exchange was founded one year later. The other four regional exchanges, Bern, Lausanne, Neuchatel, and St. Gallen, are much smaller.

Milestones in the History of the Zürich Stock Exchange

1663 Oldest known set of formal rules governing the brokerage trade.

1843 First stock price information in the Zürich newspapers.

1855 Foundation of the first Stock Exchange Association with regular weekly meetings of merchants and manufacturers.

1869 First Official Money Exchange and Security Price Record (61 securities).

1873 Official date of foundation of the Zürich Stock Exchange.

1875 First record of daily trading sessions at the stock exchange.

Table 1   Swiss Stock Exchanges in 1988

Place	Turnover		Market Share in % of Total	Number of Quotations[2]	Number of Listed Securities				
					Bonds		Stocks		
	Sfr. bn	Us\$ bn[1]			Swiss	Foreign	Swiss	Foreign	Total
Zürich	569	377	64.9	614,545	1504	880	309	226	2919
Geneva	199	132	22.7	254,313	964	878	240	242	2324
Basle	83	55	9.5	215,460	1341	876	249	225	2691
Lausanne	21	14	2.4	99,102	854	770	173	193	1990
Berne	4	2.6	0.5	23,968	918	746	113	14	1791
Total	876	580	100.0						

The exchanges at St. Galen and Neuchâtel do not publish any figures.

[1] 1 US\$ = Sfr. 1.5095 (year-end 1988)
[2] Quotations are those paid prices that are listed on the Quotations Sheet. In order to qualify for publication, a transaction involving at least one trading lot of the security concerned (Sfr. 5,000 to Sfr. 10,000) must be closed

Since the stock exchange does not record any other type of turnover data, this figure provides an approximate indication of the activity in the market sector concerned.

1876 First printed bylaws and trading rules of the Zürich Stock Exchange Assocation.

1877-
1880 Construction of the first stock exchange building.

1880 Foundation of an association for interbank delivery of securities.

1883 New legislation governing the activities of stockbrokers. Institution of state supervision.

1884 January to March: Stockbrokers' strike in protest against the new law and dissolution of the Stock Exchnge Association.——April: Foundation of the present Stock Exchange Association. Opening of the so-called "evening bourse."

1896 New Law. Banks are first admitted to trading on the stock exchange.

1897 New stock exchange trading rules.

1900 First convention on trading commissions, adopted jointly with the Basle Stock Exchange.

1912 New legislation, still valid today, to regulate the securities trade.

1914-
1916 Stock Exchange closed.

1928 Trading volume reaches an annual total of 10 billion Swiss francs for the first time.

1930 New stock exchange building opened. Ticker Service introduced.

1931 Mid-month forward transactions allowed.

1936 September 28/29: stock exchange closed because of Swiss franc devaluation.

1938 Association of Swiss Stock Exchanges founded. Elaboration of a common platform for the creation of a Swiss Admission Board.

1940 May 10-July 6: stock exchange closed.

1948 First Swiss commission rates agreement.

1954 Trading volume exceeds 10 billion Swiss francs for the first time since 1928/1929.

1961 Association of Swiss Stock Exchanges is co-founder of the International Federation of Stock Exchanges (FIBV).

1962 Guarantee insurance introduced. Implementation of Stock Exchange Television. Foundation of Telekurs AG.

1964 Installation of allotting equipment.

1965 Number of listed securities exceeds 1000.

1969 Three trading rings.—Adoption of OTC trading rules.—Introduction of Stock Exchange Telex.

1970 Foundation of SEGA, Swiss security clearing house for centralized security safekeeping.

1971 Adoption of stock exchange dues for improvement of exchange facilities.

1975 Forward trading extended to three months.

1976 Trading volume exceeds 100 billion Swiss francs for the first time.

1977 Centenary celebrations of the Zürich Stock Exchange, General Assembly of FIBV in Zürich.

1978 Exchange rate problems lead to investment ban for foreigners (lifted in 1979).

1980 Architectural competition for a new stock exchange building.

1981 Number of listed securities exceeds 2000.

1982 Introduction of "payment against delivery" system by SEGA.

1983 General reconstruction of the whole floor area.

1985 End of the rebuilding and opening of the fourth ring for trading.
Entry into force of the new agreement on commission rates.

1986 Introduction of continuous trading.
New clearing regulations.

Foundation of Association Tripartite Bourses.
Foundation of SOFFEX (Swiss Options and Financial Futures Exchange AG).

1987   Opening of the fifth ring for trading.
Start of construction work for the new stock exchange building.

List of Principal Banks

Licenses to trade in securities on the Zürich Stock Exchange have been issued to 24 banks. An additional 178 firms hold licenses to engage in the securities trade outside the stock exchange. These 24 Ring Banks form the membership of the Zürich Stock Exchange Association:

ZÜRICH STOCK EXCHANGE ASSOCIATION
Bleicherweg 5
8001 Zürich
Tel: 211 1470

ALLGEMEINE ELSASSISCHE BANKGESELLSCHAFT, SOGENAL, STRASSBURG, FILIALE ZÜRICH
Bleicherweg 1
8001 Zürich
Tel: 220 7111

AMRO BANK UND FINANZ
Bleicherweg 21
8022 Zürich
Tel: 202 5995

BANCA DELLA SVIZZERA ITALIANA, FILIALE ZÜRICH
Bleicherweg 37
8022 Zürich
Tel: 205 8111

BANK JULIUS BAER & CO AG
Bahnhofstrasse 36
8022 Zürich
Tel: 228 5111
Tix: 812154

Table 2   Members of the Zürich Stock Exchange as of January 31, 1989

| | | Zürich Stock Exchange Association | |
Year[1]	Members	Representatives and Deputies[1]	OTC Dealers[1]
1884	13		
1902	16		30
1930	34	119[2]	32[2]
1950	22	102	45
1960	25	128	59
1970	26	140	105
1975	25	146	126
1980	24	176	157
1981	24	175	163
1982	24	177	169
1983	24	193	178
1984	24	192	188
1985	25	199	200
1986	25	197	212
1987	28	219	221
1988	29	218	232

[1]   As of 1975 per January 31 of the following year.
[2]   End of 1931.

BANK CANTRADE AG
Bleicherweg 30
8038 Zürich
Tel: 481 6100

BANK HOFMANN AG
Talstrasse 27
8022 Zürich
Tel: 211 5760
Tlx: 812133

BANK LEU AG
Bahnhofstrasse 32
8022 Zürich
Tel: 211 5760
Tlx: 812133

BANK OPPENHEIM PIERSON (SCHWEIZ) AG
Uraniastrasse 28
8022 Zürich
Tel: 214 2214

BANK RINDERKNECHT AG
Bahnhofstrasse 28a
8022 Zürich
Tel: 211 1552

BANK J VONTOBEL & CO AG
Bahnhofstrasse 3
8022 Zürich
Tel: 211 8270
     488 7111
Tix: 812306

HANDELSBANK NW
Talstrasse 59
8022 Zürich
Tel: 214 5111

MAERKI, BAUMANN & CO AG
Dreikonigstrasse 8
8022 Zürich
Tel: 202 2684

OVERLAND TRUST BANCA, LUGANO
     ZWEIGNIEDERLASSUNG ZÜRICH
Todistrasse 17
8022 Zürich
Tel: 201 3111

PRIVATBANK UND VERWALTUNGSGESELLSCHAFT
Barengasse 29
8022 Zürich
Tel: 228 9111

RAHN & BODMER
Talstrasse 15
8022 Zürich
Tel: 211 3939

RUD, BLASS & CIE, INHABER BLASS & CIE BANKGESCHAFT
Talacker 21
8039 Zürich
Tel: 217 2111

RUEGG BANK AG
Waaggasse 5
8022 Zürich
Tel: 211 6267

A SARASIN & CIE BASEL ZWEIGNIEDERLASSUNG ZÜRICH
Talstrasse 66
8022 Zürich
Tel: 213 9191

SCHWEIZERISCHE BANKGESELLSCHAFT
    (UNION BANK OF SWITZERLAND)
Bahnhofstrasse 45
8021 Zürich
Tel: 234 1111
Tix: 813551

SCHWEIZERISCHER BANKVEREIN (SWISS BANK CORPORATION)
Paradeplatz 6
8021 Zürich
Tel: 223 1111
Tix: 813471

SCHWEIZERISCHE DEPOSITEN-UND KREDITBANK
Lowenstrasse 49
8021 Zürich
Tel: 211 6790
Tix: 812364

SCHWEIZERISCHE KREDITANSTALT (CREDIT SUISSE)
Paradeplatz 8
8021 Zürich
Tel: 211 6790
Tix: 812364

SCHWEIZERISCHE VOLKSBANK (SWISS VOLKSBANK)
Bahnhofstrasse 53
8021 Zürich
Tel: 228 1111
Tlx: 812575

ZÜRCHER KANTONALBANK
Bahnhofstrasse 9
8022 Zürich
Tel: 220 1111
Tlx: 812281

Transfer of Ownership

Bearer Securities

The value of these securities is embodied in the document or certificate. Consequently, the transfer does not necessitate special formalities and takes place either by handing over the security or by entries in the securities accounts of the banks (in the case of collective safecustody of the securities in-house or with the central depository SEGA). Most Swiss securities are in bearer form.

Registered Securities

The transfer of registered shares to a new holder usually requires the endorsement in blank of the registered holder on the share certificate or on a separate form (fliegende Blankozession). It also requires a signed application (Eintragungsgesuch) by the new owner giving his name, nationality, and address and declaration that he has acquired the shares for his own account. If the company has no objections to the transfer, it will alter the registration in the share register and return the old or issue a new certificate in the name of the new shareholder. Only the person entered in the share register is recognized as shareholder and is entitled to all rights deriving from the registered share(s).

Registered shares of many companies have restricted transferability (vinkulierte Namenaktien). The restrictions may be laid down specifically in the articles of incorporation, or all transfers may generally be subject to the approval by the board of directors of the company. The board may refuse a transfer without giving any reasons or make it dependent on the fulfillment of certain conditions. As a rule, only individuals of Swiss nationality residing in Switzerland and Swiss majority controlled corporations will be accepted as registered shareholders.

Table 3 Number of Listed Bonds by Issuers and Types

Issuers	Straight Bonds		Convertible Bonds		Warrant-linked Bonds		Issues with Variable Interest Rates		Swiss Franc Bonds with Interest in Foreign Currency		Issues in Foreign Currency		Total	
	Sec.	Iss.	Sec.	Iss.	Sec.	Iss.	Sec.	Iss.	Sec.	Iss.	Sec.	Iss.	Sec.	Iss.*
Switzerland/Liechtenstein														
Federal government	40	1											40	1
Cantons	167	19			1	1							168	20
Municipalities	72	22			1	1							73	22
Transportation companies	10	3			6	5	3	1					19	6
Mortgage Bond Institutions	109	2											109	2
Central Issuing Institutions	79	4											79	4
Cantonal Banks	301	21			3	3							304	21
Commercial Banks	178	28	5	3	36	20	4	3					223	41
Finance Companies	97	34	6	6	34	29							137	63
Power Plant and Elec. Comp.	226	54	1	1	4	4							231	54
Industrial Comp. and Misc.	86	49	2	2	24	19							112	55
Insurance Companies			4	3	5	4							9	4
Total	**1365**	**237**	**18**	**15**	**114**	**86**	**7**	**4**					**1504**	**293**

Table continues

Foreign Bonds

States and Cities	116	34					2	2			2	2	120	34
Transportation Companies	26	17	1	1	1	1	2	2					30	21
Internat. Development Banks	100	5											100	5
Banks and Finance Companies	263	147	16	13	34	31	10	10	3	3	32	27	358	218
Industrial Companies	232	123	23	16	6	6	2	2	4	4	5	4	272	145
Total	**737**	**326**	**40**	**30**	**41**	**38**	**16**	**16**	**7**	**7**	**39**	**33**	**880**	**423**
Total Bonds	**2102**	**563**	**58**	**45**	**155**	**124**	**23**	**20**	**7**	**7**	**39**	**33**	**2384**	**716**

*Since certain issuers appear under two or more headings, the total does not correspond to the sum of the figures.

Table 4   Number of Listed Stocks by Issuers and Types of Shares

Issuers	Bearer Shares	Registered Shares	Participation Certificates	Dividend-Right Certificates	Total Stocks	Total Issuers
Switzerland/Liechtenstein						
Banks	21	9	15		45	27
Finance Companies	54	26	31	1	112	62
Insurance Companies	4	11	11		26	13
Industrial Companies	42	25	27		94	46
Transportation Companies	4	2	1	2	9	5
Mutual Funds					23	8
Total	125	73	85	3	309	161
Foreign Countries						
USA and Canada	118				118	118
Germany	35	1			36	33
Netherlands	16				16	16
United Kingdom	12	2			14	12
France	8				8	8
South Africa	8	2			10	8
Japan	7	1			8	8
Other Countries	15	1			16	16
Total	219	7			226	219
Total Stocks	344	80	85	3	535	380

Table 5   Number and Market Value of Listed Securities 1877-1988

Year	Bonds					Stocks				Total
	Switzerland/ Liechtenstein	Market Value Sfr. bn	Foreign Countries	Market Value Sfr. bn	Total	Switzerland Liechtenstein	Market Value Sfr. bn	Foreign Countries	Total	
1877	34		1		35	42		6	48	83
1890	41		23		64	65		8	73	137
1900	93		24		117	69		13	82	199
1910	202		76		278	102		34	136	414
1920	337		89		426	80		40	120	546
1930					482				152	634
1940	329		103		432	92		41	133	565
1950	276		95		371	87		38	125	496
1960	398		137		535	98		60	158	693
1970	971		253		1224	130		91	221	1445
1980	1412	68.1	397	27.3	1809	176	75.6	166	342	2151
1981	1464	70.3	460	31.3	1924	183	68.9	168	351	2275
1982	1516	82.0	554	42.5	2070	180	77.3	163	343	2413
1983	1406	83.5	635	51.0	2041	184	96.1	170	354	2395
1984	1397	85.9	716	61.9	2113	188	103.6	181	369	2482
1985	1406	96.2	776	71.1	2182	205	174.6	190	395	2577
1986	1425	103.7	870	89.0	2295	254	208.9	200	454	2749
1987	1489	107.2	866	94.7	2355	300	170.1	217	517	2872
1988	1504	111.1	880	106.4	2384	309	211.1	226	535	2919

Table 6   Market Value of Listed Swiss Stocks as of Year-End 1988

	Sfr. Millions*	Percent of Total
Banks	53,170.86	25.2
Finance Companies	48,978.33	23.2
Insurance Companies	23,116.44	10.9
Industrial Companies	68,552.44	32.5
Transportation Companies	3,381.27	1.6
Mutual Funds	13,874.99	6.6
Market Value	211,074.33	100.0

*Participation certificate capital and unlisted portions of capital are included.

Some companies use "one-way" certificates for their registered shares, with no coupon sheets attached. A new certificate is issued at every change of ownership. One single certificate may represent the entire holding of a shareholder. The transfer can be further facilitated by including a power of attorney in the application form, authorizing the company to endorse the certificate on behalf of the shareholder. Such a power of attorney is valid until revocation and simplifies transfer formalities, in the case of the sale of the shares or of the shareholder's death.

Stock Exchange Rules and Practices

As there are no laws or regulations in Switzerland requiring securities to be traded through the intermediary of a stock exchange, exchange members are quite free to buy and sell stocks and bonds on or off the floor. This permits all transactions to be carried out in a most practical and efficient manner. In particular, the off-the-floor trade enables banks internally to offset customers' buying and selling orders against each other. Therefore, many orders are carried out off the floor. Settlement takes place at official prices, thus fully safeguarding the clients' interests. Formally, most orders are executed by the banks acting as principals.

Table 7   Market Value of the Largest Swiss Companies Listed in Zürich as of Year-End 1988

Company	Stock Capital Sfr. Millions[1]	Price on 29.12.1988[2]	Market Value Sfr. Millions	Percentage[3]
1. Nestlé AG	353.0	7240 I, 6690 N, 1310 PS	24173.7	11.4
2. Schweizerische Bankgesellschaft	2433.8	3200 I, 621 N, 114.5 PS	15329.7	7.3
3. Schweizeischer Bankverein	3899.4	339 I, 300 N, 292 PS	12150.4	5.8
4. Ciba-Geigy AG	541.4	2645 I, 2130 N, 2100 PS	11848.0	5.6
5. Sandoz AG	364.9	9575 I, 7500 N, 1585 PS	11380.7	5.4
6. Schweizerische Kreditanstalt	2051.5	2700 I, 525 N	10023.2	4.7
7. «Zürich» Versicherungs Gesellschaft	201.3	4310 I, 3480 N, 1700 PS	7294.5	3.5
8. Jacobs Suchard AG	375.6	6815 I, 1400 N, 580 PS	5054.4	2.4
9. . «Winterthur» Versicherungs-Ges.	140.0	4210 I, 3390 N, 670 PS	4978.4	2.4
10. Schweiz. Rückversicherungs-Gesellschaft	154.0	9125 I, 7440 N, 1520 PS	4684.7	2.2
The 10 Largest Companies			**106917.7**	**50.7**
11. BBC Brown Boveri AG	791.5	2750 I,620 N, 442 PS	4221.2	2.0
12. Schweizerische Volksbank	736.5	1760 N, 166 PS	2571.6	1.2
13. Elektrowatt AG	445.0	2850 I, 299 PS	2452.5	1.2
14. Inspectorate International AG	133.3	2110 I, 228 PS	2373.2	1.1
15. Surveillance Holding SA	14.5	4675 N. 4775 GS	2291.8	1.1
16. «Holderbank» Financière Glarus AG	231.0	5125 I, 940 N, 402 PS	2235.5	1.0
17. Schweizerische Aluminium AG	599.3	835 I, 402 N, 68.5 PS	1933.6	0.9
18. «Swissair» Schweiz, Luftverkehr-AG	615.4	1080 I, 1000 N, 180 GS	1918.2	0.9
19. Bank Leu AG	343.3	3200 I, 2550 N, 650 N, 415 PS	1820.8	0.9
20. Adia SA	43.1	8740 I, 4350 N, 675 PS	1796.9	0.8
The 20 Largest Companies			**130533.0**	**61.8**
21. Pargesa Holding SA	1193.5	1630 I	1768.6	0.8
22. Oerlikon-Buhrle Holding AG	429.0	1070 I, 368 N, 318 PS	1704.3	0.8
23. Báloise-Holding	70.0	2600 N, 2195 PS	1698.5	0.8
24. Soc. Internationale Pirelli SA	660.2	253 I, 220 PS	1583.2	0.8
25. Ascom Holding AG	162.9	4860 I, 4200 N, 1170 N, 740 PS	1522.9	0.7
26. Gebrüder Sulzer AG	301.4	4750 I, 420 PS	1371.2	0.7
27. Landis & Gyr AG	214.0	1500 N, 192 PPS	1327.8	0.6
28. SMH Schweiz. Ges. für Mikroelektr.	345.0	381 N, 415 PS	1322.1	0.6
29. Schindler Holding AG	·136.9	4850 I, 900 N, 755 PS	1176.1	0.6
30. BSI-Banca della Svizzera Italiana	231.0	2700 I, 580 N, 320 PS	1116.0	0.5
The 30 Largest Companies			**145123.7**	**68.8**

[1] Participation certificates and non listed parts of the capital included.
[2] I = Bearer shares, N = Registered shares, PS = Participation certificates, PPS = Priority participation certificates, GS = Dividend-right certificates.
[3] Percentage of the total market value of Swiss stocks.

Table 8 Market Value of Listed Bonds as of Year-End 1988*

Issuers	Straight Bonds		Convertible Bonds		Warrant-Linked Bonds		Issues with Variable Interest Rates		Sfr.–Bonds with Interest in Foreign Currency		Issues in Foreign Currency		Total	
	Sfr. m	%	Sfr. m	%	Sfr. m	%	Sfr. m	%	Sfr. m	%	Sfr. m	%	Sfr. m	%
Switzerland/Liechtenstein														
Federal Government	9,900.58	10.0											9,900.58	8.9
Cantons	10,564.67	10.7			46.00	0.5							10,610.67	9.6
Municipalities	2,884.05	2.9			86.00	1.0							2,970.05	2.7
Transportation Companies	633.03	0.6			203.70	2.4	270.80	45.7					1,107.53	1.0
Mortgage Bond Institutions	14,475.70	14.6											14,475.70	13.0
Central Issuing Institutions	5,156.46	5.2											5,156.46	4.6
Cantonal Banks	13,794.72	13.9			174.12	2.0							13,968.84	12.6
Commercial Banks	16,976.22	17.1	764.76	28.4	3,310.33	38.3	321.45	54.3					21,372.76	19.2
Finance Companies	7,772.56	7.9	565.74	21.0	2,211.18	25.6							10,549.48	9.5
Power plants and Electricity Companies	12,868.63	13.0	44.46	1.7	362.40	4.2							13,275.49	12.0
Industrial Comp. and Misc.	4,107.60	4.1	304.95	11.3	1,486.75	17.2							5,899.30	5.3
Insurance Companies			1,014.19	37.6	760.86	8.8							1,775.05	1.6
Market Value	99,134.22	100	2,694.10	100	8,641.34	100	592.25						111,061.91	100 51.1
Par Value	99,815.40		2,035.32		9,655.00		590.00						112,095.72	
Foreign Bonds														
States and Cities	14,326.00	16.8	755.00	10.0	695.00	9.4	256.49	24.0			125.55	3.2	14,708.04	13.8
Transportation Companies	3,419.76	4.0					150.00	14.1					5,019.76	4.7
Internat. Development Banks	12,962.24	15.2											12,962.24	12.2
Banks and finance Companies	28,346.37	33.2	2,511.05	33.4	5,921.88	80.1	483.54	45.3	454.00	40.4	3,369.13	35.7	41,085.97	38.6
Industrial Companies	26,287.62	30.8	4,251.83	56.6	774.75	10.5	176.93	16.6	670.50	59.6	436.22	11.1	32,597.85	30.7
Market Value	85,341.99	100	7,517.88	100	7,391.63	100	1,066.96	100	1,124.50	100	3,930.90	100	106,373.86	100 48.9
Par Value	86,605.03		4,656.00		6,804.62		1,088.00		1,750.00		4,505.63		105,409.28	
Total Market Value	184,476.21		10,211.98		16,032.97		1,659.21		1,124.50		3,930.90		217,435.77	100
Total Par Value	186,420.43		6,691.32		16,459.62		1,678.00		1,750.00		4,505.63		217,505.00	

*Total issues originally listed, irrespective of partial redemptions.

Figure 1   Trading Volumes and Number of Quotations 1883—1988

	Trading volumes in Swiss Francs* / Quotations	Trading volumes in billions Swiss Francs / Number of quotations in 1000 (scale: 50 100 150 200 250 300 350 400 450 500 550 600)
1883	6318	
1905	39,567	
1913	1,657,000,000	
	27,316	
1927	9,454,000,000	
	110,736	
1940	1,798,953,386	
	40,298	
1945	2,985,585,688	
	55,372	
1950	4,969,233,424	
	74,653	
1955	13,262,318,667	
	107,528	
1960	19,483,687,717	
	153,344	
1965	19,045,708,972	
	124,753	
1970	35,702,594,249	
	168,037	
1975	82,941,555,997	
	250,687	
1980	132,597,227,143	
	298,004	
1981	147,104,509,230	
	296,375	
1982	190,831,996,133	
	326,570	
1983	266,092,716,066	
	396,041	
1984	308,337,034,786	
	389,883	
1985	451,703,322,678	
	475,120	
1986	558,232,665,364	
	508,333	
1987	636,353,467,505	
	624,059	
1988	568,619,683,116	
	614,545	

Trading volume liable to duty in the Canton of Zürich. Due to restatement of trading volume liable to duty as from June 30, 1974 (in connection with the revision of Federal Stamp Duty), trading volumes after 1974 are not strictly comparable with earlier figures.

Table 9   Volume Percentages of Spot, Forward and Premium Trades 1893–1988[1]

| | Stocks | | | | | | | Bonds |
	Spot	%	Forward	%	Premium	%	Total	Total[2]
1893	908	5	12,846	77	2,909	18	16,663	
1927	42,660	51	35,809	43	4,976	6	83,445	27,291
1950	36,686	76	6,378	13	4,594	1	47,658	26,995
1960	76,980	65	29,365	25	12,191	10	118,536	34,808
1970	70,239	69	26,074	26	5,664	5	101,959	66,078
1975	93,467	67	41,007	29	5,334	4	139,808	110,879
1980	119,581	65	58,435	32	6,395	3	184,411	113,593
1981	110,749	66	51,872	31	4,644	3	167,265	129,110
1982	108,531	67	48,636	30	4,348	3	161,515	165,055
1983	141,998	63	77,559	34	6,352	3	225,909	170,132
1984	141,477	64	72,576	33	6,141	3	220,194	169,689
1985	189,356	65	95,146	33	5,955	2	290,457	184,663
1986	199.682	66	94,146	32	5,891	2	300,396	207,937
1987	268,561	69	111,626	29	5,834	2	386,021	238,038
1988	281,368	78	77,353	21	3,138	1	361,859	252,686

[1] In number of quotations
[2] Spot only

Types of Transactions

Cash Transactions

Most of the transactions are cash or spot transactions (Komptantgeschäft) that account in Zürich for about 70% of the volume.

Fixed Forward Transactions

Shares and the most important Swiss warrants can also be traded "ultimo" (Termingeschäft). The investor who buys (sells) a security "ultimo" (with the month of settlement specified) is engaged to buy (sell) the security concerned at the price fixed at the time when the transaction was concluded with value date at the end of the month concerned.

The buyer (seller) may also sell (buy) the same number of securities with the same value date before having delivered the securities of the first deal.

Table 10   Swiss Companies with Highest Number of Quotations in 1988

Company	Quotations in 1988	Year end 1987 Sfr. m	Market Value Year end 1988 Sfr. m	Change %
1. Nestlé AG (N, I, PS)	11,657	18,593.2	24,173.7	+30.1
2. Ciba-Geigy AG (N, I, PS)	10,174	8,317.7	11,848.0	+42.4
3. Schweizerischer Bankverein (N, I, PS)	9,244	12,312.9	12,150.4	− 1.3
4. Schweizerische Bankgesellschaft (N, I, PS)	9,183	14,501.4	15,329.7	+ 5.7
5. BBC Brown Boveri AG (N, I, PS)	7,850	2,349.2	4,221.2	+79.7
6. Sandoz AG (N, I, PS)	6,557	8,798.7	11,380.7	+29.3
7. Schweizerische Kreditanstalt (N, I)	6,470	8,987.2	10,023.2	+11.5
8. «Zürich» Versicherungs-Ges (N, I, PS)	6,385	6,189.0	7,294.5	+17.9
9. «Winterthur» Schweiz, Versicherungs-Ges (N, I, PS)	5,833	4,242.0	4,978.4	+17.4
10. Jacobs Suchard AG (N, I, PS)	5,790	4,736.3	5,054.4	+ 6.7
11. Schweizerische Rückversicherungs-Ges. (N, I, PS)	5,582	4,614.4	4,684.7	+ 1.5
12. Oerlikon-Bührle Holding AG (N, I, PS)	5,327	1,284.0	1,704.3	+32.7
13. Schweizerische Aluminium AG (N, I, PS)	5,023	974.3	1,933.6	+98.5
14. Adia SA (N, I, PS)	4,998	998.9	1,796.9	+79.9
15. Bank Leu AG (N, I, PS)	4,656	1,583.1	1,820.8	+15.0

N = registered shares
I = bearer shares
PS = participation certificates

Table 11   Market Indices: Year-End Figures 1984–1988

	1984	1985	1986	1987	1988	Change in % 1987/88
Swiss Index						
SPI General Share Index	608.8	982.3	1077.7	769.4	942.5	+22.5
Bearer shares	609.4	954.1	1,092.9	771.5	847.4	+ 9.8
Registered shares	599.3	1,020.8	1,042.9	822.6	1,184.9	+44.0
Bearer shares and participation Certificates	613.1	962.4	1,094.7	747.3	831.9	+11.3
Participation certificates	622.5	984.3	1,098.8	682.0	787.6	+15.5
SPI Services	598.8	1,004.0	1,167.0	725.7	841.1	+15.9
Banks	669.4	1,097.1	1,216.0	774.0	820.3	+10.3
Insurances	530.0	934.9	1,180.1	786.0	951.4	+21.0
Transport	705.3	1,263.3	947.0	863.0	1,044.9	+21.0
Retailers	402.8	767.8	1,022.4	663.8	797.7	+20.2
Misc. services	410.5	663.5	978.5	577.4	750.9	+30.0
SPI Industrials	620.3	960.4	982.1	819.1	1,058.0	+29.2
Metals	973.6	978.9	760.2	698.3	1,384.6	+98.3
Machinery	633.9	876.6	964.2	741.3	983.7	+32.7
Utilities	690.6	923.3	998.5	860.5	856.7	− 0.4
Chemicals and pharma	612.5	1,046.0	967.7	842.9	1,147.6	+36.1
Food and luxury goods	599.5	927.3	1,013.2	866.8	1,059.0	+22.2
Electrical engineering and electronics	653.5	954.1	1,004.1	656.9	958.3	+45.9
Building contractors and materials	587.7	814.7	936.1	862.9	1,113.7	+29.1
Misc. industrials	535.2	820.3	983.1	758.6	891.3	+17.5
SBC Price Index	405.2	636.1	666.4	467.3	559.8	+19.8
SKA Index	320.1	504.7	558.1	416.4	524.4	+25.9
SNB Index	195.9	302.5	314.8	224.8	269.9	+20.1

Moreover, the buyer may carry the transaction over from the originally agreed settlement date (Reportgeschäft), with the buyer selling the securities spot to the bank participating in the transaction, paying the contango (interest or lending fee), and buying the securities back as of the next closing date. A seller may also postpone the delivery of the shares (Deportgeschäft) with the buyer's consent and payment of a premium to the latter.

Premium Trading

This is a special type of contingent or optional transaction whereby the buyer can withdraw from taking delivery by paying a premium agreed upon at the time of conclusion of the transaction (Prämiengeschäft). As a rule, the forward price of the securities exceeds the cash price prevailing on the same day by approximately the amount of the premium (this difference being called "ecart").

**Table 12   Swiss Performance Index
Stocks—Market Value and Weighting of the Companies
Included in the Index per March 31, 1989
(Number of Companies = 213)**

Structure	Market Value Mio Sfr	%	Number of Securities	%	Index
General Index	**224,202.4**	**100.0**	**391**	**100.0**	**998.1**
Bearer Shares	104,575.9	46.6	177	45.3	870.8
Registered Shares	86,126.4	38.4	103	26.3	1,280.9
Bearer Shares and Participation Certificates	138,075.9	61.6	288	73.7	869.6
Participation Certificates	33,500.0	14.9	111	28.4	857.7
Services	**104,417.2**	**46.6**	**188**	**48.1**	**861.3**
Banks	54,173.0	24.2	60	15.3	833.5
Insurances	24,648.1	11.0	31	7.9	1,019.2
Transport	2,645.4	1.2	14	3.6	1,042.5
Retailers	4,680.1	2.1	23	5.9	757.4
Misc. Services	18,270.4	8.1	60	15.4	759.2
Industrials	**119,785.1**	**53.4**	**203**	**51.9**	**1,154.9**
Metals	2,948.0	1.3	13	3.3	1,530.8
Machinery	9,598.6	4.3	49	12.5	1,082.6
Utilities	5,525.5	2.5	18	4.6	864.8
Chemicals and Pharma	44,463.8	19.8	19	4.9	1,378.7
Food and Luxury Goods	32,833.5	14.6	33	8.5	1,067.5
Electrical Engineering and Electronics	10,521.5	4.7	24	6.1	1,012.8
Building Contractors and Materials	6,024.4	2.7	23	5.9	1,144.0
Misc. Industrials	7,869.5	3.5	24	6.1	940.6

On option day, which is the fourth trading day before the end of the month, the buyer has the possibility either to accept delivery of the securities in paying the price agreed upon on the transaction day or to pay the premium and decline delivery. The premium usually amounts to between 3% and 10% of the price of the security involved.

Only fully-paid shares are traded on a forward basis. For shares of banks and insurance companies and for units of investment trusts there is no forward and premium trading.

Figure 2   Performance of Bearer Shares and Participation Certificates as against Registered Shares 1968–1988

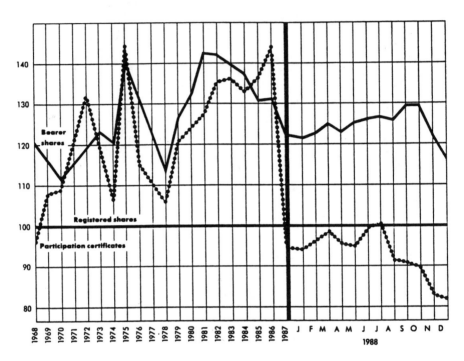

Fixing of the Price

The Zürich Stock Exchange has five separate rings in the form of a circular counter where, according to an established order, bonds, Swiss shares, and foreign shares are dealt. Each of the ring banks has its own ringside place where the representative of the individual member operates and notes down details of all transactions. Inside the ring, the Stock Exchange Commissioner, an official of the Canton of Zürich, who supervises the trading, and a stock exchange clerk are seated. The clerk has the task of calling out the individual securities in the order in which they appear on the official quotation list for the respective dealings to begin. No security may be traded until it has been called by the clerk. Shares are read out in succession twice a day (second reading called "Reprise") but bonds are read only once daily.

Table 13 Types of Securities

	Term in English	Term in German	Comments
Shares	Bearer share	Inhaberaktie	Most Swiss shares are in bearer form with a coupon sheet attached, but many Swiss companies have issued both bearer and registered shares. The par value of Swiss shares must be at least Sfr. 100 (usual practice: Sfr. 100 for registered shares and Sfr. 500 for bearer shares).
	Registered Share	Namenaktie	Share made out in the name of the owner who is entered in the register of shareholders of the company concerned. Usually, the transfer of registered shares is reserved to Swiss citizens and Swiss controlled companies and is subject to approval by the board of directors. In general, registered shares have a lower nominal value than bearer shares. The principle "one share one vote" thus allows Swiss control despite possible minority of Swiss ownership in terms of equity.
	Dividend-Right Certificate	Genussschein	Security incorporating the right to participate in the net profit and the liquidation proceeds of a company as well as the right to subscribe to new shares in the case of a rights issue. However, the holder has no membership rights, in particular he cannot attend shareholder meetings. The dividend-right certificate may be in bearer or registered form.
	Participation Certificate	Partizipationsschein	Bearer security incorporating the same rights as the dividend-right certificate and thus similar to that. It is issued for the purpose of raising capital, and its nominal value is part of the equity of the company.
	Warrant	Option	Warrants are normally issued together with so-called warrant or option bond issues and usually entitle the bearer to subscribe to new shares or bonds of specific conditions. Warrants can be traded separately from the warrant issues.
	Swiss Certificate	Schweizer Zertifikat	Original share certificate of a foreign company, mainly originating in the United States, the U.K. or Canada, which is quoted on a Swiss Stock Exchange and is registered in the nominee name of a specified Swiss Nominee endorsed in blank. For dividend payments or participation in corporate actions it must be stamped by the nominee company.

Table continues

Table 13 (continued)

	Term in English	Term in German	Comments
Bonds	Straight Bond	Anleihens- obligation	All bonds in Switzerland are in bearer form with coupon sheets attached. The minimum denomination for bonds is usually Sfr. 5,000, but in the case of certain issues Sfr. 1,000.
	Federal Bond	Anleihens- obligation der Eidge nossenschaft	Bond issued and backed by the full faith and credit of the Swiss Government.
	Public Authority Bond	Anieihens- obligation einer öffent lich-recht- lichen Körperschaft	Bond issued and backed by the full faith of a canton or municipality of Switzerland.
	Convertible Bond	Wandel-obligation	Bond that may be converted by the holder into shares or participation certificates of the same or of another company within a specified time period and at a specified price.
	Warrant issue	Optionsanleihe	Bond issue with warrant(s) attached embodying the right to purchase shares or participation certificates of the issuing company at a stipulated price within a certain period or to buy or sell determined values respectively.
	Swiss Franc Bond of Foreign debtor	Sfr.-Auslandsanleihe	Bond issues placed on the Swiss capital market by foreign borrowers (companies, government agencies or states). The issues are divided into debentures of Sfr. 5,000 and Sfr. 100,000 each. Swiss franc bonds of foreign debtors are exempt from the 35% withholding tax.
Units	Investment Trust Unit	Anteilschein	Share evidencing participation in an investment trust (mutual fund) in which investors pool their capital for joint investment. The assets are held and managed by a bank (or managed by a special management company) for account of the investors. In Switzerland, only open-end investment trusts are allowed. They are permitted to issue new shares continuously and are obligated to redeem shares at net asset value. Although a trust may stop issuing new shares, it is still obligated to redeem them.

Table 14

Trading takes place from Monday to Friday with the following schedules:

A.M.	**Swiss Bonds**
9:30	Opening of trading in unlisted bonds
10:15	Opening of official trading in listed bonds
11:30	Opening of official trading in convertible and warrant-linked bonds

A.M.	**Foreign Bonds**
9:15	Opening of trading in unlisted bonds
10:15	Opening of official trading in listed bonds

A.M.	**Swiss Stocks**
9:30	Opening of official trading in listed stocks (continuous trading at least until 1:15 p.m.)

P.M.	
Approx. 1:20	Opening of trading in unlisted stocks

A.M.	**Foreign Stocks**
10:30	Opening of official trading (continuous trading at least until 1:15 p.m.)

Minor changes of the trading hours may be made on short notice at any time. Except for continuously traded stocks, there are no closing hours for the regular securities trade, and trading times vary substantially, depending upon trading volumes.

Table 15

The minimum number of shares that can be traded varies with the market price:

Market Price in Sfr.		Trading Lot
From	To	
1	5	1,000
5	10	500
10	50	100
50	200	50
200	500	25
500	2,000	10
2,000	5,000	5
5,000	10,000	2
10,000 and more		1

The minimum number of bonds that can be traded is Sfr. 5,000 nominal value.
Odd lots in shares and bonds are traded at prices that may slightly differ from the official quotation.

The shares of the most important domestic and foreign companies, however, are traded continuously regardless of the quotation list's order. Therefore trading session starts with the continuously traded equities.

Dealings are effected and prices determined on the exchange by the "a la criee" system, whereby bargaining is carried out directly and verbally between ring representatives. The ring representatives have to make known to the clerk all prices bid (Geld), asked (Brief), and paid during the official trading hours. In addition to calling out the securities, the stock exchange clerk has to call out and write down all prices, whether bid, asked, or paid, as called out by the ring traders.

When a security is called for trading, a cash opening price is generally set. This is then followed in arbitrary sequence by additional cash transactions or by forward or premium deals for different settlement dates. Orders on hand before the opening of the market are normally executed at a price paid in the first reading.

Once a trading is in progress, a dealer is free to revert to a security that has been called earlier to execute additional orders coming in during trading hours. This is permissible, however, only within well defined groups, such as banks and industrials. An electronic alloting machine is used in those cases where there are several buyers to one offer or several offers to one buyer.

Unofficial Trading

Unofficial trading is carried out immediately after the closing of the normal market session at the ring. Regulations are similar to those governing the official sessions. The trade concentrates mainly in some medium and many smaller sized companies that do not comply with the reporting requirements of the stock exchange (or have not yet applied for the listing). The unofficial trading also includes bonds for which the certificates have not yet been printed and delivered and, therefore, are not yet officially admitted. The trading is supervised by the Stock Exchange Association.

Generally, securities may be admitted to the unofficial trading only if they have been regularly dealt over the counter.

Over-the-Counter Trading

Over-the-counter trading takes place in shares that are neither listed nor unofficially traded on the stock exchange.

Settlement of Cash Transactions

Securities of cash deals must be delivered and paid for at the earliest on the third business day (Valutatag) and no later than on the tenth business day following the trade date. Settlement in Switzerland "delivery against payment" carried out by SEGA, the Swiss depository and clearing organization, usually takes three working days.

Settlement of Forward Transactions

Fixed forward deals are settled on the last business day of a month, which may be the last day of the current month or of the next month or of the month after. At the time the deal is closed, all terms (price of the securities and the period of the contract) are agreed upon. Payment for and delivery of eligible securities takes place through the SEGA, which acts as a central clearing house. For these securities, the system of instructions of conformity, with delivery against payment, is applied.

For premium trades, on the fourth before the last business day of the month (Prämienerklärungstag), it must be declared whether the delivery of the securities will be accepted or the premium paid. Paying-in and delivery-in occurs two days after declaration of premium; paying-out and delivery-out occurs three days after declaration of premium, i.e., on the last trading day of the month (ultimo).

In the case of forward trades, the purchaser is neither entitled to the title of the securities nor may he vote or take part in a shareholder meeting of the company concerned. If, between the date of the transaction and the date of settlement coupons are due, the seller cashes them, but sets them off against the price.

In the case of transactions involving registered shares, which are not eligible for SEGA, the security sheets have to be sent directly to the company concerned with the new shareholder's registration.

Financial Newspapers

Finanz and Wirtschaft, Weberstrasse 8-10, PO Box, CH-8021 Zürich
Neue Zürcher Zeitung, Falkenstrasse 11, PO Box, CH-8021 Zürich
Schweizerische Handelszeitung, Seestrasse 37, PO Box CH-8027 Zürich.

SOFFEX

The successful development of options exchanges in numerous international financial centers and the strong demand for standardized options on Swiss shares led to the foundation of a Swiss options exchange, known as SOFFEX AG, a

Table 16   Transaction Costs on Swiss Stock Exchanges

Tax	Securities of Domestic Borrowers	Securities of Foreign Borrowers
Federal Stamp duty	0.075%	0.15 %
Cantonal securities transfer tax*	0.01 %	0.01 %
Stock exchange*	0.005%	0.005%
Withholding tax on interest	35%	—

*Official charges are: Sfr. 0.10 and Sfr 0.05, respectively, for each Sfr 1000.– of market value or fraction thereof.

Excerpt from the Agreement on Commission Rates of The Association of Swiss Exchanges

The following tariffs apply to transactions in Switzerland and are graduated according to the gross value per transaction:

Domestic Shares and Similar Securities:
– Up to Sfr. 50,000.–	0.8%
– for the next Sfr. 40,000.–	0.7%
– for the next Sfr. 50,000.–	0.6%
– for the next Sfr. 150,000.–	0.5%
– for the next Sfr. 300,000.–	0.4%
– for the next Sfr. 400,000.–	0.3%
– for the next Sfr. 1 million	0.2%
– for the amount exceeding Sfr. 2 miooion	negotiable

Foreign Shares and Similar Securities:
– up to Sfr. 50,000.–	1.0%
– for the next Sfr. 50,000.–	0.9%
– for the next Sfr. 50,000.–	0.7%
– for the next Sfr. 150,000.–	0.5%
– for the next Sfr. 300,000.–	0.4%
– for the next Sfr. 400,000.–	0.3%
– for the next Sfr. 1 million	0.2%
– for the amount exceeding Sfr. 2 million negotiable	

Trust Units:
– up to Sfr. 500,000.–	0.3%
– for the next Sfr 500,000.	0.2%
– for the next Sfr 1 million	0.1%
– for the amount exceeding Sfr 2 million	negotiable

Swiss Franc Bonds:
– up to Sfr. 50,000.	0.6%
– for the nest Sfr. 50,000.	0.4%
– for the next Sfr. 200,000.–	0.3%
– for the next Sfr. 700,000.	0.2%
– for the next Sfr. 1 million	0.1%
– for the amount exceeding Sfr. 2 million	negotiable

Table 16   Continued

Foreign Currency Bonds
– up to Sfr. 50,000.–	0.6%
– for the next Sfr. 50,000	0.5%
– for the next Sfr. 50,000.–	0.4%
– for the next Sfr. 150,000.–	0.3%
– for the next Sfr. 700,000.–	0.2%
– over Sfr. 1 million (ceiling)	wholly negotiable

Minimum Amounts
a) transactions in Switzerland:	
– shares and Swiss franc bonds	minimum Sfr. 30.–
– trust units	minimum Sfr. 10.–
b) transactions in foreign currency bonds,	minimum Sfr. 80.–
notes and promissory notes	

Minimum amounts can be fixed at will for all transactions having a gross value of less than Sfr. 250.–.

privately owned corporation with the Basel, Geneva, and Zürich exchanges and the five largest Swiss banks as shareholders.

Compared to other options exchanges, its most important distinguishing feature is that a fully automated screen-based trading system has replaced the traditional open-outcry pit. The pillar of the new trading process is a very comprehensive computer system that is linked to the screens in the trading departments of the participating banks and brokerage firms via the most rapid network in the world. SOFFEX, thereby, guarantees *quick and efficient trading*. It

Table 17   Bond Yields: Year-End Figures 1984 – 1988

	1984	1985	1986	1987	1988
SBC Bond Yields					
Swiss Bonds	5.09	4.89	4.70	4.61	4.76
Federal	4.83	4.66	4.41	4.20	4.30
Cantons	4.90	4.67	4.37	4.14	4.44
Municipalities	4.95	4.73	4.46	4.15	4.48
Banks	5.11	4.91	4.74	4.70	4.88
Finance Companies	5.52	5.20	4.95	4.97	4.95
Power Plants	5.12	4.97	4.75	4.69	4.78
Industrial Companies	5.41	5.07	5.18	4.91	4.91
Foriegn Bonds	5.76	5.48	5.62	5.35	5.20

Table 18

Foreign taxes withheld at source for residents of Switzerland (as of 31 December 1988)

Countries [*] Countries with which Switzerland has concluded no double taxation agreement[1]	Dividends			Interest		
	Normal rate %	Relief[2] %	Net tax[3] %	Normal rate %	Relief[3] %	Net tax[3] %
Australia	0[4]	[4]	[4]	10[5]	0	10
Austria[6]	25	15	5	10[7]	5	5
Belgium	25	10	15	25	15	10
for holdings of at least 25%	25	15	10			
Canada	25	10	15	25[8]	10[8]	15[8]
Denmark	30	30	0			
Finland						
Individuals	25	15	10	30	30	0
Legal entities	25	20	5	30	30	0
France[9]						
in general	25	[10]	[10]	25[11]	15[12]	10[12]
for holdings of at least 20% by Swiss companies	25	20[13]	5[13]			
Dividends from capital investment companies	25	10	15			
Interest on credits, savings books, current accounts etc.				45[14]	35	10
Germany[15]						
in general	25	10[16]	15[16]	10[17]	10[17]	
Frontier power stations	25	20	5			
Interest on credits				0		
Great Britain	0	[18]	[18]	27	27	0
Ireland	0	[19]	[19]	35	35	0
Italy	32.4	17.4	15[20]	12.5[21]	0	12.5
Bank balances				25	12.5	12.5
Interest on credits				15	2.5	12.5
Japan	20	5	15	15	5	10
for holdings of at least 25%	20	10	10			
Luxembourg*	15[22]	0	15	0[23]		0
Profit-sharing bonds				15	0	15
Netherlands	25	10	15			
for holdings of at least 25%	25	25	0			
Profit-sharing bonds				25	20	5
Norway[24]	25	20	5			
South Africa	15	7.5	7.5	0		
Spain	20	5	15	20	10	10
for holdings of at least 25%	20	10	10			
Sweden	30	25	5			
USA	30	15	15	30[25]	25	5
for holdings of at least 95%	30	25	5[26]			

TAX INFORMATION

According to the Swiss Federal Decree on the Abuse of Double Taxation Agreements, Swiss companies in which aliens hold a substantial interest may claim relief from foreign withholding taxes only on the fulfilment of certain conditions. The decree states inter alia that: a) no more than 50% of the income subject to such taxes is used to satisfy the claims of persons not privileged under the double taxation agreement (e. g. payment of credit interest to aliens), and b) at least 25% of gross earnings is to be distributed as dividends annually. Family foundations, the majority of whose founders or beneficiaries are resident outside Switzerland, are completely excluded from relief from foreign withholding taxes.

[10] As is the case with French shareholders, Swiss shareholders may claim from the French authorities a tax credit ('avoir fiscal') of 50% on declared dividends, resulting in a total dividend of 150% (100% declared dividend + 50% tax credit). However, a tax of 15% is withheld from the total dividend of 150% (= 22.5% of the declared dividend). This gives the following picture for Swiss shareholders receiving French dividends:

Declared dividend		100.—
Less 25% withholding tax at payment		25.—
Net dividend paid out by the company		75.—
plus refund from French tax authorities 25% withholding tax		25.—
Tax credit	50.—	
less 15% on 100.— + 50.— (= 22.5%)	22.50	27.50
Total income of Swiss shareholders		127.50

For the 22.5% not refunded, claim may be made in Switzerland for its application against the complete income tax.

[11] In the case of interest on private sector bonds, issued before 1 January 1965: 12%; issued between 1 January 1965 and 1 January 1987: 10%; issued after 1 January 1987: 0% (insofar as non-French domicile proved). In the case of interest on government bonds, issued before 1 January 1965: 12%; issued between 1 January 1965 and 1 October 1984: 10%; issued after 1 January 1984: 0%. Interest on loans concluded abroad after 18 June 1988: 0%.

[12] The refund on bonds issued prior to 1965 is only 13%, so that the net tax is 12%.

[13] In the case of Swiss companies under predominantly foreign control the relief is only 10% and the net tax 15%, as long as the shares of neither company are listed on the stock exchange or traded over the counter. In both cases (refund of 20% or 10%) refund will be made of the 'précompte' paid by the French company, with a deduction of 5% or 15% withholding tax respectively.

[14] Bank balances of persons not resident in France are exempt from withholding tax with retroactive effect from 1 January 1985.

[15] Persons who do not pay the normal Swiss taxes on all their German income cannot claim either a refund in Germany or tax relief in Switzerland. Persons coming from Germany who settle in Switzerland have during the first 5 years merely the right to claim net tax withheld against total income tax, but are not entitled to a refund from Germany. – For foreign-controlled Swiss companies and foundations limitations are similar to those applicable in France (see footnote 9).

[16] On the basis of the new corporate tax law which came into force as of 1 January 1977, Germany grants a tax credit of 9/16 on declared dividends to shareholders of German companies who are resident in Germany. Shareholders not resident in Germany may not claim this advantage.

[17] No claims for refund are possible in the case of investment fund distributions.

[18] The Swiss shareholder is entitled to the tax credit granted to the British shareholder,

[1] Switzerland has in addition concluded double taxation agreements with the following countries: Greece, Hungary, Malaysia, New Zealand, Pakistan, Portugal, Singapore, South Korea, Sri Lanka, Tobago, Trinidad and Egypt. The agreements with Indonesia and Iceland are not yet ratified.

[2] Tax relief is generally effected through subsequent refund of taxes withheld. In some cases, exemption at source is possible.

[3] In the case of Australia, Austria, Belgium, Canada, France, Germany, Great Britain, Ireland, Italy, Japan, the Netherlands, Spain, South Africa and Sweden, net tax withheld may be claimed against total income tax, up to the percentage of the income tax on the earnings involved.

[4] As a rule, in the case of dividends from 1 July 1987 onwards (previously: 30% withholding tax).

[5] Under Australian law, interest on loans granted before 19 May 1983 to Australian-owned companies is tax-free. Under certain circumstances, the interest on certain categories of bonds may be exempted from tax.

[6] Persons paying blanket-rate income tax in Switzerland may not claim these advantages.

[7] Foreign investors are as a rule exempt.

[8] Interest paid on certain government bonds, bonds issued by the provinces and local authorities as well as bonds having a maturity of more than five years, issued between 23 June 1975 and 1 January 1990, are tax-free. Also, interest paid on the said government bonds etc. is granted complete relief from Canadian withholding tax.

[9] For Swiss companies with predominant foreign control, the agreement stipulates essentially identical restrictions as the aforementioned Swiss Federal Decree on the Abuse of Double Taxation Agreements. In addition, Swiss legal entities in which persons not residing in Switzerland have a controlling interest, by way of participation or other means, may claim exemption from French withholding taxes on interest and licensing fees only if they do not enjoy tax privileges in the Swiss canton in which they are domiciled. Family foundations are not entitled to the tax advantages deriving from the agreement if the founder or the majority of beneficiaries do not reside in Switzerland and if more than one-third of the dividends and interest originating in France is paid, or scheduled to be paid, to persons not resident in Switzerland.

Table continues

Table 18   (continued)

TAX INFORMATION

which has been repeatedly readjusted and, with effect from 6 April 1988, amounts to ²⁵⁄₇₅. From this tax credit, which is paid by the British tax authorities, a 15% withholding tax is deducted on the dividend distributed plus tax credit. The situation for the Swiss shareholder as regards dividends due from 6 April 1988 onwards is as follows:

Distribution by the company before withholding tax deduction	100.—
+ tax credit from the British authorities, ²⁵⁄₇₅	33.33
less 15% withholding tax on 100.– + 33.33	19.99 _13.34_
Total distribution to the Swiss shareholder	113.34

The remainder of the tax credit not refunded, amounting to 19.99, may be claimed against total income tax in Switzerland.

According to the revised agreement concluded on 8 December 1977 and ratified on 7 September 1978, companies with a holding of 10% or more are entitled to claim refund of half the tax credit retroactive to 6 April 1975. This results in a 5% tax deduction (instead of 15%). In respect of the rate applying as from 6 April 1988 this presents the following picture:

Distribution by the company (without withholding tax deduction)	100.—
+ tax credit from the British authorities ½ tax credit = ½ of ²⁵⁄₇₅	16.66
less 5% withholding tax on 100.– + 16.66	5.83 _10.83_
Total income of Swiss company	110.83

In this instance too, the remainder of the tax credit not refunded may be claimed against income tax.

¹⁹ Since 25 April 1984, and with retroactive effect from 6 April 1976, Swiss shareholders are entitled to a tax credit similar to that available in Great Britain (however, here this amounts to ²⁵⁄₇₅) and may claim the unrefunded remainder against total income tax in Switzerland (see footnote 18). Swiss companies holding at least 25% of voting rights receive the dividend tax-free without entitlement to a tax credit.

²⁰ Under Italian law, a further reduction to 10.8% may be granted, subject to certain conditions.

²¹ This rate only applies to bonds of private sector borrowers issued on or after 1 January 1984. The full tax rate applicable to interest on bonds of private sector borrowers issued between 1 January 1974 and 30 September 1982 is, as a rule, 21.6%, while that for bonds issued between 1 October 1982 and 31 December 1983 is generally 10.8%. Issued from 1 January 1984 onwards: 12.5%. Interest on Treasury notes and domestic public sector bonds, issued before 1 October 1986, is exempt from tax. Issued between 1 October 1986 and 1 October 1987: 6.25% withholding tax. Issued after 1 October 1987: 12.5%. Interest on private sector bonds issued up to 31 December 1973 is exempt from tax.

²² No tax is to be withheld at source on dividends from holding companies.

²³ Income tax on interest from mortgages.

²⁴ The revised agreement, which is signed but not yet ratified, provides a relief of 15% on dividends and of 10% on holdings of 25% and above.

²⁵ The withholding tax on interest on US private sector and government bonds, issued since 18 July 1984, has been abolished.

²⁶ The reduction to 5% is only granted under quite exceptional circumstances.

Swiss taxes withheld at source for residents of other countries (as of 31 December 1988)

Countries	Dividends			Interest⁴		
* Countries with which Switzerland has concluded no double taxation agreement¹	Normal rate	Relief³	Net tax⁴	Normal rate	Relief²	Net tax⁴
	%	%	%	%	%	%
Australia	20	15		25	10	
Austria	30	5		30	5	
Belgium for holdings of at least 25%	20 25	15 10		25	10	
Canada	20	15		20⁵	15⁵	
Denmark	35	0		35	0	
Finland Individuals Legal entities	25 30	10 5		35 35	0 0	
France⁶	30⁷	5⁷		25	10	
Germany⁸ in general Frontier power stations	20 30	15 5		35	0	
Great Britain for holdings of at least 25%	20 30	15 5		35	0	
Ireland for holdings of at least 25%	20 25	15 10		35	0	
Italy	20	15		22.5	12.5	
Japan for holdings of at least 25%	20 25	15 10		25	10	
Luxembourg*	0	35		0	35	
Netherlands for holdings of at least 25%	20 35	15 0		30	5	
Norway	30	5		30	5	
South Africa	27.5	7.5		0⁹	35⁹	
Spain for holdings of at least 25%	20 25	15 10		25	10	
Sweden	30	5		30	5	
USA¹⁰ for holdings of at least 95%	20 30¹¹	15 5¹¹		30	5	

(The two columns labelled "35% withholding tax" appear vertically between the Dividends and Interest sections of the table.)

¹ Switzerland has in addition concluded double taxation agreements with the following countries: Greece, Hungary, Malaysia, New Zealand, Pakistan, Portugal, Singapore, South Korea, Sri Lanka, Tobago, Trinidad and Egypt.

² Including interest on bank balances, savings accounts, etc.

³ Procedure: generally, retroactive refund.

⁴ In most countries listed, the net tax can be credited against local income tax. Some exceptions: for example Finland, Italy, Norway.

⁵ Interest paid on federal government bonds, bonds issued by the cantons and municipalities as well as certain other bonds is granted relief from the total withholding tax of 35%.

⁶ In the case of foreign-controlled French companies, limitations on claims for benefits provided by the agreement are similar to those applying to Swiss companies with predominant foreign control (see footnote 9, 'Foreign taxes withheld at source for residents of Switzerland').

⁷ For foreign-controlled French companies which have at least 20% holdings in the

Swiss company paying dividends, the tax relief is only 20% (and the net tax thus 15%), unless the shares of one of the companies are listed on the stock exchange or traded over the counter.

⁸ For foreign-controlled German companies and foundations, limitations are similar to those contained in the treaty with France (see footnote 6).

⁹ No relief as long as South Africa imposes no tax on foreign interest paid to South African creditors; should South Africa introduce such taxation in future, the relief will be 25% and the net tax 10%.

¹⁰ Swiss citizens resident in the USA who are not also American citizens must first request that the full Swiss withholding tax be credited against their US taxes; the Swiss Tax Office will only refund that part of the tax which is not accepted for credit against US taxes.

¹¹ The reduction to 5% is only granted under quite exceptional circumstances.

aims to achieve a Swiss-wide solution and, not being fixed in any one particular location, should be able to maintain adequate liquidity.

Transparency of trading is significantly enhanced because all members are required to place all their orders through the computer system. All together, SOFFEX membership comprises over 50 members, a number of which have market-making responsibility.

Contrary to what happens in many foreign exchanges, SOFFEX AG also has a clearing function in that it acts as a counterparty for every transaction and therefore ensures that the obligations of a SOFFEX contract are always fulfilled. To accomplish this, SOFFEX sets high standards of integrity for its clearing members.

These may be divided into three categories:
- Direct Clearing Member (DCM)
- General Clearing Member (GCM)
- Non-Clearing Member (NCM)

A DCM must have at least 50 million Swiss francs of his or her own capital and has to pay one million Swiss francs into SOFFEX's Clearing Fund. Its own and client transactions are settled directly with SOFFEX.

A GCM should possess at least 500 million Swiss francs of its own capital and is obliged to contribute five million Swiss francs, as collateral against credit risk, to the Clearing Fund. In addition to its own and client transactions, it also executes those of NCM's.

NCM's must settle their business with at least one GCM by means of a prescribed SOFFEX contract.

The Swiss Stock Market: Heading for New Horizons?

Size and Structure of the Swiss Stock Market

The first decision to be taken when considering an investment in shares is how to spread one's commitment among the various stock markets. Frequently, the total market value of listed stocks is taken as a guideline; yet, on this basis, Switzerland's share of the total value of listed stocks worldwide is a mere 1.7%.

Why is it that the Swiss share index, after adjusting for inflation, is still 22% below the benchmark of 20 years ago? Why have other stock markets, such as Japan, the U.S., Canada, France, Holland, and Sweden, already left pre-crash prices far behind them, whereas Switzerland has only been able to make up half of the ground?

Figure 3   Size of Major Stock Markets

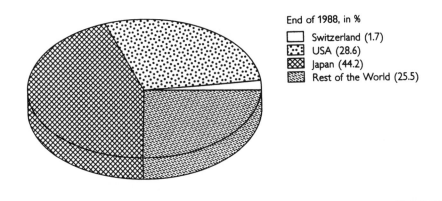

End of 1988, in %

- Switzerland (1.7)
- USA (28.6)
- Japan (44.2)
- Rest of the World (25.5)

Are prospects for the Swiss economy and corporate profits really as gloomy as the depressed share quotations would seem to suggest? In fact, quite on the contrary, and we are convinced that the presence of favorable underlying factors will sooner or later lead to the Swiss stock market seeing considerable upward revaluation.

In Europe, however, Switzerland's share is no less than 8%.

Although a large-scale investor might find a figure of SFr. 200 billion somewhat modest as the total value of listed stocks, one should bear in mind that Switzerland is the tenth largest stock market in the world, and the fourth largest

Figure 4   Size of European Stock Markets

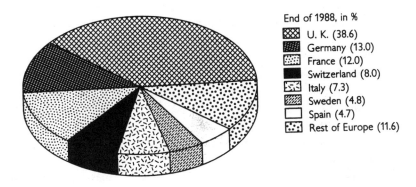

End of 1988, in %

- U. K. (38.6)
- Germany (13.0)
- France (12.0)
- Switzerland (8.0)
- Italy (7.3)
- Sweden (4.8)
- Spain (4.7)
- Rest of Europe (11.6)

Table 19   Market Weighting

End of 1988 in %

Market	Capitaliza-tion	GDP	Earnings	Cash Flow	Net Asset Value
France	2.6	7.3	3.8	4.0	3.4
Germany	2.8	9.5	3.3	5.1	3.5
Italy	1.6	6.3	2.0	3.7	2.1
Netherlands	1.0	1.8	1.7	1.8	1.9
Spain	1.0	2.5	1.2	2.0	2.0
Switzerland	1.7	1.5	2.2	2.0	2.8
United Kingdom	8.3	5.7	13.8	10.5	11.9
Rest of Europe	2.4	5.5	3.1	2.9	3.2
Europe	**20.9**	**40.1**	**31.1**	**32.0**	**30.8**
Australia	1.5	1.5	2.5	1.9	2.4
Hong Kong	0.9	0.3	1.3	0.7	1.3
Japan	44.2	21.1	16.2	22.5	22.3
Rest of Far East	0.7	0.5	0.7	0.5	1.0
Far East	**45.2**	**23.4**	**20.7**	**25.6**	**27.0**
Canada	2.5	3.3	4.0	3.5	3.9
U.S.A.	28.6	33.2	43.6	38.4	38.0
North America	**31.1**	**36.5**	**47.6**	**41.9**	**41.9**
S.A. Gold	0.2	–	0.5	0.5	0.3
World	**100.0**	**100.0**	**100.0**	**100.0**	**100.0**

in Europe. Indeed, the Swiss stock market is roughly the same size as all the Scandinavian stock markets put together. In fact, it is ideally suited to the needs of the institutional investor because the lion's share of its total stock value is accounted for by a small number of large corporations. The ten largest companies account for roughly 60% of total stock value (20 corporations make up 70% of the market value, and the top 30 cover no less than 75%). Or, to put it another way, 18% of the 414 listed stocks or 13% of the 231 listed companies constitute 75% of the value of total stocks listed.

Admittedly, trading is hindered because the stocks of most companies are allocated to three different classes of shares, but fundamental changes to this structure may be forthcoming over the next few years. At year-end 1988, bearer shares comprised 47.6% of total stock value, registered shares 37.6% and non-voting participation certificates 14.7%.

There's No Halting Liberalization

The fundamental changes just mentioned refer to the ongoing liberalization of the Swiss stock market. Liberalization got under way on November 17, 1988, the day Nestlé agreed to accept foreign investors as limited registered shareholders.

At the time, reactions on the Swiss stock market were very swift. Rumors of further announcements of liberalization measures led to both a collapse in the price of numerous other companies' bearer shares and an upswing in prices for registered shares. Within a very short time, the average premium on bearer shares fell from 47% (the day before Nestlé's decision) to below 20%; those on participation certificates fell from 17% to 0%. We believe that to date 90% of the adjustments for premiums and discounts have already been made.

Even though most companies are presently opposed to liberalization, it seems unlikely that the clock can be turned back. Companies that refuse to accept this trend will sooner or later have to pay the price for such a stance in the market. They will find that it is no longer possible to sell bearer shares to foreign investors at market prices, and every increase in their capital will inevitably hinge on the weakest link in the chain. Should this be the form of participation certificates with a high discount, then the price to be paid for the new capital will simply be that much higher. The vigorous takeover activities of Swiss firms abroad will sooner or later give rise to a call for reciprocity. After all, it is precisely by

---

Figure 5   Structure of the Swiss Stock Market by Class of Shares

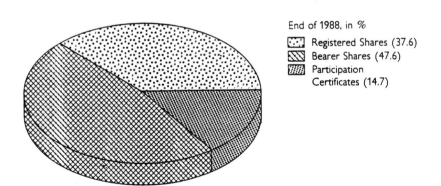

End of 1988, in %

Registered Shares (37.6)
Bearer Shares (47.6)
Participation
Certificates (14.7)

**Figure 6   Liberalization of Swiss Stock Market
January 1985 - February 1989**

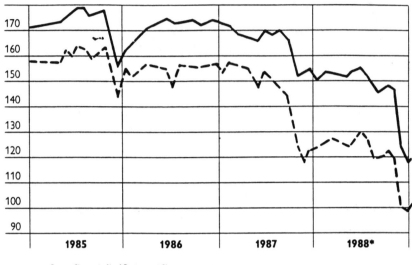

Bearer Shares in % of Registered Shares
Participation Certificates in % of Registered Shares   incl. January/February 1989

means of acquisitions both at home and abroad that numerous Swiss companies have expanded to the point at which their financing requirements can no longer be met by the limited resources of the Swiss capital market.

In the long term, liberalization should result in a reduction in the number of different classes of stock traded on the Swiss exchanges. Such a step would improve the marketability of many companies. Incidentally, the regulations on transfer, which are in many cases still restrictive, are a clear indication that current stock market prices by no means reflect the true value of companies. If the share prices were in fact too high, there would be no need to fear takeover offensives.

Benefits of Liberalization

For those companies wishing to open their doors to a wider circle of investors, the question arises as to how they can at the same time protect themselves against takeover bids. Since there are no laws or supervisory authorities in Switzerland to prevent such acquisitions, the only genuine long-term defense against unwanted bids is to be quoted at the correct market price. Yet how can Swiss companies force up the prices of their stock in order to deter would-be take-overs?

High corporate productivity must be the first line of defense. Poorly deployed capital has always attracted raiders. And a company's good performance must be readily visible, which means improving the standard of year-end company reporting. However, in many cases, this is still unsatisfactory. In this context, prominence should be given to providing consolidated accounts (some firms still publish figures for the parent company only) and interim reports. In the medium term, it would be desirable to bring Swiss valuation methods and company reporting into line with EC norms.

A further possible course of action would be to adopt a more dynamic policy on dividends. In recent years, the growth in dividends paid out by most companies lagged well behind increases in profits. The dividend rate of more than a few companies even dropped below the 20% mark. Yet Swiss institutions in particular are dependent on a regular cash flow. It may be too early to tell whether the sizeable 30% dividend increase at Ciba-Geigy signals the initiation of a new trend. However, it is our view that companies will in the future pay more attention to the question of dividends.

In the medium term, therefore, liberalizing shareholding regulations will have a favorable effect on share prices.

Currency Gains in the Offing for Swiss Firms

Given that the influx of funds depends on market capitalization, it is a sad fact that expensive markets demand a relatively large commitment of funds, whereas markets with lower prices are automatically underfunded. Although this procedure is actually illogical, it is, unfortunately, the order of the day.

This is probably an important reason for the rise in popularity of the GDP weighting as a criterion for deciding on the allocation of funds. However, this makes little difference to the weighting of the Swiss market. At 1.7%, Switzerland still counts as one of the small fry, its GDP weighting being no more an adequate gauge of its special situation than of the total value of its stocks.

In 1987, the 10 largest Swiss industrial companies achieved only 4% of their group turnover in Switzerland, and with the top 60, the respective figure was 14%. The 72 largest industrial companies alone recorded total annual turnover greater than Switzerland's GDP. Alongside these major industrial companies, one should also consider the major banks and insurances as well as 250,000 other medium-sized and smaller businesses. Last year, taking foreign subsidiaries into account, Swiss insurance companies saw a total premium volume of SFr. 63

billion, of which only 35% was generated within Switzerland; overseas operations probably account for roughly half of the business done by major banks.

These figures clearly show that, for many companies, the state of the Swiss economy is of secondary importance. All the same, it is worth mentioning at this point the encouraging buoyancy of the economy, as can be seen from the following key indicators:

Key Data on the Swiss Economy

	1988	1989	1990
Growth in GDP in real terms	3.0	2.5	2.3
Inflation	1.9	2.5	3.0
Unemployment	0.7	0.6	0.7
Current account surplus as percentage of GDP	3.4	3.5	3.5
Budget surplus as percentage of GDP	0.5	0.3	0.3

There are undoubtedly countries with a higher real growth rate; but can any of them boast such low inflation, virtually no unemployment, the world's highest current account and a budget surplus compared to GDP? As might be expected from such a high level of overseas activity, many companies' earnings are decisively influenced by exchange rate movements. Figure- 5 shows a breakdown of sales of the 10 largest Swiss industrial groups in terms of most important market regions.

The chart clearly indicates that the U.S. dollar and the European currencies have a substantial influence on Swiss corporate profits. However, the export pic-

Figure 7   Sales of 20 Largest Swiss Industrial Companies by Region

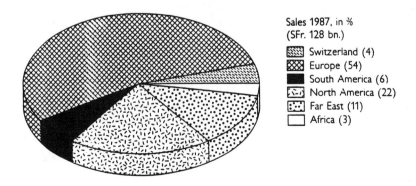

Sales 1987, in %
(SFr. 128 bn.)

Switzerland (4)
Europe (54)
South America (6)
North America (22)
Far East (11)
Africa (3)

Figure 8   **Currencies: January 1980—January 1989**
December 31, 1979 = 100

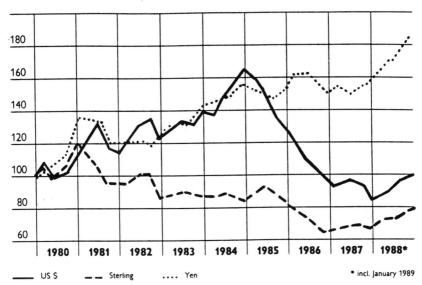

Figure 9   **Currencies: January 1980—January 1989**
December 31, 1979 = 100

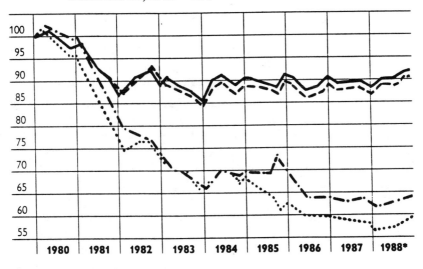

ture tells a completely different story, given that only 9% of goods exported from Switzerland are sold on the North American market. Exchange rate prospects for Swiss firms in 1989 are very rosy, following a year in which the Swiss franc proved to be the weakest of the major dealing currencies.

In terms of trade weighting, in the 12 months from January 31, 1988, the nominal trading value of the Swiss franc fell by 7%, and by 9% in real terms. The first company reports from industry show, however, that 1988 was not a year for currency gains because the nominal rate of the Swiss franc in mid-year had only weakened by 0.9%, or 1.9% in real terms. Nonetheless, the fact that for the first time in several years Swiss multinationals have suffered virtually no currency losses was enough to ensure a considerable increase in profits posted. We consequently also expect an increase in industrial earnings for the past year of roughly 20%. The exchange rate situation in the first half of 1989 should have an even more favorable impact, provided the rates of the major foreign currencies remain steady. Assuming this to be the case, the following comparisons between exchange rates for the first and second quarters of 1988 can be made as follows:

	1st Quarter 1989	2nd Quarter 1989
$	13.8	18.8
DM	4.1	7.1
£	11.8	8.6
FF	3.5	7.7
LIt	4.5	8.8
Yen	14.6	11.4

Corporate Profits Continue to Rise

Calculated for the year as a whole and assuming unchanging exchange rates, the value of the trade-weighted Swiss franc would decline by 3.5%—the largest drop on record. Earnings therefore look set to continue growing in 1989, especially as the banks and insurance companies are also looking confidently to the future. Following last year's 17% growth, we expect the private sector as a whole, i.e., industrial and commercial enterprises, banks and insurance companies, to record a further increase of 14%.

The P/E ratio of a stock market is a reflection not only of the level of earnings, but also of the growth in corporate profits. Switzerland is in this respect in particular the subject of numerous false preconceptions. Even high-ranking Swiss government and Swiss National Bank representatives were so rash as to make statements after the stock market crash that, in most instances, cannot be backed up by hard figures. The fact that the stock exchange indices had reached

Table 20   Corporate Profits—Major Quoted Companies

	Reported Figures		Estimated True Figures	
Year	Growth %	P/E	Growth %	P/E
1981	2.0	14.1	N.A.	N.A.
1982	−18.5	19.6	N.A.	N.A.
1983	36.4	20.0	N.A.	N.A.
1984	47.5	14.7	N.A.	N.A.
1985	18.4	20.6	N.A.	N.A.
1986	5.5	22.8	N.A.	14.2
1987	22.4	13.7	9.0	9.7
1988E	16.6	14.7	14.5	16.2
1989E	14.0	13.3	11.7	9.8
1990E	10.0	12.1	10.0	8.9
Average 10 Years	14.7	16.5	N.A.	N.A.

E = Estimate
P/E = End of year

1989/90: Valuation based on prices of April 1989

an all-time high on October 9, 1987, was probably the reason for claims that Swiss shares had been overvalued prior to the crash. Yet such claims are largely unfounded unless one takes the corresponding profits of the companies into consideration.

In Switzerland, a country with a high, if not the highest, standard of living, it appears to be more difficult to achieve the kind of growth rates found, for example, in Southern Europe, where markets are ostensibly still not saturated. This view is based on several misconceptions frequently aired.

As mentioned above, the majority of Swiss companies has a strong foreign slanting. Of the stocks of 75 of the largest Swiss companies quoted on the stock exchange, only 12 can be said to be typical domestic enterprises. The Swiss market is therefore secondary. Of far greater importance is the state of the European and U.S. economies. In this respect, the latest forecasts for the current year give cause for optimism. Growth, by which we mean corporate profits, is based on nominal values that are, furthermore, expressed in one currency only. Anyone wishing to compare growth rates should therefore view the matter through at least two pairs of spectacles to adjust for distortions in vision: one pair for inflation and the other for exchange-rate fluctuations.

In order to demonstrate the effect exchange rates and inflation have on the rate at which profits grow, let us take the example of Ciba-Geigy. Expressed in Swiss francs, Ciba-Geigy's profits over the past decade (1978-1988) increased by 13.7% p.a., or 10.1% after adjusting for inflation. The U.S. pharmaceutical company with the highest growth rate, Merck, increased its profits by 14.8% per year during the same period, yet this shrinks to only 8.2%, allowing for U.S. inflation. Calculated in Swiss francs, Merck's growth rate would thus be 12.5%, i.e., less than the annual increase of 13.7% achieved by Ciba-Geigy.

Based on estimated profits for 1989, the average P/E ratio for the three classes of Ciba-Geigy securities is roughly ten, compared with 16 for Merck.

Ciba-Geigy was not the only firm to show an impressive level of growth. According to our calculations, annual growth in Swiss corporate profits, including banks and insurance companies, has been over 13% since 1980. The Swiss stock market was among those hardest hit by the crash of October 19, 1987, and although the bourse has made 28% good on its post-crash low, the SBC index would need to rise another 26 points to reach once again the all-time high of October 9, 1987. Allowing for exchange rate factors, the Swiss stock market, with the exception of shares in gold mines, has thus far made the poorest recovery of all the international stock exchanges. Since corporate profits have continued to rise, the 1989 P/E ratio of only 9.3, calculated on the basis of estimated real figures, shows that the valuation of Swiss stocks has now sunk to a level unheard of in the past. Indeed, even on the basis of the figures set out above, today's valuation must be regarded as favorable.

We can also see the Swiss market's truly attractive rating if we turn our attention to the risk premium afforded by Swiss stock compared to alternatives in the area of fixed-interest securities. Risk premium is the difference between the

---

Table 21   Annual Growth in Profits (in %)
(Average for 10 Years)

	Merck (U.S.A.)	Ciba-Geigy (Switzerland)
In Local Currencies	14.8%	13.7%
In Real Terms	8.2%	10.1%
In SFr	12.5%	13.7%
P/E Ratio	16x	10x

Table 22   Swiss Stock Market Valuation
(As of February 28, 1989)

	1988	1989	1990
P/E Ratio (published figures)	14.8	13.9	12.5
P/E Ratio (estimated real figures)	10.3	9.3	8.5
Price/Cash Flow Ratio	5.0		
Price/Book Value	0.9		
Yield (%)	2.3	2.5	

earnings yield and the average yield on government bonds. The Swiss stock market can boast a higher risk premium than any other international stock market. And historically speaking, today's premium is probably at a record level.

Growing Institutional Demand for Swiss Shares

Admittedly, a favorable rating does not in itself trigger off movements in prices. The Swiss stock market generally requires stimulus in the form of demand from large institutional investors abroad.

Table 23   Risk Premiums on the International Stock Markets
(As of January 31, 1989) in %

Switzerland (real figures)	6.3
(published figures)	2.7
Netherlands	2.9
West Germany	0.3
U.S.A.	–0.3
France	–0.4
U. K.	–0.9
Canada	–1.3
Japan	–2.5
Spain	–3.7
Italy	–4.1

Table 24   Investments of Swiss Institutions (End of 1988/Estimates)

In SFr. bn	Stocks	Bonds	Mortgages	Real Estate
Pension Funds	14	70	10	20
Insurances				
Life	1	25	17	12
Non-Life	5	19	2	5
State	0	10		
Investment Funds	2	2		9
Banks	7	28	280	
Other Swiss	91			
		246	6	254
Foreign Investors	80			
Swiss (incl. banks)		200		
Foreign (incl. notes)		200		
Market Size	**200**	**400**	**315**	**300**
Annual Growth	3-5	45-55	12-15	5
Swiss (incl banks)		15-20		
Foreign (incl. notes)		30-40		

Single European Market—In the Short Term, Benefits Outweigh Disadvantages

Frequently, foreign investors rely on the fact that Switzerland is not a member of the EC as a reason for not committing funds to the Swiss stock market. In 45 months' time, however, when the Single European Market becomes a reality, Switzerland will be strongly represented within the Community, considering that last year over 40%, or nearly SFr. 100 billion, of the turnover of the 60 largest Swiss industrial groups was achieved in EC countries. Whereas other companies, even those headquartered within the EC, are still having to build up capacity and are, at the same time, ever more prone to intensified competition on their own domestic markets, Swiss companies will be able to strengthen their positions by building on the foundations they have already laid. Switzerland ranks second only to the U.S. as the EC's biggest customer, accounting for roughly 10% of the community's exports; for example, in 1988, Switzerland bought more than twice as many EC products as did Japan. A trade surplus of roughly $11 billion with Switzerland enables the EC to cover approximately half of its deficit with Japan. We do not believe that the EC is interested in penalizing its second largest customer with trade barriers. There are even quite a number of areas where the Swiss stock market will benefit from the community's future shape—standardization of taxes and company reporting requirements are but two examples.

Most shareholders will surely welcome EC regulations being implemented to force Swiss corporations to improve their company reporting in the near future, making the real figures visible even to the layman. Whatever the case, the quality of company reporting in Swiss industry has been improving from year to year, even without the influence of the Single European Market, as is shown in Figure 10.

Even today, there are clear examples of ways in which the EC has been beneficial to Swiss industry: the whole of Europe is having to rationalize and modernize. It comes as no surprise that in Swiss mechanical engineering, our most important export sector, the order books as of year-end 1988 reached record size. How does Switzerland stand in terms of rationalization and innovation? Over the past five years, Swiss industry has also invested vast amounts in plant and equipment. This time span saw investments in manufacturing capacity increase by nearly 60% in real terms. For a number of years now, Switzerland's propensity to invest, measured as a percentage of GDP, has been 27%, which places Switzerland second only to Japan among the major industrial nations. The large European industrialized countries spend somewhere between 18% and 22% of their GDP on capital expenditure, whereas in the U.S., the figure is only around 15-16%. This order is reversed when it comes to ranking countries in terms of economic problems, for the cost of a failure to make investments is inevitably a steady decline in competitiveness and an accompanying rise in budget deficits.

Despite the considerable rise in interest rates compared with the previous year, we expect investment in Switzerland to continue at its present level, since at year-end 1988, capacity utilization attained a record high of 88.5% and domestic manpower resources were virtually depleted. The Swiss government has also contributed to this ongoing investment boom by planning or recently going ahead with major infrastructural projects, such as Railways 2000 or the Alpine Transverse programs.

In our opinion, a stock market in which companies are prepared to make such vast investments deserves to be accorded much more than a mere 1.7% weighting in an international portfolio.

Figure 10 Quality of Company Reporting 1975—1988

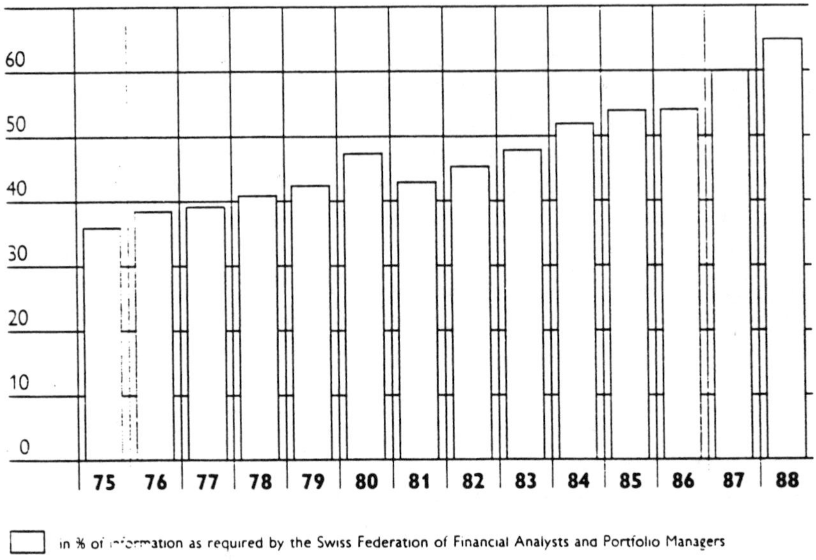
60
50
40
30
20
10
0
75 76 77 78 79 80 81 82 83 84 85 86 87 88
in % of information as required by the Swiss Federation of Financial Analysts and Portfolio Managers

Despite the level of investment and acquisition activity, major Swiss companies have high liquid resources, a consequence both of the favorable course of business over the years and also of the inexpensive Swiss capital market. Even after the latest increase, interest rates on the Swiss capital market are, in real terms, still the lowest of all the major industrialized nations. The liquid funds of the 10 most solvent Swiss industrial companies probably amount at present to roughly SFr. 30 billion—or the equivalent of the total volume of domestic bond issues over two years. A number of companies are therefore in a strong position to accelerate growth in the current year and in the near future, be it in the form of takeovers or joint ventures.

The favorable conditions underlying the Swiss stock market are soon likely to attract foreign capital back to the Swiss exchanges. However, in the long term, we also expect domestic institutional investors to play a noticeable part in stimulating trade. The most important playground of the domestic institutions, the real estate market, will sooner or later run up against the limitations of population growth. The average density of occupation per dwelling has fallen from 2.9 occupants in 1970 to only 2.2 today. Seen in conjunction with prevailing population forecasts, even today's volume of only 40,000 new houses and apartments

Figure 11   Structure of the Swiss Stock Market by Sector

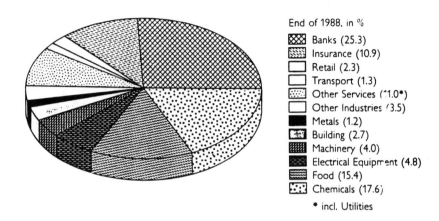

End of 1988, in %

- Banks (25.3)
- Insurance (10.9)
- Retail (2.3)
- Transport (1.3)
- Other Services (11.0*)
- Other Industries (3.5)
- Metals (1.2)
- Building (2.7)
- Machinery (4.0)
- Electrical Equipment (4.8)
- Food (15.4)
- Chemicals (17.6)

* incl. Utilities

per annum—which is only half the output achieved in the record years of 1972/73—would lead to a density of only 1.7 occupants per dwelling in 20 years' time, an unrealistic figure from today's point of view. Furthermore, given current property prices, real estate frequently no longer offers the investor attractive yields. What is more, the bond market is not in a position to cover fully the future investment needs of domestic institutions, as the total annual volume of domestic issues is already smaller than the annual growth of funds held by the pension schemes and insurance companies. For want of an alternative, domestic institutions will sooner or later be forced to focus on the Swiss stock market.

Nestlé's liberalization of shareholding policy has also had a favorable effect on institutional demand for shares. Numerous Swiss institutions have awakened to the opportunities that might have been missed in the registered share sector of the market. There may conceivably have been an excuse for missing out on the boom in Nestlé's registered shares, but many a pension fund administrator may find himself in trouble if he allows other opportunities to pass him by. It can only be hoped that more and more people will come to realize that bolstering the equity capital levels of Swiss firms is a substantial means by which to guarantee the value of pensions.

SNB Policy a Major Source of Uncertainty

The sky above the Swiss Bourse is, of course, not entirely cloudless. We have in the past all too often learned that currency gains can suddenly turn into losses.

The world's enormous trade and budget imbalances as well as the sovereign debt problems are all far from being solved. However, it is the Swiss National Bank's (SNB) monetary policy that is likely to be the most important single element of uncertainty affecting the Swiss stock market for some time to come.

When setting the money supply target for last year, the SNB undoubtedly faced major problems, stemming primarily from economic uncertainty that followed the crash of October 1987, as well as from the introduction of both new liquidity regulations and the interbank clearing system. Nonetheless, the sharpness with which the SNB further tightened its already restrictive strategy in the second half of 1988—which eventually led to a rise in mortgage rates at the end of January—surely leaves its monetary policy open to question. The SNB has in the past seriously underestimated Switzerland's economic growth without learning its lesson with respect to the money supply. Last year, for example, it forecast 1% growth in real terms, whereas in fact the economy grew by 3%; instead of the targeted 3% increase in the money supply, this actually contracted by 3.9%.

Conceivably, the assumptions on which the Swiss National Bank has based its policy may once again prove to be incorrect, and the stricter course adopted would then be overdoing things. We fully concur with the SNB in regarding inflation—caused by exchange-rate-related price increases on important goods (which accounts for 30% of the consumer price index), by higher prices for raw materials as well as rising prices among the domestic service industries—as a serious danger. We estimate that inflation will run at between 2.5% and 3% for the current year. Even if the price index does not rise any further, the effect on the statistical base will still result in an annual inflation rate of 1.9%. However, it remains to be seen whether the SNB has acted wisely in imposing such severe restrictions. Initially, the mortgage rate increase is more likely to force inflation up rather than slow it down.

Fortunately, the major Swiss companies are relatively immune to interest rate increases, owing to the vast liquid resources at their disposal. Indeed, the current year is likely to see a further substantial rise in more than a few companies' financial income. Sadly, the stock market seldom rewards this side of economic prosperity.

High interest rates will continue to impair the stock market until such a time as the situation returns to normal. We believe that a slight reduction in interest rates in the second half of the year is clearly within the bounds of the possible, given the fact that the pressure of inflation is expected to ease. This would also result in the general monetary climate again making shares more favorable. A first indication that the monetary situation is returning to normal was the mid-

Figure 12   SBV General Index

_____ Actual

_ _ _ _ 200 Day Moving Average

March SNB statement, which does not foresee any further tightening of monetary policy.

In connection with the Single European Market, however, the question arises as to whether the reserve banks of the individual EC member countries will coordinate their respective monetary policies even more closely in the future. This would have the medium-term effect of smoothing out the uneven levels of inflation that have repeatedly led to exchange rate adjustments in the past; exchange rates would, as a consequence, become more stable. This being the case, the Swiss National Bank might then also try at some point to stabilize the rate of the Swiss franc against the major European currencies. This would only be viable, however, if interest rates were simultaneously raised to match EC levels. We cannot, therefore, rule out the possibility of Switzerland's low interest rates becoming a thing of the past.

Summary

There are 10 reasons for believing that prices on the Swiss stock market will continue to recover:

1. Currency gains are in the offing.
2. The Swiss economy is sailing full steam ahead.
3. Corporate profits are expected to grow by another 12% in 1989.
4. The market valuation is at an all-time low.
5. The risk premium of the Swiss stock market is higher than in any other country and than ever before.

6. Swiss companies are well prepared for 1992 and the Single European Market.
7. The improvement in company reporting will reveal the true corporate figures.
8. Liberalization of the stock market will enhance the marketability of many companies.
9. For want of alternatives, domestic institutions will in the long term be forced to buy more shares.
10. The normalization of the monetary situation could stimulate the continuing recovery of the Swiss stock market.

13

Italian Equity Market

Marco Santi
KPMG Peat Marwick Fides s.n.c., Milan

Introduction

In the last few years the existing conditions in the Italian stock market and the outlook for an international integration have considerably changed. In fact, new issues of bonds and shares have increased, as well as the total capital managed by investment funds. And, beginning in 1985 the EEC Authorities have strongly accelerated the unification process in the European market. These changes have strengthened the need for renewing the Italian stock market.

Brief History

The stock exchanges in Italy began in different years: the one in Venice (Circa 1600) and the one in Trieste (1775) are the oldest. Much later Rome (1802), Milan (1808), and Naples (in the 1850s), set up their stock exchanges. Now ten stock exchanges are working in Italy, the most important being Milan, Turin and Rome; the other exchanges are in Genova, Venice, Trieste, Bologna, Florence, Naples and Palermo.

The Milan Stock Exchange made a rather slow and hesitant start, but beginning from the second half of 1800, with the development of industrial activities, the first shares began to be traded. At the end of the century an enormous development of the stock market turnover and of the propensity to save and invest in securities took place. In these and in the following years companies, such as

Pirelli, Montecatini and Edison, Falck and Fiat, which are now blue chips on the stock exchange, were set up.

Recent Years

Between 1980 and 1984 considerable changes occurred in the composition of financial flows among macroeconomic sectors by means of stockholdings. In fact, the market opened to new classes of stockholders, especially to private savers.

Italian companies, whose traditional problem has always been the lack of equity in comparison with an excessive presence of debt (predominantly short-term borrowings from commercial banks), began to join the stock market and in a few years' time their structure has become more capitalized.

As a consequence of the increase in the stock exchanges' activities, in 1985 and 1986 shares' prices have considerably increased, and so did the traded volumes. The MIB, for example, index reached its top value on May, 1986, then it slowly began to decrease. The quotations continued to go in a downward direction during 1987, but this negative trend was strengthened in the last months of that year as a consequence of the "Black Monday crash." The demand for stock equities considerably decreased because of having been formerly supported by mutual funds, which, after the crash, received a lot of requests for reimbursement by subscriptors. As a consequence, joining the equity market was again difficult for Italian companies. In the first four months of 1988, although shares prices slightly increased, the volumes traded did not. In addition, the market conditions did not allow companies to raise new capital from the market.

Italian Stock Exchange Structure and Related Indices

Italian Stock Exchange Structure

The Italian stock exchanges are controlled by the Ministry of Treasury. Their operations and organizations depend upon the National Companies and Stock Exchange Commission, or CONSOB, which was set up by law in 1974. CONSOB may delegate its powers to the local stock exchange bodies, such as trading chambers, stock exchange councils, and the stockbrokers managing committees.

The Italian equities market is divided in three distinct sections: the "listino" (first market), the "mercato ristretto" (second market), and the "terzo mercato" (over the counter).

Listino is the name of the official market, in which the shares officially listed in the stock exchanges are traded. These shares are public securities and those equities that obtained the official listing after a previous examination by CON-SOB. The "Listino ufficiale" (Official List) is the document drawn by the "Comitato direttivo degli Agenti di Cambio" (Stockbrokers Managing Committee). This committee reports the official quotations of securities.

In the "mercato ristretto" shares of minor companies that are awaiting the listing in the first market are traded. The "Ristretto" was originated by law (law 23/2/1977 n.49) and is controlled by CONSOB. This market, which is currently present in Milan, Rome, Genova, Turin, and Naples, occupies the same premises of the stock exchange but operate during different trading hours.

The "terzo mercato" is the over-the-counter market and is not officially ruled by law. It operates by the spontaneous trading of shares of companies not admitted to the listing in the two major markets. Related prices are published by economic papers for information only.

The Main Market Index: MIB

The formula for calculating this index is a weighted arithmetic average based on elementary price indices. Note that this calculation uses 1,000 as opposed to 100 as the index base (in order to avoid any recourse to decimals).

$$
I_t = \frac{\displaystyle\sum_{i=1}^{n} C_{0,i}\, \frac{p_{t,i}}{p_{0,i}}}{\displaystyle\sum_{i=1}^{n} C_{0,i}} \times 1{,}000
$$

$C_{0,i}$ represents the stock exchange capitalization on the date as the index base, and $p_{t,i}$ refers to the average price of the "i" security on the "t" Bourse meeting.

MIB index is calculated both as a current index and as a historical index; the difference is that the current index changes its base at the outset of each year, while the historical one has set its historical base equal to 1,000 on January 2, 1975.

Five-Year Performance

Milan Stock Exchange General Historical (MIB) Index (base 2/1/75 = 1000), US dollar, and deutschemark exchange rates from 1984–1988 are shown in Table 1.

Table 1

	1984	1985	1986	1987	1988
Yearly average MIB	3,186.00	4.998.0	10,590.0	10,056.0	8,101.0
Lit/$ (year-end data)	1,935.9	1,678.0	1,351.1	1,169.2	1,305.8
Lit/DM (year-end data)	614.2	682.2	696.5	738.5	737.3

Table 2   Price Earnings Ratios

Shares	P/ER's
Fiat	9.7
Generali	49.8
Olivetti	12.3
Montedison	9.4
Fiat privilegiata	6.0
CIR	24.6
RAS	56.0
Mediobanca	33.9
SME	20.8
Gemina	19.9
SAI	41.0
Assitalia	46.2
Stet	9.6
I.F.I. privilegiata	6.2
Snia BPD	51.5
Cartiere Burgo	12.8
Sip	9.9
Montedison di risparmio n.c.	4.6
Ferruzzi	5.0
Pirelli SPA	35.2
La Fondiaria	53.4
Comit	9.9
Ausonia Assicurazioni	39.0
Fiat di risparmio	5.8
Latina Assicurazioni	25.1
Sirti	10.8
Italcementi	16.0
Italmobiliare	8.3

**Figure 1   Milan Stock Exchange General Historical (MIB) Index
(basis 2/1/75 = 1000): end-month data, 1988**

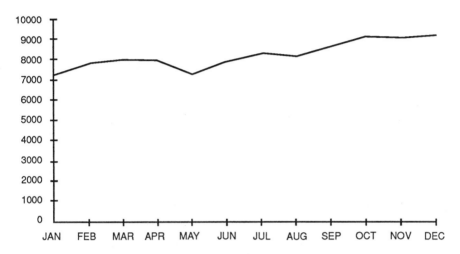

Italian Stock Exchanges

Opening Hours

Trading hours on the Italian stock exchanges are:

- "primo mercato": from 10 a.m. to 13.45 p.m.

- "mercato ristretto": from 15.30 p.m. (Milan)

- bonds: from 11 a.m.

Names and Addresses

Dealers' Committee - Genova Stock Exchange
Via Boccardo, 1
16121 - GENOVA
tel.: 010/20941 (412)
telex: 226599 (Commis)
fax: 010/2094397

Dealers' Committee - Naples Stock Exchange
Via S. Aspreno, 2
80133 - NAPOLI
tel.: 081/207100
telex: 710644
fax: 081/287124
         206248

Dealers' Committee - Rome Stock Exchange
Via de' Burro, 147
00186 - ROMA
tel.: 06/6792701
6790895-6791735
telex: 612155
fax: 06/6795648

Dealers' Committee - Turin Stock Exchange
Via S. Francesco da Paola, 28
10123 - TORINO
tel.: 011/547743 - 04
telex: 220614
fax: 011/5612193

Dealers' Committee - Milan Stock Exchange
Via Camperio, 4
20123 - MILANO
tel.: 02/85341
telex: 321430
fax: 02/8534.4640

Commissione per il listino - Bologna Stock Exchange
Piazza della Costituzione, 8
Palazzo degli Affari
40128 - BOLOGNA
tel.: 051/359331
telex: 510240 C.C
fax: 051/371229

Commissione per il Listino - Florence Stock Exchange
Piazza Mentana, 2
50122 - FIRENZE
tel.: 055/2795285
        2795239
telex: 570406 C.C.
fax: 055/2795285

Commissione per il Listino - Palermo Stock Exchange
Via E. Amari, 11
90139 - PALERMO
tel.: 091/587923
telex: 910216 C.C.
fax: 091/528262

Commissione per il Listino - Trieste Stock Exchange
Via Cassa di Risparmio, 2
34121 - TRIESTE
tel.: 040/64758
telex: 460165 C.C.
fax: 040/365425

Commissione per il Listino - Venice Stock Exchange
Via XXII Marzo, 2034
30124 - VENEZIA
tel.: 041/5289522
        5228838
telex: 410662 C.C.
fax: 041/786330

Market Size

Number of Listings and Market Value

All of the following figures are related to the Milan Stock Exchange, representing about 93% of the total Italian trading activities. At the end of 1988, 317 shares issued by 211 companies were listed on the Milan Stock Exchange. The total market capitalization at the end of the year was Lit. 176,827,000 million.

Number of listed companies, Milan Stock Exchange, 1984–1988

1984	143 plus 10 suspended
1985	147 plus 18 suspended
1986	184 plus 18 suspended
1987	204 plus 20 suspended
1988	211 plus 17 suspended

Number of listed shares, Milan Stock Exchange, 1984–1988

1984	213 including 14 suspended shares
1985	235 including 21 suspended shares
1986	306 including 20 suspended shares
1987	339 including 23 suspended shares
1988	339 including 22 suspended shares

Market value (stock market capitalization), Milan Stock Exchange, 1984–1988 (in millions of lire)

1984	49,793,000
1985	98,195,000
1986	190,472,000
1987	140,721,000
1988	176,827,000

New shares issues, 1988

Total nominal value in millions of lire	Total number of shares
2,344,480	28 (including 4 relistings)

Market Value by Industry

The insurance industry is by far the most important sector, accounting for 27.8% of total market capitalization. The other relevent industries are invrestment 18.2%), engineering and motors (17%) and banking (11.4%).

**Table 3   Market Value by Industry, December, 1988
(Stock Market Capitalization)**

Sector	Market value (Lit million)
Insurance	49,992,334
Investment	32,672,258
Engineering and Motors	30,447,715
Banking	20,207,161
Chemicals	13,566,908
Communications	9,416,893
Cement, Ceramics Etc.	4,018,144
Paper and Printing	3,886,816
Textiles	3,239,797
Building and Property	2,354,689
Electrical Engineering	1,692,292
Silos and Stores	1,609,696
Foods and Groceries	1,446,279
Mining and Metals	1,370,142
Miscellaneous	905,420
Total	176,826,564

Largest Quoted Companies (Rank)

Table 4   Largest Quoted Companies, December 1988[*]

Ranking	Company	Market Capitalization (Lit. billion)
1	Generali	23,299
2	Fiat	19,420
3	Stet	6,557
4	RAS	5,685

Table continues

Table 4   (continued)

Ranking	Company	Market Capitalization (Lit. billion)
5	La Fondiaria	5,123
6	Montedison	5,022
7	Sip	4,530
8	Olivetti	4,472
9	Mediobanca	4,081
10	Ferfin	3,715
11	Comit	3,515
12	Alleanza	3,507
13	SAI	3,007
14	Credit	2,801
15	CIR	2,570
16	Assitalia	2,448
17	Pirelli SPA	2,346
18	Italcementi	2,318
19	Gemina	2,118
20	Sirti	1,980
21	Toro	1,838
22	Fidis	1,712
23	Benetton	1,711
24	Ferruzzi A.F.	1,471
25	Snia BPD	1,448
26	Cofide	1,444
27	Mondadori	1,379
28	Nba	1,337
29	Bna	1,332
30	Sme	1,291

Total	123,477
Other Companies	53,350
Total Market Capitalization	176,827

[*] The 30 largest quoted companies on the Milan Stock Exchange in December 1988 account for 69.83% of total market capitalization.

Trading Volumes

At the end of 1988 share trading value reached at Lit. 41,269,000 millions, showing a slight decrease over the year, while trading volumes increased from 8,489,000 millions of shares traded in 1987 to 10,911,000 millions of shares in 1988.

Table 5

Year	Number of Shares Traded	Market Value in Millions of Lire
1984	5,194,753,100	7,143,000
1985	9,750,047,950	26,315,000
1986	11,672,802,650	66,661,000
1987	8,488,931,950	41,967,000
1988	10,911,428,875	41,269,000

The most actively traded shares by value in 1988 belonged to Engineering & Motors (24.76%), Investment (23.62%) and Insurance (21.70%) industries.

Table 6   **Total Turnover in 1988 per Industry**

Industry	Market Value of Share Turnover (Millions of Lire)
Engineering and Motors	10,218,900
Investment	9,746,666
Insurance	8,956,350
Chemicals	4,763,645
Banking	2,574,665
Communications	1,226,650
Paper and Printing	975,531
Cement, Ceramics, etc.	662,411
Silos and Stores	528,927
Textiles	398,838
Building and Property	350,587
Miscellaneous	281,936
Food and Groceries	274,465
Electrical Engineering	191,150
Mining and Metals	118,515
Total	41,269,236

Rank of the Most Actively Traded Shares

Table 7   The 30 Most Actively Traded Shares for Calendar Year 1988[*]

Shares	Traded Value (Lit. Millions)
Fiat	4,843,516
Generali	3,548,066
Olivetti	2,538,705
Montedison	2,435,714
Fiat privilegiata	1,700,056
C.I.R.	1,416,438
R.A.S.	925,308
Mediobanca	908,345
SME	812,456
Gemina	782,024
Iniziativa Me. T.A.	771,801
S.A.I.	710,578
Assitalia	649,853
Stet	641,394
I.F.I. privilegiata	609,080
Snia BPD	541,321
Cartiere Burgo	517,874
Buitoni	503,946
Sip	470,852
Montedison di risparmio n.c.	467,453
Ferruzzi Agricola	467,053
Pirelli S.p.A.	436,423
La Fondiaria	425,207
Comit	384,974
Ausonia Assicurazioni	351,820
Fiat di risparmio	347,961
Latina Assicurazioni	345,980
Sirti	327,934
Italcementi	295,190
Italmobiliare	289,391
Total	29,466,713

Lit. 29,466,713 million represents 71.40% of total 1988 trading value.

Types of Shares

The following categories of shares may be traded on the Italian stock exchanges: ordinary shares, preferred shares, deferred shares ("azioni di godimento"), savings shares ("azioni di risparmio"), debentures with rights of pre-emption in respect of new shares, convertible bonds, and warrant debenture bonds.

Preferred Shares

Preferred shares grant major rights in the distribution of profits or surplus assets on liquidation. They bear voting rights only in the extraordinary meeting of shareholders. The possibility to issue preferred shares is limited to the maximum percentage of 50% of the company's capital.

Deferred Shares

In case of equity decrease, the company may repay the nominal value of the shares owned by stockholders. It may then replace them by "azioni di godimento," which takes a deferred position in respect to distribution of profits or surplus assets on liquidation. These shares are non-voting. In addition, they are not very popular on the Italian Stock Exchanges. (no one is listed at December 1988.)

Saving Shares

Savings shares were created by lawn. 216/1974. They have no voting rights, but the owners of these shares may contest the company's decision in special general meetings. These shares, called "Azioni di risparmio," take the form of shares with preferred dividends or surplus assets on liquidation sharing rights. They are the only kind of bearer shares in Italy. The global amount of limited voting-rights and non-voting shares cannot be greater than 50% of company's equity.

Pre-emption Rights

The pre-emption right assigns to all stockholders and to holders of convertible bonds the right to underwrite, in case of equity increase, a number of shares proportional to the shares already in their hands. This right is incorporated in all kinds of shares and convertible bonds.

Convertible Bonds

Convertible bonds are bonds that may be converted in shares at maturity date. These bonds are interest bearing until conversion.

Warrants

Warrants are bonuses that award holders the right to underwrite shares or bonds issued by the same company or by other companies.

Trading System

There are two types of members on the Italian Stock Exchange: authorized brokers and other operators.

The only authorized brokers are stockbrokers ("agenti di cambio"), appointed by decree of the President of the Republic on the basis of a pass-list called by the Minister of Treasury and members of the Stockbrokers Managing Committee (Comitato Direttivo degli Agenti di Cambio). Authorized brokers are principally engaged in buying and selling securities on the exchange, but they are prohibited from dealing on their own account.

Other stock exchange operators are the ones who make their buy or sell orders to authorized stockbrokers. They are financial companies, banks, investment funds, previdential funds, speculators, or simply savers.

Stock exchange sessions take place at the same time in every Italian stock exchange. The beginning of auction is 10:00 a.m. The speakers call every share in a predetermined order. There is only one call auction ("chiamata a listino") for each share. When the share is called, operators make their order for buying or selling it. The equilibrium price, arising from demand and supply, is the closing price, the official price of listing. The calling of shares, which is named closing call, continues until 13:45 p.m.

The trading of shares is carried out on the basis of typical contracts, with predetermined clauses. The basic method of securities trading in the stock exchange is the open outcry method ("alle grida"). Using this method, stockbrokers show their willingness to buy or sell securities, crying the price and quantity of securities to trade.

Only stockbrokers and their employees ("procuratori," three for every stockbroker) may handle securities in the corbeilles ("recinto delle grida"), which is a part of floor fixed by the banisters. Banks, brokerage, and financial companies, if they wish, may enter in the stock exchange premises, but they cannot enter in the corbeilles. They also have to pass their orders to stockbrokers.

Transactions are complete when bid-prices meet offer-prices. Orders are conveyed through a computer order-routing system, or by telephone. The prices arising from transactions are disclosed through the Reuter system at the proper page. At the moment, an official continuous trading mechanism based on a computerized circuit hasn't yet been set up. Some shares (about ten among the most important) are currently traded on a continuous system as a consequence of a private agreement among a few institutions.

According to CONSOB rules, in order to prevent any speculative purpose on the stock market, operators purchasing forward must deposit a cash collateral of 100% of the value of securities traded, while the operators who sell forward must deposit the money value of the securities to be sold or place on deposit the securities themselves. In Italy a percentage of 60–70% of trading in shares takes place within the banking system. In fact, banks join the stock exchange market only when they need to match balances in their overall securities position (i.e., the banks' own trading portfolio plus sell and buy orders from banks' clients), otherwise they prefer to carry out all the transactions in the name of their customers by themselves. For example, if a customer wants to sell 1000 shares and another one wants to buy the same 1000 shares, the two operations are arbitraged by the bank and are not traded in the stock exchange. As a consequence, the prices resulting from stock exchange transactions are from a small portion of the total transactions.

List of Principal Brokers

Aletti Francesco
Aletti Urbano
Via S. Spirito, 14
Milano tel. 02-77121

Boffa Massimo
Solbiati Michele
Via della Posta, 10
Milano tel. 02-878618

Fumagalli Ettore
Soldan Giovanni
Via Meravigli, 16
Milano tel. 02-801545

Giubergia Guido
Via S. Maria Segreta, 6
Milano tel. 02-867633

Legnani Giuliano
Via dell'Ambrosiana, 22
Milano tel. 02-8692437

Zaffaroni Mario Vittorio
Zaffaroni Renzo
Via del Bollo, 4
Milano tel. 02-862651

Arnaboldi Renzo
Belloni Maurizio
De Gresti di San Leonardo
Via San Vittore al Teatro, 3
Milano tel. 02-806144

Belloni Leonardo
Pedercini Luigi
Via della Posta, 8
Milano tel. 02-809566

Crippa Edgardo
Mach di Palmstein Amedeo
Rivosecchi Maurizio
Via Brisa, 3
Milano tel. 02-872391

Albertini Alberto
Albertini Isidoro
Azzoni Paolo
Gamba Gianpaolo
Via Borromei, 5
Milano tel. 02-85731

Milla Gianluigi
Via V. Hugo, 1
Milano tel. 02-4980841

Sommariva Antonio
Sommariva Domenico
Sommariva Paolo
Via Dogana, 3
Milano tel. 02-860151

Agnese Savino
Bertolini Patrizio
Gabrielli Vittorio
Pastorino carlo
Via Nirone, 8
Milano tel. 02-85971

Buffa Ezio
P.za Borromeo, 10
Milano tel. 02-867829

Settlement and Transfer

On the Italian securities stock exchanges there are two kinds of transactions: cash and forward (one-month maturity). Both are settled by means of the Stock Exchange Clearing House ("Stanza di Compensazione"). The clearing house service is provided by the Bank of Italy for Members, which are stockbrokers, banks, financial companies, and trust companies.

The "Montetitoli Spa" is a society whose responsibilities are to facilitate and to give efficiency to the exchanges in bonds and securities. It clears the largest number of transactions and keeps in custody a broad variety of bonds on behalf of a multitude of banking system members. The Montetitoli Spa embodies a clearing system itself and has widely improved Italian settlement features. It is difficult to determine the precise exchanges volume handled by "Montetitoli." Because the depositary handles about 75% of the total equity and 27% of the total debt (excluding government bonds) on market, it is deemed that settled transactions volume should be in the same percentage too.

In terms of the settlement of cash transactions, the due date is on the third business day following the day of the contract, or, in the case of "contante a giorni" transactions, within ten business days. As a rule in bonds, a daily offset is carried out by the clearing house for cash transactions.

Spot contracts are rarely used for shares and convertible bonds. These are normally traded by means of forward transactions, which are settled according to the stock exchange schedule. The exchange schedule for forward trading sets up the accounting periods around the year.

The accounting period, which lasts for a month, is formed as follows:

- The option declaration day ("risposta premi") as a rule, falls on the last day but two or the day before the end of the accounting period.

- The contango day ("riporti") is the last day contracts will be settled at the end of the current stock exchange month (trading "per fine corrente"). Transactions carried out on the following day will be settled at the end of the following stock exchange month (trading "per fine prossimo"). The contango day falls around the middle of the month.

- The offsetting day ("compensi") is dedicated to the offsetting of transactions made with different operators. On this day the stockbrokers should fix the making-up price ("prezzo di compenso," a weighted mean of the quotations of the last stock exchange sessions). However, this price is fixed at the end of the contango day. The making-up day follows the contango day.

- The day of the errors correction is the day the clearing house points but the errors made by operators when recording the transactions and during the offsetting; corrections are then made.

- The day of securities delivery, which falls near the end of the calendar month is the day the effective offsetting of the debit and credit in securities takes place by the delivering of securities in the Stock Exchange Clearing House.

- The settlement day is the day balances are paid in cash. As a rule, this day is on the second day after delivery of securities.

Taxation

Witholding Tax on Foreign Dividends

Italian corporation dividends paid to foreign shareholders are subject to Italian witholding tax at 30% of their gross amount. Reduced tax treaty rates may apply if the shareholder is a resident in a country with which Italy has a reciprocal tax treaty. These rates range from 5 to 25%, depending on the country.

When an Italian corporation issues stock dividends or distributes retained earnings to the shareholders at liquidation, the witholding tax will apply as in Table 8.

Non-resident investors may demand that the Italian government reimburse 2/3 of the tax paid in Italy, providing they can demonstrate they have already paid taxes on that income.

Capital Gain Transaction

At the moment, the capital gains of an individual or a non-resident entity are not subject to taxation; on the contrary, Italian corporations are subject to the Italian corporate tax rate (ILOR plus IRPEG for a total taxation percentage of 46.368%).

Control System

CONSOB (National Companies and Stock Exchange Commission)

CONSOB supervises the stock exchanges, company's information, and listed companies. The commission is authorized to (among other powers of inspection and control):

- Suspend from quotation those securities influenced by excessive speculative tensions.

- Carry on the quality controls over audit firms' work related to listed companies.

Obligations by Law

- Audit: the law requires all listed companies to have their accounts audited by a recognized independent audit firm.

- Reporting to CONSOB: listed companies have to furnish CONSOB with the audited financial statement and with a semi-annual report within four months from the end of the first half year and with resolutions regarding any interim dividend. The semi-annual reports are usually publicized also by the financial press and are unaudited.

Listed companies are also required by CONSOB to prepare and publish consolidated financial statements (where applicable), which are usually audited (although no obligation exists on the matter).

Table 8

	Rate of Dividend Witholding Tax Percent
Residents in Non-Treaty Countries	30
Residents in Treaty Countries	
Austria	15
Belgium	15
Brazil	15
Canada	15
Czechoslovakia	15
Denmark	15
Egypt	(1)
France	15
Greece	25
Hungary	10
Ireland	15
Japan	10-15
Luxembourg	15
Morocco	10-15
Netherlands	(1)
Portugal	15
Romania	10
Singapore	10
Spain	15
Sweden	10-15
Switzerland	15
Tanzania	10
United Kingdom	5-15
United States of America	5-10-15
West Germany	(1)

(1) Special rules are stated.

THE FAR EAST
EQUITY MARKETS

Japanese Equity Market

Andrew Ballingal
Barclays de Zoete Wedd, Tokyo

Introduction

1990—A Year of Reckoning

1990 represented a watershed for the Japanese stock market. It was a year when investors grown accustomed to effortless capital gains re-learned the painful lesson that stocks can go down as well as up. The myth of Tokyo's infallibility, which so many had come to believe in after the 1987 Crash, proved to be just that—a myth. Tokyo became once again, just another stock market. In nine months the market fell almost 50%, taking the index back to levels first seen some four years previously.

The main factor pushing stock prices lower was the confrontation between, on the one hand, Japan's notoriously extended p/e multiples, and on the other, rapidly rising interest rates and the deteriorating corporate profit outlook. This threatened a collapse in the bubble economy—the explosive rise in asset prices that followed the yen's surge and four years of easy monetary policy. The invasion of Kuwait and the resultant mini-oil shock, while not key factors, hardly helped.

From being the world's largest stock market—at one point in late 1988, it was almost one and a half times the size of the U.S. market—Tokyo's market capitalization crumbled back into the No. 2 slot, where it remains today. Activity fell as fast as prices, with average daily turnover in 1990 down almost 50% on 1989, and back at 1986 levels, and new issues down 60%.

1991—Another Difficult Year

The final months of 1990 saw a rebound from the oversold position reached at the end of the third quarter, assisted by a powerful rally in the bond market. Going into 1991 however, the stock market still confronts many of the problems that daunted it in 1990.

Leaving aside the uncertainties arising from the Middle Eastern situation, the stock market—which still sells on 40 times earnings—faces a rapidly slowing economy and a deteriorating outlook for the corporate sector, with confidence, liquidity and profits all under pressure.

Bankruptcies have risen sharply in the last few months, and more will follow in 1991. Profits, which will have fallen by some 10% in FY90, will fall by another 10 to 15% in FY91. While interest rates have further to fall, particularly at the short-end of the yield curve, inflation persisting around 3% means that a repetition of the early Eighties collapse in rates is not in the cards.

This leaves the market looking fully-valued in the short-term, and no great bargain for the long-term either. Experienced investors in Japan will know that while the long-haul gains have been impressive, there have been long periods, such as the first half of the Sixties and much of the Seventies, when returns from Japanese stocks were either unexceptional, or negative.

1991 may be dull, and after 1990 many investors would be grateful for a little dullness. But while a 1990-style collapse is unlikely (but by no means impossible), so too are the vintage returns of the Golden Late Eighties.

A Little History

Early Days

Following the enactment of the Stock Exchange Ordinance in 1878, stock exchanges were established in Tokyo and Osaka. Initially only national bonds were traded, but trading in company stocks began in the 1890's. The dominant role played by the banks and zaibatsu (conglomerates such as Mitsubishi and Mitsui) in financing industry stifled new issues and the development of a serious secondary market; for a long time the stock market thus remained little more than a casino.

However, the capital demands of World War I and the rapid expansion of heavy industry, together with the increased listing of zaibatsu company shares, allowed the stock market to grow rapidly in the inter-war years. World War II resulted first in the unification of all eleven stock exchanges then existing into a single entity, and subsequently its effective closure.

Post-War Aftermath

After the war, the market was officially closed, with transactions only taking place at brokers' offices and on unofficial markets. In 1947, following the disbanding of the zaibatsu, the Securities Coordination Liquidation Committee released huge quantities of stocks previously held by the zaibatsu. As intended by the Occupying Forces, individuals availed themselves of this "Securities Democratization Movement", and by 1950 they owned almost 70% of shares outstanding - in marked contrast to the corporate ownership that dominated both prior to the War...and again now.

Enacted in April 1948, the Securities and Exchange Law, patterned on the American Securities Act (1933) and the Securities and Exchange Act (1934), provided for the re-establishment of stock exchanges. The next year the Tokyo, Osaka and Nagoya stock exchanges reopened.

Korean War Kickstart

After a slow start in the face of the austerity of the Dodge Line, the economic boom in Japan resulting from the Korean War and the introduction of margin trading and investment trusts in 1951, galvanized the market. Prices surged almost five-fold from 85 in 1950 (i.e. below the 1949 base of 100) to 474 in early 1953. At this point, the first post-war bull market was stopped in its tracks by Stalin's death and the end of the Korean War.

Late Fifties Boom

With the successive Jimmu and Iwato booms spanning the last half of the Fifties, the stock market rose over four-fold, reaching 1830 in mid-1961. Average daily volume increased more than ten times, from 13m shares in 1955 to 161m in 1961. The primary market was buoyant too—in 1961 731bn was raised compared with just 86bn in 1955. Driving the bull market was the rapid growth in investment trust assets, which soared from 60bn in 1955 to 1027bn in 1961.

Other developments in this period included the resumption of bond trading on the Tokyo and Osaka exchanges (1956); the establishment of Securities Finance companies (1956), and of separate Investment Trust companies (1960); the establishment of bond investment trusts (1961); and the opening of Second Section markets in Tokyo, Osaka and Nagoya (1961).

Early Sixties Bust

Inflation pressures from rapid economic growth resulted in a progressive credit squeeze starting in 1961, and boom soon turned to bust. Initial support operations to bolster the stock market were successful, but distressed sales of equity by corporations in both the primary and secondary markets soon proved overwhelming, and from early 1963 retail selling of both equity and mutual funds fuelled the downward spiral in prices.

Renewed joint bank/broker efforts to stabilize the market failed in early 1964, and again in early 1965, and it was only with the effective bankruptcy of one of the Big Four brokers and the intervention of the Bank of Japan that the four-year bear market came to an end. By July 1965 the Nikkei index had fallen 44% from its July 1961 high of 1830 to just 1020.

Back on Track

The recovery in the Japanese economy that began in 1965 heralded a new boom—the fabled Izanagi expansion—and this provided a suitable backdrop to a recovery in the stock market. New regulations covering securities companies, investment trusts, margin positions, and accounting procedures were introduced to ensure that the disasters of the early Sixties were not repeated.

A remarkable industrial resurgence, an improving balance of payments, and heavy investment by foreign investors, got things moving again by the final years of the Sixties, and the bull market continued— despite interruptions from the IOS collapse (1970) and the Nixon shock (the end of the Bretton Woods agreement in 1971)—through into early 1973.

Not only did stock prices soar—by its January 1973 peak at 5359 the Nikkei index stood over five times higher than in 1965—but activity surged to unprecedented levels, over 450m shares a day in 1972 compared with less than a third this amount in 1967.

The First Oil Shock

While it is convenient to lay the blame on the first oil shock, the stock market correction that took place in 1973 and 1974 was at least as much the inevitable result of the preceding speculative frenzy as of the subsequent economic contraction.

The oil shock merely exacerbated the liquidity squeeze already in place aimed at curbing the inflation pressures resulting from the rapid economic growth and asset price rises of the late Sixties and early Seventies. Interest rates rose significantly, corporate profits collapsed, and bankruptcies soared. By October 1974, the Nikkei index had fallen 37% to 3355.

While the worst was over, the stock market had suffered a severe blow, and neither prices nor activity recovered 1972 levels, even in nominal terms, until six years later, in 1978. The only consolation for the securities industry was the rapid growth in the bond market, as Japanese fiscal policy turned expansive in an attempt to resuscitate the sluggish economy. In 1972, turnover in the bond market was just 17tn—by 1978, this had risen to 203tn.

Another Oil Shock

The second oil shock had far less impact on either Japan's economy of financial markets that its predecessor, and while both activity and prices were depressed for a while, new highs of over 8000 on the Nikkei were achieved in 1981. From this point stock prices fell again, reflecting both global and domestic economic difficulties—at its October 1982 low, the Nikkei had fallen 15% to 6850.

Thereafter, falling oil prices, inflation and interest rates, and a recovery in economic activity worldwide, saw the Japanese stock market participating in the global bull market. By the end of 1984, the Nikkei had gained 70% to reach 11577, and average daily volume had recovered to almost 450m shares. But the best was yet to come . . .

Triple Merit

The final collapse in oil prices, together with the September 1985 Plaza accord to support the yen, set in train the events that came to be known as the Triple Merit bull market—collapsing energy prices, plummeting interest rates, a soaring yen, and an explosion in both real estate and stock prices.

From a base around 11500 in early 1985, the Nikkei more than doubled by October 1987 to 26646 on a tide of excess liquidity. P/E multiples, which had averaged around 25 for most of the Seventies and Eighties, soared to over 80. Corporations and institutions with excess cashflow piled money into the stock market, while mutual funds saw huge inflows. Only foreign investors—steady sellers through this period—were immune to the speculative fever.

While for many other markets the Crash of 1987 signalled the end of an era, for Tokyo it was little more than a pause. With the economy and profits growing strongly, the market shrugged off higher interest rates, and by the end of 1989 had reached 38915, almost six times higher than the low of early 1982.

Capital Shock

The events of 1990 (see above) showed just how soundly based these gains had been. As the cost of capital steadily rose, the market had to face up to reality once more. Multiples of 65 in the face of bonds yielding 7 or 8% made no sense, and stock prices had only one way to go . . . down. As we go the press, the market is still almost 40% down from its late 1989 peak, and volume remains subdued.

Table 1   Market Size and Structure

End December	1980	1985	1986	1987	1988	1989	1990
TSE 1							
Companies Listed	960	1058	1079	1101	1130	1161	1191
Issues Listed	966	1058	1079	1102	1135	1165	1197
Shares Listed - bn	199.8	249.3	258.2	271.0	285.3	303.2	316.5
Market Cap - ¥tn	73.2	182.7	277.1	325.5	462.9	590.9	365.2
- US$bn	360.6	910.8	1730.5	2667.9	3694.9	4130.8	2684.0
The Average TSE 1 Company							
Share Price - *	367	733	1073	1201	1622	1949	1154
Shares Listed - bn	208	236	239	246	252	261	266
Market Cap - ¥tn	76	173	257	296	410	509	307
US$bn	376	861	1604	2423	3270	3558	2254
TSE 2							
Companies Listed	442	424	424	431	441	436	436
Issues Listed	443	429	425	431	441	437	437
Shares Listed - bn	8.41	9.31	9.50	9.79	10.10	10.63	10.60
Market Cap - ¥tn	3.9	7.4	8.4	11.2	14.0	20.2	14.1
- US$bn	19.0	37.0	52.6	92.0	111.4	141.5	103.5
The Average TSE 2 Company							
Share Price - ¥	458	798	885	1147	1381	1905	1328
Shares Listed - bn19	19	22	22	23	23	24	24
Market Cap - ¥tn	9	18	20	26	32	46	32
- US$bn	43	87	124	214	253	325	237
TSE 1 & 2							
Companies Listed	1402	1482	1503	1532	171	1597	1627
Issues Listed	1409	1487	1504	1533	1576	1602	1634
Shares Listed - bn	208.2	258.6	267.7	280.7	295.4	313.8	327.1
Market Cap - ¥tn	77.1	190.1	285.5	336.7	476.8	611.2	379.2
- US$bn	379.6	047.8	1783.1	2759.9	3806.3	4272.3	2787.4
The Average TSE Company							
Share Price - ¥	370	735	1066	1199	1614	1947	1159
Shares Listed - bn	148	175	178	183	188	197	201
Market Cap - ¥tn	55	128	190	220	304	383	233
- US$bn	271	640	1186	1801	2423	2675	1713

Table 2   Structure—Breakdown of TSE 1 Market Capitalization by Section

End December	1980	1985	1986	1987	1988	1989	1990
Fishery	0.19%	0.13%	0.14%	0.16%	0.15%	0.18%	0.16%
Mining	0.78%	0.30%	0.19%	0.21%	0.20%	0.32%	0.29%
Construction	3.77%	3.24%	4.15%	3.84%	3.54%	4.39%	4.96%
Food & Drink	3.25%	2.77%	3.02%	3.43%	2.63%	2.67%	2.65%
Textiles	2.16%	2.24%	1.78%	1.87%	1.67%	1.85%	1.95%
Paper	0.78%	0.60%	0.59%	0.75%	0.99%	0.92%	0.95%
Chemicals/Health	8.22%	8.33%	8.32%	8.34%	6.72%	6.63%	6.77%
Oil	2.62%	1.08%	1.09%	0.88%	1.01%	1.05%	0.91%
Rubber	0.56%	0.32%	0.33%	0.44%	0.44%	0.51%	0.45%
Glass & Ceramics	1.94%	1.82%	1.61%	1.66%	1.59%	1.67%	1.45%
Steel	4.86%	2.23%	1.70%	2.64%	4.42%	3.89%	3.54%
Non-Ferrous Metals	1.60%	1.91%	1.54%	1.43%	1.38%	1.53%	1.60%
Metal Products	0.50%	0.41%	0.38%	0.57%	0.56%	0.77%	1.01%
Machinery	4.21%	2.87%	2.10%	2.32%	2.50%	3.45%	3.51%
Electricals	14.52%	13.92%	11.37%	10.28%	9.39%	9.15%	10.21%
Autos/Shipbuilding	7.68%	5.40%	4.79%	4.49%	5.74%	5.52%	5.57%
Precisions	1.61%	1.54%	1.04%	0.91%	0.86%	0.94%	1.02%
Other Products	1.18%	1.55%	1.54%	1.52%	1.37%	1.48%	1.94%
Retail Trading	7.57%	6.38%	6.40%	6.01%	6.20%	7.74%	7.66%
Finance/Insurance	19.7 %	28.48%	29.32%	32.11%	31.31%	29.70%	29.39%
Real Estate	1.16%	1.71%	2.14%	1.49%	1.74%	1.65%	1.28%
Railways/Trucking	2.41%	2.64%	3.34%	2.89%	3.33%	3.68%	2.91%
Shipping	1.41%	0.50%	0.41%	0.49%	0.70%	0.88%	0.59%
Airlines	0.69%	0.97%	0.97%	1.26%	1.12%	1.08%	1.02%
Warehousing	0.27%	0.27%	0.26%	0.25%	0.25%	0.30%	0.28%
Communications	0.31%	1.16%	0.86%	3.16%	2.60%	1.81%	1.85%
Electric Power/Gas	5.57%	6.31%	9.66%	5.74%	6.78%	5.24%	4.96%
Services	0.61%	0.88%	0.94%	0.88%	0.81%	1.01%	1.12%
TOTAL	100.00%	100.00%	100.00%	100.00%	100.00%	100.00%	100.00%
Materials	24.02%	19.27%	17.54%	18.78%	18.98%	19.14%	18.92%
Technology	29.21%	25.29%	20.85%	19.52%	19.86%	20.54%	22.25%
Consumer	11.62%	10.16%	10.50%	10.48%	9.79%	11.60%	11.59%
Infrastructure	4.92%	4.95%	6.29%	5.33%	5.28%	6.04%	6.24%
INDUSTRIAL	69.76%	59.66%	55.18%	54.11%	53.91%	57.32%	59.00%
FINANCIALS	19.57%	28.48%	29.32%	32.11%	31.31%	29.70%	29.39%
TRANSPORT	4.78%	4.38%	4.97%	4.88%	5.40%	5.94%	4.80%

Table continues

Table 2   Structure—Breakdown of TSE 1 Market Capitalization by Sector (Continued)

End December	1980	1985	1986	1987	1988	1989	1990
UTILITIES	5.89%	7.47%	10.52%	8.90%	9.38%	7.05%	6.81%
TOTAL	100.00%	100.00%	100.00%	100.00%	100.00%	100.00%	100.00%
Manufacturing	64.42%	55.11%	49.76%	49.02%	49.21%	51.42%	52.47%
Non-Manufacturing	35.58%	44.89%	50.98%	50.98%	50.79%	48.59%	47.53%

Table 3   Structure—Fifty Largest Companies by Market Capitalization 31 December 1990

	Company	Sector	¥bn	$bn	% of TSE
1	NTT	Communications	15288	112.4	4.19%
2	Industrial Bank of Japan	Banks	7760	57.0	2.13%
3	Fuji Bank	Banks	7062	51.9	1.93%
4	Mitsui Taiyo Kobe Bank	Banks	6294	46.3	1.72%
5	Sumitomo Bank	Banks	6250	45.9	1.71%
6	Daiichi Kangyo Bank	Banks	6084	44.7	1.67%
7	Mitsubishi Bank	Banks	5979	43.9	1.64%
8	Toyota Motor	Autos	5907	43.4	1.62%
9	Sanwa Bank	Banks	5593	41.1	1.53%
10	Tokyo Electric Power	Electric Power	4889	35.9	1.34%
11	Hitachi	Electricals	3694	27.2	1.01%
12	Nomura Securities	Securities	3470	25.5	0.95%
13	Long-term Credit bank	Banks	3373	24.8	0.92%
14	Matsushita Electric Inds	Electricals	3327	24.5	0.91%
15	Nippon Steel	Steel	3086	22.7	0.85%
16	Tokai Bank	Banks	2895	21.3	0.79%
17	Kansai Electric Power	Electric Power	2868	21.1	0.79%
18	Mitsubishi Trust	Banks	2344	17.2	0.64%
19	Toshiba	Electricals	2261	16.6	0.62%
20	Mitsubishi Heavy Inds	Shipbuilding	2244	16.5	0.61%
21	Bank of Tokyo	Banks	2154	15.8	0.59%
22	Mitsubishi Corp	Trading	2141	15.7	0.59%
23	Chubu Electric Power	Utilities	2044	15.0	0.56%

Table continues

Table 3   (continued)

	Company	Sector	¥bn	$bn	% of TSE
24	Tokio Marine & Fire	Insurance	2039	15.0	0.56%
25	Nintendo	Electricals	1983	14.6	0.54%
26	NEC	Electricals	1983	14.6	0.54%
27	Sony	Electricals	1975	14.5	0.54%
28	Sumitomo Trust	Banks	1964	14.4	0.54%
29	JAL	Airlines	1830	13.5	0.50%
30	Nippondenso	Electricals	1793	13.2	0.49%
31	Daiwa Bank	Banks	1787	13.1	0.49%
32	Fujitsu	Electricals	1773	13.0	0.49%
33	ANA	Airlines	1759	12.9	0.48%
34	Nissan	Autos	1758	12.9	0.48%
35	Mitsui Trust	Banks	1749	12.9	0.48%
36	Yasuda Trust	Banks	1742	12.8	0.48%
37	Seibu Railway	Railways	1603	11.8	0.44%
38	Tokyo Gas	Utilities	1588	11.7	0.43%
39	Nippon Credit Bank	Banks	1544	11.3	0.42%
40	Daiwa Securities	Securities	1529	11.2	0.42%
41	Kirin Brewery	Food & Drink	1516	11.1	0.42%
42	Kajima	Construction	1513	11.1	0.41%
43	Fuji Photo	Chemicals	1483	10.9	0.41%
44	Ito-Yokado	Retail	1454	10.7	0.40%
45	Asahi Glass	Glass & Ceramics	1434	10.5	0.39%
46	NKK Corp	Steel	1416	10.4	0.39%
47	Takeda	Health & Household	1397	10.3	0.38%
48	Seven-Eleven Japan	Retail	1396	10.3	0.38%
49	Sumitoto Metal Inds	Steel	1382	10.2	0.38%
50	Mitsubishi Electric	Electricals	1363	10.0	0.37%

Companies				
1—5	42,654	314	11.68%
1—10	71,106	523	19.47%
1—15	88,056	647	24.11%
1—20	100,668	740	27.57%
1—25	111,029	816	30.41%
1—30	120,574	886	33.02%
1—35	129,400	951	33.44%
1—40	137,406	1,010	37.63%
1—45	144,809	1,064	39.56%
1—50	151,763	1,115	41.56%

Table continues

Table 3   (continued)

Companies	¥bn	$bn	% of TSE
1—5	42,654	314	11.68%
6—10	28,452	209	7.79%
11—15	16,950	125	4.64%
16—20	12,612	93	3.45%
21—25	10,361	76	2.84%
26—30	9,545	70	2.61%
31—35	8,826	65	2.42%
36—40	8,006	59	2.19%
41—45	7,403	54	2.03%
46—50	6,954	51	1.90%
1—10	71,106	523	19.47%
11—20	29,562	217	8.10%
21—30	19,906	146	5.45%
31—40	16,832	124	4.61%
41—50	14,357	106	3.93%
TSE 1	365,154	2,684	100.00%

Table 4   Ownership—Breakdown of TSE Market Capitalization by Investor Group

End March	1986	1987	1988	1989	1990
Breakdown by Value—%					
Public Sector	0.5%	0.9%	0.5%	0.3%	0.3%
Financial cost	41.5%	43.6%	44.8%	45.6%	45.6%
(Institutions)	n/a	26.6%	27.6%	27.9%	27.9%
Insurance Companies	16.4%	16.8%	16.4%	15.8%	15.8%
Life	12.3%	12.4%	12.4%	11.8%	11.8%
Non-Life	4.1%	4.0%	4.0%	4.0%	.0%
Banks	20.9%	22.2%	23.5%	25.5%	25.9%
Banking Accounts	5.0%	14.9%	14.9%	15.7%	15.7%
Trust Accounts	n/a	7.3%	8.6%	9.8%	10.2%
Investment Trusts	n/a	1.9%	2.6%	3.1%	3.7%
Pension Trusts	1.7%	1.0%	1.1%	1.0%	0.9%

Table continues

Table 4   (continued)

End March	1986	1987	1988	1989	1990
Other Trusts	n/a	4.3%	4.9%	5.7%	5.6%
Other Institutions	2.4%	2.5%	2.6%	2.0%	1.9%
Securities Companies	1.8%	2.1%	2.3%	2.3%	2.0%
Non-Financial Companies	28.8%	30.1%	30.2%	29.0%	29.5%
Individuals	22.2%	20.1%	20.4%	19.9%	20.5%
Foreigners	7.0%	5.3%	4.1%	4.3%	4.2%
Total	100.0%	100.0%	100.0%	100.0%	100.0%

Table 5   Share Prices—Recent Trends

Calendar Year		1980	1985	1986	1987	1988	1989	1990
TSE 1								
Av Price	– End	367	733	1073	1201	1201	1949	1154
	– YoY		14.9%	46.5%	11.9%	35.1%	20.1%	–40.8%
TSE 1 Index	– End	491	1049	1556	1726	2357	2881	1734
	– YoY		16.4%	48.3%	10.9%	36.6%	22.2%	–39.8%
	– Av	474	998	1324	2134	2134	2569	2178
	– YoY		16.1%	32.7%	48.3%	8.7%	20.4%	–15.2%
	– High	498	1058	1583	2259	2357	2885	2868
	– Low	449	917	1026	1557	1690	2364	1523
TSE 2								
Av Price	– End	458	798	885	1147	1381	1905	1328
	– YoY		11.7%	10.9%	29.5%	20.5%	37.9%	–30.3%
TSE 2 Index	– End	858	1874	2048	2376	2794	3939	3344
	– YoY		16.9%	9.3%	16.0%	17.6%	41.0%	–15.1%
	– Av	760	1792	2079	2325	2857	3181	3717
	– YoY		18.7%	16.0%	11.9%	22.9%	11.3%	16.8%
	– High	858	1925	2337	2792	3106	3939	4477
	– Low	706	1645	1857	2015	2361	2774	2711
TSE 1 & 2								
Av Price	– End	370	735	1066	1199	1614	1947	1159

Table continues

Table 5   (continued)

Calendar Year		1980	1985	1986	1987	1988	1989	1990
TSE 1 & 2 (Continued)								
	– YoY		14.7%	45.1%	12.5%	34.6%	20.6%	–40.5%
Price Index	– End	509	1082	1571	1748	2370	2916	1794
	– YoY		16.3%	45.2%	11.2%	35.6%	23.1%	–38.5%
	– Av	488	1029	1347	1975	2155	2590	2235
			16.1%	30.9%	46.7%	9.1%	20.1%	–13.7%
Nikkei 225								
Price Index	– End	7116	13113	18701	21564	30159	38916	23894
	– YoY		13.0%	42.6%	15.3%	39.9%	29.0%	–38.7%
	– Av	6870	12566	16402	23248	27039	34059	29441
	– YoY		12.8%	30.5%	41.7%	16.3%	26.0%	–13.6%
	– High	7188	13129	18936	26648	30159	38916	38713
	– Low	6476	11545	12882	18544	21217	30184	20222

Table 6   Market Indices

Index	Calculation Method	Base	Constituents
TSE 1 Index	Market Cap Weighted	1968	All First Section Companies
TSE 2 Index	Market Cap Weighted	1968	All First Section Companies
TSE Sector Indices	Market Cap Weighted	1968	28 Industrial Sectors, All First Section
Nikkei 225	Arithmetic Price Weighted	1949	225 First Section Companies
Nikkei 500	Arithmetic Price Weighted	1972	599 First Section Companies
Nikkei Sector Averages	Arithmetic Price Weighted	1972	Industrial Sectors, Nikkei 500 Companies

Table 7   Activity—Primary Market

Calendar Year	1980	1985	1986	1987	1988	1989	1990	YoY
TSE Listings								
New Listings	10	33	29	37	40	27	31	15%
DeListings	6	1	6	4	1	1	1	0%
Net New Listings	4	32	23	33	29	26	30	15%
Equity Issuance – ¥bn								
Private Placements	72	32	27	102	76	89	284	218%
Shareholder Offers	84	166	49	417	749	690	751	9%
Public Offers	842	437	356	1326	2428	5646	1753	–69%
Primary Market	998	634	432	1844	3253	6425	2788	–57%
Exercise of CB/WBs	108	129	371	1054	1280	2105	611	71%
Total – ¥bn	1106	763	803	2898	4533	8529	3400	–60%
– US$m	5249	3206	4776	20056	35362	61753	23502	–62%
Equity-Linked Debt Issuance—¥bn								
Domestic CBs	40	1862	2706	5154	6468	6770	2703	–60%
Overseas CBs	575	1298	414	980	817	1533	586	–62%
CBs	615	3159	3120	6134	7285	8303	3289	–60%
Domestic WBS	0	10	116	30	0	385	915	138%
Overseas WBs	0	680	1939	3085	3503	9160	2845	–69%
WBs	0	690	2055	3115	3503	9545	3760	–61%
Total – ¥bn	615	3850	5175	9249	10787	17848	7049	–61%
– US$m	2917	16171	30797	63995	84144	129222	48729	–62%
Equity & Equity—Linked Debt Issuance								
Total – ¥bn	1720	4613	5977	12147	15321	26377	10448	–60%
– US$m	8166	19377	35573	84051	119506	190975	72231	–62%

Note: The table above excludes Government sales of NTT and JAL shares in
1987 and 1988. If these are included, the totals are as follows:

				1987	1988		
NTT/JAL Sales – ¥bn				7951	2850		
– US$m				55017	22231		
Equity Total – ¥bn		763	803	10849	7383	8529	3400
– US$m		3206	4776	75072	57593	61753	23502
E + E-L Debt – ¥bn		4613	5977	20098	18171	26377	10448
– US$m		19377	35573	139067	141737	190975	72231

Table 8   Activity—Secondary Market

		1980	1985	1986	1987	1988	1989	1990	YoY
Trading Days		285	285	279	274	273	249	246	–1%
TSE 1—Total Traded									
Shares	– bn	100.2	118.2	193.6	259.4	278.6	218.4	119.0	–45%
Value	– ¥bn	35.4	75.5	155.9	245.6	279.7	325.8	176.3	–46%
Value	– US$bn	168.0	317.0	927.8	1699.2	2182.0	2182.0	1218.9	–48%
TSE 1—Daily Average Traded									
Shares	– m	351.6	414.8	693.9	946.8	1020.5	876.9	483.9	–45%
Value	– ¥bn	124.2	264.7	558.8	896.3	1024.7	1308.5	716.7	–45%
Value	– US$m	589.6	1112.2	3325.5	6201.6	7992.8	9474.0	4954.8	–48%
TSE 2—Total Traded									
Shares	bn	2.0	3.7	4.1	4.2	4.0	4.2	4.1	–4%
Value	– ¥tn	1.1	3.3	3.9	5.2	5.8	6.8	10.4	53%
Value	– US$bn	5.2	13.7	23.4	35.7	45.1	49.2	71.6	46%
TSE 2—Daily Average Traded									
Shares	– m	7.1	12.8	14.7	15.3	14.8	17.1	16.5	–3%
Value	– ¥bn	3.8	11.4	14.1	18.8	21.2	27.3	42.1	54%
Value	– US$m	18.1	48.0	83.9	130.4	165.3	197.4	291.0	47%
TSE 1 & 2—Total Traded									
Shares	– bn	102.2	121.9	197.7	263.6	282.6	222.6	123.1	–45%
Value	– ¥bn	36.5	78.7	159.8	250.7	285.5	332.6	186.7	–44%
Value	– US$bn	173.2	330.6	951.2	1735.0	2227.2	2408.2	1290.5	–46%
TSE 1 & 2—Daily Average Traded									
Shares	m	358.8	427.6	708.6	962.1	1035.3	894.0	500.4	–44%
Value	¥bn	128.0	276.2	572.9	915.1	1045.9	1335.8	758.8	–43%
Value	US$m	607.7	1160.2	3409.4	6332.0	8158.1	9671.4	5245.8	–46%

Table 9   Breakdown of TSE1 Turnover (Value) by Sector in 1989

	¥bn	% of TSE	vs Mkt Cap
Fishery	954	0.29%	1.62
Mining	2,118	0.65%	2.03
Construction	41,951	12.84%	2.92
Food & Drink	7,592	2.32%	0.87
Textiles	7,788	2.38%	1.29
Paper	3,572	1.09%	1.19
Chemicals/Health	29,206	8.94%	1.35

Table continues

Table 9   (continued)

	¥bn	% of TSE	vs Mkt Cap
Oil	4,230	1.29%	1.23
Rubber	2,465	0.75%	1.48
Glass & Ceramics	6,778	2.07%	1.24
Steel	27,851	8.52%	2.17
Metal Products	3,173	0.97%	1.26
Machinery	19,453	5.95%	1.73
Electricals	38,381	11.75%	1.28
Autos/Shipbuilding	22,890	7.01%	1.27
Precisions	5,208	1.59%	1.70
Other Products	3,724	1.14%	0.77
Retail/Trading	23,926	7.32%	0.95
Finance/Insurance	17,556	5.27%	0.18
Real Estate	10,517	3.22%	1.95
Railways/Trucking	13,588	4.16%	1.13
Shipping	5,330	1.63%	1.85
Airlines	2,064	0.63%	0.58
Warehousing	1,059	0.32%	1.08
Communications	3,102	0.95%	0.52
Electric Power/Gas	8,280	2.53%	0.48
Services	3,135	0.96%	0.95
Total	326,730	100.00%	1.00
Materials	98,022	30.00%	1.57
Technology	89,656	27.44%	1.34
Consumer	35,607	10.90%	0.94
Infrastructure	52,468	16.06%	2.66
INDUSTRIAL	275,753	84.40%	1.47
FINANCIALS	17,556	5.37%	0.18
TRANSPORT	22,040	6.75%	1.14
UTILITIES	11,381	3.48%	0.49
Total	326,730	100.00%	1.00
Manufacturing	227,594	69.66%	1.35
Non-Manufacturing	99,136	30.34%	0.62

Table 10   Fifty Largest Companies by Turnover (Value) in 1989

	Company	Sector	¥bn	$bn	% of TSE
1	Mitsubishi Heavy Inds	Shipbuilding	4653	33.7	1.43%
2	Nippon Steel	Steel	4478	32.4	1.37%
3	Sony	Electricals	4438	32.1	1.36%
4	Toshiba	Electricals	4238	30.7	1.30%
5	Tokyu Corp	Railways	3857	27.9	1.18%
6	Sumitomo Metal Inds	Steel	3730	27.0	1.14%
7	Taisei	Construction	3669	26.6	1.12%
8	Fujita	Construction	3120	22.6	0.96%
9	NKK Corp	Steel	2967	21.5	0.91%
10	Kawasaki Heavy Inds	Shipbuilding	2868	20.8	0.88%
11	Mitsui Real Estate	Real Estate	2712	19.6	0.83%
12	Fuji Photo	Chemicals	2683	19.4	0.82%
13	Shimizu	Construction	2683	19.4	0.82%
14	Sato Kogyo	Construction	2648	19.2	0.81%
15	Kobe Steel	Steel	2567	18.6	0.79%
16	Obayashi	Construction	2535	18.4	0.78%
17	Kumgai Gumi	Construction	2455	17.8	0.75%
18	IHU	Shipbuilding	2277	16.5	0.70%
19	Hitachi	Electricals	2275	16.5	0.70%
20	Kawasaki Steel	Steel	2253	16.3	0.69%
21	Nisshin Steel	Steel	2186	15.8	0.67%
22	NTT	Communications	2103	15.2	0.64%
23	Nippon Oil	Oil	2081	15.1	0.64%
24	Tokyo Electric Power	Electric Power	2068	15.0	0.63%
25	Mitsubishi Electric	Electricals	2040	14.8	0.63%
26	Ibara	Machinery	1935	14.0	0.59%
27	Kajima	Construction	1925	13.9	0.59%
28	Fanuc	Electricals	1841	13.3	0.56%
29	Nissan	Autos	1807	13.1	0.55%
30	Nishimatsu	Construction	1804	13.1	0.55%
31	Daiwa House	Construction	1785	12.9	0.55%
32	Kansai Electric Power	Electric Power	1783	12.9	0.55%
33	Sekisui House	Construction	1710	12.4	0.52%
34	Marubeni	Trading	1705	12.3	0.52%
35	Canon	Precisions	1689	12.2	0.52%
36	Sumitomo Realty	Real Estate	1689	12.9	0.52%
37	Aoki	Construction	1687	12.2	0.52%
38	Tokyo Steel	Steel	1659	12.0	0.51%
39	Sumitomo Metal Mining	Non-Ferrous Metals	1644	11.9	0.50%
40	Nippon Express	Trucking	1609	11.6	0.49%
41	Mitsui Zosen	Shipbuilding	1609	11.6	0.49%

Table continues

Table 10   (continued)

	Company	Sector	¥bn	$bn	% of TSE
42	Mitsubishi Metal	Non-Ferrous Metals	1576	11.4	0.48%
43	Daikyp	Real Estate	1567	11.3	0.48%
44	Matsushita Electric Inds	Electricals	1559	11.3	0.48%
45	Amada	Machinery	1544	11.2	0.47%
46	Nippon Yusen	Shipping	1523	11.0	0.47%
47	Keisei Electric Railway	Railways	1435	10.4	0.44%
48	Okumura	Construction	1427	10.3	0.44%
49	Hazama	Construction	1426	10.3	0.44%
50	Pioneer	Electricals	1401	10.1	0.43%

Companies	¥bn	$bn	% of TSE
1 – 5	21,664	156.8	6.64%
1 – 10	38,018	275.3	11.65%
1 – 15	51,311	371.5	15.72%
1 – 20	63,106	456.9	19.34%
1 – 25	73,584	532.8	22.55%
1 – 30	82,896	600.2	25.40%
1 – 35	91,568	663.0	28.06%
1 – 40	99,856	723.0	30.60%
1 – 45	107,711	779.8	33.00%
1 – 50	114,923	832.1	35.21%
1 – 5	21,664	156.8	6.64%
6 – 10	16,354	118.4	5.01%
11 – 15	13,293	96.2	4.07%
16 – 20	11,795	85.4	3.61%
21 – 25	10,478	75.9	3.21%
26 – 30	9,312	67.4	2.85%
31 – 35	8,672	62.8	2.66%
36 – 40	8,288	60.0	2.54%
41 – 45	7,855	56.9	2.41%
46 – 50	7,212	52.2	2.21%
1 – 10	38,018	275.3	11.65%
11 – 20	25,088	181.6	7.69%
21 – 30	19,790	143.3	6.06%
31 – 40	16,960	122.8	5.20%
41 – 50	15,067	109.1	4.62%
TSE 1	326,370	109.1	4.62%

Table 11   Activity—Breakdown of TSE 1 Client turnover by Investor Group

	1980	1985	1986	1987	1988	1989	1990	YoY
Value – ¥bn								
Insurance Cos	0.56	0.94	1.91	2.77	3.30	4.23	4.80	13.4%
Banks	1.73	9.52	33.62	68.95	85.71	55.79	49.04	−12.1%
Investment Trusts	3.04	5.65	13.82	23.65	31.57	51.06	30.57	−40.1%
Financial Cos	.33	16.11	49.35	95.37	120.58	111.08	84.40	−24.0%
Non-Financial Cos	3.60	8.71	25.92	43.52	58.02	62.77	30.69	−51.1%
Corporations	8.93	24.82	75.26	138.89	178.60	173.85	115.10	−33.8%
Individuals	21.55	43.96	78.92	112.25	118.41	138.53	72.46	−47.7%
Domestic Investors	30.48	68.78	154.19	251.14	297.01	312.38	187.56	−40.0%
Foreigners	3.63	15.49	29.44	43.72	35.28	49.66	32.82	−33.9%
Total Clients	34.12	84.27	183.63	294.85	332.29	362.04	220.38	−39.1%
% of Total								
Insurance Cos	1.7%	1.1%	1.0%	0.9%	1.0%	1.2%	1.2%	1.0%
Banks	5.1%	11.3%	18.3%	23.4%	25.8%	15.4%	22.3%	6.8%
Investment Trusts	8.9%	6.7%	7.5%	8.0%	9.5%	14.1%	13.9%	−0.2%
Vinancial cos	15.6%	19.1%	26.9%	32.3%	36.3%	30.7%	38.3%	7.6%
Non-Financial Cos	10.5%	10.3%	14.1%	14.8%	17.5%	17.3%	13.9%	−3.4%
Corporations	26.2%	29.5%	41.0%	47.1%	43.7%	48.0%	52.2%	4.2%
Individuals	63.2%	52.2%	43.0%	38.1%	35.6%	38.3%	42.9%	−5.4%
Domestic Investors	89.4%	81.6%	84.0%	85.2%	89.4%	86.3%	85.1%	−1.2%
Foreigners	10.6%	18.4%	16.0%	14.8%	10.6%	13.7%	14.9%	1.2%
Total Clients	100.0%	100.0%	100.0%	100.0%	100.0%	100.0%	100.0%	0.0%

Table 12   Activity—Breakdown of Turnover by Stock Exchange

	1980	1985	1986	1987	1988	1989	1990	YoY
Shares Traded—m								
Tokyo	102,245	121,862	197,699	263,611	282,636	222,599	123,098	–44.7&
Osaka	12,453	18,295	29,028	37,133	31,690	25,096	17,186	–31.5%
Nagoya	3,316	5,151	10,394	13,199	12,485	7,263	4,323	–40.5%
Kyoto	105	245	363	444	373	331	416	25.7%
Hiroshima	347	155	117	160	192	189	169	–10.6%
Fukuoka	109	151	190	236	246	267	203	–24.0%
Niigata	270	329	437	512	527	397	245	–38.3%
Sapporo	82	110	124	143	158	151	194	28.5%
Total	118,931	146,301	238,354	315,441	328,311	256,296	145,837	–43.1%
% of Shares Traded								
Tokyo	85.97%	83.30%	82.94%	83.57%	86.09%	86.85%	84.41%	–2.44%
Osaka	10.47%	12.51%	12.18%	11.77%	9.65%	9.79%	11.78%	1.99%
Nagoya	2.79%	3.52%	4.36%	4.18%	3.80%	2.83%	2.96%	0.13%
Kyoto	0.09%	0.17%	0.15%	0.14%	0.11%	0.13%	0.29%	0.16%
Hiroshima	0.29%	0.11%	0.05%	0.05%	0.06%	0.07%	0.12%	0.04%
Fukuoka	0.09%	0.10%	0.08%	0.07%	0.07%	0.10%	0.14%	0.04%
Niigata	0.23%	0.22%	0.18%	0.16%	0.16%	0.15%	0.17%	0.01%
Sapporo	0.07%	0.08%	0.05%	0.05%	0.05%	0.06%	0.13%	0.07%
Total	100.00%	100.00%	100.00%	100.00%	100.00%	100.00%	100.00%	0000%
Value Traded—¥tn								
Tokyo	36,490	78,711	159,836	250,737	285,521	332,617	186,669	–43.9%
Osaka	4,370	12,536	25,181	34,670	34,504	41,679	35,813	–14.1%
Nagoya	995	2,885	7,307	9,503	11,349	10,395	7,301	–29.8%
Kyoto	37	123	221	367	375	443	70	73.8%
Hiroshima	117	82	71	138	180	235	261	11.1%
Fukuoka	39	93	118	195	233	330	405	22.7%
Niigata	84	155	249	376	445	475	334	–29.7%
Sapporo	29	54	76	125	149	221	286	29.4%
Total	42,161	94,640	193,059	296,111	332,757	386,395	231,837	–40.0%
% of Value Traded								
Tokyo	86.55%	83.17%	82.79%	84.68%	85.80%	86.08%	80.52%	–5.56%
Osaka	10.37%	13.25%	13.04%	11.71%	10.37%	10.79%	15.45%	4.66%
Nagoya	2.36%	3.05%	3.78%	3.21%	3.41%	2.69%	3.15%	0.46%
Kyoto	0.09%	0.13%	0.11%	0.12%	0.11%	0.11%	0.33%	0.22%
Hiroshima	0.28%	0.09%	0.04%	0.05%	0.05%	0.065	0.11%	0.05%
Fukuoka	0.09%	0.10%	0.06%	0.07%	0.07%	0.09%	0.17%	0.09%
Niigata	0.20%	0.16%	0.13%	0.13%	0.13%	0.12%	0.14%	0.02%
Sapporo	0.07%	0.06%	0.04%	0.04%	0.04%	0.06%	0.12%	0.07%
Total	100.00%	100.00%	100.00%	100.00%	100.00%	100.00%	100.00%	0.00%

Chapter 14

Table 13   Sales & Profits—Corporate Performance

Year to March	1984	1985	1986	1987	1988	1989	1990
Sales	3.3%	8.3%	3.4%	−8.6%	5.5%	8.5%	15.5%
Operating Profits	4.3%	14.3%	−8.1%	−15.1%	13.6%	19.7%	7.0%
Recurring Profits	11.2%	23.0%	−2.4%	−9.9%	16.6%	24.3%	10.1%
Net Profits	4.0%	17.8%	1.5%	−14.8%	21.7%	26.2%	15.5%
Dividends	6.7%	6.6%	4.6%	4.6%	4.9%	9.6%	10.7%
Payout	36.7%	33.5%	33.0%	24.8%	29.2%	28.1%	27.0%
RoE	8.5%	8.9%	8.6%	7.7%	8.6%	8.6%	8.5%

Note: The table above excludes financial companies.

Table 14   Valuations

End December	1980	1985	1986	1987	1988	1989	1990
Interest Rates							
Long Bond	8.81%	5.82%	4.61%	4.28%	4.16%	5.87%	7.06%
TSE 1—TSE Basis							
P/B Ratio	2.2	2.9	3.4	3.7	4.2	5.4	2.9
Dividend Yield	1.48%	1.03%	0.70%	0.59%	0.49%	0.43%	0.76%
P/E Ratio	20.4	35.2	47.3	58.3	58.4	70.6	39.8
Earnings Yield	4.90%	2.84%	2.11%	1.72%	1.71%	1.42%	2.51%
E'gs Yield Gap	3.91%	2.98%	2.50%	2.56%	2.45%	4.45%	4.55%
E'gs Yield Ratio	55.6	48.8	45.9	40.1	41.2	24.1	35.6
TSE 2—TSE Basis							
P/B Ratio	2.4	3.1	3.2	3.7	4.0	5.2	3.1
Divident Yield	1.36%	0.69%	0.62%	0.47%	0.49%	0.35%	0.48%
P/E Ratio	21.4	39.0	48.3	58.5	56.2	57.4	41.2
(vs TSE 1)	(1.05)	(1.11)	(1.02)	(1.00)	(0.96)	(0.81)	(1.04)

Appendix I
Principal Stock Exchanges in Japan

Tokyo Stock Exchange
2-1-1 Nihonbashi-Kayabacho
Chuo-ku, Tokyo 103
Tel: (03) 3666 0141

Osaka Securities Exchange
2-1 Kitahama
Higashi-ku, Osaka 541
Tel: (06) 203 1151

Nagoya Stock Exchange
3-3-17 Sakae
Naka-ku, Nagoya 460
Tel: (052) 241-1521
Hours 09.00 - 11.00
       13.00 - 15.00

Appendix II
Principal Securities Companies in Japan

Domestic

Cosmo Securities
Daiichi Securities
Daiwa Securities
Kankaku Securities
Kokusai Securities
Marusan Securities
New Japan Securities
Nikko Securities
Nomura Securities
Okasan Securities
Sanyo Securities
Tachibana Securities
Taiheiyo Securities
Tokyo Securities

Universal Securities
Yamaichi Securities
Wako Securities

International

Barclays de Zoete Wedd Securities (Japan)
Baring Securities (Japan)
Cazenove & Co (Japan)
CS First Boston Pacific
Goldman Sachs (Japan)
James Capel Pacific
Jardine Fleming (Securities)
Kleinwort Benson International
Lehman Bros Asia
UBS Phillips & Drew International
S.G. Warburg Securities (Japan)
W.I.Carr Overseas (WICO)

Appendix III
Commission Rates on Japanese Equity Transactions

Value—¥m		Commission Terms		Commission Rate			Commission—¥ooo		
		%	Plus	Lo	Av	Hi	Lo	Av	Hi
~	1.00	1.150%		1.15%	1.15%	1.15%		6	12
1.00 ~	4.99	0.900%	2,500	1.15%	0.98%	0.95%	12	29	47
5.00 ~	9.99	0.700%	12,500	0.95%	0.87%	0.83%	48	65	82
10.00 ~	29.99	0.575%	25,000	0.83%	0.70%	0.66%	83	140	197
30.00 ~	49.99	0.375%	85,000	0.66%	0.59%	0.55%	198	235	272
50.00 ~	99.99	0.225%	160,000	0.55%	0.44%	0.39%	273	329	385
100.00 ~	299.99	0.200%	185,000	0.39%	0.29%	0.26%	385	585	785
300.00 ~	499.99	0.125%	410,000	0.26%	0.23%	0.21%	785	910	1,035
500.00 ~	999.99	0.100%	535,000	0.21%	0.17%	0.15%	1,035	1,285	1,535
1,000.00 ~		0.075%	785,000	0.15%			1,535		

Value—US$ooo (@ ¥125/$)		Commission Terms		Commission Rate			Commission—$		
		%	Plus	Lo	Av	Hi	Lo	Av	Hi
~	8	1.150%			1.15%	1.15%		46	92
8 ~	40	0.900%	20	1.15%	0.98%	0.95%	92	236	379

Table continues

Value—US$ooo (@ ¥125/$)		Commission Terms		Commission Rate			Commission$		
		%	Plus	Lo	Av	Hi	Lo	Av	Hi
40 ~	80	0.700%	100	0.95%	0.87%	0.83%	380	520	659
80 ~	240	0.575%	200	0.83%	0.70%	0.66%	660	1,120	1,580
240 ~	400	0.375%	680	0.66%	0.59%	0.55%	1,580	1,880	2,180
400 ~	800	0.225%	1,280	0.55%	0.44%	0.39%	2,180	2,630	3,080
800 ~	2,400	0.200%	1,480	0.39%	0.29%	0.26%	3,080	4,680	6,280
2,400 ~	4,000	0.125%	3,280	0.26%	0.23%	0.21%	6,280	7,280	8,280
4,000 ~	8,000	0.100%	4,280	0.21%	0.17%	0.15%	8,280	10,280	12,280
8,000 ~		0.075%	6,280	0.15%			12,280		

Appendix IV
Useful Publications & Sources of Information

TSE Publications

Annual Statistics		Monthly
Annual Fact Book		Annual
Key Statistics for the Securities Market & Economy in Japan		Annual
A Profile of the TSE		
Constitution		
Listing Regulations		

Other Publications

Japan Company Handbook (TSE 1 & TSE 2 Volumes)	Toyo Keizai	Quarterly
Tokyo stock market Quarterly Review	Daiwa Secs	Quarterly
Daiwa Analysts Guide	Daiwa Secs	Annual
Analysis of Japanese Industry for Investors	Nikko Secs	Annual
Industrial Groupings in Japan	Dodwells	Annual
Investors Guide	Daiwa Secs	Monthly
Toyo Keizai Monthly Statistics	Toyo Keizai	Monthly
Economic Statistics Monthly	Bank of Japan	Monthly
Economic Statistics Annual	Bank of Japan	Annual
Japan Economic Almanac	Nikkei	Annual
Securities Markets in Japan—1990	JSRI	Biannual
Outlines of Foreign Exchange Control in Japan	Bank of Japan	
Guide to Japanese Taxes	Zaikei Shohosha	
Doing Business in Japan	Price Waterhouse	
Handbook of Japanese Accounting Practice	Chuo Keizaisha	

English Language Journals

Japan Times		Daily
Financial Times		
Asian Wall Street Journal		
Japan Economic Journal	Nikkei	Weekly
The Economist		

English Language Journals (continued)
Far East Economic Review
Business Tokyo   Keizaikai   Monthly
Tokyo Business Today   Toyo Keizai
Asiamoney   Euromoney

Databases & On-Line Information Systems
Datastream
Nikkei NEEDS
Nikkei Telecom
Daiwa PMS
Nikko ISS
Nomura CAPITAL
Yamaichi TIS

Australian Equity Market

Bruce Rolph and Charles Wall
Baring Securities (Australia) Limited, Sidney

Introduction

The Australian sharemarket is the third largest market in the Asian Pacific region. Its significant position reflects the Australian economy's unique characteristics; for example, it is an English speaking, politically stable, highly industrialized, and resource rich nation, in an increasingly important time zone.

Unlike other markets in Asia and the Pacific, the Australian sharemarket is relatively unique because it can be split into two general categories, one covering resource companies and the other covering non-resource, or industrial companies. The non-resource market is the larger of the two and covers about two thirds of the value of total market turnover. Companies in the non-resource market include banks, retailers, and manufacturing companies. Companies in the resource sector include oil, gold, coal, and aluminium producers.

While the Australian sharemarket has always been popular with international investors for both its resource and currency characteristics, substantial deregulation of the Australian financial system since 1983 has placed the Australian market in an even more attractive position to capture the growing flow of international investment funds into the region.

Significant among the financial deregulation was the floating of the Australian dollar in 1983, the removal of most interest rate restrictions, and the opening of the banking and stockbroking sectors to 100% foreign-owned corporations. In addition, Australia has a large and successful history in the development of derivative products, highlighted by the rapid development and spread of both futures and exchange traded option instruments.

Market Fundamentals

Size

While the Australian market is relatively small compared to the United States and Japanese equity markets, it is a major market when compared to other markets in the Asian-Pacific area. The Australian sharemarket is the second largest market open to foreign investors in the Asian-Pacific region. In fact, the market capitalization is more than double the size of the Hong Kong market, to which it is often compared by international investors.

In terms of market capitalization and turnover, the size of the Australian equity market rose dramatically through the 1980's until the stock market crash in October 1987. Since the crash the market has temporarily decreased in size. While market capitalization has more than tripled since 1984, it decreased by one percent over the last year. Similarly, while the value of market turnover in 1988 was over five times its level in 1984, turnover had decreased by over sixty percent in 1989 compared with the previous year.

The number of delistings in 1989 was nearly double that of the previous year and was a direct result of the fallout of the October crash.

Table 1   Market Capitalization

Country	Market Capitalization (US$ billion)	Percent of Non-Japan Regional Market Capitalization
Australia	182	51
Japan	3750	n/a
United States	2785	n/a
Taiwan*	197	n/a
Korea*	103	n/a
Hong Kong	64	21
Singapore	28	9
Malaysia	24	9
Thailand	13	5

* Not available to foreigners.

Exhibit 1   Value of Turnover

$ Million

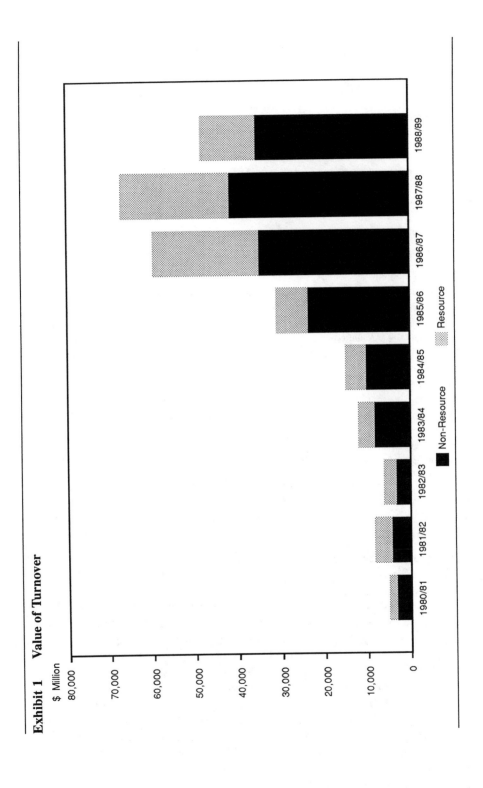

Table 2   Market Size

Year Ended June 30	1984	1988	1989
Turnover Value (A$ billion)			
Non-resource	7.80	41.88	36.32
Resource	4.55	26.32	13.18
Turnover Volume (billion)			
Non-resource	3.47	18.77	15.40
Resource	6.53	18.83	11.23
Daily Average Equity Turnover			
Value (A$ million)	48.8	269.5	105.3
Volume (million)	39.5	148.6	195.6
Capital Raisings by Main Board			
Equity and Debt (A$ billion)	3.88	14.59	12.01
Main Board			
New Listings	61	201	73
Delistings	54	77	137
Number of Companies	1000	1510	1446
Market Capitalization			
(A$ billion)	60.01	212.02	208.96

Concentration

Of Australia's ten largest listed companies seven are non-resource companies and three are resource companies; as a group, they represent around 30% of the total market capitalization.

Australia's largest listed company is Broken Hill Proprietary (BHP) (see Table 3), a diversified resource company. Its activities include exploration, mining, mineral processing, and steel making. The next largest company in Australia is Elders IXL (EXL), a diversified industrial company with activities covering brewing, agribusiness, and finance. Within the top ten companies are three banks—Westpac (WBC), National Australia Bank (NAB), and ANZ (ANZ). BTR Nylex (BTR) has activities in packaging and building and News Corporation (NCP) is a large multinational media company. Both CRA (CRA) and Western Mining (WMC) are resource companies. CRA has activities in aluminium, copper, iron ore, and coal. Western Mining has gold, nickel, and uranium activities.

Table 3   Australia's Largest Companies

	Market Capitalization (A$ million)	Percentage All Ords
Broken Hill Proprietary	12609	6.0
Elders IXL	6711	3.2
BTR Nylex	5689	2.7
News Corporation	5526	2.6
Westpac Banking Corporation	5287	2.5
National Australia Bank	5021	2.4
CRA	4978	2.4
Western Mining Corporation	4655	2.2
Coles Myer	4372	2.1
ANZ Banking Group	4190	2.0

The number of resource companies in the top level of companies is shown in Table 4.

Key Indicators

The broad indicator of market performance is the all ordinaries index. The all ordinaries index is calculated using the market prices of approximately three hundred Australian companies. The market value of these companies totals nearly 90% of the value of all shares traded on the Australian stock exchange. The all ordinaries index is a weighted index of the share prices of the companies included in the index. Each stock is weighted by the companyies market capitalization, so the larger companies exert more influence on the movement of the index.

It is important to distinguish between the all ordinaries index and the all ordinaries accumulation index. The accumulation index is adjusted to account for dividends paid by companies in the index sample.

Table 4   Number Of Resource Companies

Top 10	3
Top 50	14
Top 100	17

Market Performance

Historical Perspective

A long-run chart of the Australian share market from 1980 is given in Exhibit 2; a shorter period starting in 1987 is presented in Exhibit 3.

The Australian sharemarket had a strong bull market run from 1982 until the October 1987 crash. After the crash, the market rose again until mid-1988 and then traded in a flat range for over a year until July 1989. The market has still not traded above its pre-crash high.

The main reason for the dull performance of the market during 1988–1989 was the high and rising interest rate environment in Australia. The federal government in an attempt to increase domestic demand had been raising interest rates since April 1988. Ninety-day bank bills had risen from 11.5% to 18.0% over the period of April 1988 to August 1989, and ten year bond yields had increased from 11.5% to 13.6% over the same period.

As is shown in Table 5 the resource sector has under performed the non-resource sector over both 1987–1988 and 1988–1989. A major factor for the underperformance was that resource companies are export orientated and, as a result, are affected by exchange rate movements. The appreciation of the Australian dollar against the US dollar from 72 cents in January 1988 to 88 cents in January 1989 had been a negative factor for the resource sector.

In addition non-resource companies were favored by the change in tax laws in May 1988, which encouraged companies to pay fully franked (no tax payable) dividends. As a result, domestic investors purchased equity in those companies that paid high fully franked dividends in order to minimize their tax payable.

The Australian market is concentrated at the upper end with the twenty largest companies making up 50% of all the ordinaries index and the top fifty companies making up nearly three-quarters of the index. As shown in Table 5 during 1900–1989, the top twenty companies outperformed the general market by rising 3.2%, while the general market fell 2.2%. One reason for this outperformance was the flight to quality blue chip stocks after the sharemarket crash.

Exhibit 2   Australian All Ordinaries Index (Monthly Average January 1980–September 1989)

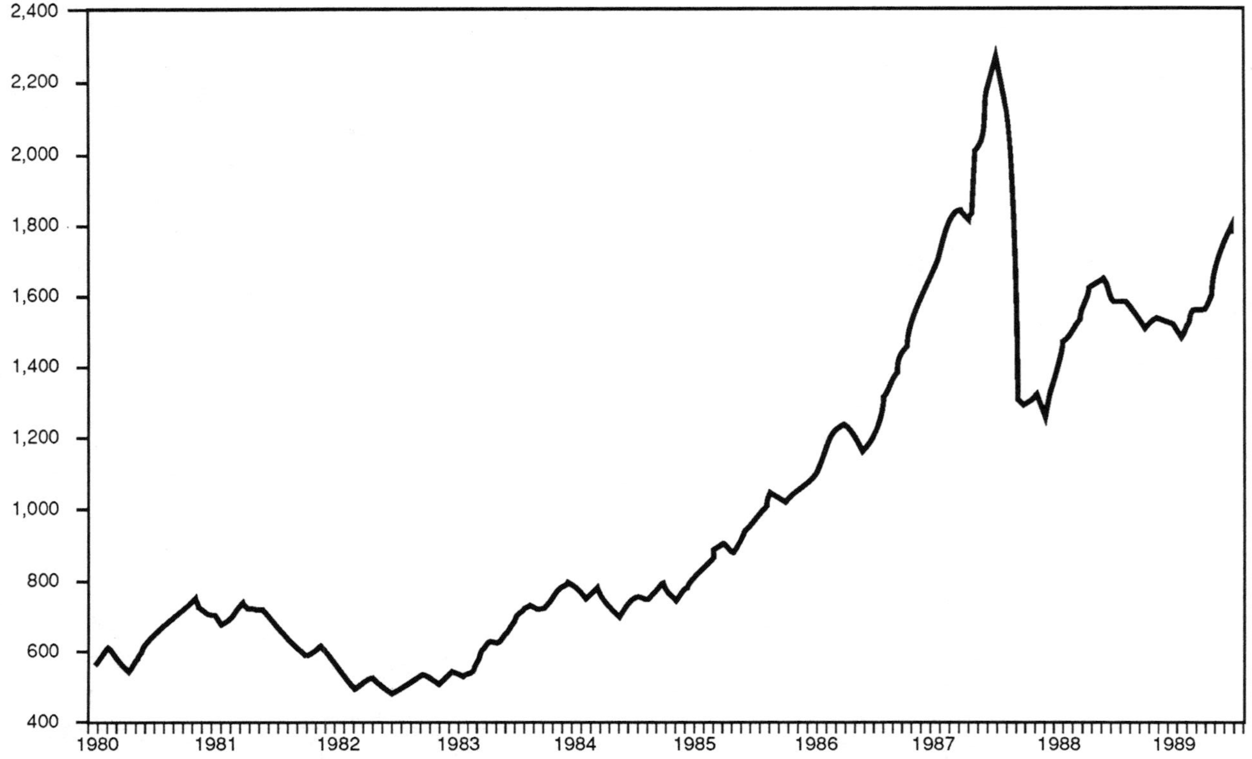

Exhibit 3   Australian All Ordinaries Index (Daily 1 September 1987–30 September 1989)

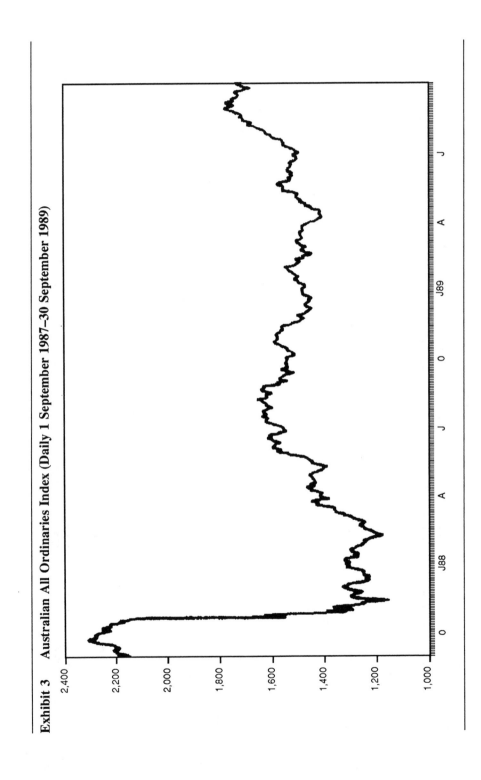

Exhibit 4   Australian All Industrials Relative to the All Resources Index
(Daily 1 September 1987–30 September 1989)

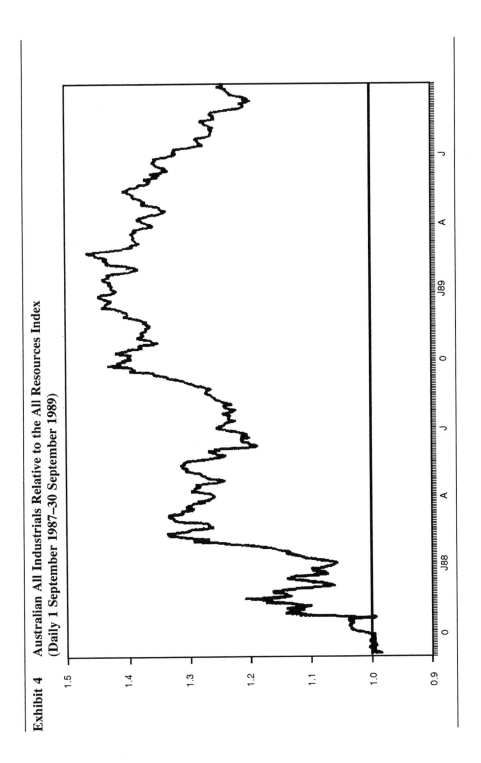

Table 5   Market Performance

Group	Percent Change 1987/8	Percent Change 1988/9	Percent All Ordinaries
All Ordinaries	−11.9	−2.2	100.0
All Mining	−24.2	−11.6	19.8
All Resources	−24.2	−5.8	32.7
All Industrials	−4.6	−0.3	67.3
20 Leaders	−8.9	+3.2	50.2
50 Leaders	−7.2	+0.8	74.2

Table 6   Market Sub-Sector Performance

Group	Percentage All Ords Index	Percentage Change 1987/8	Percentage Change 1988/9
Gold	10.7	−34.5	−22.3
Other Metals	8.9	−2.7	−4.7
Solid Fuels	1.2	−22.3	+17.0
Oil and Gas	3.7	−34.1	−5.4
Diversified Resources	10.4	−21.4	+7.7
Developers and Contractors	3.0	−15.4	−25.2
Building Materials	5.3	−1.6	−3.8
Alcohol and Tobacco	2.0	+7.6	+0.2
Food and Household Goods	3.4	−8.2	+2.0
Chemicals	2.2	+45.4	−3.0
Engineering	1.6	+11.0	+4.5
Paper and Packaging	1.4	+3.7	−2.2
Retail	4.1	+15.0	+2.7
Transport	3.1	+7.0	+16.7
Media	3.3	−7.2	+2.0
Banks and Finance	8.3	+28.3	+3.3
Insurance	1.3	−17.3	−30.1
Entrepreneurial Investors	7.1	−43.4	+3.5
Investment and Financial Services	2.0	−21.6	−13.1
Property Trusts	3.3	−9.4	−9.8
Miscellaneous Services	1.9	−11.0	+0.9
Miscellaneous Industrials	1.8	−6.9	−17.7
Diversified Industrials	10.0	+6.0	+8.9

Exhibit 5   Performance of the All Ordinaries Index Relative to the Dow Jones Index (4 January 1988-9)

**Exhibit 6   Performance of the All Ordinaries Index Relative to the
Dow Jones Index (January 1980-9)**

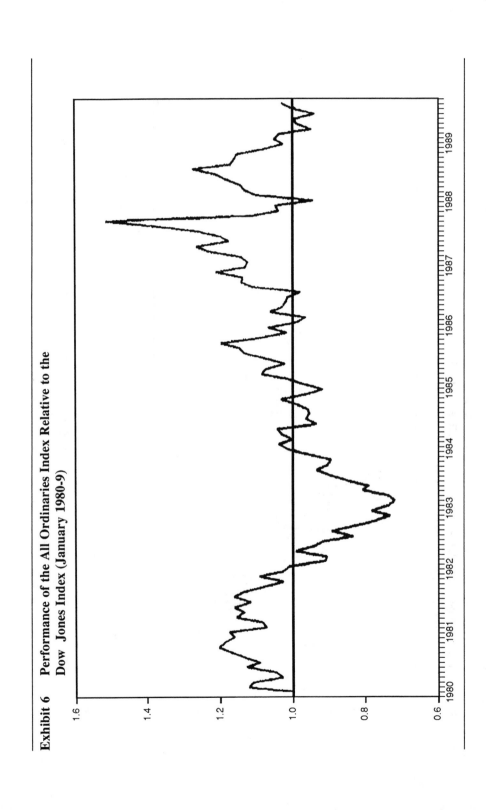

Exhibit 7   All Ordinaries Price Earnings Ratio

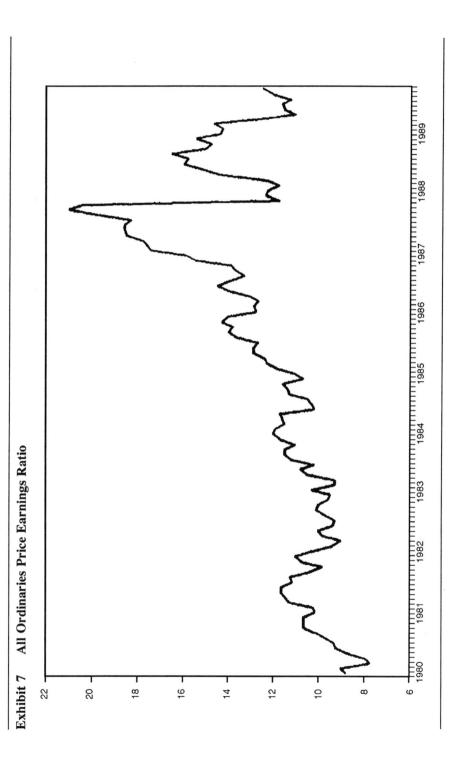

Exhibit 8   All Ordinaries Dividend Yield

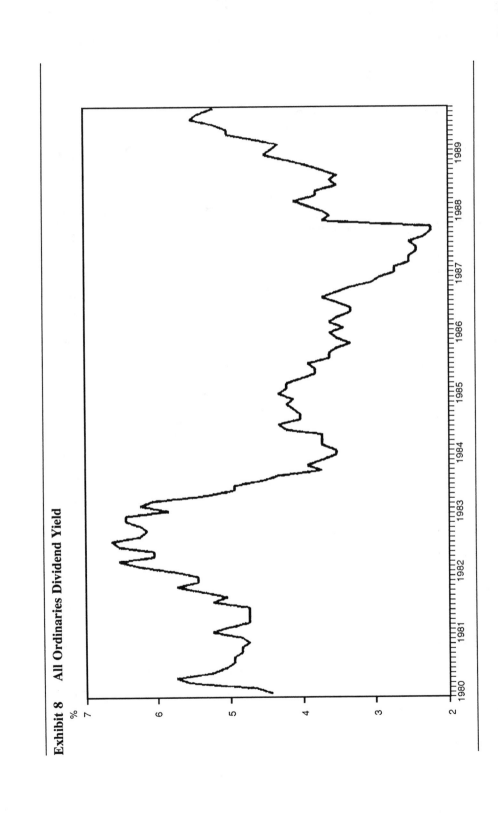

Market Structure

Location

Stocks are traded in six cities in Australia: Sydney, Melbourne, Brisbane, Perth, Adelaide, and Hobart. The Australian Stock Exchange is an amalgamation of the six state stock exchanges that have formed a national body in 1987. The Australian Stock Exchange is owned by its members, both corporate and natural person members who in turn elect a board of directors to manage the affairs of the exchange. The addresses of each of the exchanges are given below:

Sydney Stock Exchange
Exchange Centre
20 Bond Street
NSW 2000
Tel: 2-227 0000

Adelaide Stock Exchange
55 Exchange Place
SA 5000
Tel: 8-212 3702

Melbourne Stock Exchange
Stock Exchange House
351 Collins Street
VIC 3000
Tel: 3-617 8611

Perth Stock Exchange
68 St. George's Terrace
WA 6000
Tel: 9-327 0000

Brisbane Stock Exchange
Riverside Centre
123 Eagle Street
QLD 4000
Tel: 7-831 1499

Hobart Stock Exchange
10th Floor AMP Building
86 Collins Street
TAS 7001
Tel: 02-34 7333

The most important exchanges are Sydney and Melbourne, where over 90% of floor traded turnover occurs. Trading hours are from 10:00 A.M. to 12:15 A.M. and then from 2 P.M. until 4 P.M., local time. Because Perth is further west of Sydney, Melbourne, and Brisbane, it closes two to three hours after these exchanges.

Type of Shares

There are several types of equities traded on the stock exchange.

Ordinary Shares   Ordinary shares are those shares for which the par value has been fully paid. When they are first issued through the primary market generally the par value is paid in full, which may also include a premium. Ordinary shares have full voting rights.

Contributing Shares   A contributing share is one in which the par value and any premium has not been fully paid to the company. The company will make a call in the future for all or part of the remaining amount. Contributing shares participate on a pro-rata basis for any dividends and rights issues.

Preference Shares   These shares have a fixed dividend rate expressed as a percentage of the par value. They are known as preferred shares because they rank above ordinary shares for claims on assets, earnings, and dividends but rank below creditors, debenture, and note holders.

Convertible Notes   A convertible note is a cross between a loan and a share. It is similar to a loan in that it has a fixed interest rate and a specific repayment date. Recently there has been a trend towards issuing updated or perpetual convertible notes. The note may be converted to a share, and for this reason it is listed among the equities. A noteholder has the choice of selling the notes through the market, converting to shares on specified dates, or redeeming them at par on maturity. The notes accrue bonus and cash issues. As it is an unsecured loan, the convertible note ranks after secured loans and before preference and ordinary shares for claims on company assets. The Australian convertible note market makes up around 1.7% of the total market capitalization.

Company Options   In addition to the exchange traded option market, which is discussed further on, stock options are traded on the Australian Stock Exchange. These options are very similar to warrants in that they are long-dated call options over stock. Presently, there over 300 options attached to 300 stocks with the distribution favoring mining stocks. Stock options are primarily issued to sweeten a new issue or to establish new stock for a company. The company option market makes up around 0.3% of the total market capitalization.

Property and Equity Trusts   An investment in a property trust is an investment in a property or a group of properties that is administered by a management company and watched over by a trustee. An investment in an equity trust is an investment in a company that uses the funds to buy and sell shares on the equity market. Subscribers hold units in the trust and are paid distributions out of the earnings. Trusts usually have specific charters that restrict the type of properties or equities in which they may invest.

Derivative Markets

Exchange Traded Options Market

The Australian options market was established in 1976, when it became the first listed options market outside Canada and the United States. The number of option contracts traded has increased dramatically over recent years, and research has indicated that option related equity transactions account for in excess of 50% of turnover in the Australian equity market.

Call and put options are quoted over the next three consecutive quarters for twenty-seven leading stocks (see Table 7). Call options are the most preferred option type. All options are similar to American options in that they can be exercised before the expiry date. Buyers of call options who wish to participate in dividends, bonus shares, and rights issues must exercise their option before the last trading day on which the underlying shares are quoted cum the benefit.

In regard to limits, there is no position limit on option buyers or "scrip-covered" call writers. However "cash-covered" writers are limited to 500 contracts per series. There is also an overall limit on the number of contracts written in any class to 10% of the total ordinary issue capital underlying the security. Exercise limits restrict the exercising of options by a client to 1% of ordinary fully paid issued capital within 15 consecutive business days.

Registered traders are present in each stock, and they are obligated to make a market in any maturity or strike when asked. This obligation ensures continuity in trading and that appropriate price relationships are established in each option series.

Share Price Index Futures

A share price index contract is traded at the Sydney Futures Exchange. Share price index futures began trading in 1983, and options on share price index futures began in 1985. The futures contract provides investors with the ability to hedge their equity exposure and information about future sharemarket levels. The share price index futures contract trades from 9:30 A.M. to 12:30 A.M. and from 2:00 P.M. until 4:10 P.M. Contracts are quoted for March, June, September, and December up to eighteen months ahead, with the nearest two contracts being the most heavily traded.

The SPI futures contract is based on the all ordinaries index. The unit of the futures contract is a sum of money equal to the all ordinaries index multiplied by $100. Deposits are subject to change depending on contract volatility; however, they are presently set at A$6000, which is around three to four percent of the contract value. The expiry date is the last business day of the contract

Table 7   Option Traded Stocks

Aust and New Zealand Bank	Lend Lease Corporation
Broken Hill Proprietary	Mount Isa Mines
BHP Gold Mines	National Aust Bank
Bougainville Copper	North Broken Hill
Boral	News Corporation
BTR Nylex	Pacific Dunlop
Coles Myer	Pioneer International
CRA	QCT Resources
CSR	SA Brewing
Elders IXL	Santos
FAI Insurance	TNT
Fletcher Challenge	Westpac Bank
Goodman Fielder Wattie	Western Mining Corp.
Industrial Equity	

month and the contract is cash settled. It should be noted that the all ordinaries index is simply a price index, excluding dividends. Holding futures contracts based on the index is not an exact substitute for holding the shares on which it is based.

Market Mechanics

Trading System

All equity transactions must be conducted through a member organization of the Australian Stock Exchange. These organizations may then transact equity trades through either of the stock exchange's trading systems:

1. The trading floor.
2. Stock Exchange Automated Trading System (SEATS).

Trading in floor traded stocks is based on the open outcry system. Bids and offers for shares are recorded on the trading boards, and brokers' operators negotiate as to the price and volume of the shares they are prepared to trade. This information is then recorded on sales slips, which are entered in the exchange's computers and makes up the market information published by the exchange and various news agencies. This also forms the basis of broker-broker accounting.

The screen trading system (SEATS) began operation in October 1987. SEATS terminals can be used to enter bids and offers, and to watch the market. The number of companies on SEATS is gradually increasing. There are now over 1200 companies on SEATS, covering approximately 25% of the daily turnover. All exchanges have access to SEATS terminals.

The trading principles on SEATS terminals are slightly different from those on the trading floor. During normal hours, overlapping bids and offers are executed at each successive price level in the order in which they were entered into the market. On the trading floor overlapping bids and offers are shared. At the opening, bids and offers with overlapping prices are shared among all participants as long as stocks are available.

Settlement and Transfer

Settlement in Australia is on a rallying basis, whereby an institution contacts the broker through which it has transacted business to arrange settlement of a transaction. This is generally within five business days of the trade taking place.

Once a buy transaction is settled with a broker the shares are registered into the name of the buyer. The buyer may take physical delivery of the scrip or may have the scrip registered into the name of a custodian or agent bank. With an agent bank, stock will be registered into the name of the agent. The agent will then effect settlement on behalf of the broker and the agent bank's mutual client.

Regulation

There has been a gradual trend of deregulation in both financial and other markets in Australia during the 1980's. Some of the more significant events are outlined below.

Recent Deregulation Events

1983

    December   Floating of the Australian dollar.

1984

    April   Fixed commissions for stockbrokers services abolished in favor of negotiable rates.

| December | Foreign interests allowed to own 50% of a stockbroking business. |

1985

| February | Approval given for sixteen foreign banks to commence business. |

1986

| April | Removal of the interest ceiling on new home loans. |

1987

| April | Foreign interests allowed to own 100% of a stockbroking business. |
| October | Withdrawal of control over aircraft imports, capacity, air fares, and route entry as part of deregulation to take effect in 1990. |

1988

| January | Australian crude oil market deregulated. |

1989

| July | Domestic wheat market deregulated. |

Australian Commonwealth legislation governs both the stock exchange and its members. In addition, each of the six states pass subsequent matching legislation. The main pieces of legislation, which are of direct relevance to the equity market, are the National Companies and Securities Commission Act 1979, the Securities Industry Act 1980, and Companies (Acquisition of Shares) Act 1980. Other legislation that impinges on the equity market is the Trade Practices Act.

Consumer/shareholders protection comes largely from the Companies Act, Securities Industry Act, Futures Industry Act, and Acquisition of Shares Act. These various pieces of legislation address issues, such as licensing of brokers and their representatives, prohibition of insider trading, stock exchange regulations, and the conduct of securities businesses. This legislation forms a cohesive protection package whereby the National Companies and Securities Commission addresses national policy, legislative, and prosecution issues. Their policy decisions are then acted on by the NCSC's state delegates—the Corporate Affairs Commission. In many cases, the Australian Stock Exchange acts in conjunction with the NCSC and CAC in matters relating to public companies.

The stock exchange policies the listing rules for public (Listed) companies. The ASX also maintains surveillance and regulation and compliance departments

to police the activities of its members to govern disputes between member organizations and to administer the Membership of Exchanges. The Regulation &
Compliance Department also has a close relationship with the State Corporate
Affairs Commissions and the National Companies and Securities Commission as
part of their surveillance roles in the finance industry.

Tax

Witholding Tax

Withholding tax applies to foreign investors with regard to interest income
earned and unfranked dividends received. This tax is levied at the rate of 10%
where a double-tax agreement exists between Australia and the relevant country;
where such an agreement does not exist, withholding tax is levied at the rate of
30%.

Double-tax agreements exist between Australia and United Kingdom,
South Ireland, Canada, United States, New Zealand, Singapore, Japan, Papua
New Guinea, West Germany, France, Netherlands, Belgium, Switzerland, Den-
mark, Malaysia, Sweden, Korea, Norway, Malta, Italy, and Austria.

Capital Gains Tax

Capital gains tax does not apply to foreign investors where they are a foreign
owned, foreign controlled, and foreign registered entity.

Where the investor is not foreign controlled or foreign registered, then the
corporate must pay capital gains tax at the prevailling corporate rate, which is
currently 39%. Capital gains tax on any such sale is based on a CPI adjusted
value of the initial purchase price.

Korean Equity Market

Thae S. Kwarg
Baring Brothers & Co., Ltd., Seoul

Introduction

The Korean stock market has enjoyed a boom that began in late 1985, as the high levels of liquidity from rising current account surpluses fed into the market. As strong growth of exports fuelled a double-digit real GNP growth for the past three years, the domestic savings ratio, which surpassed the domestic investment ratio for the first time in 1986, has remained strong at 35.8% in 1987 and 37.8% in 1988.

Today, after years of rapid expansion, a market which was capitalized at just $7.5bn at end-1985, a mere 0.2% of the then total market capitalization of the world markets (Morgan Stanley Capital International Indices), is now worth over $140bn and 1.4% of the world market capitalization. The number of listed companies has jumped from 342 to 586. Korean companies, which traditionally favored the loan market to the capital market as a source of their funds, are expected to raise $21.6bn through the stock market in 1989.

The government is keen on using the stock market to recycle the huge current account surpluses and making the Korea Stock Exchange an integral part of the domestic capital market. It sees equity financing as a means of increasing the competitiveness of Korean companies. This is done primarily through the reduction of the traditionally high debt-equity ratios of Korean companies, and the spreading of wealth and power through the public ownership of the many family-controlled chaebols, i.e., conglomerate business groups, and government-owned entities. Increased foreign competition will give an added incentive to local companies to reduce further their debt-equity ratios, which have already come down from as high as 500% to the current 220% level.

Recent Stock Market Performance

The recent performance of the Korean stock market has been quite remarkable (See Table 1). As of September 30, 1989, the index had surpassed the 940-point mark, a leap of 601% over the last five years and 477% since end-1985. Similarly, average daily trading volume mushroomed, reaching $435m for the first nine months in 1989, up 549% over the last five years, and 964% since the end of 1985.

During this period, the local currency, Won, weakened against the US$ and Japanese Yen in 1984 and 1985. As Table 2 shows, however, the Won has steadily appreciated against the US$ since the G-5 Plaza Accord in late 1985. In 1988 it appreciated at an even faster pace, reaching +15.8%. Starting in 1988 the Won has been appreciating against the Yen as well, rising by 17.3% by the end of the year. The strong appreciation of the Won has provided an additional bonus to foreign investors in the overseas Korean investment vehicles. The currency is now stabilizing against the US$, rising only 2.1% in the first nine months. Due to the strength of the US$, however, the Won has appreciated 13.6% against the Yen during the same period.

Stock Market Structure

The Korea Stock Exchange

History   Although some public subscriptions and bond offerings occurred in Korea as far back as the 1880's, in 1911 the Japanese formed the first organized securities exchange. Japanese firms dominated listings in those early days and Japanese brokers carried most of the trading. This market disintegrated at the end of World War II.

Revived in 1956 under the name of Daehan Stock Exchange, the KSE did not get off the ground very quickly. The country's entrenched system of family business ownership made shareholders deeply suspicious of public listings. In addition, regulations did not draw adequate distinctions between equity and loan finance and required public firms to pay dividends, which, as a percentage of par value, were equal to time deposit rates. These were sometimes as high as 20-25%.

The Park Chung-Hee regime's First Five-Year Plan from 1962 to 1966 helped to expand the KSE. Because of the stress it imposed on the mobilization

Table 1   Stock Market Index and Average Daily Trading Volume
(1984 - September 1989)

Year	KCSPI	Daily Trading Volume (US$ m)	Year	KCSPI	Daily Trading Volume (US$ m)
1984			1987		
1	124.1	11.0	1	310.2	53.6
2	129.7	20.8	2	335.0	57.2
3	132.4	11.4	3	405.1	96.5
4	135.6	18.1	4	358.6	49.5
5	130.5	13.7	5	388.0	62.6
6	132.1	11.2	6	411.8	56.1
7	134.7	14.8	7	485.5	120.0
8	135.3	11.7	8	474.0	127.6
9	134.4	8.9	9	485.4	83.2
10	130.3	6.9	10	509.1	96.4
11	135.3	11.2	11	475.6	84.2
12	142.5	19.9	12	525.1	144.2
1985			1988		
1	138.9	16.4	1	633.6	277.9
2	134.7	9.6	2	612.4	252.3
3	136.5	10.5	3	656.5	151.5
4	134.2	10.5	4	647.2	148.7
5	134.1	7.4	5	717.4	261.5
6	136.6	12.4	6	702.8	246.8
7	137.4	9.0	7	721.1	262.3
8	136.5	11.8	8	664.4	234.3
9	138.9	8.4	9	677.5	143.5
10	140.9	15.2	10	729.8	280.2
11	150.2	20.9	11	831.1	467.5
12	163.4	40.9	12	907.2	649.9
1986			1989		
1	160.4	27.3	1	884.3	392.5
2	175.9	14.2	2	917.9	443.4
3	199.8	50.8	3	1003.3	684.5
4	202.9	47.7	4	940.5	488.3
5	231.1	39.9	5	932.8	264.5
6	243.4	55.0	6	854.6	275.3
7	273.8	47.3	7	895.7	326.1
8	264.6	30.2	8	975.3	571.8
9	253.5	23.4	9	942.4	469.0
10	240.8	16.5			
11	269.0	33.0			
12	272.6	46.2			

Source: *Stock*, Korea Stock Exchange.

Table 2   **Won/$ and Won/Yen Exchange Rate**
              (1984 - September 1989)

	Won vs.			Won vs.	
Year	US$	Yen	Year	US$	Yen
1984			1987		
1	799.30	340.53	1	875.20	557.53
2	793.30	339.81	2	854.80	557.97
3	791.80	352.78	3	846.90	579.18
4	797.60	351.60	4	834.10	600.08
5	798.30	345.07	5	822.70	572.32
6	803.40	338.56	6	808.90	551.21
7	811.40	330.24	7	808.00	540.47
8	808.70	335.22	8	807.70	569.52
9	815.20	330.45	9	805.70	549.66
10	817.40	333.42	10	801.40	579.05
11	821.10	333.45	11	796.40	596.56
12	827.40	330.57	12	792.30	642.32
1985			1988		
1	830.60	326.31	1	781.60	610.39
2	842.80	325.19	2	760.80	592.75
3	850.30	339.45	3	746.20	596.96
4	865.90	343.55	4	740.00	591.30
5	871.00	346.12	5	732.90	586.79
6	873.80	351.63	6	728.30	549.04
7	876.30	370.14	7	723.80	543.40
8	886.80	370.97	8	722.00	535.41
9	891.70	408.48	9	719.00	534.88
10	892.20	420.06	10	701.40	558.33
11	889.10	439.28	11	687.50	564.59
12	890.20	443.66	12	684.10	547.72
1986			1989		
1	888.70	461.67	1	680.60	523.36
2	883.80	490.46	2	673.10	530.67
3	885.20	492.33	3	671.90	509.02
4	885.10	526.69	4	666.30	500.98
5	889.80	509.34	5	666.70	467.86
6	886.60	536.20	6	667.20	462.21
7	885.00	568.77	7	677.40	479.41
8	880.20	571.75	8	669.20	463.44
9	877.00	571.15	9	670.00	482.02
10	873.20	541.69			
11	865.00	534.45			
12	861.40	538.38			

Source: Monthly Bulletin, Bank of Korea.

of savings for capital expenditure of industries until 1967, only two dozen companies were listed, many of which were government-owned enterprises. Furthermore, a series of speculative booms and busts undermined public confidence in the stock market.

The market's most rapid development occurred from 1972 onwards. Because of the impact of a crash in 1970, high levels of activity in the Curb market (private, uncontrolled money market), and an insufficient number of companies raising funds through the stock market, the government introduced the August 3 Emergency Decree and the Going Public Encouragement Act in 1972. The former act was an attempt to eliminate the curb market, while the latter enabled the Ministry of Finance to force companies to go public. The latter act also required designated corporations to give employees preference to subscribe up to 10% of new shares offered to the public.

The result of these and other measures was a surge in the number of public offerings and secondary distributions. Between 1972 and 1976 the number of new public offerings leapt from a meager 6 to 56, while the amount raised on the primary market rose from Won 11bn to Won 262.2bn over the same period. The number of listed companies rose to 274 from 66. In addition, in 1974 the first investment trust company was formed.

In 1977 the Securities Exchange Commission and its enforcement arm, the Securities Supervisory Board, were formed. With the exception of major corrections in 1980 and 1982, the market has continued to grow steadily in all respects. The growth has most notably been since 1985, due to government policies aimed at assisting its successful progress.

Another factor contributing to the growth of the stock market in the recent years has been the internationalization of the Korean capital market. In December 1988, the government announced a detailed timetable, calling for foreign direct investment to be phased during 1991–1992. The market opening theme is expected to continue to contribute to the stock market growth for the foreseeable future. (*See* Internationalization.)

Location; Operating Hours The KSE is located in southern Seoul, on Yoido, a large island in the Han River, which the government wants to develop as the Wall Street of Korea. At present the KSE is the country's only stock exchange, though Pusan, Korea's second largest city, did have a bourse for some time until 1978 when it was closed due to inactivity.

Established under the ownership of securities firms in 1956, the KSE became a government-controlled special corporation in 1963. The authorities held 68% of the shares of the KSE; the member securities firms held the remaining 32%. In 1988 the KSE was re-privatized and is now 100% owned by the 25-member securities firms.

The exchange is open Monday through Saturday. Trading from Monday through Friday is divided into a morning session from 9:40 to 11:40, and an afternoon session from 1:20 to 3:20. On Saturday there is a morning session only. The exchange is closed for public holidays and for five days at the end of the year.

First Section   Like the Tokyo Stock Exchange, the KSE is divided into two sections. As of September 30, 1989, there were 357 companies with 615 issues listed on the First Section, accounting for 75% of the total market capitalization of the KSE. There were 229 companies with 399 issues listed on the Second Section. Compared to the Second Section companies, the First Section companies have more mature profit records, trading performance, and ownership structure, as described below:

- An initial listing of at least six months on the Second Section

- Net profit for the preceding financial year of 5% or more of its paid-in capital; this requirement is waived if shareholders' equity is two times or more of paid-in capital

- Dividends paid at least two out of the last three financial years

- Monthly average trading volume equal to 0.3% or more of floating shares

- A maximum of 51% of all outstanding stock owned by one majority shareholder

- A minimum of 40% of the floating stock owned by minority shareholders

- The following minimum number of minority shareholders:

Capital of less than Won 5 billion	300
Capital of Won 5-15 billion	400
Capital of over Won 15 billion	500

Companies that have paid-in capital of Won 5 billion or more, or shareholders' equity of Won 10 billion or more, are expected to satisfy all the criteria for the First Section listing within three years of their listing on the Second Section. If they fail to do so they are subject to delisting.

Second Section The Second Section consists of companies with all new listings; firms less recently listed, but not yet meeting the criteria for the First Section listing; and firms removed from the First Section for failing to meet its criteria.

Administrative Section The Administrative Section consists of a small number of companies that have suffered severe financial difficulties or have fallen within the delisting criteria. As of September 30, 1989, there were 22 companies with 25 issues each in this Section. These stocks are normally very low-priced and, as such, are often targets of speculative buying. They are subject to tighter daily price fluctuation limits than First and Second Section stocks. Any First Section issue designated as an administrative issue is reassigned to the Second Section.

Supervised Issues Issues are placed under supervision when they exhibit unusual trading patterns, suggesting that they may be the subject of speculative manipulation. The "supervised" status normally lasts just a few weeks and is mostly aimed at cooling off overheated share price movements. Sometimes threats of investigations are announced as an issue gets placed under supervision. Supervised stocks stay in their usual listing section but become subject to even tighter price limit fluctuations than the Administrative Section stocks.

New Issues and Pricing Until recently, going public meant selling common stock equal to the value of paid-in capital at par Won500 or Won1000. This was perhaps appropriate in the days when share prices were driven by dividend yields. However, as prices began to dramatically rise after 1985, the obsolescence of this system and its disincention to issuers became manifest. The regulations governing new issue pricing were thus changed in 1987. The new system is an improvement on the old but still contains flaws. Public offerings do not take place at what Western investors would consider to be fair market value, and the concept of comparative earnings multiples does not enter the process.

Companies must meet several requirements before going public, including the following:

- Companies must have been in operation for at least three years.

- Paid-in capital must be over Won1bn, and the number of shares issued over 100,000.

- The earnings-related value and asset-related value must exceed the par value.

- The return on paid-in capital in the most recent fiscal year must exceed the current one-year time deposit rate. The return on paid-in capital in the previous two years must exceed 50% of the one-year time deposit rate for each of those years.

- Companies must have reported a recurring and net profit for the previous three consecutive years.

To determine the issue price, an appraisal value is then calculated. This acts as an effective cap on the issue price, which may not exceed the appraisal value and, in fact, is frequently below it. This happens because the government intervenes and imposes what it considers to be a "fair" price, rounded up to the nearest Won100. The appraisal value is assessed as follows:

1. Calculate Earnings-Related Value (ERV)

$$\left\{ \frac{(\text{First-Year Income} \times 3) + (\text{Second-Year Income} \times 2)}{5} \right\} \Big/ \left\{ \frac{\text{shares outstanding post-listing}}{\text{current one-year time deposit rate}} \right\}$$

If second-year income is less than first-year income, the average of the two is divided by the time deposit rate.

2. Calculate Asset-Related Value (ARV)

$$= \frac{\text{net asset value post listing}}{\text{shares outstanding post-listing}}$$

Both the above calculations can be used for determining the issue price, but generally the higher value of the two calculations is used.

Rights Issues and Pricing Offerings of new shares are made on a pre-emptive basis to current stockholders, but the rights are not tradeable. Stockholders are thus faced with a stark choice: subscribe, sell, or take ex-rights losses when the price adjusts. Alternatively, one may dispose of a portion of shares cum-rights to finance the subscription to the rest. Very rarely, however, do investors have second thoughts about rights issues. Shares do not adjust fully for dilution, creating an automatic profit opportunity that drives stock prices higher whenever a capital increase is rumoured or announced. However, the margin of profit is in the process of being reduced.

Until 1983, it was compulsory to offer at par, i.e., at a large discount to market value. Shareholders benefitted from this system but companies were placed at a disadvantage. To rectify this situation, in 1983 the KSE introduced above-par issuance. Large discounts to the market nonetheless remained the rule, since this made investors more cooperative and minimized the cash call on majority shareholders. High rights issue prices might force them to sell shares to finance subscription, thus diluting their stake.

In mid-1988 the KSE announced a new system designed to force more rapid cuts in discounting. Announcement of the new system ushered in a prolonged spell of bearishness on the exchange. The bearishness of the market made the authorities add an additional calculation in July 1989. It established a base value for rights issue prices, which is the lower among:

Value A:

$$\frac{\text{Latest 30--day weighted average price} + \text{latest 6--day weighted average price} + \text{final cum--rights price}}{3}$$

Value B:

The share price on the fifth day before allotment.

Value C:

$$\frac{\text{The one month average price before the 7th day of subscription} + \text{the 7th day price before the subscription date}}{2}$$

The result of this calculation is compared with the seventh day price before the subscription date.

The allowed discount from the base value was 20% in 1988; in 1989 it had fallen to 10%.

Underwriting and Initial Public Offerings Underwriting public offerings can be a very profitable business in Korea. With the government intervening to assure "fair" prices, i.e., above par but still below market, underwriters can collect large fees without having to bear much risk.

Rights issues, which are automatically subscribed and do not carry tradeable rights, do not require underwriting in the first instance. In the rare cases where stockholders do not take up rights, syndicates can be formed to repackage the new shares and offer them through public subscription.

Underwriting is carried out by twenty-four of the twenty-five securities companies. The country's first merchant bank (KMBC) and its first short-term finance corporation (KIFC) are also allowed to engage in this business.

Underwriting fees as of 1989 were liberalized so as to allow companies to decide after discussion, with management and the synidcation group, what fees should be charged. Generally, 3% is charged for underwriting.

Underwriting fees are allocated as shown:

Management Group	40%
Underwriting Syndicate	40%
Subscription Agent Group	??

The minimum requirements for an initial public offering are:

- Incorporation for at least three years, without suspension of business

- Paid-in capital of Won 1bn

- A minimum 100,000 shares to be listed

- A minimum 30% of outstanding shares offered to the public

- Qualified or unqualified CPA opinion

As part of its pressure on companies to go public, the government requires corporations to register for eventual listing once they have attained a certain business standing. At present there are around 1,600 registered companies. The conditions that trigger this process are various combinations of the following:

- Shareholders' equity of Won 10 bn or paid-in capital of Won 5 bn

- Debt/equity ratio must be lower than the average debt/equity ratio for all listed companies

- Return on paid-in capital must be above the highest one-year time deposit rate

Over-the-Counter Market The government established an OTC market in April 1987, recognizing it as an important way for smaller companies to raise funds. Criteria for an OTC listing are:

- Incorporation for at least two years

- Paid-in capital of Won 200 million or more

- Minimum of 10% of stock offered to public within six months preceding registration or held by sponsoring brokers

- Positive net worth in the most recent financial statements

So far this market has been inactive, with only 37 companies with 54 issues listed as of September 30, 1989. Starting in 1989, however, the OTC market has become much more active, with trading volume during the first nine months increasing 195% YoY in terms of the number of shares traded and 183% YoY in terms of the amount. It was estimated that close to 50 companies would be listed on the OTC by end-1989 and 100 companies by end-1990. Bid/offer mismatches on OTC shares are very common. Shares traded on the OTC market are not subject to daily price fluctuation limits.

Index The Korea Composite Stock Price Index (KCSPI) is a weighted aggregate indicator composed of all companies listed on the exchange. On trading days it is made available every ten minutes. Computation of the index consists of dividing the latest market capitalization by the previous day's market capitalization. The base market value is adjusted for capitalization changes, such as new listings or rights issues in order to reflect only the market price movement. The base date for the index is January 4, 1980, and the base index is 100.

New issues enter the index one month after listing. There are 34 industry sub-indices and another three indices based on the size of the companies' capital base. For example, small companies have a paid-in capital of below Won 5bn; medium companies have between Won5bn and 15bn; and large companies have above Won 15bn. These indices are computed in the same way as the KCSPI. Starting in 1988, the KSE publishes another stock price index, the industrials index. It has the same base date and the same index as the KCSPI.

Equity Market

Market Information Information on the market is abundant. The KSE makes comprehensive real-time and historical data available through a computer terminal network that accepts subscribers. Market price information is also broadcast to branches of brokers. The KSE also publishes monthly and annual statistical books on the market, as do a number of the regulatory agencies and industry associations. Also, the Korea Securities' Dealers Association publishes a daily paper that lists the previous day's closing prices, turnover, company announcements, and other useful information on the market.

Market P/E; Corporate Earnings Growth   The KSE has had a reputation for having one of the lowest P/E's in the world. Based on the KSE's official figures the average P/E for the entire market during 1980-1987 ranged from 2.6 in 1980 to a high of 10.9 in 1987. However, the method employed by the KSE in figuring out the market P/E yields a much lower number than the weighted P/E calculation method used by Western analysts.

The KSE derives the average P/E by simply dividing the sum of the closing prices of all listed stocks by the sum of the EPS of all listed stocks. The KSE also excludes those companies that have reported losses.

For our computation of P/E's for the twenty-eight top companies, we followed the historical P/E, based on the 1988 financial year results of 30.6x. The prospective P/E for 1989 was 31.5x. Both results were on a weighted basis, using share prices as of September 4, 1989. In comparison, the KSE's published historical P/E for the market, based on the 1988 financial year results and share prices as of September 4, 1989, was 14.2x.

Although this makes the Korean market more expensive than many other markets, including New York and London, domestic investors and government officials both believe that the market is still too undervalued for opening to foreign investors. In addition, many Korean companies understate their true earnings. This perception is caused in part, of course, by the lower P/E published by the KSE, but more importantly because they think that the Tokyo market is an appropriate yardstick.

Dividend Yields   In earlier days the Korean market was a relatively high-yield market, as befitted an exchange where stocks were valued by the relationship between dividend rates and interest rates on bank time deposits. But starting in 1982, yields began to fall, as the plunge in time deposit rates exceeded that of stock prices and a large number of companies reduced dividends due to financial difficulties.

The declining yield trend has accelerated in recent years. At present, the dividends are set as a percentage of par value, which is Won 5,000 for all KSE listed companies. Since share prices have gone up strongly while the dividend rates have remained roughly the same, yield rates have obviously come down. It is possible that the present system of setting dividend amounts as a percentage of par value will change to a new system based on current share prices.

Turnover and Liquidity As so much stock is tightly held by majority shareholding families and friends, the free float is estimated to be only around 25%. This is offset in part by the high turnover rate. The average daily trading volume was 0.31% of the total market capitalization in 1988, up significantly from a mere 0.016% in 1980.

Table 3 below shows the trading value of the twenty-five most actively traded shares on the KSE.

Composition of Market Capitalization Table 4 shows the composition of the KSE as of September 30, 1989.

Table 3   **The 25 Most Actively Traded Shares on the KSE in 1988**

Rank	Company Name	Trading Value (Won bn)	% of Total Mkt Turnover
1	The Commercial Bank of Korea	2,326	4.0
2	Daewoo Corp.	1,954	3.4
3	Cho-Hung Bank	1,914	3.3
4	Bank of Seoul & Trust	1,859	3.2
5	Hyundai Engineering & Const.	1,739	3.0
6	Korea First Bank	1,708	2.9
7	Hanil Bank	1,575	2.7
8	Goldstar	1,210	2.1
9	Daewoo Electronics	1,155	2.0
10	The Chungbuk Bank	902	1.6
11	Daewoo Heavy Ind.	831	1.4
12	Tong Il	765	1.3
13	Daegu Bank	727	1.3
14	Kia Industrial	695	1.2
15	Kyunggi Bank	669	1.2
16	Daewoo Securities	643	1.1
17	Yukong	640	1.1
18	Sammi Corp.	618	1.1
19	Daelim Industrial	614	1.1
20	Daeshin Securities	601	1.0
21	Lucky	595	1.0
22	Lucky Securities	576	1.0
23	Dongsuh Securities	523	0.9
24	Dong-Ah Construction	486	0.8
25	Coryo Securities	484	0.8
	Total	25,811	44.4
	Total Market Turnover	58,121	100.0

Source: Korea Stock Exchange.

Table 4   KSE Composition (30 September 1989)

Industry	Market Cap. Won bn	US$ bn	% of Total Mkt. Cap.
Fisheries	373.3	0.56	0.40
Mining	137.0	0.20	0.15
Foods & Beverages	1,398.3	2.09	1.50
Textiles & Apparel	2,500.2	3.73	2.68
Wood (& Prods.)	327.2	0.49	0.35
Paper (& Prods.)	805.6	1.20	0.86
Chemicals	6,640.9	9.91	7.12
Rubber	753.7	1.12	0.81
Pharmaceuticals	863.4	1.29	0.93
Non-Metalic Minerals	1,635.9	2.44	1.75
Iron & Steel	5,669.3	8.46	6.08
Non-Ferrous Metals	761.3	1.14	0.82
Fabricated Metals	740.7	1.11	0.79
Machinery	1,770.3	2.64	1.89
Electronics	8,793.9	13.13	9.43
Transport Equipment	4,747.5	7.09	5.09
Other Manufacturing	194.6	0.29	0.21
Utilities	14,052.5	20.97	15.07
Construction	4,954.6	7.39	5.31
Wholesale & Retail Trade	4,633.0	6.91	4.97
Transport & Storage	1,442.5	2.15	1.54
Banks	13,469.0	20.10	14.44
Short-Term Finance	3,461.4	5.17	3.71
Securities	11,913.3	17.78	12.77
Insurance	1,230.0	1.84	1.32
Recreational Services	6.1	0.01	0.01
Total Market Cap.	93,275.5	139.2	100.0

Source: Korea Stock Exchange.

As of September 30, 1989, the twenty-five largest quoted companies on the KSE accounted for 52% of the total market capitalization. See Table 5.

Types of Shares

In addition to ordinary shares and beneficiary certificates, quasi-equities and preference shares are also listed on the KSE.

Quasi-Equities: Domestic Convertible and Warrant Bonds   The convertible and warrant bond markets are very underdeveloped, due to public ignorance of

Table 5   The 25 Largest Companies on the KSE, 30 September 1989

Rank	Company Name	Market Value (Won bn)	% of Total Mkt Value
1	KEPCO	14,053	15.1
2	Pohang Iron & Steel	3,029	3.2
3	Hanil Bank	1,937	2.1
4	Samsung Electronics	1,907	2.0
5	Korea First Bank	1,818	1.9
6	The Commercial Bank of Korea	1,806	1.9
7	Bank of Seoul	1,799	1.9
8	Cho-Hung Bank	1,795	1.9
9	Hyundai Motor	1,718	1.8
10	Goldstar	1,516	1.6
11	Daewoo	1,457	1.6
12	Yukong	1,379	1.5
13	Daewoo Securities	1,359	1.4
14	Daeshin Securities	1,241	1.3
15	Lucky Securities	1,216	1.3
16	Daewoo Electronics	1,188	1.3
17	Hyundai Engineering & Const.	1,166	1.2
18	Kia Motors	1,143	1.2
19	Daewoo Heavy Ind.	1,135	1.2
20	Lucky	1,129	1.2
21	Dongsuh Securities	1,070	1.1
22	Korean Air	998	1.1
23	Ssang Yong	978	1.0
24	Coryo Securities	730	0.8
25	Hyundai Securities	715	0.8
	Total	48,280	51.8
	Total Market Value	93,276	100.0

Source: Korea Stock Exchange.

these instruments. Although the terms and conditions are very attractive, the lack of understanding of these instruments results in a very illiquid market. Towards the end of September 1989, typical terms were as follows: CB conversion and BW warrant exercise price set at a discount of 5%; coupons of about 6.5%; payment of the full coupon in the year of conversion or exercise; a guaranteed annual yield of 12.5% upon redemption. CB's were first issued in 1963, but no real activity occurred until 1987. Even so there were only twenty offerings, with a total value of Won 218bn. In 1988 they increased to thirty-seven offerings,

+85% YoY, worth Won 332bn, +52% YoY. During the first nine months of this year, they increased to 44 offerings, +16% YoY, worth Won 770bn, +168% YoY.

Activity in warrant bonds have been even more circumscribed. As of September 30, 1989, there were only seven issues outstanding, worth Won 149bn. Besides the same problem of public ignorance as in the case of convertibles, the fact that the warrants are not detachable explains the lack of activity.

CB's and BW's nonetheless have their attractions for the issuer. They are an interesting alternative to a rights issue since majority shareholders do not have to worry about raising funds for new subscriptions, as in the case of rights issues.

Preference Shares   Korean preference shares are similar to those in foreign markets. They are non-voting but carry higher dividends and rank ahead of common stock in the event of company liquidation. Dividends of preference shares, as a fraction of par, are usually one percentage point higher than common stock dividends. At time of break up preference, shareholders receive par value plus the annual dividend. Preference shares are usually cumulative, although some recent issues are non-cumulative.

Prices of preference shares are usually 10% lower than common shares, and show prolonged periods of relative underperformance, possibly due to the lack of public understanding of this instrument. In connection with large rights issues in the first quarter of 1989, many securities companies issued preference shares as they offered a means of increasing capital without diluting the shareholding of majority shareholders. Many companies, both in the financial and non-financial sectors, are now issuing preference shares in connection with rights issues. As of September 30, 1989, 83 companies had preference shares outstanding. We expect the number of preference share issuances to increase even more in the near future both as the large shareholding families come to realize the benefits of preference shares and as public understanding improves.

Dealing Procedures

Dealing System   All transactions of listed equities must be carried out through the KSE. Off-floor trading is allowed. The KSE runs a continuous auction system. The auction principles are based on priorities of price, time, customer orders (over member firms' orders for their own account), and order size. Treating all bids and offers submitted prior to a certain point in time as simultaneous orders determines the opening prices and first price after a trading halt or suspension. The mid-price level is set so that all bids above and all offers below that price can be filled. A computerized on-line system for matching orders was put into full operation in February 1983. As of September 30, 1989, as much as 62% of all trading was carried out through the computerized matching system.

The KSE's plans call for 70-80% of executions being computerized by end-1989 and 100% by 1991.

The KSE does not have market-makers or specialists, and orderly trading is ostensibly maintained through a system of daily price limits. All orders must be at a stated bid or offer within these limits.

Board Lots Board lots are generally ten shares. Small orders are handled by brokers off-floor. Orders for shares priced below Won 10,000 are made in units of Won 10 and shares priced at Won 10,000 or higher in units of Won 100. Convertible and warrant bonds are quoted in units of Won 1.

Daily Price Limits Table 6 shows the daily price fluctuation limits.

Table 6   Daily Price Limits

(Unit : Won)

	Previous Day's Closing Price	Daily Price Change Limits
First & Second Section Limits	Less than 3,000	100
	3,000 to 4,999	200
	5,000 to 6,999	300
	7,000 to 9,999	400
	10,000 to 14,999	600
	15,000 to 19,999	800
	20,000 to 29,999	1,000
	30,000 to 39,999	1,300
	40,000 to 49,999	1,600
	50,000 to 69,999	2,000
	70,000 to 99,999	2,500
	100,000 to 149,999	3,000
	150,000 or more	4,000
Supervised Issue Limits	The same price range as above	50% of the above limit
Administrative Section Limits	Less than 500	10
	500 to 999	20
	1,000 to 1,999	30
	2,000 to 2,999	40
	3,000 to 4,999	50
	5,000 or more	100

Source: The Korea Securities Dealers Association.

Commissions, Fees, Transaction Tax Since 1989, KSE commissions have been deregulated and are negotiable within a band of 0.2-0.4%. Despite the deregulation, most brokers charge the same standard commission rates as Table 7 shows.

Besides commissions, a transaction tax of 0.5% of the value of the shares is levied on the seller. If the share price is below par, no transaction tax is levied. This rate may be reduced to 0% by the government if necessary to foster the market.

Settlement and Registration Share transactions are generally settled through the so-called "regular way," which calls for payment on the second day from the contract date. The only exception is the administrative issues that are settled within fourteen days from the contract date. Under the regular way transaction cash equal to a certain percentage of the contract value must be on deposit in the customer's account before an order can be placed. This collateral cash requirement is frequently adjusted in the range of 30%-100% by the KSE, often at the instruction of the Ministry of Finance, as a means of boosting or cooling off the market as deemed appropriate. However, institutional investors may be exempted from this requirement.

Settlement of all share transactions is carried out by the Korea Securities Settlement Corporation (KSSC), which is a wholly-owned subsidiary of the KSE. KSSC is the sole transfer and custodial agent of the KSE. Brokers are required by law to maintain accounts there. Transactions are then settled through electronic bookkeeping entries in brokers' names on the basis of net balances rather than through physical delivery. Brokers keep their own records of client accounts and, when they receive dividends or rights and bonus issue notifications, re-allocate them accordingly.

The settlement system is highly efficient. Client registration of stock certificates is not necessary. Accordingly, most share certificates never leave the KSSC's three underground vaults in Yoido.

Customer Accounts At present, clients may open accounts either in real name or street name. Street name accounts are hit with a withholding tax on

Table 7   Standard Commission Rates

Contract Value (Won m)	Board Lot Rate (%)	Old Lot Rate (%)
below 200	0.4%	0.4%
200-500	0.3% + Won 200,000	0.4%
above 500	0.2% + Won 700,000	0.4%

dividend income at four times the levels of taxes on real name accounts. Despite higher taxes, street name accounts are still popular. As of September 30, 1989, 2% of all accounts were in street names. There are three major reasons for this phenomenon:

a) keeping the full extent of one's financial assets hidden from tax authorities

b) Enabling majority-shareholding families and their agents and nominees to maintain ownership of companies above statutory limits

c) Enabling political campaign funds to be raised secretly through the stock market

Recently the street name account system has been used to open accounts for foreigners in order to hide the source of the "hot" money. Prior to the market opening, the government seemed eager to abolish this account system, but a strong resistance can be expected from wealthy families and public figures.

Rights and Bonus Issues Shareholders owning stock on the last cum-rights or cum-bonus day are eligible for offers of new shares. The issue process is a long-drawn-out one due to cumbersome paperwork requirements imposed on the issuer. There is approximately one month between announcement and the ex-rights or ex-bonus date, another month for payment in the case of subscriptions, and sometimes up to two months for listing.

Rights and bonus issues, or "new shares," are listed separately from old shares. This is because they are not eligible for the full dividend. They receive just a fraction of the payment, pro-rated according to when they were subscribed during the year. The system applies to each individual capital increase made in the course of the year, and it is not uncommon for a company to have two or three issues of new shares outstanding ("First New," "Second New"). The parallel listing continues until the last trading day of the relevant company's fiscal year. At that point old and new shares are combined, and counters re-open at an "ex-dividend" price.

Theoretically, the difference between the price of a new share and an ordinary share should be equal to the difference between expected dividends, and, in fact, this is often roughly the case. However, when trading in a counter becomes brisk and scrip shortage develops, this relationship often breaks down. Then the new shares' price may on occasion exceed that of the common stock.

Dividends Korean companies pay an annual dividend that is usually declared at the general shareholders' meeting 90 days after the fiscal year-end. Corporations do not have to pay the dividend for another 60 days thereafter. Despite these delays, the market makes its own adjustment to share prices on the trading day of the new year when stocks go "ex-dividend" on the basis of the expected DPS.

Dividends are paid to shareholders owning stock on the last day of the company's fiscal year. Companies in financial difficulty are all owed to give lower dividends to large shareholders (loosely defined as having 1% or more of stock) than to other investors.

Margin Transactions; Short-Selling Margin trading is allowed on shares of all First Section companies with paid-in capital of over Won 1bn, except securities company shares and supervised issues. Margin trading is estimated to account for 7% of turnover in eligible shares and 6% of total market turnover.

Margin requirements are another means by which the MoF influences the market. If a boost is desired, the margin requirements will be lowered and vice versa if MoF wishes to cool off a bull run. As of September 30, 1989, the margin requirement stood at 40%. The settlement period is 150 days and the loan limit is 150% of a broker's net worth and Won 50m per customer.

Short-selling is allowed by the KSE, but it is a much less common practice than margin buying, accounting for perhaps 0.12% of turnover of eligible shares and 0.09% of total market turnover. The same shares that are eligible for margin trading are eligible for short-selling. The settlement period is 150 days, with a loan limit of 50% of a broker's net worth and Won 20m per customer. Margin buying is also limited to 20% of an eligible company's shares, while short-selling is limited to 10%. Brokers may extend credit to their customers by using either their own funds or shares or by borrowing from the Korean Securities Finance Corporation, the only institution specializing in securities financing in Korea.

Investors

Investor Overview

According to official statistics, the largest category of investors is individuals, holding 66% of outstanding shares at the end of 1988. At the end of 1988, 6.1% of the population were investors in the market. The government, which used to be the biggest investor in the market, is now the smallest, having yielded its share over the past twenty years to individuals and other institutions. The breakdown of share ownership by investor is shown in Table 8.

Table 8   Investors (%)

	Gov't	Banks	Brokers	Other Institutions	Individuals	Foreigners
1965	56.4	8.6	6.7	7.3	20.8	0.2
1975	13.9	8.1	6.3	17.7	52.9	1.0
1985	0.4	7.1	7.4	30.0	52.5	2.6
1986	0.2	7.0	6.7	30.6	52.4	3.0
1987	0.1	5.6	2.6	26.0	62.3	3.3
1988	1.4	6.5	3.1	3.3	63.0	2.7

Securities Companies

There are twenty-five member firms of the Korea Stock Exchange. The types of business in which they may engage is restricted by the size of their paid-in capital, as shown in Table 9.

The top member firms in Fiscal Year 1989, ending 31 March, are shown in Table 10. With the exception of Daishin Securities, all member firms are subsidiaries of major business groups.

Although the number of securities companies remains fixed at twenty-five, the number of branches is being deregulated for companies that meet certain

Table 9   Business Restrictions on Securities Companies

Capital	Incremental Activities
Won 500m or more	Dealing only
Won 2bn or more	Retail broking of stocks and bonds
Won 5bn or more	Underwriting of guaranteed bonds
Won 7bn or more	Underwriting of stock issues and non-guaranteed bonds
Won 20bn or more	International business, overseas CB issues CD's, bond guarantee

| **Table 10** | **Comparison of Top 15 Securities Companies (in FY89, ending 31 March 1989)** | | | | |

Company	Revenues (Won bn)	Net Profit (Won bn)	Capital (Won bn)	Branches	Employees
Daewoo*	268.5	73.3	182.8	52	2,828
Daishin*	185.0	46.4	180.8	50	2,500
Lucky*	173.1	36.1	180.0	56	2,100
Dongsuh*	179.9	37.7	165.0	53	2,200
Ssangyong*	144.6	35.6	158.3	36	1,306
Hyundai*	128.1	34.0	107.4	35	1,276
Hanshin*	95.1	21.8	80.0	37	1,228
First*	83.3	17.5	81.3	24	883
Coryo*	99.8	25.9	118.0	31	1,287
Tongyang*	85.2	15.4	80.4	24	861
Hanheung*	67.5	13.1	41.6	17	632
Dongbang*	61.9	13.1	67.8	25	823
Shinyoung*	54.5	13.7	55.8	13	468
Dongnam*	47.2	11.8	47.7	15	527
Korea Inv.	32.6	7.1	29.6	12	347

* Licensed for International Business.

financial criteria. The government is urging these companies to set up provincial branches rather than more branches in Seoul.

All firms are allowed to buy and sell stocks for their own account. Investment is limited to a certain percentage of net worth, depending on how the Ministry of Finance wishes to influence trading. As of September 30, 1989, the limit is 60%, although it has ranged from 0% to 100%. Brokers do not have a large proportion of share ownership, but at any given time their influence in individual counters and on market trends can be telling.

Although research is still not an important operation at Korean securities firms, it is increasing in terms of both quantity and quality. Securities houses have set up economic research institutes to take charge of their research.

Brokers' earnings are roughly derived as follows: 45% from commissions, 30% from stock trading, 30% from interest received, 15% from underwriting, 5% from other activities, and a negative 20% from built-in losses on bond trading in the primary market.

Before the bull market, the securities companies were financially shaky and somewhat disreputable outfits, but since 1985 they have dramatically expanded their capital, revenues, profits, and staff. Salaries in the business have soared, and employment at a securities firm is now one of the most sought-after positions among university graduates.

Investment Trust Companies

There are three main investment trust companies in Korea as shown in Table 11.

In the autumn of 1989, five regional investment trust companies were established, each with a paid-in capital of Won150bn. The investment trust companies offer bond and equity funds. Any fund that can contain even one share of equity is called an equity fund. Most equity funds are mixed funds with a portfolio of equity and bonds and are usually closed-ended. Participation is through beneficial certificates that are traded on the KSE.

The major restrictions on the trust companies' activities are that they may neither invest more than 15% of trust assets in one corporation nor hold more than 20% of the shares of a listed corporation.

Trust companies were set up at government behest and are owned by commercial banks and securities companies. They often serve as an instrument of MoF policy when the ministry wants to influence trading in a certain way. On these occasions they will receive blunt instructions to buy or sell a specified number of stocks.

Investment Advisory Companies

Starting in the early part of 1988, the authorities permitted establishing investment advisory companies. At the present time, they are not allowed to manage either commingled or segregated accounts. Their activity is limited to providing advice to institutional and individual clients. It is very likely that they will eventually be permitted to manage segregated accounts. As of September 30, 1989, there were 29 such companies. Only five of the companies were independent

Table 11   Investment Trust Companies

(Unit : Won bn)

Company Name	FY89 Revenues	FY89 Net Profit	30-9-89 Bond Holdings	30-9-89 Stock Holdings
Korea Investment Trust	183.5	48.3	4,509.3	2,034.5
Daehan Investment Trust	153.3	45.2	2,487.0	4,075.5
Citizens' Investment Trust	70.6	23.3	962.5	1,378.8

Note: Fiscal Year ends on March 31.

companies; the remainder were affiliates or subsidiaries of brokers, investment trusts, and large business groups.

The first one and one-half year of operation has seen all the investment advisory companies suffering losses. This is due in part to the start-up costs, and, more importantly, strict staffing requirements. Currently, they are required to have a minimum of 11 professional staff members, who have high academic and professional experience.

Other Institutions

There are various other institutions operating in the securities market, whose activities are summarized in Table 12.

Individuals

Individuals are the most active participants in the market, most of whom are short-term traders. Stock ownership is becoming a standard form of personal investment, and the government, through its privatization program, is actively encouraging the trend. The number of individual investors has expanded dramat-

---

Table 12   Other Institutional Investors

Institutions	Remarks
Commerical Banks	Nine banks, all firmly government-controlled; may invest up to 25% of demand deposits in stocks; manage special trust accounts.
Regional Banks	Twelve banks, may invest up to 25% of demand deposits in stocks; manage special trust accounts.
Merchant Banks	Six houses, all foreign joint ventures; allowed to manage bond and equity trust funds and invest for own account.
Short-Term Finance Companies	32 houses, mainly discount CP's issued by medium-sized corporations; may invest up to 35% of net worth in stocks.
Life Insurance Companies	18 firms; may invest 30% of total assets (excluding deferred assets) in stocks; no limits on guaranteed bonds.
Non-Life Insurance Companies	15 firms; may invest 30% of total assets (excluding deferred assets) in stocks; no limits on guaranteed bonds.
Pension Funds	Corporate pension funds still developing; The government has a Government Employee Retirement and National Pension funds that now invest only a small portion of their funds through trust companies, but will expand activities in coming years.

---

ically in recent years and is currently estimated by the KSE at 10m. However, these figures probably overstate the case, for many so-called individuals are simply multiple alias or nominee accounts of majority shareholders, who have dispersed their stock to give the appearance of meeting statutory ownership limits.

Their number rose dramatically in 1988 with the government's privatization program. The Pohang Iron & Steel (POSCO) issue, for example, was subscribed to by an estimated 3.2m individual investors. Most were first time investors from low income brackets who received up to seven shares each. The number rose further in 1989 with the privatization of the Korea Electric Power Corporation.

Table 13   Number of Shareholders and Percent of Population

Year	Number of Shareholders* (Persons)	Number of Population (1,000 Persons)	Percent of Population
1965	14,820	28,705	0.1
1966	31,767	29,436	0.1
1967	33,064	30,131	0.1
1968	39,986	30,838	0.1
1969	54,318	31,544	0.2
1970	76,276	32,241	0.2
1971	81,923	32,883	0.2
1972	103,266	33,505	0.3
1973	199,699	34,103	0.6
1974	199,613	34,692	0.6
1975	290,678	35,281	0.8
1976	568,105	35,849	1.6
1977	395,275	36,412	1.1
1978	963,049	36,969	2.6
1979	872,075	37,534	2.3
1980	753,290	38,124	2.0
1981	696,276	38,723	1.8
1982	682,175	39,326	1.7
1983	708,510	39,910	1.8
1984	723,734	40,406	1.8
1985	772,471	40,806	1.9
1986	1,410,507	41,184	3.4
1987	3,102,303	41,575	7.5
1988	8,541,253	41,975	20.3

Note: * Gross number of investor accounts.
Source: Korea Stock Exchange. Economic Planning Board.

A large number of investors are also participants through employee stock ownership programs. By law, 20% of every rights issue must be offered to employees, and as much as 3.1% of the market is held under such schemes.

Internationalization

Korean Stock Market Opening Schedule

In December 1988, the government proposed a revised timetable for future market opening. The contents were as follows:

1989

- Funds for overseas investors will be expanded

- Restrictions on overseas issues by Korean companies will be relaxed. In addition to convertible bonds, Korean companies will be permitted to issue other Euro equities, such as BW's and DR's.

- Overseas investors will be permitted to convert their bonds and to trade these shares over the counter.

- Limits on foreign ownership of Korean securities companies will be revised to permit up to 40% foreign ownership from 10% at present. Individual holdings will be limited to 10%, up from 5% at present.

1990

- A "Matching Fund" will be established, which will invest both domestically and overseas. It will be sold to domestic and overseas investors.

- Overseas issues by Korean companies will be further expanded.

- Guidelines will be announced to permit foreign securities companies to open branches and establish joint ventures with Korean securities companies from 1991.

1991

- Limited direct investment by foreigners will be permitted as overseas investors will be allowed to invest funds raised from selling converted shares into other listed shares.

Overview

Foreign investors have only been able to invest in the Korean stock market in a restricted manner since 1981, when the government announced a four-stage plan for market-opening. This was a gradual plan aimed at gaining direct foreign investment by the late 1980's, envisioned concomitant freeing of the Won and the start-up of overseas business and investment by Korean institutions.

The years 1981 through 1985 saw issues to overseas investors of five Korean-managed closed-end unit trusts and two offshore listed, offshore managed country funds. Several of these vehicles were subsequently allowed to have second tranches, and two venture capital funds were launched. Issues of Euro-convertible bonds also began in 1985.

Unexpectedly strong surpluses in the balance of payments from 1986, threatening monetary stability, caused the internationalization process to stall. Only five Euro-convertible bonds and one Bond with Warrants have so far been issued. Severe restrictions exist on the use of funds from convertibles, requiring that these instruments be issued exclusively for the purpose of overseas investment or repayment of offshore debt and that all funds raised by them stay offshore.

At the end of 1988, there were a total of 15 vehicles available for indirect investment in the Korean stock market. Their market capitalization stood at about US$3.2bn. Reflecting the scarcity value of these instruments, they are trading at premiums in the 70-200% range.

- Foreign securities companies will be permitted to open branches and establish joint ventures with Korean securities companies.

1992
- Foreign investors will be permitted to invest directly in the Korean market, within certain limits, regardless of their CB holdings.

Korean Overseas Securities Business and Investment

Korean securities companies have been allowed to maintain overseas representative offices since 1984 and to participate in various types of capital market business. From July 1988, certain institutions have been allowed to have foreign exchange accounts up to the following limits:

Securities companies:	US$30m
Insurance companies:	US$10m
Investment trust companies:	US$10m

This put possible overseas investment at US$880m, but institutions moved slowly. They remained wary of Won appreciation and did not like the opportunity costs involved in forsaking high domestic bond yields and the booming local stock market. The only significant overseas investments were made by brokers. This was primarily for the purpose of underwriting. With the stable Won and a weaker domestic market, however, the Korean institutional investors are actively increasing their portfolio investments. As of December 1988 only US$200m was invested overseas.

The government has proposed the following timetable for future overseas business and investment:

1989
- A fund for overseas investment by domestic securities institutions will be established.

- Limits on overseas investment by institutions will be increased.

- Korean securities companies will be permitted to establish more overseas representative offices.

1990
- Domestic corporations, in addition to financial institutions, will be permitted to invest overseas with certain limitations.

- Limits on foreign exchange holdings by institutional investors will be completely abolished.

- More funds for overseas investment will be established, including the "Matching Fund."

1991
- Limits on overseas investment by domestic corporations will be relaxed.

- Korean securities companies will be permitted to establish branches overseas.

1992
- Individuals will be permitted to invest overseas, within certain limits.

Investment Vehicles

Unit Trusts KITC's Korea International Trust and DITC's Korea Trust, both launched in November 1981 with original capitalizations of $15m each, were the first legal opportunity for foreign investors to invest in the Korean stock market. They were to be managed domestically by investment trust companies, although they were specifically designed for foreign investors. Strong foreign demand resulted in the size of both trusts being increased by $10m each, KIT in 1983 and KT in 1984.

In 1985 the Korea Growth Trust was introduced by the third investment trust company, CITC, with an initial capitalization of $30m. Unlike KIT and KT, which were designed to invest solely in equities, 30% of KGT's funds were to be invested in bonds, falling to 20% after 1985.

Seoul International Trust and Seoul Trust were also launched in 1985 and were managed by KITC and DITC respectively. They were followed by two venture capital trusts, much smaller with funds of $5m, each aiming to invest the majority in unlisted equities.

Market capitalization of these trusts on September 30, 1989, stood at $1.4bn. These issues cannot be increased in size by investor demand. Permission to increase the number of units can only be granted by the government. Although there have recently been reports that the authorities are considering granting such permission, concrete plans have yet to be announced.

Offshore Funds The Korea Fund, a closed-end fund managed abroad and listed on the New York Stock Exchange, was set up in August 1984. It was initially capitalized at $60m, but a second tranche of $40m in June 1986 and a third tranche of $50m in August 1989 boosted the fund's size to $150m.

The Korea Europe Fund, launched in April 1987, aimed to give European investors the opportunity to invest in Korean securities. The initial size was $30m, increasing to $60m in June 1988. KEF also is listed on the London Stock Exchange.

The Korea Fund is not permitted to invest in more than 5% of the total outstanding shares of a listed company, for Korea Europe Fund, the figure is 3%. Neither fund may invest more than 5% of its total net asset value in one stock nor have more than 25% of its NAV invested in one industrial sector.

Convertible Bonds Samsung Electronics was the first Korean company to issue overseas convertible bonds, raising $20m on the Euromarket in December 1985. In 1986 this action was followed by similar issues from Daewoo Heavy raising $40m, and Yukong raising $20m. Goldstar issued a $30m convertible in 1987, and Saehan Media had a $30m issue in 1988. To date only Sammi Steel has issued an overseas Bond with Warrants, raising US$50M on the Euromarket

Table 14 Korean Convertible and Warrant Bonds

	Samsung Electronics	Daewoo Heavy Industries	Yukong	Gold Star	Saehan Media	Sammi Steel
Issue Date	Dec. 3, 1985	May 8, 1986	June 30, 1986	July 24, 1987	Sept. 23, 1988	Oct. 17, 1989
Amount	US$ 20m	US$ 40m	US$ 20m	US$ 30m	US$ 30m	US$ 50m
Coupon Rate	5% p.a.	3% p.a.	3% p.a.	1.75% p.a.	1.75% p.a.	1.25% p.a.
Premium at Issue	30%-100%	50%	55%	115%	65%	145%
Fixed US$ FX Rate	Won 889.7	Won 886.1	Won 884.6	Won 808.1	Won 719.8	Won 671.5
Conversion Price	Won 16,048	Won 11,162	Won 37,166	Won 32,646	Won 51,171	Won 45.992
Final Maturity	Dec. 31, 2000	Dec. 31, 2001	Dec. 31, 2001	Dec. 31, 2002	Dec. 31, 2003	Nov. 8, 1994
Conv. Period Begins	Oct. 19, 1987	Nov. 23, 1987	Jan. 15, 1988	Feb. 11, 1989	April 4, 1990	May 8, 1991
Listed	Luxembourg	Luxembourg	Luxembourg	Luxembourg	Luxembourg	Luxembourg
Interest Paid on	December 31	December 31	December 31	December 31	December 31	December 31

in October. The Samsung bond will be the first to become convertible, following the vote for conversion by bondholders in April. Other bonds will likely follow suit.

Tax and Foreign Exchange Regulations

Taxation

Dividends Dividend income received by a minority (less than 10%) shareholder of listed equities is subject to a 10% final withholding tax. In other words, the dividend income is not included in the recipient's gross income tax. On top of the withholding tax, the recipient must pay a residence tax in the amount of 7.5% of the withholding tax amount. In addition, there are two special taxes, defense (10% of the tax amount) and education (5% of dividend income) taxes, which are due to expire in 1990 and 1991 respectively. In any event, the entire tax burden at the moment is 16.75% of the dividend income. If an account is in a street name, the entire tax burden is 52%.

The taxation of non-residents depends on their status. If a non-resident has a "permanent establishment" in Korea, he or she is subject to the same tax rates as Korean nationals. If, on the other hand, the non-resident does not have a permanent establishment in Korea, he is levied a final withholding tax of 25%, unless reduced by an applicable tax treaty. A residence tax surcharge is added to this amount to raise the total tax burden to 26.875%. Defense and education taxes are not levied on non-residents who do not have a permanent establishment in Korea.

Table 15 sets forth the countries with which Korea has tax treaties and the tax rates currently applicable on dividend income and capital gains.

Capital Gains Capital gains from securities transactions are not taxed. The government presumably will be imposing a capital gains tax on securities transactions starting in 1991 as a part of introducing a comprehensive tax system.

A non-resident who does not have a permanent establishment in Korea is subject to capital gains tax at the rate of 26.875% of the amount of capital gains or 10.75% of the gross proceeds of sale, whichever is lower. This capital gains tax is reduced to zero in most cases for residents of countries that have tax treaties with Korea. Furthermore, recent indications show that tax authorities will not levy a capital gains tax on portfolio investments.

Corporate and Institutional Investors Corporate shareholders are exempt from withholding. Dividend income and capital gains, however, constitute corporate revenues and are thus taxed at the corporation's normal income tax rate.

Table 15   Countries with which Korea Has Tax Treaties and Taxation Rates

Country	Interest (%)	Dividend (%)	Capital Gains
Australia	15	15	Normal rate
Austria	10	10 or 15 [3]	0 or Normal rate [4]
Bangladesh	10	10	0
Belgium	15	15	0
Canada	16 1/8 [1]	16 1/8 [1]	0 or Normal rate [4]
Denmark	15	15	0
Finland	10	10 or 15 [3]	0
France	15	10 or 15 [3]	0 or Normal rate [4]
India	10 or 15 [2]	15 or 20 [3]	0
Japan	12	12	Normal rate
Luxembourg	10	10 or 20 [3]	0
Malaysia	15	10 or 15 [3]	0
Netherlands	12.5	10 or 15 [3]	0
New Zealand	10 or 15 [2]	15	0
Norway	10	15	0
Pakistan	10	10 or 12.5 [3]	0 or Normal rate [4]
Philippines	10 or 15 [2]	10 or 15 [3]	0
Singapore	10	10 or 15 [3]	Normal rate
Sri Lanka	10	10 or 15 [3]	0
Sweden	10 or 15 [2]	10 or 15 [3]	0
Switzerland	10	10 or 15 [3]	0
Thailand	10 3/4 [1]	10 3/4 or 21 1/2 [1,3]	Normal rate
Turkey	10 or 15 [2]	15 or 20	0
United Kingdom	10 or 15 [2]	10 or 15	0
United States	12.9 or Normal rate [1,5]	10 3/4, 16 1/8 or Normal rate [1,3,5]	0 or Normal rate [5]
West Germany	10 or 15 [2]	10 or 15 [3]	Normal rate

[1]   The tax treaties with Canada, the United States, and Thailand do not exempt resident's tax and thus tax rate above has been increased.

[2]   Rates vary depending on the term of the loan or debenture in the main.

[3]   Rates vary depending on whether the dividend paying company is owned over a particular percentage by the dividend receiving company (the range of share ownership is from over 10 to 25 percent: Austria 10, Finland 25, France 25, India 20, Luxembourg 25, Malaysia 25, Netherlands 25, Pakistan 20, Philippines 25, Singapore 25, Sri Lanka 25, Sweden 25, Switzerland 25, Thailand 25, United States 10, West Germany 21).

[4]   No capital gains tax is payable unless the shares sold are of a corporation in which the seller owns 25 percent or more of the shares.

[5]   Normal rates will apply if the company receiving the interest, dividends, or capital gains is owned 25 percent or more (directly or indirectly) by individuals who are not residents of the United States and by reason of special measures the tax imposed on such company by the United States with respect to such interest, dividends or capital gains is substantially less than the tax generally imposed by the United States on corporate profits.

Institutions classified as institutional investors can benefit from certain tax deductions.

Foreign Exchange Regulations

Inflow and outflow of foreign capital are tightly controled by the government under the Foreign Capital Inducement Law and the Foreign Exchange Control Law. With the large current account surpluses in recent years, inflow of foreign capital has come under even tighter controls.

In connection with the internationalization of its capital market, the Korean government plans to internationalize the Won. The initial steps, which could take place sometime in early 1990, would allow non-residents to open interest-bearing Won accounts at foreign branches of Korean banks. At the moment, however, all remittances or repatriation of funds into or out of Korea require the permission of the government.

Regulatory Framework

Reporting Requirements

The Securities and Exchange Law requires filing a registration statement and prospectus at the time of initial listing and filing annual and semi-annual reports and non-periodic reports after listing. Annual reports must be filed within 90 days after the close of each financial year. Unaudited semi-annual reports must be filed within 45 days after the close of the first six months of each financial year.

In addition, listed companies are required to make public announcements through the SEC and KSE any event that has a material impact on the company.

Shareholder Protection

The Korean stock market is under the control of the Ministry of Finance. Under the umbrella of the MoF the SEC acts as a central regulatory agency, with the Securities Supervisory Board acting as its executive organ. All members of the KSE are also governed by the rules of the Korea Securities Dealers Association, a self-regulatory trade organization.

The Securities and Exchange Law contains the main body of regulations designed to protect investors. Although regulations are modeled after U.S. securities regulations, enforcement is not nearly as strict as in the United States. To prevent insider trading by those with superior knowledge and information about the market, all employees of securities firms and investment trust companies are prohibited from investing in the stock market. It is common knowledge, however, that most of them actively invest in the market through accounts in the name of relatives or friends and in street name accounts.

This situation often leads to self-dealing. In the fall of 1988, several employees of Daewoo Securities, Korea's largest securities house, were caught making more favorable share allocations for accounts in which the employees had a beneficial interest. Since securities and investment trust companies are allowed to invest for their own account, the potential for conflict of interest is enormous.

On the whole, since the government is very keen on improving both the size and quality of the stock market, continuous development on Korean corporate and securities laws can be expected.

Sources of Information

Besides the various sources for our data mentioned throughout this guide the following materials were consulted.

1. Korea Stock Exchange, October 1988, published by the Korea Stock Exchange.
2. Securities Market in Korea, October 1988, published by the Korea Securities Dealers Association.
3. Stock, published monthly by the Korea Stock Exchange.
4. Securities Statistics Yearbook, published yearly by the Korea Stock Exchange.
5. Monthly Bulletin, published monthly by the Bank of Korea.
6. Securities Regulation in Korea, by Dr. Young Moo Shin, Shin & Kim, attorneys-at-law.
7. Korean Securities Regulations and Internationalization Policy, by Kim & Chang, attorneys-at-law.

Taiwan Equity Market

Sam Chang
Blue Chip Capital Associates, Taipei

Ted Chao
Cathay International, New York

Value and Performance of the Taiwan Stock Market

The Taiwan Stock Exchange's total trading volume in 1988 was US$279 billion, the fourth highest in the world behind Tokyo, New York, and London. The stock market achieved such volume with only a total of 163 companies listed as of the end of 1988. Total market capitalization of US$120 billion at the end of 1988 was about the same as the island's GNP. The price movements in Taiwan's stock market often seems to defy logical analysis. In 1987 and 1988, Taiwan stock market underwent two major cycles of boom and bust without major changes in Taiwan's economic performance. The Weighted Price Index shot up 350% from 1039.11 at the end of 1986 to 4673.14 on October 1, 1987; on November 14, 1987, it crashed 48% to 2448.66. By September 24, 1988, however, it had surged to a record 8789.78, a 275% rise from the beginning of that year. The government's surprise announcement of re-imposition of capital gains tax then sent the market into a virtually volume-less 19-day crash of 3174.45 points, or 36%. It climbed in November 1988 to 7458.97 but came down again to close at 5119.11 at the end of the year. Market P/E and yield from 1984 to 1988 has been as follows[1]:

Table 1   Stock Market Key Data

Market capitalization (year end 1988)	US$ 120 billion
Trading volume (1998)	US$ 279 billion
Listed companies (year end 1988)	163
Market index (year end 1988)	5119.11
One year change	+119%

Source: Taiwan Stock Exchange.

Table 2   Basic Economic Indicators

GNP (1988)	US$ 120 billion
GNP per capita	US$ 6045
CPI change (1988 average)	1.3%
Prime rate (year end 1988)	6.75%
Exchange rate (year end 1988)	US$ 1 = NT$ 28.17
M1B growth (1988)	27.8%
Exports (1988)	US$ 60.6 billion
Imports (1988)	US$ 49.7 billion
Surplus (1988)	US$ 10.9 billion
Foreign exchange reserve (year end 1988)	US$ 74 billion
Population (Nov., 1988)	19.9 million
Unemployment (1988)	1.7%

Source: Department of Statistics, Ministry of Economic Affairs; Central Bank.

	1984	1985	1986	1987	1988
Price/earnings ratio	14	21	15	23	38
Indicated dividend yield	2.9%	2.4%	2.6%	2.2%	1.0%

In addition to the usual macroeconomic issues that affect the economy and the microeconomic conditions that impact individual firms, a number of factors collectively explain much of the behavior of Taiwan's stock market, including Taiwan's excess money, limited float, and 5% price fluctuation limit.

Excess Money

The most important driving force behind the stock market's rise in 1987 and 1988 was the excess liquidity in Taiwan's economy. Continued strong trade surplus has led to a rapid accumulation of foreign exchange reserve that totaled about US$74 billion at the end of 1988, the second highest accumulation in the world after Japan. The resulting liquidity has essentially two legitimate channels of investment in the local economy—the stock market and real estate. Both have seen prices rising in multiples over the last two years.

Limited (Supply of Shares)

Only 130 companies were listed at the end of 1986. Recent rises in the market has enticed 37 new listings over the last two years, more than the total new listings of the previous six years. Nevertheless, the supply of shares is still relatively small. In addition, most listed companies are still largely owned and tightly controlled by the founding families or, in the case of financial institutions, by the government. Float is often 40% or less of the outstanding shares. The limited float along with excess liquidity lead to misleading "market" valuation. The most glaring example is perhaps Taiwan Machinery, which at the end of 1988 had the highest market capitalization of US$14 billion but only US$1.5 million in trading volume for the year. Another example is International Commercial Bank of China, which has a float of less than 2%, a P/E ratio of 100^2, and price/book ratio of 22. The bank has 22 domestic branches and 9 overseas branches, yet its market value of US$8.7 billion at the end of 1988 is higher than that of Citicorp (US$8.6 billion). Thirteen financial institutions are listed on the exchange, and they commanded an average P/E ratio of 84 at the end of

---

Table 3

	Real GNP Growth	Trade Surplus (US$ billion)	Foreign Exchange Reserve (US$ billion)	M1B Growth
1984	10.5%	8.5	15.7	9.3%
1985	5.1%	10.6	22.6	11.8%
1986	11.6%	15.6	46.3	47.3%
1987	11.9%	18.7	76.8	38.3%
1988	7.5%	10.9	74.0	27.8%

Source: Domestic & Foreign Express Report of Economic Statistics Indicators.

1988.[3] These companies make up 8% of all companies listed but account for 34% of the total market capitalization. The price movement of these stocks, therefore, often dictates the direction of the Weighted Price Index.

5% Price Fluctuation Limit

In its desire to limit market volatility, the government has imposed a 5%[4] daily limit on price change from the previous close. The restriction has led to several predictable results, including a reduction in liquidity, increase in trading risk, and easier price manipulation. Since trading is restricted to a narrow price range each day, it is often not possible to buy when prices are heading up and to sell when prices are going down. Small float plus this 5% price limit then enable manipulators to bid up an individual stock to its daily ceiling quickly. At the closing seconds of the trading session, such players often load the market with large bid orders to reinforce the illusion that many bids for the stock are unfulfilled. Unsophisticated investors, following tips and rumors, then chase after such shares, often unsuccessfully for several days, until they finally are able to buy it when the majors are ready to unload. Similar tactics can drive prices down.[5]

The 5% limit does the most damage when stock prices are going down. An investor, regardless of sophistication or size, is always threatened with the risk that he may not be able to convert his stock holding to cash even if he is willing to take a loss. The need or desire for liquidity can then aggravate the pressure to sell when prices go down.

The daily percentage limit also creates a misleading impression among the unsophisticated investors. These investors think that they may, with luck or following the right tip, earn 5% profit per day, compared to the yearly bank deposit interest of 5%. They also think that when the market turns sour, the government should take steps to protect the investors against losses, since the government has set a limit to protect the investors.

Structure of the Taiwan Stock Market

Brief History [6]

The origin of the securities market in Taiwan stemmed from the 1953 Land Reform. To compensate the landowners who were required to distribute their land to the tillers under the "Land-to-the-Tiller" program, the government issued land bonds and shares of four large government-owned enterprises.[7] Gradually, sporadic markets and brokerage companies for trading these stocks and bonds were formed.

The Securities and Exchange Commission (SEC) was established on September 1, 1960, to supervise and control all aspects of securities market operations. The Taiwan Stock Exchange (TSE) began operations on February 9, 1962. Provisional regulations and other rules governing securities dealers were instituted before the formal promulgation of the Securities and Exchange Law (SEL) on April 30, 1968.

At the end of 1962, shares of eighteen corporations were listed on the exchange with a total market capitalization of NT$6.9 billion (about US$ 170 million).

Market Size

There were 171 stocks listed on the Taiwan Stock Exchange issued by 163 companies at the end of 1988. Total market capitalization at the end of 1988 was NT$ 3,383 billion (US$120 billion), up 130% from a year ago. The listed companies are classified as either First Category or Second Category[8] according to their capital size, profitability, financial structure, and distribution of shares. First Category shares accounted for 84% of total market capitalization as of December 29, 1988; Second Category accounted for 16%.

The Banking and Insurance sector dominates the market with 34% of the total capitalization, followed by Electric Machinery and Machinery at 14% and Steel Industry at 10%.

Trading Volume

Total trading value in 1988 was NT$7,881 billion (US$279 billion). Daily trading volume averaged US$967 million in 1988. It ranged from a low of US$4.7 million on October 1, following the government's surprise announcement of re-

Table 4   Number of Listed Companies and Market Value

	1984	1985	1986	1987	1988
Listed Companies					
1st Category	66	65	67	80	103
2nd Category	57	62	63	61	60
Total	123	127	130	141	163
Market Value (NT$ billlion)					
1st Category	$299	$370	$471	$1,307	$2,829
2nd Category	$91	$46	$78	$79	$554
Total	$390	$416	$548	$1,386	$3,383

Source: Taiwan Stock Exchange.

Exhibit 1   TSE Index—Monthly Close

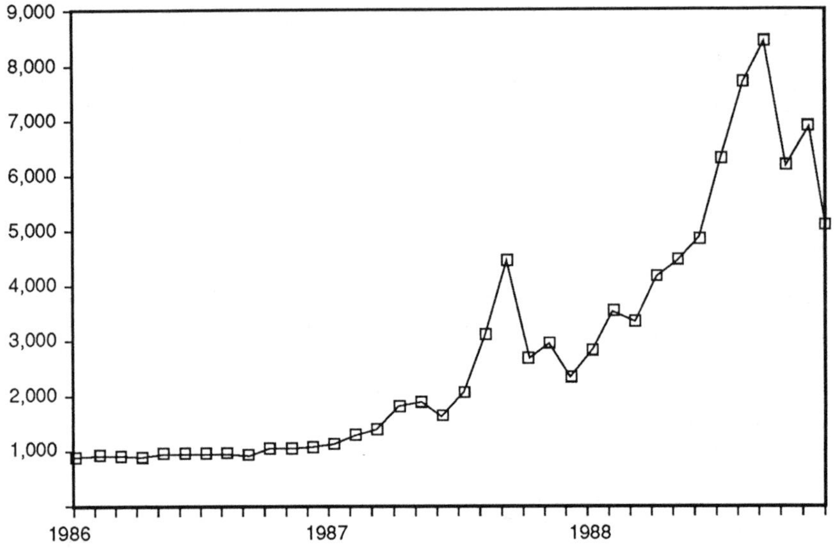

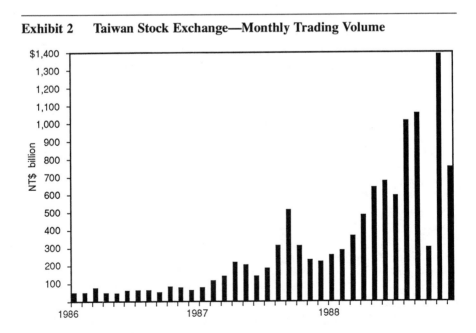

Exhibit 2   Taiwan Stock Exchange—Monthly Trading Volume

Exhibit 3   NT\$ per US\$

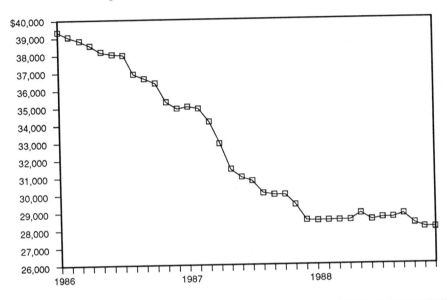

Exhibit 4   Prime Rates

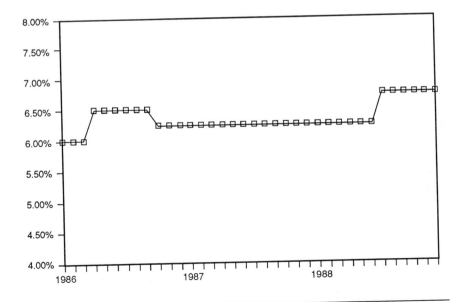

Table 5   Market Value by Sector

	1988 Market Value	Market Value Height	Number of Companies
Banking and Insurance	$1,167,397	34.5%	13
Electric Machinery and Machinery	$463,340	13.7%	5
Steel	$355,121	10.5%	7
Plastic	$292,109	8.6%	10
Textile	$285,198	8.4%	25
Cement	$163,210	4.8%	6
Pulp and Paper	$89,497	2.6%	7
Electric Appliance and Wires	$74,710	2.2%	8
Foods	$70,756	2.1%	13
Electronics	$62,041	1.8%	10
Transportation	$59,396	1.8%	3
Automibile	$58,254	1.7%	3
Chemical	$56,103	1.7%	10
Construction	$49,425	1.5%	5
Rubber	$39,819	1.2%	5
Glass and Porcelain	$31,045	0.9%	2
Department Stores	$25,041	0.7%	4
Tourism	$15,261	0.5%	5
Other	$25,557	0.8%	22
Total	$3,383,280	100.0%	163

Source: Securities & Exchange Commission.

imposition of capital gains tax for stocks purchased after 1988, to a high of US$3 billion on November 16. The most actively traded sectors by value were bank & insurance at 27%, plastic at 12%, and textile at 11%.

Types of Shares

Types of shares traded are predominantly common shares. Six preferred shares of five companies are also listed on the exchange but accounted for only 0.3% of total volume traded in 1988.

Investors

The Taiwan stock market is dominated by individuals, which accounts for half of the capital contributed but more than 98% of turnover by volume. Total num-

Table 6   Top 10 Companies by Market Value

Company	Year End 1988 Market Value (NT$ million)	Year End 1988 Market Value (US$ million)	Market Value Height
1 Taiwan Machinery	$404,307	$14,352	12.0%
2 China Steel	$349,485	$12,406	10.3%
3 Int. Comm. Bank of China	$245,243	$8,706	7.2%
4 Cathay Life Insurance	$243,962	$8,660	7.2%
5 First Bank	$179,194	$6,361	5.3%
6 Hwa Nan Bank	$171,763	$6,097	5.1%
7 Chang Hwa Bank	$170,700	$6,060	5.0%
8 Formosa Plastic	$78,937	$2,802	2.3%
9 Nan Ya Plastic	$77,234	$2,742	2.3%
10 Formosa Chemical & Fibre	$75,076	$2,665	2.2%
Top 10 Total	$1,995,899	$70,852	59.0%
Market Totasl	$3,383,280	$120,102	100.0%

Source: Securities & Exchange Commission.

Table 7   Trading Volume 1984–1988

	Volume (shares million)	Value (NT$ billion)	Turnover Rate
1984	18,164	$324	95.4%
1985	14,534	$195	68.1%
1986	39,041	$676	162.1%
1987	76,857	$2,669	267.5%
1988	101,350	$7,868	332.6%

Source: Securities & Exchange Commission.

ber of accounts opened at brokerage houses rose 34% in 1987; at the end of 1988 it rose another 150% to 1.6 million.

Table 8   Trading Volume by Sector

	1988 Trading Volume (NT$ million)	Trading Volume Height
Banking and Insurance	$2,117,306	26.9%
Plastic	$916,674	11.7%
Textile	$889,733	11.3%
Cement	$521,421	6.6%
Foods	$456,958	5.8%
Electric Appliance and Wires	$407,376	5.2%
Chemical	$347,547	4.4%
Pulp and Paper	$331,429	4.2%
Rubber	$330,850	4.2%
Construction	$319,831	4.1%
Electric Machinery and Machinery	$279,544	3.6%
Electronics	$213,358	2.7%
Transportation	$127,465	1.6%
Automobile	$126,253	1.6%
Steel	$116,797	1.5%
Department Stores	$113,400	1.4%
Tourism	$95,459	1.2%
Glass and porcelain	$34,992	0.4%
Other	$121,631	1.5%
Total	$7,868,024	100.0%

Source: Securities & Exchange Commission.

Operations

Trading

Trading sessions are 9:00 A.M. to 12:00 noon, Monday through Friday and 9:00 A.M. to 11:00 A.M. on Saturday. The minimum unit of trading is 1000 shares. Daily price movements of stocks are not allowed to be up or down more than 5% from the closing price of the preceding day. Trading is carried out by the Computer-Assisted Trading System of the exchange. Only brokers and traders are allowed to trade on the exchange. The broker or trader enters the volume and price of the stock to be bought or sold through his terminal into the main computer of the exchange. The trading clerks at the exchange will then match the order according to price and time priority. When a transaction is consummated, the broker or dealer will immediately receive the trade report via an office computer printer. The broker will then confirm the trade with his customer.

Table 9   Top 10 Companies by Market Value

Company	1988 Trading Volume (NT$ million)	1988 Trading Volume (US$ million)	1988 Trading Volume (million shs)	Turnover
1 Chang Hwa Bank	$370,792	$13,153	723.0	241.0%
2 First Bank	$289,552	$10,271	568.7	174.2%
3 Hwa Nan Bank	$284,483	$10,092	536.4	177.4%
4 Shihlin Electric & Engineering (B)	$255,954	$9,080	4681.7	479.3%
5 Formosa Plastic	$228,806	$8,117	1994.1	204.6%
6 Nan Ya Plastic	$226,406	$8,031	2499.9	234.7%
7 China Develop Corp.	$214,262	$7,601	1021.8	973.1%
8 Cathay Life Insurance	$205,493	$7,290	184.5	65.3%
9 Taiwan Synthetic Rubber	$179,771	$6,377	2492.5	1045.9%
10 Formosa Chemical & Fibre	$150,788	$5,349	2029.4	154.1%

Source: Securities & Exchange Commission.

Table 10   Share Ownership by Investor Type

	1984	1985	1986	1987
Domestic individuals	40.53%	41.09%	40.27%	43.52%
Government agencies	25.96%	25.99%	27.11%	25.94%
Domestic financial institutions	9.43%	8.54%	7.50%	5.78%
Domestic trust funds	0.39%	0.10%	0.32%	0.48%
Corporations	11.21%	11.68%	11.85%	11.73%
Other jurdicial persons	3.71%	3.50%	3.32%	3.08%
Foreign financial institutions	0.11%	0.13%	0.08%	0.08%
Foreign jurdicial persons	2.64%	3.09%	3.68%	4.62%
Foreign trust funds	0.24%	0.59%	0.77%	0.46%
Foreign individuals	5.77%	5.29%	5.10%	4.31%

Source: Taiwan Stock Exchange.

Table 11   Trading Volume by Investor Type

	1984	1985	1986	1987	1988
Domestic individuals	87.85%	91.51%	92.02%	94.37%	97.84%
Domestic jurdicial person	11.66%	8.05%	7.61%	5.37%	2.09%
Foreign individual	0.49%	0.41%	0.34%	0.24%	0.06%
Foreign jurdicial person	0.01%	0.03%	0.04%	0.03%	0.01%
Total	100.00%	100.00%	100.00%	100.00%	100.00%

Source: Taiwan Stock Exchange.

Brokers and Traders

Prior to the revision of the Securities Exchange Law in January 1988, there were 28 brokers and 10 traders. Revision of the law lifted the ban on licensing of new firms. By the end of 1988, 74 new brokerage companies were formed, eight of which were integrated securities firms that were licensed to be a broker, a dealer, and an underwriter. A brokerage license permits the firm to trade for its customers only. A licensed trader may transact in securities for his own account. Brokers and dealers may neither accept deposits or extend loans nor borrow or lend securities. It is interesting to observe that new brokerage companies are still being organized and that there are nearly as many brokers as listed companies.

Table 12   Number of Accounts Opened at Brokerage Companies (Thousand)

1984	384
1985	400
1986	474
1987	634
1988	1606

Source: Taiwan Stock Exchange.

Table 13   Top 10 Brokerage Companies

Name	1988 Market Share
1 Jin-Sun Securities Co., Ltd.	9.4%
2 Ting Kong Securities Co., Ltd.	7.5%
3 Yuen Ta Securities Co., Ltd.	4.9%
4 Asia Securities, Inc.	4.9%
5 Shin Kuang Securities Co., Ltd.	4.8%
6 Yung Li Securities Co., Ltd.	4.7%
7 Well-Phone Securities Co., Ltd.	4.4%
8 Sheng Hoh Securities Co., Ltd.	4.4%
9 First Securities Co., Ltd.	4.1%
10 Jen Hsin Securities Co., Ltd.	4.0%
Total	53.1%

Source: Taiwan Stock Exchange.

Some brokerage houses are formed by major investors (including owners of listed companies) and often focus trades of favored stocks through their own brokerage firms.

Fuh-Hwa Securities Finance Co., Ltd., a quasi-government company, is the only company licensed to provide securities finance. Investors may purchase stocks on margin or sell short through their brokers after opening accounts with Fuh-Hwa. Because of the restrictive limits placed on margin purchase and short sell[9], however, a substantial number of such transactions goes to underground financiers. Official data indicates that margin purchase and short selling accounted for 7% and 0.3%, respectively, of the total trading volume in 1988.[10]

Settlement

Settlement is made on the third business day following the day of transaction. A customer must deliver stock certificates or pay cash to his broker the next business day after selling or buying so as to enable the broker to make deliveries to the exchange for settlement. The broker, after completing the settlement on the exchange, delivers the securities purchased or the proceeds of securities sold to his customer. Consequently, the customer can't receive the securities purchased or cash offered until the third business day following the buying or selling. Same day canceling trades are prohibited.

Fuh-Hwa Securities Finance Co. also renders the service of centralized depository of securities. Most investors, however, still prefer to take physical possession of the share certificates rather than depositing their stock holdings with Fuh-Hwa.

Commissions and Other Transaction Costs

The brokerage commission rate for stocks are fixed at 0.15% of the trading value of the stocks. In addition, a seller of shares must also pay a securities transfer tax of 0.15% beginning in 1989, down from 0.3% in 1988.

Taxation

For Individuals Combined cash dividends and interest income are exempt from taxes up to a household maximum of NT$360,000 per year. Stock dividends valued at *par value* are exempt from taxes up to NT$120,000 per year. Stock dividends representing a distribution of capital surplus or an asset revaluation surplus are not subject to income tax. Stock dividends representing a distribution of earnings are subject to income tax that is payable on receipt or, in certain cases, on disposal of the stock dividends. Capital gains tax on sale of listed stocks, suspended since 1976, was re-imposed at the beginning of 1989[11]. Stocks purchased prior to and during 1988 are permanently exempt from capital gains tax. Capital gains tax on stock sales are taxed as ordinary income. Exemption applies to gains of each individual whose value of stock *sales* total less than NT$10 million in a year. This exemption applies for two years through December 31, 1990. For stocks held for more than one year, half of the gains are taxed.

For Corporations 80% of dividend income for corporations are exempt from taxes. Dividends and capital gains are taxed as ordinary income; corporate income tax is taxed at a rate of 25%.

For Foreigners Since foreigners are only allowed to purchase mutual funds and gains on mutual funds, they are exempt from taxes through 1990.[12] There is also no capital gains tax for foreigners. Dividends paid to non-residents are subject to withholding tax of 35% but may be reduced to 20% if investments are approved under the Statue for Investment by Foreign Nationals.

Market Indices

The Taiwan Stock Exchange's Weighted Price Index is derived from each day's total market value by the base period's[13] total market value. In addition, the Exchange also provides a weighted price index exclusive of the banking and insurance issues, indices for First Category and Second Category stocks, and eight indices by industry sector. Beginning in January 1989, the Exchange is also providing two additional market indices (retroactive to January 1987), calculated in similar manner as the Dow Jones average and Nikkei-Dow average. One index is a composite of 30 companies representing 17 industry sectors, and the other is a composite of 20 industrial companies.

Foreign Exchange Control

The Central Bank of China keeps a tight control of foreign exchange in Taiwan. The NT dollar is not traded in international markets and not freely traded in Taiwan. Although foreign exchange control has been liberalized significantly since July 15, 1987,[14] there has been little change for foreign investors who wish to invest in Taiwan's stock market. To supplement the control on inward remittance under the Central Bank's Regulations for Non-governmental Inward Remittance, the SEC instructed the Taiwan Stock Exchange and securities firms not to permit foreign nationals' and corporations' application for opening trading accounts, unless they are to be opened for selling their holdings.[15]

Opportunities For Foreign Institutional Investors

Current Opportunities

Present available channels for investment in Taiwan's stock market by foreign institutional investors is very limited. Foreign investors are allowed to participate only indirectly by purchasing the foreign funds managed by the four licensed securities investment trust companies—mutual fund management companies. All four companies have minority international owners.[16] Each sponsors a foreign fund and two domestic funds (one open-end and the other closed-end) for investment in Taiwan stocks and an international fund to invest in non-Taiwan securities. Trading by the 12 Taiwan mutual funds represent less than 1% of the total trading volume. Of the four foreign funds, only the Taiwan Fund is closed-end, the other three are open-end funds.[17] The four funds have been permitted to invest a total of US$156 million into the Taiwan market. The open-end funds all carry a one-year restriction on redemption. The four management companies and their respective foreign funds are located in Table 14.

Outlook for Foreign Investors

While the Taiwan government is committed to internationalization of its capital market, near term prospect for direct foreign investment in Taiwan's stock market will remain restrictive. With foreign exchange reserves of US$74 billion (about US$3,700 per capita), Taiwan is still faced with a problem of having too much cash. Eliminating the existing barriers may invite greater capital inflow to Taiwan, further compounding the problem of excess liquidity. Although the NT$ has appreciated more than 40% against the U.S. dollar over the last two years, it is still widely expected to appreciate significantly as trade surplus continues. Even without the inflationary pressure from excess foreign exchange reserves, the government is not likely to allow foreign institutions to be able to transfer money freely into and out of Taiwan to purchase or to sell local securities for fear of the disturbance that might be caused by large capital flows that foreign institutional investors are capable of affecting.

Further deregulation on participation of foreign institutional investors in the stock market is likely to be implemented gradually in terms of controlling the type of investors (i.e., those who have offices in Taiwan to provide services and products) and the absolute dollar amount that may be invested.

For example, the proposed change will allow foreign insurance companies licensed to operate in Taiwan to invest in Taiwan securities up to 35% of their branch capital and reserves. In 1989, the combined amount was NT$200 million (US$7 million), too small to be of any significance to the market or the investing company. Interestingly, the announcement of this proposal came on the heel of the near volume-less market crash in October 1988, while no indication of recovery was in sight.

Speculative fever continues to plague Taiwan's stock market in 1989. The TSE Index on January 5 was 4873.18—its lowest point for the year—it reached its peak of 10,773.11 on September 25, and closed the year at 9624.18. Bowing to investor pressure, the government again suspended capital gains tax indefinitely beginning in 1990. Transaction tax, however, was raised to 1.5% beginning in 1990. Trading volume rose 223% in 1989 to NT$25.4 trillion (nearly US$1 trillion), or about US$3.4 billion per day. Listed companies rose to 181

Table 14

Management Company	IIT	Kwang Hwa	NITC	China Securites
Fund	Taiwan (ROC) Fund	Formosa Fund	Taipei Fund	Taiwan Fund
	open-end	open-end	open-end	closed-end
Initial date	10/27/83	3/13/86	5/22/86	12/27/86
Initial units	7,495,000	2,500,000	2,500,000	25,000,000
NAV per unit (NT$)				
Initial	$401	$390	$383	$36
Year-end 1986	$594	$447	$413	$36
Year-end 1988	$1,767	$1,729	$1,548	$115
1988 Year-end Units	2,963,000	1,241,000	1,069,000	22,017,565
1988 Year-end NAV				
NT$ million	$5,235	$2,146	$1,654	$2,524
US$ million	$185.9	$76.2	$58.7	$89.6

Table 15   Management Companies' Addresses

International Investment Trust Company Limited
17/F No. 167 Fu Hsing N. Road
Taipei, Taiwan
Republic of China
Telephone: (02) 713-7702

Brokers:
London:
Robert Fleming Securities Ltd.
25 Copthall Avenue
London EC2R 7DR, England
Telephone: (01) 638-5555

Citicorp Scrimgeour Vickers International Ltd.
Cotons Centre
P.O. Box 200, Hay's Lane
London SEI 2QT, England
Telephone: (01) 634-3000

CSFB Investment Management
22 Bishopsgate
London EC2N 4BQ, England
Telephone: (212) 912-7000

New York:
Eberstadt Fleming Inc.
Two World Trade Center, 32nd Floor
New York, New York 10048, U.S.A.
Telephone: (212) 912-7000

Vickers da Costa Securities Inc.
320 Park Avenue
New York, New York 10022, U.S.A.
Telephone: (212) 906-1600 or (212) 509-0315

Kwang Hwa Securities Investment & Trust Co., Ltd.
11F, 658 Tun-Hua South Road
Taipei, Taiwan
Republic of China
Telephone: (02) 708-8201
Fax: (02) 705-2698

Broker:
Hoare Govett Asia Limited
3001 Edinburgh Tower
The Landmark, Hong Kong
Telephone: (5) 868-0368
Fax: (5) 810-4932

Table continues

Table 15   (continued)

National Investment Trust Company Limited
17F First Commercial Bank Building
Taipei, Taiwan
Republic of China
Telephone: (02) 361-1551

Brokers:
Prudential-Bache Capital Funding (Equities) Limited
9 Devonshire Square
London EC2M 4HP, England

China Securities Investment Trust Corporation
Room 1201
125 Nanking East Road Section 5
Taipei, Taiwan
Republic of China
Telephone: (02) 760-6123
Fax: (02) 768-3951

Taiwan Fund is listed on the New York Stock Exchange and may be purchased through brokers as other stocks.

firms, with aggregate market value of NT$6.2 trillion (US$ 232 billion). In December 1989, for the first time, equity shares were traded in the OTC market and the trading volume was NT$1.4 billion (US$ 51 million).

Financial Reporting and Sources of Information

Disclosure Requirements

Listed companies are required to submit a prospectus in the standard format prescribed by the SEC that includes information on company history, organization, business scope and facilities available, capital structure and share distribution, record of corporate bond issues, plans and business prospects, audited financial statements, etc. The prospectus must be submitted on the initial public offering and when capital stock is increased. Otherwise it need not be renewed on a regular basis.

Listed companies must publish monthly reports that include the sales volume of the preceding month and financial statements on a quarterly basis. The semi-annual and annual financial statements shall be fully audited and certified. Following the annual meeting of shareholders, a listed company must file the resolution, operating reports, and financial statements with the exchange. In addition, a listed company is required to report to the exchange and make public immediately any event that might affect significantly its shareholders' interest or securities prices. All reports filed by the listed companies are kept by the exchange for reference by the general public.

Publications Issued by the Taiwan Stock Exchange

1. *The Status of Securities on the Taiwan Stock Exchange* (monthly)
2. *Stock Exchange Monthly Review*
3. *Taiwan Stock Exchange Statistical Data* (monthly)
4. *An Introduction to The Taiwan Stock Exchange* (annual)
5. *Taiwan Stock Exchange Trading Volume, Value and Stock Price Index* (annual)
6. *Taiwan Stock Exchange Fact Book* (annual)
7. *Taiwan Stock Exchange Annual Report*

Taiwan Stock Exchange
7-10 Fl., 85 Yen Ping S. Rd.
Taipei, Taiwan
Republic of China
Telephone: (02) 311–4020
Fax: (02) 391–5591

Publications Issued by the Securities & Exchange Commission

1. *SEC Statistics* (annual)
2. *Annual Report of Securities Management in R.O.C.*
3. *Securities Management* (bi-monthly)

Securities & Exchange Commission
Ministry of Finance
12th Fl., 3 Nan-Hai Road
Taipei, Taiwan
Republic of China
Telephone: (02) 341–3101

Newspapers, Magazines

1. *China Post* (daily)
2. *The Economic News* (weekly)
3. *Asian Wall Street Journal* (daily)

Endnotes

[1] P/E is based on year-end market value divided by actual earnings (or estimated earnings for the year 1988) of all listed companies for the year. Taiwan companies pay dividends on an annual basis. Indicated yield is based on actual or estimated cash dividends paid in the following year divided by market value at year-end.

[2] Based on 1988 year end price and estimated after tax earnings for 1988 by Ting Kong Securities.

[3] Id.

[4] The limit was reduced to 3% on Oct. 27, 1987, following the world-wide crash. It was restored to 5% on November 14, 1988, after the market recovered from its second crash.

[5] Insider trading and market manipulation are illegal but enforcement has been less than satisfactory.

[6] *Source:* Taiwan Stock Exchange.

[7] The four companies are Taiwan Cement Co., Ltd.; Taiwan Paper Co., Ltd.; Agriculture and Forestry Co., Ltd.; and Industrial and Mining Co., Ltd.

[8] Included in Second Category are 19 companies in financial distress and further classified as "stocks requiring full delivery." These shares account for 0.4% of the total market capitalization. Settlement in trading for these shares must be on the same day as the transaction day instead of the usual three business days hence the term "full delivery." Stocks may also be classified as Third Category for Over-the-Counter trading, but to-date, no company has chosen to apply for listing in the Third Category due to concerns for image and liquidity.

[9] Margin loan is limited to NT$1.2 million per stock up to NT$3 million per person. Maximum margin percentage is 50% for First Category shares and

40% for Second Category shares and is based on a complex formula reflecting market index, market value, and book value of each stock such that effective percentage is often less than 30%. Short sell amount is limited to a maximum of NT$400,000 per person.

10 *Source:* Securities & Exchange Commission.

11 Capital gains tax on unlisted stocks has been re-imposed since 1985.

12 It is not clear whether the government would extend the exemption beyond 1990.

13 1966 average = 100.

14 One of the most notable changes is that any resident may remit outward up to US$5 million per year.

15 *Securities Regulation Review (Cheng Chuan Kuan Li Tsa Chih)*, Vol. 5, No. 6, at 77 (November, 1987).

16 The foreign partners are as follows:

IIT:
Credit Suisse First Boston (Asia) Ltd.; Vickers da Costa International Ltd.; Robert Fleming (H.K.) Ltd.; Wardley Investment Services, Citicorp International Ltd.; Gartmore (H.K.) Ltd.; Lazard Brothers & Co., Ltd.; Nikko International Capital Management Co. (American) Inc.; and United Merchant Bank Ltd.

Kwang Hwa:
Interallianz Bank Zurich, AG, Hoare Govett (Far East) Ltd., and MIM (Asia Pacific) Holdings, Ltd.

NITC:
Prudential-Bache Securities; G.T. Management; Daiwa Securities; and B.T. Foreign Investment Corporation, an affiliate of Bankers Trust.

China Securities:
Merrill Lynch, Fidelity, Yamaichi Securities, and Bangkok Bank.

17 Redemption was suspended for all open-end funds during the volume-less crash in October 1988.

COUNTRY FUNDS

Closed-End Country Funds Review

Michael T. Porter
Smith Barney, Harris Upham & Co., New York

ASA LTD. (ASA)

Listing: NYSE
Launched: September 1958
Offering Price: $28.00
Investment Manager: ASA Ltd.
Total Shares: 9,600,000
Total Net Assets: $566 million
Market Capitalization: $481 million

Expense Ratio: 0.19%

Recent Dividends: $0.75 paid 08/25/90
$0.75 paid 05/26/90
$0.75 paid 02/24/90

INVESTMENT OBJECTIVE:
Long-term capital appreciation through investment of more
than 50% of its assets in equity securities of gold mining
companies in South Africa, and the balance in other South
African companies.

Current Disc./Prem.: −15%
52-Week Range: −13% to −27%
Avg. Discount/Premium: −21%

SECTOR BREAKDOWN: August 31, 1990:

Industry	% of Assets
Gold Mining	72.6
Coal, Diamond & Platinum Mining, Other	24.1
Cash	3.3
Total	100.0

TOP TEN HOLDINGS: August 31, 1990:

Company	Industry	% of Net Assets
Driefontein Consolidated Ltd.	Gold Mining	20.4
Kloof Gold Mining Co. Ltd.	Gold Mining	12.8
Vaal Reefs Exploration & Mining Co.	Gold Mining	12.4
Southvaal Holdings Ltd.	Gold Mining	10.6
De Beers Consolidated Mines	Diversified Mining	6.1
Winkelhaak Mines Ltd.	Gold Mining	5.9
Rustenburg Platinum Holdings	Diversified Mining	5.2
Hartebeestfontein Gold Mining Co.	Gold Mining	4.2
Anglo American Coal Corporation	Gold Mining	3.3
Zandpan Gold Mining Co.	Gold Mining	2.7
		83.5

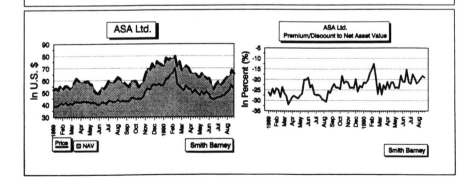

ALLIANCE NEW EUROPE FUND (ANE)

Listing: NYSE
Launched: April 1990
Offering Price: $12.00
Investment Manager: Alliance Capital Management
Total Shares: 21,009,000
Total Net Assets: $196 million
Market Capitalization: $155 million

Management Fees: 1.10% up to $100 million, 0.95% on
next $100 million, 0.80% thereafter.

Expense Ratio: 1.43%
Recent Dividends: None

INVESTMENT OBJECTIVE:
Long-term capital appreciation through investment primarily
in the equity securities of companies based in Europe.

Current Disc./Prem.: –21%
52-Week Range: +8% to –21%
Avg. Discount/Premium: –9%

ASSET ALLOCATION: May 31, 1990:

	% of Assets
Common Stock	50.5
Preferred Stock	2.1
Convertible Bonds	0.4
Cash	45.9
Other	1.1
Total	100.0

COUNTRY ALLOCATION: May 31, 1990:

	% of Assets
Germany	17.7
United Kingdom	12.3
Netherlands	6.0
United States	2.8
Austria	2.8
Italy	2.4
Denmark	2.1
Switzerland	2.1
France	1.6
Spain	1.0
Norway	0.5
Total	51.3

TOP TEN HOLDINGS: May 31, 1990:

Company	Country	% of Net Assets
Springer A. Verlag	Germany	2.2
Volkswagen AG	Germany	1.9
Mannesmann AG	Germany	1.8
Bayer AG	Germany	1.6
Nestor-BNA	United Kingdom	1.6
Dresdner Bank AG	Germany	1.4
Continental AG	Germany	1.3
La Rochette	France	1.2
FAG Kugelfischer	Germany	1.1
Norit NV	Netherlands	1.1
		15.2

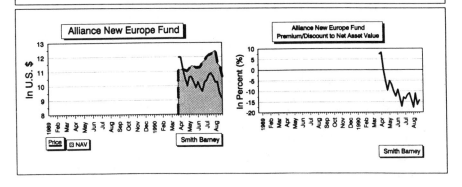

ASIA PACIFIC FUND (APB)

Listing: NYSE
Launched: April 1987
Offering Price: $10.00
Investment Manager: Baring International
Total Shares: 8,662,520
Total Net Assets: $100 million
Market Capitalization: $87 million

Management Fees: 1.1% of first $50 million, 0.9% of next $50 million, and 0.7% on excess.

Expense Ratio: 2.69%
Recent Dividends: $0.18 paid 01/12/90
                  $0.66 paid 06/29/90

INVESTMENT OBJECTIVE:
Long-term capital appreciation through investment primarily in equity securities of companies in the Asia Pacific countries. These countries are Hong Kong, South Korea, Malaysia, the Philippines, Singapore, Taiwan and Thailand.

Current Disc./Prem.: –14%
52-Week Range: +43% to –23%
Avg. Discount/Premium: –2%

COUNTRY ALLOCATION: July 31, 1990:

Country	% of Assets
Thailand	25.7
Hong Kong	24.4
Singapore	20.0
Malaysia	19.6
Korea	8.4
Philippines	1.9
Taiwan	0.0
	100.0

TOP TEN HOLDINGS: July 31, 1990:

Company	Country
Daewoo Heavy Industry (CB)	South Korea
Development Bank of Singapore	Singapore
Hutchison Whampoa	Hong Kong
Jardine Matheson	Hong Kong
Keppel Corporation (Warrants 1993)	Singapore/Malaysia
Siam Cement	Thailand
Swire Pacific "A"	Hong Kong
Thai Farmers Bank	Thailand
Thai Wah Company	Thailand
UMW Holdings	Malaysia

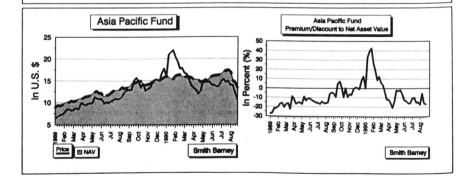

AUSTRIA FUND# (OST)

Listing: NYSE
Launched: August 1984
Offering Price: $12.00
Investment Manager: Alliance Capital
Total Shares: 8,259,000
Total Net Assets:$94 million
Market Capitalization: $71 million

Management Fees: 1.00% of average net assets for first
$50 million, and 0.9% of excess.

Expense Ratio: 1.88%
Recent Dividends: $0.65 paid 01/12/90

INVESTMENT OBJECTIVE:
Long-term capital appreciation through investment primarily
in equity securities of Austria companies.

Current Disc./Prem.: -24%
52-Week Range: +85% to -23%
Avg. Discount/Premium: +10%

SECTOR BREAKDOWN: May 31, 1990:

Industry	% of Assets
Basic Industries	28.5
Financial Services	21.9
Capital Goods	16.5
Consumer Products & Services	9.0
Utilities	8.9
Multi-Industry	2.7
Cash and Other Assets/Liabilities	12.5
Total	100.0

TOP TEN HOLDINGS: May 31, 1990:

Company	Industry	% of Net Assets
Erste Allgemeine Versich	Insurance	8.6
OeMV	Energy	8.1
Creditanstalt-Bankverein	Banking	5.8
Verbund	Utilities	5.6
Wienerberger Baustoff Industrie	Engineering & Construction	5.4
Radex Heraklith AG	Mining & Metals	5.3
Papierfabrik Laakirchen	Paper	4.6
Universale Bau AG	Engineering & Construction	4.3
Oest Landerbank	Banking	3.7
Lenzing AG	Chemicals	3.5
Total		54.9

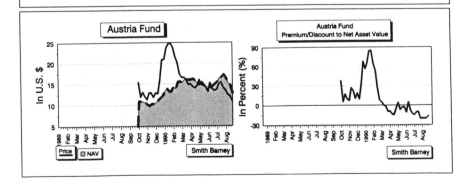

BRAZIL FUND (BZF)

Listing: NYSE
Launched: April 1988
Offering Price: $12.50
Investment Manager: Scudder, Stevens & Clark
Total Shares: 12,041,019
Total Net Assets: $115 million
Market Capitalization: $96 million

Management Fees: 1.25% of average net assets.

Expense Ratio: 2.12%
Recent Dividends: $3.07 paid 01/23/90
$0.12 paid 03/30/90

INVESTMENT OBJECTIVE:
Long-term capital appreciation through investment in securities, primarily equity securities, of Brazilian companies.

Current Disc./Prem.: –16%
52-Week Range: +27% to –55%
Avg. Discount/Premium: –22%

SECTOR BREAKDOWN: June 30, 1990:

Industry	% of Assets
Forest Products	17.2
Mining	12.7
Food and Beverages	11.0
Chemicals	9.1
Petroleum	5.7
Tobacco	5.7
Retailing	4.8
Textiles and Apparel	4.4
Electrical Equipment	4.3
Glass	2.6
Iron and Steel	2.3
Cash and Other Assets/Liabilities	20.2
Total	100.0

TOP TEN HOLDINGS: June 30, 1990:

Company	Industry	% of Net Assets
Aracruz Celulose S.A. "B"	Forest Products	8.9
Companhia Vale do Rio Doce	Mining	6.9
Petroleo Brazileiro S/A	Petroleum	5.7
Companhia Souza Cruz Industria de Comeric	Tobacco	5.7
Companhia Suzano de Papel e Celulose	Forest Products	5.5
S.A. Mineracao da Trindade	Mining	4.6
Sadia Concordia S/A	Food and Beverage	4.4
COPENE Petroquimica do Nordeste S.A.	Chemicals	4.3
S/A White Martins	Chemicals	4.3
Metal Leve S.A.	Auto Parts	3.4
		53.6

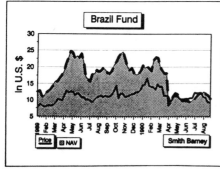

CENTRAL FUND OF CANADA (CEF)

Listing: ASE
Launched: September 1983
Offering Price: $8.50
Administrator: The Central Group Ltd.
Total Shares: 16,824,300
Total Net Assets: $86 million
Market Capitalization: $83 million

Recent Dividends: $0.01 paid 11/15/89

INVESTMENT OBJECTIVE:
Central Fund of Canada is a holding company whose
investment objective is to hold the vast majority of its
assets in gold and silver bullion, primarily in bar form.

Current Disc./Prem.: –3%
52–Week Range: +9% to –7%
Avg. Discount/Premium: +1%

SECTOR BREAKDOWN: August 31, 1990:

	Ounces	% of Assets
Gold Bar	116,205	53.6
Gold Certificates	13,000	6.0
Silver Bar	6,138,615	35.2
Silver Certificates	221,750	1.3
Cash		3.9
		100.0

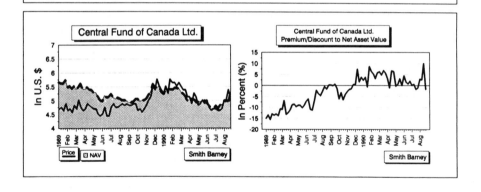

CHILE FUND (CH)

Listing: NYSE
September 1989
Offering Price: $15.00
Investment Manager: BEA Associates
Total Shares: 5,374,674
Total Net Assets: $85 million
Market Capitalization: $62 million

Management Fees: 1.20% of first $50 million, 1.15% of next $50 million, and 1.10% of excess.

Expense Ratio: 1.81%

Recent Dividends: $0.34 paid 01/12/90

INVESTMENT OBJECTIVE:
Total return, consisting of capital appreciation and income, to be achieved by investing primarily in Chilean equity and debt securities.

Current Disc./Prem.: –26%
52-Week Range: +30% to –18%
Avg. Discount/Premium: +8%

SECTOR BREAKDOWN: June 30, 1990:

Industry	% of Assets
Electric Utilities	21.1
Telecommunications	12.7
Investments	9.8
Paper & Cellulose	9.7
Basic Metals	8.2
Forestry	7.4
Beer, Beverages, Liquor & Tobacco	2.6
Other	14.1
Cash & Other Assets/Liabilities	14.4
	100.0

TOP TEN HOLDINGS: June 30, 1990:

Company	Industry	% of Net Assets
Cartones	Paper Products	8.9
Telefonos de Chile	Telecommunications	8.7
Copec de Chile	Forestry	7.4
Cap	Basic Metals	7.2
Enersis	Electric Utility	6.7
Chilgener	Electric Utility	4.7
Endese de Chile	Electric Utility	4.4
Entel	Communications	4.0
Antofagasta Holdings	Investments	3.6
Chilectra	Electric Utilities	3.2
		58.8

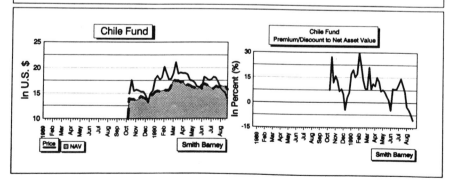

EMERGING GERMANY FUND (FRG)

Listing: NYSE
Launched: March 1990
Offering Price: $12.00
Investment Manager: ABD Securities Corporation
Investment Advisor: Asset Mgmt. Advisors for Dresdner Bank
Total Shares: 14,000,000
Total Net Assets: $124 million
Market Capitalization: $98 million

Management Fees: 0.30% of average weekly net assets up to $100 million and 0.20% of excess.

Advisory Fees: 0.70% of average weekly net assets up to $100 million and 0.60% of excess.

Recent Dividends: None

INVESTMENT OBJECTIVE:
Long-term capital appreciation by investing primarily in equity and equity-linked securities of medium- and smaller-sized West German companies.

Current Disc./Prem.: –21%
52-Week Range: +1% to –23%
Avg. Discount/Premium: –12%

SECTOR BREAKDOWN:

NEW FUND
DATA UNAVAILABLE

TOP TEN HOLDINGS:

NEW FUND
DATA UNAVAILABLE

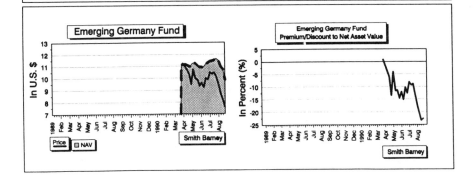

Emerging Germany Fund

Emerging Germany Fund
Premium/Discount to Net Asset Value

THE EUROPE FUND (EF)

Listing: NYSE Launched: April 1990 Offering Price: $15.00 Investment Manager: Warburg Investment Management Total Shares: 8,3450,000 Total Net Assets: $106 million Market Capitalization: $86 million	Management Fees: 0.75% of first $250 million, and 0.65% of excess Expense Ratio: 1.52% Recent Dividends: None

INVESTMENT OBJECTIVE: Long-term capital appreciation through investment primarily in equity securities of European companies that will benefit from the trends emerging in Europe over the next few years.	Current Disc./Prem.: −19% 52-Week Range: +9% to −23% Avg. Discount/Premium: −4%

GEOGRAPHIC BREAKDOWN: June 30, 1990

	% of Assets
France	6.2
Italy	5.6
The Netherlands	5.7
Norway	1.8
Portugal	1.3
Spain	5.8
Switzerland	8.4
U.K.	17.8
West Germany	5.2
CASH	25.6
OTHER ASSETS	16.6
	100.0

TOP TEN HOLDINGS: June 30, 1990

Company	Industry	% of Net Assets
Ciba Geigy	Pharmaceuticals/Chemicals	2.5
Fomento de Obras Y Constucciones	Construction	2.5
Ahold	Food Retailer	2.0
British Petroleum	Energy	1.6
Polly Peck International	Fresh Fruit	1.6
Veba	Utility	1.3
Stet	Telecommunications	1.3
GKN	Auto Components/Industrial Services	1.2
Pirelli & Cie.	Holding Company	1.2
Thorn EMI	Leisure	1.1
		16.3

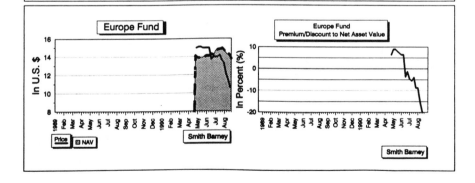

EUROPEAN WARRANT FUND (EWF)

Listing: NYSE
Launched: July 1990
Offering Price: $12.00
Investment Advisor: Julius Baer Securities
Total Shares: 6,000,000
Total Net Assets: $56 million
Market Capitalization: $44 million

Advisory Fees: 1.25% of average weekly net assets.

Recent Dividends: None

INVESTMENT OBJECTIVE:
Long-term capital appreciation through investment primarily in equity warrants of Western European issuers.

Current Disc./Prem.: –22%
52-Week Range: +5% to –22%
Avg. Discount/Premium: –10%

PORTFOLIO INFORMATION: September 27, 1990:

Net Asset Value: $9.30
Percentage of Assets Invested: 54.5%
Percentage of Derivatives: 35.2%
Weighted Average Life of Derivatives: 713.2 days
Weighted Average Yield on Cash: 7.34%
Pctg. of Foreign Exchange Hedge to Invested Assets: 98.8%

MARKET WEIGHTINGS: September 27, 1990:

Country	% of Assets
Germany	20.1
France	10.5
United States	6.4
Italy	5.7
Switzerland	5.3
United Kingdom	4.4
Netherlands	1.5
Norway	0.6
Cash	45.5
Total	100.0

TOP TEN HOLDINGS:

NEW FUND
DATA UNAVAILABLE

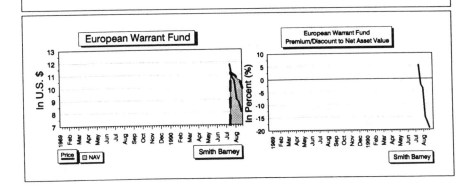

European Warrant Fund

European Warrant Fund
Premium/Discount to Net Asset Value

FIRST AUSTRALIA FUND (IAF)

Listing: ASE
Launched: December 1985
Offering Price: $10.00
Investment Advisor: EquityLink Australia
Total Shares: 6,019,274
Total Net Assets: $60 million
Market Capitalization: $45 million

Advisory Fees: 1.10% on first $50 million, 0.9% on next
$50 million, and 0.7% on excess.

Expense Ratio: 2.54%
Recent Dividends: $0.49 paid 01/12/90
                               $0.13 paid 06/13/90

INVESTMENT OBJECTIVE:
Long-term capital appreciation through investment primarily
in equity securities of Australian companies.

Current Disc./Prem.: -25%
52-Week Range: +20% to -24%
Avg. Discount/Premium: -10%

SECTOR BREAKDOWN: April 30, 1990:

Industry	% of Assets
Natural Resources	33.0
Diversified Industrials	20.3
Services	9.5
Property-Related	2.9
Cash	34.3
Total	100.0

TOP TEN HOLDINGS: April 30, 1990:

Company	Industry	% of Net Assets
CRA Ltd.	Natural Resources	6.3
BTR Nylex Ltd.	Diversified Resources	5.4
Western Mining Corp.	Natural Resources	4.2
M.I.M. Holdings Ltd.	Natural Resources	4.0
Renison Goldfields	Natural Resources	4.0
Pacific Dunlop	Diversified Resources	3.6
Broken Hill Proprietary	Natural Resources	3.4
Westpac Banking Corp.	Services	2.4
National Australia Banking	Services	2.0
Santos Limited	Natural Resources	1.8
		37.1

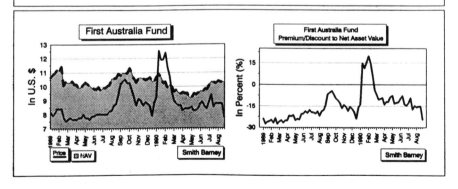

FIRST AUSTRALIA PRIME INCOME FUND (FAX)

Listing: ASE
Launched: April 1986
Offering Price: $10.00
Investment Manager: EquityLink International
Total Shares: 85,954,618
Total Net Assets: $913 million
Market Capitalization: $800 million

Management Fees: 0.65% on first $200 million, 0.60% on next $300 million, 0.55% on next $400 million, and 0.50% on excess.

Expense Ratio: 2.77%
Dividend Rate: $0.09 monthly, $0.127 paid 01/12/90.

INVESTMENT OBJECTIVE:
Current income through investment primarily in debt securities (rated "A" or better) of Australian issuers, including obligation of Australian banks and state governmental entities, and corporations. The fund may also invest in U.S. govt. securities and corporate and bank securities of U.S. issuers rated "A" or better.

Current Dis./Prem.: -12%
52-Week Range: +1% to -15%
Avg. Discount/Premium: -5%

COUNTRY BREAKDOWN: April 30, 1990:

Country	% of Assets
Australia	96
United States	4
New Zealand	0
Total	100

MATURITY PROFILE: April 30, 1990:

	% of Assets
under 1 year	24
1 year to less than 6 years	49
6 years to less than 9 years	19
9 years and over	8
Total	100

Average Maturity of the Portfolio: 4 years

SECTORIAL COMPOSITION: April 30, 1990:

	% of Assets
Government	28
State and Semi-Government	44
Corporate	11
Commercial Banks	17
Total	·100

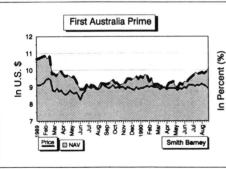

First Australia Prime

Price □ NAV   Smith Barney

First Australia Prime
Premium/Discount to Net Asset Value

Smith Barney

THE FIRST IBERIAN FUND (IBF)

Listing: ASE
Launched: April 1988
Offering Price: $10.00
Investment Manager: Iberian Cap. Gestion BV
Total Shares: 6,511,000
Total Net Assets: $57 million
Market Capitalization: $46 million

Expense Ratio: 3.38%

Recent Dividends: $0.201 paid 01/12/90
$0.05 paid 07/13/90

INVESTMENT OBJECTIVE:
Long-term capital appreciation through investment primarily
in equity securities of Spain and Portugal.

Current Disc./Prem.: -19%
52-Week Range: +87% to -17%
Avg. Discount/Premium: +20%

COUNTRY ALLOCATION: March 31, 1990:

Country	% of Assets
Spain	98
Portugal	6
United States	1
Total	104

ASSET ALLOCATION: March 31, 1990:

	% of Asset
Equity Securities	85
Fixed-Income Securities	18
Cash	1
Total	104
Less:Other Assets/Liabilities:	4
	100

SECTOR BREAKDOWN: March 31, 1990:

Industry	% of Assets
Utilities	15.4
Building Materials & Equipment	13.0
Banking	11.5
Machinery & Equipment	8.6
Transportation	6.4
Holding Companies	6.5
Food Wholesalers	4.7
Real Estate	4.5
Insurance	2.4
Other	12.4
	85.4

TOP TEN HOLDINGS: March 31, 1990:

Company	Industry	% of Net Assets
Sistemas Financieros	Holding Company	5.3
Zardoya Otis, S.A.	Machinery & Equipment	5.2
Banco Popular Espanol	Banking	3.3
Portland Valderrivas, S.A.	Building Materials & Equipment	3.3
Asland, S.A.	Building Materials & Equipment	3.1
Sevillana de Electricidad	Utilities	2.7
Vallehermoso	Real Estate	2.7
Autopistas, C.E.S.A.	Transportation	2.6
Banco Zaragozano	Banking	2.6
Banco Interontinental Espanol	Banking	2.4
		33.4

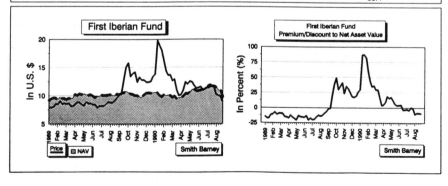

First Iberian Fund — Price / NAV — In U.S. $ — Smith Barney

First Iberian Fund Premium/Discount to Net Asset Value — In Percent (%) — Smith Barney

FIRST PHILIPPINE FUND (FPF)

Listing: NYSE
Launched: November 1989
Offering Price: $12.00
Investment Manager: Clemente Capital
Total Shares: 8,970,000
Total Net Assets: $87 million
Market Capitalization: $58 million

Management Fees: 1.35% of average net assets

Expense Ratio: 1.87%

Recent Dividends: $0.08 paid 01/12/90

INVESTMENT OBJECTIVE:
Long-term capital appreciation through investment primarily in equity securities of Philippines companies.

Current Disc./Prem.: -33%
52-Week Range: +61% to -29%
Avg. Discount/Premium: -1%

SECTOR BREAKDOWN: June 30, 1990:

Industry	% of Assets
Telecommunications	4.5
Food & Beverage	4.3
Drug & Personal Health Care	3.9
Mining	3.3
Investment & Finance	2.6
Light Industry	1.2
Electronics	0.4
Ship Repair	0.3
Real Estate Development	0.2
Banking	0.1
Tires	3.7
Time Deposits/Cash	75.5
	100.0

TOP TEN HOLDINGS: June 30, 1990:

Company	Industry	% of Net Assets
Philippine Long Distance Telephone	Telecommunications	4.3
San Miguel Corp.	Food & Beverage	4.2
Metro Drug, Inc.	Drug & Personal Health Care	3.9
Sime Darby Tire Philipinas, Inc.	Tires	3.5
Ayala Corp.	Investment & Finance	2.6
Dizon Copper-Silver Mines	Mining	1.8
Jardine Davies, Inc.	Light Industry	1.1
Philex Mining Corp.	Mining	1.0
Benguet Corp.	Mining	0.4
Precision Electronics	Electronics	0.4
		23.2

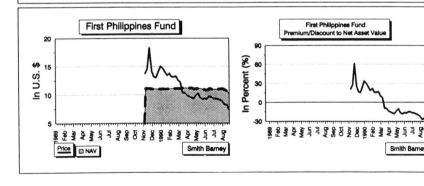

First Philippines Fund

First Philippines Fund
Premium/Discount to Net Asset Value

FRANCE GROWTH FUND (FRF)

Listing: NYSE
Launched: May 1990
Offering Price: $12.00
Advisor: Indosuez International Investment Services
Total Shares: 11,509,000
Total Net Assets: $120 million
Market Capitalization: $88 million

Management Fees: 0.90% of assets up to $100 million, 0.80% of assets thereafter.

Expense Ratio: 1.47%
Recent Dividends: None

INVESTMENT OBJECTIVE:
Long-term capital appreciation through investment primarily in equity securities of French companies.

Current Disc./Prem.: –27%
52–Week Range: +22% to –33%
Avg. Discount/Premium: –7%

SECTOR BREAKDOWN: June 30, 1990:

Industry	% of Assets
Services (Hotel, Real Estate and Other)	7.5
Financial Services	5.7
Distribution Services	3.0
Building Materials	2.8
Other Consumer Non–Durables	2.4
Food & Beverage	1.8
Air & Space	1.7
Consumer Durables	1.4
Advertising	1.2
Chemicals	1.1
Civil Engineering	1.1
Construction	0.8
Other	3.2
Cash	66.5
Total	100.0

TOP TEN HOLDINGS: June 30, 1990:

Company	Industry	% of Net Assets
Bon Marche	Distribution Services	1.4
Poliet	Building Materials	1.3
L'Oreal	Consumer Products	1.1
Spie Batignolles	Civil Engineering	1.1
Air Liquide	Chemicals	1.1
BHV	Department Store	1.1
Generale Occidentale	Communications	1.1
BSN	Food & Beverage	1.0
CGE	Electrical & Electronics	0.9
Elf Aquitaine	Oil & Gas	0.9
		11.0

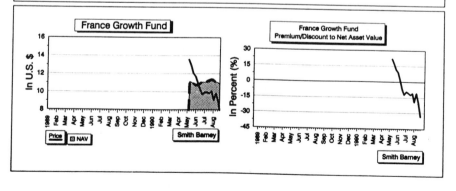

FUTURE GERMANY FUND (FGF)

Listing: NYSE
Launched: February 1990
Offering Price: $18.00
Investment Manager: DB Capital Management International
Investment Advisor: DB Capital Management International
Total Shares: 12,927,674
Total Net Assets: $169 million
Market Capitalization: $135 million

Management Fees: 0.65% of average weekly net assets up to $100 million and 0.55% of excess.

Advisory Fees: 0.35% of average weekly net assets up to $100 million and 0.25% of excess.

Recent Dividends: None

INVESTMENT OBJECTIVE:
Long-term capital appreciation through investment primarily in equity and equity-linked securities of West German companies.

Current Disc./Prem.: -20%
52-Week Range: +8% to -26%
Avg. Discount/Premium: -11%

SECTOR BREAKDOWN: July 31, 1990:

Industry	% of Assets
Chemical	14.6
Automotive	14.3
Utilities	12.1
Engineering/Plant Construction/Other	10.7
Steel Manufacturing	8.1
Retailing	8.1
Insurance	7.6
Electrical	5.8
Pharmaceuticals	2.8
Machinery/Machine Tools	2.6
Non-Ferrous Metals	1.9
Other	6.3
Cash	6.7
Total	101.6
Less: Other Assets/Liabilities	1.6
Total	100.0

TOP TEN HOLDINGS: July 31, 1990:

Company	Industry	% of Net Assets
Allianz Holding	Insurance	5.9
Rheinisch-Westfalisches Elektrizitatswerke	Utilities	5.2
Siemens	Electrical	4.6
Bayer	Chemical	4.5
Volkswagen	Automotive	4.2
Thyssen	Steel Manufacturing	3.8
Daimler-Benz	Automotive	3.4
VIAG	Utilities	3.2
Bayerische Motoren Werke	Automotive	3.0
Hoechst	Chemical	3.0
		40.8

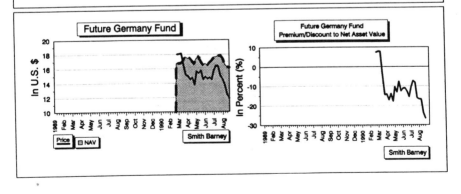

GERMANY FUND (GER)

Listing: NYSE
Launched: July 1986
Offering Price: $10.00
Investment Manager: Deutsche Bank Capital Corp.
Total Shares: 13,075,593
Total Net Assets: $134 million
Market Capitalization: $139 million

Management Fees: 0.65% on first $50 million, and 0.55% on excess.

Expense Ratio: 1.47%
Recent Dividends: $0.06 paid 01/05/90
$0.19 paid 02/01/90

INVESTMENT OBJECTIVE:
Long-term capital appreciation through investment primarily in equity securities of West German companies.

Current Disc./Prem.: +4%
52-Week Range: +100% to -8%
Avg. Discount/Premium: +25%

SECTOR BREAKDOWN: June 30, 1990:

Industry	% of Assets
Automotive	15.9
Retail/Consumer	9.6
Chemical	10.7
Utilities	9.8
Engineering/Construction	9.2
Electrical	7.8
Banking	7.7
Insurance	6.9
Steel	6.1
Engineering/Machinery	5.2
Pharmaceutical	2.1
Glass	1.0
Cash	8.0
Total	100.0

TOP TEN HOLDINGS: June 30, 1990:

Company	Industry	% of Net Assets
Allianz Holding	Insurance	5.3
Siemens	Electrical	5.2
Thyssen	Steel Manufacturing	4.9
Daimler-Benz	Automotive	4.1
Volkswagen	Automotive	3.7
Bayer AG	Chemicals	3.7
Bayerische Hupothekenund	Banking	3.2
Linotype	Engineering/Machinery	3.0
Linde	Engineering/Plan Construction	2.7
Wella	Cosmetics	2.7
		38.5

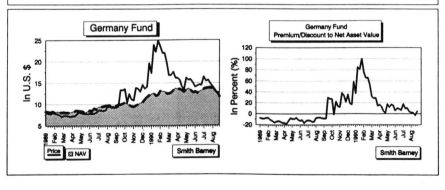

GROWTH FUND OF SPAIN (GSP)

Listing: NYSE
Launched: February 1990
Offering Price: $12.00
Investment Manager: Kemper Financial Services
Total Shares: 17,759,000
Total Net Assets: $173 million
Market Capitalization: $125 million

Management Fees: 1.0% of average weekly assets.

Expense Ratio: 1.48%
Recent Dividends: None

INVESTMENT OBJECTIVE:
Long-term capital appreciation through investment primarily in equity securities of Spanish companies.

Current Disc./Prem.: -28%
52-Week Range: -3% to -22%
Avg. Discount/Premium: -15%

PORTFOLIO COMPOSITION: May 31, 1990:

	% of Assets
Common Stocks	69.7
Convertibles	1.1
Cash & Equivalent - Net	29.2
	100.0

SECTOR ALLOCATION: May 31, 1990:

	% of Asset
Energy Sources	23.3
Construction	13.4
Banking	11.4
Food & Beverage	6.4
Real Estate & Development	6.1
Diversified	5.0
Other	5.2
	70.8

TOP TEN HOLDINGS: May 31, 1990:

Company	Industry	% of Net Assets
Repsol	Energy	5.6
ENDESA	Utility	5.0
Uralita	Construction	4.7
Corporacion Financiera Alba	Diversified	3.8
Acerinox	Construction	3.3
Vallehermosa	Real Estate	3.1
Banco Popular	Banking	3.1
Iberduerdo	Utility	3.0
Dragados y Construcciones	Construction	2.9
Banco Intercontinental	Banking	2.8
		37.3

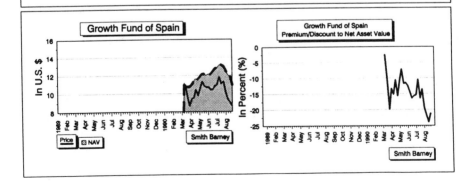

GT GREATER EUROPE FUND (GTF)

Listing: NYSE
Launched: March 1990
Offering Price: $15.00
Invest. Mgr.: G.T. Capital Management, Inc.
Total Shares: 16,007,100
Total Net Assets: $179 million
Market Capitalization: $146 million

Management Fees: 1.25% of average weekly assets

Recent Dividends: None

INVESTMENT OBJECTIVE:
Long-term capital appreciation through investment primarily in a broad range of securities of European issuers in both established and emerging markets.

Current Disc./Prem.: -18%
52-Week Range: +8% to -18%
Avg. Discount/Premium: -2%

GEOGRAPHIC BREAKDOWN OF EQUITY PORTFOLIO: August 10, 1990

Country	% of Assets
Austria	3.4
France	13.2
Germany	29.0
Hungary	0.7
Italy	4.2
Netherlands	18.0
Norway	1.8
Poland	0.5
Spain and Portugal	14.4
Sweden	1.3
Switzerland	3.6
Turkey	2.3
U.K.	5.0
Total	97.4

TOP TEN HOLDINGS: August 10, 1990

Company	Country	% of Net Assets
Pittler Maschinen	Germany	2.9
Cubiertas	Spain	2.8
Bergemann	Netherlands	2.7
Germany City Estates	Netherlands	2.7
Herlitz	Germany	2.7
Canal Plus	France	2.4
Vestel Elektronic Sanayi	Turkey	2.3
Hunter Douglas	Netherlands	2.2
Schering	Germany	2.2
Aux De La Construction	Spain	2.2
		25.1

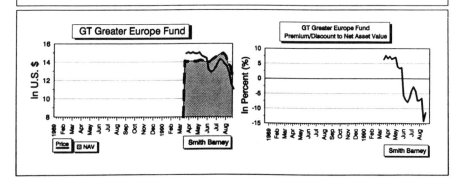

INDIA GROWTH FUND (IGF)

Listing: NYSE
Launched: August 1988
Offering Price: $12.00
Investment Manager: Unit Trust of India
Total Shares: 5,014,348
Total Net Assets: $95 million
Market Capitalization: $71 million

Management Fees: 0.75% of first $50 million, 0.6% on next $50 million, 0.46% thereafter.

Expense Ratio: 3.27%
Recent Dividends: $1.10 paid 01/26/90

INVESTMENT OBJECTIVE:
Long-term capital appreciation through investment primarily in equity securities of Indian companies.

Current Disc./Prem.: –25%
52-Week Range: +47% to –21%
Avg. Discount/Premium: +17%

SECTOR BREAKDOWN: June 30, 1990:

Industry	% of Assets
Automobiles & Auto Ancillaries	15.6
Textiles	12.8
Consumer Products	7.5
Fertilizers & Pesticides	7.5
Tea & Plantation	6.4
Aluminum	6.4
Steel & Steel Products	6.3
Paper	5.6
Chemicals & Dyes	4.9
Shipping	3.5
Petrochemicals	3.4
Other	11.4
Cash	13.0
Total	104.3
Less: Other Assets/Liabilities	4.3
	100.0

TOP TEN HOLDINGS: June 30, 1990:

Company	Industry	% of Net Assets
TELCO	Automobile & Parts	7.6
GSFC	Fertilizers & Pesticides	5.5
TISCO	Steel	5.2
INDALCO	Aluminum	4.9
Century Textiles	Textiles	4.8
Tata Tea	Tea & Plantation	3.9
Colgate Palmolive (India)	Consumer Products	3.7
Grasim Industries	Textiles	3.7
Century Enka	Textiles	3.0
Escorts	Automobile & Parts	2.9
		45.2

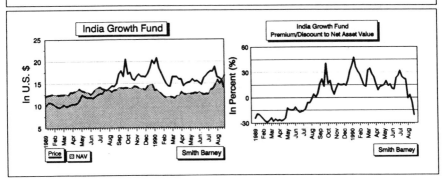

THE INDONESIA FUND (IF)

Listing: NYSE
Launched: March 1990
Offering Price: $15.00
Investment Manager: BEA Associates
Total Shares: 4,607,169
Total Net Assets: $56 million
Market Capitalization: $44 million

Management Fees: 1.0% of average monthly assets.

Expense Ratio: 1.91%

Recent Dividends: None

INVESTMENT OBJECTIVE:
Long-term capital appreciation by investing primarily
in Indonesian securities.

Current Disc./Prem.: –21%
52-Week Range: +19% to –16%
Avg. Discount/Premium: +3%

PORTFOLIO COMPOSITION: June 30, 1990:

	% of Assets
Common Stocks	63.4
Cash & Equivalent – Net	36.6
Total	100.0

COUNTRY ALLOCATION: June 30, 1990:

	% of Assets
Indonesia	40.9
Malaysia	10.0
Thailand	7.5
Singapore	4.4
Philippines	0.6
Total	63.4

TOP TEN HOLDINGS: June 30, 1990:

Company	Industry	% of Net Assets
Astra International	Indonesia	5.8
Pakuwon Jati	Indonesia	4.4
Semen Cibinong	Indonesia	3.2
PT Inco	Indonesia	3.2
Petaling Gardens	Malaysia	2.9
Siam Cement	Thailand	2.8
Hotel Sahid Jaya International	Indonesia	2.6
Ficorinvest	Indonesia	2.4
Malayan Weaving Mills	Malaysia	2.4
Mathichon Publishing	Thailand	2.4
		32.1

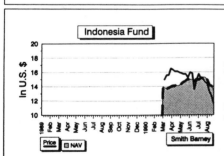

THE IRISH INVESTMENT FUND (IRL)

Listing: NYSE
Launched: March 1990
Offering Price: $12.00
Investment Manager: Bank of Ireland Asset Management
Total Shares: 5,009,000
Total Net Assets: $46 million
Market Capitalization: $34 million

Management Fees: 0.75% of average weekly net assets, annualized and paid monthly.

Expense Ratio: 1.87%
Recent Dividends: None

INVESTMENT OBJECTIVE:
Long-term capital appreciation through investment primarily in equity securities of Irish companies.

Current Disc./Prem.: −27%
52−Week Range: +8% to −28%
Avg. Discount/Premium: −14%

PORTFOLIO COMPOSITION: April 30, 1990:

	% of Assets
Common Stocks	21.5
Other – Net	78.5
	100.0

TOP TEN HOLDINGS: April 30, 1990:

Company	Industry	% of Net Assets
Allied Irish Bank	Bank	5.2
CRH	Construction	3.7
European Leisure	N/A	2.0
Inish Tech	Industrial Holding Company	1.6
Independent Newspapers	Publishing	1.6
James Crean	Diversified Holding Company	1.3
Waterford Wedgwood	Tableware	1.1
Seafield	Property	0.8
Power Corporation	Property	0.8
Jefferson Smurfit	Paper & Packaging	0.8
		18.9

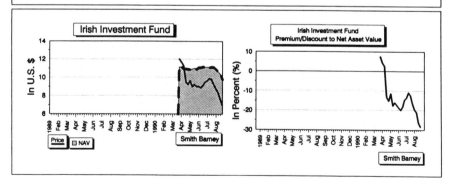

ITALY FUND (ITA)

Listing: NYSE
Launched: February 1986
Offering Price: $12.00
Advisor: Shearson Lehman Gbl. Asset Mgmt.
Total Shares: 6,334,901
Total Net Assets: $84 million
Market Capitalization: $63 million

Management Fees: 0.75% of avg. monthly assets

Expense Ratio: 1.90%
Recent Dividends: $0.15 paid 12/29/89

INVESTMENT OBJECTIVE:
Long-term capital appreciation through investment primarily
in equity securities of Italian companies.

Current Disc./Prem.: -24%
52-Week Range: +38% to -34%
Avg. Discount/Premium: +1%

SECTOR BREAKDOWN: April 30, 1990

Industry	% of Assets
Holding Companies	13.0
Insurance	13.1
Communications	10.5
Banking	9.6
Construction and Property	6.6
Mechanical Engineering	4.8
Cement and Ceramics	4.4
Chemicals and Pharmaceuticals	3.6
Transportation and Auto Parts	3.5
Retailing	2.9
Other	6.7
	78.7

TOP TEN HOLDINGS: April 30, 1990

Company	Industry	% of Net Assets
Italcementi	Cement	4.4
Cofegar	Construction	3.7
STET	Holding Company	3.7
Sirti	Communications	3.4
Danieli & Co.	Engineering	3.0
La Rinascente	Transportation	2.9
Fiat S.p.a.	Automobiles	2.7
Assicurazioni Generali	Insurance	2.6
Mediobanca	Banking	2.5
SAI	Insurance	2.5
		31.4

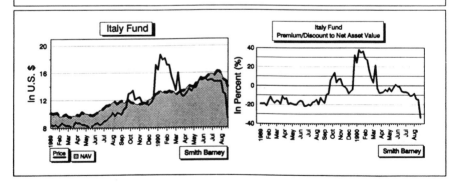

THE JAKARTA GROWTH FUND (JGF)

Listing: NYSE
Launched: April 1990
Offering Price: $12.00
Inv. Manager: Nomura Capital Management, Inc.
Total Shares: 5,000,000
Total Net Assets: $48 million
Market Capitalization: $33 million

Management and Other Fees: 1.10% of avg. weekly assets

Expense Ratio: N.A.
Recent Dividends: None

INVESTMENT OBJECTIVE:
Long term capital appreciation through investment
primarily in equity securities of Indonesian
companies and non-Indonesian companies that derive
a significant proportion of their revenue from
Indonesia.

Current Disc./Prem.: -30%
52-Week Range: +26% to -20%
Avg. Discount/Premium: +5%

SECTOR BREAKDOWN:

NEW FUND
DATA UNAVAILABLE

TOP TEN HOLDINGS:

NEW FUND
DATA UNAVAILABLE

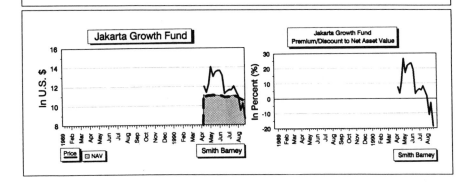

JAPAN OTC EQUITY FUND (JOF)

Listing: NYSE
Launched: March 1990
Offering Price: $12.00
Investment Manager: Nomura Capital Management
Total Shares: 8,500,000
Total Net Assets: $81 million
Market Capitalization: $67 million

Management Fees: 1.10% of average weekly net assets of $50 million or less, 1.00% of same assets in excess of $50 million but less than $100 million, and 0.90% in excess of $100 million.

Recent Dividends: None

INVESTMENT OBJECTIVE:
Long-term capital appreciation through investment primarily in equity securities traded in the Japanese over-the-counter market.

Current Disc./Prem.: −17%
52-Week Range: +48% to −25%
Avg. Discount/Premium: +9%

SECTOR BREAKDOWN:

NEW FUND
DATA UNAVAILABLE

TOP TEN HOLDINGS:

NEW FUND
DATA UNAVAILABLE

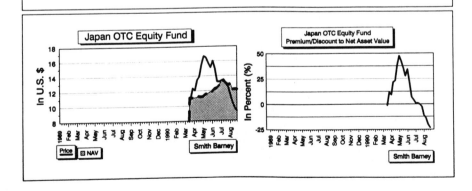

KOREA FUND (KF)

Listing: NYSE
Launched: August 1984
Offering Price (adj.): $4.00
Investment Manager: Scudder, Stevens & Clark
Total Shares: 20,966,704
Total Net Assets: $231 million
Market Capitalization: $257 million

Management Fees: 1.05% of average net assets

Expense Ratio: 1.44%
Recent Dividends: $0.49 paid 01/23/90
                  $1.45 paid 09/25/90

INVESTMENT OBJECTIVE:
Long-term capital appreciation through investment primarily in equity securities of South Korean companies.

Current Disc./Prem.: +11%
52-Week Range: +120% to +16%
Avg. Discount/Premium: +65%

SECTOR BREAKDOWN: June 30, 1990:

Industry	% of Assets
Basic Industry	32.7
Consumer Cyclical	17.0
Technology	14.5
Consumer Nondurable	13.2
Financial	9.4
Media & Services	4.4
Energy	2.6
Health	2.3
Producer Durables	1.9
Utilities	0.6
Cash	1.4
Total	100.0

TOP TEN HOLDINGS: June 30, 1990:

Company	Industry	% of Net Assets
Samsung Electronics Co., Ltd.	Technology	8.1
Lucky Ltd.	Basic Industry	6.2
Korea Long Term Credit Bank	Financial	4.8
Samsung Co., Ltd.	Media & Services	4.3
Daelim Industrial Co., Ltd.	Basic Industry	4.2
Korean Airlines Co., Ltd.	Consumer Cyclical	4.1
Hyundai Motor Services Co. Ltd.	Consumer Cyclical	3.7
Samsung Electromechanics Co., Ltd.	Technology	3.7
Hyundai Motor Co., Ltd.	Consumer Cyclical	2.9
Cheil Food & Chemical	Consumer Nondurables	2.8
		44.6

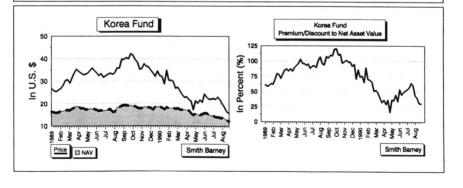

LATIN AMERICA INVESTMENT FUND# (LAM)

Listing: NYSE
Launched: July 1990
Offering Price: $15.00
Investment Manager: BEA Associates, Inc.
Sovereign Debt Advisor: Solomon Bros. Asset Mgmt.
Total Shares: 4,000,000
Total Assets: $51 million
Market Capitalization: $37 million

Management and Other Fees: 1.25% of first $100 million, 1.15% of next $50 million and 1.05% of excess.

Expense Ratio: N.A.
Recent Dividends: None

INVESTMENT OBJECTIVE:
Long-term capital appreciation through investment primarily in Latin American debt and equity securities. The Fund intends to have at least 65% of its total assets in Mexico, Chile and Brazil.

Current Disc./Prem.: –28%
52-Week Range: +5% to –28%
Avg. Discount/Premium: –14%

GEOGRAPHIC BREAKDOWN:

NEW FUND
DATA UNAVAILABLE

TOP TEN HOLDINGS:

NEW FUND
DATA UNAVAILABLE

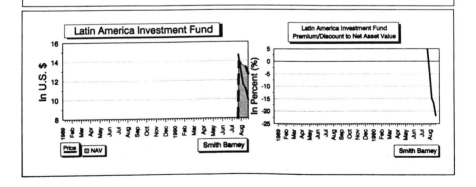

MALAYSIA FUND (MF)

Listing: NYSE
Launched: May 1987
Offering Price: $12.00
Investment Manager: Arab-Malaysian Consultant
Total Shares: 7,259,233
Total Net Assets: $84 million
Market Capitalization: $83 million

Management Fees: 0.84% of average net assets
Sub-Advisory Fee: 0.22% of average net assets

Expense Ratio: 1.77%
Recent Dividends: $0.11 paid 01/16/90

INVESTMENT OBJECTIVE:
Long-term capital appreciation through investment in equity
securities of Malaysian companies.

Current Disc./Prem.: -1%
52-Week Range: +75% to -9%
Avg. Discount/Premium: +18%

SECTOR BREAKDOWN: June 30, 1990:

Industry	% of Assets
Industrial & Commercial	70.7
Finance Companies	12.5
Property & Development	7.3
Dollar Rubbers & Plantations	2.6
Oil Palms	2.3
Tin & Mines	1.8
Cash	2.8
Total	100.0

TOP TEN HOLDINGS: June 30, 1990:

Company	Industry	% of Net Assets
Sime Darby	Industrial & Commercial	5.6
Malayan Banking	Finance Company	5.1
Malaysian International Shipping	Industrial & Commercial	4.5
Genting	Industrial & Commercial	4.4
Malaysian Airlines System	Industrial & Commercial	4.0
Perlis Plantations	Industrial & Commercial	3.6
Rothmans of Pall Mall	Industrial & Commercial	3.5
Tan Chong	Industrial & Commercial	3.4
Amalgamated Steel Mills	Industrial & Commercial	2.9
Public Bank	Finance Company	2.7
		39.7

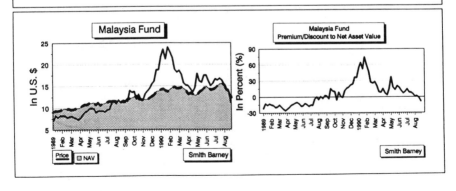

MEXICO FUND (MXF)

Listing: NYSE
Launched: June 1981
Offering Price: $12.00
Investment Manager: Impulsora de Funda Mexico S.A.
Total Shares: 19,718,204
Total Net Assets: $266 million
Market Capitalization: $227 million

Management Fees: 0.85% on first $200 million and 0.70% on excess.

Expense Ratio: 1.60%

Recent Dividends: $0.28 paid 08/31/90.
$0.039 paid 05/31/90
$0.063 paid 01/31/90

INVESTMENT OBJECTIVE:
Long-term capital appreciation through investment primarily in equities of Mexican companies.

Current Disc./Prem.: −15%
52-Week Range: +14% to −20%
Avg. Discount/Premium: −4%

SECTOR BREAKDOWN: May 31, 1990:

Industry	% of Assets
Development Companies	21.1
Retail Trade	11.7
Mining	10.0
Electronics	9.3
Construction	8.8
Chemicals & Petrochemicals	7.0
Communications	6.8
Consumer Goods	6.2
Banks	6.0
Paper	6.0
Other	1.1
Cash	6.0
Total	100.0

TOP TEN HOLDINGS: May 31, 1990:

Company	Industry	% of Net Assets
CIFRA	Retail Trade	8.4
Telefonos de Mexico, S.A.	Communications	6.8
Grupo Industrial Minera Mexico, S.A.	Mining	6.5
Kimberly-Clark de Mexico, S.A.	Paper	5.4
Vitro, S.A.	Development Company	5.3
Cemex, S.A.	Construction	5.2
Grupo Industrial Alfa, S.A.	Development Company	5.0
Grupo Condumex, S.A.	Electronics	4.5
Desc Sociedad de Fomento Industrial, S.A.	Development Company	4.3
Teleindustrial Ericsson, S.A.	Electronics	3.9
		55.2

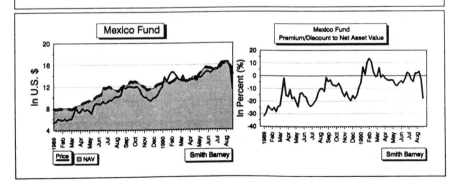

MEXICO EQUITY AND INCOME FUND (MXE)

Listing: NYSE
Launched: August 1990
Offering Price: $12.00
Local Advisor: Acci Worldwide, S.A.
U.S. Co-Advisor: Advantage Advisors, Inc.
Total Shares: 6,000,000
Total Net Assets: $69 million
Market Capitalization: $57 million

Management Fees: 0.998% of average monthly assets.

Expense Ratio: N.A.

Recent Dividends: None

INVESTMENT OBJECTIVE:
High total return from capital appreciation and current income through investment in convertible debt securities issued by Mexican companies and equity and other debt issued by Mexican issuers. The Fund will invest at least 50% in convertible debt securities issued by Mexican companies.

Current Disc./Prem.: –17%
52-Week Range: +2% to 0%
Avg. Discount/Premium: +1%

SECTOR BREAKDOWN:

NEW FUND
DATA UNAVAILABLE

TOP TEN HOLDINGS:

NEW FUND
DATA UNAVAILABLE

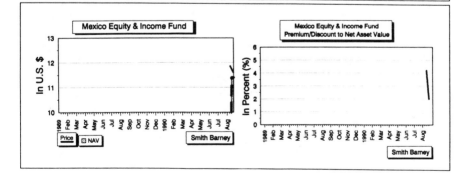

NEW GERMANY FUND (GF)

Listing: NYSE
Launched: January 1990
Offering Price: $15.00
Investment Manager: DB Capital Management International
Total Shares: 28,757,169
Total Net Assets: $341 million
Market Capitalization: $280 million

Management Fees: 0.65% of weekly assets up to $100 million and 0.55% of assets over $100 million.

Recent Dividends: None

INVESTMENT OBJECTIVE:
Long-term capital appreciation through investment primarily in equity securities of West German companies.

Current Disc./Prem.: -18%
52-Week Range: +51% to -21%
Avg. Discount/Premium: -1%

SECTOR BREAKDOWN: June 30, 1990:

Industry	% of Assets
Engineering/Specialists	9.3
Retailing/Apparel	8.2
Engineering/Plant Construction/Other	8.2
Chemical	8.1
Electrical	7.9
Steel Manufacturing	6.7
Insurance	6.4
Utilities	6.2
Automotive	6.0
Consumer Goods/Cosmetics	5.6
Construction/Construction Materials	4.0
Food	3.4
Non-Ferrous Metals	2.8
Machinery/Machine Tools	2.5
Pharmaceuticals	2.2
Other	4.2
Cash	8.3
	100.0

TOP TEN HOLDINGS: June 30, 1990:

Company	Industry	% of Net Assets
Siemens	Electrical	3.5
Allianz Holdings	Insurance	3.4
Volkswagen	Automotive	3.2
Munchener Ruckversicherung	Insurance	2.9
Douglas Holding	Retail	2.8
Kaufhof	Retail	2.5
GEA	Engineering/Plant Construction	2.4
Hoesch	Steel Manufacturing	2.4
Bayer AG	Chemicals	2.3
Moksel	Food	1.6
		27.0

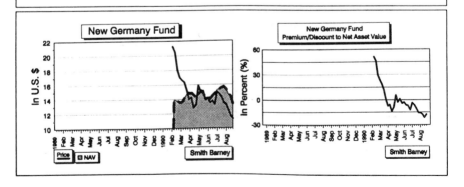

PACIFIC–EUROPEAN GROWTH FUND (PEF)

Listing: NYSE Launched: April 1990 Offering Price: $12.00 Investment Advisor: Piper Capital Management Total Shares: 3,000,000 Total Net Assets: $27 million Market Capitalization: $26 million	Advisory Fees: 1.00% of average weekly net assets up to $100 million, 0.875% between $100 and $200 million, and 0.75% of excess. Dividends: None

INVESTMENT OBJECTIVE: Long-term capital appreciation through investment primarily in equity securities of companies in the Pacific Basin (Hong Kong, Malaysia, Singapore and Thailand), or in Europe (including Eastern Europe).	Current Disc./Prem.: –3% 52–Week Range: +16% to –10% Avg. Discount/Premium: +3%

COUNTRY BREAKDOWN: July 1990:

	% of Assets
Austria	1.0
Belgium	0.9
France	6.6
Germany	7.6
Hong Kong	17.8
Indonesia	4.2
Italy	3.0
Korea	1.6
Malaysia	10.9
Netherlands	3.3
Norway	0.7
Philippines	1.3
Singapore	4.2
Spain	2.2
Sweden	0.5
Switzerland	2.2
Thailand	6.3
Cash	25.7
Total	100.0

TOP TEN HOLDINGS:

NEW FUND
DATA UNAVAILABLE

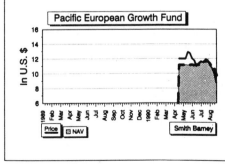

PORTUGAL FUND (PGF)

Listing: NYSE
Launched: November 1989
Offering Price: $15.00
Investment Manager: BEA Associates
Total Shares: 5,297,253
Total Net Assets: $61 million
Market Capitalization: $46 million

Management Fees: 1.20% of first $50 million, 1.15% of next $50 million, and 1.10% of amounts over $100 million.

Expense Ratio: 1.98%

Recent Dividends: $0.84 paid 12/29/89

INVESTMENT OBJECTIVE:
Long-term capital appreciation through investment primarily in equity securities of Portugese companies.

Current Disc./Prem.: –26%
52–Week Range: +40% to –28%
Avg. Discount/Premium: +6%

SECTOR BREAKDOWN: June 30, 1990:

Industry	% of Assets
Chemicals & Petroleum Products	8.9
Construction & Public Works	8.8
Banks	7.3
Retail Trade	7.1
Metal Products	7.0
Non-Metallic Mineral Products	6.4
Financial Institutions	6.1
Real Estate & Services	5.9
Transports & Warehousing	5.3
Wood & Cork	5.3
Communications	2.1
Cash & Other Investments	29.8
Total	100.0

TOP TEN HOLDINGS: June 30, 1990:

Company	Industry	% of Net Assets
Continente SA	Retail Trade	5.6
Corticeira Amorim	Wood & Cork	5.3
Banco Commercial Portuguese	Banking	4.3
Tertir Terminais de Portugal	Transports & Warehousing	4.1
Soares da Costa	Construction	3.5
Banco Portuguese de Investimento	Banking	3.2
Jeronimo Martins	Chemicals & Petroleum	3.0
Sociedad Financeira Locacao Sofinloc	Financial Institution	2.9
Cerexport, Ceramica de Exportacao	Non-Metallic Products	2.7
Mota e Companhia	Construction & Public Works	2.6
		37.2

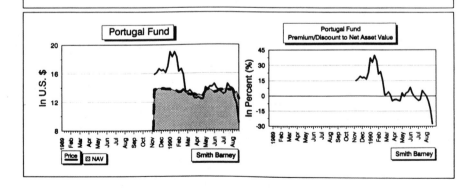

SCUDDER NEW ASIA FUND (SAF)

Listing: NYSE
Launched: June 1987
Offering Price: $12.00
Investment Manager: Scudder, Stevens & Clark
Total Shares: 7,026,245
Total Net Assets: $105 million
Market Capitalization: $87 million

Management Fees: 1.15% of first $50 million, 1.10% of next $50 million, and 1.00% of excess.

Expense Ratio: 1.84%
Recent Dividends: $1.38 paid 01/23/90
$0.18 paid 03/30/90

INVESTMENT OBJECTIVE:
Long-term capital appreciation through investment primarily in equity securities of Asian companies, including, in particular, equity securities of smaller Japanese companies.

Current Disc./Prem.: -18%
52-Week Range: -4% to -25%
Avg. Discount/Premium: -16%

SECTOR BREAKDOWN: June 30, 1990:

Industry	% of Assets
Financial	19.3
Technology	16.1
Basic Industry	14.6
Consumer Nondurables	13.7
Producer Durables	9.3
Utilities	8.0
Media & Service	6.5
Consumer Cyclical	6.3
Health	0.1
Cash and Other Short-Term Investments	6.1
Total	100.0

COUNTRY BREAKDOWN: June 30, 1990:

Country	% of Portfolio
Japan	45.0
Thailand	11.2
Hong Kong	8.3
Malaysia	6.2
India	5.5
Indonesia	4.5
The Philippines	3.2
Singapore	3.2
Korea	3.0
Other	3.8
Total	93.9

TOP TEN HOLDINGS: June 30, 1990:

Company	Industry	% of Net Assets
Japan Associated Finance	Venture Capital	4.4
MKC, Ltd.	Software	4.4
The India Fund	Investment Company	4.0
Cable & Wireless PLC	Communications	2.4
Siam Cement Co., Ltd.	Construction Materials	2.4
Dusit Thani Corporation	Hotel Operator	2.2
Asatsu	Advertising	2.2
Ines Corporation	Data Processing	1.9
American Standard Sanitaryware	Bathroom Fixture Manufacturer	1.9
Nintendo Co., Ltd.	Game Equipment Manufacturer	1.8
		27.7

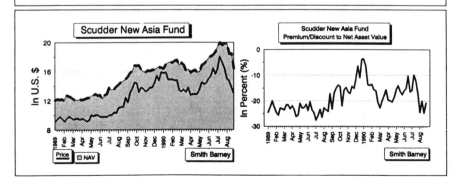

SCUDDER NEW EUROPE (NEF)

Listing: NYSE	Management Fees: 1.25% of assets up to $75 mil., 1.15% on next $125 million, 1.10 in excess of $200 million.
Launched: February 1990	
Offering Price: $12.50	
Invest. Mgr.: Scudder, Stevens & Clark, Inc.	
Total Shares: 16,008,603	Expense Ratio: 1.84%
Total Net Assets: $166 million	Recent Dividends: None
Market Capitalization: $130 million	

INVESTMENT OBJECTIVE:
Long-term capital appreciation through investment primarily in equity securities of companies traded on smaller or emerging European markets and companies that are viewed as likely to benefit from changes and developments throughout Europe.

Current Disc./Prem.: -22%
52-Week Range: +9% to -23%
Avg. Discount/Premium: -11%

SECTOR BREAKDOWN: April 30, 1990:

Industry	% of Assets
Credit and Finance	24.5
Banking	15.6
Govt. of France Bonds	8.7
U.K. T-Bills	8.6
Kingdom of Sweden Bonds	8.0
Kingdom of Belgium Bonds	6.5
Technology	6.1
Kingdom of Denmark Bonds	5.1
Republic of Ireland Bonds	4.4
Basic Industry	4.3
Producer Durables	2.7
Consumer Durables	2.5
Other	3.0
Total	100.0

COUNTRY BREAKDOWN OF EQUITIES: April 30, 1990:

Country	% of Portfolio
Austria	0.5
Finland	1.0
France	2.9
Germany	4.9
Italy	1.7
Norway	1.4
Portugal	0.5
Spain	3.8
Switzerland	2.5
U.K.	3.7
Total	22.9

TOP TEN HOLDINGS: April 30, 1990:

Company	Industry	% of Net Assets
Banco Pastor SA (Spain)	Bank	1.7
Ciga Hotels SPA (Italy)	Hotels	1.5
Phoenix Mecano (Switzerland)	Computer Components	1.4
Gluntz AG (Germany)	Plywood Products	1.4
Deutsche Bank AG (Germany)	Bank	1.2
Siemens AG (Germany)	Electrical and Electronics	1.2
Compagnie Generale d'Electricite (France)	Diversified	1.2
Sika Finanz (Switzerland)	Construction Chemicals	1.2
Mannesmann AG (Germany)	Construction and Technology	1.1
Diamond Cruise, Ltd. (Finland)	Cruise Ship Operator	1.0
		12.8

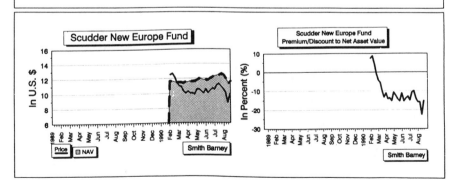

Scudder New Europe Fund

Price   NAV   Smith Barney

Scudder New Europe Fund
Premium/Discount to Net Asset Value

Smith Barney

THE SINGAPORE FUND (SGF)

Listing: NYSE
Launched: August 1990
Offering Price: $12.00
Inv. Manager: DBS Asset Management Pte. Ltd
Total Shares: 5,009,000
Total Net Assets: $54 million
Market Capitalization: $41 million

Management and Other Fees: 1.2% of assets up to $50 mil,
1.0% of excess

Expense Ratio: N.A.
Recent Dividends: None

INVESTMENT OBJECTIVE:
Long term capital appreciation through investment
primarily in Singapore equity securities.

Current Disc./Prem.: –25%
52-Week Range: +8% to –21%
Avg. Discount/Premium: –13%

SECTOR BREAKDOWN:

NEW FUND
DATA UNAVAILABLE

TOP TEN HOLDINGS:

NEW FUND
DATA UNAVAILABLE

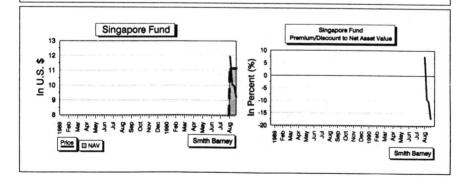

SPAIN FUND (SNF)

Listing: NYSE
Launched: June 1988
Offering Price: $12.00
Investment Manager: Alliance Capital Management
Total Shares: 10,010,356
Total Net Assets: $114 million
Market Capitalization: $108 million

Management Fees: 1.00% up to $50 million, 0.9% of next $50 million, and 0.8% of excess.

Expense Ratio: 1.93%
Recent Dividends: $0.98 paid 01/12/90

INVESTMENT OBJECTIVE:
Long-term capital appreciation primarily through investment in equity securities of Spanish companies.

Current Disc./Prem.: –5%
52–Week Range: +145% to –6%
Average Discount/Premium: +60%

SECTOR BREAKDOWN: May 31, 1990:

Industry	% of Assets
Utilities	17.0
Finance	15.9
Energy	8.9
Capital Goods	8.3
Consumer Services	8.2
Consumer Manufacturing	8.1
Basic Industries	7.5
Consumer Staples	6.7
Health Care	1.6
Technologies	0.8
Cash/Other Investments	17.0
Total	83.0

TOP TEN HOLDINGS: May 31, 1990:

Company	Industry	% of Net Assets
Repsol S.A.	Petroleum	6.6
Antena 3 Radio	Broadcasting & Cable	6.4
Tabacalera S.A.	Tobacco	4.2
Corporacion Mapfre	Insurance	3.9
Compania Telefonica Nacional de Espana	Telephone Utility	3.8
FOSCA	Engineering & Construction	3.2
Aumar	Utilities	2.9
Hidroelectric Iberica	Utilities	2.9
Antena 3 Television	Broadcasting & Cable	2.9
Huarte S.A.	Engineering & Construction	2.3
		39.1

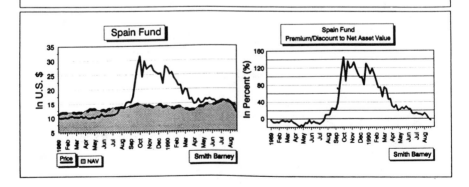

SWISS HELVETIA FUND# (SWZ)

Listing: NYSE
Launched: August 1987
Offering Price: $15.00
Investment Manager: Helvetia Capital Corp.
Total Shares: 8,007,168
Total Net Assets: $100 million
Market Capitalization: $90 million

Management Fees: 1.0% of first $60 million, 0.9% of next $40 million, and 0.8% of excess.

Expense Ratio: 1.85%
Recent Dividends: $0.05 payable 10/30/90.

INVESTMENT OBJECTIVE:
Long-term capital appreciation through investment primarily in equity securities of Swiss companies. The Fund has large holdings in Swiss registered and bearer shares.

Current Disc./Prem.: -10%
52-Week Range: +16% to -13%
Avg. Discount/Premium: 0%

SECTOR BREAKDOWN: June 30, 1990:

Industry	% of Assets
Pharmaceuticals	18.6
Machinery & Metals	14.8
Food & Beverage	13.0
Insurance	12.2
Chemicals	8.5
Miscellaneous Services	7.3
Banks	6.8
Miscellaneous Industries	4.5
Other	6.2
Cash	8.1
	100.0

TOP TEN HOLDINGS: June 30, 1990:

Company	Industry	% of Net Assets
Roche Holdings	Pharmaceuticals	13.7
Nestle AG	Food & Beverage	13.0
Ciga Geigy AG	Chemicals	7.3
Sandoz AG	Pharmaceuticals	4.9
BBC Brown Boveri Ltd.	Machinery & Metals	4.7
Union Bank of Switzerland	Bank	4.6
Surveillance	Inspection	4.1
Zurich Insurance	Insurance	2.8
Holzstoff Holding AG	Paper Manufacturing	2.7
Lindt & Spruengli AG	Confectionary	2.6
		60.4

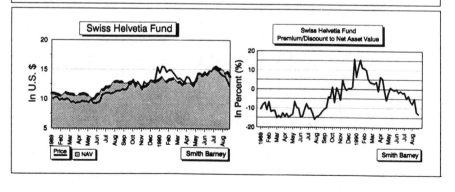

THE TAIWAN FUND (TWN)

Listing: NYSE
Launched: December 1986
Offering Price: $12.00
Investment Manager: China Securities Investment Trust
Total Shares: 4,214,561
Total Net Assets: $68 million
Market Capitalization: $61 million

Management Fees: 1.50% of average assets.

Expense Ratio: 1.21%
Recent Dividends: $1.69 paid 06/26/90.
$14.75 paid 01/26/90

INVESTMENT OBJECTIVE:
Long-term capital appreciation through investment primarily
in equity securities of Taiwan companies.

Current Disc./Prem.: –10%
52-Week Range: +98% to –23%
Avg. Discount/Premium: +19%

SECTOR BREAKDOWN: June 30, 1990:

Industry	% of Assets
Chemicals	8.8
Textiles & Apparel	3.7
Electrical & Electronics	3.6
Banking	3.3
Building Materials/Components	2.4
Food & Household Products	2.1
Transportation – Shipping	1.0
Forest Products & Paper	0.8
Construction & Housing	0.7
Automobiles	0.5
Other	1.0
Cash & Other Assets/Liabilities – Net	72.1
	100.0

TOP TEN HOLDINGS: June 30, 1990:

Company	Industry	% of Net Assets
Nan Ya Plastic	Chemicals	2.1
Formosa Chemical & Fibre	Chemicals	2.0
Formosa Plastic	Chemicals	2.0
President Enterprises	Food & Household Products	1.9
Tatung	Electrical & Electronics	1.8
Teco Electric & Machinery	Electrical & Electronics	1.6
Formosa Taffeta	Textiles & Apparel	1.5
Far East Textile	Textiles & Apparel	1.4
Taiwan Synthetic Rubber	Chemicals	1.2
Asia Cement	Building Materials/Components	1.1
		16.5

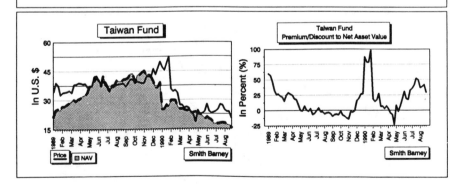

THAI FUND (TTF)

Listing: NYSE
Launched: February 1988
Offering Price: $12.00
Investment Manager: Mutual Fund Co. Ltd.
Total Shares: 9,835,108
Total Net Assets: $153 million
Market Capitalization: $173 million

Management and Other Fees: 1.3% of first $50 million, 0.95% of next $50 million, 0.7% thereafter.

Expense Ratio: 1.79%

Recent Dividends: $2.45 paid 01/16/90

INVESTMENT OBJECTIVE:
Long-term capital appreciation through investment primarily in equity securities organized under the laws of the Kingdom of Thailand.

Current Disc./Prem.: +14%
52-Week Range: +91% to –8%
Avg. Discount/Premium: +30%

SECTOR BREAKDOWN: June 30, 1990:

Industry	% of Assets
Financial	37.8
Construction Material	24.3
Commercial	8.4
Textile and Clothing	4.7
Food and Beverage	3.7
Hotel	2.9
Mining	2.5
Other	12.6
Debentures	0.4
Cash	2.7
	100.0

TOP TEN HOLDINGS: June 30, 1990:

Company	Industry	% of Net Assets
Siam Cement	Construction	10.5
The Siam Commercial Bank	Construction	5.6
The Siam City Cement Co.	Construction	4.8
National Finance & Securities Co.	Finance	4.3
Phatra Thanakit Co.	Finance	3.7
Bangkok Bank Ltd.	Finance	3.6
The Thai Farmers Bank	Finance	3.3
Dhana Siam Finance and Securities Co.	Finance	3.3
Thai Investment and Securities Co.	Finance	3.3
Thai-German Ceramic Industry Co.	Construction	3.1
		45.3

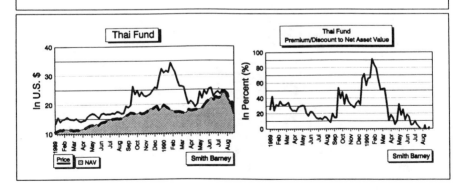

TEMPLETON EMERGING MARKETS FUND (EMF)

Listing: NYSE
Launched: February 1987
Offering Price: $10.00
Investment Manager: Templeton, Galbraith & Hansberger
Total Shares: 11,510,753
Total Net Assets: $159 million
Market Capitalization: $135 million

Management Fees: 1.25% on average net assets

Expense Ratio: 2.03%
Recent Dividends: $0.18 paid 12/28/89
$0.15 paid 10/31/89

INVESTMENT OBJECTIVE:
Long-term capital appreciation primarily through investment
in equities of emerging markets around the world. Currently,
the geographic distribution of assets is broken down as follows:
Asia (65%); Latin America (17%); Middle East & Mediterranean
(11%); and 10% in other emerging market areas such as Africa.

Current Disc./Prem.: -15%
52-Week Range: +14% to -19%
Avg. Discount/Premium: -2%

SECTOR BREAKDOWN: May 31, 1990:

Industry	% of Assets
Multi-Industries	15.2
Telecommunications	12.3
Banking & Financial Services	11.5
Food & Household	7.8
Real Estate	7.0
Building Materials & Components	5.6
Transportation	4.4
Merchandising	3.2
Energy Sources	2.4
Chemicals	2.2
Automobiles	2.1
Industrial Components	1.3
Other	10.7
Cash & Other Investments	14.3
Total	100.0

COUNTRY BREAKDOWN: May 31, 1990:

Country	% of Assets
Hong Kong	26
Mexico	2
Turkey	8
Thailand	4
The Philippines	6
Malaysia	5
Greece	5
Chile	4
Argentina	3
Nigeria	2
Brazil	1
Other	14
Total	80

TOP TEN HOLDINGS: May 31, 1990:

Company	Industry	% of Net Assets
Telefonos de Mexico, S.A.	Telecommunications	9.6
Jardine Matheson Holdings	Multi-Industries	4.6
Dairy Farm International	Food & Household Products	3.3
Hutchison Whampoa Ltd.	Multi-Industries	3.1
Antafagasta Holdings PLC	Transportation	2.9
Hong Kong & Shanghai Bank	Banking & Financial Services	2.9
Cheung Kong Holdings	Real Estate	2.5
CIFRA SA	Merchandising	2.4
Siam Cement	Building Materials	2.4
Swire Pacific Ltd.	Multi-Industries	2.4
		36.1

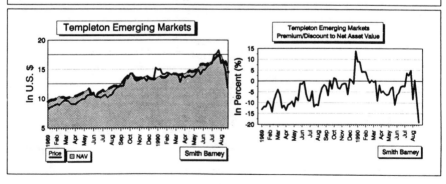

THAI CAPITAL FUND (TC)

Listing: NYSE
Launched: mAY 1990
Offering Price: $12.00
Investment Manager: The Mutual Fund Co., Ltd.
Total Shares: 6,009,000
Total Net Assets: $50 million
Market Capitalization: $38 million

Management Fees: 1.20% of avg. assets

Expense Ratio: 1.75%
Recent Dividends: None

INVESTMENT OBJECTIVE:
Long term capital appreciation through
investment primarily in equity
securities of Thai companies.

Current Disc./Prem.: -24%
52-Week Range: +10% to -19%
Avg. Discount/Premium: -3%

SECTOR BREAKDOWN: June 30, 1990

Industry	% of Assets
Construction Materials	9.6
Financial	8.1
Food and Beverage	4.2
Commercial	3.7
Electrical Equipment	3.4
Services	1.4
Automotive	1.2
Mining	0.8
Packaging	0.5
Hotel	0.3
Other	5.3
CASH	61.5
	100.0

TOP TEN HOLDINGS: April 30, 1990

Company	Industry	% of Net Assets
The Siam Cement Co.	Construction Materials	3.1
The Siam Commercial Bank, Ltd.	Financial	2.5
Land and House Co., Ltd.	Real Estate	1.9
Thai Wire Products Co.	Construction Materials	1.9
The Serm Suk Co.	Food and Beverage	1.8
Thai-German Ceramic Industry Co.	Construction Materials	1.7
The Thai Farmers Bank	Financial	1.6
Ayudhya Insurance Co., Ltd.	Financial	1.6
Bank of Ayudhya, Ltd.	Financial	1.6
M.K. Real Estate Development Corp.	Real Estate	1.5
		19.3

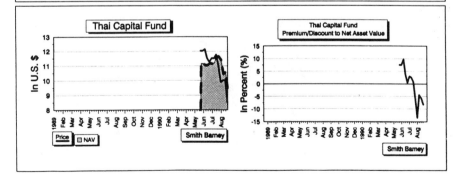

Thai Capital Fund

Thai Capital Fund
Premium/Discount to Net Asset Value

Price NAV

Smith Barney

Smith Barney

TURKISH INVESTMENT FUND (TKF)

Listing: NYSE
Launched: December 1989
Offering Price: $12.00
Investment Manager: Morgan Stanley Asset Management
Total Shares: 7,023,431
Total Net Assets: $106 million
Market Capitalization: $71 million

Management Fees: $0.95% of first $50 million of average weekly assets, 0.75% in excess of $50 million and 0.55% over $100 million.
Advisory Fees: 0.20% of first $50 million of average weekly assets, 0.10% in excess of $50 million and 0.05% over $100 million.
Expense Ratio: 1.72%
Recent Dividends: $0.03 paid 01/16/90

INVESTMENT OBJECTIVE:
Long-term capital appreciation through investment primarily in equity securities of Turkish corporations.

Current Disc./Prem.: –33%
52-Week Range: +8% to –33%
Avg. Discount/Premium: –19%

ASSET ALLOCATION: April 30, 1990:

	% of Assets
Equities	67.4
Temporary Cash Investments	25.0
Foreign Currency on Deposit	7.3
Other Assets/Liabilities	0.3
Total	100.0

TOP TEN HOLDINGS: April 30, 1990:

Company	Industry	% of Net Assets
Otosan	Auto	15.2
Eregli Demi Celik	Steel	14.3
Celik Halat	Steel	6.0
Izmir Demir Celik	Steel	5.0
Maret	Food	4.1
KAV	Match Manufacturer	4.0
Arcelik	Household Appliances	3.5
Rabak	Metals	2.8
Turk Tubourg	Brewery	2.4
Cukurova Elektrik	Utility	2.1
		59.4

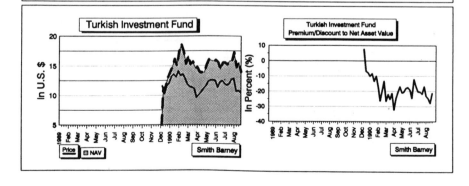

UNITED KINGDOM FUND (UKM)

Listing: NYSE
Launched: August 1987
Offering Price: $12.50
Investment Advisor: Warburg Investment Management
Total Shares: 4,008,602
Total Net Assets: $42 million
Market Capitalization: $35 million

Expense Ratio: 1.86%

Recent Dividends: $0.435 paid 01/12/90
$0.16 paid 07/16/90

INVESTMENT OBJECTIVE:
Long-term capital appreciation through investment primarily in equity securities of United Kingdom companies.

Current Disc./Prem.: -17%
52-Week Range: -5% to -24%
Avg. Discount/Premium: -13%

ASSET ALLOCATION: July 31, 1990:

	% of Assets
Stocks	87.0
Sterling-Denominated Cash	12.9
Dollar-Denominated Cash	0.1
Total	100.0

TOP TEN HOLDINGS: July 31, 1990:

Company	Industry	Approximate Dollar Value
Cable & Wireless	Electrical	2.8
Porter Chadburn	Industrial	2.7
Blue Circle Industries	Building Materials	2.6
ASDA Group	Food, Groceries	2.3
Alexander Proudfoot	Industrial	2.3
ASW Holdings	Engineering	2.3
BAT Industries	Tobacco	2.2
General Electric	Electrical	2.1
Great Universal Stores	Stores	2.0
Westpool Investment Trust	Finance	1.8
Total		23.1
Percentage of Total Equities		55.0%
Percentage of Total Net Assets		47.8%

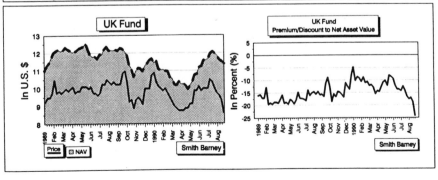

APPENDIX I: WORLD MARKET PERFORMANCE DATA (LOCAL CURRENCY TERMS)
(PRICED AS OF 9/30/90)

PRICE PERFORMANCE OF MAJOR WORLD MARKETS (IN LOCAL CURRENCY)
(RANKED BY % CHANGE SINCE 08/01/90.)

	PRICE AS OF 09/30/90	% CHG SINCE 08/01/90	PRICE AS OF 06/30/90	% CHG SINCE 06/30/90	PRICE AS OF 12/31/89	% CHG SINCE 12/31/89	PRICE AS OF 12/31/88	% CHG SINCE 12/31/88	52 WEEK RANGE HIGH	LOW	% CHG SINCE HIGH	% CHG SINCE LOW	1980-1990 RANGE HIGH	LOW	% CHG SINCE HIGH	% CHG SINCE LOW
INDIA	706	26.4%	439	60.9%	419	68.5%	340	NA	730	369	-3%	91%	730	100	-3%	606%
GOLD: BULLION	405	8.4%	353	14.7%	401	0.9%	410	-1.3%	423	346	-4%	17%	835	285	-52%	42%
NORWAY	787	-13.0%	826	-4.6%	687	14.6%	468	68.3%	915	606	-14%	30%	915	94	-14%	738%
AUSTRALIA	1,398	-11.9%	1,501	-6.8%	1,649	-15.2%	1,487	-6.0%	1,776	1,385	-21%	1%	2,306	443	-39%	216%
SOUTH AFRICA	2,660	-12.6%	2,968	-10.4%	2,768	-3.9%	1,954	36.1%	3,211	2,306	-17%	15%	3,208	457	-17%	482%
CANADA	3,159	-11.5%	3,544	-10.9%	3,970	-20.4%	3,390	-6.8%	4,038	3,159	-22%	0%	4,038	1,346	-22%	135%
DENMARK	332	-13.8%	377	-12.1%	363	-8.7%	272	22.0%	388	322	-15%	3%	388	58	-15%	472%
UNITED STATES	306	-13.9%	358	-14.5%	353	-13.4%	278	10.2%	369	301	-17%	2%	369	98	-17%	212%
MEXICO	522,083	-10.0%	615,333	-15.2%	418,925	24.6%	211,531	146.8%	679,665	368,021	-23%	42%	679,665	480	-23%	108577%
HOLLAND	168	-15.8%	199	-15.6%	203	-17.4%	166	1.1%	208	168	-19%	0%	211	51	-20%	232%
HONG KONG	2,761	-20.4%	3,278	-15.8%	2,837	-2.7%	2,687	2.7%	3,560	2,602	-22%	6%	3,950	676	-30%	308%
UK	1,990	-14.9%	2,375	-16.2%	2,423	-17.9%	1,793	11.0%	2,464	1,990	-19%	0%	2,464	509	-19%	291%
NEW ZEALAND	1,469	-18.5%	1,762	-16.6%	1,988	-26.1%	1,840	-20.2%	2,327	1,456	-37%	1%	3,969	357	-63%	311%
KOREA	598	-13.4%	720	-17.0%	910	-34.3%	907	-34.1%	943	566	-37%	6%	1,006	93	-41%	542%
BELGIUM	3,009	-20.1%	3,770	-20.2%	4,003	-24.8%	3,538	-14.9%	4,211	2,981	-29%	1%	4,215	704	-29%	327%
MALAYSIA	459	-27.4%	585	-21.5%	562	-18.4%	357	28.5%	633	456	-27%	1%	631	170	-27%	169%
FRANCE	415	-21.0%	545	-23.8%	554	-25.0%	416	-0.1%	565	410	-26%	1%	565	77	-26%	439%
SWITZERLAND	512	-23.4%	682	-24.8%	661	-22.5%	560	-8.5%	698	512	-27%	0%	734	264	-30%	94%
ITALY	558	-22.7%	754	-26.0%	687	-18.9%	590	-5.5%	764	554	-27%	1%	908	82	-39%	580%
SINGAPORE	1,099	-29.5%	1,527	-28.0%	1,481	-25.8%	1,039	5.8%	1,607	1,099	-32%	0%	1,607	430	-32%	156%
IRELAND	1,208	-22.9%	1,689	-28.5%	1,766	-31.6%	1,378	-12.3%	1,893	1,208	-36%	0%	1,893	1,000	-36%	21%
GERMANY	1,629	-30.1%	2,297	-29.1%	2,190	-25.6%	1,652	-1.4%	2,414	1,629	-33%	0%	2,414	650	-33%	151%
SPAIN	209	-29.0%	296	-29.2%	297	-29.5%	274	-23.7%	326	209	-36%	0%	329	39	-36%	437%
SWEDEN	3,179	-30.0%	4,599	-30.9%	4,275	-25.7%	3,444	-7.7%	4,661	3,179	-32%	0%	4,661	335	-32%	849%
AUSTRIA	402	-39.4%	604	-33.5%	493	-18.5%	219	83.2%	703	371	-43%	8%	703	99	-43%	309%
JAPAN	20,984	-32.0%	31,940	-34.3%	38,916	-46.1%	30,159	-30.4%	38,916	20,984	-46%	0%	38,916	6,476	-46%	224%
THAILAND	642	-43.9%	1,060	-39.5%	879	-27.0%	384	67.1%	1,144	614	-44%	4%	1,131	102	-43%	529%
PHILIPPINES	733	-44.1%	1,230	-40.4%	1,585	-53.8%	950	-22.9%	2,009	730	-64%	0%	2,009	102	-64%	617%
TAIWAN	2,705	-53.1%	5,157	-47.6%	9,624	-71.9%	5,119	-47.2%	12,425	2,597	-78%	4%	12,495	421	-78%	542%

APPENDIX II: WORLD MARKET PERFORMANCE DATA (IN U.S. $ TERMS)
(PRICED AS OF 9/30/90)

PRICE PERFORMANCE OF MAJOR WORLD MARKETS (IN U.S. DOLLAR TERMS)
(PRICED AS OF 9/30/90. RANKED BY % CHANGE SINCE 08/01/90.)

	% CHG SINCE 8/01/90	% CHG SINCE 6/30/90	% CHG SINCE 3/31/90	% CHG SINCE 12/31/89	% CHG SINCE 12/31/88	52-WEEK HIGH	52-WEEK LOW	1980-1990 % CHG SINCE HIGH	1980-1990 % CHG SINCE LOW
INDIA	22.1%	56.2%	60.7%	55.9%	72.4%	-3%	81%	-3%	156%
GOLD: BULLION	8.4%	14.7%	9.5%	-0.4%	-1.3%	-4%	17%	-52%	42%
TORONTO GOLDS	-1.4%	7.2%	-4.2%	-12.9%	22.6%	-19%	17%	-29%	172%
AUSTRALIA	-8.3%	-2.7%	-0.2%	-12.4%	-9.1%	-17%	7%	-32%	165%
NORWAY	-11.5%	0.7%	4.1%	26.5%	82.2%	-12%	49%	-12%	880%
CANADA	-11.7%	-9.9%	-12.0%	-19.4%	-3.9%	-21%	0%	-21%	163%
SOUTH AFRICA	-11.8%	-6.8%	-7.5%	-4.2%	27.3%	-18%	20%	-18%	203%
DENMARK	-12.4%	-6.7%	-5.7%	1.8%	40.1%	-13%	25%	-13%	482%
KOREA	-13.7%	-17.1%	-30.9%	-37.7%	-37.5%	-41%	6%	-45%	498%
UNITED STATES	-13.9%	-14.5%	-10.0%	-12.3%	10.2%	-17%	2%	-17%	212%
UK	-14.1%	-10.0%	0.7%	-4.3%	14.9%	-15%	14%	-15%	240%
HOLLAND	-14.5%	-10.4%	-8.7%	-10.3%	14.7%	-15%	5%	-15%	383%
NEW ZEALAND	-15.5%	-12.5%	-9.0%	-23.7%	-21.9%	-33%	1%	-64%	158%
BELGIUM	-18.8%	-18.1%	-16.3%	-19.4%	-4.7%	-20%	1%	-20%	422%
FRANCE	-19.6%	-18.7%	-13.7%	-16.6%	15.4%	-22%	2%	-22%	491%
SWITZERLAND	-20.0%	-18.0%	-5.7%	-7.7%	5.9%	-21%	3%	-21%	222%
HONG KONG	-20.4%	-15.3%	-7.2%	-5.1%	3.5%	-22%	8%	-29%	339%
IRELAND	-21.5%	-23.8%	-25.1%	-24.6%	-0.1%	-30%	0%	-30%	396%
ITALY	-23.2%	-22.8%	-13.6%	-11.8%	5.3%	-24%	2%	-24%	372%
MALAYSIA	-27.5%	-21.1%	-20.6%	-17.9%	29.1%	-28%	1%	-28%	162%
JAPAN	-27.6%	-27.7%	-20.3%	-44.4%	-37.1%	-44%	0%	-44%	500%
SINGAPORE	-27.9%	-24.9%	-25.7%	-20.6%	16.7%	-28%	0%	-28%	217%
SPAIN	-28.9%	-25.9%	-8.8%	-21.1%	-11.6%	-30%	0%	-30%	549%
GERMANY	-29.0%	-24.6%	-27.0%	-17.9%	11.6%	-30%	12%	-30%	301%
SWEDEN	-29.2%	-27.6%	-13.5%	-18.5%	-1.9%	-30%	0%	-30%	584%
AUSTRIA	-38.2%	-29.1%	-35.8%	-8.3%	107.7%	-39%	28%	-39%	726%
THAILAND	-43.4%	-38.2%	-23.1%	-24.6%	64.2%	-43%	5%	-43%	428%
PHILIPPINES	-47.8%	-46.1%	-58.0%	-60.2%	-35.3%	-69%	0%	-69%	457%
TAIWAN	-53.8%	-48.3%	-75.5%	-72.7%	-46.7%	-79%	4%	-79%	370%

APPENDIX III: SELECTED DATA
(PRICED AS OF 9/30/90)

REGIONAL AND SPECIALIZED CLOSED-END COUNTRY FUNDS

SELECTED DATA

	LISTING/ SYMBOL	WHEN ISSUED	PRICE AS OF 09/30/90	NAV AS OF 09/30/90	% PREMIUM/ DISCOUNT	# SHARES OUTSTANDING (IN MILLIONS)	TOTAL ASSETS (IN MILLIONS)	MARKET CAPITALIZATION (IN MILLIONS)	EXPENSES/AVG NET ASSETS RATIOS
SPECIALIZED FUNDS									
ASA LTD	NYSE-ASA	1958	50.13	58.99	-15%	9.6	$566	$481	0.19%
CENTRAL FUND OF CANADA	ASE-CEF	08/05/87	4.94	5.09	-3%	16.8	86	83	NA
CLOSED-END BOND FUNDS									
FIRST AUSTRALIA PRIME INC.	ASE-FAX	04/17/86	9.31	10.62	-12%	86.0	913	800	2.77%
EQUITY FUNDS -- REGIONAL									
ALLIANCE NEW EUROPE FUND	NYSE-ANE	03/26/90	7.38	9.33	-21%	21.0	196	155	1.43%
ASIA PACIFIC FUND	NYSE-APB	04/24/87	10.00	11.57	-14%	8.7	100	87	2.69%
EUROPE FUND	NYSE-EF	04/26/90	10.38	12.74	-19%	8.3	106	86	1.52%
EUROPEAN WARRANT FUND	NYSE-EWF	07/17/90	7.25	9.30	-22%	6.0	56	44	NA
GT GREATER EUROPE FUND	NYSE-GTF	03/22/90	9.13	11.16	-18%	16.0	179	146	NA
LATIN AMERICA INV. FUND#	NYSE-LAM	07/27/90	9.25	12.86	-28%	4.0	51	37	NA
PACIFIC EUR. GROWTH FUND	ASE-PEF	04/20/90	8.75	9.01	-3%	3.0	27	26	NA
SCUDDER NEW ASIA FUND	NYSE-SAF	06/18/87	12.38	15.00	-18%	7.0	105	87	1.84%
SCUDDER NEW EUROPE FUND	NYSE-NEF	02/09/90	8.13	10.40	-22%	16.0	166	130	1.84%
TEMPLETON EMERGING MKT. FUND	NYSE-EMF	02/27/87	11.75	13.84	-15%	11.5	159	135	2.03%

PREMIUM/DISCOUNT ANALYSIS

	PREM/DISC AS OF 09/30/90	PREM/DISC AS OF PREV WEEK	PREM/DISC AS OF 06/30/90	PREM/DISC AS OF 03/31/90	PREM/DISC AS OF 12/31/89	PREM/DISC AS OF 12/31/88	52-WEEK HIGH	52-WEEK LOW	52-WEEK AVERAGE PREM/DISC	26-WEEK AVERAGE PREM/DISC
SPECIALIZED FUNDS										
ASA LTD	-15%	-14%	-28%	-25%	-24%	-27%	-13%	-27%	-21%	-21%
CENTRAL FUND OF CANADA	-3%	-5%	2%	6%	4%	-17%	9%	-7%	1%	1%
CLOSED-END BOND FUNDS										
FIRST AUSTRALIA PRIME INC.	-12%	-12%	-5%	1%	-6%	-15%	1%	-15%	-5%	-5%
EQUITY FUNDS -- REGIONAL										
ALLIANCE NEW EUROPE FUND	-21%	-11%	-13%	8%	NA	NA	8%	-21%	-9%	-9%
ASIA PACIFIC FUND	-14%	-5%	-16%	-12%	12%	-27%	43%	-23%	-2%	-11%
EUROPE FUND	-19%	-18%	-4%	NA	NA	NA	9%	-23%	-4%	-4%
EUROPEAN WARRANT FUND	-22%	-15%	NA	NA	NA	NA	5%	-22%	-10%	-10%
GT GREATER EUROPE FUND	-18%	-11%	-7%	8%	NA	NA	8%	-18%	-2%	-2%
LATIN AMERICA INV. FUND#	-28%	-26%	NA	NA	NA	NA	5%	-28%	-14%	-14%
PACIFIC EUR. GROWTH FUND	-3%	-5%	2%	NA	NA	NA	16%	-10%	3%	3%
SCUDDER NEW ASIA FUND	-18%	-19%	-16%	-16%	-3%	-26%	-4%	-25%	-16%	-17%
SCUDDER NEW EUROPE FUND	-22%	-18%	-13%	-13%	NA	NA	9%	-23%	-11%	-14%
TEMPLETON EMERGING MKT. FUND	-15%	-12%	-2%	-2%	14%	-16%	14%	-19%	-2%	-5%
AVERAGE PREM/DISC:	-16.09%	-13.11%	-8.09%	-5.04%	-0.53%	-21.25%				

REGIONAL AND SPECIALIZED CLOSED-END COUNTRY FUNDS

PRICE PERFORMANCE

SPECIALIZED FUNDS	PRICE AS OF 09/30/90	% CHANGE SINCE PREV.WEEK	PRICE AS OF 06/30/90	% CHG SINCE 06/30/90	PRICE AS OF 03/31/90	% CHG SINCE 03/31/90	PRICE AS OF 12/31/89	% CHG SINCE 12/31/89	PRICE AS OF 12/31/88	% CHG SINCE 12/31/88	52-WEEK RANGE HIGH	LOW	% CHG FROM HIGH	LOW
ABA LTD	$50.13	3.4%	$40.50	23.8%	$52.88	-5.2%	$55.5	-10%	$37.9	32%	$73	$41	-31%	21%
CENTRAL FUND OF CANADA	4.94	5.3%	4.81	2.6%	5.25	-6.0%	5.5	-10%	4.8	4%	6	5	-19%	7%
CLOSED-END BOND FUNDS														
FIRST AUSTRALIA PRIME INC.	9.31	0.0%	9.13	2.1%	9.00	3.5%	8.9	5%	9.1	2%	10	8	-7%	12%
EQUITY FUNDS -- REGIONAL														
ALLIANCE NEW EUROPE FUND	7.38	-14.5%	10.25	-28.0%	12.00	-38.5%	NA	NA	NA	NA	12	7	-39%	0%
ASIA PACIFIC FUND	10.00	-15.8%	13.75	-27.3%	13.88	-27.9%	17.8	-44%	6.4	57%	23	10	-56%	3%
EUROPE FUND	10.38	-3.5%	13.75	-24.5%	NA	NA	NA	NA	NA	NA	15	10	-31%	1%
EUROPEAN WARRANT FUND	7.25	-10.8%	NA	NA	NA	NA	NA	NA	NA	NA	12	7	-40%	0%
GT GREATER EUROPE FUND	9.13	-11.0%	13.50	-32.4%	15.13	-39.7%	NA	NA	NA	NA	15	9	-40%	0%
LATIN AMERICA INV. FUND#	9.25	-5.1%	NA	NA	NA	NA	NA	NA	NA	NA	15	9	-37%	0%
PACIFIC EUR. GROWTH FUND	8.75	-2.8%	11.38	-23.1%	NA	NA	NA	NA	NA	NA	13	8	-33%	6%
SCUDDER NEW ASIA FUND	12.38	-6.6%	15.63	-20.8%	13.75	-10.0%	15.9	-22%	8.9	39%	18	12	-33%	5%
SCUDDER NEW EUROPE FUND	8.13	-7.1%	10.63	-23.5%	10.00	-18.8%	NA	NA	NA	NA	14	8	-41%	0%
TEMPLETON EMERGING MKT. FUND	11.75	-8.7%	15.75	-25.4%	13.875	-15.3%	15.3	-23%	7.9	49%	19	12	-36%	2%

NET ASSET VALUE (NAV) PERFORMANCE

SPECIALIZED FUNDS	NAV AS OF 09/30/90	% CHANGE SINCE PREV.WEEK	NAV AS OF 06/30/90	% CHG SINCE 06/30/90	NAV AS OF 03/31/90	% CHG SINCE 03/31/90	NAV AS OF 12/31/89	% CHG SINCE 12/31/89	NAV AS OF 12/31/88	% CHG SINCE 12/31/88	52-WEEK RANGE HIGH	LOW	% CHG FROM HIGH	LOW
ABA LTD	$58.99	4.6%	$56.51	4.4%	$70.20	-16.0%	$72.81	-19%	$51.60	14%	$80	$52	-26%	13%
CENTRAL FUND OF CANADA	5.09	2.6%	4.72	7.8%	4.96	2.6%	5.30	-4%	5.72	-11%	6	5	-9%	8%
CLOSED-END BOND FUNDS														
FIRST AUSTRALIA PRIME INC.	10.62	0.6%	9.58	10.9%	8.95	18.7%	9.49	12%	10.68	-1%	11	9	0%	19%
EQUITY FUNDS -- REGIONAL														
ALLIANCE NEW EUROPE FUND	9.33	-3.3%	11.75	-20.6%	11.16	-16.4%	NA	NA	NA	NA	12	9	-25%	0%
ASIA PACIFIC FUND	11.57	-7.1%	16.28	-28.9%	15.69	-26.3%	15.78	-27%	8.76	32%	17	12	-33%	0%
EUROPE FUND	12.74	-2.8%	14.34	-11.2%	NA	NA	NA	NA	NA	NA	15	13	-15%	0%
EUROPEAN WARRANT FUND	9.30	-3.0%	NA	NA	NA	NA	NA	NA	NA	NA	11	9	-17%	0%
GT GREATER EUROPE FUND	11.16	-3.4%	14.44	-22.7%	14.04	-20.5%	NA	NA	NA	NA	15	11	-25%	0%
LATIN AMERICA INV. FUND#	12.86	-2.1%	NA	NA	NA	NA	NA	NA	NA	NA	14	13	-8%	2%
PACIFIC EUR. GROWTH FUND	9.01	-4.5%	11.19	-19.5%	NA	NA	NA	NA	NA	NA	12	9	-23%	0%
SCUDDER NEW ASIA FUND	15.00	-8.4%	18.70	-19.8%	16.30	-8.0%	16.36	-8%	12.04	25%	20	15	-25%	0%
SCUDDER NEW EUROPE FUND	10.40	-2.4%	12.19	-14.7%	11.52	-9.7%	NA	NA	NA	NA	13	10	-18%	0%
TEMPLETON EMERGING MKT. FUND	13.84	-5.3%	16.12	-14.1%	14.15	-2.2%	13.40	3%	9.36	48%	17	13	-21%	7%

REGIONAL AND SPECIALIZED CLOSED-END COUNTRY FUNDS

AVERAGE DAILY TRADING VOLUME — AUGUST 1989 THROUGH AUGUST 1990
(000's)

	AUG '90	JUL	JUN	MAY	APR	MAR	FEB	JAN	DEC	NOV	OCT	SEP	AUG '89
SPECIALIZED FUNDS													
ASA LTD	1,478	574	672	871	550	876	2,267	1,488	805	1,423	739	394	412
CENTRAL FUND OF CANADA	415	161	246	201	168	245	404	455	311	556	251	163	174
CLOSED-END BOND FUNDS													
FIRST AUSTRALIA PRIME INC.	899	601	500	543	605	624	624	686	735	569	677	701	941
REGIONAL FUNDS													
ALLIANCE NEW EUROPE FUND	607	511	588	777	1,312	974	NA	NA	NA	NA	NA	NA	NA
ASIA PACIFIC FUND	218	227	156	266	416	290	299	1,422	324	337	465	790	375
EUROPE FUND	104	68	177	135	426	NA	NA	NA	NA	NA	NA	NA	NA
EUROPEAN WARRANT FUND	238	495	NA	NA	NA	NA	NA	NA	NA	NA	NA	NA	NA
GT GREATER EUROPE FUND	170	101	159	458	586	254	NA	NA	NA	NA	NA	NA	NA
LATIN AMERICAN INV. FUND#	303	631	NA	NA	NA	NA	NA	NA	NA	NA	NA	NA	NA
PACIFIC EUROPEAN GROWTH FUND	34	18	22	26	14	NA	NA	NA	NA	NA	NA	NA	NA
SCUDDER NEW ASIA FUND	208	98	97	125	109	163	186	199	142	93	189	282	163
SCUDDER NEW EUROPE FUND	487	309	390	476	486	690	3,042	NA	NA	NA	NA	NA	NA
TEMPLETON EMERGING MKT. FUND	311	184	133	143	92	140	124	205	144	108	241	210	181

SINGLE-COUNTRY CLOSED-END FUNDS

SELECTED DATA

EUROPE

	LISTING/ SYMBOL	WHEN ISSUED	PRICE AS OF 09/30/90	NAV AS OF 09/30/90	% DISCOUNT/ PREMIUM	# SHARES OUTSTANDING (IN MILLIONS)	TOTAL ASSETS (IN MILLIONS)	MARKET CAPITALIZATION (IN MILLIONS)	EXPENSES/AVG NET ASSETS RATIOS
AUSTRIA FUND#	NYSE-OST	09/21/89	8.63	11.33	-24%	8.3	94	71	1.88%
EMERGING GERMANY FUND#	NYSE-FRG	03/29/90	7.00	8.83	-21%	14.0	124	98	NA
FIRST IBERIAN FUND	ASE-IBF	04/12/88	7.13	8.80	-19%	6.5	57	46	3.38%
FRANCE GROWTH FUND	NYSE-FRF	05/11/90	7.63	10.40	-27%	11.5	120	88	1.47%
FUTURE GERMANY FUND	NYSE-FGF	02/27/90	10.50	13.10	-20%	12.9	169	135	NA
GERMANY FUND	NYSE-GER	07/18/86	10.63	10.26	4%	13.1	134	139	1.47%
GROWTH FUND OF SPAIN	NYSE-GSP	02/14/90	7.00	9.73	-28%	17.8	173	125	1.48%
IRISH INVESTMENT FUND#	NYSE-IRL	03/30/90	6.75	9.24	-27%	5.0	46	34	1.87%
ITALY FUND	NYSE-ITA	02/25/86	10.00	13.24	-24%	6.3	84	63	1.90%
NEW GERMANY FUND#	NYSE-GF	01/24/90	9.75	11.87	-18%	28.8	341	280	NA
PORTUGAL FUND	NYSE-PGF	11/01/89	8.63	11.59	-26%	5.3	61	46	1.98%
SPAIN FUND	NYSE-SNF	06/21/88	10.75	11.34	-5%	10.0	114	108	1.93%
SWISS HELVETIA FUND#	NYSE-SWZ	08/19/87	11.25	12.54	-10%	8.0	100	90	1.85%
TURKISH INVESTMENT FUND	NYSE-TKF	12/05/89	10.13	15.09	-33%	7.0	106	71	1.72%
UK FUND	NYSE-UKM	08/06/87	8.63	10.44	-17%	4.0	42	35	1.86%

ASIA & PACIFIC RIM

	LISTING/ SYMBOL	WHEN ISSUED	PRICE AS OF 09/30/90	NAV AS OF 09/30/90	% DISCOUNT/ PREMIUM	# SHARES OUTSTANDING (IN MILLIONS)	TOTAL ASSETS (IN MILLIONS)	MARKET CAPITALIZATION (IN MILLIONS)	EXPENSES/AVG NET ASSETS RATIOS
FIRST AUSTRALIA FUND	ASE-IAF	12/12/85	7.50	9.96	-25%	6.0	60	45	2.54%
FIRST PHILIPPINES FUND	NYSE-FPF	11/08/89	6.50	9.69	-33%	9.0	87	58	1.87%
INDIA GROWTH FUND	NYSE-IGF	08/12/88	14.25	18.98	-25%	5.0	95	71	3.27%
INDONESIA FUND	NYSE-IF	03/01/90	9.63	12.19	-21%	4.6	56	44	1.91%
JAKARTA GROWTH FUND	NYSE-JGF	04/10/90	6.63	9.51	-30%	5.0	48	33	NA
JAPAN OTC EQUITY FUND	NYSE-JOF	03/14/90	7.88	9.53	-17%	8.5	81	67	NA
KOREA FUND	NYSE-KF	08/22/84	12.25	11.00	11%	21.0	231	257	1.44%
MALAYSIA FUND	NYSE-MF	05/08/87	11.50	11.59	-1%	7.3	84	83	1.77%
SINGAPORE FUND	NYSE-SGF	08/01/90	8.13	10.87	-25%	5.0	54	41	NA
TAIWAN FUND	NYSE-TWN	12/17/86	14.50	16.09	-10%	4.2	68	61	1.21%
THAI CAPITAL FUND	NYSE-TC	05/22/90	6.38	8.39	-24%	6.0	50	38	1.75%
THAI FUND	NYSE-TTF	02/17/88	17.63	15.51	14%	9.8	153	173	1.79%

LATIN AMERICA

	LISTING/ SYMBOL	WHEN ISSUED	PRICE AS OF 09/30/90	NAV AS OF 09/30/90	% DISCOUNT/ PREMIUM	# SHARES OUTSTANDING (IN MILLIONS)	TOTAL ASSETS (IN MILLIONS)	MARKET CAPITALIZATION (IN MILLIONS)	EXPENSES/AVG NET ASSETS RATIOS
BRAZIL FUND	NYSE-BZF	03/31/88	8.00	9.58	-16%	12.0	115	96	2.12%
CHILE FUND	NYSE-CH	09/27/89	11.63	15.77	-26%	5.4	85	62	1.81%
MEXICO FUND	NYSE-MXF	06/11/81	11.50	13.48	-15%	19.7	266	227	1.60%
MEXICO EQUITY & INC. FUND	NYSE-MXE	08/14/90	9.50	11.42	-17%	6.0	69	57	NA

Within the last three years, Smith Barney, Harris Upham & Co. Inc. or one of its affiliates was the manager (comanager) of a public offering of this company.

PREMIUM/DISCOUNT ANALYSIS

SINGLE-COUNTRY CLOSED-END FUNDS

	PREMIUM/ DISCOUNT AS OF 09/30/90	PREMIUM/ DISCOUNT AS OF PREV.WEEK	PREMIUM/ DISCOUNT AS OF 06/30/90	PREMIUM/ DISCOUNT AS OF 03/31/90	PREMIUM/ DISCOUNT AS OF 12/31/89	PREMIUM/ DISCOUNT AS OF 12/31/88	52-WEEK HIGH	52-WEEK LOW	52-WEEK AVERAGE PREM./DISC.	26-WEEK AVERAGE PREM./DISC.
EUROPE										
AUSTRIA FUND #	-24%	-10%	-13%	-10%	68%	NA	85%	-23%	10%	-11%
EMERGING GERMANY FUND #	-21%	-16%	-12%	NA	NA	NA	1%	-23%	-12%	-12%
FIRST IBERIAN FUND	-19%	-14%	-3%	4%	27%	-16%	87%	-17%	20%	1%
FRANCE GROWTH FUND	-27%	-19%	-12%	NA	NA	NA	22%	-33%	-7%	-7%
FUTURE GERMANY FUND	-20%	-19%	-15%	-14%	NA	NA	8%	-26%	-11%	-13%
GERMANY FUND	4%	4%	7%	15%	58%	-9%	100%	-8%	25%	10%
GROWTH FUND OF SPAIN	-28%	-25%	-16%	-20%	NA	NA	-3%	-22%	-15%	-15%
IRISH INVESTMENT FUND #	-27%	-26%	-15%	8%	NA	NA	8%	-28%	-14%	-14%
ITALY FUND	-24%	-16%	-7%	-8%	32%	-17%	38%	-34%	1%	-9%
NEW GERMANY FUND #	-18%	-21%	-12%	1%	NA	NA	51%	-21%	-1%	-8%
PORTUGAL FUND #	-26%	-27%	-3%	-5%	23%	NA	40%	-28%	6%	-4%
SPAIN FUND	-5%	-7%	13%	47%	130%	-5%	145%	-6%	60%	18%
SWISS HELVETIA FUND #	-10%	-4%	-2%	-1%	16%	-12%	16%	-13%	0%	-3%
TURKISH INVESTMENT FUND	-33%	-36%	-17%	-21%	-8%	NA	8%	-33%	-19%	-22%
UK FUND	-17%	-8%	-14%	-16%	-8%	-14%	-5%	-24%	-13%	-13%
ASIA & PACIFIC RIM										
FIRST AUSTRALIA FUND	-25%	-22%	-15%	-9%	-16%	-24%	20%	-24%	-10%	-13%
FIRST PHILIPPINES FUND	-33%	-29%	-15%	-10%	25%	NA	61%	-29%	-1%	-18%
INDIA GROWTH FUND	-25%	-26%	26%	20%	44%	-24%	47%	-21%	17%	12%
INDONESIA FUND	-21%	-14%	-1%	19%	NA	NA	19%	-16%	3%	3%
JAKARTA GROWTH FUND	-30%	-24%	5%	NA	NA	NA	26%	-20%	5%	6%
JAPAN OTC EQUITY FUND	-17%	-26%	4%	12%	NA	NA	48%	-25%	9%	9%
KOREA FUND	11%	35%	52%	32%	85%	65%	120%	16%	65%	42%
MALAYSIA FUND	-1%	-16%	10%	9%	36%	-16%	75%	-9%	18%	9%
SINGAPORE FUND	-25%	-22%	NA	NA	NA	NA	8%	-21%	-13%	-13%
TAIWAN FUND	-10%	22%	33%	7%	27%	13%	98%	-23%	19%	21%
THAI CAPITAL FUND	-24%	-19%	0%	NA	NA	NA	10%	-19%	-3%	-3%
THAI FUND	14%	-2%	6%	11%	71%	15%	91%	-8%	30%	9%
LATIN AMERICA										
BRAZIL FUND	-16%	-19%	3%	-39%	-32%	-39%	27%	-55%	-22%	-5%
CHILE FUND	-26%	-22%	8%	11%	5%	NA	30%	-18%	8%	3%
MEXICO FUND	-15%	-8%	3%	1%	-9%	-32%	14%	-20%	4%	-3%
MEXICO EQUITY & INC. FUND	-17%	-9%	NA	NA	NA	NA	2%	-8%	1%	1%

Within the last three years, Smith Barney, Harris Upham & Co. Inc. or one of its affiliates was the manager (comanager) of a public offering of this company.

	09/30/90	PREV.WEEK	03/31/90	12/31/89	12/31/88
AVG. PREM/DISC SINGLE-COUNTRY	-17.93%	-14.33%	1.69%	30.26%	-8.36%
AVG. PREM/DISC RGNL & SPCLZD	-16.09%	-13.11%	-5.04%	-0.63%	-21.25%
AVG. PREM/DISC ALL FUNDS	-17.38%	-13.97%	-0.04%	22.09%	-12.23%

SINGLE-COUNTRY CLOSED-END FUNDS

PRICE PERFORMANCE

	PRICE AS OF 09/30/90	% CHANGE SINCE PREV.WEEK	PRICE AS OF 06/30/90	% CHG SINCE 06/30/90	PRICE AS OF 03/31/90	% CHG SINCE 03/31/90	PRICE AS OF 12/31/89	% CHG SINCE 12/31/89	PRICE AS OF 12/31/88	% CHG SINCE 12/31/88	52-WEEK RANGE HIGH	LOW	% CHG FROM HIGH	LOW
EUROPE														
AUSTRIA FUND#	8.63	-21.6%	13.00	-33.7%	14.50	-40.5%	20.5	-58%	NA	NA	25	9	-65%	0%
EMERGING GERMANY FUND#	7.00	-9.7%	9.88	-29.1%	11.25	-37.8%	NA	NA	NA	NA	12	7	-41%	4%
FIRST IBERIAN FUND	7.13	-10.9%	11.13	-36.0%	10.00	-28.8%	13.4	-47%	7.8	-8%	20	7	-64%	0%
FRANCE GROWTH FUND	7.63	-10.3%	9.75	NA	NA	NA	NA	NA	NA	NA	14	7	-44%	9%
FUTURE GERMANY FUND	10.50	-6.7%	14.50	-27.6%	15.13	-30.6%	19.3	-45%	7.5	42%	19	11	-45%	0%
GERMANY FUND	10.63	-6.6%	14.13	-24.8%	15.88	-33.1%	NA	NA	NA	NA	25	9	-58%	18%
GROWTH FUND OF SPAIN	7.00	-8.2%	10.75	-34.9%	8.63	-18.8%	NA	NA	NA	NA	14	7	-50%	0%
IRISH INVESTMENT FUND#	6.75	-1.8%	9.50	-28.9%	12.00	-43.8%	17.0	-41%	8.1	23%	12	7	-44%	2%
ITALY FUND	10.00	-11.1%	14.75	-32.2%	12.38	-19.2%	NA	NA	NA	NA	19	9	-46%	11%
NEW GERMANY FUND#	9.75	-1.3%	13.00	-25.0%	15.00	-35.0%	17.0	NA	8.1	1%	25	10	-61%	1%
PORTUGAL FUND	8.63	-2.8%	13.38	-35.5%	12.50	-31.0%	17.00	-49%	NA	NA	20	9	-57%	0%
SPAIN FUND	10.75	-4.4%	17.00	-36.8%	18.50	-41.9%	31.8	-66%	10.6	1%	39	11	-72%	0%
SWISS HELVETIA FUND#	11.25	-10.0%	14.50	-22.4%	12.50	-10.0%	15.1	-26%	9.6	17%	18	11	-36%	5%
TURKISH INVESTMENT FUND	10.13	1.3%	12.88	-21.4%	11.50	-12.0%	12.0	-16%	NA	NA	15	10	-32%	5%
UK FUND	8.63	-9.2%	10.00	-13.8%	8.75	-1.4%	10.8	-20%	9.4	-8%	12	8	-25%	5%
ASIA & PACIFIC RIM														
FIRST AUSTRALIA FUND	7.50	-4.8%	8.38	-10.4%	8.63	-13.0%	8.8	-14%	8.1	-8%	13	8	-41%	0%
FIRST PHILIPPINES FUND	6.50	-7.1%	9.38	-30.7%	10.13	-35.8%	13.75	-53%	NA	NA	18	7	-64%	12%
INDIA GROWTH FUND	14.25	2.7%	16.00	-10.9%	15.25	-6.6%	19.5	-27%	9.3	54%	21	13	-32%	0%
INDONESIA FUND	9.63	-11.5%	14.88	-35.3%	16.50	-41.7%	NA	NA	NA	NA	17	10	-43%	0%
JAKARTA GROWTH FUND	6.63	-10.2%	11.50	NA	NA	NA	NA	NA	NA	NA	15	7	-54%	0%
JAPAN OTC EQUITY FUND	7.88	-1.6%	13.25	-40.6%	12.38	-36.4%	NA	NA	NA	NA	17	8	-53%	0%
KOREA FUND	12.25	-14.8%	22.13	-44.6%	22.88	-46.4%	34.4	-64%	26.3	-53%	43	12	-72%	7%
MALAYSIA FUND	11.50	4.5%	15.63	-26.4%	15.25	-24.6%	18.8	-39%	7.5	53%	25	11	-54%	0%
SINGAPORE FUND	8.13	-4.4%	NA	-37.6%	NA	NA	NA	NA	NA	NA	12	8	-33%	0%
TAIWAN FUND	14.50	-25.2%	23.25 (B)	-37.6%	26.00 (B)	-44.2%	49.8	-71%	34.8	-58%	41	15	-64%	0%
THAI CAPITAL FUND	6.38	-5.6%	11.25	-43.3%	NA	NA	NA	NA	NA	NA	13	6	-50%	0%
THAI FUND	17.63	17.5%	23.75	-25.8%	20.00	-11.9%	32.3	-45%	11.8	50%	36	14	-50%	26%
LATIN AMERICA														
BRAZIL FUND	8.00	-3.0%	10.25 (A)	-22.0%	11.00 (A)	-27.3%	12.9	-38%	7.9	2%	15	8	-45%	0%
CHILE FUND	11.63	-7.9%	17.63	-34.0%	19.13	-39.2%	15.6	-25%	NA	NA	23	12	-48%	0%
MEXICO FUND	11.50	-10.7%	15.25	-24.6%	13.13	-12.4%	11.4	1%	5.4	114%	17	9	-33%	35%
MEXICO EQUITY & INC. FUND	9.50	-8.4%	NA	NA	NA	NA	NA	NA	NA	NA	12	10	-20%	0%

(A) Return does not include $3.07 dividend paid in January 1990.
(B) Return does not include $14.75 dividend paid in January 1990.

NET ASSET VALUE (NAV) PERFORMANCE

SINGLE-COUNTRY CLOSED-END FUNDS

	NAV AS OF 09/30/90	% CHANGE SINCE PREV. WEEK	NAV AS OF 06/30/90	% CHG SINCE 06/30/90	NAV AS OF 03/31/90	% CHG SINCE 03/31/90	NAV AS OF 12/31/89	% CHG SINCE 12/31/89	NAV AS OF 12/31/88	% CHG SINCE 12/31/88	52-WEEK RANGE HIGH	52-WEEK RANGE LOW	% CHG FROM HIGH	% CHG FROM LOW
EUROPE														
AUSTRIA FUND#	11.33	-7.1%	14.98	-24.4%	16.03	-29.3%	12.21	-7%	NA	NA	17	10	-34%	15%
EMERGING GERMANY FUND#	8.83	-4.0%	11.28	-21.7%	11.16	-20.9%	NA	NA	NA	NA	12	10	-24%	-10%
FIRST IBERIAN FUND	8.80	-4.9%	11.48	-23.3%	9.61	-8.4%	10.57	-17%	9.21	-4%	12	9	-26%	-7%
FRANCE GROWTH FUND	10.40	-0.4%	11.08	NA	NA	NA	NA	NA	NA	NA	11	11	-8%	-3%
FUTURE GERMANY FUND	13.10	-5.8%	17.14	-23.6%	17.65	-25.8%	12.15	-16%	8.23	25%	18	15	-27%	-13%
GERMANY FUND	10.26	-6.0%	13.24	-22.5%	13.79	-25.6%	NA	NA	NA	NA	14	9	-26%	8%
GROWTH FUND OF SPAIN	9.73	-4.1%	12.73	-23.6%	10.75	-9.5%	NA	NA	8.23	NA	13	11	-26%	-8%
IRISH INVESTMENT FUND#	9.24	-0.6%	11.12	-16.9%	11.16	-17.2%	NA	NA	NA	NA	11	9	-17%	-2%
ITALY FUND	13.24	-1.4%	15.82	-16.3%	13.40	-1.2%	12.86	3%	9.83	35%	16	11	-16%	17%
NEW GERMANY FUND#	11.87	-4.8%	14.81	-19.9%	14.88	-20.2%	NA	NA	NA	NA	16	13	-24%	-11%
PORTUGAL FUND	11.59	-4.3%	13.72	-15.5%	13.11	-11.6%	13.79	-16%	NA	NA	14	12	-17%	-6%
SPAIN FUND	11.34	-6.0%	15.10	-24.9%	12.58	-9.9%	13.82	-18%	11.23	1%	16	12	-29%	-6%
SWISS HELVETIA FUND#	12.54	-3.5%	14.79	-15.2%	12.65	-0.9%	13.05	-4%	10.99	14%	16	12	-19%	5%
TURKISH INVESTMENT FUND	15.09	-3.6%	15.51	-2.7%	14.63	3.1%	13.01	16%	NA	NA	19	11	-19%	35%
UK FUND	10.44	0.6%	11.58	-9.8%	10.36	0.8%	11.67	-11%	10.94	-5%	12	10	-15%	5%
ASIA & PACIFIC RIM														
FIRST AUSTRALIA FUND	9.96	-1.1%	9.81	1.5%	9.49	5.0%	10.41	-4%	10.65	-6%	11	9	-12%	9%
FIRST PHILIPPINES FUND	9.69	-1.1%	11.01	-12.0%	11.20	-13.5%	11.03	-12%	NA	NA	11	10	-14%	-3%
INDIA GROWTH FUND	18.98	1.1%	12.70	49.4%	12.72	49.2%	13.54	40%	12.24	55%	19	12	1%	62%
INDONESIA FUND	12.19	-3.9%	14.99	-18.7%	13.86	-12.0%	NA	NA	NA	NA	15	13	-20%	-6%
JAKARTA GROWTH FUND	9.51	-2.4%	10.92	-12.9%	NA	NA	NA	NA	NA	NA	11	10	-15%	-6%
JAPAN OTC EQUITY FUND	9.53	-12.1%	12.70	-25.0%	11.08	-14.0%	NA	NA	NA	NA	13	11	-29%	-14%
KOREA FUND	11.00	3.3%	14.60	-24.7%	17.36	-36.6%	18.55	-41%	15.93	-31%	19	11	-43%	0%
MALAYSIA FUND	11.59	-11.3%	14.26	-18.7%	14.03	-17.4%	13.77	-18%	8.98	29%	16	12	-25%	-2%
SINGAPORE FUND	10.87	-0.7%	NA	NA	NA	NA	NA	NA	NA	NA	11	11	-3%	-1%
TAIWAN FUND	16.09	1.2%	17.50	-8.1%	24.33	-33.9%	39.12	-59%	30.73	-48%	45	16	-64%	3%
THAI CAPITAL FUND	8.39	0.2%	11.20	-25.1%	NA	NA	NA	NA	NA	NA	12	9	-20%	-9%
THAI FUND	15.51	1.4%	22.46	-30.9%	18.07	-14.2%	18.88	-18%	10.24	51%	24	16	-37%	-6%
LATIN AMERICA														
BRAZIL FUND	9.58	-5.7%	9.91	-3.3%	18.11	-47.1%	18.85	-49%	12.90	NA	25	8	-61%	13%
CHILE FUND	15.77	-3.0%	16.29	-3.2%	17.18	-8.2%	14.79	7%	NA	NA	18	14	-10%	16%
MEXICO FUND	13.48	-3.8%	14.87	-9.3%	13.03	3.5%	12.50	8%	7.89	71%	16	11	-16%	16%
MEXICO EQUITY & INC. FUND	11.42	0.4%	NA	NA	NA	NA	NA	NA	NA	NA	11	11	0%	1%

Latest available data.

SINGLE-COUNTRY CLOSED-END FUNDS

AVERAGE DAILY TRADING VOLUME — AUGUST 1989 THROUGH AUGUST 1990
(000's)

EUROPE

	AUG '90	JUL	JUN	MAY	APR	MAR	FEB	JAN	DEC	NOV	OCT	SEP	AUG '89
AUSTRIA FUND #	240	252	188	272	214	323	518	1,735	599	186	579	NA	NA
EMERGING GERMANY FUND #	396	242	316	375	566	830	NA	NA	NA	NA	NA	NA	NA
FIRST IBERIAN FUND	89	82	64	113	123	102	145	787	118	173	857	2,053	311
FRANCE GROWTH FUND	498	314	507	2,533	NA	NA	NA	NA	NA	NA	NA	NA	NA
FUTURE GERMANY FUND	528	476	431	504	705	1,066	3,085	NA	NA	NA	NA	NA	NA
GERMANY FUND	511	467	300	601	424	513	1,085	5,470	2,586	787	503	1,990	137
GROWTH FUND OF SPAIN	521	661	577	801	898	1,129	5,307	NA	NA	NA	NA	NA	NA
IRISH INVESTMENT FUND #	192	101	90	147	254	443	NA	NA	NA	NA	NA	NA	NA
ITALY FUND	151	158	172	273	186	208	133	995	284	111	504	917	110
NEW GERMANY FUND #	764	670	515	821	689	764	4,001	9,276	NA	NA	NA	NA	NA
PORTUGAL FUND	87	84	60	170	117	99	226	451	301	1,043	NA	NA	NA
SPAIN FUND	126	97	99	137	121	114	249	279	203	228	694	3,361	1,124
SWISS HELVETIA FUND #	155	210	144	294	136	126	274	1,029	329	172	497	235	169
TURKISH INVESTMENT FUND	352	161	184	355	245	254	446	1,222	1,244	NA	NA	NA	NA
UK FUND	65	66	115	130	77	70	54	214	114	78	103	123	56

ASIA & PACIFIC RIM

	AUG '90	JUL	JUN	MAY	APR	MAR	FEB	JAN	DEC	NOV	OCT	SEP	AUG '89
FIRST AUSTRALIA FUND	212	151	115	94	106	141	184	736	185	70	143	338	209
FIRST PHILIPPINES FUND	147	123	100	90	122	165	354	549	1,139	3,106	NA	NA	NA
INDIA GROWTH FUND	102	76	100	49	68	76	159	206	174	183	131	247	220
INDONESIA FUND	100	96	136	143	164	1,102	NA	NA	NA	NA	NA	NA	NA
JAKARTA GROWTH FUND	94	41	155	669	NA	NA	NA	NA	NA	NA	NA	NA	NA
JAPAN OTC EQUITY FUND	227	146	299	921	2,163	2,647	NA	NA	NA	NA	NA	NA	NA
KOREA FUND	426	361	469	944	462	349	282	355	413	325	390	467	572
MALAYSIA FUND	206	176	137	262	305	220	480	1,430	504	421	366	661	206
SINGAPORE FUND	197	472	NA	NA	NA	NA	NA	NA	NA	NA	NA	NA	NA
TAIWAN FUND	193	270	263	411	221	293	338	378	272	303	138	155	92
THAI CAPITAL FUND	157	126	351	434	NA	NA	NA	NA	NA	NA	NA	NA	NA
THAI FUND	283	187	219	371	312	210	369	912	384	326	687	1,408	385

LATIN AMERICA

	AUG '90	JUL	JUN	MAY	APR	MAR	FEB	JAN	DEC	NOV	OCT	SEP	AUG '89
BRAZIL FUND	349	625	354	273	630	591	518	1,276	749	199	503	476	238
CHILE FUND	113	106	166	125	107	208	297	503	378	217	543	NA	NA
MEXICO FUND	1,229	937	1,180	1,165	308	652	790	2,162	429	493	1,097	874	933
MEXICO EQUITY & INC. FUND	343	NA	NA	NA	NA	NA	NA	NA	NA	NA	NA	NA	NA

APPENDIX IV: NEW ISSUE GRAPH

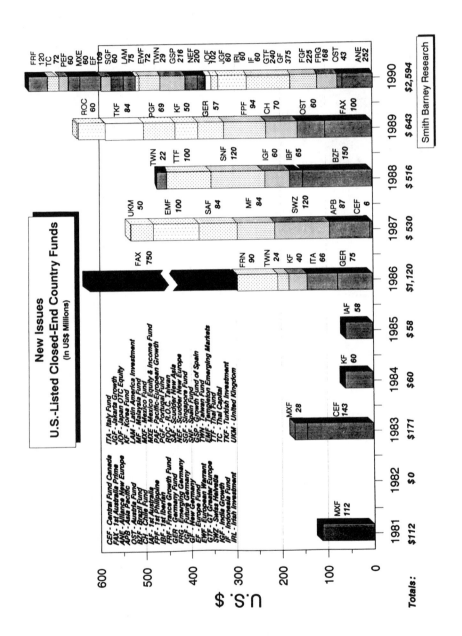

New Issues
U.S.-Listed Closed-End Country Funds
(in US$ Millions)

Smith Barney Research

APPENDIX V: AVERAGE PREMIUM/DISCOUNT GRAPH

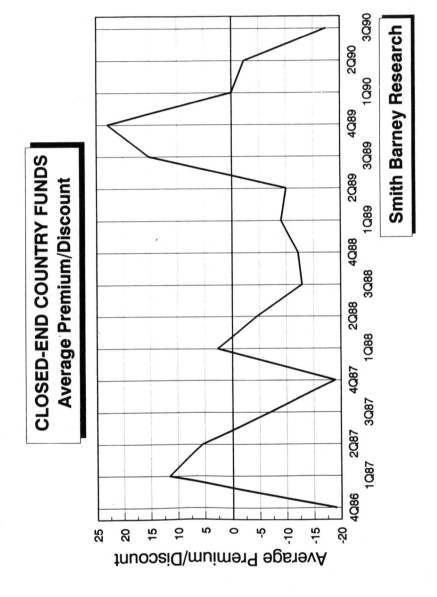

CLOSED-END COUNTRY FUNDS
Average Premium/Discount

Smith Barney Research

GLOBAL EQUITY
INVESTMENT STRATEGIES

Analyzing International Financial Statements

Dr. Vinod B. Bavishi
Center for International Financial Analysis and Research, Inc. (CIFAR), Kobe, Japan

Introduction

Users in the financial community would like to compare a vast number of companies internationally. However, a complete restatement of each foreign company's accounts in a particular user's accounting conventions would be neither cost effective nor timely. Since users in the investment community are particularly interested in the relative differences found through examining the performances of companies, the approaches discussed in this chapter are meant to identify differences among annual reports worldwide and provide suggestions for resolving some of these differences.

Research Objectives

The objective of this paper is to address the following research questions:

1. What are the major difficulties users face in analyzing international financial statements?
2. What are the major accounting differences among leading companies in 24 countries?

3. How do annual reports of non-U.S. companies prepared under local accounting standards compare to reports of non-U.S. companies prepared under U.S. accounting standards?
4. How can users of international financial statements reconcile accounting differences and overcome other difficulties encountered in analyzing international financial statements?
5. How can users of international financial statements use capital market-generated information?

Research Design

Data sources include the *Worldscope Database,* jointly developed by CIFAR and Wright Investors' Service, of Bridgeport, Conn., and CIFAR's reference library of over 10,000 international annual reports.

The problems encountered in undertaking research and analyzing international annual reports have been divided into four sections:

- Administrative problems

- Problems with procedural accounting matters

- Differences in accounting standards

- Difficulties in merging fundamental accounting data with capital market- generated information

In each category we identify problems, discuss why these problems make international financial analysis more difficult, and provide suggestions, where possible, for resolving some of these difficulties.

We have drawn from research performed elsewhere in this study in order to provide a comprehensive examination of the issues involved in analyzing international financial statements.

Administrative Problems

In undertaking any international research, one is bound to encounter some general difficulties. In this section, these difficulties are identified as they pertain to the analysis of international financial statements.

Identification of a Global List of Companies

PROBLEMS:

- There is no single source that provides a comprehensive list of traded securities worldwide; this makes it difficult for a given user to systematically select a set of companies to employ in analysis. (Table 1 provides the number of domestic companies listed on selected exchanges in 24 countries.)

- In some instances, subsidiaries, whose reports are more difficult to analyze due to various transactions with parent companies, are also listed on stock exchanges.

- Stock exchange listings change considerably every year.

- In Europe, many prominent companies are not listed or are government-owned.

SOLUTIONS:

- Leading company listings, as well as company directories, are available for most stock exchanges.

- Stock exchange publications provide comprehensive information on the companies listed.

- One can construct a database, with a few key variables (such as country, company name, industry classification, sales, assets, and market value of shares), to produce a global list of traded companies. Non-traded companies should also be included in such a list so that major companies in a given industry are analyzed together, even though the user's focus may be on traded companies.

Difficulties in Obtaining Information

PROBLEM:

In general, the availability of published corporate data on local companies is quite good, but information sources on foreign companies is not readily available.

**Table 1   Extent of Listings on Stock Exchanges Worldwide
for Common Shares**

Country	Stock Exchange	Number of Domestic Companies Listed
North America		
Canada	Toronto	1147
Mexico	Mexico City	197
United States	American	818
	New York	1575
Asia/Pacific		
Australia	Sydney	1785
Hong Kong	Hong Kong	264
Japan	Tokyo	1532
Korea, South	Seoul	389
Malayasia	Kuala Lumpur	287
New Zealand	Wellington	274
Singapore	Singapore	127
Europe		
Austria	Vienna	69
Belgium	Brussels	192
Denmark	Copenhagen	272
Finland	Helsinki	49
France	Paris	481
Germany, West	Frankfurt	234
Italy	Milan	204
Netherlands	Amsterdam	226
Norway	Oslo	148
Spain	Madrid	312
Sweden	Stockholm	150
Switzerland	Zurich	166
United Kingdom (& Ireland)	London	2135
Africa/Middle East		
South Africa	Johannesburg	531
Total		13,564

SOLUTIONS:

- One potential way to improve the accessibility of information on international companies is to establish collections of international annual reports at leading public and academic libraries. In addition,

users in need of annual reports from specific foreign firms may want to obtain them directly from companies of interest. Directories of foreign companies are available in the reference sections of major public and academic libraries worldwide.

- Another possible solution involves using any of the international financial data services listed in Table 2.

Delays in Receiving Financial Information

PROBLEM:

Companies in many countries take longer than three months after the fiscal year-end date to publish financial statements.

Some of the reasons for this delay are:

- Stock exchanges and government authorities in many countries allow a longer lead time to file annual reports.

- An English-language version of a foreign annual report is produced later than the local language version.

- Similarly, the consolidated version of an annual report is available later than the non-consolidated version.

Table 3 provides a classification of countries in terms of the average number of days elapsed between the year-end date of the financial statements and the date of the annual report's publication. Our information is based on our experience in receiving international annual reports for fiscal year 1987.

SOLUTIONS:

- The application of competitive pressure on companies worldwide, where the investment community demands timely information, may cause them to publish more quickly.

- Users may want to use press releases and news clippings to obtain key information, as these sources are available much sooner than the full text annual financial statements. Possible sources for this type of information are the Financial Times, The Economist and The Wall Street Journal, as well as other leading financial and business publications worldwide.

Table 2   Selected Sources of International Company Information

Services	Contact Address and Phone Number	Coverage	Format and Variabales Availabale
Extel International Card Service	37–45 Paul Street London EC2A 4PB United Kingdom Ph: (01) 253-3400	22 Countries Over 4,500 Companies	Details of each company are published on an annual card, which shows a chairman's statement, identifies members of the board, and depicts profit and loss account, balance sheet, company capital (with history), subsidiaries and activities, dividend records, yields, earnings, etc. Cumulative news cards are issued regarding the anouncement of dividends, interim or preliminary results or any other event concerning the company's capital, activities, or organization. A monthly index and update is provided with the service.
Morgan Stanley Capital International Perspective	Mortan Stanley 1633 Broadway New York, NY 10019 USA Ph: (212) 703-2965	21 Countries 2,100 Companies	Published monthly and quarterly. Presents, in booklet form, share price information for the world's largest companies. Provides selected items from the balance sheet and income statement, and share data. National, regional and industry indices are also included.
Moody's International Manual	Moody's Investors Service 99 Church Street New York, NY 10007 USA Ph: (212) 553-0300	Over 90 Countries excluding the US Nearly 5,000 Companies	Published annually in two volumes. Countries are listed alphabetically. Each section includes a brief country profile followed by corporate profiles in xhich data from the income statement and balance sheet, financial and operating information, capital structure and capital stock data, company history, and name of key managers are included. The coverage vaaries depending on whether a listed company pays for a detailed profile.

Table continues

Table 2   (continued)

Service	Contact Address and Phone Number	Coverage	Format and Variables Available
Worldscope Industrial Company Profiles and Worldscope Financial Service Profiles	CIFAR 601 Ewing Street Suite C-16 Princeton, NJ 08540 USA Ph: (609) 921-0910 and Wright Investors' Service 10 Middle Street Bridgeport, CT 06609 USA Ph: (203) 333-6666	5,000+ Companies in 24 Countries	Published in finv-volume (Industrial Companies) and three-volume (Financial and other Service Companies) sets with quarterly updates. Provides comprehensive financial and capital market information, financial statement data, financial ratios, growth rates, per share data and investment ratios, five-year annual growth rates, and identification of accounting practices used on a company-specific basis. Other features include a guide on how to analyze international financial statements. Also provides country and industry averages and company rankings worldwide within a country, within a country by industry and within an industry.

- An increasing number of European companies publish preliminary annual results that provide key financial data and information on major developments long before their annual report is published.

PROBLEM:

- Of the 5,000 non-U.S. annual reports reviewed for this study, approximately 30% were not published in English.

- As English is becoming an accepted common denominator in international financial communication, international users may experience difficulty in using annual reports that are not published in English.

Table 4 identifies the availability of annual reports in English by country.

Table 3   **Timeliness of Publication of Annual Reports**
Average Number of Days Elapsed between Fiscal Year-End and
Publication of Annual Reports
Fiscal Year 1987 Reports

Country	60–150 Days	151–180 Days	181 and above
North America			
Canada	X		
Mexico		X	
United States	X		
Asia/Pacific			
Australia	X		
Hong Kong		X	
Japan	X		
Korea, South	X		
Malaysia		X	
New Zealand	X		
Singapore	X		
Europe			
Austria			X
Belgium			X
Denmark		X	
Finland	X		
France			X
Germany, West			X
Italy			X
Netherlands		X	
Norway		X	
Spain		X	
Sweden		X	
Switzerland		X	
United Kingdom	X		
Africa/Middle East			
South Africa	X		

SOLUTIONS:

- Use accounting dictionaries or lexicons to translate foreign-language accounting terms into English.

- Set up a computerized table to permit the printing of financial statements in multiple languages.

Table 4   Availability of English Language Financial Statements Fiscal Year 1987

Country	All Companies Reporting in English	More than 50% Reporting in English	Less than 50% Reporting in English
		1987	
North America			
Canada	X*		
Mexico			X
United States	X		
Asia/Pacific			
Australia	X		
Hong Kong	X		
Japan		X	
Korea, South			X
Maylasia	X		
New Zealand	X		
Singapore	X		
Europe			
Austria			X
Belgium			X
Denmark		X	
Finland		X	
France			X
Germany, West			X
Italy			X
Netherlands		X	
Norway		X	
Spain			X
Sweden		X	
Switzerland			X
United Kingdom	X		
Africa/Middle East			
South Africa	X		

* Less than 1% of Canadian companies publish annual reports only in French.

- Use professional translators to translate key financial pages.

- Recruit multilingual colleagues. In our experience of recruiting from business schools in the U.S. and in Europe, we have been able to locate business graduates with multilingual expertise. Many MBA programs have an international focus and require foreign language skills in order for students to complete their degrees.

Financial Statements Expressed in Domestic Currency
PROBLEM:

Expressing figures in annual reports in domestic currency is another perceived information barrier. In the present study, almost 100% of the financial statements studied were expressed in local currency.

SOLUTIONS:

Financial ratios that transform nominal measurements to percentage relationships are independent of currency denomination. A current ratio computed from ABC Plc's balance sheet in pounds or from a Spanish balance sheet expressed in pesetas is no different from a current ratio computed from ABC Plc's financial statements translated into Japanese yen.

For readers preferring a single currency framework, foreign currency translations can be accomplished simply by restating foreign currency balances in a user's domestic currency equivalents, using a rate equal to the exchange rate prevailing at the financial statement date. Such a translation would also allow users to rank companies worldwide in a given industry by sales, assets, or market value.

To judge the true performance of an entity in a particular country, local currency results are preferable, as they are more useful in analyzing the financial history of a company vis-a-vis local competitors as well as in analyzing financial trends.

Different Fiscal Year-end Dates
PROBLEM:

Calendar year-end dates are not widely used as fiscal year-end dates in many countries. This makes it difficult to compare the reporting periods of companies, causing a problem in analysis if a user is studying a cyclical industry.

Table 5 provides a list of year-end dates used by companies in different countries.

SOLUTION:

The use of companies' quarterly reports may facilitate standardization, where quarterly results from the previous year can be subtracted and quarterly results of the current year can be added to obtain results for a common reporting period between various firms being analyzed.

Problems with Procedural Accounting Matters

This section focuses on accounting differences involved in the process of preparing financial statements. The difficulties arising from the application of differing accounting standards are discussed in the next section.

Inadequate Disclosures

PROBLEM:

International financial statements vary in terms of what they disclose.
For example:

- A cash flow statement is not available in many countries.

- Segment and geographic information is widely available in North America, somewhat in Europe, and minimally in the Asia/Pacific region.

- Information on subsidiaries is extensive in Europe, but not as extensive in North America.

- Footnotes are extensive in reports from Commonwealth countries and Scandinavia but are not widely used in Japan or Continental Europe.

Table 6 lists key disclosure differences by industrial companies.

SOLUTION:

- Disclosing more information in financial statements depends on management's view of the user's needs. Therefore, capital market persuasion would improve disclosures.

- Local government agencies are demanding more disclosures. Government filings, which are in the public domain, such as Japanese companies' filings with the Japanese Ministry of Finance and American companies' filings with the U.S. Securities and Exchange Commission, usually provide more financial disclosure than those provided to shareholders.

Table 5 Year-End Dates Used Fiscal Year 1987
Classification of Companies by Fiscal Year-End Dates

Country	Number of Companies	% of Companies with Year-End Dates Between:			
		Jan. 1 to March 31	April 1 to June 30	July 1 to Sept. 30	Oct 1 to Dec. 31
North America					
Canada	444	13%	5%	9%	73%
Mexico	34	–	6	12	82
United States	3,483	12	12	10	66
Asiz/Pacific					
Australia	157	10	64	11	15
Hong Kong	145	28	17	3	52
Japan	510	75	7	6	12
Korea, South	51	21	18	4	57
Malaysia	70	20	21	6	53
New Zealand	34	50	32	9	9
Singapore	44	7	5	13	75
Europe					
Austria	67	–	–	–	100
Belgium	115	5	3	7	85
Denmark	96	2	6	6	86
Finland	85	4	1	7	88
France	317	3	1	3	93
Germany, West	548	2	4	8	86
Italy	158	2	3	1	94
Netherlands	252	3	2	5	90
Norway	84	2	1	–	97
Spain	72	–	3	–	97
Sweden	142	1	1	3	95
Switzerland	183	4	2	4	90
United Kingdom	702	29	9	11	51
Africa/Middle East					
Sourth Africa	173	21	39	17	23
Total	7,966	16%	10%	8%	66%

Table 6   Key Disclosure Differences: Industrial Companies

By Selected Countries	5–10 Years Financial Summary	Comparative Income Statement	Comparative Balance Sheet	Statement of Changes in SE Equity
North America				
Canada	E	2 Years	2 Years	E
Mexico	M	2 Years	2 Years	E
United States	E	2–3 Years	2 Years	M
Asiz/Pacific				
Australia	E	2 Years	2 Years	L
Hong Kong	E	2 Years	2 Years	L
Japan	E	2 Years	2 Years	E
Korea, South	L	1–2 Years	1–2 Years	E
Malaysia	E	2 Years	2 Years	L
New Zealand	E	2 Years	2 Years	L
Singapore	E	2 Years	2 Years	L
Europe				
Austria	E	1–2 Years	1–2 Years	R
Belgium	E	2 Years	2 Years	M
Denmark	E	2 Years	2 Years	L
Finland	E	2 Years	2 Years	L
France	E	2 Years	2 Years	E
Germany, West	M	1–2 Years	1–2 Years	L
Italy	M	2 Years	2 Years	M
Netherlands	E	2 Years	2 Years	L
Norway	E	2 Years	2 Years	L
Spain	E	2 Years	2 Years	L
Sweden	E	2 Years	2 Years	M
Switzerland	E	2 Years	2 Years	L
United Kingdom	E	2 Years	2 Years	L
Africa/Middle East				
Sourth Africa	E	2 Years	2 Years	L

Key:
E   Extensively Disclosed
M   Moderately Disclosed
L   Less Frequently Disclosed

Table continues

Table 6   (continued)

By Selected Countries	Statement of Cash Flow	Notes to Financial Statement	Segment Information	Geographic Information
North America				
Canada	E	E	S/OI/TA	S/OI/TA
Mexico	E	E	MP	MP
United States	E	E	S/OI/TA	S/OI/TA
Asiz/Pacific				
Australia	E	E	S/OI/TA	S/OI/TA
Hong Kong	M	E	MP	S/OI
Japan	L	M	S/OI/TA	S/OI/TA
Korea, South	L	M	MP	MP
Malaysia	E	E	MP	S/OI/TA
New Zealand	E	E	S/OI/TA	S/OI/TA
Singapore	E	E	MP	S/OI/TA
Europe				
Austria	L	M	TA	MP
Belgium	L	M	S/OI	S/OI/TA
Denmark	M	M	S/OI	S/OI
Finland	E	E	S/OI	S/OI
France	M	M	S/OI	S/OI
Germany, West	L	M	S/OI	S/OI
Italy	M	M	S/OI	MP
Netherlands	M	E	S/OI/TA	S/OI
Norway	E	E	S/OI/TA	S/OI
Spain	M	M	S/OI	MP
Sweden	M	E	S/OI	S/OI
Switzerland	L	M	S/OI	S/OI
United Kingdom	E	E	S/OI	S/OI
Africa/Middle East				
Sourth Africa	E	E	MP	S/OI/TA

Key:
S/OITA   Sales, Operating Income and Total Assets by Product Line or by Area
S/OI   Sales and Operating Income by Product Line or by Area
TA   Total Assets by Product Line or by Area

E   Extensively Disclosed
M   Moderately Disclosed
L   Less Frequently Disclosed

- International governmental organizations (e.g., the Organization for Economic Cooperation and Development and the United Nations' Center on Transnational Corporations) are recommending that multinational corporations provide more financial information to users.

Differences in Auditing Standards and Audit Reports

PROBLEM:

Independent auditors help assure the integrity of financial information by reviewing financial statements and attesting to their reliability, fairness, and general quality. National variations in auditing standards and practices are common and result primarily from differences in legal, political, and economic factors.

It is important for international users, who may depend extensively on published financial statements, to understand these differences and their implications for reliance on the statements.

Table 7 highlights key differences in the auditors' reports included in the annual reports of companies from 24 countries.

SOLUTION:

The international expansion of large public accounting firms represents a further harmonizing influence on local auditing practices. Table 8 shows the percentage of clients audited by international accounting firms in 24 countries.

Recent efforts toward the harmonization of auditing standards suggest that gaps in standards will narrow, at least in the major industrial nations. The European Community (EC), in its Fourth Directive, now requires all large public and private corporations to undergo an annual audit. The auditor is expected to disclose whether the annual accounts give a true and fair view of the financial position and of profit or loss. Recent efforts toward the harmonization of auditing standards have also been made by the International Federation of Accountants (IFAC).

Lack of Interim Data

PROBLEM:

As summarized in Table 9, interim reports are published on a varied frequency internationally, making a global comparison of the financial performance of companies in a given industry very difficult.

Table 7   Key Characteristics of Auditors' Reports

Country	Key Conclusion Words Used			Audit Report Coverage		Percentage of Audit Reports Qualified
	True and Fair View	In Conformity With the Law	Fair and Conforms with GAAP	Identified Sections Only	Entire Report Covered	
North America						
Canada			X	X		35%
Mexico			X	X		33
United States			X	X		4
Asiz/Pacific						
Australia *				X		48
Hong Kong	X		X	X		4
Japan			X	X		21
Korea, South			X	X		0
Malaysia	X			X		0
New Zealand	X			X		0
Singapore	X			X		4
Europe						
Austria		X			X	0
Belgium			X	X		13
Denmark	X				X	0
Finland	X				X	0
France	X			X		12
Germany, West		X			X	0
Italy			X	X		10
Netherlands			X	X		0
Norway	X				X	4
Spain			X	X		37
Sweden	X				X	2
Switzerland		X		X		0
United Kingdom	X			X		3
Africa/Middle East						
Sourth Africa	X			X		1

* Autitors' reports in Australia use "Properly Drawn Up" as the key conclusion phrase.

Interim financial statements often include several items from the income statement, but very few balance sheet items.

**Table 8   Percentage of Companies Audited by
Leading International Accounting Firms**

Country	% of Clients Audited by	
	Sixteen International Accounting Firms	Audit Firms not Affiliated with Sixteen International Accounting Firms
North America		
Canada	97%	3%
Mexico	96	4
United States	100	0
Asiz/Pacific		
Australia	95	5
Hong Kong	96	4
Japan	71	29
Korea, South	70	30
Malaysia	70	30
New Zealand	87	13
Singapore	99	1
Europe		
Austria	53	47
Belgium	45	55
Denmark	76	24
Finland	97	3
France	70	30
Germany, West	88	12
Italy	96	4
Netherlands	99	1
Norway	91	9
Spain	97	3
Sweden	95	5
Switzerland	56	44
United Kingdom	97	3
Africa/Middle East		
Sourth Africa	97	3

SOLUTION:

Capital market initiatives or regulatory changes requiring more frequent disclosure of financial data may persuade companies to provide interim information to users.

**Table 9   Frequency of Interim Financial Statements
Fiscal Year 1988**

Country	Majority Practice Quarterly	Every Four Months	Semi-Annually	Interims Published by Few companies
North America				
Canada	X			
Mexico				X
United States	X			
Asiz/Pacific				
Australia			X	
Hong Kong			X	
Japan			X	
Korea, South				X
Malaysia			X	
New Zealand			X	
Singapore			X	
Europe				
Austria				X
Belgium				X
Denmark			X	
Finland		X		
France			X	
Germany, West			X	
Italy			X	
Netherlands	X			
Norway		X		
Spain	X			
Sweden		X		
Switzerland				X
United Kingdom			X	
Africa/Middle East				
South Africa			X	

Differences in the Account Form of Financial Statements
PROBLEM:

Differences in international balance sheet and income statement formats can prove troublesome. Table 10 summarizes the differences in the 24 countries studied.

Income statement presentations appear standarized throughout most of the world. Differences occur primarily in a few European countries where the debit/credit format is commonly employed.

SOLUTION:

Because of the pervasiveness of the double-entry bookkeeping system internationally, similarity in the underlying structure of financial statements allows format differences to be reconciled readily. For example, current liabilities can be added back to net working capital to obtain current assets in an Australian company's balance sheet.

Variance in Definition of Accounting Terms
PROBLEM:

Some accounting terms have different meanings in various countries, leading to confusion.

For example:

North America Commonwealth Countries
Inventories Stock
Stock Investments
Sales Turnover
Leased Assets Hired Purchased Assets
Accounts Receivable Debtors
Accounts Payable Creditors

SOLUTION:

The construction of a table of key terms and further familiarization with international reports usually resolves this problem.

The difficulties identified in this section are not insurmountable. With proper insight and experience, most of these problems can be overcome, as many of

Table 10   Differences in the Form of Financial Statements
Industrial Companies

	Balance Statement			Income Statement		
Country	TA = TL + SE	FA + NWC Less LTD = SE	FA + NWC = LTD + SE	Sales Less Expenses	Debit = Credit	Op. Prof. Less Int. & Tax Exp.
North America						
Canada	X			X		
Mexico	X			X		
United States	X			X		
Asiz/Pacific						
Australia		X				X
Hong Kong		X				X
Japan	X			X		
Korea, South	X			X		
Malaysia		X				X
New Zealand	X					X
Singapore		X				X
Europe						
Austria	X				X	
Belgium	X				X	
Denmark	X			X		
Finland	X			X		
France	X			X	X	
Germany, West	X			X		
Italy	X			X	X	
Netherlands	X			X	X	
Norway	X			X		
Spain	X			X	X	
Sweden	X			X		
Switzerland	X			X		
United Kingdom		X				X
Africa/Middle East						
Sourth Africa						

Key:
TA = TL = SE   Total Assets = Total Liabilities + Shareholders' Equity
FA + NWC – LTD = SE   Fixed Assets + Net Working Capital – Long-Term Debt
                                     = Shareholders' Equity
FA + NWC = LTD + SE   Fixed Assets + Net Working Capital = Long-Term Debt
                                     + Shareholders' Equity
Op Prof. – Int. & Tax Exp.   Operating Profits – Interest and Tax Expenses

them are mechanical in nature. In the next section, differences in accounting standards, which are more difficult to mitigate, are discussed.

Differences in Accounting Standards

On the surface, a user may find many accounting differences while reviewing the annual reports of companies worldwide. All of these differences, however, may not necessarily have an impact on earnings and balance sheet totals. Some of the differences can be easily reconciled.

The awareness of major differences in the underlying accounting principles of companies located in different countries is an important prerequisite for the analysis of international financial statements. With such knowledge, a user of financial statements may be able to at least take into account the magnitude of such differences.

To facilitate the comparison of companies internationally, the discussion of accounting differences has been divided into four sections:

A. Format differences
B. Accounting differences with a small impact on earnings/valuation
C. Accounting differences with a large impact on earnings/valuation
D. Methods of reconciling accounting differences

Format Differences

PROBLEMS:

- Due to the double entry bookkeeping system, which is widely accepted around the world, the income statement format is standardized as revenues minus expenses. However, expense classifications vary considerably. For example, the cost of goods sold is not defined consistently, and earnings per share are computed using different earnings numbers.

- The balance sheet has many such format differences from country to country.

Some examples:
- Contra accounts such as accumulated depreciation and treasury stock may or may not be netted out.

•   Contingent liabilities are sometimes included on both sides of the balance sheet, and as a result, assets and liabilities are overstated.

•   Sub-classifications, such as current assets and current liabilities, are not comparable.

Tables 11A through 11E report some of the format differences found in the annual reports of companies in selected countries.

SOLUTIONS:

Restate numbers to make them format compatible. For example, depreciation reserves can be subtracted from fixed assets; treasury stock can be subtracted from current assets, thereby effectively reducing shareholders' equity. Thus, format differences do not involve many changes in the figures. (The figures are regrouped into a format that will conform to the reporting practices of other countries.)

For example, U.S. companies show earnings per share as net income minus preferred dividends, divided by the average number of common shares outstand-

---

Table 11A   Format Differences in Reporting from Selected Countries
Cost of Goods Sold (COGS) in Income Statement

Item:

Australia	– No cost of goods sold is disclosed. Trading profit from operations before taxation is disclosed. Trading profit from operations before taxation is disclosed. COGS is sometimes disclosed in the footnotes.
Canada	– Cost of sales provided. Also administration and depreciation expenses are provided separately.
France	– COGS not given. In its place a company will disclose operating expense accounts that include depreciation and interest expense. Other operating expenses may not be included but disclosed elsewhere.
W. Germany	– Not given. A list of operating expense accounts is given and can be used to approximate COGS. These expenses include depreciation.
Italy	– COGS not given, but a list of operating expense accounts is provided.
Japan	– Provided.
Sweden	– Not given, but a list of operating expense accounts that include depreciation is given.
Switzerland	– Not given, but a list of operating expenses is provided.
U.K.	– Usually provided, and is the actual cost of the goods sold; does not include interest expense and depreciation.
U.S.	– Provided.

Table 11B   Format Differences in Reporting from Selected Countries Earnings per Share (EPS)

Item:

Australia	– Disclosed in financial highlights, not in I/S*. Basis of computation usually not disclosed. Computed after extraordinary items are considered.
Canada	– Usually basic EPS are disclosed but could also be fully diluted. Based on weighted average number of shares. Calculated before and after extraordinary items.
France	– Basic EPS. Calculated after preferred dividends. Effect of extraordinary items is included. Calculated on the basis of total shares outstanding.
W. Germany	– Basic EPS. Calculated after preferred dividends and extraordinary items and based on wieghted average number of shares.
Italy	– Rarely disclosed.
Japan	– Basic EPS. Based on weighted average number of shares. Could be stated per unit of 100 shares. Computed after effect of extraordinary items.
Sweden	– Basic EPS. Calculated after preferred dividends (though preferred equity is rare), but before extraordinary items. Based on weighted average number of shares.
Switzerland	– Not disclosed on I/S—disclosed in financial summary. Basis of computation is usually disclosed.
U.K.	– Basic EPS. Calculated after preferred dividends but before extraordinary items. Based on weighted average number of shares.
U.S.	– Basic and diluted EPS calculated after preferred dividends; before and after extraordinary items. Weighted average shares are used.

* I/S = Income Statement

Table 11C   Format Differences in Reporting from Selected Companies Current Assets

From

Australia	– Shown in descending order of liquidity. Individual accounts are net of valuation or contra items.
Canada	– Shown in descending order of liquidity. Net of valuation or contra accounts.
France	– Shown in descending order of liquidity. Valuation accounts may be shown on liability side. Inventory may be shown as separate item.
W. Germany	– Shown in ascending order of liquidity. No netting, valuation accounts are on liability side. Could include treasury stock.
Italy	– Shown in descending order of liquidity. Individual accounts in gross amount, valuation or contra accounts on liability side.
Japan	– Shown in descending order of liquidity. Individual accounts are net of valuation or contra accounts. May include treasury stock.
Sweden	– Shown in descending order of Liquidity. Valuation accounts netted out.
Switzerland	– Shown in descending order of liquidity. Net of valuation or contra accounts.
U.K.	– Shown in ascending order of liquidity. Shown net of current liabilities.
U.S.	– Shown in descending order of liquidity. Individual accounts are net of any valuation or contra accounts.

**Table 11D   Format Differences in Reporting from Selected Countries
Property, Plant and Equipment**

Item:

Australia	– Shown net. Accumulated depreciation shown in footnotes.
Canada	– Shown net. Accumulated depreciation disclosed in footnotes.
France	– Shown gross with accumulated depreciation. Subject to revaluation. Accumulated depreciation may be shown under liabilities.
W. Germany	– Shown gross on asset side with accumulated depreciation on liability side.
Italy	– Shown gross; accumulated depreciation on liability side.
Japan	– Shown gross, but accumulated depreciation is deducted to arrive at net fixed assets.
Sweden	– Shown net of accumulated depreciation.
Switzerland	– Shown gross with accumulated depreciation, additions and disposals.
U.K.	– Shown net of accumulated depreciation.
U.S.	– Shown gross, but accumulated depreciation is deducted to arrive at net figure.

**Table 11E   Format Differences in Reporting from Selected Countries
Treasury Stock**

Item:

Australia	– Reduction of shareholders' equity.
Canada	– Reduction of shareholders' equity.
France	– Not disclosed.
W. Germany	– Included in current assets.
Italy	– Included in current assets.
Japan	– Reduction of shareholders' equity in consolidated version. Included in current assets in unconsolidated version.
Sweden	– Reduction of shareholders' equity.
Switzerland	– Included in current assets.
U.K.	– Reduction of shareholders' equity.
U.S.	– Reduction of shareholders' equity.

---

ing. U.K. companies, on the other hand, take net income before extraordinary items, and then divide that by the average number of total shares outstanding. An extraordinary loss would decrease the net income figure but would not show up in earnings per share. Comparing earnings per share for U.K. and U.S. companies, therefore, simply means recalculating for extraordinary items.

Varying Application of Uniform Accounting Standards
PROBLEM:

Though accounting differences between companies worldwide are numerous, there are certain uniform accounting standards. However, differences still exist in the application of these standards.

For instance, the amortization of goodwill is common among all countries. However, there may be differences in the length of the period over which amortization takes place. European and other countries use a maximum of ten years. The United States prescribes a maximum period of forty years, but many U.S. companies have used periods that fall substantially below forty years. It is clear, then, that the impact of yearly amortization expense on net income does vary, but not necessarily substantially.

Table 12 provides a list of a few of the accounting standards in this category.

SOLUTION:

The effect of accounting differences in this category are not of a large magnitude, and we believe that over a longer time period their effect would be nullified.

Major Differences in Accounting Standards
PROBLEMS:

Differences in international accounting standards that can have a great impact on earnings and various balance sheet totals are a major barrier for users of international financial statements. Some of these major differences in accounting policies are:

1. Depreciation Methods: Depreciation methods differ from industry to industry, country to country, and even within a country.
2. Inventory Methods: Although FIFO is widely accepted, companies in some countries use the weighted average or LIFO method for inventory valuation.
3. Deferred Taxes: Accounting rules differ from tax rules in some countries. The difference between the tax expense and the tax liability can be substantial.
4. Consolidation Principles: Quite frequently, only domestic or significant subsidiaries are consolidated. In addition, the cost basis of accounting

Table 12 Accounting Differences with a Small Impact on Earnings/Valuation Industrial Companies from Slected Countries

Standard	Australia	Canada	France	West Germany	Italy	Japan	Nether-lands	Sweden	Switzer-land	U.K.	U.S.
R&D Costs Expensed Currently?	Yes	Yes	Yes	ND	ND	ND	ND	ND	ND	Yes	Yes
Pension Fund Contributions Provided Regularly	Yes	Yes	Yes	Yes	Yes	Yes	Yes	Yes	ND	Yes	Yes
Accounting for Investments Less than 20% —Cost Method?	Mixed	Yes	ND	Yes	Mixed	Yes	Yes	Mized	ND	ND	Yes
Acquisition Method —Purchase?	Yes	Yes	Yes	Yes	ND	Yes	Yes	Yes	Yes	Yes	Yes
Accounting for Goodwill —Amortized?	Yes	Yes	Yes	Mixed	ND	Yes	Mixed	Yers	ND	No	Yes
Accounting for Minority Interest —Before Bottom Line on Income Statement; Excluded from Stock-holders' Equity?	Yes	ND	Yes	Yes	Yes	Yes	Yes	Yes	Yes	Yes	Yes

Key:

Yes – most common practice
No   – not commonly adhered to; small number may adhere to standard
Mixed – more than one method used considerably
ND   – not disclosed; majority of companies do not disclose method.

for investments is used in many countries for investments of greater than 20% in a subsidiary.

5. Discretionary Reserves: In many countries, allocations to and from reserves, which can often distort income, can be made at management's discretion. For banks and insurance companies, allocations to such reserves constitute a large percentage of operating revenues.

6. Inflation Adjustments: The periodic revaluations of fixed assets and inventories are common in some countries, resulting in a revaluation reserve in the balance sheet and extra charges in the income statement.

7. Foreign Currency Gains/Losses and Translation Method: The current rate method is widely accepted, but currency translation gains and losses may either be reflected in the income statement or recorded as a change in reserves in the balance sheet.

8. Valuation of Fixed Income and Equity Securities: For banks and insurance companies, alternative methods of valuing their security portfolios are used (i.e., cost, market, or lower of cost or market).

Table 13 provides a summary of these major accounting differences among industrial companies in 24 countries.

Table 14 provides a summary of these major accounting differences among banks in 22 countries.

Table 15 provides a summary of these major accounting differences among insurance companies in 22 countries.

SOLUTIONS:

The ideal solution would be to have the leading companies in global industries prepare financial statements under a single accounting convention. Since this will not occur in the near future, we would like to suggest some practical approaches to the analysis of companies across national boundaries.

The user should exercise caution since all of these adjustments do not necessarily make annual reports completely comparable internationally. However, the approaches suggested in this section do minimize the impact of accounting differences so that a global view can be taken in evaluating companies:

1. Use Stock Market-Determined Financial Ratios:

The investment community is very conversant with financial indicators derived from stock market data items, such as market price per share, dividend per share, and the risk identification of each security. Stock market averages are also available on each of these items:

Table 13   Major Accounting Differences Among Countries: Industrial Companies

Country	Revaluation Allowed	Consolidated Financial Date	Valuation Long-Term Investments 20%—50%	Inventory Valuation Methods	Deferred Income Taxes	Discretionary and/or Non-Equity Reserves	Currency Translation G/L Taken To	Depreciation Methods
North America								
Canada	Yes	M	Equity	FIFO	Used	Not Used	IS/Defer	SL
Mexico	Yes	M	Equity	Rep Cost	Used	Not Used	ND	SL
United States	No	E	Equity	FIFO	Used	Not Used	IS/SE	SL
Asia/Pacific								
Australia	Yes	E	Eq/PC	FIFO	Used	Not Used*	IS/SE	SL
Hong Kong	Yes	E	Cost/Eq	FIFO	Used	Not Used*	IS/SE	SL
Japan	No	M	Cost/Eq	Average	Not Used	Not Used*	IS/Defer	AM
Korea, South	Yes	L	Cost	Average	Not Used	Not Used*	IS/Defer	AM
Malaysia	Yes	E	Cost/Eq	FIFO	Used	Not Used*	IS	SL
New Zealand	Yes	M	Equity	FIFO	Used	Not Used*	IS/SE	SL
Singapore	Yes	E	Equity	Average	Used	Not Used*	IS	SL
Europe								
Australia	Yes	L	Cost	Not. Disc	Not Used	Used	ND	SL
Belgium	Yes	L	Cost/Eq	Mixed	Not Used	Used	IS/SE	SL
Denmark	Yes	M	Equity	FIFO	Used	Used	IS/SE	SL
Finland	Yes	M	Cost	FIFO	Not Used	Used	IS/Defer	SL
France	Yes	M	Equity	FIFO	Used	Used	IS/SE	SL
Germany, West	Yes	M	Cost	Average	Not Used	Used	IS/SE	Mixed
Italy	Yes	L	Cost/Eq	Mixed	Not Used	Used	IS/Defer	SL
Netherlands	Yes	E	Equity	FIFO	Used	Not Used	IS/SE	SL

Norway	Yes	M	Cost/Eq	FIFO	Used	Used	IS	SL
Spain	Yes	L	Cost/Eq	Average	Not Used	Used	IS/Defer	SL
Sweden	Yes	E	Cost/Eq	FIFO	Not Used	Used	IS/SE	SL
Switzerland	Yes	M	Cost/Ez	Average	Not Used	Used	SE	SL
United Kingdom	Yes	E	Equity	FIFO	Used	Not Used*	IS/SE	SL
Africa/Mid-East								
South Africa	No	E	Equity	FIFO	Used	Not Used*	IS/SE	SL

* Specific items such as replacement reserves or excess depreciation used.

Key:

Consolidated financial Data
E   Extensively Disclosed
M   Moderately Disclosed
L   Less Frequently Disclosed

Valuation of Long-Term Investments 20—50%

Eq/PC Equity Method; partially consolidated
Cost/Eq Cost Method or Equity Method

Inventory Valuation Methods
FIFO   First in First out
Rep. Cost Replacement Cost
Average Average Cost
Mixed   No Majority Practice, one of several methods used

Depreciation Methods
SL   Straight Line Method
AM   Accelerated Method

Currency Translation Gains/Losses Taken to:

IS   Income Statement
SE   Shareholders' Equity
IS/Defer Income Statement and/or Deferred
IS/SE   Income Statement and/or Shareholders' Equity
ND   Not Disclosed

Table 14   Major Accounting Differences Among Countries: Banks

Country	Valuation of Marketable Securities	Allow. Loan Losses fixed by Law	Valuation of Long-Term Investment	Hidden or Non-Equity Reserves	Customers' Liability for Acceptances	Interest Inc/Exp Disclosed	Commissions Earned/Paid Disclosed
North America							
Canada	MV	Yes	PP	No	TA	Gross	ND
United States	MV	No	PP	No	TA	Gross	Gross
Asia/Pacific							
Australia	MV	No	PP	No	TA	Gross	Net
Hong Kong	LCM	Yes	PP/Amort	No	TA	ND	ND
Japan	LCM	Yes	PP	No	TA	Gross	Gross
Korea, South	LCM	Yes	PP	No	TA	Gross	Gross
Maylasia	LCM	No	PP/Amort	No	TA	ND	ND
Singapore	LCM	No	PP/MV	No	TA	ND	ND
Europe							
Austria	LCM	ND	PP	Sep'd	TA/pt	Gross	Net
Belgium	HC	No	PP	No	FN	Gross	Gross
Denmark	MV	No	MV	SE	TA/pt	Gross	Net
Finland	LCM	Yes	PP	Sep/d	FN	Gross	Net
France	LCM	Yes	PP	Sep'd	FN	Gross	Gross
Germany, West	LCM	Yes	PP	Sep'd	TA/pt	Gross	Gross
Italy	LCM	Yes	PP	Sep'd	FN	Gross	Gross

Netherlands	MV	No	MV	SE	FN	Net	Net
Norway	LCM	Yes	PP	Sep'd	FN	Gross	Net
Spain	LCM	Yes	PP/MV	Sep'd	FN	Gross	Net
Sweden	LCM	Yes	MV	Sep'd	FN	Net/FN	Gross
Switzerland	LCM	Yes	MV	No	FN	Gross	Gross
United Kingdom	MV	No	LCM	No	FN	Net/FN	Net
Africa/Mid-East							
South Africa	MV	No	MV	No	TA	ND	ND

Key

Valuation of Marketable Securities

MV   Market Value
HC   Historical cost
LCM Lower of Cost or Market
ND   Not Determinable

Valuation of Long-Term Investments

PP   Purchase Price
PP/Amort Purchase Price Adjusted by Amortization of Premiums or Discounts
PP/MV   Purchase Price Adjusted by Market Value
LCM   Lower of Cost or Market

Hidden or Non-Equity Reserves

NO   Do Not Exist
Sep'd Exist and Separately Accounted for
SE   Exist and Accounted for as a Part of Shareholders' Equity

Customers Liability for Acceptances

TA   As a Part of Total Assets
TA/pt Partially as a Part of Total Assets
FN   Disclosed Only in a Footnote

Commissions Earned/Paid Disclosed

Gross   Gross Amounts on Income Statement
Net   Net Amounts on Income Statement
Net/FN Net Amounts on Income Statement and Gross Amounts in a Footnote
ND   Not Disclosed Separately

Table 15   Major Accounting Differences Among Countries: Insurance Companies

Country	Life/ Non-Life by the Same Company	Fixed Income Securities Valuation	Equity Securities Valuation	Reinsurance Business	Under-writing Expenses Disclosed	Hidden or Non-Equity Reserves
North America						
Canada	No	AC	HC	ND	GAE	ND
United States	Yes	AC	MP	Net	Sep	NE
Asia/Pacific						
Australia	No	HC	MP	Gross	Sep	ND
Hong Kong	No	LCM	HC	Net	GAE	NK
Japan	No	LCM	LCM	Gross	GAE	NE
Korea, South	No	AC	LCM	Gross	GAE	NE
Malaysia	Yes	HC	MP	Net	Sep	NE
Singapore	Yes	HC	MP	ND	Sep	NE
Europe						
Austria	Yes	ND	ND	Net	Sep	Sep
Belgium	Yes	LCM	MP	Gross	Sep	Sep
Denmark	Yes	AC	MP	Net	GAE	ND
Finland	Yes	AC	MP	Gross	Sep	Sep
France	Yes	HC	HC	Net	Sep	Sep
Germany, West	Yes	AC	LCM	Net	Sep	ND
Italy	Yes	LCM	LCM	Net	Sep	ND
Netherlands	Yes	AC	MP	Gross	Sep	Sep
Norway	Yes	LCM	LCM	Net	GAE	Sep
Spain	Yes	HC	LACM	Net	Sep	Not Sep
Sweden	Yes	LCM	LCM	Net	GAE	Sep
Switzerland	yes	LCM	LCM	Net	GAE	ND
United Kingdom	Yes	MP	MP	Gross	GAE	NE
Africa/Mid- East						
South Africa	No	AC	MP	Net	GAE	ND

Key:

Fixed Income and Equity Securities Valuation

AC	Amortized Cost
HC	Historical Cost
MP	Market Price
LCM	Lower of Cost or Market
ND	Not Disclosed
LACM	Lower Cost and Partial Adjustment to Market

Reinsurance Business

Gross	Gross Amounts on Individual Accounts are Disclosed
Net	Only Net Reinsurance Results are Disclosed

Underwriting Expense Disclosed

GAE	Part of General Administrative Expenses
SEP	Separately Disclosed

Hidden or Non-Equity Reserves

NE	Do Not Exist
Sep	Exist and Separately Accounted for
Not Sep	Exist but Not Separately Accounted for
ND	Not Disclosed

a. Dividend Yield = Total cash dividends to common shareholders
Total market capitalization

b. Annual Rate of Return to Stockholders =
Dividend Yield ± Appreciation or Loss

c. Excess Returns =

Annual Rate of Return Less Risk	Adjusted Rate of Return
to stockholders on a	on that company
given company	

Users can easily compare the financial performance of large international companies by using the above financial ratios.

This approach is advantageous because the results are unaffected by accounting differences. In addition, financial analysis by users is facilitated by the availability and timeliness of the data.

A major disadvantage of this approach, however, is that the underlying fundamental characteristics of each firm will not be evaluated.

2.   Use Growth-Related Financial Ratios:

Financial ratios, which are not affected by accounting differences, can be used. Year to year growth in sales, operating income, dividends, net worth, total assets, earnings per share, dividends per share, and book value per share can be computed. This approach allows for easier computation of global industry averages, thus facilitating global evaluation of international companies.

The argument in favor of such an approach would be that large companies do not change their accounting standards each year. Therefore, year to year changes in key accounts can provide important signals about a particular firm's financial performance and position.

A problem with this approach would be that in several countries, due to various tax incentives, companies report a very low net income. Thus, a percentage change in earnings may not reflect actual performance.

3.   Use Cash Flow Statements:

Use cash flow statements where charges to discretionary reserves and other non-cash expenses, such as depreciation, can be added back to net income to obtain true cash generated by the company and, thereby, minimize the influence of accounting differences.

The financial community has recently expressed a preference for cash flow- related indicators, such as cash flow per share and cash flow generated as a percentage of sales, as unbiased indicators of a firm's performance.

4.   Obtain Annual Reports Restated in User's GAAP.

In an attempt to better serve the information needs of foreign investors, a number of multinational companies have begun to experiment with alternative reporting modes. For example, in reporting to their U.S. shareholders, Philips of the Netherlands not only presents English translations of its annual reports, but also restates the key items of its balance sheet and income statement according to U.S. GAAP. Many large multinational firms in Japan go a step further and entirely restate their financial statements according to U.S. GAAP. Swedish companies provide a reconciliation of the cost method of accounting for investments with the equity method to reflect international accounting standards.

We obtained and analyzed the restatements of financial statements into U.S. GAAP, which were published by selected companies in the United Kingdom, Sweden, and Japan. Though only a few companies from these countries published financial statements according to U.S. GAAP, the comparisons may be of use in identifying differences between the accounting standards of the U.S. and each of these countries.

a. United Kingdom

The major reconciliation items, compared with the general practice in the United States, are summarized in Table 16.

The financial results of five U.K. companies under two sets of accounting standards are illustrated in Table 17. Shareholders' equity is significantly different when a company has very high foreign operations or purchases a business, which result in foreign currency translation adjustments and goodwill, respectively. Thus, the effects of the differences in standards can be either favorable or unfavorable.

b. Sweden

The major differences in accounting practices between Sweden and the United States are summarized in Table 18 and the financial results for selected companies in Table 19. The most significant differences in accounting practices between Sweden and the United States are the appropriation of earnings to untaxed reserves and related items in the balance sheet.

c. Japan

The restatements of Japanese companies are slightly different from those analyzed in the United Kingdom and Sweden. Japanese restatements focus mainly on the consolidated financial statements. Consolidation of financial data is a recent accounting practice in Japan. Since the 1970's, the Securities Exchange Law of Japan has required public companies to report consolidated financial statements based upon guidelines provided by the Japanese Institute of Certified Public Accountants. About 50% of the companies listed in

Table 16   Major Differences in Accounting Standards between the United Kingdom and the United States

Items	United Kingdom GAAP	United States GAAP
1. Deferred Income Taxes		
• Method Used	• Liability Method	• Deferral Method
• Coverage	• Partially Used (Only if probable to be payable in forseeable future)	• Fully Used
2. Property Revaluation	• Allowed Under Certain Circumstances	• Not Allowed
3. Dividends	• Proposed Amounts	• Declared Amounts
4. Gain or Loss on Foreign Currency Forward Exchange Contracts	• Not Allowed	• Allowed
5. Extraordinary Items	• Broad definition	• Narrow Definition
6. Discontinued Operation	• Part of Extraordinary Items	• Separate Item
7. Foreign Currency Translation of Income Statement Items	• Fiscal Year-End Rate	• Average Rate
8. Goodwill	• Write-down Against Reserve	• 40 Years of Amortization
9. Convertible Cumulative Redeemable Preferred Shares	• As a Part of Shareholders' Equity	• Separate Item
10. Capitalization of Interest Expenses on Long-Term Contracts	• Not Capitalized	• Deferred and Amortized
11. Exceptional Pension Contributions	• Charged when Payable	• Deferred and Amortized

Table 17   Major Financial Items under United Kingdom and United States Accounting Standards for Selected U.K.-Based Companies—Fiscal Year 1987

U.K.-based Companies	Net Income (£ in MM)		Earnings £ Per Share		Shareholders' Equity (£ in MM)	
	U.K. GAAP	U.S. GAAP	U.K. GAAP	U.S. GAAP	U.K. GAAP	U.S. GAAP
British Airways	148	155	.205	220	605	410
Beecham Group Plc	199	189	.271.	.250	1,276	1,372
Glaxo Holdings Plc	496	481	.670	.650	1,450	1,460
Reuters Holdings Plc	109	93	.260	.221	218	384
Saatchi & Saatchi Co. Ltd	67	33	.459	.215	40	628

Table 18   Major Differences in Accounting Standards between Swedish GAAP and U.S. GAAP

Items	Swedish GAAP	United States GAAP
1. Special Reserves and Provisions (Allocations to untaxed reserves)	• Allowed	• Not Allowed
2. Deferred Income Taxes	• Not Allowed	• Allowed
3. Classification of Accumulated Foreign Currency Translation Adjustment	• Distribute Them Between Restricted and Unrestricted Retained Earnings	• Separate Item as a Part of Shareholders' Equity
4. Revaluation of Assets	• Allowed in Certain Circumstances	• Not Allowed
5. Valuation of Investment Assets	• Write-up and Write-down	• Only Write-down
6. Capitalization of Interest Expenses for Construction	• Not Allowed	• Allowed
7. Early Termination Benefits	• Capitalized and Amortized	• Expensed in the Year
8. Revenue Recognition of Long-Term Contracts	• Completion Method	• Percentage of Completion
9. Equity Earnings of Associated Companies (20–50%)	• Generally Cost Method (recently some use equity method)	• Equity Method
10. Earnings Per Share Calculation	• Income Before Extraordinary Items	• After Extraordinary Items

Table 19   Major Financial Items under Swedish and United States Accounting Standards for Selected Swedish Companies Fiscal Year 1987

Swedish Companies	Net Income (In Millions of Swedish Kronor)		Earnings (Per Share in Swedish Kronor)		Shareholders' Equity (In Millions of Swedish Kronor)	
	Swedish GAAP	U.S. GAAP	Swedish GAAP	U.S. GAAP	Swedish GAAP	U.S. GAAP
Atlas Copco AB	459	634	15.40	27.00	3,258	3,820
Electrolux AB	1,282	1,833	25.6*	25.0*	9,914	11,340
Ericsson (LM) Telefon AB	495	657	17.90	17.22	7,468	8,684
SKF AB	739	288	20.90	10.65	9,632	9,125
Volvo AB	3,291	1,345	57.80	59.70	12,264	20,092

*Fully Diluted

Consolidation of financial data is a recent accounting practice in Japan. Since the 1970's, the Securities Exchange Law of Japan has required public companies to report consolidated financial statements based upon guidelines provided by the Japanese Institute of Certified Public Accountants. About 50% of the companies listed in the first section of the Tokyo Stock Exchange filed consolidated financial statements in 1987. However, the guidelines for consolidation have some flexibility. About 20% of the consolidated financial statements are restated to help foreign users understand them better, especially in terms of U.S. GAAP. The restated financial statements are reported to the Ministry of Finance, as well as to the foreign users of English reports, together with unconsolidated financial statements.

A few companies provide two different consolidated financial statements: consolidation under pure Japanese accounting standards for the Ministry of Finance, and consolidation under the accounting standards partially modified to U.S. GAAP for the foreign users of English-language reports. The most important items modified are summarized in Table 20. However, the modification of a few accounting standards is insufficient to explain the current norm of a higher price-earnings ratio for Japanese companies. For example, depreciation expense, which is a major expense in manufacturing companies, is based upon the accelerated depreciation method for both financial and tax reporting as permitted by Japanese tax regulations. Deferred income tax will also be affected by the depreciation method if a straight-line method, which is common in the U.S. or EC countries, is applied for financial reporting purposes.

Table 21 illustrates the differences between the financial results of a few companies that report two different consolidated financial statements. It is difficult to draw a definite conclusion from the table.

Table 22 approaches the problem from a different angle. Thirty-one companies were selected from the electronics industry, of which 15 companies report consolidated financial information under Japanese GAAP, while the other 16 companies report under adjusted U.S. GAAP. The latest financial information, taken from annual reports for fiscal years ending as recently as April 1988, has been analyzed. It is assumed that these companies have similar types of assets since they are in the same industry.

Depreciation expense-related ratios are similar for these two groups, with the result that they use the same method to calculate depreciation expenses.

Table 20   Accounting Standards Modification to U.S. GAAP
for Foreign Users of the Consolidated Financial Statements
in Japan

Items	Japanese GAAP	Adjustments to U.S. GAAP
1. Deferred Income Taxes	• Not Used	• Partially Applied
2. Compensated Absences	• Expensed when Paid	• Partially Accrued
3. Foreign Currency Translation Adjustments	• Modified Temporal Method	• MainlyCcurrent Rate Method
4. Valuation of Marketable Equity Securities	• Lower of Cost or Market (Individual Basis)	• Lower of cost or Market (Aggregate Basis)
5. Classification of Business Tax	• As a Part of Selling, General, and Administrative Expenses	• As a Part of Income Taxes
6. Appropriation for Special Reserves	• Allowed	• Not Allowed

---

Table 21   Major Financial Items under Japanese Accounting Standards
and U.S. GAAP Modification for Selected Japanese Companies
1987 Operating Results

Japanese Companies	Net Income (In Millions of Japanese Yen)		Earnings Per Share (In Japanese Yen)		Shareholders' Equity (In Millions of Japanese Yen)	
	Japan	U.S. GAAP	Japan	U.S. GAAP	Japan	U.S. GAAP
Denny's Japan Co. Ltd	2,557	2,528	95.63	94.50	33,964	26,584
Nitto Electric Ind.	8,275	8,107	56.22	52.91	117,173	115,545
Seven-Eleven Japan	18,390	18,937	150.49	155.00	82,757	85,107
Sumitomo Corp.	28,924	30,184	37.22	37.01	342,368	335,580
Uny Co. Ltd.	9,672	8,454	62.90	52.36	128,776	130,746

Deferred income tax is not used under Japanese GAAP, but is used under U.S. GAAP. For example, in the United States, an accelerated depreciation method is used for tax purposes and a straight-line depreciation method for financial reporting purposes. This is not the case in Japan.

Pension expenses are another issue, but their significance to the cost of goods sold and selling, general and administrative expenses is very small. It is difficult to say whether the use of different ac-

Table 22   Comparison of Financial Data between Companies under Pure Japanese GAAP and U.S. GAAP Adjustments for Selected Companies in the Electronics Industry

Financial Data	Japanese GAAP* Average	U.S. GAAP Adjustment** Average
1. Depreciation Expenses		
Depreciable Assets/Total Assets	19.5%	17.5%
Accumulated Depreciation/ Gross Depreciable Assets	59.9%	60.6%
Depreciation Expense/COGS and SGA	5.5%	58.3%
2. Effective Tax Rate	63.3%	58.3%
3. Operating Margin	4.2%	8.6%
4. Cumulative Foreign Currency Adjustments to Shareholders' Equity	–0.88%	–3.7%
5. Return on Assets	1.87%	2.9%
6. Return on Equity	4.8%	6.3%
7. Price/Earnings	78.1 Times	45.1 Times
8. Price/Book Value	3.18 Times	2.61 Times

Key:

* Average of 15 Japanese Electronics Companies' Financial Statements Prepared under Japanese Accounting Standards.

**Average of 16 Japanese Electronics Companies' Financial Statements Prepared under U.S. Accounting Standards

Alps Electric Company, Ltd.
Citizen Watch Co., Ltd.
Hattori, Seiko Co., Ltd.
Konica Corp.
Matsushits Electric Works Ltd.
Minolta Camera Co. Ltd.
Nikon corp.
Nippondenso Co., Ltd.
Oki Electric Ind. Co. Ltd.
Sharp Corporation
Sumitomo Electric Industries, Ltd.
Tokyo Electric Co. Ltd. (TEC)
Victor Company of Japan Ltd.
Yamaha Corporation
Yokagowa Electric Corp.

Canon Inc.
Casio Computer Company Ltd.
Fuji Photo Film Co., Ltd.
Hitachi Ltd.
Makita Electric Works Ltd.
Matsushita Electric Industrial Co.
Mitsubishi Electric Corporation
Murata Manufacturing Co. Ltd.
NEC Corporation
Olympus Optical co., Ltd.
Omron Tateisi Electronics Co. Ltd.
Ricoh Co. Ltd.
Sanyo Electric Co. Ltd.
Sony Corporation
TDK Corporation
Toshiba Corporation

the shareholders' equity negatively in recent years, particularly for companies under U.S. GAAP.

Operating results under U.S. GAAP are much higher than those under Japanese GAAP in terms of return on assets or return on equity. Price to earnings or price over book value per share ratios are also realistic compared to averages in other countries.

To summarize, Japanese adjustments to U.S. GAAP are published only for outside users. The adjustments are done partially. Further research in the areas of depreciation expense, pension expenses, inclusion of smaller subsidiaries, and related accounting practices will be necessary to fully reconcile Japanese GAAP to U.S. GAAP.

5.   Create Subtotals of Key Accounts that are Format Compatible:

Users can minimize differences in accounting terminology, stock price format, statement format, and language through the use of standardized company profile accounts. Research into the accounting standards and practices of each country can be done prior to the actual extraction of financial data. Efforts can then be made to streamline the coding of accounts to make them comparable across countries for each company. Valuation provisions/charges and contra items that tend to inflate or deflate total assets can be adjusted against the respective asset accounts, thereby reducing the effect of over or understatement. Although this approach does not eliminate accounting differences, it does make key accounts such as operating income, current assets, total assets, and owners' equity more comparable internationally.

6.   Restate Financial Statements of Companies in a Given Industry Worldwide:

Identify specific differences in accounting principles between companies of interest and determine the direction and magnitude of the impact of these accounting changes on the earnings and valuations of the companies. As an illustration, we have highlighted such differences in Table 23 for selected companies in the electronics industry.

Following are some suggestions regarding the adjustment of key accounting differences:

a. Depreciation:

To harmonize discrepancies, an equalization method can be utilized whereby equal percentages are applied to depreciate assets when an equal number of years is taken for the estimated asset life.

b. Differences in Income Tax Expense & Deferred Taxes:

To compensate for tax differences, one may want to ignore taxes altogether and focus on pre-tax income in order to compare true operating income.

Table 23   Accounting Differences with Large Impact on Earnings Selected Companies in the Electronics Industry

Accounting Standards	France Thomson	West Germany Siemens	Italy Olivetti	Japan Hitachi Ltd.	Netherlands Phillips	U.K. Plessey	U.S. Hewlett-Packard
Financial Statement Cost Basis:							
– Historical Cost?	Yes	Yes	No	Yes	No	No	Yes
Historical Cost with Revaluation of Assets?	No	No	Yes	No	Yes	Yes	No
Depreciation:							
– Straight Line Method?	Mixed	Mixed	Yes	Accel.	Yes	Yes	Accel.
– Excess Deprecia tion Used	No	Yes	No	No	No	No	No
Accounting for Long-Term Investments Greater than 50%:							
–Full Consolidation?	Yes	No	Yes	No	Yes	Yes	Yes
Accounting for Loang-Term Investments between 21–50%:							
– Equity Method	No, at Cost	No, at Cost	Yes	Yes	Yes	Yes	Yes
Inventory Cost Method?	Mixed	Not Discl.	Mixed	Mixed	Current Cost	Not Discl.	FIFO
Deferred Taxes Reported?	Yes	No	Not Discl.	Yes	Yes	Yes	Yes
Discretionary Reserves Used?	Yes	Yes	Not Disscl.	Yes	Yes	Yes	No
Currency Translation:							
– Current Method?	Yes	Temporal	Yes	Mixed	Yes	Yes	Not Discl.
– Gains/Losses Reflected in Current Income?	Yes	Yes and/or deferred	Yes	Yes, and to S/E	Yes, and to S/E	Yes, also in S/E	Yes

c. Discretionary Reserves:
   To neutralize this variable, a user can either focus on income before reserves, or add the reserves back to pre-tax income.

d. Inventory Cost Methods:
   Many companies adopt one inventory approach, but footnote what the costs would have been had they used another formula. This procedure allows for easy comparison.

   If alternative inventory cost numbers are not reported, one can compare the results of companies that use different inventory costing methods by calculating the cost of goods sold as a percentage of sales.

 e. Results of Non-consolidated Subsidiaries:

  Many companies in Europe disclose key financial variables of non-consolidated subsidiaries (i.e. sales, net earnings, total assets) in their parent company reports.

  To restate parent company statements for non-consolidated subsidiaries, the user should subtract the dividend earnings of non-consolidated subsidiaries from the parent company report and add back the total earnings of non- consolidated subsidiaries. If there are any minority holdings in these subsidiaries, an appropriate portion of earnings should be subtracted to reflect the share of minority holders.

 7. Keep Abreast of International Accounting Developments:

  Regular users of international financial statements may want to keep abreast of international accounting developments so that the impact of various changes in international accounting standards can be reflected in their analysis. Table 24 provides various sources of information on current international accounting developments.

Difficulties in Merging Fundamental Accounting Data with Capital Market-Generated Information

Users need to combine accounting information with additional information from capital markets in order to complete their assessment of a foreign company's performance. There are some difficulties in obtaining this information and combining it with company-specific accounting data. This section discusses those difficulties.

Inconsistent Reporting of International Stock Prices

PROBLEM:

 A principal difficulty we have found is that the format for the reporting of stock prices worldwide is not always consistent.

- • Though most newspapers list companies in alphabetical order, some newspapers list individual companies under industry classifications (e.g., Financial Times and some Japanese newspapers), thus requiring prior knowledge about the industry classification of companies of interest.

Table 24   International Accounting Publications/Conferences

A. *International Accounting Organizations:*

    1. *IASC News:*
      International Accounting Standards Committee (IASC)
      41 Kingsway
      London WC 28 6 YU
      United Kingdom

    2. *IFAC News & Annual Report:*
      International Federation of Accountants (IFAC)
      540 Madison Avenue
      New York, NY 10020

B. *Governmental Organizations Involved in*
   International Accounting Standards

    1. *Bulletin of the European Communities*
      Official Journal of the Eurppean communities:
      (Please contact the nearest EC office)
      or write to:
         Commission of the European Community
         200 Rue de la Loi
         B1040 Brussels
         Belgium

    2. *OECD Observer:*
      Organization for Economic Cooperation and Development
      (Please contact the nearest OECD office)
      or write to:
         OECD
         2 Rue Andre Pascal
         75775 Paris Cedex 16
         France

    3. *CTC Reporter:*
      United Nations Centre on Transnational Corporations
         (UNCTC)
      Room DC 2-1312
      New York, NY 10017
      USA

Table continues

Table 24   (continued)

C. Monthly International Accounting Publications

    1. International Accounting Bulletins
        Lafferty Publications Ltd.
        Axe & Bottel Court, &70 Newcomen St.
        London SE1 YT
        United Kingdom

    1. International Accounting Bulletin:
        Lafferty Publications Ltd.
        Axe & Bottel Court, 70 Newcommen St.
        London SE1 1UYT
        United Kingdom

    2. World Accounting Report:
        Financial Times Business Information Ltd.
        Tower House
        Southhampton Street
        London WC2E 7HA
        United Kingdom

D. Publications of International Accounting Firms:
Many of the sixteen international accounting firms studied in this research project publish reference manuals and newsletters on international accounting and auditing standards as well as individual country guides, although the frequency of publication is not regular. We recommend that users request current publications on international accounting topics from the local offices of international accounting firms.

E. *Conferences of Academic Organizations:*

    1. *Newsletter: International Accounting Section:*
        American Accounting Association
        5717 Bessie Drive
        Sarasota, FL 34233
        USA
        (Annual conference usually held in August)

Table continues

Table 24   (continued)

2. *Center on International Education &*
   Research in Accounting Newsletter:
   Center for International Education & Research in Accounting
   University of Illinois at Champaign-Urbana
   320 Commerce Building (West)
   1206 South Sixth Street
   Urbana, IL 61820
   USA
   (Annual conference usually held in April)

3. *EAA Newsletter:*
   European Accounting Association (EAA)
   c/o EFMD
   40 Rue Washington
   B-1050 Brussels
   Belgium
   (Annual conference usually held in April)

• Identification of different securities (i.e., common stock, preferred stock, long-term securities) is sometimes not clear.

• In some cases, dividends are reported before taxes and, in other cases, they are reported after taxes.

Table 25 summarizes the information listed in the stock price sections of the leading newspapers of 24 countries.

SOLUTION:

The preparation of an in-house guide on how to use reported stock prices will improve financial analysis of international companies.

Table 25   Variations in Stock Price Reporting Found in Newspapers from Selected Countries

Country/ Newspaper	Yearly High/ Low	Amount of Last Dividend Paid	Dividend Yield %	P / E	Previous Day's Volume	Previous Day's High/ Low	Previous Day's Closing Price	Net Change
Australia *Sydney Morning Herald*		X	X	X	X	X	X	X
Austria *Die Presse*					X		X	
Belgium *Le Soir*							X	
Canada *Financial Times of Canada*	X	X	X	X	X		X	X
Denmark *Berlinske Tidende*	X	X	X	X	X	X	X	X
Finland *Helsingin Sonomat*			X	X	X	X	X	X
France *Le Monde*							X	X
West Germany *Frankfurter Allgeme- ine Zeitung*		X					X	
Hong Kong *South China Morning Post*	X	X	X	X	X	X	X	X
Italy *Corriere della Sera*	X				X		X	X
Japan *The Japan Times*							X	X
Korea, South *Korea Herald*				X	X		X	X

Australia — Yearly data based on calendar year. Includes closing buy/sell offers.

Austria — Also includes closing price from two most recent trading sessions.

Belgium — Lists the closing price from two most recent trading sessions.

Canada — Also discloses dates on which latest interim and fiscal year earnings were declared.

Denmark — Yearly high and low prices are based on the calendar year. Also includes total capitalization.

Finland — Includes final "buy" and "sell" offers, par value of share.

France — Also lists the closing price from two most recent trading sessions.

West Germany — Also includes closing price from two most recent trading sessions.

Hong Kong — Gross yield disclosed; yearly comparisons based on calendar year to date.

Italy — Two days previous closing price also listed.

Japan — No other information disclosed.

Korea, South — No other information disclosed.

Table continues

Table 25   (continued)

Country/ Newspaper	Yearly High/ Low	Amount of Last Dividend Paid	Dividend Yield %	P / E	Previous Day's Volume	Previous Day's High/ Low	Previous Day's Closing Price	Net Change
Malaysia *New Straits Times*	X				X		X	X

Yearly High and low prices are for calendar year to date.

Mexico *Excelsior*							X	X

Final "Buy" and "sell" offers for day's trading also included.

Netherlands *De Volksrant*	X					X	X	

Closing price for previous year and dates of high/low prices also included.

New Zeland *The Evening Post*					X		X	X

No other information disclosed.

Norway *Aftenposten*	X				X	X	X	X

Includes final "buy" and "sell" offers. Also includes return over last 12 months.

Singapore *The Straits Times*	X		X		X	X	X	X

Yearly high and low prices are for the calendar year.

South Africa *Die Burger*		X			X	X	X	X

Also includes EPS figures and closing "buy" and "sell" offers.

Spain *El Pais*	X				X	X	X	

Par value of share, closing price for two days previous also disclosed. Yearly high/low prices given for calendar year. Number of days traded for current year given.

Sweden *Svenska Dagbladet*	X	X	X		X	X	X	X

Also disclosed are 12 and 24-month percentage changes in price and 5-year average growth rates in price, dividend, and EPS.

Switzerland *Neue Zuercher Zeitung*							X	

Also disclosed is closing price for two days previous.

United Kingdom *Financial Times*		X	X				X	

Other disclosures include date last divident paid, total market capitalization.

United States *The Wall Street Journal*	X	X	X	X	X	X	X	X

Yearly high and low prices are for the preceding 52-week period.

Lack of Capital Change Information

PROBLEM:

Information about capital changes of international companies (stock splits, stock dividends and rights offerings) is not readily available on a timely basis.

SOLUTION:

- Multiple sources must be utilized to compile this information, such as:

    - printed services on corporate news worldwide
    - the financial press - stock exchange bulletins
    - databases on international stock prices

- Users should persuade stock markets to publish capital change information regularly.

Multiple Classes of Common Stock

PROBLEM:

- More than one type of common stock is permitted in several countries, which makes computation of stock-related ratios difficult. Table 26 provides a general overview of the various classes of common stock in existence in selected countries.

- In many of these countries, one class of common stock may be "more common" than another. In most cases, the annual report includes selected information for the class which should be considered "common" (such as the earnings per share computations). The other "common shares" are mostly held by related parties and are not traded regularly.

SOLUTION:

Compute common stock-related ratios (such as price/earnings, price/book value, dividend yield and dividend payout), based on the aggregate value of the shares of the different classes of stocks traded.

Table 26   Characteristics of Multiple Classes of Common Stocks for Selected Companies

	Belgium	Denmark	Finland	Mexico	Spain	Sweden	Switzerland
Total Companies Studied	49	47	41	15	45	83	44
Number of Companies with Multiple Classes of Common Stocks	24	18	15	4	5	42	35
% of Companies with Multiple Stocks	49	38	37	27	11	51	80
Characteristics of Multiple Classes of Common Stocks							
Number of Different Classes	4	2	7	2	2	4	4
Different Voting Rights	No	Yes	Yes	No	No	Yes	Yes
Different Dividends Paid	Yes	Yes	Yes	No	ND	No	ND
Different Tax treatment	Yes	No	No	No	No	ND	No
Different Market Prices	Yes	ND	Yes	ND	ND	Yes	Yes
Different Par Values	Yes	No	ND	No	No	ND	Yes
Different Ownership Rights	No	ND	ND	Yes	Yes	Yes	Yes

ND   Not Disclosed

Lack of Information on Local Capital Market Behavior

PROBLEM:

The final problem in this category is that little information is available on domestic capital market preferences. In other words, it is difficult to know how key players in each market use financial data.

The following questions will help illustrate this problem:

- When do companies in different countries increase dividends? An examination of dividend growth vs. earnings growth, will reveal different trends in different countries. For example, U.S. companies tend to reward stockholders sooner, while Japanese companies usually increase dividends only after earnings growth has been maintained.

- Which financial ratios are important in which markets? Current ratios and interest coverage are very important in the U.S. but not as important in Japan.

- What would be an acceptable limit to the amount of debt companies carry? Japanese and European companies have high leverage ratios compared to U.S. companies.

Tables 27, 28 and 29 provide selected financial ratios for companies from selected countries in the industrial, banking, and insurance sectors.

SOLUTIONS:

- Familiarity with the financial environment of the company whose financial ratios are being examined is a logical remedy to the problem of capital market differences. Again, using Japan as an example, an understanding of the locally accepted business practice of banks serving both creditors and stockholders and the practice of interlocking ownership enables readers to interpret Japanese financial statement ratios more intelligently. While direct experience with a country is an invaluable means of acquiring environmental familiarity, reading programs (e.g., country guides, articles in the financial press, etc.), and continuing education seminars provide alternative sources of information.

Table 27   Capital Market Differences: Selected Ratios Industrial Companies—Fiscal Year 1987

Oper. Margin %	Eff. Tax Rate %	Return on Assets %	Return on Equity %	Total Assets Turnover	Country	No. of Companies	Current Ratio	Common Equity % Assets	Price/ Earnings Ratio	Price/ Book Value Ratio	Dividend Payout %
					North America						
9.2	44.3	4.7	12.8	1.0	Canada	151	1.5	34.3	15.0	1.9	27.9
19.2	28.8	17.0	42.1	0.5	Mexico	15	1.9	44.0	8.5	1.2	6.0
10.1	43.8	5.6	13.7	1.1	United States	1270	1.6	39.2	15.2	2.0	48.6
					Asia/Pacific						
9.5	37.4	5.8	14.4	0.9	Australia	48	1.3	42.1	14.9	1.8	42.5
19.5	14.0	13.6	21.8	0.4	Hong Kong	20	1.4	63.7	7.8	1.3	26.6
2.6	58.9	1.5	5.8	1.3	Japan	300	1.2	25.9	54.9	2.9	79.9
5.0	30.5	2.4	13.6	1.8	Korea, South	14	0.9	17.8	8.2	0.9	23.0
8.4	45.1	3.9	7.0	0.6	Malaysia	25	1.4	54.5	20.8	1.4	63.4
10.8	15.3	9.1	22.2	0.8	New Zealand	20	1.6	41.8	10.5	1.7	17.1
10.1	29.2	6.1	10.2	0.5	Singapore	18	1.8	57.8	19.6	1.8	30.3
					Europe						
-1.2	42.1	0.9	4.4	1.1	Austria	16	1.4	20.2	23.7	1.0	114.6
5.7	34.2	3.9	13.1	11.3	Belgium	33	1.4	32.3	14.8	1.8	47.8
4.3	33.4	3.7	12.1	1.3	Denmark	28	1.5	31.0	11.0	1.3	40.7
6.3	17.5	2.9	16.7	0.9	Finland	32	1.5	18.1	15.7	2.1	26.6
3.9	42.4	3.6	20.0	1.2	France	126	1.3	19.9	9.7	1.6	21.5
2.7	52.8	2.7	10.2	1.4	Germany, West	151	1.8	26.1	22.1	2.2	45.1
7.6	24.6	4.7	17.7	0.8	Italy	42	1.3	21.4	8.0	1.4	23.7
5.5	21.6	4.5	14.2	1.3	Netherlands	42	1.5	20.8	6.1	0.9	34.6

Table continues

Table 27 (continued)

Oper. Margin %	Eff. Tax Rate %	Return on Assets %	Re-turn on Equity %	Total Assets Turnover	Country	No. of Companies	Current Ratio	Common Equity % Assets	Price/ Earnings Ratio	Price/ Book Value Ratio	Dividend Payout %
					Europe (Continued)						
4.4	29.9	2.7	17.2	1.1	Norway	28	1.2	15.1	10.8	1.8	36.9
5.5	21.3	3.1	8.0	0.9	Spain	25	1.3	40.7	18.8	1.2	38.8
6.4	34.6	3.4	19.9	1.2	Sweden	63	1.6	19.0	18.9	3.1	31.3
16.3	71.8	4.3	9.1	0.9	Switzerland	25	2.2	48.5	11.1	1.0	25.9
8.7	36.6	7.4	17.5	1.2	United Kingdom	232	1.5	42.9	12.1	2.0	35.4
					Africa/Middle East						
13.1	39.6	8.5	18.2	1.1	South Africa	60	1.6	47.7	12.3	2.0	43.3

Source: *Worldscope Financial and Service Company Profiles* (1988)

Table 28 Capital Market Differences: Selected Ratios Banks—Fiscal Year 1987

Country	Return on Assets %	Return on Equity %	Eff. Tax Rate %	Total Int. Inc. % Earning Assets	Reserve for Loan Loss-% Total Loans	No. of Companies	Earning Assets % Total Assets	Equity % Total Assets	Price/ Earnings Ratio	Price/ Book Value Ratio	Dividend Payout %
North America											
Canada	-0.3	-8.6	36.9	9.0	1.8	5	89.0	3.5	NC	1.0	NC
United States	-0.3	-6.1	N/A	10.5	3.3	88	84.4	4.5	NC	1.0	NC
Asia/Pacific											
Australia	0.6	13.6	51.4	17.1	1.7	5	75.6	4.7	15.0	1.7	34.5
Japan	0.3	12.5	54.4	6.3	0.9	68	72.5	2.1	76.1	8.4	21.9
Korea, South	0.1	5.0	34.2	6.9	1.5	6	65.6	2.9	30.9	1.3	45.4
Europe											
Denmark	0.5	8.3	21.7	11.1	N/A	8	74.5	6.4	8.3	0.6	36.4
France	0.3	13.0	35.7	10.7	5.3	14	93.5	2.6	9.1	1.0	22.4
Germany, West	0.2	6.6	54.3	6.8	N/A	19	91.4	3.1	29.1	1.8	69.0
Italy	0.5	11.9	40.7	9.9	3.6	16	81.4	4.4	9.4	1.0	27.2
Netherlands	0.4	10.5	27.5	2.2	N/A	5	95.8	4.0	10.1	0.9	47.4
Spain	0.9	19.0	20.8	12.3	4.2	8	80.8	4.8	15.3	2.7	34.1
Sweden	0.4	30.6	38.2	2.5	0.5	5	93.3	1.3	16.8	4.1	53.3
Switzerland	0.5	7.9	33.3	5.3	N/A	6	89.5	6.0	19.5	1.4	65.9
United Kingdom	Nom	-0.6	N/A	12.5	4.4	8	86.1	5.0	NC	0.9	NC
Africa/Middle East											
South Africa	0.7	12.7	41.7	N/A	N/A	5	80.9	4.4	8.9	1.2	42.1

Source: *Worldscope financial and Service Company Profiles* (1988)

NC = Not computed due to negative earnings per share

Table 29   Capital Market Differences: Selected Ratios Insurance Companies—Fiscal Year 1987

Return on Assets %	Return on Equity %	Eff. Tax Rate %	Net Premium Written % Equity	Benefit & Loss Reserve % Total Cap	Country	No. of Companies	Equity % Total Assets	Equity Sec. & Real Estate % Inv't Assets	Price/ Earnings Ratio	Price/ Book Value Ratio	Dividend Payout %
					North America						
0.2	0.1	16.6	286.5	721.3	Canada	7	7.1	15.8	N/A*	N/A*	N/A*
2.4	16.6	12.5	224.5	183.3	United States	47	13.5	7.2	7.7	1.2	26.2
					Asia/Pacific						
0.2	25.9	88.7	1590.0	N/A	Australia	5	1.1	79.6	N/A	N/A	N/A
0.3	3.2	20.1	285.1	24.6	Japan	19	10.6	41.2	73.9	1.9	33.6
					Europe						
0.6	6.8	37.9	115/2	552.1	Denmark	5	9.7	9.2	15.7	1.0	18.3
2.1	21.7	12.0	386.0	627.7	France	7	8.6	42.3	7.0	1.3	15.6
0.4	8.7	47.2	498.3	920.3	Germany, West	17	5.0	29.3	106.3	7.7	51.5
1.6	12.5	35.9	228.6	344.1	Italy	5	12.9	31.9	71.5	8.6	36.0
1/0	9.8	24.6	157.9	410.6	Netherlands	5	9.8	18.4	19.4	1.8	51.2
0.6	7.6	28.1	399.8	760.1	Switzerland	7	7.9	20.2	77.2	5.1	57.8
1.0	16.9	30.9	364.9	287.5	United Kingdom	14	5.9	57.4	16.7	2.6	48.2

Source: *Worldscope financial and Service Company Profiles* (1988)

* N/A = not applicable

- Cross-tabulate historical results to identify patterns, such as growth in assets vs. growth in net worth, to see to what degree growth is financed by equity.

In summary, international users of company-specific financial data need to analyze a company's stock market performance vis-a-vis the performance indicated by accounting variables, such as earnings per share, return on equity, etc. Many users prefer combining both sources of information by computing the price/earnings ratio or market/book value ratio. Though the preparers or auditors are not responsible for providing capital market- related variables, it is useful to discuss these difficulties as they relate to the interpretation of international financial statements.

Summary and Conclusions

The "answers" provided in this paper represent specific approaches to international financial statement analysis. Ultimately, a more coherent, systematic approach to financial analysis at the international level must be developed.

After the accounting numbers of companies from different countries in a given industry have been made comparable, it is easier to construct industry averages within a region or worldwide. A practical framework is needed for users to analyze the financial statements of companies in a given industry across national boundaries. The following steps are suggested to aid in the development of a comprehensive global industry analysis system:

A. Develop a standard chart of accounts to facilitate format compatibility of data internationally.
B. Compile company-specific accounting practices so accounting differences can be analyzed by company, industry, and country.
C. Compute financial ratios by: - Industry within country - Country averages - Industry within region - Regional averages - Industry globally
D. Develop computer software logic to allow users to convert financial data on any company from one country's accounting standards, currency, and language, into another country's accounting standards, currency, and language.

In conclusion, this chapter has attempted to provide some suggestions on how to compensate for accounting differences internationally. Further research is needed to empirically document the impact of accounting differences on earnings and balance sheet accounts in order for users to restate financial statements fully in the accounting conventions of their home country.

Prospective Equity Returns in a Disinflationary Environment

Richard T. Coghlan
Strategic Investment Services, Wayne, Pennsylvania

As we entered the 1980s there were serious doubts expressed as to whether stock prices really could keep up with inflation. In an earlier time, the standard view had been that equities were the perfect hedge against inflation. The argument was simple enough: corporations charged consumer prices, which brought in revenues. Consequently, both rose together.

In the 1970's, as inflation accelerated and stock prices fell further behind, stocks were viewed as a poor hedge against inflation. Theories followed the fact and provided belated justification for what was happening. Unfortunately, these theories had more of the characteristic of ex-post rationalization than predictive theory that could explain market behavior over different periods and different countries. These criteria are too often neglected in the attempt to explain particular circumstances. The development of specific theories, or explanations, is not unique to the stock market, but can be found in most areas of market behavior, economics, politics, and life itself. However, general applicability should provide the ultimate test of any such model. While the main emphasis here is on the United States, examples from other countries are also used. The proposed explanation of the relationship between the stock market and inflation is general enough to cover a wide range of different experiences without being a tautology.

An interesting aspect of the serious alternatives that explain why the stock market was not a good hedge against inflation was that nearly every case concluded that decelerating inflation would be bullish for stocks. For that reason, it is relevant to review the main theories that were proposed and to discover how stock prices have performed with inflation at different times and places.

Another school of thought deemed that the stock market had caught some terminal disease from which it would never recover. However, while such views had some popular supporters, they did not receive widespread acceptance. There are still some who hold this position today, but it has become increasingly difficult to sound convincing as the market continues to rise.

In judging prospects for the stock market for the 1990s, it is necessary not only to have a view about how inflation or disinflation will affect the stock market, but also what the inflation outlook is likely to be. It should also be clear that a view about inflation is not enough, since there will always be a variety of other forces at work. Putting the market theory and the inflation forecast together provides a market forecast for the remainder of this decade.

An Outline Model

Before discussing how inflation might affect stock prices, it will be helpful if we first create a framework on which the arguments can be based. The intention is not to capture all the intricacies of stock market behavior but aim at only the more modest objective of identifying the major elements in a stock valuation model. The starting point is to define the expected return on equities (re) as equal to the current dividend yield (d/p) plus the rate at which these dividends and earnings are growing (g).

$$re = d/p + g \qquad\qquad (i)$$

Underlying this equation is the assumption that the dividend yield is constant into infinity. There is, therefore, no cyclicality to earnings and no risk. Needless to say, this is hardly a perfect representation of reality. However, it is slightly less unrealistic for the market as a whole, which is averaging a variety of companies, than it is for any individual stock.

It is reasonable to state that the observed rate of interest (rb) consists of a real rate of interest (i) and the expected rate of inflation (x).

$$rb = i + x \qquad\qquad (ii)$$

In a state of equilibrium, it can be assumed that the expected return on equity will be equal to the default free return on bonds, plus a risk premium (R).

Figure 1   Inflation and Market Yields

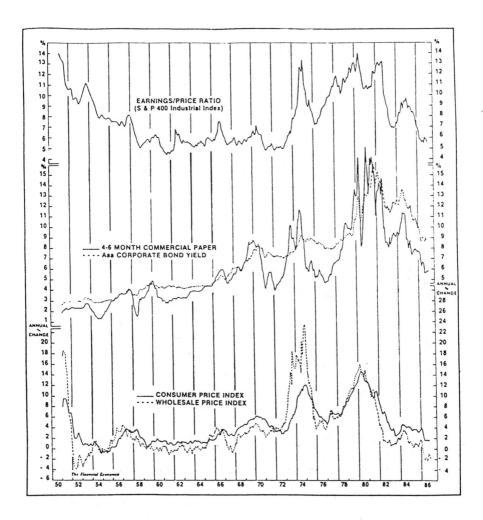

$$re = rb + R \qquad \text{(iii)}$$

Putting these three equations together produces:

$$p = d/i + x + R - g \qquad \text{(iv)}$$

and

$$e/p = (i + x + R - g)/a \qquad \text{(v)}$$

Where "e" is earnings, "a" represents the dividend payout ratio and "e/p" is the earnings yield, the inverse of the price earnings ratio. While somewhat unrealistic, the final equations do help to identify the major influences on stock prices and provide a useful starting point for analysing the effect of inflation and disinflation on stock prices. A model of this type underlies the main theories of how inflation affects market prices.

Inflation and the Stock Market

In proposing a general explanation for the failure of stock prices to keep up with inflation in the 1970's, one should be aware of the other proposed explanations that have failed to meet this criterion. The explanations vary from the assumption of irrationality on the part of investors to rationality in the face of deteriorating conditions.

The different explanations considered here have each emphasized their own distinguishing characteristics. This has helped to conceal the common thread running through all of them; namely, that the earnings yield, as defined above, has fluctuated with nominal interest rates and inflation, as shown in Figure 1. A problem arises because the earnings yield (or price/earnings ratio) ought to be much more stable if, as is generally accepted, the rate at which corporate earnings are discounted is a real rate of return, and the real rate of interest is fixed. The essence of this argument as seen in equation (v), can be stated as follows: If with a fixed payout ratio, a fixed real rate of interest, and no change in the risk premium, the earnings grow at the same rate as inflation (plus a fixed margin), then the earnings yield should remain unchanged in the face of accelerating inflation.

One reason for the failure of stock prices to keep up with inflation is that adjusted corporate earnings also did not keep up with inflation. Nominal earnings as reported may have kept up, but the quality of the earnings deteriorated because of the effect of rapid inflation on inventory valuation and depreciation adjustments. This deterioration implies that the increases in earnings were unsustainable. In fact, however, the earnings were sustained, as shown by their ability to keep up with inflation. There has been endless debate on the quality of earnings, and this debate is likely to continue without ever being resolved.

Others have argued that if a true adjustment is made, including the benefits of fixed interest debt issued at lower yields, then re-adjusted earnings have in fact kept up with inflation. In this case, alternative explanations are required for the failure of stock prices to keep up, one of which has been based on the assumed irrationality of investors. There are inherent problems with this explanation. For example, why does the irrationality persist? And why have investors not always been irrational when faced with rapid inflation, since there are plenty of examples when stock prices have kept up with inflation?

Another alternative explanation has been that the dividend payout ratio declined as a direct result of inflation. In this case, there would be an increase in retained earnings that might be expected to raise the growth of earnings and dividends in the future. After all, Japanese companies have very low payout ratios and yet are also highly priced. A higher growth rate should actually have the effect of reducing the dividend yield, not raising it. The greatest weakness in this explanation is its failure to account for the rise in the dividend yield along with the earnings yield. A different explanation of the observed reduction in the payout ratio is possible which reverses the casualty. A reduction in the share price relative to earnings, for some other reason, raises the cost of borrowing. It, therefore, becomes sensible to retain a higher proportion of earnings for investment purposes.

The final specific explanation of the rising earnings yield puts the blame on increases in the risk premium. Certainly that would do it, but no justification has been provided as to why the risk premium should move so closely with interest rates. An even greater problem with the argument that there is some automatic link between the risk premium and inflation in the United States in the 1970's is that in other countries and at other times the relationship has been absent. This is the problem with all those explanations that seek to establish an automatic link between inflation and the earnings yield.

What is needed is an explanation that covers all behavior and that allows stock prices to go up with inflation under some circumstances, but which also explains why sometimes, particularly in the developed countries, stock prices fail to keep up. The possibility has to be considered that it is not inflation that is holding back stock prices, but something else. The key factor is whether the inflation is unrestrained or whether attempts are being made to control it. In the first case, money is pumped in to keep the level of activity up and fuel further price increases. Under these circumstances of easy credit, stock prices will keep up with inflation. If, on the other hand, the monetary authorities are trying to restrain inflation so that credit becomes expensive and real interest rates increase, then stock prices will lag behind inflation. This explanation is consistent with the facts and is general enough to explain behavior in different countries and over different times.

The previous assumption and the assumption generally made by economists is that the real rate of interest is very stable, with wide fluctuations only in nominal yields. This alternative view of the way in which inflation affects the stock market lifts that assumption and allows the real rate of interest to vary. That, in turn, would also explain increases in the earnings yield, but not automatically with inflation and only when monetary policy is tight.

In addition, there is likely to be a systematic relationship between risk and attempts to control inflation, as distinct from inflation itself. Once it becomes clear that the monetary authorities are going to push interest rates up in order to bring inflation under control, we can expect weakening economic activity, falling profits, and increasing possibility of bankruptcies. Rather than wait for this to happen, investors are likely to anticipate events by lowering the price they are prepared to pay for the present inflated stream of profits. Therefore, since earnings are still rising with inflation, the earnings yield will be pushed up even faster. Instead of assuming that investors are irrational, this approach assumes a very rational form of behavior.

For all these theories, a fall in inflation is good for the stock market. However, there is an important distinction between the general explanation suggested here and the alternative theories. In the latter cases, declining inflation is all that is needed to bring down the earnings yield. According to the former view, falling inflation only creates the conditions for the relaxation of monetary policy, and it is this that will bring down the earnings yield. The distinction may seem slight, but, as discussed later, can be very important, as, for example, in the period from 1980 to 1982.

Some Examples of Inflation

Looking at the way stock prices have moved at times of very rapid inflation contradicts the theories that say the process of inflation inherently requires stock prices to lag behind. What we find, in fact, is that stock prices have typically kept up easily. In Israel, over the five years from 1980 to 1984, consumer prices rose 56 times, which definitely counts as high inflation, and stock prices rose 57 times.

The classic inflation period occurred in Germany after the First World War. As proven at that time, stock prices will rise with general prices no matter how fast inflation accelerates; after all, why not exchange rapidly depreciating paper money for claims on real assets? This period also showed that there must be sufficient liquidity available. The stock market was disorientated by the war and the chaos that followed produced major fluctuations in prices.

In 1920, stock prices outpaced wholesale price inflation and the depreciation of the mark by a substantial margin. In 1921, although the increase in stock prices fell just short of the decline in the exchange rate, it still did better than wholesale prices and substantially better than consumer prices. 1922 produced a very different response. Share prices ended the year 12 times higher than they had been at the start, but wholesale prices and the dollar/mark exchange rate had risen 40 times. There was, therefore, a substantial decline of share prices in real terms.

Costantino Bresciani-Turroni in *The Economics of Inflation* noted that at this time the Daimler car company had a total market value equivalent to only 327 cars. The economy was weak, with production 30% below what might have been considered normal, but the undervaluation of corporations was clearly extreme. Bresciani-Turroni stated that whereas there had been easy money through 1921, conditions tightened considerably in 1922. Bank credit slowed, and the quantity of money increased only 65% over the first seven months of the year. At the same time the government had tried reducing expenditures and raising taxes. The discussion above suggests that this restriction in money growth was even more significant than allowed for by Bresciani-Turroni.

Towards the end of the year, there was a dramatic shift in monetary conditions. Note issues increased rapidly and the flood-gates were opened wide. During 1923, stock prices increased an incredible 83,000 times, compared with an increase in the cost of living of only 16,500 times. A buying panic developed, encouraged by foreign exchange constraints. In November 1923, the gold price of shares had risen above the pre-war level for the first time; the ratio of the share price to gold was 39.4 compared with only 16 in July of the same year and 18 in October 1921. At this point stock prices had clearly become overpriced, given the fragile economic structure.

In reviewing these experiences, one can conclude that stock prices will rise at times of rapid inflation by an equal, or even greater amount, as long as monetary policy is easy and credit is readily available. Runaway inflation is no problem for real stock values. However, attempts to stop inflation will typically lead to high real interest rates and uncertainty about future profitability. It is these attempts that will prevent stock prices from keeping up with inflation.

Why Inflation Will Be Down

The apparent political awareness that it is not possible to buy your way to sustained high growth is one reason for expecting the trend of inflation to remain down. Governments around the world have been cutting back on their spending and bringing budget deficits down. This deficit reduction has happened even as unemployment has risen to post-war records levels in many industrial countries. And there are no signs yet that this new attitude has changed, despite the reduction in inflation.

The United States has lagged in this general trend. Government expenditure has increased, and the budget deficit has soared. This lag might suggest that the United States is still out of control, with only a desperate rear-guard action being fought by the Federal Reserve. That interpretation has actually been made, but it is not justified. Certainly, monetary policy has been forced on the defensive by easy fiscal policy, but real interest rates would have had to rise anyway. More important is the widespread recognition that a greater contribution is required from fiscal policy. The increasingly pro-business attitude by governments, for example, is an additional benefit for stock prices.

Fiscal policy in the United States has been out of control, but that is in the past. The momentum from now on will be in the opposite direction. The Gramm-Rudman-Hollings bill exemplifies the widespread concern to bring the budget under control. The political momentum is still in the direction of achieving a better fiscal balance. Even the Democratic party has pinned its flag to the same post, differentiating that position in the past only by being prepared to increase taxes.

Wherever you look, Belgium, France, the United Kingdom, Germany, etc., there is a persistent drive to restore a better balance in government finances and to prevent inflation accelerating again. In Japan, the government has for some time been under strong international and domestic pressure to stimulate the domestic economy, but still it is only moving slowly in that direction. The Japanese economy is relatively weak, and consumer inflation is very low and significantly negative at the wholesale level. Normally these circumstances would have produced a greater reaction towards stimulus, but here also there is evidence of a much more cautious approach by the government and central bankers. For this reason, more than any other, one should expect the trend towards lower inflation to be maintained. The collapse of oil prices is important, but this itself is a result of the more responsible attitude being adopted by governments around the world.

Real Comparisons

The crash of 1929 and the subsequent depression of stock prices and the economy continues to exercise a fatal fascination on many people. Comparisons with that period have been used to justify an impending crash for many years. As each corner is turned and the expected crisis fails to materialize, the argument is discarded, only to resurface soon afterward in a slightly different, but similar form.

Figure 2   Real International Stock Market Indexes

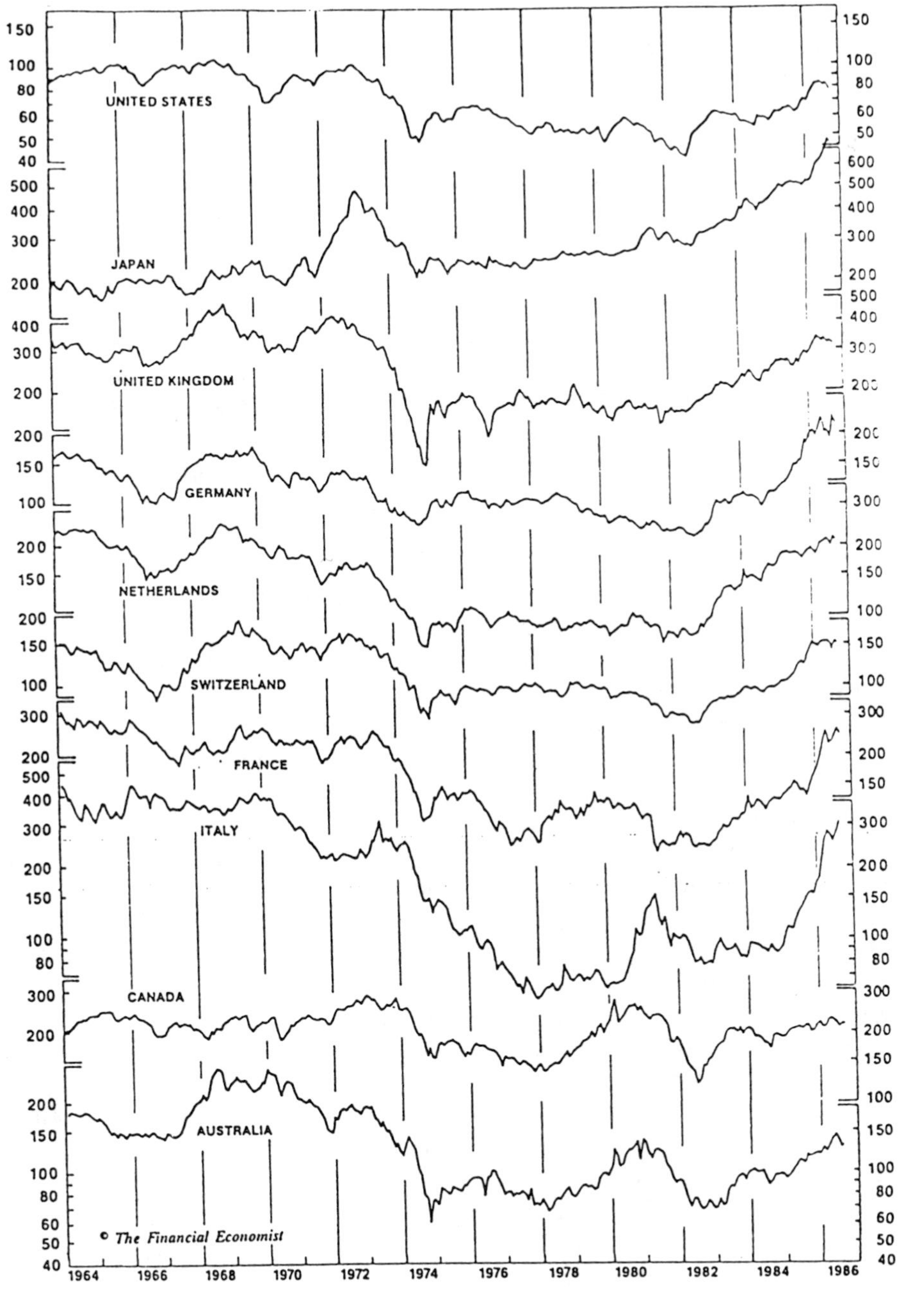

© The Financial Economist

The extent and duration of the stock market decline of 1974 came as a surprise to most people. As inflation continued through the second half of the decade, the resultant instability was widely seen as the precursor to some greater catastrophe. The potential fragility of the financial system became increasingly obvious through this time and into the 1980's, with first the S & Ls, then the money center banks with their loans to the developing countries, the farmers' loans, and finally oil loans coming into question. To many, it seemed as if the end of the world was coming, and, for a while, the Kondratieff long-wave became a popular explanation of events and portent of doom.

Despite all this, inflation came down, the economy recovered, and stock prices soared, not only in the United States but around the world. Once more the end of the world was postponed, and the crisis scenario was placed on a back burner along with Kondratieff. Recently there have been signs that the heat is being turned back up, on the basis of comparisons between present market action and that in the period leading up to and including 1929. All of a sudden charts are appearing that show how similar the current period is with that historical period. These same historical charts can, however, be used to draw a very different conclusion.

A number of comparisons for example, have been made between the behavior of the stock market in the period 1912—1929 and the more recent period starting in 1970. Both of these periods are shown in Figure 2, which shows the trend of stock prices monthly since 1900. There is supposed to be a close similarity, but that seems to be very much in the eye of the beholder, since there is really little correspondence except for the very recent run-up in prices. It is also possible to show that the 1950's was similar in this respect but was not followed by a crash. Any of the comparisons are equally good, and none are very good; they certainly do not stand up to close statistical scrutiny.

An even greater failing with the comparisons that have been made, however, is that they are in nominal terms. Comparisons of stock prices across time or country only make sense in real terms, after taking out the effect of inflation. It is clearly illogical to argue that a 400% increase in stock prices in Brazil is better than, say, a 20% increase in the United States, if inflation is 500% in Brazil, but only 5% in the United States. A 1200% increase in stock prices, as in Germany in 1922, did not mean that the stock market was doing well for investors, since inflation was 4000%, and about to get spectacularly worse.

Comparing stock prices in real terms makes a lot of difference. A plot of real stock prices is included in Figure 2 along with measures of nominal and real economic activity. High inflation through the 1970's produced a much worse performance in real terms than is indicated by the nominal numbers. In real terms, it becomes hard to justify the argument that a major correction is due because the market has come such a long way. Stock prices have recovered strongly, but, in real terms, still remain well below their 1968 peak and have only recently crossed above the level reached in 1929.

Figure 3 shows the major foreign stock markets in real terms, i.e., after allowing for changes in consumer prices. Everyone knows what has been happening in nominal terms, but comparisons in real terms have been significant only by their neglect. They show that on that basis the markets do not look overvalued. In Italy, where stock prices have advanced strongly since 1984, the index in real terms only exceeded its 1980 level at the end of 1985, and it remains substantially below the 1960's highs. This is an extreme example, but the story is similar in most other countries.

As a rule of thumb, the higher the trend rate of inflation and the more depressed the real stock price has been, the further the real index will be from its old highs. The only two countries where the stock indices have crossed their old 1960's peaks are Japan and Germany. The Japanese index crept above first, then went sideways for a year before again advancing strongly. The German market only moved above the old record at the end of 1985. The U.K. and U.S. markets still have a long way to go to get back that far.

In terms of a long-wave view of history, it is reasonable to conclude that the market "crash" has already occurred. An extended correction in real terms from the peak in 1968 down to the low in July 1982 has been observed. This interpretation of the recent past is completely opposite to the view of those who are still anticipating a repeat of 1929.

The problem lies in looking for exact replicas of the past. However, because lessons were learned from history, this has changed reactions in the present. There have been plenty of opportunities over the past ten years to create a financial panic, a sharp liquidation, and a contraction of output had the government and Federal Reserve followed the policies of their 1920's and 1930's predecessors.

The mistakes were not repeated; however the resulting inflationary correction that avoided a sharp collapse, was dragged out, much longer than it should have been. We have now come to an end of this correction period and are still in the early stages of an extended recovery. Now is not the time to look back in despair but to gather encouragement from the past.

The Outlook for Stock Prices

There are many ways to analyze market behavior. The Dow industrials and transports moving to new highs and prices crossing above their moving average are two popular technical indicators of a rising market. Clearly it follows that stock prices must be strong under such circumstances, although it is not always

Figure 3   Stock Market Index and the Economy—Real and Nominal

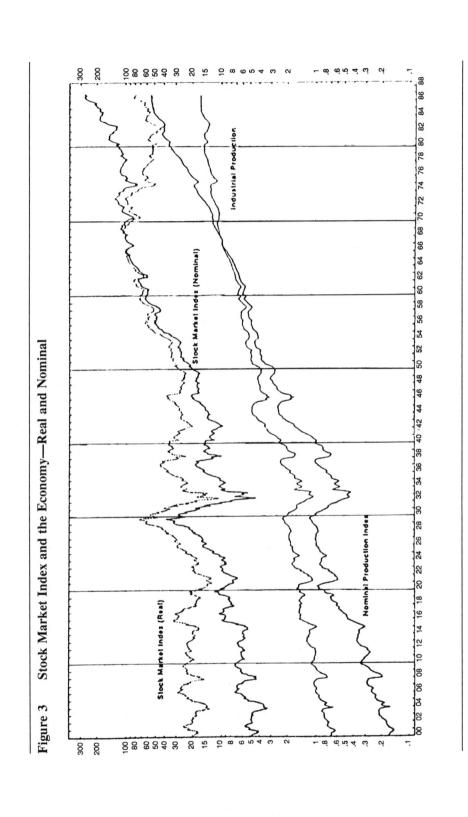

the case that they will continue that way. More importantly, these observations do not explain why market prices should rise or fall the way they do.

The basic starting point for a fundamental view of the market is that stock prices rise with earnings. The two key influences are the level of earnings themselves and the growth of earnings. A high level of earnings provides justification for a high stock price. However, if growth is slow this will tend to produce a relatively higher earnings yield, i.e., a lower price-earnings ratio. Alternatively, rapid growth of earnings will generally produce even faster appreciation of the share price, and, therefore, a rising P/E, even if there is no dividend payment at all.

It is not at all unreasonable that lower growth will produce a higher earnings yield. If earnings actually fall, that is likely to result in an even greater drop in price, and an even greater increase in the earnings yield, which will exaggerate the weakness coming from the lower earnings. What is more, the stock market will not wait for these events to happen but will typically lead them by six to nine months. It should, therefore, not be considered unusual to observe rising inflation and falling stock prices, or at least prices not keeping up with inflation. The persistence of this experience came from the continual attempts to bring inflation under control, until they were finally successful.

As inflation came down this produced the conditions for an explosive rally in stock prices. This did not happen immediately when inflation came down, contrary to the predictions of most inflation theories, but only when interest rates dropped sharply in 1982. Falling inflation created this possibility, since it allowed the anti-inflationary policies to be relaxed. However, it was not until that point was reached that stock prices reacted. Up until then, there was still too much uncertainty. The situation can be compared with a wound when the blood loss is stopped but the circulation is not restored until the tourniquet is removed; the one is a precondition for the other, and both are necessary to maintain a healthy blood flow.

The new environment of disinflation has not been fully accepted by investors, and this has kept real interest rates high. Over time, as inflation has remained low, there has been a gradual improvement in the outlook. Despite the influence of rational expectations on theoretical models, expectations in the real world are still slow to adjust and are based on hard news rather than abstract theories. The decline in oil prices has accelerated this process, encouraging an optimistic outlook for inflation. Oil prices are probably more important for expectations than inflation itself.

More than just inflation, falling oil prices also raise the expectation of faster economic growth. The slowdown in world economic growth in the 1970's has often been blamed on the shift of resources to OPEC. In fact, the OPEC price hikes were really a symptom of the overexpansion in demand that was taking place. The economic slowdown was the result of the rise in real interest rates designed to bring the situation back under control. Now growth is likely to accelerate, and the fall in oil prices will certainly help. The truth is, however, that it is really the general improvement in inflation that is responsible. Stock prices stand to benefit both from a fall in the earnings yield as real interest rates come down and reasonably strong profit growth that should average around 10% per year. These two forces combined should produce price appreciation on the average of 16% to 17% a year over the four years from the end of 1985, which in turn implies a Dow of around 3000 by 1990.

In addition, there are dividend returns to add in, and when this is done an average annual return of 20% certainly seems possible. The high return is based on two things. First, the catch up from past distortions as real interest rates come down, and secondly, on improved conditions for economic growth. The 1980's are the 1970's in reverse. There will be cyclical setbacks, and inflation will strengthen in the United States in reaction to the declining dollar, but these reversals to the main trend should prove temporary. Those sectors that stand to benefit most are the same ones that suffered the greatest loss of competitiveness from the high dollar.

European Investment Opportunities

Richard T. Coghlan
Strategic Investment Services, Wayne, Pennsylvania

Europe in the 1990s

The rapid turn of events in Europe over recent years has focused attention on this corner of the world. First, there was the accelerating trend towards economic integration, as embodied in the 1992 deadline. Then came the dramatic events in Eastern Europe that added a whole new dimension. When this chapter was first written in the early part of 1989, the main focus was on the potential created by European integration. This remains a major consideration, but it has subsequently become necessary to take account of the wide ranging implications of the collapse of Communism. Suddenly the game has changed to such an extent that even the boundaries of "Europe" have become the subject of debate.

The spectacular disintegration of the communist machine across Eastern Europe has opened up opportunities and introduced new risks. The ramifications extend beyond the borders into the West. Now, even more than before, Western Europe wants to accelerate the process of integration. The dream of German unification has become a reality. What had seemed impossible at the start of 1989, had become a virtual certainty by the end of the year.

This chapter will focus on the investment potential provided by Europe in broad terms, setting the scene for the subsequent chapters on individual countries. It is time to re-evaluate the old world. The newer, developing countries of the Far East have provided much more excitement for investors over recent years. The old world is rapidly changing, and the speed of events is creating a much more dynamic and interesting environment for investors.

Complete economic integration between the main industrialized countries of Western Europe is still some time off. Also, it will be many years before Eastern Europe can develop free-market economies, assuming the movement toward establishing a democratic economy is allowed to continue. There can be no doubting the importance and pervasive influence of these political events. However, separate country bond and equity markets will still behave differently, depending on their own individual country characteristics.

European Integration

The European Economic Community (EEC) has been in existence since the original founding members signed the Treaty of Rome in 1957. The early years were characterized by high ideals and low achievements, but at least the foundations for the future were laid. In retrospect it is clear that a commitment to a unified Europe required participation from a greater number of countries. A significant step in that direction was taken in 1973 when the United Kingdom finally stepped over the line to become a member of EEC. Since then the number of countries has grown, encompassing the majority, but not all, of Western Europe.

The removal of barriers to trade proceeded slowly until it was decided to set a 1992 deadline for the elimination of virtually all restraints on the free movement of goods, services, people, and information within EEC countries. Finally, there was an attempt to create a single, unified market of 320 million people.

The changes required in each country are involved and time consuming, and the 1992 deadline is bound to be missed in some instances. However, by setting such an objective, the architects of the new Europe have concentrated the collective mind and quickened the pace of change. Even more, it has captured the imagination of people around the world, making the idea of a united Europe more real than ever before.

Significant benefits are supposed to flow from all of these changes, substantially boosting living standards within the combined economy. Various estimates have been made about the size of these benefits. The Cecchini Report, published by the European Commission in 1988 (The European Challenge: 1992, by Paolo Cecchini; Wildwood House), estimated that the real standard of living in Europe would rise by between 2.5% and 6.5% as a result of unifying markets. Another report by Richard Baldwin for the Center for Economic Policy Research, claims that these estimates only cover the static, one-time, benefits. Once the dynamic effects are taken into account, the estimates of the improvement in living standards will increase to between 3.5% and 19.5%.

One of the main benefits for unifying the European economy is the elimination of bureaucratic paperwork at the operating level. This shows up most dramatically in the transporting of goods across country boundaries. The Cecchini Report calculated that at its worst a truck driver would spend a third of his time dealing with 200 pieces of paper in the process of traveling across Europe, adding as much as 2% to the cost of the product.

One major barrier to trade is differences in technical specifications, including safety standards, which partly explains shipping delays. A complete solution would require the adoption of universal standards. In some cases this is what is happening; in others there is simply the acceptance by each country of alternative specifications. The Cecchini Report estimates that the elimination of technical barriers will save 2% of GDP.

The changes taking place are extremely significant from a political viewpoint. Governments are giving up sovereignty over parts of their economy, legal system, and social structure. Force has been the driving factor in most unifications in history, and Europe has had its share of such attempts. The continent has been torn apart over centuries, as individual fiefdomes, and then countries, fought for supremacy.

Currently governments are attempting to bring countries together, through peaceful discussion and agreement. It is quite remarkable how much agreement has been achieved so far, considering that unanimous agreement is required from all countries on any major change. Restraints on the free movement of goods, capital, and labor will be eliminated by 1992, and are largely gone already. By then, it will be possible to sell anything, including insurance and financial services anywhere within Europe. Of course, there are major differences in local conditions, tastes, preferences, and language and these will continue to form a barrier to common goods and services. However, the worldwide expansion of McDonald's and Coca-Cola demonstrates that tastes do adapt over time. It also shows that non-European companies are also likely to benefit from the opening up of the internal markets.

Much attention has also been given to the question of unifying taxes. Emphasis has generally been on the conflicts that exist. However, countries are moving VAT rates closer together. Germany raised VAT rates in 1989, while France and the Netherlands reduced rates. Further demands are being made for greater coordination of the rest of the tax system. This is a sensible move, but is not essential to economic integration, and is certainly not a precondition as often suggested. The market will take care of any anomalies that remain. Free markets will impose a discipline on tax policies far more effective than any number of debates. Countries will adjust taxes in order to protect market share.

Far more important to the case of full integration is the adoption of a single currency, which will eliminate any exchange rate uncertainty. Without the option of currency devaluations, domestic policies will have to move much closer together. The details of how policy coordination is to be achieved do not matter, and such debate is largely missing the point. It is necessary only to maximize competition. The way to do that is through a single currency. Prime Minister Margaret Thatcher opposes such a move, but on this she is alone among the twelve leaders of the EEC countries.

Monetary union has been an objective from the start, but has steadily moved to center stage. The Werner Plan in 1970 set a timetable for Economic and Monetary Union by 1980, but that was derailed by the oil crisis and subsequent recession. The European Monetary System, established in 1979, had a more limited objective of a stable currency zone. This is separate from the European Currency Unit, which is a basket of all the currencies of the countries within the EEC, and is discussed below in the section on bonds.

Jacques Delors, currently president of the EEC Commission, has been pushing hard for monetary union and a single European central bank as a condition for economic union. Mrs. Thatcher in the United Kingdom has been pushing back just as hard, recognizing the loss of sovereignty involved. If this political opposition was removed, full scale economic integration might become a reality. The European summit in December 1989 overrode Mrs. Thatcher's objections and set a timetable for negotiations for full monetary union. The startup date for these negotiations was put at the end of 1990, which is after the German elections. This provides enough time for Mrs. Thatcher to find a way around, over, or through negotiations.

From a political aspect, the countries are building a bloc that is capable of standing up to the other economic and political superpowers. There are 320 million people in the EEC, and the combined GNP is greater than that in the United States. Some people are worried this will result in greater trade protection against the excluded countries. This seems unlikely. The unification of tariffs, etc., will result in adjustments, and should open more markets. It will, however, strengthen the bargaining position of the combined group of countries. While this may seem to raise the possibility of getting into a trade war, it could have exactly the opposite effect and act as a deterrent. Fear of "Fortress Europe" should actually cause other countries to be less ready to raise barriers than otherwise.

Of course, not all of Europe is within the new superpower. Austria has stated its desire to join the EEC, but the member countries are no longer keen to expand. Including more countries adds to the compromises that have to be made and makes it more difficult to progress further. The other countries of Western

Europe still outside are Switzerland, Norway, Sweden, and Finland. There is a debate over whether Turkey is within Europe or not; this has to be settled before membership can be considered.

Excluding Turkey, these other countries are all members of the European Free Trade Association (EFTA) which already enjoys a special relationship with the EEC. It is likely that, much to the desire of the EEC, this special relationship will be expanded and reinforced. If Austria is accepted into the club then conditions will become more difficult, eventually leading to other EFTA countries requesting membership. The last bastion of independence and exclusivity is likely to be Switzerland. EFTA countries are likely to adapt to the EEC changes in rules and regulations anyway. Being small, these countries have always had to adapt to the conditions and specifications of others. Their success is shown in generally good trade performance. As a result, there will continue to be good investment opportunities in these countries, although there is likely to be an intense political debate.

Unification requires some loss of independence, as rules have to be set by the centralized European parliament, which also tries to ensure compliance. In economic terms, such changes offer tremendous potential for improvements in efficiency for large economies. In reality, however, there is bound to be a transition period characterized by a massive duplication of effort. The short-term cost is worth paying to earn the longer-term benefits, but these should not be ignored when it comes to making investment decisions.

The Changing Face of Europe

In the summer of 1989, the main discussion for future prospects within Europe would have concentrated on the proposals for market integration by 1992. However, events moved rapidly in the second half of the year, and the opening of Eastern European economies became the focus of attention. These two movements are not totally independent. Economic integration had emphasized the size and wealth of the European market and the potential that created. This was in sharp contrast to the impoverished state of affairs existing across the borders in the East and emphasized the need for change. At the same time the unraveling of the communist web of controls and restrictions has accelerated the movement towards unifying the markets of Western Europe.

It is important to recognize that an economic revolution is taking place. This is a revolution in computer technology, information, and communications. As a result the importance of geographical barriers is being broken down. The EEC responded to the pressures and incentives being created by removing increasing obsolete physical restraints. High living standards grew even higher during the 1980's, with the prospect of going much higher in the future. At the same time, it became harder and harder for the communist regimes to conceal the truth from their repressed populations. The comparison revealed the lumbering inefficiency of the centralized system, and also the widespread corruption. Communism as it worked in practice seemed to be less "by the people, for the people," as "by the people in charge, for the people in charge." Communism in most cases was nothing more than justification for dictatorship.

While the accelerating pace of change was a force for change within the Eastern bloc countries, so the overthrow of communism has provided an added incentive for integration within Western Europe. Until very recently, the concept of Europe was clearly defined. The EEC was changing the rules within a clearly defined area. Now it has become difficult to say where Europe as an economic entity begins and ends. The most striking example is German reunification, which brings East Germany within the EEC. If that has happened, then what about Czechoslovakia, Hungary, and Poland?

With events moving so rapidly, it is clearly dangerous to make forecasts on such matters. While most people agree that the old ties will continue to bind for some time to come, there is no certainty about it. The European leaders want to accelerate the process of integration so that when or if such questions arise the framework of a united Europe will already be firmly in place.

There are a number of motives for wanting to settle the rules. One is German reunification. Fears of a resurgence of German militarism are overstated, but the French and many others will feel a lot happier with Germany within rather than outside the EEC. The poorer members of the EEC had hoped to obtain substantial aid from fellow members to develop their economies. Now competing claims have been generated across the eastern borders. In theory, the more integrated the political and economic systems become, the greater these countries will have in the management of community resources. Rising demands for scarce capital will also make it more expensive.

There is a tendency to think of President Mikhail Gorbachev as the father of the peaceful revolution that is taking place. That is natural enough, and there is no doubt that he has played a pivotal role. But he is more in the position of the jailor who has opened the door than the leader of the revolution. The leaders appeared years ago in Hungary, Poland, and Czechoslovakia and were overthrown by Russian intervention.

The Gorbachev reforms were a necessary condition for the changes in the rest of Eastern Europe, but they only released the pent up pressure that had been building over the years. Gorbachev went from country to country, turning the key and opening the doors. Since then, however, he quickly acquired the role as leader of reform. Having offered freedom, he then had no choice but to watch as the communist parties were pushed into the background.

Glasnost started in the Soviet Union, but democracy will take root most easily in the East-European satellite countries. Ultimately, there is no half way measure between suppression and freedom. Freedom is an addictive drug. However, free markets will only be achieved after a long period of transition. Allowing the people to spend their money any way they wish would create an economic crisis of gigantic proportions. Imports would flood into the countries, and the currencies would collapse. Progress necessarily has to be slow, but new markets will open up, and these countries will also offer new competition. It cannot be a one-way street. However, the overall pie will be growing, potentially faster than at any time in history.

Western Europe should benefit from the transition taking place. In the short-term, West Germany is in the best position to take advantage of what is happening. There is the potential for cheaper labor, both through the influx of East Germans, and the potential for locating production in East Germany. The likelihood of higher consumption might hurt some countries' balance of payments, but West Germany has the strongest current account in the world at this point.

The prospect of higher demand within Germany, and a higher exchange rate will help to bring down the huge trade surplus and provide a solution to what was becoming a major problem. Since the majority of the growing surplus has been with the rest of Europe, this will smooth down an increasing source of friction. The rest of Europe also stands to benefit, through satisfying demand in the East, and using eastern labor and facilities as low cost sources of production. These benefits will not show up overnight, but will provide a steady source of additional growth through the 1990's. Always assuming, of course, that the peaceful revolution is allowed to continue.

The real benefits are long term rather than short term. There are now substantial investment opportunities which should be capable of supporting economic growth in the future. There is little likelihood of a shortage of demand, assuming progress is made in opening up these markets. Rather the problem will be to keep domestic demand within western Europe under control. Paradoxically, the first couple of years of the new decade are likely to be below par, as an economic slowdown finally seems to be approaching. However, the potential exists for Europe to dominate the decade of the 1990s.

The further the ex-communist countries move towards free markets and free elections, the greater the potential for everyone, but also the greater the risk if the process were to be suddenly reversed. At this stage there is little investment and little to lose, but that will change. The retying of the communist straight jacket already seems inconceivable, but then it is from the unexpected that comes the greatest risk. There are some commentators who have emphasized the risks involved. This is quite the wrong way to view these events.

Risk and return are closely related, and that is the same here. There is risk that the Soviets will march in and reestablish hard line communism, that the new governments will default on loans in the future or confiscate foreign investments. There is also the risk that the governments will spend scarce resources on frivolous or wastful projects. All these risks are worth taking into consideration, but they seem relatively slight compared with the potential that exists. The Russians are having trouble getting control of regions within the Soviet Union; it is beyond belief that they should simultaneously march into East Germany, Poland, Hungary, and Czechoslovakia and reestablish the old order. The risk of default or confiscation exists but lies somewhere in the distance. However, the risk is far less than for the LDC borrowers, as shown by the Latin American debacle. At the same time, there is real demand for open government and investment in raising living standards. Conspicuous consumption by the State seems to be the furthest things from the minds of the new emerging governments.

Pessimism is not the right approach to the historic events taking place. Equally, unbounded optimism is clearly going too far. There are risks, and these need to be recognized. They should not, however, be allowed to blind observers to the potential rewards. We are standing on the threshold of one of the greatest movements in history, and the economic potential is truly spectacular.

Country Possibilities

European markets provide some of the greatest opportunities for international diversification. This is true not only from an American or Japanese perspective but also for individual countries within Europe. Many European fund managers are happier over-weighting neighboring countries than markets further away. This can be justified on the grounds that what is physically near or culturally close is more easily understood. So far, this has been included as international diversification. As the EEC becomes more closely integrated, however, this will appear more like the parochialism of which U.S. investors have often been accused.

Some countries are so small that domestic investors have to look beyond their country borders in order to invest in a wide spread of industries. In all cases, opportunities are increased through international diversification. That, of course, is always true, but clearly the importance is greater the smaller the country is.

For a long time there were controls on capital flows from many countries within Europe. These were totally removed by 1990 as part of the evolution towards market integration. The move in this direction would have continued anyway and is one of many examples of European integration following already established world trends. The most dramatic change came in 1979 when Mrs.

Thatcher removed all restrictions on outward investment from the United Kingdom under no immediate pressure from fellow community members.

As it happens, this unshackling of international capital flows from the United Kingdom resulted in much greater flows to the United States than into Europe; a trend that has continued up to the present. In fact, this is a general trend. So despite the great perceived advantage provided by European integration, there are still greater investment flows outward to America than are flowing in the other direction. U.K. investment in taking over companies within the EEC has been rising steadily and hit a record in 1988. However, the dominant trend has still been towards North America. Over the three years to 1988, roughly 80% of all overseas takeovers by U.K. companies was on the other side of the Atlantic.

Direct investment flowing into and within Europe will continue to grow as a result of the perceived opportunities there. Companies will consolidate within industries in order to enjoy economies of scale that were not possible before, which will provide entry into local markets. Investors from outside will also buy into existing facilities and markets, as well as set up new operations. Companies outside the EEC, e.g., American, Japanese, and Swiss, are keen to establish a foothold in the expanded EEC market and are also seeking agreements in Eastern Europe. Investment into the United States will not disappear but is likely to slow down, as a result of the increased alternatives available.

Equity Markets

Diversification opportunities in equities are created because various countries are in different stages of development, and because different cultural, economic, geographical, and political conditions have favored certain sectors and types of company. In addition, each country has its own tax regime, and changes can have an important impact on profitability. Foreign demand is likely to magnify any such effects, as investors outside the country try to anticipate the domestic reaction. The more integrated the economies become, the closer the markets should be expected to move together, as reflected in the correlations existing between the major European stock markets over two separate periods, 1971–1979 and 1980–1988. These can be seen in Table 1.

Table 1 shows that there has been some increase in the correlation between the European markets over this period. For example, the correlations are higher for the second period, even though the differences are slight. This sort of evidence might be used to show the closer ties produced by the move towards economic integration. To test the validity of this conclusion, the United States and Japan have been included in the table. What this shows is that higher correlations are not only apparent between countries within Europe but also show up between these countries and the United States and Japan.

Table 1   European Equity Market Correlations

1971–1979

	France	Germany	Italy	U.K.	Japan	U.S.
France	1					
Germany	0.474	1				
Italy	0.403	0.340	1			
U.K.	0.520	0.363	0.371	1		
Japan	0.374	0.489	0.350	0.314	1	
U.S.	0.426	0.309	0.167	0.493	0.290	1

1980–1988

	France	Germany	Italy	U.K.	Japan	U.S.
France	1					
Germany	0.617	1				
Italy	0.449	0.358	1			
U.K.	0.511	0.454	0.421	1		
Japan	0.450	0.369	0.392	0.417	1	
U.S.	0.440	0.422	0.270	0.559	0.607	1

A more general conclusion seems to be that there has been a closer integration of world economies. Part of the improved cooperation within Europe is a reflection of this trend. It could be argued that the European integration has accelerated over the past few years and that this is not fully reflected in these comparisons. Certainly, it is likely that EEC equity markets will move closer together over time, but significant diversification opportunities are likely to remain through the 1990s.

Another factor to bear in mind regarding European equity markets is how few companies are represented. The exception is the United Kingdom, where the ratio of market capitalization to GDP is nearly 90%. By comparison the ratio is below 20% in Germany and France. In these countries, there are a large number of medium-sized companies that remain under family control. This is likely to change over the 1990s. This is partly due to the Europeanization of markets, which is raising competition by breaking down regional barriers, as in the case of local brewers. There is also the influence of changing laws and the problems of inheritance. It will remain a gradual process, but these equity markets should play an increasing role over time. In addition, this situation provides opportunities for cross-border expansion within Europe and from outside. This mainly involves direct investment by companies rather than individual or institutional investors.

Bonds

Individual countries also have their own bond markets, each with its own particular characteristics. These provide different investment returns to investors in any year, often varying by large amounts. Closer integration will produce more similar returns, but differences will exist as long as the shift to a single currency is resisted. Once prices are denominated in the same currency, interest rates will move into line. Regional differences in inflation will remain, as are found in the United States, but these will not always be in the same direction. For domestic holders of the currency, only the average rate of inflation would then be relevant, while there would only be a single exchange rate affecting the return to foreign holders.

The single greatest influence on bond yields is the rate of inflation, which is why yields are so much higher in the United Kingdom or Italy than they are in Germany. However, that is not the only influence, and changes in fiscal policy can also have an important effect. The fiscal surplus in the United Kingdom over the latter years of the 1980s was instrumental in holding down bond yields despite the sharp rise in inflation in 1988 and 1989.

Inflation rates have moved closer within Europe over recent years, as the higher inflation countries—United Kingdom, France, Italy—have brought their rates down closer to those in Germany. The improvement has been particularly noticeable in France. Even more importantly for the future, success has reinforced the desire for further improvement. Here again, the commitment to greater economic integration has received most of the credit for the reduced spread of inflation rates. While this has been a factor, more important has been the general shift of sentiment towards greater financial and fiscal responsibility and lower inflation. It so happens that while Japan has been even more successful in bringing down the rate of inflation, the United States and Canada have experienced relatively low inflation for a number of years.

The only real guarantee of achieving and maintaining the same inflation rates within Europe is for the individual countries to adopt the same currency. This requires countries to relinquish sovereignty over monetary policy, and also requires the establishment of a central bank for Europe. Many countries are uncertain about such a move.

The closest moving bond markets within Europe are those that have the least movement in exchange rates, such as those in Germany and the Netherlands. More similar inflation rates and greater stability in exchange rates will eventu-

---

Table 2   European Bond Market Correlations

1969–1979

	France	Germany	Italy	U.K.	Japan	U.S.
France	1					
Germany	−0.022	1				
Italy	0.135	0.150	1			
U.K.	0.144	0.196	0.174	1		
Japan	0.063	0.285	0.062	0.097	1	
U.S.	−0.039	0.247	0.049	0.209	0.120	1

1980–1988

	France	Germany	Italy	U.K.	Japan	U.S.
France	1					
Germany	0.396	1				
Italy	0.370	0.199	1			
U.K.	0.144	0.260	0.084	1		
Japan	0.149	0.434	0.065	0.401	1	
U.S.	0.123	0.550	0.106	0.423	0.453	1

---

ally produce closer bond yields, but only long experience will prove convincing in the absence of a single currency. Table 2 shows the correlations between the various bond market returns. The story is the same as for the equity markets. Correlations between the individual European markets have increased over time, but the same trend is also apparent between the countries of Europe and Japan and the United States.

It is, however, already possible to invest in representative European bonds. The European Currency Unit (ECU) is made up from a basket of European currencies, weighted according to relative size and economic importance. Reweighting takes place every five years. The U.K. government conducts regular bill auctions in ECU, while Italy issues short-term and variable rate instruments. ECU bonds have become much more widely available over recent years, as acceptability has increased. The more there are (up to a point) the more acceptable they are, and vice versa. There is an initial threshold to be overcome but this now seems to have been reached. Liquidity is less than in the major domestic bond markets but has improved considerably over recent years.

At certain times the ECU yield moves out of line with the underlying markets. An example occurred during 1988, when ECU bond yields remained significantly below the yield that could be obtained by buying bonds in the underlying markets in the same proportions. The anomaly was removed in the first quarter of 1989. Alternatively, there have been times when ECU yields have been substantially above the theoretical yield, as for example, during 1983, when ECU yields were over a full point higher than they should have been. It is possible to calculate the underlying theoretical yield and institutions can arbitrate the basket of securities and the ECU if the market yield moves too far out of line. As the market matures such arbitrage opportunities are likely to be reduced significantly.

Investment Prospects in the 1990s

Europe seems to offer attractive investment opportunities over the upcoming decade, both in bonds and equities. There are a number of favorable influences, and these are reinforced by the closer economic integration associated with 1992 and the opening up of the Eastern bloc countries.

The changes that are taking place will have a generally positive effect. However, by improving competition, there will clearly be winners and losers. Some of the winners will have a strong base with Europe but may ultimately be owned abroad. And even importers into Europe will benefit from the improved distribution network. One possibility would be the importing of American made automobiles. This may seem unrealistic, but even that may happen in response to larger, more unified markets. So far little attention has been paid to this aspect of the dramatic changes that are taking place.

Before summarizing the potential in the markets, a word of caution is due. Apart from the risk of an attempted reimposition of the communist hard line approach, there is the possibility of expectations running ahead of the reality. This can be seen, for example, by the shift in perceptions about Europe during the 1980s. In the early part of the decade, "Eurosclerosis" became a popular term to describe the economic difficulties and stagnation within Europe, and in particular, the seizing up of the mighty German economic machine. According to discussions at the time, the economies of Europe were in a state of terminal decline, and nothing would help. At that time, the American economy was held up as a shining example of success.

This deep pessimism has now been replaced with high optimism about the seemingly boundless opportunities that face a unified Europe. Reality lies on a plain that runs between these hills and valleys. Seen in the right perspective, the true potential is represented more accurately by gradual slopes.

The differences can be important, and the longer-run implications of a truly unified and expanded Europe is highly significant. However, exaggerated expectations or fears serve only to confuse and mislead and do nothing to improve understanding. Many non-European companies will benefit from greater integration of markets within Europe, while the prospects for many domestic companies and bonds will continue to be dominated by conditions within the individual countries for years to come.

As far as bonds are concerned, there is still a general trend towards lower inflation. Inflation accelerated at the end of the 1980s, but this represented a normal cyclical phenomenon. The peak will be lower than those experienced in the 1970s and will average lower over the next few years. Inflation may not disappear altogether, but confidence should return that the lower trend has come to stay. In that case, real yields should fall, given lower inflation that will also result in far lower nominal yields and a significant rise in bond prices.

Reinforcing this trend is the continued drive by governments within Europe to reduce budget deficits and the growth of government spending. The United Kingdom has already achieved this objective, actually running substantial budget surpluses in 1988 and 1989. A weaker economy and the growing need for increased spending on infrastructure should eliminate the surplus fairly soon. The principle and the improving trend, however, will remain. Circumstances are quite unlike the 1970s when the basic political attitude was to keep on spending. Greater control over the public purse strings should have the effect of lowering inflationary expectations during the next business cycle.

Real interest rates should continue to fall over time, but the timing has been extended by the opening of Eastern Europe to trade and investment. This development has suddenly created a whole new range of opportunities. The potential is enormous. Developing markets and production in these countries will be capable of providing a new impetus to the whole world. In order to realize this potential, these countries will require huge injections of capital. Part will be provided by aid, some from bank lending, and some from direct investment. These financing needs are likely to hold up bond yields, since real returns available have increased. As a result real interest rates are likely to fall more slowly than they would otherwise. However, the news is not all bad; capital gains on bonds may be delayed, but that means that high real returns will be available for a longer time.

Lower nominal and real interest rates will also give a boost to the equity markets. Costs will be reduced, and there is the prospect of more stable business conditions. The technological revolution referred to earlier is not confined to Europe, and the beneficiaries of closer integration will not be confined to European companies. AT&T is finally making inroads in Europe; IBM has had a presence for a very long time, as have the other major computer companies. Electronic communications are breaking down the importance of physical barriers, an example of which is the widespread use of fax machines. It may seem that this process has already gone a long way, but there is still much further to go, and the pace is accelerating. The ultimate beneficiaries will not be restricted to the large information technology companies. As communication improves, this enhances the capability of other, smaller companies to provide goods and services. In an earlier age, the building of roads opened whole new markets to farmers and merchants. The present revolution will have a similar effect on the general economy.

Does the Current State of the Korean Equity Market Indicate What Lies Ahead of the Other Asian Emerging Markets in the 1990s?

Keith Park
Global Strategies Group, New York

Introduction

As the world equity markets become further globalized in the 1990s, we will continue to see the ever-increasing outflow of investment into the foreign equity markets. According to an estimate by Salomon Brothers in the summer of 1989, the international equity trading, which was forecasted then to be some $1.40 trillion in 1989, will grow to $3.9 trillion by the year 2000. Furthermore, many U.S. pension fund managers expressed in 1989 their interest in increasing the international portion of their portfolio to 20-25% from the current average of 4% in ten years. This interest is probably fueled by excellent investment opportunities overseas such as the Asian emerging equity markets.

From the U.S. institutional fund managers' point of view, the low correlations of the Pacific Rim emerging equity markets with the U.S. market have served as a superb means for achieving a solid diversification of their portfolio, and consequently, lowering the risk of their portfolio—see Table 1. Moreover, as we can see in Exhibit 1A and 1B, five out of the seven Asian emerging equity markets outperformed the U.S. market in the 1980s both in local currency and U.S. dollar terms.[1] Consequently, international fund managers were able to fur-

Table 1 Correlations Amoung EAFE Index, USA and Asian Emerging Equity Markets (From 1985–1989)

	USA	EAFE	India	Korea	Malaysia	Pakistan	Philippines	Taiwan	Thailand
USA	1.00								
EAFE	0.42	1.00							
India	−0.04	−0.05	1.00						
Korea	0.22	0.15	−0.03	1.00					
Malaysia	0.53	0.20	−0.03	−0.06	1.00				
Pakistan	−0.09	0.12	0.24	0.13	−0.15	1.00			
Philippines	0.20	0.20	−0.13	0.19	0.21	−0.06	1.00		
Taiwan	0.14	0.14	−0.05	−0.19	0.15	−0.03	−0.18	1.00	
Thailand	0.26	0.15	−0.01	−0.23	0.44	0.16	0.03	0.46	1.00

Source: International Finance Corporation.

Exhibit 1A   Market Performance of U.S. and Asian Emerging Markets in the 80s (in local currency)

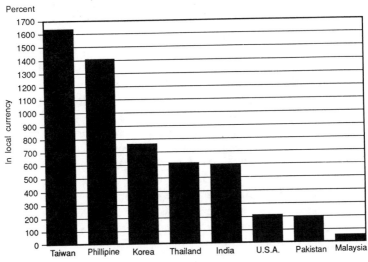

Source: International Finance Corporation.

Exhibit 1B   Market Performance of U.S. and Asian Emerging Markets in the 80s (in U.S. dollars)

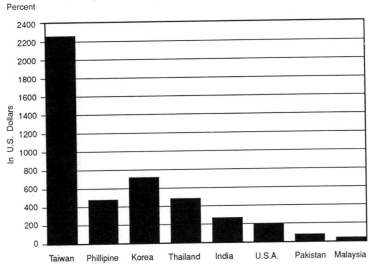

Source: International Finance Corporation.

ther enhance the return of their portfolio by participating in the Asian emerging markets.

In the 1990s, the continuing economic expansion of the Asian economies will further fuel the robust growth of the equity markets in the region. For instance, as we can see in Exhibit 2B, at the end of 1989 80% of the world emerging equity markets were located in Asia—according to Exhibit 2A, the aggregate market capitalization of the Asian equity markets, which was some 20% of the total world equity market in 1980, grew to some 44% at the end of 1989; the market capitalization of Europe grew from 18% to 22% of the world total during the same period of time.

In the 1990s, Korea and Taiwan, two of the best performing emerging equity markets in the 1980s, will be liberalized to direct foreign investment—during the second half of the 1980s, the equity market of Korea has risen some 540% and that of Taiwan, some 1100%. Starting in 1992, the U.S. institutional investors will be able to directly own a piece of the miracle economic machines of Korea which have transformed the once war-destroyed country into a newly-emerging industrial powerhouse—the definite time schedule for the Taiwanese market opening has yet to be finalized by the local government.[2]

However, despite the rosy expectation for the performance of the Asian equity markets in general, the Korean equity market will be beginning the 1990s with various uncertainties and difficulties. The final year of the 1980s was quite disappointing for the international investors holding the Korean papers. The Korea Composite Stock Price Index, which stood at 100 in early 1980, broke 1000 briefly in April 1989 but drifted lower since then to finish the year with a 1.1% loss. As its currency appreciated and labor costs rose, Korea's exports faltered in 1989 and the export-oriented economy grew at half the rate of the previous three years.

The early 1990s will become the most crucial period for the Korean economy, which is currently going through the metamorphosis into an advanced industrial economy. Moreover, as we expect some of the Asian developing economies to make a transition to become an advanced industrial economy in the 1990s, the current uncertainties and problems of the Korean economy might indicate what lies ahead of the other developing Asian economies in the 1990s.

This chapter will examine the current state of the Korean economy, and the consequent implications for the Korean equity market. In addition, the close examination of the Korean equity market might break the myth that the fundamental norms of an established equity market are not applicable to the Asian equity markets, and convince some of us to reconsider their valuation of the Asian emerging markets. Also, given the current volatility and uncertainty of the Korean market, the chapter will explore the opportunities for the U.S. institutional fund managers and investment banking firms in Korea upon the liberalization of 1992 and also, in the other Asian markets in the 1990s.

Exhibit 2A   Market Capitalization of World

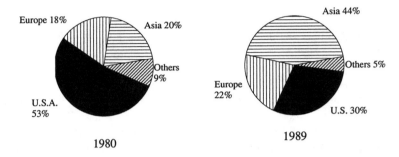

1980

1989

Source: International Finance Corporation.

Exhibit 2B   Regional Market Capitalization of All Emerging Markets

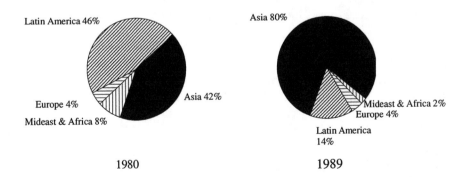

1980

1989

Source: International Finance Corporation.

Economic Overview

Impressive Past Growth

In 1985, Korea had $46 billion of external debt—the fourth largest among the developing countries behind Mexico, Brazil and Argentina. However, at the end of 1988 the Ministry of Finance of Korea made the last payment for the loan from the International Monetary Fund. As a sign of the further turnaround for the Korean economy, two state-owned Korean banks, Korea Development Bank and KEB (Asia) Finance Ltd. which is the Hong Kong subsidiary of Korea Exchange Bank, announced in November 1989 that they would be participating as lead managers in a major sovereign loan syndication, which would lend $400 million to Indonesia. Since only one U.S. bank, Chemical, was involved in the syndication, the Korean participation impressed a number of foreign bankers. This dramatic metamorphosis of Korea from a borrower to an arranger of major international loans has been made possible by its fast-growing trade surplus.

The export-oriented industrial strategy has transformed Korea into a manufacturing power house which exports steel, petrochemicals, textiles, consumer electronics, automobiles, ships, computers, and semiconductors. This industrial strategy enabled Korea to achieve the stupendous real growth rates of gross national product: 12.9%, 12.8% and 12.2% in 1986, 1987 and 1988 respectively. As Table 2 shows, these growth rates far exceeded those of major industrialized countries.

At the same time, the export growth brought about $4.2 billion, $9.9 billion and $14.2 billion current account surpluses in 1986, 1987 and 1988 respectively—current account measures trade in goods and services as well as some unilateral transfers. This impressive economic growth fueled the Korean equity market, which rose some 540% between 1985 and 1988.

Table 2   Comparison of Real GNP Growth Rates

	1986	1987	1988	1989
Korea	12.9%	12.8%	12.2%	6.5%
United States	3.1	3.0	2.8	2.5
Japan	4.0	4.3	4.8	5.2
West Germany	2.4	1.4	2.7	3.9
Britain	3.1	5.2	3.0	2.1
France	2.1	2.5	2.8	3.7

Source: The Economist, Salomon Brothers, Lucky Securities.

Without a doubt, the 1980's has been a significant and giant step forward for the Korean economy—the per capita GNP of Korea, which was mere $87 in 1962, grew to some $4,040 in 1988. However, it is not that the Korean economy does not have its own share of problems, which have been elicited by the rapid economic expansion in the 1980's. For instance, 1989 has been a very tough year for Korea. The trade surplus is expected to be mere $4.3 billion in 1989, which is a 63% drop from $11.6 billion of 1988. Also, the real GNP growth rate will slow down to 6.5% in 1989 from the two digit growth rates of the previous three years—the 6.5%, however, is still far greater than 3.6% of the average GNP growth rate of 24 OECD member economies in 1989. As the performance of an equity market is closely tied to that of its own economy, the Korea Composite Stock Price Index, which is the market capitalization weighted index of all the companies listed at the Korean Stock Exchange, ended 1989 with a 1.1% loss.

Current Problems

The Korean economy exported $33.9 billion, $46.2 billion, and $59.6 billion in 1986, 1987 and 1988 respectively; the corresponding nominal GNP's were $102.7 billion, $128.4 billion and $169.2 billion. Korea exported about one third of its GNP each year since 1985, and in 1988, became the 10th largest trading nation in the global economy. The trade surplus in 1988 grew to $11.6 billion from $4.2 billion of 1986—by the way, this was relatively small compared to $95 billion of Japan in 1988. As its trade surplus mushroomed, trade friction with the U.S. and Europe has become a sensitive and sticky issue.

In 1989, Korea was told by the U.S. and western Europe that its growing significance in the world economy makes it no longer feasible to further rely on an unbalanced large trade surplus for its economic expansion, and that its large trade surplus creates a distorting impact on the world economy. Furthermore, in 1989 Korea was accused of: 1) artificially manipulating its currency in order to make its manufactured products unfairly competitive in the global marketplace; and 2) fortressing its domestic market with trade barriers in order to protect internationally uncompetitive domestic industries and constrain imports.

The U.S. pressure for the rectification of the accused unfair trade policies has been most demanding and vocal. Nonetheless, thanks to its well-orchestrated lobbying on Capitol Hill, Korea was able to spare itself from the trade sanctions of the so-called Super 301 clause of the 1988 trade bill, which named Japan, Brazil and India as unfair trading partners. However, Korea came to a rude awakening in 1989 that its unbalanced export-oriented strategy would be no longer a viable industrial policy in the 1990s.

Under the heavy pressure from the U.S. and Europe, the Korean won has appreciated some 25% against the U.S. dollar since the end of 1985. Most of the appreciation, some 14%, occurred in 1988. Combined with the currency appreciation, the hike in labor cost which rose some 20% annually in the previous three years has elicited the declining competitiveness of Korean manufactured goods in major world markets.

As Korea more widely embraces democracy, the labor activism, which had been severely repressed under the previous authoritarian regimes of Presidents Park and Chun, has become more and more vocal. During the first half of 1989, there were numerous labor strikes demanding higher wages and broader rights of workers. These strikes had such a crippling impact on normal manufacturing operation that it was estimated to cost the Korean economy more than $1 billion of export in the first half of 1989. Furthermore, according to a recent survey, the currency appreciation and wage increase forced some 400 Korean companies to fold in 1988.

According to the Bank of Korea, if wage increases coupled with labor disputes and currency appreciation continues to weaken the international competitiveness of Korean firms in 1990, the Korean economy will expand at the annual rate of 7%, which is higher than 6.5% of 1989 but much lower than some 12% of 1986, 1987 and 1988. Also, the central bank of Korea predicts that the trade and current account surpluses will continue to decline to $3.2 billion and $3.4 billion in 1990 from $11.4 billion and $14.2 billion of 1988.

The industrial development of the Korean economy has been a classical case of how the Asian NICs (Newly Industrialized Countries) such as Korea, Taiwan, Hong Kong and Singapore have upstaged advanced, western industrial nations. After initially achieving highly efficient economies of scale in their domestic markets which were heavily protected from foreign competition, the firms from the Asian NICs have entered the major world markets in the 1980's. Subsequently, they have enlarged their market shares by driving the established firms of advanced industrial nations out of the market by undercutting prices, which has mainly been possible by their cheap domestic labor. The dominance of the Asian NICs' manufacturers has usually been in low-end manufacturing sectors. However, the Korean manufacturers came to realize in 1989 that this strategy would not work any longer.

Remedies

The effective strategic response of the low-end manufacturing firms of advanced industrial nations, when their markets were flooded with cheap goods exported from the Asian NICs, was to move into more specialized, higher-technology manufacturing sectors. This is what the Korean manufacturers have to undertake now—it seems that history always repeats herself. Otherwise, it is bound to happen that the Korean manufacturers will lose out to the new Asian NICs, which are Indonesia, Malaysia, the Philippines and Thailand—the four members of the Association of South East Asian Nations (ASEAN).

The upscaling of the Korean manufacturing industries has already begun. Rhee Sang Hee, Minister of Science, announced in February 1989 that the government would invest $1.5 billion (Won 1 trillion) next five years in electronics, information technology and biotechnology research and development. Furthermore, the government is pushing manufacturers to increase their spending on R&D. It is planning to raise investment in R&D from 2% of GNP in 1987 to 3% in 1991.

This urgency to increase capital investment in R&D in the 1990s will require the Korean equity market to play a critical role in assisting the growth— maybe, the survival—of the Korean economy. It must be able to provide low-cost capital which the Korean manufacturers badly need to upscale their products.

However, the current state of the Korean equity market, which is quite anachronistic in many respects in contrast to the rapid and successful modernization of its economy, keeps it far from being an efficient source of capital. However, the government has been making a serious attempt to nurture a solid equity market by imposing heavy pressure on corporations to move away from bank loans and rely more on equity financing. Furthermore, the government, which does not want the corporate financing of the Korean firms to be limited to the shallow pocket of the domestic equity market, has been steadily masterminding the liberalization of the market despite its somewhat ineffectiveness.

The Korean Equity Market

Past Corporate Financing

In the English-speaking countries such as the U.S., Britain and Australia, the well developed equity markets have been the traditional source of corporate financing. And shareholders have exerted strong control over the governance of corporations. In contrast, West German and Japanese firms have often relied on loan financing provided by banks, which in turn, have maintained a strong relationship with the management of the borrowing corporation. Until the first half of the 1980s, the Korean corporation raised capital in a way somewhat similar to their West German and Japanese counterparts. Their corporate financing need was mostly met by the low-cost bank loans subsidized by the government, which in turn, had a strong say in the management and destiny of corporations.

In the 1970s, the government formulated an industrial development policy to nurture chemical and heavy industries. Following the policy of the government, the state-owned commercial banks provided huge low-cost loans to major business conglomerates called chaebol in order for them to implement the industrial planning of the government. This government subsidy combined with the high inflation of the 1970s enabled the chaebols to fund their growth with negative real interest rates.

However, some of the development projects subsidized by the government turned out to be embarrassing disasters, and incurred a massive amount of nonperforming loans in the books of the state-owned commercial banks—as of June 1989, it was estimated that the top five commercial banks had some $3.8 billion bad and doubtful loans in their books. These problematic loans, in turn, have elicited high interest rates which are well above the world average. Ironically, the government subsidy which funded the initial expansion of the Korean conglomerates are now haunting the beneficiaries by creating such a high financing cost. Because the Korean corporate borrowers have to put up a large amount of interest free deposit to be eligible for bank loans, the Korean firms are estimated to pay real interest rates three times as high as those paid by their foreign competitors.

Changes in Corporate Financing

Consequently, the government has attempted to reduce the chaebols' reliance on bank loans by pressuring them to use equity financing to meet their urgent need for investment in R&D. Also, the chaebols have been told to deleverage their balance sheets which are loaded with huge debt due to the easy, low-cost credit provided by the government in the past—the average debt amount of the chaebols is estimated to be 450% of their equity. They are unbelievably high, compared to those of other countries as shown in Table 3.

In 1988, the Ministry of Finance of Korea required 177 companies with debts of more than $30 million (Won20 billion) to repay debts through equity financing.

**Table 3   Comparison of Debt and Equity Ratios
(Corporate Debt as % of Equity)**

Korea	450%	as of 1989
United States	45	as of 1987
Japan	75	as of 1985
West Germany	29.7	as of 1987
Britain	15.1	as of 1986
France	22.8	as of 1986

Source: *The Economist, The Financial Times, The Korean Times Daily.*

As a further move to wean the chaebols from dependence on the govern-ment-subsidized bank loans, the Ministry ordered 598 of the chaebols' affiliated companies to repay bank debts with funds to be raised in the capital markets in 1989. Also, the banking regulations have been amended in several ways that will force large corporations to raise money directly in the capital markets. For instance, the borrowing limit has been lowered to 50% of equity capital from 75%. Moreover, large corporations will not be allowed to acquire a controlling interest in banks.

The efforts of the government to nurture the equity market has brought about some solid results. For instance, the Korean firms raised $11 billion through equity issuance in 1988 which was more than a ten-fold increase from $970 million of 1986, and the number of the listed companies at the Korean Stock Exchange grew from 355 to 502 in the same time period. Also, the rising equity market had created an ideal environment for the Korean firms to raise capital by issuing shares. For instance, the Korean corporations met 63% of their 1988 corporate financing need in the equity market. Before then, the equity financing hovered around 20-30% of the total, annual corporate financing.

Internationalization of Corporate Financing

The domestic equity market has not been the only source from which the Korean corporations have tried to raise capital. In addition to the high cost of the domestic bank loans, there had always been a severe shortage of capital in the domestic capital markets because the Korean economy did not begin generating trade and current account surpluses until 1986. As a result, the Korean corporations used to have no choice but to substantially rely on foreign bank loans for their growth. Consequently, they have been trying to tap the international capital markets as a cheaper and more efficient source of corporate financing. For instance, as early as November 1981, Korea International Trust—an investment trust—was established to encourage foreign investors to indirectly participate in the Korean equity market.

Until 1985, the majority of foreign investment in the Korean equity market had been established through investment trusts managed by the three Korean investment trust companies—Korea Investment Trust Co (KITC), Daehan Investment Trust Co (DITC), and Citizens Investment Trust Management Co (CITMC). Table 4 details the investment trusts managed by the above three for foreign investors. Most of the funds are traded in the form of International Depository Receipts.

Most of the investment trusts are open-end funds. However, they are actually closed-end funds because the managers do not have freedom to issue new units at will. The managers have to wait until the pre-existing units are redeemed before issuing new units. Because the Korean government currently determines

---

**Table 4   Issuing Details of Korean Investment Trusts for
Foreign Investors**

Name	Value	Date	Manager	Underwriter	Type*	Premium 3/19/90
Korea Int'l Trust	$25m	11/81	KITC	CS First Boston	O	36.91%
Korea Trust	$25m	11/81	DITC	Merrill Lynch	O	37.88%
Korea Growth Fund	$30m	3/85	CITMC	Jardine Fleming	O	35.64%
Seoul Int'l Trust	$30m	4/85	KITC	Vickers da Costa /Baring Brothers	O	35.07%
Seoul Trust	$30m	4/85	DITC	Prudential Bache	O	36.12%
Korea Small Companies Trust	$5m	12/85	KITC		C	
Korea Emerging Companies	$5m	3/86	DITC		C	

* "O" for open-ended and "C" for close-ended.

Source: Baring Securities, Dong-Suh Securities.

the amount of foreign investment entering into the Korean equity market, the funds will not truly become open-ended until the liberalization of the market, which is currently planned to occur in 1992.

The most well known vehicles for indirect foreign investment in the Korean equity market are the two closed-end funds: the Korea Fund at the New York Stock Exchange, and the Korea Europe Fund at the London Stock Exchange. Table 5 contains information on the above close-end funds. The Korea Fund is not allowed to hold more than 5% of the total outstanding shares of a listed company; the Korea Europe Fund, 3%. Both funds may not invest more than 5% of their net asset value in one share, or more than 25% of their NAV in one industrial sector.

In December 1985, the Korean corporations whose operation had become more international began raising cash abroad and repatriating the funds by issuing convertible bonds in the Eurobond market. Table 6 details the issuance history of the Korean convertible and warrant bonds offered to foreign investors.

The high premium of the indirect investment vehicles can be attributed to the following historical factors: 1) the scarcity value of financial instruments for

Table 5   Offshore Korean Close-End Funds for Foreign Investors

Name	Date	Manager	Initial Capital	Changed Capital	Date	Premium 3/19/90
Korea Fund	8/84	Scudder	$60m	$100m	6/86	42.15%
Korea Europe Fund	3/87		$30m	$60m	6/86	29.17%

Source: Baring Securities, Dong-Suh Securities.

Table 6   Korean Convertible and Warrant Bonds in the Eurobond

Name	Date	Coupon Rate	Conversion Begins	Premium 3/19/90	Amount
Samsung Electronics	12/85	5% p.a.	10/19/87	81.71%	$20m
Daewoo Heavy Industries	5/86	3% p.a.	11/23/87	53.94%	$40m
Yukong	6/86	3 p.a.	01/15/88	77.02%	$20m
Gold Star	8/87	1.75% p.a.	02/11/89	63.66%	$30m
Saehan Media	9/88	1.75% p.a.	04/04/90	79.48%	$50m
Sammi Steel (Warrant Bond)	10/89	1.25% p.a.	05/08/91	157.62%	$50m

Note: The above are all listed at Luxemburg Stock Exchange.
Source: Baring Securities, Dong-Suh Securities.

foreign investment in Korea; 2) the rising stock market; 3) the superb economic growth; 4) the appreciation of the Korean won. Probably, the premium is justifiable only if the Korean stock market rises at least more than the current premium due to the inflow of foreign capital upon the liberalization. At the end of 1989, the foreign ownership via indirect investment accounted for 2% (or $1.9 billion) of the total Korean equity market capitalization.

So far, due to the tight constraints imposed by the government, the Korean corporations' access to the international capital markets has been on a limited scale. This limited access, the Korean government understands, puts the Korean firms at a substantial disadvantage vis-à-vis their foreign competitors. Whereas their counterparts can raise capital in New York, London, Tokyo and Frankfurt wherever an efficient opportunity arises, Korean firms are basically constrained to the domestic capital markets which are not as deep as the global capital markets. As a result, the Korean government has tried to liberalize its capital markets.

Liberalization Outline

At the end of 1988, the government announced the following outline for the capital markets liberalization plan.

However, after the announcement of the plan, the implementation of the liberalization had to be immediately delayed due to the rapid increase in money

---

Table 7   Liberalization Schedule

1989

1. Investment funds for foreigners will be expanded.
2. The regulations on the issuance of the convertible bonds (CBs) in the Eurobond market by Korean firms will be relaxed.
3. Korean firms will be allowed to issue bonds with warrants (BWs) and depository receipts (DRs).
4. Foreign investors will be permitted to trade stocks converted from CBs in the over-the-counter market.
5. The limit on foreign ownership of Korean securities firms will be raised to 40% from the present 10%.

1990

1. The matching funds for investment in domestic and foreign markets will be established and sold to both domestic and foreign investors.
2. The overseas issuance of securities by Korean firms will be further expanded.
3. Domestic corporations will be permitted to increase investment in foreign markets.
4. The guidelines for opening branches and setting up joint ventures with Korean securities firms by foreign securities firms from 1991 will be established.

1991

1. The holders of the Euro-CBs will be permitted to trade stocks converted from CBs on the Korean Stock Exchange; however, the trading will be subject to certain restrictions.
2. Foreign securities firms will be authorized to open branches and set up joint ventures with Korean securities firms.

1992

1. Foreign investors will be permitted to directly invest in the Korean equity market within an as-yet-unspecified limit.
2. The restricted investments in foreign markets by individual Korean investors will be permitted.

Source: Baring Securities.

supply in the Korean economy. As the trade surplus rose, the excessive liquidity began to exert a severe upward pressure on inflation. Consequently, the government tried to limit the inflow of foreign capital by delaying the liberalization.

Reactionary Knee-Jerk Government Policies

In the beginning of 1989, the Korean government realized that the accelerating money supply was creating a severe inflationary pressure in the economy. Its mounting trade surplus was mainly responsible for the 18.8% growth of M2 in 1988 which was 11.8% in 1985—M2 includes cash in circulation, savings and time deposits.

In 1988, the consumer price index jumped 7%, which was a two-fold increase from 3% in 1987. The relatively strict foreign exchange controls, which prevented the trade surplus from flowing outward, did not help lessen the excessive liquidity despite the government's tight reign on money supply. Alarmingly, in the first 25 days of January 1989, M2 increased at an annualized rate of 19.9%.

In order to restrain money growth, the government reversed its earlier position on the market liberalization and imposed strict restrictions on the Korean corporations' new issuance of convertible bonds in Europe. The government even required the capital raised from floating the Euro-CBs to be used only for overseas operations.

Whereas it blocked the Korean corporations' access to the international capital markets, in the beginning of 1989 the Korean government actively encouraged corporations to take advantage of the domestic equity market. Maybe, the Korean government believed that the pocket of the domestic equity market was deep enough to fund the corporate financing need of 1989. The Korean firms raised some $21 billion in the equity market in 1989, which is about twice that of 1988. Also, the number of the listed companies at the Korean Stock

Table 8   Comparison of M2 Growth Rates

	1987	1988	1989
Korea	18.8%	18.8%	19.5%
Japan	11.7%	10.0%	11.5%
United States	5.9%	5.9%	3.2%
West Germany	6.3%	6.9%	5.3%
Britain	22.2%	21.7%	18.2%
France	7.6%	7.1%	8.4%

Source: Baring Securities, Dong-Suh Securities, the Economist.

Exchange increased to 626 in 1989 from 502 of 1988. However, the bull market did not last forever.

In the first three months of 1989, the Korea Composite Price Index impressively rose about 11%, but after the first quarter, headed south. As the Korean economy stumbled due to lackluster exports, the stock prices began reflecting the bleak outlook for Korean corporations. In November 1989, the government heavily intervened in order to prop up the slowing economy and sagging equity market. Despite the inflationary threat, the Bank of Korea lowered the discount rate, and the government decided to offer $1.5 billion (Won1 trillion) low interest loans to companies. However, it did not bring about the intended economic cure, and instead, the stock market continued to sag.

Now, the Korean government believed that the oversupply of shares was responsible for the downward trend of the equity market, and ordered the brokerage houses to postpone new share issuances until 1990. It reversed its earlier position that actively encouraged the domestic equity financing. Due to the shrinking trade surplus, there was less money available to flow into the stock market. Furthermore, as the Korean corporations, which relied heavily on export for their growth, struggled, the shares of the Korean firms were no longer a good investment choice. Despite the repeated intervention of the government, the invisible hand of Adam Smith dominated the market. Discounting the realities of the Korean economy and corporations, share prices continued their downward trend.

In mid December 1989, the equity market hit its yearly low, and the Korea Composite Price Index closed at 844.76, which was about negative 7% change from the close of 1988. As the stock market appeared to collapse, the government once again aggressively intervened. It announced that an unlimited amount of bank funds would be supplied to investment trust firms intending to purchase stocks. Furthermore, in order to bring back investors, the Korean government increased the discount on newly floated shares to 30% from 10%.

As for foreign investors, the government indicated that it would enlarge the Korea Europe Fund to $110 million from $60 million, and allow three new domestic investment trusts—$30 million each—to be created for foreign investors. Also, it announced its intention to encourage the Korean corporations to issue more convertible bonds and bonds with warrants in the Eurobond market. Furthermore, the Ministry of Finance even hinted that it might liberalize the market to direct foreign investment before the targeted 1992. Basically, the government decided to reverse its policy again after less than twelve months. Now, it realized that the pocket of the domestic equity market was not deep enough to sustain the market rally of the 1980s, and that the domestic market does indeed need foreign capital.

Aided by the active support from the government which wanted to see the market finish the year higher than the previous year's close, the market briefly surged. However, showing no sign of reversing its gradual downward trend, the stock market ended 1989 with a 1.1% loss.

The Korean equity market showed in 1989 that it had grown too big to be managed by the bureaucrats of the government. Despite the government's effort to prop up the equity market, the market continued its bearish trend. The market continued to signal its loss of confidence in the Korean corporations' ability to sustain their previous export-oriented growth as the currency appreciation and rising labor cost adversely affected their global competitiveness.

Furthermore, the economy managed by the government showed its limitations as well. The foreign exchange controls, which restricts the free outflow of capital, elicited a severe inflationary pressure as the mounting trade surplus brought about an excessive liquidity.

Inevitability of a Freer Market System

Rather than zigzagging its policy, the Korean government should make an effort to nurture a more self-sufficient, freer market. This will solve many of the current economic problems. As the closed domestic market became a less favorable place to raise necessary equity financing, the market opening will definitely enhance the depth of the domestic equity market, and make it easier for Korean firms to raise necessary financing for upscaling their operations and sustaining their global competitiveness.

Furthermore, Korean corporations should be actively encouraged to use the Euromarket if a cheaper corporate financing is available. Also, the inflow of foreign capital would not worsen the rapid money growth if the current foreign exchange controls are further loosened and if the freer outflow of capital is permitted. Currently, Korean securities firms are allow to invest up to $50 million, and institutional investors such as insurance companies and banks, up to $30 million.

Despite its merits, the market liberalization presents the dilemma of losing corporate ownership to foreigners. The Korean firm are particularly worried that the Japanese will be gobbling them up. However, it has been estimated that the undisclosed family- and cross-share holdings by the Korean conglomerates reduce the liquid market capitalization by half. Consequently, the immediate loss of control is implausible despite the market liberalization. Furthermore, appropriate measures can be installed to prevent the realization of the Korean corporations' fears.

For instance, like the Swiss counterparts, the Korean firms can create three categories of shares: bearer shares (voting common shares for foreign investors), registered shares (voting common shares for domestic investors), and participation certificates (non-voting common shares for foreign investors). This will effectively make it implausible to acquire a controlling interest in a Korean firm.

However, the Korean firms will one day find the above limitation on foreign investment an inefficient measure. For instance, Nestlé of Switzerland decided that the domestic market would not be able to support its global expansion, and that it should have a full access to the global equity markets. It made its registered shares available to foreign investors in November 1988. Since then, a few Swiss firms have followed Nestlé's decision to make their corporate financing more competitive and efficient in preparation for the 1992 integration of the European economies.

In order to open the market in 1992, Korea needs to consolidate the rapid growth of the 1980s and develop a stable and mature freer market structure. It has definitely outgrown the infrastructure of its old self.

Is the Market Ready for the Liberalization?

First, in order to attract international investors the Korean firms need to practice more credible corporate accounting and reporting. For instance, the listed firms at the Korean Stock Exchange with assets in excess of $450 million (Won3 billion) are currently required to be audited by an external public accountant. However, many corporations have showed reluctance and resistance to comply with the regulation. Understanding the need to establish better corporate reporting for development of a mature equity market, the government announced that it would impose a strict auditing system beginning January 1990.

Another problem with the Korean equity market is the casino-like speculative frenzy engulfing investors—whether they are institutional or individual investors. The rapid economic expansion of the 1980's has brought about a fast-achieved prosperity, and substantially contributed to fostering a mentality of accumulating wealth overnight. The extremely short-sighted investment horizon usually leads investors to massive purchasing and selling at the slightest rumor. This has created severe market volatility. Due to the thinness of the market, for instance, a massive selling elicits an abrupt fall of share prices.

Moreover, irresponsible individual investors blame brokerage houses and the government for falling stock prices. Last October, as the market drifted lower, the investors expressed their disappointment and grievances by showing up at the brokerage offices and turning off the electronic display boards. At the just opened regional branch offices, managers had to stay away from their offices to avoid protesting investors.

Furthermore, rampant market manipulation persists despite the well-publicized intention of the government to strictly enforce its law against illegal trading. As lately as last November, the government arrested ten including the employees of Hanshin Securities which is one of the top tier securities houses, and a few Big Hands who are the big time individual investors in Korea. They reaped handsome profits by collaborating to spread a groundless rumor that a silverware manufacturer/exporter was planning a rights issuance in the near future.

Potential Problems for the 1990s

Japanese firms were extremely successful in coping with the dramatic appreciation of Yen and the rising trade barriers abroad. They have upscaled their products and transplanted manufacturing around the globe. The Japanese automakers are a good example. In contrast, the Korean chaebols displayed an enormous inertia in 1989 to cope with the changes in the global trading place.

Basically, they are confronting the same problems which Japanese firms have had to resolve. However, their bloated size has created bureaucracy that does not help them to be responsive and innovative. Furthermore, their will to transform themselves into globally competitive, upscaled operations does not seem as sincere as they claim. According to the 1989s probe by the Office of National Taxation, the 30 largest chaebols own a substantial amount of real estate and securities despite their highly-leveraged balance sheets. Table 9 details the five major chaebols' holding of real estate and securities.

When the labor dispute was at its peak during the first half of 1989, the chaebols appealed to the workers to moderate their demands, citing the difficulties due to the appreciation of the Korean won and the rising trade barriers abroad. Furthermore, claiming the hardships in meeting their corporate financing needs, the chaebols have insisted that the government lowers interest rates and provides more bank loans. However, it seems that their commitment to investing in R&D and upscaling their products has not been as strong as that to speculating in real estate and the stock market.

Table 9   Chaebols' Real Estate and Securities Holdings (in million U.S. dollar)

Chaebols	Bank Loan	Debt/Equity	Real Estate	Securities
Samsung	3,132	502.4%	2,239	731
Hyundai	2,060	429.1%	2,388	1,360
Lucky Goldstar	1,976	407.6%	1,874	852
Daewoo	1,816	488.2%	1,524	1,305
Sunkyung	1,168	354.5%	607	408

Real Estate and Securities as of June 1989.

Source: *The Korea Times Daily.*

Another problem preventing the chaebols from aggressively innovating through investment in R&D is their hesitancy to use equity financing. The chaebols, which have become multinational during the last two decades, are still controlled by the first-generation entrepreneurs. They find the idea of diluting ownership control by issuing more shares unacceptable. However, the rapid growth of the chaebols in the 1980s mandates them to develop a modern structure of corporate governance in order to meet their global expansion need and maintain their competitiveness in major world markets.

How the Korean stock market fares in the 1990s will depend on how well the Korean firms strategically position themselves to stay competitive. As the currency appreciates and labor costs rise, the stock market will not support the companies which try to cling to the status-quo despite the rapidly changing market environments.

Outlook for the 1990's and Consequent Implications for International Fund Managers and Investment Banks

The problems which the Korean economy currently confronts depict what could lie ahead of the fast-growing economies of Asia in the 1990s as they try to become advanced industrial economies. Definitely, the developing Asian economies are not a homogeneous economic group. However, some of Korea's economic problems will be commonly seen during their transitional period. Moreover, we will also observe the similar type of uncertainties and volatilities seen at the Korean bourse in the other Asian emerging equity markets during their transitional period.

The transformation the Korean economy has to make in the 1990s will not be an easy task. However, its equity market can surely assist the transformation if a constructive environment and leadership could be provided by the government. The Korean equity market is no longer an up-and-coming market, but rather a came-and-to-be-seen one.

Concerning the investment opportunities in Korea, Global Strategies Group sees that the current uncertainty and bearish trend have created interesting buying opportunities for savvy investors. A wise and selective buying of undervalued shares will bring about handsome returns when the dust settles down. Investors should look for the companies which are making a solid progress in transforming themselves to high-end manufacturers. Also, the companies which have been gearing themselves to take advantage of booming domestic consumption for their future growth will do well in the 1990s as the Korean economy becomes more consumption-oriented and less export-oriented.

Naturally, foreign institutional investors will not be able to directly buy the above shares until 1992. However, as the current Korean equity market continues its bearish trend and the Korean won steadily depreciates vis-à-vis the U.S. dollar, the Korean institutional investors will be interested in international investing more than ever before. As a result, international fund managers and investment banks will see the growing Korean demand for their expertise on international investing, in particular their quantitative investment and trading technologies. Considering some $35 billion of the current account surpluses accumulated during the second half of the 1980s, the international investment by the Korean institutional investors in the 1990s will not be an insignificant amount. This demand will also occur in the other Asian emerging markets in the 1990s as their trade surplus grows and as the local investors subsequently seek to diversify some of their assets into the developed financial markets as a hedge against the political and economic instability of their domestic market. Given the size of their accumulated trade surplus, the Taiwanese will probably emerge as the second most voracious international investor of Asia after the Japanese in the 1990s.

Differing from Taiwan, Singapore and Hong Kong, the Korean economy has nurtured a significant number of substantial-sized multinational corporations. Consequently, these Korean companies, who have achieved significant economies of scale, are better prepared for the global competition of the 1990s. As a result, in the long run they will outperform the small-sized Taiwanese, Singaporean and Hong Kong companies. Furthermore, Global Strategies Group would like to note that the democratized Eastern Europe will not emerge as a serious competition against Korea in the 1990s because they do not even have necessary industrial infrastructure and political stability. In contrast, the mid-range manufacturing technologies of the Korean firms will be highly demanded by Eastern Europe for their economic reform. This will create additional demand for exports from Korea, which have met various trade barriers in the other parts of the globe. Therefore, the current economic problems, if they are properly resolved, will end up making the Korean firms more efficient and competitive, and better prepared for the global competition in the 1990s.

Endnotes

[1] Some emerging equity markets such as India, Korea and Taiwan are accessible to foreign investors only through the country funds specially set up for foreign investors. Table F1 details the performance of the country funds of the Asian emerging markets since their inception.

Table F1   Performance of Country Funds for Asian Emerging Equity Markets

Fund Name	Market Listed	Date of Inception	Compound Annual Return (%)
			As of Dec. 1989
INDIA			
India Fund	London	July 1986	14.2
India Growth Fund	NYSE	Aug. 1988	38.3
INDONESIA			
Indonesia Fund Inc.	—	Mar. 1989	28.3
Jakarta Fund	London	Aug. 1989	−2.8
Nomura Jakarta Fund	Hong Kong	Sep. 1989	1.2
KOREA			
Korea Fund (I, II, III)	NYSE	Aug. 1984	39.5
Korea Growth Trust	Hong Kong	Mar. 1985	48.2
Korea Int'l Trust (I, II)	—	Nov. 1981	36.3
Korea Trust (I, II)	—	Nov. 1981	32.9
Korea Europe Fund (I, II)	London	Mar. 1987	65.7
Seoul Int'l Trust	—	Apr. 1985	49.8
Seoul Trust	—	Apr. 1985	48.7
MALAYSIA			
Malaysia Fund	NYSE	May 1987	18.9
Malaysia Growth Fund	—	Apr. 1989	38.8
Malacca Fund	London	Jan. 1989	46.4
PHILIPPINES			
Manila Fund	London	Oct. 1989	−80.9
First Philippine Fund	NYSE	Nov. 1989	412.2
TAIWAN			
Formosa Fund	London	Mar. 1986	91.9
Taipei Fund	London	May 1986	86.5
Taiwan Fund (I, II)	NYSE	Dec. 1986	32.4
R.O.C. Taiwan Fund	NYSE	Oct. 1983	4.2
THAILAND			
Bangkok Fund (I, II, III)	London	Aug. 1985	59.1
Siam Fund	—	Feb. 1988	47.6
Thai Fund, Inc.	NYSE	Feb. 1988	62.2
Thailand Fund	London	Dec. 1986	51.4
Thai Euro Fund	London	May 1988	50.3
Thai Prime Fund	Singapore	Sept. 1988	98.1
Thai Int'l Fund	London	Nov. 1988	77.8

Source: International Finance Corp.

2   Currently, foreign investors can invest in the equity markets of India, Korea and Taiwan by purchasing the country funds which have been established for foreign investors. Table F2 states the present status of the accessibility of the Asian emerging equity markets.

Table F2   Accessibility of the Far Eastern Emerging Markets

Accessibility	Repatriation of:	Income	Capital
FREE ENTRY			
Indonesia		Free	Free
FREE ENTRY			
Malaysia		Free	Free
RELATIVELY FREE ENTRY			
Thailand		Free	Free
RESTRICTED BY NATIONALITY			
Pakistan		Only after 1 year	
SPECIAL CLASSES OF SHARES			
Philippines		Free	Free
SPECIAL FUNDS ONLY			
India		Some restrictions	
Korea		Free	Free
Taiwan		Free	Free

Tactical Asset Allocation

Tactical Asset Allocation

Jane Buchan
Collins Associates, Newport Beach, California

Tactical Asset Allocation

Interest in tactical asset allocation as an investment strategy has exploded. Domestically, tactical asset allocation principles are used in shifting among stocks, bonds, and cash. Internationally they are used in shifting among countries and asset classes within individual markets. Regardless of the technique, the objective in using the strategy is to earn a higher rate of return for a given level of risk than otherwise possible. If the goal is to outperform the equity market, the level of risk is high; in other models, the goal is defensive in nature, thus the risk level is low. While the recent popularity of tactical asset allocation may make it appear to be a new type of strategy, it is, in fact, the resurgence of market timing.

Philosophy

Most tactical asset allocation strategies are variants on the old adage "buy low, sell high." Ideally, the tactical asset allocator invests in an asset class when it is "cheap" (in effect, purchasing a high-yielding asset class). Conversely, the tactical asset allocator reduces exposure to an asset class when it is "rich" (implying that the yield or expected return is low). In theory the idea works as follows.

Exhibit 1 illustrates the dividend yield of the S&P 500 Index from 1929 through March 1989. Market peaks are indicated by a "P," and troughs are indi-

Exhibit 1   S&P 500 Dividend Yield
March 1929 through March 1988

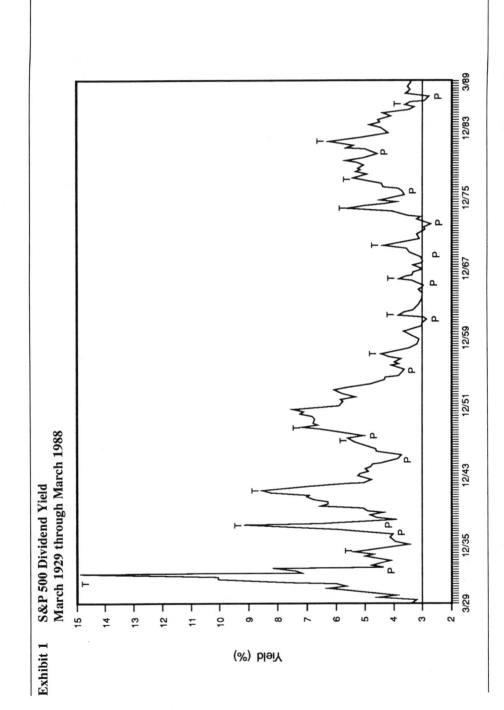

cated by a "T." The chart indicates that except for the mid-1950's through the mid-1970's and the mid-1980's, the market was near a peak when the dividend yield was below 4%. In addition, the market was always near a peak when interest rates were below 3%, which occurred in 1929, 1961, 1966, 1968, 1973, and 1987. Thus, if an investor would have reduced his stock holdings when the dividend yield was below 4% and eliminated them when it was below 3%, he would have outperformed in the ensuing bear market. This is an example of the rationale behind a tactical asset allocator's "sell high" strategy.

Focusing on yield or expected return forces the tactical asset allocator to buy the asset class before it appreciates greatly and to reduce exposure when the expected return is lackluster.

Model Structure

The primary task of the tactical asset allocator is to determine the expected return of asset classes. After the estimates of expected return have been formulated, the tactical asset allocator will synthesize them into an "optimum" asset mix. There are a variety of models in use. One traditional method involves measuring the risk premium. Another more modern method is to use a mean-variance, efficient frontier methodology.

Risk Premium

A risk premium is defined as the expected return of the risky asset less the expected return of the riskless asset. Therefore, a high equity risk premium indicates that stocks are more attractive than usual when compared with cash. When the equity risk premium is high, a tactical asset allocator will increase his commitment to equities. A simple stock/cash risk premium tactical asset allocation model can be illustrated as follows.

Exhibit 2 illustrates the equity risk premium as calculated by our internal risk premium tactical asset allocation model. Some tactical asset allocators include into their calculations of the equity risk premium economic variables, such as the inflation rate and Gross National Product; financial variables, such as investor sentiment, market liquidity; and price momentum.

Exhibit 3 indicates the corresponding percent invested in equities. The benchmark in this example is a 60% equity, 40% cash portfolio. The rule used in the above model is based on the step function in Exhibit 4.

In risk premium models, the degree of desired risk is controlled typically by adjusting the upper and lower bounds of the percent in the risky asset class as well as the corresponding step function.

Exhibit 2   Equity Risk Premium
July 1970 through March 1989

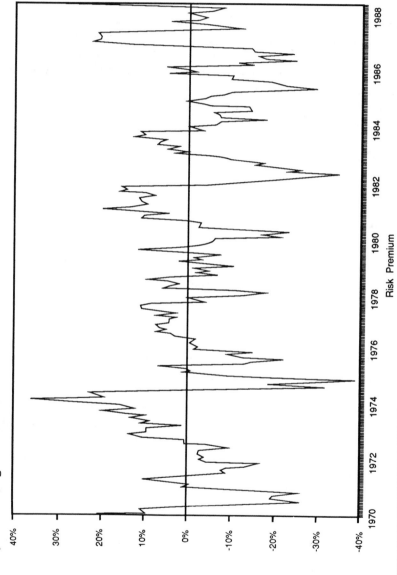

Exhibit 3   Stock, Cash Efficient Frontier Rolling Yearly Periods 1973–1988

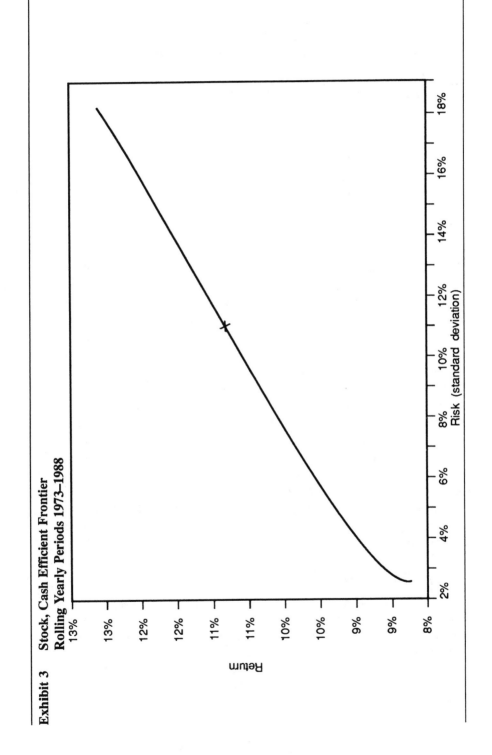

Exhibit 4   Equity Risk Premium, Percent in Equities

Equity Risk Premium	Percent in Equities
–40% to –30%	20%
–30% to –20%	30%
–20% to –10%	40%
–10% to 0	50%
0 to 10%	60%
10% to 20%	70%
20% to 30%	80%
30% to 40%	90%

Most tactical asset allocators use more than two asset classes. If the tactical asset allocator is using a risk premium methodology, adjustments need to be made to the procedure previously outlined in order to accomodate the additional asset classes. There are two common methods in use for dealing with the multiple asset class framework. The first involves making a sequence of decisions between asset classes often in order of the highest long-term rate of return asset class first. For example, in a stock, bond, cash model the allocator will first decide on the stock/bond mix since stocks have a higher long-term expected rate of return. After this decision, the allocator will then invest the remaining funds in the same proportion as the bond/ cash decision indicates. The other method for allocating among many asset classes in a risk premium framework involves adjusting a normal mix in proportion to the difference between the current risk premium and some equilibrium value. For example, assume the normal mix is 60% stock, 30% bond, and 10% cash. If the equity risk premium is 10% higher than its historical average, the tactical asset allocator would increase his equity exposure by 10% to 66% in equities. The other asset classes are adjusted in a similar fashion.

Mean-Variance Methodology

Another common method of tactical asset allocation is based on mean-variance analysis. Typically, in this methodology, the allocator observes the current yields-to-maturity for long bonds and cash and uses a dividend discount model to calculate the appropriate expected return for stocks. The decisive factor in this model is the procedure used to combine the expected return estimates into the best asset mix for each level of risk. The expected return (mean) and the expected volatility (variance) of each asset class and the relationships (correlation) among the asset classes are used as inputs. The resulting asset mixes reflect not only the differentials among the return estimates but also the allocator's confidence in his return estimates and his predictions of the expected relative behavior of each asset class. The mean-variance methodology will produce a set of "efficient" portfolios. The sponsor can then elect the portfolio deemed correct for the level of risk he wishes to bear.

In Exhibit 5, the line represents various mixes of stocks and cash based on the inputs in Exhibit 6.

As an example, the point labeled 60/40 represents a portfolio containing 60% stock and 40% cash. Assuming that the estimates will reflect the future, if one held the 60/40 portfolio, then one would expect to earn an average return of 10.9%, with a standard deviation of returns of 11 percentage points. The expected return and standard deviation of return for a portfolio are computed as follows for the two and three asset class cases.

Two asset class case:

$$E(R) = w_1\ E(R_1) + w_2\ E(R_2)$$

$$E\ (\sigma) = w_1{}^2\ (E(\sigma_1))^2 + w_2{}^2\ (E(\sigma_2))^2 + 2w_1w_2\ \text{corr}_{12}\ E(\sigma_1)\ E(\sigma_2)$$

$$\text{where } w_1 + w_2 = 1$$

Three asset class case:

$$E(R) = w_1\ E(R_1) + w_2\ E(R_2) + w_3\ E(R_3)$$

$$\begin{aligned} E\ (\sigma) = &\ w_1{}^2\ (E(\sigma_1))^2 + w_2{}^2\ (E(\sigma_2))^2 + w_3{}^2\ E(\sigma_3))^2 \\ &+ 2w_1w_2\ \text{corr}_{12}\ E(\sigma_1)\ E(\sigma_2) + 2w_2w_3\ \text{corr}_{23}\ E(\sigma_2)\ E(\sigma_3) \\ &+ 2w_1w_3\ \text{corr}_{13}\ E(\sigma_1)\ E(\sigma_3) \end{aligned}$$

$$\text{where } w_1 + w_2 + w_3 = 1$$

Note that the average rates of return used in the above equations must be simple arithmetic averages.

Tactical asset allocators generally recompute the expected return assumptions on a monthly basis, the exception being a major market move. For many tactical asset allocators, intramonth evaluation is not useful since consensus estimates of earnings are not available on a more frequent basis. While this may result in 12-15 paper recalculations per year, the actual number of shifts averages two to three times per year, with the average shift being a transfer of 10% of total portfolio value.

Exhibit 5   Percent Invested in Equities
July 1970 through March 1989

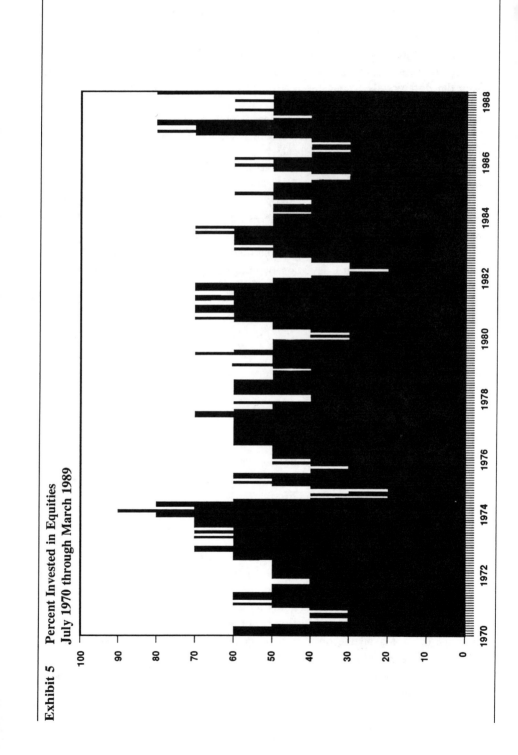

Exhibit 6   Rolling Yearly Periods: 1973–1988

	Average E(R)	Volatility (Standard Deviation) E(σ)	Correlation Corr$_{12}$
Stocks	12.65%	18.38%	−.03%
Cash	8.17%	2.64%	−.03%

Characteristics

Implicit in tactical asset allocation are several characteristics that may or may not be desirable depending upon the investor's tolerances. Tactical asset allocation is *anticipatory*. Thus, a tactical asset allocator has made a guess as to how the market will behave in the future. Even if an allocator's expected return calculations are based on historical data, his forecast implies that the markets will move to "historical" levels. Certainly, most tactical asset allocators' forecasts and combination methodologies allow for a variety of possible market outcomes; nevertheless, the allocator must choose the one allocation that reflects his best prediction of the future.

Tactical asset allocation is *inherently contrarian*. Buying when the market is undervalued and selling when the market is overvalued implies a change in the market direction. However, a market reversal may not occur for quite some time. An example of this occurred in 1987. Early in the year, most tactical asset allocators significantly reduced their equity exposure. The market continued to rise, and at one point, several tactical asset allocators were under the market by more than 20 percentage points. It would have been very easy to declare the low percentages held in stocks a mistake and thus force re-investment. If this had happened, it would have been disastrous for the tactical asset allocator, for he would have participated in the downside, not in the upside.

How Does Tactical Asset Allocation Fit Into an Investment Program?

The return pattern for tactical asset allocation is different from that of an index manager. While an equity index manager may have a high rate of return, he will also have a high degree of volatility in the return pattern. Since a tactical asset allocator is invested in several asset classes, the relationships among the asset classes will stabilize the return pattern. Theoretically, given the same level of return, a good tactical asset allocator will have a lower level of volatility in his return pattern.

The efficient frontier is the common paradigm for evaluating risk and return on a long-term time horizon as well as on the short term. The efficient frontier for the S&P 500, small capitalization stocks, long government bonds, and cash using rolling yearly data from 1973–1987 is shown in Exhibit 7.

The line represents the highest possible return that one could have earned over the time period for that given level of risk or volatility. The further to the right a point is on the horizontal axis, the riskier an investment is considered; the higher a point is on the vertical axis, the more return one expects to earn. The point labelled 1/56/7/36 represents a 1% S&P 500/ 56% small capitalization stocks/ 7% long governments bond/ 36% cash portfolio. The diamond represents the actual risk/return tradeoff realized by a tactical asset allocator during this period.

On the surface, if one evaluates managers on a yearly basis, the tactical asset allocator is slightly superior to that static 1/56/7/36 mix. However, if an investor lengthens his time horizon to three years, the efficient frontier shifts backwards. A strategy that might seem risky on a yearly basis no longer.

For example, notice that even the 100% small capitalization portfolio has shifted to a lower risk level than that of the 1/56/7/36 portfolio evaluated on a yearly basis. Moreover, when examining rolling three year data, the tactical asset allocator no longer looks as attractive. In Exhibit 8, the rolling three year tactical asset allocator's return is denoted by the triangle.

Tactical asset allocation is a viable strategy for an investor with a relatively short time horizon, since it allows a higher than average exposure to equities than would otherwise be indicated. An investor with a long-time horizon will achieve a higher overall rate of return by holding a static, equity dominated asset mix.

Exhibit 7   Efficient Frontier
Based on Rolling Yearly Data, 1973–1987

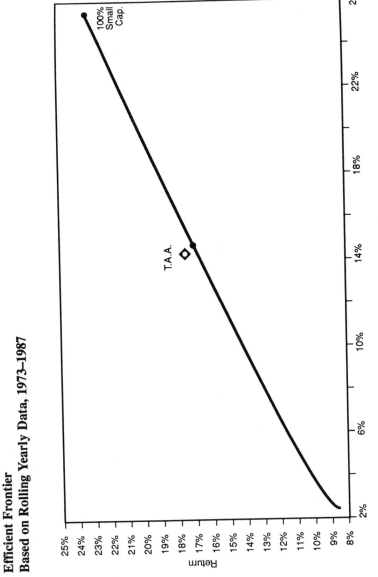

Exhibit 8   Efficient Frontier
Based on Rolling 3-Year Data, 1973–1974

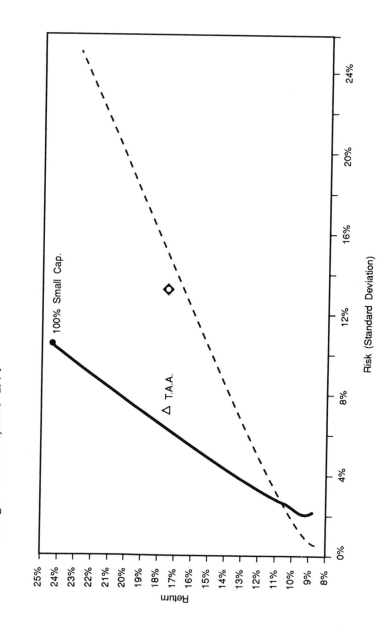

23B

Global Tactical Asset Allocation

Edgar E. Peters
PanAgora Asset Management
Boston, Massachusetts

Bruce E. Clarke
PanAgora Asset Management
London, England

Introduction

Global Tactical Asset Allocation (GTAA) is the shifting of assets between the major stock, bond and cash markets around the world. Its production is an exciting development as it represents the culmination of extensive work in several investment fields. As the name suggests, it evolved from the investment philosophies of domestic (U.S.) Tactical Asset Allocation and International (non-U.S.) Tactical Country Allocation. Its process draws upon quantitative and structured investment concepts as well as the recent development of comprehensive international databases.

GTAA is a relatively new and complex investment concept. Interest is growing rapidly for a variety of different reasons including:

- Continued high growth in international investments: Intersec Research estimates that non-U.S. assets of tax-exempt U.S. plans have grown to $70 billion. Most of this growth is occurring in the quantitative area which includes index funds and model-driven allocation strategies.

• Failure of traditional active strategies: The Frank Russell Company, which monitors the performance of a variety of active managers and active management styles, reports that nearly all active international equity managers have underperformed the Morgan Stanley Capital International EAFE index over the past five years. Although, on the other hand, international fixed-income managers have been more successful in outperforming the Salomon Brothers World Government Bond Index.

• The asset and/or country allocation decision is the most important investment decision in an international portfolio. The majority of an individual stock's return, and almost all of a fixed-income security's return, is due to the return from its market. Knowing which asset class to be invested in is far more important than which issues to be in.

By focusing on the asset class decision, GTAA offers an innovative and predictable approach to adding value in a global or international portfolio while maintaining strict control over the risk of the portfolio.

Global Tactical Asset Allocation: The Theory Market Efficiency and Tactical Asset Allocation

All Tactical Asset Allocation (TAA) strategies follow one basic assumption: Markets are efficient in the long term and inefficient in the short term. This means that while markets can be mispriced, this mispricing will eventually correct itself. The market is, in fact, self-regulating and self-adjusting. Tactical Asset Allocation measures value and takes advantage of those periods where the consensus is wrong.

TAA in this regard is no different to any other value-based investment strategy. In stock-picking and bond-picking styles of asset management, the purpose is to recognize value before the consensus does. Once the consensus realizes that mispricing has occurred, it moves to profit from the market's mistake and corrects the price.

Profiting from the mispricing of individual securities is a very uncertain business. Besides the vast amount of data and the nonmarket risk that this type of strategy involves, there is a high level of transaction costs as well, particularly for non-U.S. equity securities. These factors make the opportunity for a significant payoff from stock picking very small. The greatest and most easily exploitable inefficiencies, and so the largest opportunities, lie between asset classes and across countries. As shown in Exhibits 1 and 2, there has been a tremendous

Exhibit 1   Best/Worst Global Equity Markets

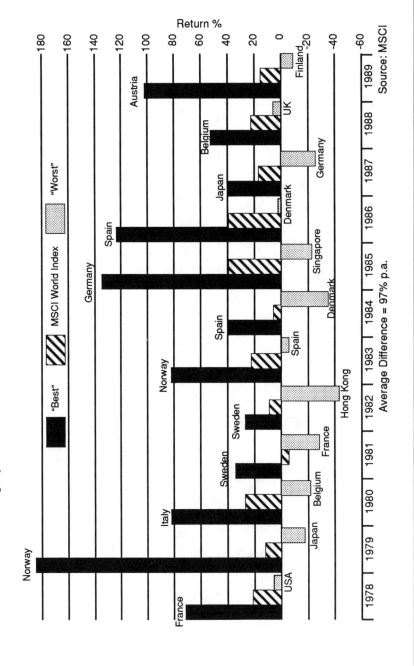

Source: MSCI

Exhibit 2   Best/Worst Global Fixed Income Sectors

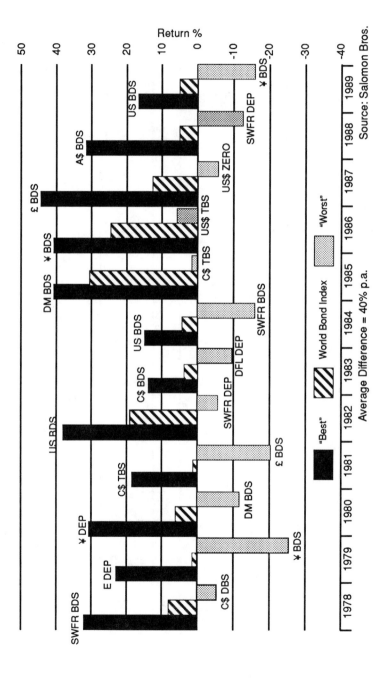

Source: Salomon Bros.

disparity in returns from different equity, bond and cash markets in each of the last 12 years.

The range between best and work-performing equity markets can be dramatic: in 1988, a year of "tight" returns, the range was 48%, while in 1985, a year of widely diverging returns, the range was over 157%. The average difference in return has been 97% in the last 12 years.

In the case of the bond and cash markets, the average difference in return has been 40% with a high of 52% in 1987 and a low of 24% in 1983.

Of even greater interest and surprise are the names of the countries that make it to the top and bottom of annual lists. There appears to be no pattern in the ratings—no region or country has dominated as either the best performing or worst performing market. All types of markets, some predictable, others unpredictable, have made it to the top and bottom of the lists. Who would have guessed that Japan was the best performing equity market in only one of the last 12 years and was the worst performing market in 1979?

Risk/Return Tradeoff: Successful Active Strategies Must Be Able to Overcome High Costs and Control Risks

Much of the underperformance reported by traditional active managers of international equity portfolios is due to the high cost of trading and their inability to control the overall risk of the portfolio.

While in a period of decline, transaction costs in foreign markets remain very high (see Exhibit 3). This is due both to higher average commissions and significant taxes in most countries. For example, in Japan, which is by far the largest foreign market, there is a stamp tax of 0.35% on all sales. In the UK, the stamp tax is 0.5% on purchases. In Sweden there is a stamp tax of 1% on both sales and purchases.

In the case of the bond markets, while transaction costs are lower, a much higher percentage of the return for a fixed-income security is due to its market return, so that there is less to be potentially gained by security selection.

In order to add value, an active strategy must limit the leakage from transaction costs. GTAA controls this in two ways. Firstly, turnover is kept low and, secondly, trading is usually done on a negotiated program or package basis resulting in significantly lower charges.

Risk control, the other key variable in active management, is central to GTAA strategy, but is often the poor relation in a traditional active account.

Each security in an international portfolio can be thought of as a combination of three bets: one on each of the company, the industry and the country. (Currency can be considered as a separate investment decision.) GTAA controls total portfolio risk by confining its bets to over or underweighting markets

Exhibit 3   Commission Costs for International Investing

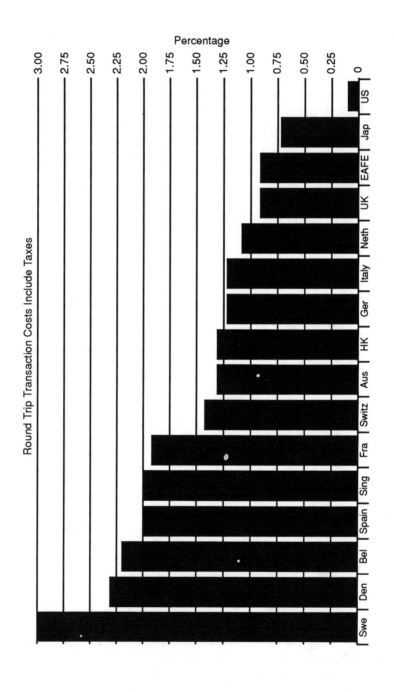

Round Trip Transaction Costs Include Taxes

Percentage

3.00 2.75 2.50 2.25 2.00 1.75 1.50 1.25 1.00 0.75 0.50 0.25 0

Swe | Den | Bel | Spain | Sing | Fra | Switz | Aus | HK | Ger | Italy | Neth | UK | EAFE | Jap | US

and/or asset classes. There are no stock selection or industry weighting risks inherent in the portfolio. The risk that is taken is monitored and controlled through a variety of techniques including country/asset class deviation limits, and portfolio optimization.

Strategic *vs.* Tactical Asset Allocation

Investors have learned over recent years the importance of establishing the proper benchmark portfolio for their international investments. A benchmark represents that portfolio to which the investor is willing to make a long-term strategic commitment. Often the choice will be made as part of a review of the existing asset mix. The benchmark plays a further important role; it is the standard of performance against which the plan sponsor will assess the value added by the active strategy being pursued.

GTAA adds value by varying the asset class weights in the portfolio from those of the benchmark. The deviations are often small in size and short in duration, depending on the level of risk allowable in the portfolio.

The benchmark chosen to measure the GTAA strategy against is important for two reasons. Firstly if the benchmark chosen is significantly different from the industry standard benchmark, (e.g., a combination of the Morgan Stanley Capital International index and the Salomon World Government Bond Index), it can have greater impact on long-term performance relative to the industry standard than the GTAA strategy, and secondly the choice of benchmark affects the amount of value that can be added by the GTAA strategy.

Country Allocation Process

The core of the country allocation process is a systematic valuation model which makes country decisions based on expected return and risk for each market. The allocation process involves two steps. First, the model generates expected returns for each country. Second, the portfolio is optimized to ensure that returns are maximized given a specified level of risk. This process is illustrated by our equity market allocation models.

Equity Models

The valuation models are based on relationships between econometric variables and equity returns. The variables, all of which are stable, proven predictors of equity market returns, include value, growth, economic and volatility measures.

For example, an important predictor of the Italian market is the dividend growth rate. In Italy, investors tend to focus on hard variables like dividends rather than earnings, which are often manipulated. In the UK on the other hand, the foreign exchange rate is important as it measures industrial competitiveness.

Since each equity market is unique, separate models have been developed for each country. The number of variables used in each model ranges from three to five. For example, in our Japan model, we have included:

1. The equity risk premium, defined as the difference between the earnings yield and the long bond yield.
2. The change in the slope of the yield curve.
3. Deviations from the average of the price/book ratio of the Japanese equity market relative to its equivalent for the World Index.

The second step of the allocation process involves optimizing the expected returns generated from the individual country models to maximize the portfolio return relative to a specified level of risk. The expected returns are adjusted for transaction costs in order to minimize undesirable turnover—an important attribute given the high cost of trading in foreign markets.

Risk control is a crucial component of the model. Portfolio risk is controlled by optimization. This involves measuring the risk of each country not only in isolation but relative to the other countries in the benchmark. Country deviation limits are imposed in the optimization process to prevent imprudent allocations and to ensure low residual risk.

Conclusion

Global Tactical Asset Allocation is a raw investment idea evolving from U.S. domestic TAA and recent advances made in international quantitative research. It works from the assumption that while markets are efficient in the long term, short term inefficiencies occur regularly and can be captured through a value-based model or process.

While the concept of asset and country allocation may be simple, its execution is far more complex, and is only possible using the latest advances in investment technology and data delivery. The process described in this article for example, requires the concurrent execution and correlation of over 25 different valuation models based on more than 100 key investment variables. Implementation then requires optimization from a pool of more than 2,000 securities. This investment in systems and data is justified, however, by the benefits of this structured approach to global investing.

Interest in GTAA is growing quickly as it provides an effective and efficient approach to adding value. By concentrating its bets (risks) on the asset class and market decision, it focuses on the most important element of an international portfolio's total return. In addition, by keeping transaction costs to a minimum, GTAA reduces the leakages from the portfolio making it easier to add value.

C H A P T E R **24**

Global Equity Indexation

24A

Introduction to Global Equity Indexation

Keith Park
Global Strategies Group, New York

Theoretical Foundation

The passive investment strategy is based on two premises: 1) the efficient market hypothesis; 2) the capital asset pricing model (CAPM) of Sharpe, Lintner and Mossin.[1] According to the efficient market hypothesis, market prices reflect all the information about the past and future expectations. Asset prices will move as new information emerges in the market. However, once this new information appears in the market, it is too late for a fund manager to utilize it for the returns superior to those of other managers. Before the fund manager acts on the new information, market prices will have already discounted this new information. In other words, perfect information exists in the efficient market, and no fund manager can outperform the market.

Furthermore, the CAPM—which assumes an efficient market where all investors have an identical expectation of the risk-return characteristics of each asset due to perfect information—maintains that the optimal portfolio in market equilibrium will be the market portfolio in which every asset outstanding is contained exactly in proportion to the fraction of its value vis-a-vis the total value of all assets. That is, the excess demand for any asset is non-existent.

Given these premises, the passive fund managers index their portfolios to the market capitalization-weighted benchmark indices such as Standard & Poor's 500 stock index

500 stock index and the Europe, Australia and Far East (EAFE) index of Morgan Stanley Capital International.

Problems with the Benchmark Market Indices

However, it is questionable that S&P 500 and the EAFE indices are the true representation of the U.S. and international asset markets respectively. As Roll claimed in his article that the market portfolio should include all the risky investment such as gold, oil and real estate; that the market indices containing only a group of common stocks do not accurately reflect the true asset market.[2]

Moreover, the critics of international indexers point out that: because the less developed equity markets such as Mexico and Malaysia are not as efficient as the U.S. or U.K. markets, the active investment strategy will do better in these countries than the passive one.

Also, in case of international equity indexation the currently available global equity indices, which are market capitalization-weighted, present a country asset allocation problem. Japan is presently given some 60% weight when a portfolio is indexed internationally, excluding the U.S. No fund manager can claim that his international portfolio has achieved an ultimate diversification by investing in 21 countries while it is weighted 60% in one country.

Practical Answers to Problems

Despite the above problems, equity indexation has been an effective investment methodology which has consistently outperformed most of actively managed domestic and international investment portfolios in the 1980s. The effectiveness of indexation can be traced to low transaction costs and high investment stability achieved by diversification. Furthermore, despite the existence of inefficiency in some of the foreign markets, the cost of poring over the financial statements of some 5000 stocks of the world stock markets is just too overwhelming for the majority of fund managers. Probably, these practical reasons have been the major factors to the increasing popularity of domestic and international equity indexation.

The index fund managers who find the weight currently given to Japan unwise have lowered the weight in their own discretion, or concocted a different approach to the country asset allocation such as Gross Domestic Product weighting scheme. Japan currently represents about 30% in a GDP-based international portfolio. On the other hand, some index fund managers have hedged against the Japanese market by purchasing OTC Nikkei put options.

New Trend in Indexation

The new trend in the indexation is that the index managers, who are no longer satisfied with the market average return of their portfolios, have been seeking to enhance their investment returns by applying active strategies to their passively-managed portfolios. These active strategies include: tilting indexed portfolios; tactical asset allocation; and the application of derivative products such as index futures and options. For instance, some 85% of the markets covered by the EAFE index offer derivative products.

Growing Acceptance

The random walk model from which the efficient market hypothesis was developed was formulated by Louis Bachelier in 1900,[3] and the efficient market hypothesis and CAPM were formulated in the 1960s. But it was not until the early 1970s that fund managers began practicing indexation.

During the U.S. bear market of 1973-74, the active managers performed poorly, and the sudden recovery of the equity market in 1975 caught them unguarded. Again in 1976, due to the market volatilities the active managers showed disappointing returns. During this period, the active practitioners significantly lagged behind the market average, and this convinced many to adopt indexation. For instance, in 1976 Fortune magazine ran an article, *Index Funds—An Idea Whose Time Is Coming* with a drawing of nine greyhounds at the dog tract—supposedly, representing the nine banks that managed the largest amounts of pension money at that time—chasing behind a rabbit which is Standard & Poor's 500 stock index.[4]

In 1989, the indexation strategy is no longer an up-and-coming idea. It has been widely embraced by institutional money managers for domestic investment, and is being further applied to international investment which came in vogue in the U.S. after the world stock market crash of 1987.

According to The Economist magazine, some 11% of the 2 trillion pension funds of the U.S., or $220 billion, was supposedly indexed as of May 1988—according to the index fund managers, $300 billion, or some 15% of the total, was a more accurate estimation. This indexed amount included both domestic and

Table 1   Major Index Investors and Managers

Major Index Investors (as of May 1989)	Indexed Portion of the Total	Dollar Valueof Indexed Portion
New York State Common Fund	100%	$12.60 billion
New York State Teachers	97	9.52
California State Teachers	80	9.29
Central States Teamsters	74	2.67
Exxon Corp.	80	1.72
Major Index Managers (as of May 1989)	**1989**	**1988**
Wells Fargo	$59,357 billion	$47,350 billion
Bankers Trust	29,524	21,291
Mellon Capital	23,850	20,000
State Street Bank	21,111	16,584
ANB Investment	9,821	8,425
Major International Index Managers (as of Oct. 1988)	**1988**	
State Street	$5.0 billion	
Wells Fargo	1.6	
Chase Investors	0.83	
Bankers Trust	0.5	
Dimensional Fund Advisors	0.5	

Source: The Wall Street Journal

international investments. 4% of this $220 billion, or $8.8 billion, is said to be internationally indexed—according to Greenwich Associates, some 21% of the domestic portfolios of the U.S. corporate pension funds are passively invested.

This is a dramatic growth for index funds, compared to the total amount of some $500 million managed by the three pioneers of index funds in 1976: the Wells Fargo Bank in San Francisco; the American National Bank & Trust Co. in Chicago; and Batterymarch Financial Management Corp. in Boston. Table 1 illustrates five major index investors and managers.

Currently, the internationally indexed funds account for a mere 8% of the total internationally invested U.S. assets. However, as the internationalization of the U.S. institutional funds continues to grow in the 1990s, we will see a further increase in international index funds—according to an estimate by Salomon

Brothers in the summer of 1989, the international equity trading, which was forecasted then to be some $1.40 trillion in 1989, will grow to $3.9 trillion by the year 2000; furthermore, many U.S. pension fund managers expressed in 1989 their interest in increasing the international portion of their portfolio to 20-25% from the current average of 4% in ten years.

Questions to Be Answered

The full implication of the growth of index funds still remains to be seen. For instance, if the majority of fund managers adopt the passive strategy, will small companies, which are excluded in the market indices used for indexation, be able to raise enough capital in the equity market? Furthermore, if all institutional funds are indexed and no analyst is doing fundamental research, will our equity market still be efficient? Also, what would happen to the responsibility of institutional shareholders if the trustees of pension funds cannot effectively voice their displeasure with a corporate management which recklessly damages our environment because the pension funds are locked into the company's stock through an indexed investment program and cannot boycott the company's stock?

Closing

This section include two other chapters: Comparison of International Indices by Investment Management Group of Bankers Trust, and Synthetic Global Index Funds by Mark Zurack and William Toy of Goldman, Sachs & Co. The editor hopes that readers will find them insightful and helpful in formulating their global investment strategies.

Endnotes

[1]   William F. Sharpe, "Capital Asset Prices: A Theory of Market Equilibrium Under Risk," Journal of Finance, Volume 19 (September, 1964), pp. 425-442.

John Lintner, "The Valuation of Risk Assets and the Selection of Risky Investments in Stock Portfolios and Capital Budgets," The Review of Economics and Statistics, Volume 47 (February, 1965), pp. 13-37.

Jan Mossin, "Equilibrium in a Capital Asset Market," Econometrics, Volume 34 (October, 1966), pp. 768-783.

[2]   Richard Roll, "A Critique of the Asset Pricing Theory's Test; Part I: On past and Potential Testability of the Theory," Journal of Financial Economics, Volume 4 (March 1977), pp. 129-176.

[3]   Louis Bachelier, "Theorie de la Speculation," Paris: Gauthier Villas, 1900. Translated and reprinted in [18], pp.17-78.

[4]   A.F. Ehrbar, "Index Funds—An Idea Whose Time Is Coming," Fortune, June, 1976, p. 144 et seq.

Comparison of International Indices

Rick Nelson
Bankers Trust Company, New York

Introduction

This chapter examines the merits of three international indices. The perspective taken is that of either a U.S. plan sponsor who is concerned with the proper benchmark for managers or the sponsor who is choosing the appropriate index for a passive portfolio. The three published indices reviewed are the Salomon-Frank Russell Europe-Asia index (SFR), the Morgan Stanley-Capital International EAFE index (MSCI), and the Financial Times Europe-Pacific Basin index (FT). The major aspects in discussing the indices are: i) the logic underlying the index construction; ii) the fundamental characteristics of the index; and iii) the practicality of investing in the index. In examining these topics, we will attempt to contrast the three indices. Not only do we look at the indices in general, but we also focus on the two countries which dominate the indicesJ—apan and the United Kingdom. Finally, some thought will be expressed regarding alternative and customized indices that might better suit plan sponsor measurement and investment needs.

Logic of Index Construction

The algorithm used in determining the composition of an index must cover the weighting of stocks, the rules for including/excluding stocks, and the method for updating the stocks in the index. There are various mathematical formulas that may be used to weight the securities in an index—equal weighting, price weighting, and capitalization weighting. Modern portfolio theory holds that the most representative, most "efficient" portfolio is one that weights issues according to their market capitalization. The greater the capitalization of a stock, the more highly valued the firm by investors, and the greater its influence on the stock market and the index.

The MSCI, the FT, and the SFR all use the optimal scheme, capitalization weighting, with some modifications. The differences arise in the rules for admittance. MSCI selects issues in an attempt to represent at least 60% of each industry in each constituent country. The securities are weighted using their full capitalization position. Among the issues allowed are those that cannot be purchased by U.S. investors (ex. Swiss registered shares and Swedish Banks). Firms that are closely held are permitted. Capitalization, however, is not adjusted to account for cross ownership.

The FT attempts to correct for the shortcomings of the MSCI. It is broader index in terms of coverage. Stocks that cannot be purchased by U.S. investors are excluded. Securities that have less than 25% of their shares publicly available are excluded. Capitalization is not adjusted to account for cross ownership.

The SFR, which goes one step further in a mathematical sense, focuses on larger capitalization issues. Stocks that cannot be purchased by U.S. investors are excluded. Securities that are closely held have their shares outstanding adjusted, as do those firms with substantial cross ownership.

In practical terms, however, the adjustments for float, cross ownership and issues not available to foreign investors may not be all that dramatic. MSCI has begun to publish an EAFE (free) index that adjusts for the Swiss and Swedish shares unpurchaseable by U.S. investors. For the month of December 1987, the "free" index performance differed from EAFE by 10 basis points.

In terms of maintaining the indices the FT has the most fair-minded technique. To determine the entry/exit of companies, the FT has the "World Index Policy Committee," an impressive monicker for the group of independent industry representatives that determine index changes. This suggests that changes will reflect investors needs and will be unbiased by any brokerage consideration. Both Salomon and Morgan have a more arbitrary system of changing the composition at their discretion. In terms of logic, the MSCI is good, but the FT and SFR are superior.

Fundamental Characteristics of the Indices

Given that there is a logic that justifies these indices, it remains to be seen what the formulas lead to in terms of stocks, coverage and characteristics. Financial theory suggests the optimal index should have broad coverage and a diversity of stocks. If one believes the market is efficient, then one should seek to hold the portfolio that represents the average of all investors—a capitalization weighted basket of all stocks. As will be seen, this equates to the FT. There are practical considerations, however, that might suggest other indices.

If the plan sponsor is choosing a bogey for active managers, the benchmark should represent the universe of issues from which the managers will select. To the extent that the managers focus more on country/currency allocations and select stocks from among well known names, a larger capitalization, narrower index may be appropriate. If the manager focuses on stock selection in particular countries, a broader index may be appropriate. If the manager focus on stock selection in particular countries, a broader index whose country components more closely reflect the local market indices of each country may be more appropriate. If the benchmark is to be used for indexing, then the sponsor must consider several items. How will the index fund fit in with the plan's other international investments? Should the index be biased toward larger issues? What industries are to be emphasized? Each index has definite attributes along these lines. If rapid asset moves are anticipated, then a more liquid index is desirable. Custody costs can be minimized by selecting a smaller index. Smaller indices also minimize tracking error (and explanations to trustees!). The FT might be the theorist's dream, but it must be examined in conjunction with reality.

The comparison illuminates four interrelated areas of the indices: a) General composition and capitalization structure; b) Breakdown of capitalization and companies by country; c) Specific studies of the two major countries, Japan and the United Kingdom; d) Risk and Return histories for the SFR, MSCI and the FT. Before embarking on this, it is useful to keep in mind the apparent intent of each vendor in creating their index. MSCI created a diversified benchmark for comparing managers and a source of research when none other existed. Indexing was not envisioned. FT wanted to create the broadest possible benchmark for comparison and research, correcting for MSCI's construction anamalies and providing an extremely diversified, yet investable, portfolio for indexing. SFR went in the opposite direction, attempting to create a benchmark with no construction anamolies to serve a benchmark for managers with larger capitalization portfolios. It's construction and composition would allow for the easier creation of index funds and the lower cost in trading them. The following sections demonstrate the success in reaching those goals.

General Characteristics

Exhibit 1 gives an informative view of the three indices. The SFR has the broadest diversification in terms of countries with 20, but this is misleading. The number of corporations is 541, encompassing $1.9 trillion in capitalization. Furthermore, as of January 1, 1988, MSIC's inclusion of New Zealand and Fin-

Exhibit 1   Comparison of Various Indices Europe and Pacific Basin

	SFR	MSCI	FT
Countries	20	16	19
Companies	541	907	1620
Capitalization (billion)	$1,920	$2,653	$3,407
Mean Capitalization (million)	$3,549	$2,925	$2,103
Median Capitalization (million)	$1,360	$939	$695

as of 12/31/87

Note: MSCI added New Zealand & Finland (37 securities) as of 1/1/88.

land plus the expansion of Spain by 13 issues brings its totals to 18 countries and 957 securities—in keeping with MSCI's committment to expand the index. MSCI extends both the number of stocks and the capitalization base. The FT, though, achieves the greatest depth and breadth. There are 1620 securities, which equal more than $3.4 trillion. The averages on capitalization bear this out. The mean is somewhat close, with SFR having the greatest big cap orientation, while the FT has the least. Note that the $3+ billion average cap is similar to that in the U.S. The median gives a more dramatic picture in the capitalization distinctions. The SFR's median is twice that of the FT's, while the MSCI is in between.

A twist is added to the capitalization profile, as Exhibit 2 sorts the indices into large, medium and small cap categories. The categories loosely correspond to the capitalization guidelines followed in the U.S. by the Russell Company. In it we see that the SFR, while having the largest percentage of companies in the large cap "bucket" ($5 billion and above), has much greater representation with respect to capitalization in the mid-cap area of $5 billion to $.5 billion. As anticipated the FT has much greater small cap exposure, both in terms of companies and capitalization coverage.

The indices do have a great deal in common. The intersection of them is displayed in Exhibit 3. The FT basically engulfs the other two indices. It contains 429 companies of the SFR and 771 stocks that are in MSCI; at least 96% of each of these indices are also in the FT. The overlap is quite extensive.

Country and Capitalization Breakdown

Given that the FT exceeds the SFR index by nearly 1100 issues, the extensive holdings by country in the FT come as no surprise (Exhibit 4). This depth in-

Exhibit 2   Capitalization Profile of the Indices

	SFR	MSCI	FT
Large Capitalization			
$5 Billion and Greater			
% Cap	65.0%	63.6%	59.4%
# of Companies	97	111	118
Medium Capitalization			
$0.5 Billion to 5 Billion			
% Cap	33.0%	33.4%	36.5%
# of Companies	294	472	827
Small Capitalization			
$0.5 Billion and Less			
% Cap	2.0%	3.0%	4.1%
# of Companies	150	324	675

Exhibit 3   Overlapping Representation in the Indices

	Base Index Overlaps "x" %		
	of	of	of
Base Index	**SFR**	**MSCI**	**FT**
SFR			
% Cap	100%	79%	48%
# of Companies	541	318	429
MSCI			
% Cap	85%	10%	59%
# of Companies	318	907	771
FT			
% Cap	97%	96%	100%
# of Companies	429	771	1620

Exhibit 4   Country Allocation by Numbers of Securities

	SFR	MSCI	FT
Japan	163	239	457
United Kingdom	70	133	332
Germany	27	57	93
France	56	87	121
Italy	30	52	94
Netherlands	13	21	37
Australia	39	58	88
Switzerland	21	50	53
Sweden	16	35	34
Hong Kong	18	32	46
Spain	20	19	43
Belgium	15	21	48
New Zealand	8	*	20
Singapore/Malaysia	14	55	62
Denmark	9	24	38
Norway	8	15	24
Ireland	4	–	14
Austria	5	10	16
Finland	2	*	**
Luxembourg	3	–	–

As of 12/31/87
*   MSCI added New Zealand (16 securities) and Finland (21 securities) as of 1/1/88.
**   FT to add in February.

sures that each country index provided by the FT will be a good proxy of local stock market activity. On the other extreme, the SFR will tend to capture only the general trend in the currency and market, due to the lack of names. Again MSCI stands on the middle ground. The surprising insight occurs in Exhibit 5, which examines the percentage of the index that resides in each country. Although Salomon has taken a dramatically different route, holding fewer names, focusing on larger issues and adjusting for cross ownership, its weightings are similar to MSCI's which are similar to the FT's. None of the indices offers any relief from the concern on the "overvalued" state in Japan and its more than 60% weight.

The observations on number of companies/country allocation lead to some predictions on the future performance of the funds. The greatest returns internationally are due to allocations among countries, as opposed to selections within

Exhibit 5   Country Allocation by Capitalization

	SFR	MSCI	FT
Japan	63.5%	61.4%	62.7%
United Kingdom	16.5	14.4	16.4
Germany	4.4	4.7	4.8
France	2.9	3.6	3.0
Italy	2.1	2.6	2.5
Netherlands	2.4	2.2	1.9
Australia	1.8	2.1	1.9
Switzerland	1.6	2.8	1.7
Sweden	0.5	1.2	0.5
Hong Kong	1.6	1.2	1.1
Spain	1.4	1.5	1.4
Belgium	0.8	0.9	0.9
New Zealand	0.2	–	0.2
Singapore/Malaysia	0.3	0.7	0.3
Denmark	0.2	0.3	0.3
Norway	–	0.2	0.1
Ireland	0.2	–	0.2
Austria	*	0.1	0.1
Finland	*	–	***
Luxembourg	*	–	–

As of 12/31/87
  MSCI added New Zealand (16 securities) and Finland (21 securities) as of 1/1/88.
  FT to add in February.
* Less than 0.05%

countries. Thus, while there will be differences in the SFR-UK, the MSCI-UK and the FT-UK index returns, they will track one another closely. Since the country weightings are very similar, the indices will have fairly similar returns.

Focus on Japan   Perhaps the best way of distinguishing among the indices is to do a detailed examination of the indices' major components. To that end we look at Japan using the BARRA model to classify risk, to say what "bets" are being made in the index. We also look at the divergence in the largest industries. (Note: all BARRA exhibits are based on 6/30/87 data).

First a few words about the BARRA model. Risk is measured in terms of standard deviations. Imagine a bell-shaped curve. On each risk attribute each security is assigned a measure ranging from –3 to +3. The market itself is neutral, thus it has a measure of zero. A simple interpretation of the standard deviation is that 95% of all firms fall between +/– 2 units of risk. The aggregation of the risk measure of all the stocks in a portfolio determines what a portfolio's risk profile is. For example, look at Exhibit 6. "Growth," risk factor 7. The SFR, with a measure of –.04 tends to be slightly less growth oriented than the market.

Exhibit 6 compares the various indices to the Tokyo Stock Exchange First Section (TSE1). This 1000+ stock index is the best measure of the broad Japan market; any index that has similar risk characteristics is well designed. Keeping that in mind we focus on the tables in Exhibit 6 and Exhibit 7, the industry comparison table, to contrast the indices versus the TSE1:

> **SFR**—The beta is significantly higher than the TSE's 1.00. There is a large difference on factor 1, Systematic Variability. Stocks with high Systematic Variability tend to react very positively with market upturns, and negatively with downturns; in this sense it is a bit like beta (see the appendix for definitions of the Japan and UK risk factors). Typically in Japan it is large capitalization stocks that are strongly tied to the market. Small caps do not necessarily move with the market and have lower betas (this is contrary to U.S. experience, except most recently). The SFR portfolio is a case in point. It is large capitalization (factor 6, Size) and quite sensitive to the market.

Exhibit 6   Comparison of BARRA Risk Factors: Japan

	TSE1	SFR	MSCI	FT
Beta	1.00	1.07	1.10	1.07
1) Systematic Variability	.21	.71	.62	.43
2) Specific Variability	–.07	–.06	–.08	–.07
3) Trading Activity	.00	–.02	–.02	–.02
4) Success	.01	–.02	.06	.02
5) Relative Price Momentum	.05	.19	.14	.12
6) Size	.17	.45	.45	.31
7) Growth	–.04	–.04	–.02	–.05
8) Value/Price	–.02	–.01	–.04	–.02
9) Sales Revenue/Price	.00	.03	–.01	–.01
10) Yield	.01	.14	.01	–.01
11) Export Revenue	–.06	.04	–.06	–.02
12) Financial Leverage	.06	.17	.06	.12
Tracking Error vs. TSE1	0.0%	2.1%	2.0%	1.6%

Also of interest is the positive measure on Relative Price Momentum (5). Japanese firms tend to be "ramped" or run up in price over a short time period, and then suffer a reversal. The SFR has a greater than average number of stocks that have had good short run returns. Finally the SFR has a positive exposure to Export Revenue (11) compared to the TSE's negative exposure. This is probably insignificant, although it suggests a somewhat greater sensitivity to dollar fluctuations.

The industry chart in Exhibit 7 gives additional interesting facts. The SFR has a 3.5% underweighting on City Banks. This is beneficial to those concerned about the recent strength of that sector. Both energy utilities and brokerage firms are overweighted versus the TSE. All of this can be reduced to one number, the predicted tracking error (Exhibit 6). After adjusting for beta, one would anticipate the SFR to be within +/- 2.1% of the TSE1 in 2 out of three years—not close by U.S. domestic index standards.

MSCI—The MSCI has a somewhat higher beta, but slightly less Systematic Variability. It too has a greater than average exposure to Relative Price Momentum, and its Size factor equals that of SFR. In terms of industries, the overweighting in City Banks stands out, +2.2% versus the TSE and +5.7% when compared to the SFR. MSCI would track the TSE1 similarly to the SFR, at +/- 2%.

FT—Of the three indices, the FT bears the most resemblance to the TSE1. Although the beta is 1.07, Systematic Variability and Size are much more in line. In terms of industries, the only puzzling item is the large City Bank position, 3.6% greater than the TSE in a sector

---

Exhibit 7   Comparison of Top 10 Industry Weightings: Japan

	TSE1	SFR	MSCI	FT
1) City Banks	24.4%	20.9%	26.6%	28.0%
2) Energy Utilities	8.5%	10.9	10.4	9.1
3) Securities Firms	6.4	11.6	7.0	6.4
4) Construction	4.0	3.1	4.2	3.8
5) Drugs	3.9	3.3	3.9	4.1
6) Land Transportation	3.7	2.9	4.1	3.9
7) Food	3.5	3.6	4.1	3.9
8) Chemicals	3.2	3.1	3.1	3.1
9) Automobiles	3.2	4.9	3.8	3.6
10) Regional Banks	3.0	0.3	0.0	0.8

about which most U.S. investors are concerned. Predicted tracking error, not surprisingly, is the tightest of the three at 1.6%. Simply stated the Financial Times Japan component comes the closest to matching the respected TSE 1 benchmark. The SFR presents the greatest distinction, particularly in terms of the City Banks.

Focus on the United Kingdom   To discuss this market, we again employ a BARRA model of risk factors and its industry classifications (Exhibits 8 & 9), this time the one developed for the U.K. market. Exhibit 8 displays the risk characteristics measured against a capitalization weighted universe of 1100 + stocks. This "U.K. Broad Market" is more extensive than the U.K. standard for indices, the FT All Shares (720 issues).

SFR—The SFR component in the United Kingdom has only 70 stocks, thus it is quite different from the U.K. broad market. The beta is somewhat more aggressive at 1.04. Size (3) is large, as anticipated. The SFR securities are not R&D oriented (4). Conversely, there is a greater than average capital investment committment (12). Although these two perhaps offset one another, it probably indicates that the firms are in a different phase of their product cycle. (For the trivia buff: BARRA is considering dropping both Research and Investment

---

Exhibit 8   Comparison of BARRA Risk Factors: United Kingdom

	U.K. Broad Market	SFR	MSCI	FT
Beta	1.00	1.04	1.04	1.01
1) Variability in Markets	.00	.01	.03	.03
2) Success	.00	−.11	.03	−.08
3) Size	.00	.57	.52	.20
4) Research	.00	−.23	−.21	.05
5) Growth	.00	−.06	−.15	−.05
6) Price/Earnings	.00	.03	.04	.03
7) Book/Price	.00	−.07	−.03	−.04
8) Earnings Variation	.00	−.13	−.15	−.07
9) Financial Leverage	.00	.04	.00	−.03
10) Foreign Income	.00	.04	.30	.09
11) Labor Intensity	.00	−.04	.05	−.02
12) Investment	.00	.35	.26	−.09
Tracking Error vs. U.K. Market	0.0%	2.7%	2.8%	2.3%

Exhibit 9   Comparison of Top 10 Industry Weightings: United Kingdom

	U.K. Broad Market	SFR	MSCI	FT
1) Oils	11.9%	9.9%	8.1%	7.5%
2) Stores	6.5%	7.9	6.1	7.8
3) Health	5.8	10.5	5.5	7.4
4) Food	4.4	2.3	11.8	5.5
5) Liqour	4.2	5.2	4.1	5.3
6) Engineering (Contractors)	4.2	4.4	3.3	4.5
7) Investment Trusts	4.0	0.0	0.0	1.5
8) Banks	3.8	8.1	4.7	4.4
9) Chemicals	3.4	4.8	4.3	4.1
10) Retail Food	3.3	5.9	5.4	4.1

as factors, and adding Relative Price Momentum and perhaps Sales to Price. Perhaps this recognizes the positive/negative condition observed above. BARRA's software reduces these factors to zero in the final output. Bankers chooses to print them in its aggregations.)

The industry distinctions of note are the underweighting in oils (1), and the substantial overweightings in the health (3) and bank (8) industries. Note the total absence of Investment Trusts, a logical choice. The tracking error of the SFR versus the U.K. market is predicted to be 2.7%.

MSCI—The MSCI U.K. index, while containing 132 issues, mirrors its SFR counterpart closely. A large distinction occurs in the Foreign Income (10) factor. This positive exposure indicates that the index will perform somewhat better in a strong U.S. dollar market. The oil segment is underweighted, while food is dramatically overstated. The upshot is an even greater tracking error versus the U.K. market of 2.8%.

FT—As was the case in Japan, the FT comes closest to representing the "market" in the U.K. Size is much more in line; the other risk factors are negligibly different from the market. Oils are underweighted by 4.4%. Predicted tracking error, while not glove like, is a tighter 2.3%.

The FT is the best broad market measure. The magnitude of difference in oils suggests that selecting the FT for a bogey or a passive strategy also has an implicit bet against oils. The MSCI and the SFR embody larger capitalization orientation; the MSCI also has greater dollar sensitivity.

Return and Risk

Having examined the characteristics of the indices the natural question is "How have they performed?" Exhibit 10 displays the return history of the three indices from 12/31/84 to 12/31/87. Note: This period was chosen to match the extent of returns available for SFR. The FT index has been reconstructed back to 1981 to create a seven year history, while MSCI has returns based on an actual index extending more than twenty-seven years.

After all is said and done, the indices are close. SFR shows the greatest distinction, differing by nearly 2%, on an annualized basis, from its counterparts. MSCI and FT are virtually identical, with annualized returns of 49.4% and 49.5%, respectively. This observation is born out in Exhibit 11. MSCI and FT have virtually identical variability of returns, and their correlation is very close to perfect. Prospectively, one could anticipate that the smaller capitalization profile of the FT would separate the indices a bit. The fact that the country weightings and risk profiles are so close, however, suggests the divergence will not be great. SFR should differ to a greater extent, although its 98% + correlation with MSCI and FT indicates that returns among the three will be very similar.

Investability

The breadth or emphasis one seeks in an index can be decided having poured over Section II. Yet that part does not discuss the practicality of investing in these indices, whether one is selecting issues for an active portfolio or creating an index fund. Investability (to manufacture a word) can be determined by look-

---

Exhibit 10   Returns of International Indices

Total Return ($)	SFR E-PAC	MSCI EAFE	FT EPB
1985	53.4%	56.9%	55.1%
1986	69.9	70.2	72.8
1987	23.6	24.8	24.7
Annualized Return	47.7%	49.4%	49.5%

Exhibit 11   Risks of International Indices

Correlation	SFR	MSCI	FTA
SFR	1.000		
MSCI	0.994	1.000	
FT	0.989	0.997	1.000
Annual Standard Deviation	21.2%	20.6%	20.8%

ing at index construction rules, number/type of issues in the indices, and by measuring the liquidity of the securities to be purchased in each index.

In the context of index rules, it was pointed out in Section I the various rules used by each index. MSCI ranks lowest on this measure, given that it contains issues not purchasable by U.S. investors, and it includes certain closely held issues that do not have much float. The legal unavailability of an issue means that it is not fair to judge a manager or index fund on that basis. The alternatives to something which cannot be purchased, such as bearer stocks in replacement of Swiss registered shares, may be bid up in response. The lack of sufficient publicly available shares is reflected in higher transaction costs. The FT is better, given that it excludes non-purchasable issues, and even more importantly it excludes issues that lack sufficient public ownership. SFR is the best, given that it takes the FT improvements and then corrects for significant cross ownership.

The capitalization profile and industry concentrations also determine the practicality of investing in an index. This aspect applies more in the case of indexation. The broader the index, the greater the difficulty in tracking and the higher the trading and custody costs.

To save costs, some indexers use a sampling approach. The larger the number of issues in an index, the greater the benefits of sampling. More extensive sampling is done in these cases. While the sampling may provide unbiased tracking error, it still is increased deviation. While sampling does reduce costs, it is inescapable that the larger index will require trades in smaller issues (higher commissions) and more tickets processed (higher custody costs).

To this end, the SFR is the best index. Having only 541 issues, it benefits in terms of tracking and costs. The index could be effectively tracked with 450 issues. MSCI is second on this measure. Bankers would use approximately 675 issues to match its 907 stock universe. The FT is the most difficult, with 900 stocks needed to replicate it. While certain optimization techniques can minimize the tracking/cost differences, the number of issues is still positively related to the costs. Industry concentration is also important to note. SFR, with its lower weighting in the often illiquid Japanese City Banks, will trade better.

The final measure of investability is to measure how well each index trades, how liquid the stocks are. The more liquid a portfolio, the lower the transaction costs. We looked at purchasing, to the extent legally possible, a $100 million portfolio in the SFR, the MSCI, and the FT. For each index we purchased each stock in its exact capitalization weighting. We then took the amount to be purchased and divided it by the average volume in that security. Thus if we needed 100,000 shares of Cadbury-Schwepps and it typically trades 1 million shares a day, then we would require one-tenth of a day's trading volume. Sum that number across all the issues in the index, and one has the percentage of average daily trading volume a $100 million purchase in the index would represent.

We calculate that such a $100 million package would have the following liquidity measures: SFR - 3.79% of average daily volume; MSCI - 4.80% of average daily volume; and FT - 8.71% of average daily volume. (NOTE: Pre-October 19th estimate) This fits with earlier comments. The SFR is a more liquid, less costly index. It is important to note though that there is a great dispersion of liquidity from stock to stock. It is not only average portfolio liquidity, but the number of outliers, the really illiquid names (say 1 day's volume and greater) that makes a portfolio purchase expensive. Indexing techniques can reduce this problem to some extent.

To quantify the costs of executing an exact duplication of each index, we estimated the costs on a $100 million hypothetical fund (Exhibit 12). We also estimated the costs of creating an index fund that employed cost reducing sampling procedures (Exhibit 13). While it is difficult to estimate dealer spreads and market impact, we used our experience and broker input for a conservative estimate. It should be noted, however, that there is a wide divergence of opinions. Commissions in general vary by broker and sense of competition. Dealer spread/impact is somewhat subjective. While the 120-180 basis point cost might get general agreement, the three brokerage houses would strongly differ on the ordering. Regarding custody costs we focused only on per ticket transaction charges. To the extent that the plan sponsor is charged an all inclusive management/custody fee that allows for unlimited holdings/transactions, this issue is irrelevant. Assuming this is not the case, the sponsor could face per ticket transaction charges of up to $50 per ticket.

In terms of dollar costs on a $100 million portfolio, exact duplication equates to $1,290.000 on the SFR, $4,450,000 on the MSCI, and $1,790,000 on the FT. The choice of the SFR could save from $260,000 to $500,000 in costs, assuming these estimates hold true.

It should be noted, however, that this need not make SFR the automatic choice. Sophisticated sampling techniques, such as Bankers stratified optimiza-

Exhibit 12   Cost of Transacting Internationally
Purchasing Entire Index - $100 Million Portfolio

	SFR E-PAC	MSCI EAFE	FT EPB
Number of Securities in Index	541	907	1620
Number Purchased	541	870	1620
Commissions and Taxes	.45%	.50%	.60%
Dealer Spread / Market Impact	.80	.90	1.10
Custody Cost (Incremental per ticket)	.03	.05	.09
Total %	1.28%	1.45%	1.79%
Total Cost	$1,280,000	$1,450,000	$1,790,000

Exhibit 13   Cost of Transacting Internationally
Sampling - $100 Million Portfolio

	SFR E-PAC	MSCI EAFE	FT EPB
Number of Securities in Index	541	907	1620
Number Purchased	450	675	900
Commissions and Taxes	.40%	.45%	.50%
Dealer Spread / Market Impact	.75	.80	.85
Custody Cost (Incremental per ticket)	.02	.04	.05
Total %	1.17%	1.29%	1.40%
Total Cost	$1,170,000	$1,290,000	$1,400,000

tion, reduce transaction costs by purchasing fewer stocks and purchasing more liquid issues. This technique reduces it proportionately more for an index such as the FT, versus an index such as the SFR. For example, BT's approach, applied to the FT, would save at least 39 basis points or $390,000 versus buying all

1620 issues. MSCI costs can be diminished by 16 basis points ($160,000). Other factors can mitigate the costs of building a portfolio. If the portfolio size is large and trading can be done over an extended time, then commissions can be negotiated downward and fixed costs diminish, while market impact can be controlled. If the portfolio is created from existing stocks instead of cash, the matrix is altered. Additionally, while trading costs are important, the investment qualities of an index such as the FT may outweigh its higher set-up costs.

A final observation: For a $100 million portfolio, if intelligent sampling is used, the difference in market impact among the indices is diminished. Liquidity only becomes an issue if the portfolio size is quite large, and the portfolio is transacted in a short amount of time, or if there is great turnover in the portfolio, perhaps caused by market timing or portfolio insurance. In that case, SFR's trading advantage would grow. Regardless of the rankings, perhaps the most important point is the high cost of international transacting, and the need to control it.

Alternative Indices

Remember that one need not restrict oneself to these three indices. For performance measurement purposes, customized benchmarks can be created. Managers' styles, both within countries and in allocating across countries, can be identified. Then "normal" portfolios that approximate these styles can be maintained on a buy and hold basis.

In terms of passive money management, several possibilities present themselves. The plan sponsor should consider strategies that create a reasonable level of comfort. This might sound obvious, but often is not followed. A common concern is the weight of Japan in any portfolio matching the SFR, MSCI, or FT. Rather than accepting that, the sponsor can direct the indexer to hold a lower weight in Japan. If a passive country allocation approach, better grounded in theory, is desired, a GNP weighting scheme offers an alternative. The stock market index in each country is replicated. Funds are allocated across countries not according to the country's capitalization weight, but according to it's GNP weight. By using a system based on economic importance, Japan is reduced to less than 40% of the index fund.

Another alternative does not alter the MSCI country weights, but changes characteristics within specific countries. In Japan, concern seems to center on high P/E's and/or the concentration in the finance sector. The use of P/E screens or the exclusion of banks and brokerage firms could eliminate these concerns.

Customized portfolios, however, cause concern among sponsors, for they are perceived to require an active judgement. As can be seen from the preceding examples, the degree of "activeness" varies a great deal. Sponsors cannot avoid some active decisions. Whether it is in selecting indices or selecting manager styles, it is done. The argument for customized passive strategies combines the cost efficiencies and structured control of indexing, with a product that is better tailored, more comfortable for the sponsor.

Conclusion

Several international indices are now available to the plan sponsor. In selecting the appropriate index, the sponsor might wish to use several points as a guide. An index needed as a performance benchmark should strike a balance. It should be consistent with financial theory. In that context, the broadest possible index (the FT) makes sense. The other consideration is that the index in some sense reflect the investable universe and the styles of the managers. Furthermore, the availability of research data, both current and historical, is a relevant point. Both the SFR and MSCI merit consideration on these other two criteria.

When the index is considered as a bogey for an index fund, several other factors become important. Each index has distinct characteristics in terms of breadth of coverage, capitalization profile, industry concentrations, and fundamental risks. If one is indexing based on a belief that managers cannot beat the market, then financial theory would again suggest the index with the greatest breadth and most logical construction. Yet indexing is generally chosen for reasons of cost as well as financial theory. An index that is less costly to transact and custody may be more practical, even if less pure. This is particularly the case if an active country allocation/passive stock selection strategy is employed.

Factors beyond financial theory and cost may enter the decision. The specific characteristics of the plan may dictate a particular index. If a South African screen is to be used, a broader index, less effected by the exclusion, makes sense. If the sponsor is not comfortable with any of the published indices, alternatives exist. Modifications of security selection within countries (i.e. P/E screen in Japan) and country allocation systems based on economic importance, not capitalization weights, are two possibilities.

When the FT and SFR were released, many people expected dramatic differences from MSCI. While this did not arise in terms of country weightings and some performance issues, definite distinctions occur. The FT is perhaps the strongest index in terms of combining breadth and construction system. Yet it is more expensive to create an index fund to match it, and several years of historical data suggests that the return differences between the FT and MSCI have not been great. SFR is a more limited index, but its lower set-up costs suggest it is appropriate in certain indexing situations. The sponsor must weigh these theoretical and practical considerations in determining the best index.

C H A P T E R **24C**

Synthetic Global Index Funds

Mark A. Zurack, C.F.A.
William W. Toy
Goldman, Sachs & Co., New York

Tracking the World with Futures

A stock portfolio that has been built to track a certain index, like the S&P 500 or the Nikkei 225, is often called an index fund. A *synthetic* index fund is a "stockless" index fund with two parts: a position in stock index futures and a cash instrument, such as a T-bill. These funds became popular with U.S. investors after the S&P 500 futures market opened. Now that other countries have stock index futures markets, you can create and manage a synthetic global index fund.[1]

The information in this chapter is derived from the FT-Actuaries World Indices™* database. The FT-Actuaries World Indices are based on information that Goldman, Sachs & Co. considers reliable, but Goldman Sachs cannot guarantee that the Indices will be at all times accurate or complete, and this should be borne in mind. While Goldman Sachs has made every attempt to obtain accurate information, there is no assurance that errors will not occur as a result of erroneous information, errors in input or failure to represent accurately certain changes, including changes in capitalization structure and other distributions of assets to shareholders of constituent securities. This material has been issued by Goldman, Sachs & Co. and has been approved by Goldman Sachs International Limited, a member of The Securities Association, in connection with its distribution in the United Kingdom and by Goldman Sachs Canada in connection with its distribution in Canada.

The FT-Actuaries World Indices™ are jointly compiled by the Financial Times Limited, Goldman, Sachs & Co., and County NatWest/Wood Mackenzie in conjunction with the Institute of Actuaries and the Faculty of Actuaries.

Table 1	**Percentage of the FT-Actuaries World Index Market Value (as of 6/30/89)**

Japan	40.72%
United States	33.26
United Kingdom	8.86
France	2.42
Canada	2.21
Netherlands	1.29
Australia	1.25
Hong Kong	.64
New Zealand	.14
Total	90.79%

This report describes how to combine stock index futures contracts to make a basket that closely tracks one of four FT-Actuaries World Indices[tm] (FT-A World Indices). All four indexes are capitalization-weighted and the largest, the FT-A World Index (or simply the World Index), covers 24 countries. Nine of those countries have stock index futures markets and together they represent close to 91% of the World Index's market value.

Why Trade Futures Instead of Stocks?

Trading stock index futures has four main advantages over trading stocks. We describe them below, and then turn to the drawbacks of using futures in the next section.

Lower Commissions and Costs

Commissions Your commission charges for stock index futures trades are, on average, one-tenth the amount you pay for stock commissions. But because futures contracts expire, you must pay out commissions whenever you roll over a futures position to extend the fund's horizon. Even so, you will find that the total futures commission cost is usually lower than commission costs for managing a portfolio of stocks over an extended period of time.

Market Impact Assuming liquid markets, market impact costs for stock index futures trades are usually lower than they are for stock trades. This holds true because, at any point in time, more traders make markets in stock index futures contracts than in any one of the stocks in the index.

Taxes and Settlement Charges Typically you pay no taxes to buy or sell futures contracts. Also, settlement charges for futures trades are lower than those for trades in the underlying stocks.

Easier Management

Every three months, it takes only a few steps to roll over a long futures position and reinvest the fund's cash. By contrast, managing a stock basket entails reinvesting dividends and adjusting the portfolio to reflect changes in the index composition, changes in market capitalization of stocks, and corporate actions such as an issuer's repurchase of stock. As an example, 262 stocks were added to or deleted from the World Index in 1988, representing about 4% of the capitalization of the index.

No Withholding Tax

If you own foreign stocks, you probably do not receive 100% of their dividend payouts since the issuer, or issuer's government, withholds some portion as tax. By contrast, no such tax is withheld from earnings on futures positions. Also, you can probably invest the cash portion of your synthetic fund in money market instruments which are usually not subject to withholding.

Easier Currency Hedging

Compared to trading foreign stocks, it's easier to gain exposure to foreign markets and minimize foreign exchange risk by trading futures. To reduce currency risk, you can keep most of your cash position in your home currency. Then your only sources of exchange rate risk are the initial and variation margins, since both must usually be met in the local currency of the futures contract. While hedging the exchange risk of the initial margin is straightforward, hedging variation margin cash flows is less certain.

In a publication entitled "Universal Hedging," Fischer Black explains why most investors should hedge some, but not all, of the currency exposure in their equity portfolios.[2] The paper also suggests hedging the same proportion of exposure in each currency represented in a portfolio. These principles also apply to a global synthetic index fund.

Drawbacks of Using Index Futures

Along with their advantages, futures markets present risks and problems that you won't encounter in stock markets.

Mispricing

The futures contracts must be trading at fair value when you establish your position in order for the returns of your synthetic index fund to match those of the index underlying the contracts. If a contract is trading above fair value, your fund will underperform the contract's underlying index.

Rollover Risk

Most trading takes place in contracts with three months or less to expiration. To extend your synthetic fund's horizon, you close out your position in the nearby contract before it expires and open a new one in the second nearby contract. Each time you roll over, you face the possibility that the spread between the two contracts is mispriced.

Tracking Error

Tracking error is a measure of how close the synthetic fund's return comes to the return of the target index. In this paper, the indexes underlying the futures contracts that form the synthetic index fund are different from the target indexes, the FT Indexes. Therefore we will be taking a close look at tracking error in later sections.

Margin Accounts

Anyone with a position in the futures markets must maintain a margin account. Most exchanges accept government securities denominated in the local currency as initial margin, but some require cash for a portion of it. If you do put cash in a margin account, be sure to include any forgone interest earnings in your costs. Likewise, if other securities are acceptable in lieu of cash, for instance T-bills, you may want to factor in an opportunity cost if you would ordinarily have invested that money in a higher yielding security.

Exhibit 1   FT-Actuaries World Index: June 30, 1989

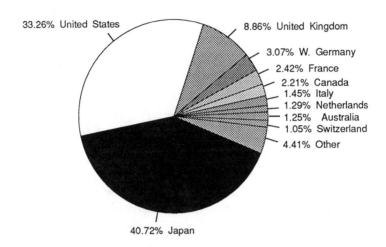

FT-Actuaries Europe-Pacific Index: June 30, 1989

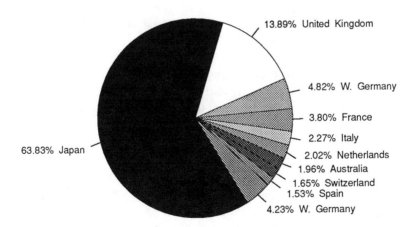

Piecing Together a Synthetic Global Index Fund

Picking the Target Index

To set up a synthetic global index fund, you must first choose your target index—the index whose returns you want to match. If, like many institutional investors, you manage your domestic and foreign equities separately, you should choose a target index that excludes domestic stocks. For example, Japanese investors might want to track the World ex. (that is, without) Japan Index, British investors the World ex. U.K. Index, and so on. On the other hand, a Middle Eastern manager may want a fund that tracks The World Index, since countries in the Middle East are not covered by an FT index at this time.

In this report we describe synthetic global index funds that are designed to track The World Index, as well as the World ex. U.K., World ex. Japan, and Europe-Pacific (Euro-Pac) indexes. All FT indexes are capitalization-weighted. The pie charts on the next page show how capitalization is distributed among the different countries in the World Index and the Euro-Pac.

Which Futures Contracts?

To create synthetic index funds that track the four FT indexes, we need to look at the available listed stock index contracts. These appear in Table 2. Note that we use the S&P 500 and TOPIX contracts for the United States and Japan. Both countries have other listed stock index contracts, but the S&P 500 and TOPIX indexes come closest to tracking the FT indexes for the United States and Japan.

For each of the nine stock index contracts, Table 2 gives the following information based on June 30, 1989 exchange rates: 1) the average daily U.S. dollar volume for the 12 months ending June 30, 1989; and 2) the open interest, in U.S. dollars, at the close of trading on June 30, 1989.

The limited number of contracts and their characteristics will affect our fund's tracking accuracy.

First, as we mentioned, 15 of the 24 countries in the World Index do not have stock index futures markets. These countries account for more than 9% of the market value of the World Index.

Second, not one of the indexes underlying the nine available contracts tracks its corresponding FT country index perfectly.

Third, the Canadian, Hong Kong and New Zealand futures markets are impractical for a synthetic global index fund: Either they represent a very small portion of the world market or they don't have enough liquidity. Therefore we won't use these three stock index contracts in our synthetic index funds.

Table 2   Average Daily Volume (7/1/88—6/30/89) and Open Interest on 6/30/89 for 9 Index Futures Contracts

	Contact	Average Daily Volume	Open Interest on 6/30/89
Japan	TOPIX*	2,941	4,377
United States	S&P 500	6,595	18,610
United Kingdom	FTSE 100	237	1,037
France	CAC-40**	73	307
Australia	All Ordinaries	133	663
Netherlands	EOE***	26	303
Canada	TSE 35	9	69
Hong Kong	Hang Seng****	11	21
New Zealand	Barclays	1	2

*Volume data from 9/6/88
**Volume data from 8/18/88
***Volume data from 10/24/88
****Open interest as of 6/29/89

Note: TOPIX futures began trading on 9/30/88, CAD-40 futures on 8/18/88, and EOE futures on 10/24/88.

Futures Index vs. the FT Country Index

Now that we have narrowed our universe of stock index contracts to six, we can start to build stock index baskets to track the four FT Indices. We begin by comparing the risk statistics for the index underlying each futures contract with the FT index for that country—for instance, Japan's TOPIX index versus the FT Japan and the S&P 500 versus the FT USA.

Table 3 lists the risk statistics. The results are based on regressions of weekly percentage changes from Jan. 4, 1988, through March 6, 1989 and of monthly changes from March 1984 through February 1989. In running the regressions we used the FT country index as the dependent variable and the futures index as the independent variable. Note that monthly data going back to March 1984 is not available for the CAC-40 and EOE indexes.

Following are a few general observations about the information in Table 3.

The S&P 500 has the lowest tracking error. More by coincidence than design, the FT U.S. Index and S&P 500 cover about the same subset of the U.S. equity market.

Table 3   FT Country Index vs. Index Underlying Futures Contract

	Index	Weekly Statistics (1/4/88—3/6/89)			Monthly Statistics (3/84—2/89)		
		Beta	R2	Tracking Error	Beta	R2	Tracking Error
Japan	TOPIX	1.03	.97	2.54	1.07	.99	1.98
United States	S&P 500	.96	.99	0.77	1.00	.99	1.09
United Kingdom	FTSE 100	.95	.97	2.35	1.00	.99	1.68
France	CAC-40	.91	.98	2.91	not available		
Australia	All Ords.	1.11	.97	3.49	1.01	.99	2.83
Netherlands	EOE	.76	.80	6.58	not availabale		

The FT Japan and FT Australia indexes cover a smaller portion of the Japanese and Australian markets than do the TOPIX and All Ordinaries indexes.

The FT France and FT U.K. indexes cover a larger portion of the French and British markets than do the CAC-40 and FTSE 100 indexes.

Compared to all of the indexes in Table 3, the EOE is the poorest substitute for its FT country index. That's because it is the only index in the table that is not capitalization-weighted. The EOE's weighting scheme is much like an arithmetically equal-weighted index.

Constructing a Basket of Futures Contracts

To decide how much weight to assign to the different stock index contracts in a basket, we ran multiple regressions. For dependent variables we used price changes in the four different FT World Indices. For independent variables we used price changes in the indexes underlying the futures contracts. All prices were converted to U.S. dollars.

We ran two sets of regressions to figure out how much money (per $100) to allocate to the different futures contracts.

The first set compares each of the four FT World Indices with a basket of the futures contracts covered by that FT index. For example, we ran the World ex U.K. against a basket of five futures contracts, not including the FTSE 100 contract. And we ran the World ex Japan against a basket of five futures contracts, not including the TOPIX.

The second set of regressions compares each of the FT World Indices with a basket of the three most active stock index futures markets—TOPIX, the S&P 500 and the FTSE-100. Here again, we designed the futures basket to cover the each of the four FT World Indices. Therefore we ran the FT World against a basket of all three contracts, but we ran the World ex Japan against a basket of the S&P 500 and FTSE 100 contracts.

To get both short- and long-term views of the results, each set of regressions covers two periods: January 4, 1988 through March 6, 1989, using weekly price changes, and March 1984 through February 1989, using monthly price changes. Because historical data for the CAC-40 and EOE indexes cover less than five years, we had to substitute the FT France and FT Netherlands indexes in the monthly data regressions. This means that tracking accuracy for the futures baskets is overstated during the five-year period.

Even though daily updates for the FT World Indices did not begin until December 31, 1985, the indexes were reconstructed back to 1981 using the component stocks in the indexes on December 31, 1985. Since this process did not incorporate additions and deletions in the indexes, the data is not the same as it would have been if the index had been updated daily between 1981 and 1985.

Table 4 shows the following information for each basket of futures contracts created to track the FT indexes listed in the left-hand column.

1) The number of dollars based on weekly prices and monthly prices that you should allocate to futures contracts in each country to obtain $100 of total exposure to the FT index.

2) The estimated tracking error (one standard deviation) for the futures basket relative to the FT index. This appears in the far right-hand column.

Note that the dollar allocations shown only held true for February 28, 1989. As markets change, the allocations should change.

From Table 4, we see that the easiest FT index to match is the World Index, followed by the World ex U.K., the World ex Japan, and the Euro-Pac. The order comes as no surprise: The indexes with large U.S. components should be easiest to match since the FT USA and the S&P 500 are so well correlated. For the same reason, the Euro-Pac, the index with no U.S. component, is the most difficult to match.

Note that you can reduce a synthetic fund's tracking error by adding stocks of countries that don't have futures markets. For example, you might want to buy German or Italian stocks since neither Germany nor Italy has a stock index market. Incidentally, both countries have plans to start stock index markets in 1990.

Table 4   Allocation of $100 in Stock Index Futures Baskets Designed to Track 4 Different FT World Indices

		Using Futures Contracts from Five or Six Countries					
	Japan	United States	Netherlands*	United Kingdom	France	Australia	Tracking Error
FT Index							
World							
Weekly	48.64	31.17	8.73	7.86	1.80	1.54	1.36
Monthly	45.07	30.93	10.90	4.80	5.37	2.96	1.39
Europe-Pacific							
Weekly	72.73		12.70	11.59	2.59	1.96	2.04
Monthly	69.56		14.78	6.04	7.27	3.80	2.73
World ex U.K.							
Weekly	53.10	34.75	8.54		2.18	1.43	1.44
Monthly	49.09	32.79	9.50		6.09	2.67	1.44
World ex Japan							
Weekly		53.29	11.02	18.02	5.23	3.89	1.55
Monthly		57.96	14.23	12.29	9.56	4.92	1.50

* In most cases, the Netherlands is the largest European component in the different funds. It turns out that Germany, Italy, and Switzerland are better correlayed with the Dutch market than with either the United Kingdom or French market. Hence, the Netherlands carries comparitively more weight in the fund.

	Using Futures Contracts from Two or Three Countries			
	Japan	United States	United Kingdom	Tracking Error
FT Index				
World				
Weekly	50.83	34.64	12.06	1.89
Monthly	50.31	40.14	10.36	2.51
Europe-Pacific				
Weekly	74.90		18.72	2.97
Monthly	76.26		21.41	4.44
World ex U.K.				
Weekly	56.93	39.35		2.11
Monthly	56.10	45.12		2.88
World ex Japan				
Weekly		57.86	26.78	3.00
Monthly		71.54	22.90	3.63

Table 5

Index	Sterling Exposure	Exchange Rate (2/28)	Local Currency Exposure	Index Close (2/28)	Contract Multiplier	No. of Contracts	Initial Margin (Per Contract)
TOPIX	53,100,000	221.301	Y 11,751,107,816	2447.23	10,000	480	Y 2,202,507
S&P 500	34,750,000	1.745	US$ 60,624,564	288.86	500	420	US$ 4,000
EOE	8,540,000	3.594	Dfl 30,691,556	263.77	200	582	Dfl 4,000
CAC-40	2,180,000	10.816	FFr 23,579,902	1480.07	200	75	FFr 20,000
All Ord.	1,430,000	2.183	A$ 3,121,701	1470.00	100	21	A$ 6,000

A Simulation

In this section we walk through an example of how to set up a synthetic global index fund with stock index futures. Then we compare the return of the target index with the simulated return of the futures basket for the same time period.

Suppose we turn the calendar back to February 28, 1989. On that day we place 100 million British pounds in a World ex U.K. synthetic index fund using five different stock index contracts. Based on the weekly figures in Table 4, we allocate funds in stock index contracts as follows:

(in British pounds)

53.10 million in TOPIX futures
34.75 million in S&P 500 futures
8.54 million in EOE futures
2.18 million in CAC-40 futures
1.43 million in All Ordinaries futures

Using closing prices and exchange rates on February 28, 1989, Table 5 shows the number of futures contracts we buy in each market and the initial margin required.

We can manage the cash portion of the fund in two ways: by buying Japanese, U.S., Dutch, French, and Australian money market securities; or by keeping most of our entire cash portfolio in U.K. money market securities and using forward contracts to gain exposure in the other currencies.

Now let's turn the calendar forward and look back at the period March 1, 1989 to June 15, 1989. Exhibit 2 compares the returns during this period for the synthetic index fund that we constructed on February 28, 1989 and the World ex U.K.

In creating the simulation we followed two trading rules. First, we invested all cash in risk-free securities in each of the five countries where the futures positions were held. Second, whenever we rolled over futures positions, we did so on the day before the contract's expiration.

Exhibit 2 shows that our synthetic index fund consistently outperformed the World ex U.K. between March 1, 1989 and June 15, 1989. We can trace most of the excess return in the synthetic portfolio to the outperformance of TOPIX relative to the FT Japan Index during that time.

Exhibit 2   Indexed Total Return for the World ex United Kingdom and the Futures Basket

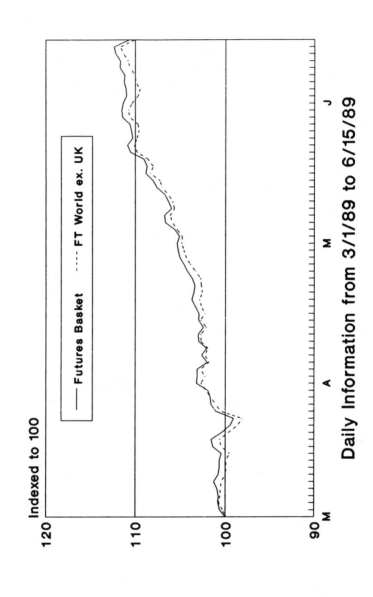

Indexed to 100

Daily Information from 3/1/89 to 6/15/89

Endnotes

[1] Two notes from our legal department: 1) The term "index fund" in this report means a stock portfolio that has been put togethere to track a certain index—not to legal entity such as a mutual fund. 2) By using the pronoun "you" in this report, we are not suggesting that all readers have permission to make the transactions we describe. Bear in mind that access to futures contracts may be restricted in some countries; also certain legal and regulatory questions may arise when investors' assets are pooled.

[2] Black, Fischer, "Universal Hedging—How to Optimize Currency Risk and Reward in International Equity Portfolios," Revised May 1989, Goldman, Sachs & Co.

The Cost of Change

Francis Enderle
Barclays de Zoete Wedd, Tokyo

Change in stock market dealing procedures and the use of basket trades have significantly reduced the costs of investment transactions. However, making a policy change in a global portfolio can still be an expensive operation. Being able to quantify the magnitude of these expenses in advance can influence the way portfolios are initially structured, and subsequently restructured in response to changes in anticipated returns from many markets and asset classes.

Global portfolio management requires extensive knowledge of the world's financial markets, and investment managers require the expertise of economists and market/currency analysts to aid the process of forecasting investment returns. In a world that gave us perfect foresight "risk" would not be a word in our vocabulary. Unfortunately, all market forecasts are subject to error and the likely outcome for some asset categories is much harder to predict than others. An illustration of this point might be the ease of predicting the return of cash in one's own domestic market against the difficulty of predicting the return to a Japanese investor of the Mexican equity market.

One of the more obvious ways of measuring or quantifying the uncertainty of a forecast is to examine the historic volatility associated with the category. This provides a benchmark against which forecasting can be made so that both expectations of return and chance of failure can be examined simultaneously.

When many asset categories are examined at the same time a computerized modeling system becomes necessary and is a valuable tool to assist investment managers in structuring (and restructuring) global portfolios. Changes in market forecasts can lead to major investment policy changes, and this can lead to significant turnover[1] within a portfolio.

The main purpose of this paper is to analyze the turnover incurred in restructuring global portfolios based on the changes in investment forecasts for various markets and asset classes.

Quantec[2] software and the associated data base was used to optimize a global portfolio which held both bond and equity investments in various markets. The only constraint was that the resulting portfolio could not have any cash. There was no upper or lower limit for any of the other asset classes. The base currency of the portfolio was Japanese yen. BZW Investment Management's forecasts for the next 12 months were applied to the time periods chosen for this analysis.

Two periods representing different market conditions were chosen to analyze turnover resulting from restructuring a global portfolio. The first period was June–July 1988. This was a period of relative quiet in the market, with nothing exceptional to make equities considerably more favorable than bonds, or vice versa. The second period was October–November 1987. This is the period covering the worldwide stock-market crash of October 1987, representing a major reappraisal of market conditions. Prior to the crash, equity markets were at high levels and investors were generally optimistic about equities. On the other hand, the outlook for bonds was considered less positive. However, after the crash investors' confidence in equities was shattered, and bond yields were expected to fall.

The Quantec optimiser assesses the risk of each market by measuring the volatility of historical returns, hence giving us a measure of uncertainty in forecasting. This historic volatility (or risk) was plotted against the forecast returns (see Exhibit 1) for different markets. By taking into account the correlations between markets, similar risk and return statistics can be calculated for every possible portfolio. The set of all pollible portfolios is bound on the graph by the "efficient frontier"—namely those portfolios which are efficient in that they offer the highest expected return at any given level of risk and the lowest for any given level of return. It is sensible that investment managers maintain efficient portfolios, and therefore the context of this analysis is based on this assumption.

The forecast returns were applied to produce a set of efficient portfolios for each time period selected. Twelve portfolios were selected along each efficient frontier in equally increasing degrees of risk (and increasing predicted return), ranging from minimum risk to maximum return. The turnover incurred in restructuring any one of these portfolios, maintaining the same absolute level of risk, was then calculated for both time periods. Exhibit 2 shows the turnover

Exhibit 1 Efficient Frontier

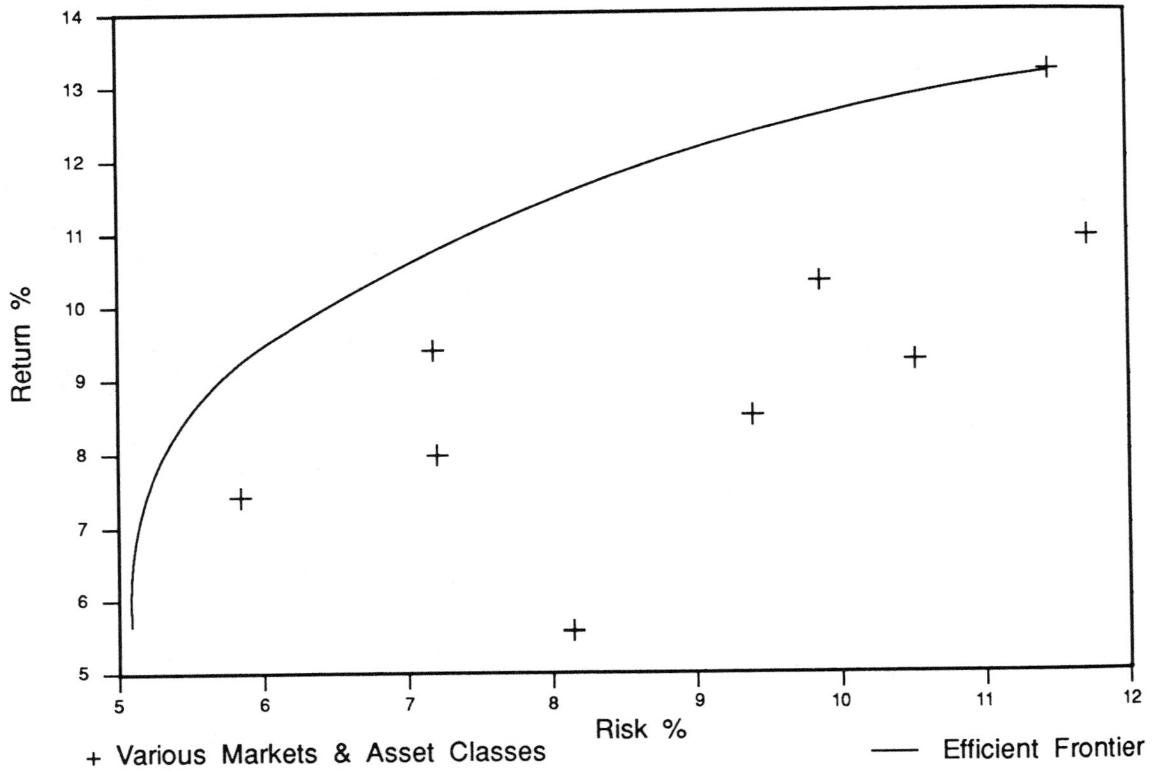
Return %
14
13
12
11
10
9
8
7
6
5
5
6
7
8
9
10
11
12
Risk %
+ Various Markets & Asset Classes
— Efficient Frontier

Exhibit 2   Measurement of Turnover

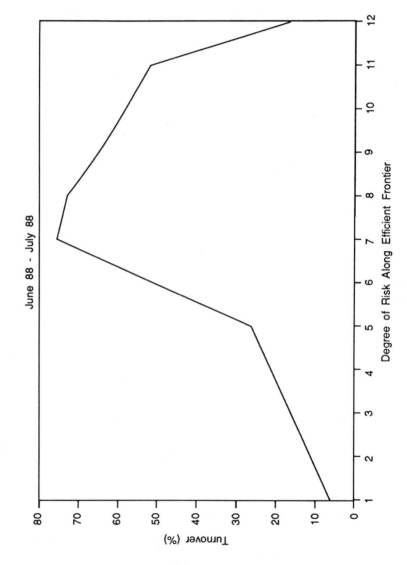

June 88 - July 88

Turnover (%)

Degree of Risk Along Efficient Frontier

incurred in going from a range of portfolios along the efficient frontier produced from the June forecasts, to portfolios, with the same level of risk, along the efficient frontier produced from the July forecasts.

The low risk portfolios generated by the optimiser are mainly risk oriented, and therefore changes in forecasts tend to not affect these portfolios very much. On the other hand, further along the "degree of risk spectrum" towards higher risk, the portfolios are more return oriented. Therefore a change in forecasts is likely to have a greater impact on them. this can be seen in Exhibit 2 as the turnover increases sharply after the 5th portfolio.

In general, equities are more volatile than bonds. Consequently, the Quantec optimiser creates portfolios that are more heavily weighted in bonds at the "low risk" end of the risk spectrum, and emphasizes the highest return asset at the other end. This can be seen in Exhibit 3. The point at which the two lines intersect usually lies around the 4th/5th point along the spectrum, representing a volatility of return of about 8% per annum.

Importantly, this does not mean that the increase in turnover towards the high risk end of the spectrum is always related to equities. It just shows how portfolios toward the high risk end of the spectrum are more return oriented. This concept is demonstrated later.

In the forecasts for the June–July period there is general increase in the expected returns from equities, and a general decrease in the returns for bonds. This was in anticipation that a strong dollar would promote confidence, equities would rise, and some of the major markets would reach new highs. In contrast, inflationary fears had grown worldwide, and the increasing possibility of higher interest rates made bonds less attractive.

The degree of bond related turnover is quite significant. This can be seen in Exhibit 4. Quite obviously, the majority of the turnover is attributable to bonds. It is interesting to look at how this bond related turnover is constituted, and why there is a sudden increase after the 5th portfolio.

Focusing on the return oriented portfolios we notice a sharp increase in bond related turnover. This is attributable to the change in forecasts for European bonds. In June Dutch bonds were forecast to have the highest return, but all bond markets other than the Japanese has a high risk factor. Therefore, the highest yielding Dutch bonds only formed a part of the more return oriented portfolios. Going into July as inflationary fears grew worldwide, all return forecasts for bonds were revised downwards except for Germany. German bonds were forecast to have the highest returns, but likewise being a risky market for a yen investor, German bonds also only formed a part of the return oriented portfolios. Therefore, the changeover from Dutch bonds having the highest return forecast

Exhibit 3 Breakdown of Portfolio

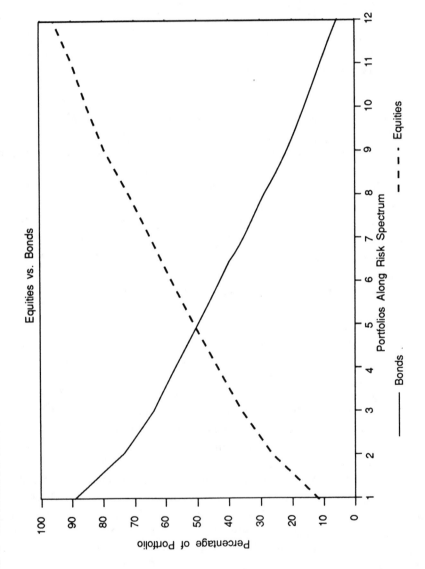

Equities vs. Bonds

Exhibit 4 Measurement of Turnover

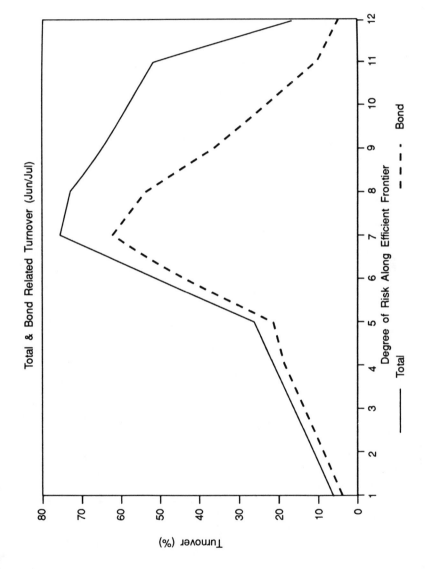

Total & Bond Related Turnover (Jun/Jul)

Degree of Risk Along Efficient Frontier

— Total   - - - - Bond

Turnover (%)

Exhibit 5   Measurement of Turnover

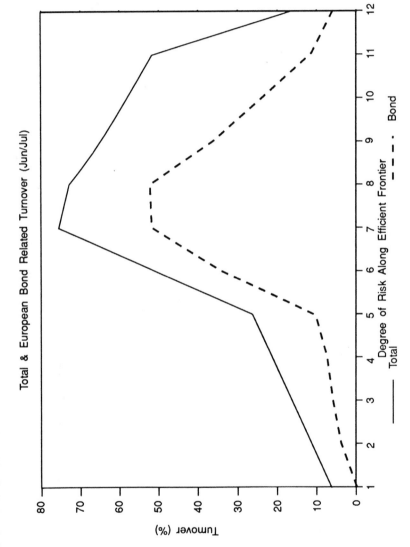

Total & European Bond Related Turnover (Jun/Jul)

in June, to German bonds in July, has caused the sharp increase in the turnover seen after the 5th portfolio (see Exhibit 5).

The equity related portion of the turnover is shown in Exhibit 6. It is interesting to note that even though this does not represent much of the total turnover, the contribution does rise sharply after the 5th portfolio.

There was also a significant change in the expected returns for Germany, especially in equities. This was due to the fact that a strong dollar against a weakening Deutsche mark had helped German exporting companies, as well as the earnings generated overseas in U.S. dollars by the branches of German companies. Earnings forecasts for the year 1987–1988 averaged zero in the first quarter for many German companies, but as these companies realized that the crash itself was an isolated event and the German economy was actually growing, they revised their earnings forecast upwards to an average of about eight percent. Along with this came improved GNP forecasts, and this all led to the significant change in the return forecast for Germany.

The impact of the above changes can be seen in Exhibit 7. The significant change in return forecasts from 1.9% to 14.0% obviously affected the more return oriented portfolios along the risk spectrum, as would be expected.

The June–July 1988 period represented one of relative stability in the world's financial markets. By way of contrast the second set of data focuses on a more volatile period. These forecasts and corresponding graphs are for the October–November 1987 period. It is interesting to observe the impact the worldwide equity crash had on the forecasts and the level of turnover that resulted.

There was a major downward revision of equity market forecasts in November, and the only exception was Hong Kong. The 12 month forecast for Hong Kong actually went up from 7.3% to 21.5%. Exhibit 8 exhibits the effect this revision had on turnover. The total turnover is considerably higher than that of the June–July period, especially towards the riskier end of the spectrum, and this is due to Hong Kong equities being favored at the expense of Japanese equities. Most of the turnover incurred for the medium risk portfolios is attributable to the impact of bonds, as detailed later.

As might have been expected, the impact of the change in forecasts for equities can be seen in Exhibit 9, especially after the 5th portfolio. From here the optimizer really starts to focus on maximizing the return of the portfolios, rather than on minimizing the risk.

A significant amount of the steep increase in equity related turnover after the 5th portfolio is attributable to the change from Japan being the highest yielding asset to Hong Kong. The turnover incurred from selling Japanese equities and purchasing Hong Kong equities can be seen in Exhibit 10, and predictably the impact of the change is more pronounced after the 5th portfolio.

Exhibit 6 Measurement of Turnover

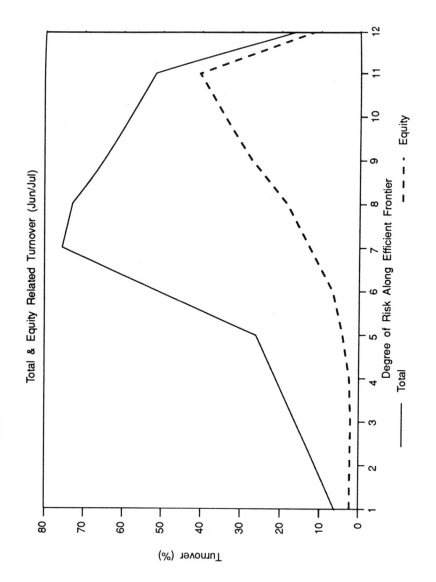

Total & Equity Related Turnover (Jun/Jul)

Exhibit 7   Measurement of Turnover

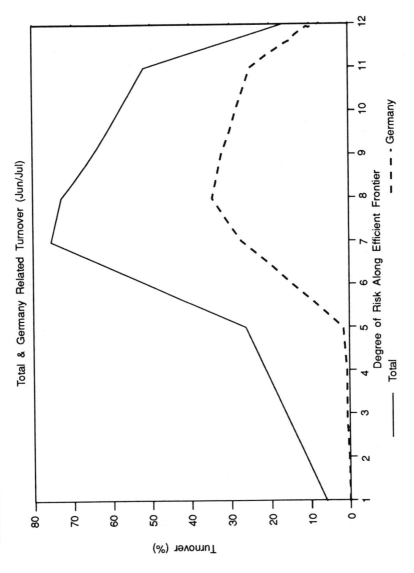

Total & Germany Related Turnover (Jun/Jul)

Degree of Risk Along Efficient Frontier

Turnover (%)

— — — Germany

——— Total

Exhibit 8   Measurement of Turnover

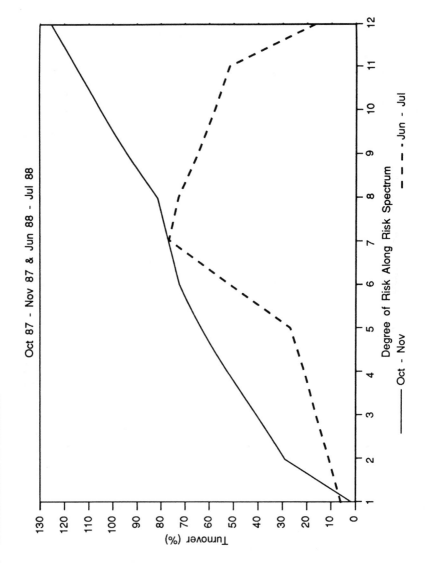

Oct 87 - Nov 87 & Jun 88 - Jul 88

Turnover (%)

Degree of Risk Along Risk Spectrum

———— Oct - Nov   – – – Jun - Jul

Exhibit 9 Measurement of Turnover

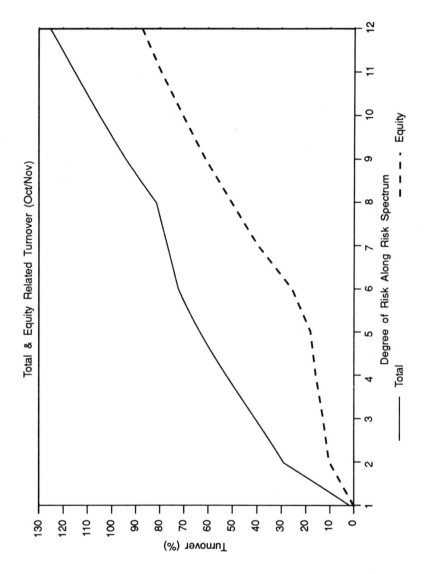

Total & Equity Related Turnover (Oct/Nov)

Turnover (%)

Degree of Risk Along Risk Spectrum

—— Total   - - - Equity

Exhibit 10 Measurement of Turnover

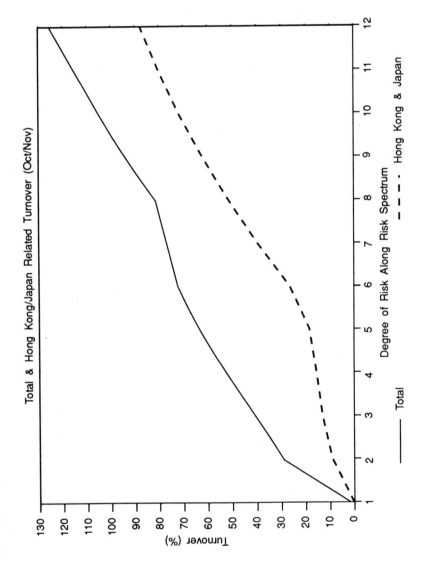

Total & Hong Kong/Japan Related Turnover (Oct/Nov)

Turnover (%)

Degree of Risk Along Risk Spectrum

—— Total   – – – Hong Kong & Japan

Bond related turnover, although not as significant as the equity contribution, is still interesting. As would be expected, it makes up a little over half the total turnover for the portfolios along the low risk end of the risk spectrum, and also a fair portion for the return oriented portfolios. This is shown in Exhibit 11.

The main reason for the significant amount of bond related turnover for low risk portfolios, and likewise for the return oriented portfolios along the risk spectrum, is due to the reatment of French bonds. The average percentage invested in French bonds for the low risk portfolios in October was 23%. This figure doubled to 46% in November. As for return oriented portfolios, the percentage invested in October was 12%, and this figure significantly rose to 43%. There are two reasons for this.

The first reason is the significant change in the return forecast for French bonds from 8.5% to 15.6%. The reason for this change is two fold. There was political uneasiness in France at time due to the elections coming up and whether or not there would be a change in government, and this caused bond yields to climb. We believed this to be an overreaction, and therefore forecast yields to come down. We also saw a downward trend in inflation in France and believed that inflation was finally under control. Hence the upward revision in return forecasts.

The second reason comes from how the November portfolio was constructed in terms of the equity/bond breakdown. We saw that the "cross over" point occurred between the 4th and 5th portfolio for June, and this was also the case for July and October. However, due to crash this cross over point shifted across the 7th portfolio for the November set of portfolios, causing the optimizer to buy heavily the most attractive bond market. The impact of the change in return forecasts for French bonds can be seen in Exhibit 12. The French bond related turnover forms most of the bond related turnover.

Summary

Risk adverse portfolios are more cost effective than aggressively managed ones. Low risk portfolios are risk oriented and therefore incur less turnover when rebalancing. On the other hand, aggressive portfolios are driven by return, and inevitably result in higher turnover. A significant rise in turnover is usually seen after the 5th portfolio, which represents a volatility of around 8% per annum. Higher turnover results in additional transaction costs, and possibly even capital gains tax for non-exempt accounts. Naturally, this has a detrimental effect on portfolio return.

Overall transaction costs will also be affected by the debt/equity split. Transaction costs for bond trades are significantly lower than for equities. Low risk

Exhibit 11 Measurement of Turnover

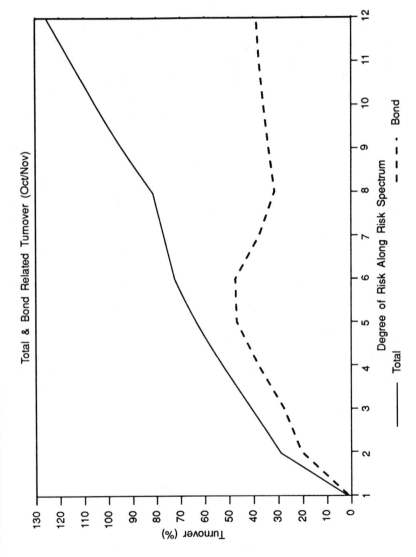

Total & Bond Related Turnover (Oct/Nov)

Turnover (%)

Degree of Risk Along Risk Spectrum

——— Total   – – – Bond

Exhibit 12 Measurement of Turnover

Total & France Related Turnover (Oct/Nov)

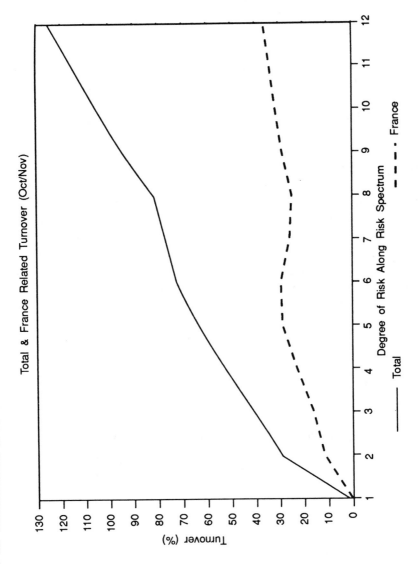

Turnover (%)

Degree of Risk Along Risk Spectrum

—— Total   — — · France

portfolios generally have a greater percentage invested in bonds, and therefore benefit from this difference in transaction costs. In contrast, the effect on portfolio return as measured by actual transaction costs will be noticeably greater for high risk portfolios than the effect measured only by turnover. High risk portfolios tend to have a larger percentage invested in equities, and this results in higher transaction costs.

Rebalancing a global portfolio is an operation which requires careful attention. A rebalanced portfolio with the same level of risk may give you a predicted return of 12% per annum, but this may be at the cost of high turnover. Another portfolio with the same level of risk with a predicted return of only 10% per annum may be an alternative, but with a very low turnover. Settling for a sub-optimal portfolio (with the same level of risk) is another specific example where turnover analysis can eliminate excessive costs.

Turnover analysis should form an integral part of the initial process of building a global portfolio, as well as the critical decision-making process of rebalancing it. A policy change can be very expensive, but prior analysis can help reduce unnecessary expenses. Both active and passive portfolio managers when initially constructing, and subsequently restructuring global portfolios have to be conscious of the implication different risk levels have on portfolio turnover. The impact of turnover on two "medium risk" portfolios can drastically differ, and result in one outperforming the other.

Endnotes

[1]   Turnover is calculated as the sum of the total value of all sales and purchases, divided by the initial portfolio value.

[2]   Quantec is a computer system which performs international risk analysis both on a global asset allocation and individual market basis.

Asian-Pacific Financial Futures and Options Markets

Steven Schoenfeld
Simcha SIMEX Trading (PTE) Ltd.
Washington, D.C.

The world's economic center of gravity is shifting toward the Asia-Pacific basin. Spectacular growth in production, trade and living standards has increased the size and importance of the region's financial markets. The growing maturity of their capital and foreign exchange markets, combined with the irrepressible globalization of financial activity, means that institutional investors can no longer ignore the region's opportunities.

With opportunity comes risk. Many Far Eastern markets are particularly volatile. Therefore, responsible institutions need risk management strategies for Asian Pacific investment. Financial futures and options are a key component of such techniques. Until recently, however, investors had few instruments to trade and inadequate liquidity in most products. The region's markets are now developing rapidly, with a widening base of users and a diverse range of instruments. Perhaps most significant is the gradual integration of Asia-Pacific exchanges and firms into the world futures industry. In the 1990s, these emerging markets will gain a role equivalent to the prominence of their economies and financial markets.

Importance of the Region for Institutions

The Asia-Pacific region has gained the attention of investors because of its stellar economic growth in the past three decades. As the economies grew, their financial markets matured, a process led by Japan, the *newly industrializing countries* (NICs), and resource-rich Australia and New Zealand. Despite cultural and valuation differences, varying levels of financial safeguards, and above-average volatility, institutions have found lucrative opportunities in the debt and equity markets of the region.

The size of Asia-Pacific equity markets has grown along with the economies. Japan's market capitalization is now the world's largest, comprising 42% of the Morgan Stanley Capital International (MSCI) World Index in mid-1989. When American stocks are excluded, Japan accounts for over 65% of international shares, as measured by MSCI's EAFE (Europe, Australia, and Far East) index. Korea and Taiwan also have very large equity markets, but foreign participation is restricted. Australia, Hong Kong, Singapore, Malaysia, and New Zealand are smaller but open to, and popular with, foreign investors. Thailand, the Philippines, Indonesia, India and others are becoming much more attractive and accessible.

The real attraction of these markets has been their remarkable performance. Over time, Asia-Pacific stock markets have provided some of the best returns in the world. Despite the devastating effect of the October 1987 crash on many institutional portfolios, most regional markets have still outperformed American and European bourses. Japan, Taiwan, Korea and Thailand all set new record highs in 1988, and continued to achieve record growth in 1989. Singapore and Malaysia also recovered substantially in 1988 and 1989.

Asia-Pacific debt markets also offer opportunities for enhanced returns, diversification and currency exposure. Deregulation, particularly in Japan, Australia and New Zealand, and maturing international trading in offshore markets in Singapore, Hong Kong and Tokyo, has opened up heretofore inaccessible or nonexistent capital markets.

Forex markets in Asia have grown dramatically in the past decade. Tokyo is now the second largest forex trading center in the world, and frequently surpasses the leader—London. Sydney, Singapore and Hong Kong also have very active international currency markets. Much activity is due to heavy local asset bases as well as "hot" and mobile capital. The other major reason for the growth of Asia-Pacific forex markets is the globalization of trading.

Overview of a Financial Revolution

The advent of around-the-clock trading—in equity, debt and forex markets—has made 24-hour risk management essential. This is the primary rational for some of the futures and options products in the region, along with their serving domestic price discovery and hedging functions. These needs sparked a financial revolution in the Asia-Pacific region.

The financial derivative markets in the area are still in their infancy. The oldest product is twelve years old, and most have been launched in the past five years. The sophistication of exchanges, members and users is growing rapidly, and volume is booming. This was not always the case.

The *first phase* of Asian-Pacific financial futures market development was from 1979 to 1984. Exchanges at the periphery introduced the new products and educated users on the concepts. The Sydney Futures Exchange (SFE) was first, in 1979, with a domestic interest rate future. In 1984, the Singapore International Monetary Exchange (SIMEX) was opened and forged the first inter-exchange link with the Chicago Mercantile Exchange. Both regional exchanges faced an uphill battle to convince skeptical players on the merits of futures. Volume growth was impressive in percentage terms, but activity levels were minuscule compared to bigger exchanges in the U.S. and London.

From 1985 to early 1987, futures and options trading was booming around the world, and the financial community recognized that Asia-Pacific was the most undeveloped sector of global futures trading. During this period, the *second phase* of development, three new markets opened in the region. The Tokyo Stock Exchange (TSE) launched yen bond futures, the New Zealand Futures Exchange (NZFE) was inaugurated, and the Hong Kong Futures Exchange (HKFE) was restructured to accommodate financial futures.

Domestic Japanese market development was restricted, and their residents were prohibited from using overseas futures markets. Other regional exchanges frantically scrambled to become the primary futures trading center in the Asian time zone before Japan liberalized. Optimistic and grandiose expansion plans and linkage proposals were promulgated and implemented. Inter-exchange rivalry was heated, and the rhetoric was often bellicose, particularly between SIMEX and the SFE.

The *third phase* began in May 1987, when the gradual liberalization of Japanese futures trading began. Japanese financial firms were allowed to trade in overseas futures and options markets for their own accounts. Orders began to flow into regional markets, and the Japanese built up their presence at foreign exchanges. That June, the Osaka Securities Exchange listed physically settled stock index futures. Meanwhile, the Japanese bureaucracy—under pressure from the domestic financial industry and foreign governments, exchanges and firms— began to lay the groundwork for substantial opening and expansion of the markets.

Regional exchanges, riding the crest of the worldwide stock market boom, enjoyed record volume and a surge of confidence. Index futures in Hong Kong,

Sydney and Singapore were attracting institutional participation from around the globe, as well as heavy retail activity.

The euphoria ended that October. The fallout from the 1987 crash varied from exchange to exchange, but with one exception, the markets suffered. Only in Japan, where the markets were unable to trade for most of October 20th, did the crash actually help a futures contract. Japanese investors—accustomed to one-way bull markets—finally recognized the need for an equity hedging mechanism. Volume in the Stock Futures 50 contract in Osaka grew substantially.

Elsewhere, the damage was severe. Australia and New Zealand suffered substantial drops in volume and terrifying volatility. SIMEX, which managed to trade throughout the turmoil, lost much business, but had no defaults. The HKFE closed for four days, and the market collapsed. A government-arranged "lifeboat fund" was needed to save the exchange.

The regional markets entered a period of introspection and restructuring. The SFE and NZFE began to look inward for growth, assuming the role of "mother market" for their countries. SIMEX continued to prospect for international business, since the Singapore domestic market is limited. The HKFE underwent a drawn out reorganization, designed to restore investor confidence.

The Japanese, however, finally aware of the need for risk management tools, accelerated their futures market development plans. The contours of the Asia-Pacific derivative scene was changing. The Japanese, using their financial muscle, were moving to the vanguard. By late 1988 the new pattern was clear. Other regional markets would have to differentiate themselves and carve out unique niches if they were to prosper alongside the Japanese.

1988 was still a remarkably successful one for most of the regions' exchanges. The SFE, SIMEX, TSE and OSE all set volume records. Investors and firms from Europe and North America resumed and even increased their participation in the markets. 1989 also witnessed healthy volume growth and an expansion of markets and products, particularly in Japan, where a new financial futures exchange was opened.

As the new decade began, Asia-Pacific futures and options markets became more integrated with the rest of the world. They are now poised for explosive growth, but will also have to compete with the new automated trading systems being developed by London and the Chicago exchanges. And while Japan may seem destined to capture the lion's share of activity, institutional investors will have the final choice of trading facility based on factors of market access, cost, liquidity, regularity, environment and sovereign risk.

Promising Areas for Institutional Investors

The expanding and maturing Asia-Pacific markets will soon be able to accommodate the same debt and equity derivative strategies that institutional investors practice in other markets. Increased liquidity, closer integration and more sophisticated local users will result in more efficient markets.

The areas of most significance are in the equity, debt and currency arenas. The trend toward indexation of portfolios has increased the institutional need for equity derivatives. Japan's predominant weighting in global and international indices—and the difficulty many fund managers have had in matching broad index performance—makes Japanese index futures and options essential tools. Australia, Hong Kong and New Zealand have relatively insignificant weightings, but those who want to include these markets may opt to use derivatives instead of a cash position. Singapore will also likely have an index product in the near future.

The large Asian cash market in government and corporate debt, as well as short-term deposits, increases hedging needs. The major U.S. dollar, Japanese yen, and Australian dollar cash debt instruments now have related futures and options markets. Growing OTC derivatives have also developed for yen and dollar interest rates.

Each developing center provides specific opportunities and has a unique structure of regulations, markets and players. As a whole, they have come a long way from the early 1980s, when financial futures and options were generally an alien concept in the region. Their greatest growth, however, lies in the future.

Japan: The Giant Awakes

The Japanese futures and options market has come the furthest in the least amount of time. A new attitude of innovation, combined with enormous latent demand has built the foundation for Asia's preeminent futures and options center. Japanese financial prowess will now expand to derivative products as exchanges and firms shift into high gear.

Until the second half of the 1980s, it was illegal for Japanese institutions to trade financial futures. Less than four years later, Japan emerged as a major power in the futures industry. By the early 1990s, it will be home to some of the most active futures and options markets in the world. In addition, the increasing sophistication and power of its budding futures industry cannot be taken lightly.

The Japanese started gingerly in the early 1980s, studying foreign markets and domestic needs. Cautious Ministry of Finance bureaucrats and intraministerial consensus-building held back innovation. External pressure and the internationalization of Japanese financial markets sped up the usual glacial pace of deregulation. Since then, the Japanese have moved with surprising speed and characteristic aggressiveness to develop markets and products.

Japanese firms are now able to act as direct brokers for overseas business, and many anticipate an expanding flow of two-way activity. Japanese and foreign exchanges, firms, regulators, and investors are all scrambling to keep pace

Exhibit 1

Overseas Financial Futures Exchange Memberships

	City Banks	Long-Term Banks	Trust Banks	Other Banks	Securities Firms
Chicago Merc Exchange	8	2	3	0	4
Chicago Board of Trade	5	2	2	0	7
LIFFE	14	3	6	1	6
SIMEX	13	2	2	0	5

(Includes standard and nonclearing memberships)

Foreign Firms Participating in the Japanese Financial Futures Markets

	Securities Houses Ordinary Membership	Securities Houses Special Membership	Banks Special Membership
Japanese government bond futures (TSE)	22	5	1
TOPIX Futures (TSE)	22	3	0
Nikkei 225 Futures (TSE)	2	4	0

Source: Nikkei Financial.

with the changes. The 1990s promises to be the decade of Japan's emergence on the world futures and options scene.

Expanding Market Structure

Japan's first experiment with financial futures began in October 1985, when the Tokyo Stock Exchange listed yen bond futures. After a shaky start, the market took off and became a vibrant component of the Tokyo debt market. Liberalization gained momentum in May 1987 when Japanese financial firms were allowed to deal for their own account in overseas futures markets. Since then, barriers have fallen rapidly, and firms and exchanges have steadily gained wider opportunities to dabble with new products.

In September 1988 Tokyo and Osaka introduced cash-settled index futures, and in mid-1989 nonfinancial corporations were allowed to use futures abroad.

In June 1989 Osaka listed index options, and a new financial futures exchange was inaugurated in Tokyo. Later the same year, Tokyo and Nagoya launched index options; and Japanese securities firms and banks were also allowed to act as brokers for overseas futures business.

The Ministry of Finance's key decision, however, was to vertically integrate regulatory authority between cash and futures instruments. This followed exhaustive studies of America's 1987 stock market crash and major "turf-battles" within the Ministry. MOF's Securities Bureau now reigns over stock index and bond futures and the connected equity and long-term debt markets. Similarly, the Ministry's Banking Bureau supervises the new Tokyo financial futures exchange, along with its traditional responsibility for short-term interest rates and interbank forex deals.

This "gentlemen's agreement" has settled the basic issue of which exchanges can list which products and which institutions can trade or broker the new instruments. The rough contours of a large and diverse futures industry are now visible. From one exchange trading one futures contract in late 1985, Japan had four exchanges trading ten different futures and options products in early 1990. Judging by recent successes, most of them will be active and healthy.

TSE: Holding the High Ground

The Tokyo Stock Exchange, the world's largest equity market, also offers Japan's broadest slate of derivatives. It was trading five distinct products in early 1990, with more on the horizon.

Japan's first and most active contract is the TSE's Ten-Year Government Bond (JGB) futures, which was launched on October 19, 1985. In late-1989 it was trading over 80,000 lots per day, with an open interest of more than 210,000 contracts. Because of its high par value of 100 million, the contract has become the most active futures contract in the world in value of trade terms.

There have always been doubts about the level of genuine activity, since most trading is for member firms' proprietary accounts. Red-hot market share competition between Japanese banks and securities firms artificially boosts volume, and cross-trading is rampant.

Some cross-trading is also for accounting purposes, since Japan's margin rules lock up access to excess equity. Members' own trading consistently accounts for close to 90% of volume, with insurance companies and nonfinancial firms taking up the bulk of remaining activity. By mid-1989 the banks took the lead in market-share, as they geared up for their new financial futures exchange. In the first quarter of that year, they generated 59% of TSE bond futures volume.

Observers estimate that less than 5% of activity is bona fide hedging. Furthermore, commissioned trades rarely account for more than 15% of volume.

Thus, over 80% of activity is dealing between members, of which probably half is cross-trading. Nevertheless, the wash trades do not negate the price discovery function of the JGB futures market, since futures market activity is more than three times that of the cash market.

The Japanese, who have been active users of T-Bond futures in Chicago since 1987, now have a nearly identical product in their own backyard. The TSE launched U.S. T-Bond futures in December 1989. Although SIMEX and the SFE failed to successfully build U.S. bond futures markets in the Asian time zone, Tokyo—home to the largest foreign investors in U.S. debt—should succeed in a modest way. Institutional investors would then have a futures pricing mechanism for bonds during all major cash trading hours.

The TSE contract is similar, but not fungible, to the Chicago Board of Trade (CBOT) future. Contract size is the same at $100,000, but the underlying instrument is the 20-year bond which is more widely held by Japanese investors. Margining and settlement procedures are also different.

Success for the TSE T-Bond is likely because of the active cash market in Japan. But the TSE has also recently experienced its first failure. In July 1988 the TSE launched a 20-year JGB contract, hoping to capture business in longer maturities. By early 1989, volume—never impressive—dried up, and the TSE admitted to being "premature." Exchange officials blamed a thin cash market, as the Ministry of Finance slowed issues at the extreme end of the yield curve. The TSE has no plans for delisting, since it is hoping that government debt structure might still shift to longer maturities.

After the launch of T-Bond futures, the TSE moved to expand its range of debt products into options. JGB futures options were launched in 1990 and have attracted healthy activity. The TSE does not, however, have a monopoly in this area as it does with yen bond futures. MOF-approved and administered Over-the-Counter bond options began trading in April 1989—with banks, securities firms and Japanese institutional investors as active participants. The TSE, which views its fixed commission rates as sacrosanct, may find it difficult to compete in this area.

Stock Index Battles

The Tokyo Stock Exchange is best known for its enormous equity market, and this is the arena with which it has the most potential for derivative products. The TSE is attempting to build on its TOPIX stock index futures with a cash TOPIX option.

TOPIX is the acronym for the TSE's First Section index, a composite of all 1,108 larger, more established companies in the exchange's top tier. While less of a household name than the Nikkei Average, TOPIX is the performance benchmark used by most fund managers and institutions.

Cash-settled futures on the index were launched in September of 1988 and have been a moderate success. In their first year of trading, daily average volume was close to 15,000 lots per day, with open interest about 30,000. A significant deepening of the market occurred in mid-1989 as longer time frame investors began participating. But TOPIX futures have not grabbed the limelight.

The TSE does not have this vibrant field to itself. A rival contract on the popular Nikkei 225 index was launched at the same time by the Osaka Securities Exchange (OSE). The OSE was Japan's pioneer with equity derivatives, having introduced a physically-settled "Stock Futures 50" product in June 1987. Although now obsolete and inactive, it boosted the exchange's reputation and brought in new domestic and foreign participants.

OSE's Nikkei contract started with a solid base of users and has successfully challenged TOPIX for top volume in Japan. Osaka led in volume and open interest for the first three months but fell behind in early 1989. It then lagged TOPIX in open interest, as more index funds were pegged to the broader TSE benchmark. Nikkei volume again surpassed TOPIX's in June 1989, and it has maintained its lead ever since, averaging over 20,000 lots per day after its first year of trading. By early 1990, Osaka overtook Tokyo in open interest and volume, and its growth rate accelerated. This competition, plus the existence of a small but well-established Nikkei futures market in Singapore, has broadened user choices and trading opportunities. The interexchange rivalry—and even fiercer corporate market share competition—has given dealers much incentive to cross trades, so it is difficult to determine how much of the volume is real. While most observers agree that the percentage of customer business has increased since the first few months, it remains small.

In the first six months of trading, securities firms proprietary deals accounted for about 90% of TOPIX and Osaka Nikkei volume and never fell below 80%. Close to half of this activity is cross-trading, particularly among Japanese houses. Market share is the prime motivation, but there are also technical consideration. As in the yen bond futures, traders often cross order to free up margin money.

Securities firms dealings also includes arbitrage activity. Foreign houses dominated this area early in the contracts' history. Until March 1989, Japanese firms were at a great disadvantage in cash/futures arbitrage because of formal and informal guidelines regarding transactions in equities undergoing financing (i.e., Eurobond issues). Foreign firms took advantage of this wide open field and often found lucrative mispricings.

The playing field is now more level, and Japanese firms are free to trade any stocks for arbitrage purposes. Restrictions against short-selling have been eased, which should result in a more stable basis relationship. Also, expiration procedures were changed so that settlement is based on the next day's opening price as a means of eliminating expiration volatility.

Exhibit 2   Japanese Equity Derivatives

	SIMEX NK	OSF 50	TOPIX	OSE NK
Trading Hours	08:00 A.M. to 2:15 P.M. Monday-Friday 8:00 A.M. to 10:15 A.M. on Saturdays when TSE open (except Singapore holidays)	9:00 A.M. to 11:00 A.M. 1:00 P.M. to 3:00 P.M. Morning session only on Saturdays	9:00 A.M. to 11:15 A.M. 1:00 P.M. to 3:15 P.M. Morning session only on Saturdays (last 15 minutes eliminated on last day of trading)	9:00 A.M. to 11:15 A.M. 1:00 P.M. to 3:15 P.M. Morning session only on Saturdays (last 15 minutes eliminated on last day of trading)
Trading System	Open-Outcry Pit Trading	Individual Auction system on OSE trading floor (same system as for stocks) best bids and offers matched by exchange specialists	Pure auction through TSE's computer-assisted Order Routing and Execution System (CORES-F)	Computerized auction through OSE computer trading system. If computer introduction delayed, will be traded by individual auction on OSE floor
Approximate Contract Value on July 12, 1988	¥14,000,000 US$106,000	¥68,500,000 US$520,000	¥22,000,000 US$166,000	¥28,000,000 US$212,000

Even discounting arbitrage activity, which helps check the one-sided nature of Japanese investors, around 40% of the volume in the new stock index futures first six months was artificial. An indicator of the depth of the market is the percentage of brokerage orders. Although by mid-1989 they have doubled over late 1988, to about 18%, much of this increase is the result of banks entering the market, and a good deal of their trading is wash deals.

The activities of institutional users—trust funds, insurance companies, investment managers, and nonfinancial corporation—is more indicative of the continuing immaturity of these two markets. Their total trading volume amounts to well under 10% of trading. Foreign customer orders have been insignificant but could rapidly expand if the Commodity Futures Trading Commission (CFTC) passes a "no action" ruling on the two contracts.

The OSE has announced in mid-1989 that it is considering plans for the world's first convertible bond futures contract. The current market capitalization of the Japanese CB market is around 16 trillion yen, with over 1,000 issues listed. CBs are popular among institutional investors, and an OSE executive claimed that a CB futures market would encourage new issues as well as offering a hedging instrument.

New Options for Investors

Many Japanese players remain wary about futures, because of both myths arising from the crash of '87 and cautious senior management. It is these investors, as well as overseas fund managers and individuals, who are attracted to options. Demand for Japanese index options could potentially dwarf that of futures. The huge Japanese equity warrant market—particularly the index warrants which have become popular in Tokyo and London since 1987—indicates a wide investor interest.

Japanese exchanges chose cash options instead of options on the existing futures contracts. Options are perceived as a safer way to hedge, and since they are trying to attract a new category of users, there was little reason to confuse the issue with options on futures. The Ministry of Finance also expressed a preference for cash options.

The Osaka Securities Exchange was again at the vanguard of equity derivatives in Japan. It launched Nikkei 225 Index Options in June 1989, months ahead of the TSE.

The specs for cash options of the same value as Nikkei futures—1,000 times the index. Four consecutive months are listed, with strike prices at intervals of 500 Nikkei points. The options are a unique modified American Style; they can be exercised before expiration, but only on a designated day each week. The minimum margin for sellers is also the same as Nikkei futures, at 9% of contract value or ¥6 million, whichever is greater. Trading was initially on the

OSE floor, but computerized dealing was started within the first year of trading. Some have questioned the near-term bias created by the availability of only four monthly options series, and initial trading has born out these fears. On most days, only the nearby expiration month trades consistently.

Others have complained about unusual exercise procedures and the inherent uncertainties of a contract where trading stops prior to expiration. The steep margin requirement for writers was also questioned, particularly since customer cross-margining with futures position will be banned.

Despite the various shortcomings of the options market structure in Japan, activity was buoyant from the start. Most foreigners have accepted the quirks as more of the idiosyncracies of doing business in Japan. A number of "gaijin" firms joined as *special members* of the OSE for futures and options trading.

Osaka's Nikkei options should develop into a healthy market with a broader mix of institutional users than the futures market. It will also serve as a training ground for trust and tokkin funds to explore new strategies.

By the end of 1989, two more index options were launched in Japan. The TSE's TOPIX options, listed on October 20, were expected to eventually capture half of the index option market. On the other hand, the Nagoya Stock Exchange's new institutional option will have a difficult struggle to carve out even a narrow market niche.

TOPIX options—like Osaka's Nikkei—have the same value as the futures contracts but will be based on the cash index. They are also of a modified American style and have a 9% margin for writers. Four consecutive months are listed at any one time, and commissions are fixed on the same schedule as Osaka's options.

Japanese market participants expect huge interest to build for the TOPIX options, since TOPIX is the primary benchmark for the majority of portfolio managers. Although Osaka's four month headstart has given it an important lead in depth and liquidity, TOPIX might prevail. This optimistic forecast has not come to pass, despite the TSE's huge equity turnover.

It was also difficult for the Nagoya Stock Exchange (NSE), Japan's third largest stock exchange. The NSE, which lags far behind Osaka in equity turnover, made a desperate bid for some of the new derivative activity. It spent about ¥4 billion to develop a new index of widely traded, high-capitalization shares. Dubbed "The Options 25," it is modeled roughly on the CBOT's Major Market Index and is designed to be useful for institutional investors.

NSE officials hope to differentiate their product and carve out a market for large hedgers. The option is therefore European style, in the hopes that the lower premium will attract buyers. Other specs are similar to TOPIX options. In fact, the NSE bases its index calculations on TSE stock quotes.

The prospects for this upstart are fair at best. The product faces very difficult competition from much larger exchanges with well-established products. It is doubtful whether institutions—for whom the new product was designed—will use the small index to hedge, particularly if liquidity is poor. Foreign firms and investors are unlikely to familiarizing themselves with such a marginal product when deep and active markets are developing in the two other index options.

Banker's New Futures Market

Nagoya may not be a significant new player in Japanese futures and options developments, but the Tokyo International Financial Futures Exchange (TIFFE) is destined to have a major impact. The TIFFE will change not only Japan's financial landscape but will also affect derivative markets in the region and the world. Trading began on June 30, 1989, with contracts on Euroyen and Eurodollar interest rates and the dollar/yen exchange rate. By virtue of the huge assets controlled by its institutional membership, the new exchange will be active despite its many inefficiencies.

The TIFFE was set up by Japan's Federation of Bankers' Associations. MOF gave the banks sovereignty over short-term interest rates and currency futures as part of 1989s turf division process. MOF has stressed the need for Japan to develop domestic futures exchanges, partly to enable it to maintain tight control of trading activity. The Federation has been striving to overcome sentiment that the TIFFE would be a "city-banks only" exchange and has drawn in membership from securities firms, long-term credit and trust banks, insurance companies, and foreign institutions.

Total membership was limited to 350 firms, with a maximum of 100 as clearing members. Net capital requirements for Japanese clearing firms was set at ¥50 billion ($350 million), but lowered to ¥5 billion for experienced foreign futures companies. The TIFFE hoped to attract skilled overseas brokers and traders to give the market an initial boost. Fewer than 20 foreign firms joined.

Enthusiasm for the exchange is lukewarm among foreigners for several reasons. Aside from the high cost of entry, many foreigners fear the market will develop as an isolated Japanese dealers' playground. The TIFFE is not linked with any other exchanges and has no intention of doing so. Differing settlement procedures make TIFFE contracts less fungible with existing markets in Chicago, London and Singapore.

A number of brokers have also questioned the viability of the TIFFE's yen futures. They cite the huge and efficient Tokyo forex spot, forward and swap markets—where volume often reaches $100 billion a day—as formidable competition. There is little incentive to use futures when the cash market is highly developed, as SIMEX discovered in the past few years. Singapore's liquid and accessible forex market has inhibited the growth of SIMEX's currency futures. The first six months of trading indicated strong interest in Euroyen, light activity in the Eurodollar, and insignificant trading in the yen futures. This pattern continued in 1990.

Inter-Market Dynamics

Of the three contracts which TIFFE offers, only the Euroyen was unique, at least until SIMEX quickly listed a similar contract in October 1989. Bank dealers see a great need for the TIFFE contract and expect it to boost liquidity in Tokyo's short-term money markets.

TIFFE's Eurodollar contract has intriguing prospects. While there is unquestionably latent demand for the product in Japan, potential users have a variety of markets to trade. In the Asian time zone, SIMEX has developed a liquid Eurodollar market which now regularly doubles Eurodollar volume at the London International Financial Futures Exchange. Tight quotes are made by SIMEX locals up to 10 months out, and open interest is almost 10% of the leading Chicago contract. Japanese banks are heavy users of the SIMEX contract. They are not likely to shift all of their business to the TIFFE.

The deciding factor in the equations might be GLOBEX. The CME-Reuters electronic trading venture might include SIMEX but has not received clear-cut approval from Japan's MOF. If GLOBEX is integrated with SIMEX, it will pose a formidable challenge to the TIFFE. If SIMEX and GLOBEX stand alone, TIFFE will have a greater chance to dominate short-term interest rate futures trading in the Asia-Pacific region.

Industry in the Making

Bitter rivalries may inject some uncertainty about the success of the TIFFE, but such competition is beneficial for the developing Japanese futures and options markets and industry. Institutional users will benefit from the expanding menu of trading vehicles. The outcome of market share battles are difficult to predict, but growth of the industry is assured. The combination of a huge and internationalizing asset base, and increasingly sophisticated financial technology, is creating the demand for new products. The contours of a huge industry are visible. With MOF's division of activity resolved, firms and exchanges are focusing on building up business. Many predict that the new markets gearing up in Japan will rival the U.S. in volume and value of business by the middle of the decade. Even if this outlook turns out to be too bullish, Japan will still be the largest source of global growth in the futures industry in the 1990s.

Booming Domestic Activity

The proliferation of markets and a new readiness to participate is most apparent in the activities of large Japanese firms within Japan. Securities houses, banks, insurance firms and even the Postal Savings System behemoth are deploying resources into the market.

Japanese life and nonlife insurance firms are beginning to unleash their huge assets. These companies have been doing their homework and picking the brains of their brokers, both foreign and domestic. They have greatly increased their trading in JGBs and are becoming more noticeable in the index futures and options markets.

The Ministry of Posts and Telecommunications (MoPT) has also begun to be a factor. This Ministry is by far Japan's largest recipient of savings. In addition to overseeing the country's enormous Postal Savings System, MoPT has under its management life insurance and annuity funds valued at about 4.5 trillion yen ($320 billion) at the end of fiscal 1988.

Beginning in April 1989, MoPT was authorized to use futures and options trading in the management of its insurance and annuity funds. The ministry hopes to increase the return on funds currently invested in equities, bonds and cash. Although proceeding gingerly, because of its size, MoPT is expected to become a major player—perhaps the biggest—and will give a major boost to volume in the markets.

Japan's Integrations

Though many in Japan hope to make Tokyo the center of the worldwide marketplace, few see it as a near-term possibility. Japan's trading systems, structure and markets are too different from the mainstream of world markets. Nevertheless, the differences are expected to narrow. There are more foreign firms active in Japanese markets than ever before, and vise versa. The net result is the integration of a growing Japanese market and industry with the world's futures and options community.

Japan will inevitably become the predominant futures and options center for the Asia-Pacific time zone and may, in fact, become the world's biggest trading arena in terms of volume. Japan's financial strength may enable it to pump huge amounts of money into its new markets, but it will not be as easy to develop true acumen and sophistication. The markets will, however, be far too significant for institutional investors to bypass.

The Australian Futures Market: Essential Risk Management for Investing Down Under

The second largest exchange in the region, and the ninth largest in the world, is the Sydney Futures Exchange. Founded in 1960, it was Asia-Pacific's first futures exchange, and also the first (in 1979) to list a financial contract. Along with New Zealand, it is the first to open the trading day—hours before Japan,

Hong Kong or Singapore. The exchange has expanded rapidly in recent years as restrictions, which formerly prevented overseas residents from trading in Australian markets, were lifted in December 1983.

The Sydney Futures Exchange (SFE) lists a unique range of Australian financial derivatives essential to the management of investments in the Australian capital markets. The SFE made a few notable attempts to launch international products, but they ended in failure. The exchange now emphasizes the domestic nature of its product range while nurturing international participation.

The demand for Australian risk management tools has supported tremendous growth at the SFE. By mid-1988, the exchange was bursting at its seams. Volume for its ten most popular financial futures and options was up by 40% in 1988 over 1987, despite a severe drop in share index products after the crash.

In February 1989, the SFE moved to new, customized premises designed to enable the exchange to reach its full potential. Volume for the first half of 1989 was about 50% higher than the year-earlier period. The Sydney exchange has literally and figuratively built a strong foundation for the 1990s.

Although Australia has an excellent geographical position, the exchange has had little success with international products like Eurodollars and T-Bonds. Nevertheless, the market is still important for institutional investors from outside Australia. Because of the relatively high yields available on the country's debt, Australian dollar bonds and bills have become a significant component of many fixed-income portfolios. Australian exchange and interest rates are notoriously volatile, thus necessitating efficient hedging mechanisms. This is where the SFE finds its widening niche.

Market Structure

At the end of 1988, there were over 380 members of the SFE, divided into three categories. *Floor membership* is the highest class of membership and provides the right to trade on behalf of clients and for proprietary accounts. This category was limited to 29 members because of space constraints on the old premises. A restructuring of membership—which will allow more firms to have a presence in the pits—is now under consideration.

Floor membership has become the preserve of the largest Australian and foreign banks and brokers. Their presence has displaced the commission houses and commodity firms. This has introduced much treasury and institutional participation into the marketplace.

There are three forms of *associate membership*. "Full associate members" trade on their own behalf or on behalf of clients, but their orders are executed by floor members. "Introducing broker associate members" can advise clients on futures and options trading but have orders executed and accounts maintained by floor members. "Market associate members" trade for their own accounts and have no floor presence.

The SFE actively nurtures its *local members,* since they provide much-needed liquidity to the markets. There are about 70 locals on the Sydney floor, with an occasional supplement of Chicago and London traders on the exchange's special local permit plan. Locals often account for up to 50% of volume in some contracts.

Sydney's futures community is regulated by federal legislation and a self-regulatory system administered by the SFE. In practice, the legislation, known as the Futures Industry Code, delegates much of the regulatory responsibility to Australian exchanges. (SFE is the only active exchange; Melbourne's Australian Financial Futures Market is dormant.) By the end of 1987, the Code was effective in all Australian states and territories.

The Australian regulatory environment received the approval of the U.S. Commodity Futures Trading Commission (CFTC) in November 1988, when SFE members were allowed to promote exchange products in the U.S. The CFTC decision was based in part on its satisfaction that SFE regulations and the federal industry code provided similar protection for clients and to those applying in the U.S.

The SFE lists ten futures contracts and five options on futures. All but two are in financial-related items. The vast bulk of institutional, local and retail activity is in the short- and long-term Australian interest rate contracts. Smaller but still significant business is done in stock index futures and options and in a revised Australian dollar contract.

The attraction of institutional investors to high-yielding Australian dollar debt has made interest rate futures the core business of the SFE. Much of the exchange's volume surge in the past four years is attributable to the increasing popularity of its 90-day Bank Accepted Bill and 10-Year Treasury Bond futures and options.

In 1987, 1988 and the first half of 1989, these four instruments accounted for over 85% of total exchange volume with over 75% for futures. In mid-1988, the SFE filled the gap in its yield curve coverage by listing 3-year Treasury Bond futures and options.

Bank-Accepted Bills were the SFE's first financial future and are its biggest. Launched in 1979, the contract has sustained steady growth in the mid-1980s. It had volume of almost three million contracts in 1988. This was up 50% form 1987, which was up 100% from 1986 levels.

One reason for such growth is the high volatility of Australian short-term interest rates. Liquidity is high; the dollar value of bank-bill futures trading is often bigger than the physical market. The futures market is deep enough to accommodate trades in distant months, up to two years out. This facilitates the creation of synthetic longer term securities, using the distant futures to bypass the quarterly rollovers on 90-day bills.

Options on bank-bill futures are available for the first four consecutive trading months. Although their underlying future is the SFE's most active contract, bank bill options trade less than one-third the volume of options on Australian government bond futures. Liquidity has improved markedly, however, with 1988 volume up over 300% and open interest up over 400%

Futures on Australian 10-Year Commonwealth Bonds were introduced in 1984 and have grown to become the SFE's number two product. Volume for 1988 was 2.7 million contracts. Since its inception, the bond contract was cash-settled, based on a poll of dealers. Restrictions on physical settlement have been lifted, but the previous system worked and was not tampered with.

Since May 1988, the contract has faced a more serious issue—a shortage of actual bonds. The Australian Treasury decided to restructure its borrowing toward short-term debt, and the previously thin cash market has gotten thinner. Futures volume is estimated at 20 times physical turnover. Expirations have been subject to manipulation, and the exchange and its members are looking at solutions.

These include changing the contract to a shorter maturity and listing a Semi-Government Contract. The latter was listed in early 1990 and further filled out SFE's yield curve coverage. The Semi-Government Bond contract is based on an index of bonds issued by the central borrowing authorities of Australian state governments and state-affiliated companies and utilities.

Institutional investors require these longer term hedging mechanisms. This explains the success of options on 10-year bond futures. These are the SFE's most popular option, trading 721,000 contract in 1988, a 90% jump from 1987. The options are an effective tool for fixed-income investors to lock in or protect the yields on Australian debt. Options on Semi-Government bond futures are also expected to be successful and will be launched concurrently with the futures in 1990.

Three-year T-Bond futures and options have been successful since their launch in mid-1988. As the supply of long-term bonds gets tighter, many investors have been forced toward the short end of the yield curve. Many market participants expect these contracts to rival the 10-year bond and bank bill in the near future.

The Australian equity market has attracted significant institutional funds since late 1983. When restrictions on foreign investments were lifted, the market became internationalized. In late 1989, Australia accounted for just over 2% of the EAFE index, although it had been higher before the October 1987 market crash.

The most popular domestic indicator of the share market is the Australian Stock Exchanges' All Ordinaries Index. The index is a capitalization-weighted group of over 250 companies listed on the Sydney and Melbourne Stock Exchange. The market value of these firms totals nearly 90% of the value of all Australian shares. The share futures contract at the SFE is based on this index, and trade in three month cycles on units of A$100 times the index.

Before the 1987 crash, all Ordinaries futures were heavily traded with broad institutional and retail participation. Volume in 1988 dropped 55% to 285,000, down from 625,00 in 1987. Volume in 1989 recovered somewhat, up about 15% from 1988 levels.

Institutions have become the primary users of the market. While less liquid than before the crash, the futures still track the market accurately and are suitable for index funds and other passive strategies.

Options on All Ordinaries futures also lost much business since the crash but remain popular with institutions. In 1988, 82,000 options were traded, down from 137,000 in 1987. The options trade two consecutive futures cycles with strike prices 26 index points apart.

One of the key elements of volatility with Australian investments is the wide movements of the country's currency. This volatility helps make the Aussie dollar the world's sixth most actively traded currently. The SFE launched revised Australian dollar futures and options in early 1988. The new contract, priced and margined in U.S. dollars, is similar but not fungible to the contract at the Chicago Mercantile Exchange. The SFE hopes to draw activity into the "mother market" but has not had outstanding success. Liquidity in both the futures and options is thin, particularly when compared with the huge spot forex trading in Australian dollars.

Earlier SFE attempts to develop internationally oriented products resulted in failure. In 1986, Sydney forged a much-publicized link with the London International Financial Futures Exchange (LIFFE) to trade Eurodollar and U.S. T-Bond futures. There was a flurry of activity in the initial months, but few international players were interested—preferring the existing Eurodollar market in Singapore and the liquid Asian cash T-Bond market.

In early 1987, following years of preparation, the SFE inaugurated its second international link with the Commodity Exchange in New York (COMEX). The COMEX 100 ounce gold contract fared only slightly better than the LIFFE interest rate futures. Although trading volume is often nil, the contract has remained listed and enables SFE members to access the COMEX market at low cost.

Both of these ventures have essentially been abandoned. The SFE, however, is secure in its role in the global and regional marketplace. The exchange has acknowledged that its strength is derived from the support of the Australian banking, institutional and brokerage community. The focus is on the "home base" of activity in Australian financial derivatives and broadening the range of users. SFE's agreement-in-principle to join the GLOBEX automated trading network is a major part of this strategy, although the exchange is relying first on its own automated trading system, SYCOM.

Australia's prime attraction for institutional investors is its currency and interest rates. The country's equity market also offers opportunities, particularly in the natural resource sector. The SFE aims to provide derivative products which will be essential to a comprehensive Australian investment strategy. With 30 years in operation and over a decade of experience with financial futures, its aim is true.

The Singapore International Monetary Exchange: Striving to Maintain Innovation

The Singapore International Monetary Exchange (SIMEX)—Asia's pioneering financial futures market—has provided institutional investors with a reliable locus for risk management since 1984. Through its innovative mutual offset link with the Chicago Mercantile Exchange, SIMEX has carved out a slice of international futures trading, particularly in Eurodollar interest rates.

The Singapore exchange has emerged from its infancy and is striving to forge an identity and find a path to continued growth. Heavy competition, from within and beyond the region, threatens SIMEX's unique niche in the Far Eastern time zone. The exchange is meeting this challenge with a three-pronged strategy which capitalizes on Singapore's regional importance and advance financial system.

SIMEX is fostering growth in its existing range of financial futures products by positioning itself to capture spillover and arbitrage activity from bigger markets like Japan. It also hopes to gain from the increased familiarity and experience with futures and options on the domestic scene and market liberalization among its immediate neighbors in Southeast Asia. Expansion of financial products will be pursued when demand is perceived and SIMEX has begun to aggressively diversify into commodity trading starting with the energy complex.

Asia's Futures Pioneer

SIMEX's history is an intriguing mixture of government initiatives, international financial market developments, and private sector reactions. When the Singapore authorities moved to reorganize the chaotic Gold Exchange in 1983, they asked the Chicago Mercantile Exchange (CME) for assistance. Officials from East and West recognized the potential of financial futures in Asia and the accelerating globalization of the industry. The Singapore exchange was revamped along CME lines and renamed SIMEX, and a unique mutual-offset system was created to link it with Chicago. Fungible contracts in Eurodollars, deutschmarks, and yen were launched in autumn 1984, and a new era in global futures trading began.

The "financial revolution" was slow to catch on. SIMEX did much ground-work to educate Asian investors and recruit locals to fill the pits. But its first full year of trading registered volume of just 538,000, a daily average of 2,150 contracts. 1986 saw the launching of contracts on Japan's Nikkei Stock Average and the British pound. Volume increased 38% but was still averaging only 3,500 lots per day.

The exchange broke out of its doldrums in early 1987. Even before the Japanese Finance Ministry permitted financial institutions to trade in overseas markets, new participants were entering the market. In May of that year, the orders from Japan flooded in and volume in the Eurodollar and Nikkei contracts surged. Unprecedented volatility, even before the crash, gave further impetus to trading activity. Daily average volume reached a healthy 8,600 contracts in 1987, with a peak of over 16,000 in October. Total volume was up 145% from 1986 to 2,142,000. Volume continued impressive growth in 1988 and 1989.

While these levels of activity were minuscule compared to Chicago's, SIMEX has played a meaningful trailblazing role in a region where futures and options were relatively mysterious. As in the West, many new contracts are dis-appointments, but in Asia each product introduced serves an educational role, even if it eventually fades away. (Such was the case with the SIMEX U.S. T-Bond contract, which also had the first night-trading session of any exchange in the world.)

SIMEX was more successful with the Nikkei. Its listing in Singapore is considered one of the major catalysts for Japan's recalcitrant bureaucrats legaliz-ing index futures. Furthermore, SIMEX served as a vital training ground for Japanese securities houses and their institutional customers.

Among the exchange's less publicized achievements is the development of its locals, a difficult task in Asian societies which value consensus over individu-alism. SIMEX is the only market in Asia with locals, and their numbers and sophistication continue to grow. SIMEX also can boast additional innovations. In late 1987 it listed the first options on futures in Asia and has been well-versed in multi-currency settlements since 1986.

Market Structure

The SIMEX market is patterned after that of its original mentor—the CME. It has nearly identical rules, compliance, audit, surveillance, membership and clearing house structure. Exchange management and committees also have a similar format. Market participants are protected by a common bond system, segregation of customer accounts, and a gross margining system. Overseas users find the structure and safeguards familiar and are comfortable doing business at the exchange.

The Mutual-Offset trading system between SIMEX and the CME enables positions established on one exchange to be transferred or liquidated on the other exchange. The extended trading hours enables futures and options participants to manage risk in different time zones within existing account structures. Transaction costs are reduced because margin must only be posted once.

As in Chicago, there are three categories of membership. *Clearing members* have the highest level of responsibility. They are members of the clearing house and are liable for all trades that pass through their firm. In late 1989 there were almost forty clearing members, each holding a minimum of three seats. Almost all the major international futures players are represented in this grouping, with the American banks and brokers having the greatest number. Singaporean, British and French firms are also represented. And in 1988, three of Japan's "Big Four" securities houses took clearing membership.

Corporate non-clearing members can have booths on the floor and traders in the pits, but must have their trades processed by clearing members. Japanese banks are the largest contingent in this category. American and British investment banks, Japanese securities firms and South East Asian companies are also well represented. A new type of nonclearing membership was added in early 1989, specifically for fuel oil futures. "Corporate associate members" need to hold only one seat, valid only for the energy complex. They may have employees on the floor but not in the pits and must process their trades through clearing members. Regional and international oil trading companies are the main users of this membership facility.

There are over 300 *individual nonclearing members,* or locals, at SIMEX. As in Chicago, they trade for their own account or execute orders in the pit for member firms. The majority of locals are Singapore citizens and ethnic Chinese, but a polyglot collection of "foreign locals" can also be found in the pits. Aside from Malaysians, Indonesians, Hong Kong Chinese, Thais and Burmese from within the region, there are members from the United States, Great Britain, France, Canada and Australia. The locals as a group have built up capital and experience and are able to support liquid markets wherever there is adequate order flow. Locals in the SIMEX Eurodollar pit have become particularly sophisticated, quoting complex spreads and deferred contracts up to three years out.

Futures market activity in Singapore is regulated under the Futures Trading Act. The Act, which was made law in 1987, confers upon the Monetary Authority of Singapore (MAS) power over the futures industry. The MAS is the city-state's central bank and overseer of financial markets. It has a reputation as a tough enforcer and protector of the large banking sector in Singapore.

Consolidation

After record-shattering volume in October 1987, SIMEX, like futures exchanges worldwide, suffered a large drop in activity in the months that followed. Reforms were enacted to boost user confidence, and the launch of options brought in some new players. By April 1988, volume returned to 1987 levels and open interest had increase 65%. Activity surpassed record marks in June and achieved new records for 1988. 1989 surpassed year-earlier levels by a wide margin, and thus the exchange ended the decade on an impressive growth track. Corporate and individual membership is growing and seat prices have reached new heights. In September 1989, SIMEX further integrated itself into Singapore's financial community by moving to new premises in the heart of the city-state's business district.

Threats from East and West

While SIMEX's statistics are impressive, it still has a dangerously narrow base of activity. Over 85% of 1988 trading was in Eurodollar and Nikkei futures, with the former taking the lion's share. The Singapore market's problems are compounded by the accelerating competition emerging from within the region and beyond. Particularly troubling is that its two "bread and butter" contracts have the most to lose or gain, depending on the contours of the newly developing markets. The biggest threat comes from Japan, which has expanded its domestic financial futures activity at a blistering pace. SIMEX prefers to view Japanese market growth as an opportunity for parallel growth, citing the interactive nature of financial markets. Whether such a synergy develops depends on SIMEX maintaining its role as regional innovator.

In the first year of Japanese stock index futures (SIF) trading, the Singapore market benefited. SIMEX Nikkei volume was about 40% higher than the previous period. Open interest, however, is well below record levels; and its value more than 80% less than Osaka's. The increased volume comes from institutions, particularly American ones, drawn to the greater liquidity that Osaka-SIMEX arbitrage has created. Arb and spread trading of two Nikkei contracts against TOPIX has boosted volume, but has also dampened volatility.

While Nikkei trading may be less exciting than before the crash, the contract is healthy, liquid and fairly priced. But it and the exchange's other products face longer term threats from Japan. U.S. investors who have boosted their activity in the Nikkei may shift their trading if and when the CFTC gives a "no action" ruling on the new Japanese SIFs. Some observers in Tokyo consider it inevitable that institutional players will shift to Japan's contracts as soon as they are able, leaving SIMEX's Nikkei in the dust. SIMEX officials paint a brighter picture, claiming that such a development may not impair the exchange's customer base—the more active users become in Japan, the more they will need Singapore's open-outcry market as a safety valve.

SIMEX had hoped to attract players with options on Nikkei futures in early 1989, but its plans were postponed because of ongoing negotiations with the CME about GLOBEX. Osaka listed options in June 1989, and thus beat SIMEX into this new and exciting niche. The smaller Singapore exchange still intends to list futures options on the Nikkei, but it is doubtful whether it will become a deep enough market for institutions.

In addition to the challenge in SIFs, new interest rate futures in Japan might drain business from the Eurodollar contract at SIMEX. The Tokyo Stock Exchange listed U.S. T-Bond futures in December 1989. Around-the-clock trading of bond futures would then be an alternative to Eurodollars for some users.

SIMEX's Eurodollar futures—its most popular contract—became exposed to direct competition on another flank. In June 1989 the Tokyo International Financial Futures Exchange began trading short-term yen deposit and Eurodollar futures as well as the yen/dollar exchange rate. In 1987, direct orders from Japan accounted for over 10% of SIMEX Eurodollar volume, with another 15% coming indirectly. In 1988 the figure was even higher. While spillover activity and arbitrage from Japan might boost volume, this major slice of business can no longer be taken for granted.

SIMEX responded in October 1989 by launching its own Euroyen deposit futures. The new contract has similar specifications as the TIFFE product and is aimed at current users of the Japanese contract and participants in Singapore's rapidly expanding offshore yen market. The exchange has set low margin requirements for Eurodollar-Euroyen spreads, facilitating an interest rate differential market.

Even if the growth of business from Tokyo slows, non-Japanese activity is likely to remain attracted to Singapore. SIMEX will continue to serve as a bridge between time zones since its contracts are fungible and its trading system is compatible with Chicago and London.

The nature of SIMEX's bridging role is likely to change dramatically by the mid-90s and the impetus for change will be, ironically, the Singapore exchange's mentor in Chicago. Ever since the CME's September 1987 announcement of its GLOBEX electronic trading venture with Reuters, the forward momentum of the SIMEX-Merc relationship has waned. And while exchange officials on both sides of the Pacific have maintained genuine cordiality, difficult negotiations have strained the connection.

The relationship is extremely important for SIMEX as about 30% of its volume comes from the U.S. via the mutual-offset system. Furthermore, the link with the Merc provides an intangible but crucial aura of security and technical sophistication. However, by all assessments from Chicago mutual-offset volume has been somewhat disappointing.

Facing the Challenge

The GLOBEX joint venture between the CME and Reuters Information Services to introduce electronic trading outside of normal Chicago hours will greatly effect SIMEX. The Singapore exchange is expected to join the system on preferential terms, but it still faces the threat of losing business in its most important contract. The transformation of the CME/SIMEX relationship will also set precedents for the integration of other markets with GLOBEX.

The exchange is clearly at an important crossroads in its short existence. SIMEX is hoping to improve activity in current products and expand with related financial contracts when the timing is right. But it is also hedging by moving into commodity futures. Singaporean officials have begun to realize that some promising trails lie close to home.

With the fate of most of its international contracts out of its hands, it is logical for SIMEX to focus on domestic and regional products. The most natural extension of its financial futures menu is an index contract for the Singapore stock market. The exchange had actually completed the much difficult groundwork by September 1987, having secured regulatory approval and completed negotiations with the Stock Exchange. A third quarter 1988 launch was targeted. The following month's crash naturally shelved the plans, and the Monetary Authority of Singapore waited for the dust to settle before giving a green light to SIMEX.

A listing is only a matter of time (and timing) since the market and regulatory environment must be right. Foreign investors have greatly increased their involvement in Singaporean equities in 1989, and greater amounts of overseas Chinese funds have shifted south in response to unrest in China and uncertainty in Hong Kong. This bodes well for a Singapore index contract, and exchange officials are optimistic about an introduction by late 1991 or early 1992.

In February 1989, SIMEX launched its long-awaited energy contract on high-sulphur fuel oil, along with inducements to attract new members. Simultaneously, the Singapore government introduced a range of tax concessions for international oil trading activities conducted in the republic.

Initial activity has been mediocre, with major cash market users reluctant to participate in large amounts. The exchange plans to move rapidly into other energy contracts. A crude oil future was next, based on Dubai Fateh, which is actively traded in Asia. Naphtha, the part of the barrel left over from fuel oil production is a probable follow-up.

The move into energy has prompted the exchange to try and revive its moribund gold contract. SIMEX's original product, 100 ounce gold futures, began trading in July 1984 but has been inactive since late 1986. Like foreign currencies, cash market gold trading in Asia is cheap and accessible, giving little natural demand for futures.

SIMEX is also exploring other commodities for listing. Singapore's re-source-rich neighbors still depend on the city-state's vital entrepôt role for their agricultural and mineral products. Coffee and rubber are the most promising areas under consideration.

Striking a Balance

In its first six years, SIMEX strived to make its mark as an international ex-change with innovative financial futures and options. It has succeeded with some of its contracts, and undoubtedly helped develop regional awareness and activity in futures. It continues to provide institutions and international traders with a valuable risk transferral facility in the Asian time zone. And it has proven its reliability in times of stress, particularly during the October 1987 crash when markets in Hong Kong, Tokyo and Osaka were closed or could not establish prices.

As new technology and competition place its role as the Asian link in 24-hour trading in jeopardy, the exchange is seeking new momentum and identity closer to home. SIMEX, like Singapore's economy as a whole, has done well in identifying niches where it can play a meaningful role. It may do so again with energy futures and local stock indices. But much work remains to be done if the exchange is to achieve a healthy balance of products, activity and participants that will carry it through the 1990s.

The Hong Kong Futures Exchange: Struggling Against Political and Financial Turbulence

Hong Kong, the Pacific Basin's second largest financial center and a bastion of free enterprise, faces great political and economic uncertainty. The imminent re-turn to Chinese sovereignty in 1997 has made investment in the British colony riskier than ever. Furthermore, while most Asian financial centers had put the crash of '87 behind them, Hong Kong was still feeling the aftereffects in 1990.

The territory's reputation was greatly damaged by a four-day exchange clo-sure, lax regulatory control, and subsequent revelations of serious corruption. In the late spring of 1989, just as the stock market was beginning to show signs of life, Hong Kong equities were rocked by political shock waves emanating from China. Asia's freewheeling economic dynamo may never regain its prominence as a regional financial market.

Institutional investors have frequently made Hong Kong a key component of their Asian portfolios. It has the highest weighting in the region (after Japan and Australia) in the major global stock indices and has been more accessible than less developed regional markets. As events in the 1980s have demonstrated,

Hong Kong can be a treacherously volatile market, stemming from political factors and the high level of participation by Hong Kong individual investors. Risk management tools for Hong Kong assets should play an important role in institutional strategies.

The territory's entrepreneurial and speculative environment would ideally provide liquidity to derivative markets on local and China-related instruments. In 1986 and 1987, these factors seemed well on their way to providing a base of activity. However, the Hong Kong Futures Exchange (HKFE) has since had great difficulty in building reliable, active and secure markets to serve institutional needs.

Hong Kong's capital market opportunities are mostly in equities, although numerous foreign firms float commercial paper and bonds in Hong Kong to finance regional operations. The unrestricted flow of information and accumulated financial know-how also means most loans to Asian countries are syndicated in the colony. Hong Kong dollar debt frequently offers yields well above prevailing rates, without a currency risk, since it is formally pegged in the U.S. unit. Hong Kong interest rates, however, fluctuate more than Eurodollar rates.

The Hong Kong equity market has approximately a 1.4% weighting in the MSCI EAFE index. For much of the 1980s, involvement in Hong Kong's markets has been rewarding. Yet in contrast to some other Asian markets, a buy and hold approach can be dangerous. Three times in the decade, stock prices had drops of over 50% in less than six months. Institutional investors thus have a serious need for risk management tools in this financial arena.

Since May 1986, one such tool has existed at the HKFE. Index futures on the colony's popular Hang Seng Index were at one time the most active stock index futures outside of the U.S. The market attracted a diverse group of users and served various institutional needs. The stock market crash of '87 devastated the contract, and the exchange has since been struggling to regain user confidence.

The exodus of overseas funds from the colony's capital markets, despite booming double-digit real GDP growth rates in 1988 and 1989, was a natural reaction to the magnitude of blunders and wrongdoing by exchange officials in October 1987. Ronald Li, then Chairman of the Stock Exchange of Hong Kong, unilaterally decided to close the market after Wall Street's 508 point plunge. Local and foreign investors were infuriated, and the wave of selling that hit the exchange when it reopened after the weekend on October 26 was much greater than if the exchange had stayed open. In just over a week, Hong Kong equities lost half their value.

The four-day suspension was also imposed on the futures market, exacerbating already critical margin difficulties. The largest default in the history of futures exchanges ensued, necessitating a government-backed HK$2 billion (U.S.$257 million) "lifeboat fund" to save the market from collapse.

Reforms and Uncertainties

Once the dust settled, but before the financial wounds had healed, investigations began. Aside from finding that Ronald Li acted out of self-interest, he and other Stock Exchange officials were arrested for taking bribes from companies seeking a listing. Recriminations and finger pointing continued through the mid-1988, all the while further damaging Hong Kong's reputation.

In response, the colonial government went into action, making sweeping changes to the regulatory system. The Securities and Futures Commission was established and was given broad powers to pursue market abuse. The pendulum swung nearly 180 degrees—while reforms were sorely needed, brokers, bankers and lawyers in Hong Kong have complained that regulation is now too tight.

Aside from tighter colony-wide controls—including the right of entry into firms' offices to check accounting practices and the elimination of a person's right to remain silent to questions asked by regulators—the Securities and Futures Commission was empowered with a direct watchdog role over the HKFE. With much input from the commission, as well as member and outside consultants, the HKFE was thoroughly reorganized, patterned on many of the best features of more established futures exchanges.

Stricter membership requirements have shifted the exchange's emphasis toward bigger players. Minimum firm capital—as little as HK$2 million ($260,000) before the crash—has been raised to a range of HK$10 million up the HK$25 million for clearing membership. More detailed and frequent financial reporting requirements were also established.

The previously independent clearing house has been brought under the exchange's domain, thus unifying position risk management and trade processing. Members are likely to be more responsible, as they are now shareholders of the clearing corporation. A further safeguard is a HK$200 million guarantee fund.

The exchange counts on more than just members' accountability to prevent another default. Rules and enforcement procedures have been upgraded to international standards. Most important is the switch to gross margins. Members' previous ability to net off client and house positions before posting margin were a primary cause of the 1987 default. Now both initial and variation margin for all open positions must be deposited in the clearing house. Exchange officials believe the new market structure will serve members and customers for a long term.

The new HKFE constitution was approved in early May 1989 and restored some confidence in the market. Buoyant Hong Kong equities in early 1989 revived interest in Hang Seng index futures, and the exchange was making plans for new products. At around the same time in May, massive student demonstrations in China were clouding Hong Kong's political future, culminating with June's brutal suppression in Tiananmen Square. Hong Kong stocks were battered almost as severely as hopes for democracy in China, with the Hang Seng Index losing over 50% and probing its lows from the crash of '87. Unlike October 1987, the HKFE remained open throughout the crisis, performing a valuable risk transferral and price discovery function and restoring confidence in the exchange's integrity and independence.

Since then, large institutional investors in Hong Kong equities have used HSI futures as a hedging mechanism. Late-1989 volume averaged about 1,000 lots/day, up over 55% from the same period in 1988. Open interest has also rebounded, to over 2,500 contracts. This level of activity remains small compared to daily volume of over 20,000 lots in mid-1987 and is only barely adequate to accommodate institutional trading strategies.

Moving Forward

Cleaning up after 1987's defaults and the subsequent restructuring required the total effort of the HKFE's new management. Only in 1989 were they able to shift their energies to developing an overall business strategy. The new structure may be the potential foundation for rebuilding, but the HKFE must both convince institutions to reenter the market and redefine its regional niche.

The exchange's stated mission is to "assert itself as one of the top Asian exchanges, while concentrating on local commercial needs. Because of Hong Kong's political status and location, we must also build a close association with China." As China's trade and investment activities expand, their business entities will become more exposed to market risk. Their hedging needs are potentially enormous, and the exchange hopes to serve them as their sophistication grows. In the near term, however, most of HKFE's opportunities remain with the traditional user groups—local and foreign financial institutions in Hong Kong.

The exchange's first test is to revitalize Hang Seng Index futures. Individual speculators, which made up almost 50% of 1987's volume, have virtually abandoned the market. Most have simply given up on futures, and many have completely withdrawn from the stock market to pursue investment and emigration plans outside the colony.

Institutions, including HKFE member firms, are still reluctant to participate in a meaningful way. Even when they are ready to do so, it will be difficult as HSI futures volume is light. One detriment to higher volume has been the "special levy" on transactions designed to pay back brokers who lent to the "lifeboat fund." But the real problem is an underlying lack of faith in the exchange due to memories of 1987.

The contract's greatest potential is due to the inability of most investors to short stock in the cash market. In addition to this latent demand, the HSI contract itself is well-designed. The 33-share Hang Seng Index is the most popular barometer of the colony's stock market and is familiar to both the old "amah" investing her hard-earned HK$5,000, and to the investment manager with a HK$500 million portfolio.

Furthermore, it is relatively simple to construct a basket of stock which accurately track the small index, making cash/futures arbitrage—and occasional market manipulation—attractive. Market participants think a critical mass of 2,000 to 3,000 lots/day would be adequate to draw major institutions back to the market.

The HKFE's continuous trading during the Stock Exchange's dislocations in May and June of 1989 restored a degree of confidence. Futures participants appreciated the HKFE's alternative facilities during the crisis.

By late 1989, there was renewed interest in the exchange from large foreign institutions, including Japanese securities house and American investment banks. The Bank of China was also rumored to be taking active steps to enter the market through some of its brokerage and corporate holdings in the colony.

One reason for the new signs of interest are the exchange's plans to list options on HSI futures. In many ways they would be more attractive than the futures, since at least for option buyers, their risk—and hence their exposure to another exchange default—is limited. Such a product will serve the extensive hedging needs of the local investment community without the perceived high-risk profile of futures.

The HKFE is negotiating with the Stock Exchange over the options' format, with a 1991 target for listing. However, hopes for a successful options launch are dependent on the further revitalizaiton of Hang Seng futures.

HIBOR Hopes

The HKFE wants to broaden its appeal beyond equity-oriented products and is thus launching a new contract designed specifically for the local corporate sector. Futures on short-term Hong Kong dollar interest rates were listed in February 1990 and were the HKFE's first new contract in over three years. The benchmark rate is the 3-month HIBOR (Hong Kong Interbank Offered Rate). Exchange officials hope that the new product will attract a different class of participants and thus improve the market's activity and image.

Hong Kong interest rates are volatile for traditional economic reasons and because the government uses its monetary powers to discipline those speculating on a revaluation of the colony's currency. Thus, banks and companies in Hong Kong face substantial variations in the cost of money and have a natural hedging need. Chinese business entities have also been assuming more interest rate risk—as they sign more joint venture agreements—and are also potential users.

The Hong Kong clearing banks and large American banks were enthusiastic about the new contract—and should be supportive since they have significant need for such a hedging tool. Companies issuing debt in the colony should also find uses for the contract. While Forward Rate Agreements have long been available in Hong Kong, their use and trading has been limited, hampered by extremely wide bid/offer spreads. HIBOR futures could greatly improve the environment for short-dated hedging instruments.

The contract specifications are similar to Eurodollar futures, with the size of HK$1 million quoted as 100 less the interest rate. Each tick of one basis point is worth HK$24, with a price limit of 250 basis points. Rates of 12 reference banks will be used to compute the cash settlement price with the highest and lowest two quotes discarded.

Market participants were optimistic about the HIBOR contract, and exchange officials hoped that success would rub off on Hang Seng futures and open up possibilities for both HSI and HIBOR options. Initial volume, however, has been extremely disappointing. While other financial products are being considered, nothing notable is on the drawing board. Although the HKFE has long wanted to list currency futures, citing Hong Kong's vibrant foreign trade, the opportunities are slim. The colony's banks offer a variety of sophisticated forex products, Singapore has an established five-year-old currency futures market, Tokyo has listed a similar contract, and the GLOBEX electronic trading system will feature currency futures.

Chinese Commodities

Any HKFE expansion beyond its current plans is unlikely to come from the financial section. Therefore, the exchange is looking toward commodities for future growth. The HKFE gold contract is essentially dead, kept alive by a daily cross of 20 to 30 lots. Hong Kong's "Loco-London" cash market in gold is Asia's largest, and extremely liquid. Major bullion dealers and traders move easily in and out of this market. Furthermore, the Hong Kong Gold and Silver Society trades tael (a traditional Asian measurement) units priced in Hong Kong dollars. This wild and unregulated market is a favorite of Hong Kong Chinese speculators, who have little incentive to switch to futures.

The HKFE is hoping to garner new business by offering a wider range of agricultural commodities which have a Chinese connection. Hong Kong currently trades futures on soybeans and sugar, priced in U.S. dollars and traded by the Japanese call method. Most participants are local trading houses, commercial users or Japanese grain dealers.

The first new contract with a Chinese connection may be rice, but it faces numerous infrastructural hurdles regarding delivery and quality. Wheat futures and an energy complex have also been discussed with Chinese officials but never made much progress.

Hong Kong's Regional Niche

Because of its tarnished international reputation, the Hong Kong Futures Exchange had no choice but to abandon its grandiose expansion plans. It has made the necessary transition away from aggressive competition with other regional exchanges and toward a complementary focus on its home environment.

HKFE leaders stress the importance of serving the "mother market" when they define Hong Kong's "natural products." For the foreseeable future, the exchange will have its hands full with the Hang Seng Index, HIBOR futures, options, and China-related commodities. If it can build active markets in these areas, the exchange will have gone a long way toward putting the crash of '87 behind it and preparing for a future under Chinese rule.

The New Zealand Futures and Options Exchange: Significance Beyond Its Size

The New Zealand Futures and Options Exchange (NZFOE) is one of the smaller regional markets, but one which has lead the way in automation. Founded in 1985, the exchange has never had a trading floor but instead provides computer-based electronic dealing facilities to its members. The market is primarily the domain of New Zealand financial institutions; however, most of its products have relevance for international investors.

New Zealand's capital markets are at the economic and geographic periphery of the world's financial markets, yet in both respects, they play a role proportionately larger than their small size. They are the first market to open each trading day, and thus the first to react to overnight and over-weekend news. The New Zealand debt market also attracts substantial foreign participation due to historically high yields. In the 1980s, the currency frequently paid ten percentage points over debt from the major industrial nations. With the high yields, however, comes volatile exchange and interest rates caused by the nation's budgetary and political situation.

Foreign institutions are also involved in New Zealand equities, even though the market comprises a minuscule .2% of the MSCI EAFE index. There are a number of world class companies listed in Auckland, and they have attracted significant investors from the U.K., U.S. and Japan.

The impetus for foreign participation in New Zealand—and the spark that unleashed domestic financial innovation—was the liberalization of the country's economy and capital markets in the early and mid-1980s. Prior to this process, New Zealand was a tightly controlled financial backwater with little foreign portfolio investment. The abolition of foreign exchange controls and deregulation of the banking and brokerage industries paved the way for the development of a futures exchange. Since then almost every sector of the New Zealand economy has used the futures and options market to offset the increased financial risk associated with the open economic environment.

Computerized Beginnings

The creation and growth of the NZFOE was innovative from the start. The exchange founders chose a fully electronic marketplace because of lower start-up costs and in response to geographic realities. None of the country's three major cities (Auckland, Wellington or Christchurch) had enough commercial activity to support a market independently. The exchange developed its Automated Trading System (ATS) with the International Commodity Clearing House Ltd. (ICCH), which also clears all trades for the NZFOE.

ATS functions by matching the buy and sell orders which members enter into terminals in their offices throughout New Zealand. If no exact opposite position is available, the system queues orders according to the dealer's instructions. The computer also generates all the documentation and accounting records for brokers and provides continuously updated information on prices and volume. ICCH has since used ATS software for the London Futures and Options Exchange (London Fox). In July 1988, ATS Mk II was launched, providing an enhanced dealing facility and multi-currency settlement capability. The system is so advanced that it is being used as the backbone for LIFFE's Automated Pit Trading System which will compete with GLOBEX.

Since there is no physical exchange building, NZFOE and its members supported "The Kerb/Futures Industry Information Centre" in Auckland to encourage public participation in the market. Many retail customers use the Centre as a base for their trading, although it has now been transfered to private operation.

There are two types of membership at NYFE: trading members and affiliate members. Changes in the membership ranks have reflected the growing trend toward futures trading as an integral part of corporate and banking treasury operations in New Zealand. The membership includes most of New Zealand's financial institutions, including 11 banks.

Trading members are all shareholders of the exchange and have direct access to ATS terminals. All business on the exchange must be transacted through one of the 17 trading members who are directly liable to the clearing house. Trading members are limited and can only be acquired by transfer from an existing member.

Affiliate members are not NZFOE shareholders and must operate through trading members. They can do so on their own behalf or for clients. Affiliate membership is not limited. In late 1989 there were 22 affiliate members.

In mid-1990, NZFOE and the New Zealand Stock Exchange began discussions exploring the possibility of merging. Leaders of both exchanges anticipate synergistic gains from such a move.

Regulation

Beyond strict membership requirements, futures trading activity in New Zealand is safeguarded by exchange self-regulation and oversight by government authority. New Zealand's Securities Law Reform Bill of 1988 provides a statutory environment similar to that in the United States and Australia. The exchange controls the activities of members and customers through its rules, internal compliance and surveillance capabilities.

Diverse Products, Narrow Activity

The NZFOE lists contracts on debt, equity, forex and agricultural products. Activity is dominated by debt contracts, particularly New Zealand Government bonds. Volume has grown steadily since 1986, to a pace of over 600,000 contracts annually in mid-1989. Although these levels are small, they are significant in the context of New Zealand. The dollar value of trading in each year since 1987 has been nearly equal or above the country's Gross National Product.

Five-Year Government Stock futures, listed in February 1986, are the NZFE's most successful contract, accounting for over half of exchange volume since late 1987. This medium-term bond contract was designed to allow corporate borrowers, lenders and institutional investors to manage the substantial interest rate risk in New Zealand. The contract was revised in May 1988 with a lower 10% coupon rate for a face value of NZ$100,000.

New Zealand financial institutions are very active in this contract, both to adjust their debt positions and in arbitrage transactions. Foreigners with Kiwi dollar fixed-income investments use this product to lock in high yields.

In the 1989, daily average volume for the Government Stock Contract (GSC) was about 1,200 lots per day. Open interest surged in 1989, to a level of about 8,000 contracts, indicating healthy market depth. GSC volume has been increasing by over 65% per year since 1988.

GSC options were successfully launched in December 1988, along with an extensive marketing and educational program. The exchange hopes that more risk-adverse corporations will be attracted to the fixed-cost of hedging with options, while institutions have welcomed the new trading vehicle.

The NZFOE's second most popular contract is the 90-Day Bank Accepted Bill future. It was listed in December 1986 to replace an existing short-term interest rate product on Prime Commercial Paper. The Bank Bill Contract (BBC) is used to control the risk associated with New Zealand's volatile call money, 30-day, and 90-day rates. The emergence of sophisticated interest rate management tools such as *FRA's, caps, collars* and *cylinders* has been fostered by NZFE's short-term rate futures.

The contract has a unit value of NZ$500,000 and is cash-settled, based on quotes from 15 approved bill dealers. In mid-1989, BBC futures were averaging 400 to 500 lots per day, with a relatively deep open interest of 4,300. Options on BBC futures are being planned to meet institutional demand as futures activity increases.

Stock index futures in New Zealand had a spectacular rise and fall since their listing in January 1987. NZFE's contract on the Barclays Share Price Index (BSI) grew rapidly in its first nine months, to a peak volume of 17,000 lots in October 1987. The crash hit New Zealand extremely hard, and the BSI was a prime casualty. Volume quickly dropped to under 1,000 lots per month and held this low level through early 1989. When New Zealand equities recovered in mid-1989, some interest came back into the futures, which average 1,500 lots per month in June, July and August 1989. Open interest for the period was a thin 250 lots.

The contract is valued at NZ$20 times the index and is cash-settled. Few international investors currently use the BSI contract as a substitute for investment in New Zealand equities because the country's small weighting in global indices. Fund managers with a desire for New Zealand exposure tend to purchase shares directly in Auckland or via ADRs.

Exchange-traded options on BSI futures were launched in February 1989. The investment community acknowledged the necessity of the product but has not heavily supported trading. Activity has been extremely thin due to inadequate market-making by member firms and slow trading in the underlying futures. Exchange officials hope to remedy both problems and attract more pension and trust funds to the market. The introduction of options on individual New Zealand shares is planned for the early 1990s.

The volatile Kiwi dollar exchange rate forces many institutions and corporates to use risk management tools. Currency futures should therefore fare well in New Zealand. The NZFE's first product was a U.S. dollar future, but it never won widespread acceptance. This was due to competition from the interbank forward market and the fact that the contract was quoted in U.S. dollar terms which was unfamiliar to major dealers.

In response, the exchange in late-1988 switched to New Zealand dollar futures (KWI), based on units of NZ$100,000. Although the Kiwi contract's format is more familiar, it has yet to attract wide interest. Volume rarely tops 100 lots per day.

Agricultural contracts played a critical role in the genesis of the New Zealand futures industry but have since become inactive. Wool futures volume dried up in 1987 and 1988 while wheat futures did not last through their first year of trading.

Looking Forward

The NZFOE, although a regional innovator, has yet to achieve prominence in the Pacific Basin financial arena. Instead of rushing to launch new products to gain worldwide attention, the exchange intends to build on existing strengths. Particular emphasis is being placed on education of members and corporate customers. In addition, ties with the stock exchange will broaden its user base.

Expansion for the New Zealand Futures and Options Exchange will be internal—through increased liquidity in its debt and equity futures and options. As these markets develop, institutional users will find them attractive for hedging and asset allocation strategies.

How to Hedge Currency Risk

Lee R. Thomas, III
Goldman Sachs International Ltd.
London, England

Evaluating the International Risk/Return Tradeoff

If you diversify your investments among international markets, you must make two key choices: What foreign securities to buy and what foreign currency exposures to bear. By using forward foreign exchange contacts, you can unbundle these decisions,[1] and you should. We recommend that you select your securities as if you intend to currency hedge, valuing each security on its own merits. Then decide separately whether to hedge, partially hedge, or over hedge each foreign holding.

The decision to hedge or not to hedge depends on how you think the currency exposures embedded in your foreign investments will affect your portfolio's risk and return. Elsewhere, we and others have demonstrated that currency hedging lowers the risk of offshore investing, as measured by return volatility.[2] The remainder of this paper focuses on the other half of the risk/return tradeoff—the impact of currency hedging on foreign investment returns. In short, what is it likely to cost you to currency hedge? Is currency hedging a "free lunch"?[3]

We will look at the cost element of your currency hedging decision from both a conceptional and an empirical perspective. Essentially, your cost of currency hedging depends on the difference between the forward and future spot foreign exchange rates. In this paper, we examine two theories of the forward/spot relationship and the implications each has for currency hedging. Then we offer a common sense synthesis and suggest what we consider to be a practical and efficient approach to managing the currency exposures in an international investment portfolio. Finally, with this in mind, we look at some historical evidence on the returns to hedged versus unhedged foreign investments.

Currency Hedging and Volatility

Currency hedging is supposed to reduce the riskiness of foreign investing. Does it, and if so how much? Exhibit 1 illustrates the effects of currency hedging in ten-year government bond markets. If you declined to currency hedge, every foreign bond was more risky than a similar maturity U.S. Treasury. But if you used one month rolling forward exchange contracts to eliminate your exchange rate exposures, your risk would have fallen in every foreign bond market.[4] On average the volatility of return fell by 47%. As a result, the average foreign ten-year bond, held currency hedged, was less risky than a ten-year U.S. Treasury bond.

Exhibit 2 shows the effect of currency hedging on a portfolio of foreign bonds. The portfolio weights are as follows: Japan, 30%; Germany, 25%; U.K.,

---

Exhibit 1   Foreign Investment Volatilities 1975–1988

Country	Bonds*		Equities**	
	Unhedged Risk	Currency Hedged Risk	Unhedged Risk	Currency Hedged Risk
U.S.	9.5	—	16.1	—
Japan	17.0	7.7	20.1	14.5
Germany	15.7	6.4	20.6	17.0
U.K.	18.3	11.3	26.8	23.1
France	13.7	5.8	26.1	22.0
Canada	11.6	9.3	20.9	18.8
Netherlands	19.6	6.8	18.9	17.8
Australia	16.0	9.1	31.8	26.7
Portfolio***	12.4	5.3	16.6	13.1

---

*   Government bonds with approximately ten years to maturity.
**   The Ft-Actuaries country indices.
*** The portfolio weights are: Japan, 30%; Germany, 25%; U.K., 15%; Canada, 10%; and the Netherlands, 5%.

Exhibit 2   Currency Hedging and Bond Volatility
10 Year Government Bonds, 1975–1988

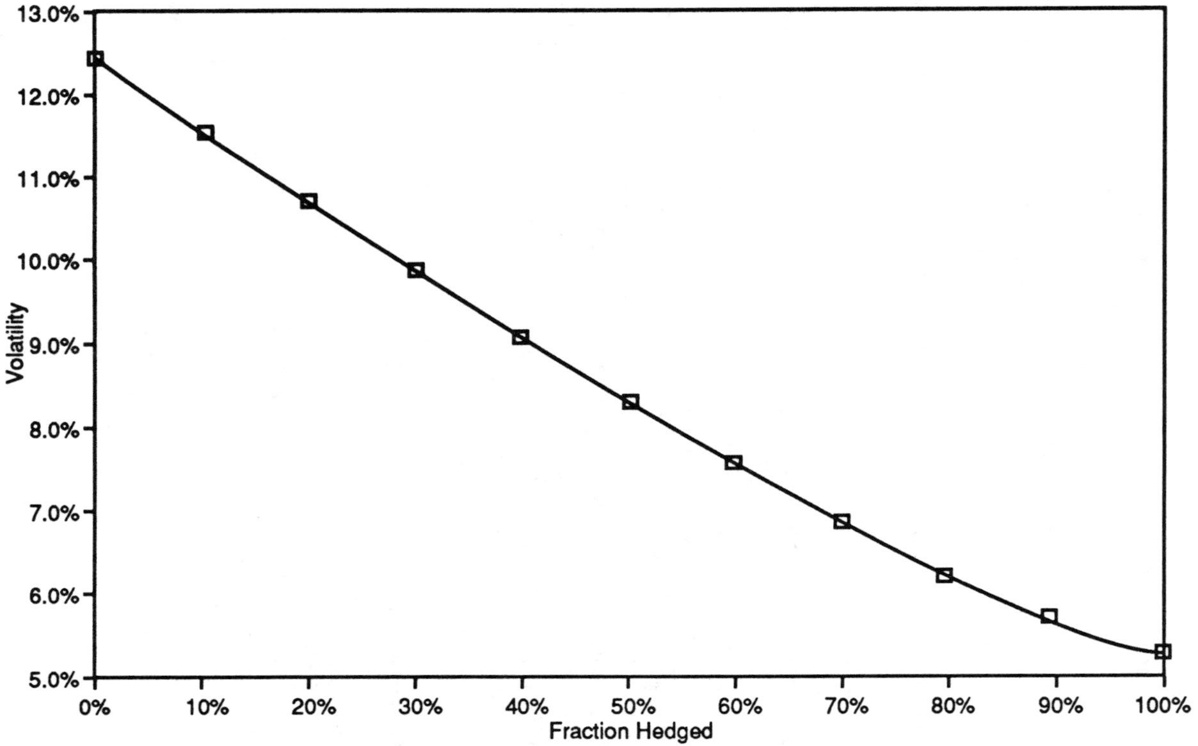

15%; France, 10%; Canada, 5%; and the Netherlands, 5%. As you can see, the more you hedged, the lower the volatility of your position. If you hedged all of your foreign bonds you could have driven your volatility down 7.1 percentage points, from 12.4% to 5.3%. This 57% decline is comparable to the risk reduction currency hedging delivered in the average individual foreign bond market.

The results for foreign equity investments are also shown in Exhibit 1. As we found in the case of bonds, currency hedging reduced the volatility of return in every foreign market we examined. However, the reductions were much smaller in the case of foreign equity investments. On average, foreign equity investment volatility declined by just 15%, compared with 47% for bond investments.

The results for a representative equity portfolio are shown in Exhibit 3. The portfolio weights are the same as they were for bonds: Japan, 30%; Germany, 25%; U.K., 15%; France, 15%; Canada, 5%; and the Netherlands, 5%. The portfolio's volatility fell by 3.5 percentage points, from 16.6% to 13.1%. This fall represents a decline of 21%.

It is significant to note that currency hedging reduced the volatility of foreign portfolios about as much as it did for investments in single foreign markets. This was true for foreign bond or equity portfolios. In Modern Portfolio Theory this finding shows that exchange rate risk is systematic, even in a portfolio of foreign securities that is well diversified internationally. That is, dividing your foreign eggs among many foreign baskets, rather than just a few, is not enough to eliminate exchange rate risk.

Gauging the Cost of Hedging

When you are deciding whether to currency hedge, a key concern will be how much expected return you will have to sacrifice, if any, to achieve the desired reduction in return volatility. The prospective decrease in expected return represents your cost of currency hedging.

Gauging the prospective, or "before-the-fact," cost may seem a bit tricky. To get a better sense of just how to go about such an evaluation, let's first consider the cost of hedging "after the fact."

After-the-Fact Hedging

Finding the cost of hedging after the fact is straightforward. We need only to compare the realized return on an unhedged foreign investment to the realized return on an otherwise identical investment that we have combined with a forward foreign exchange contract. We will assume that you use a simple hedging strategy: Sell forward (one month) the beginning-of-period foreign currency

**Exhibit 3   Currency Hedging and Equity Volatility
1975–1988**

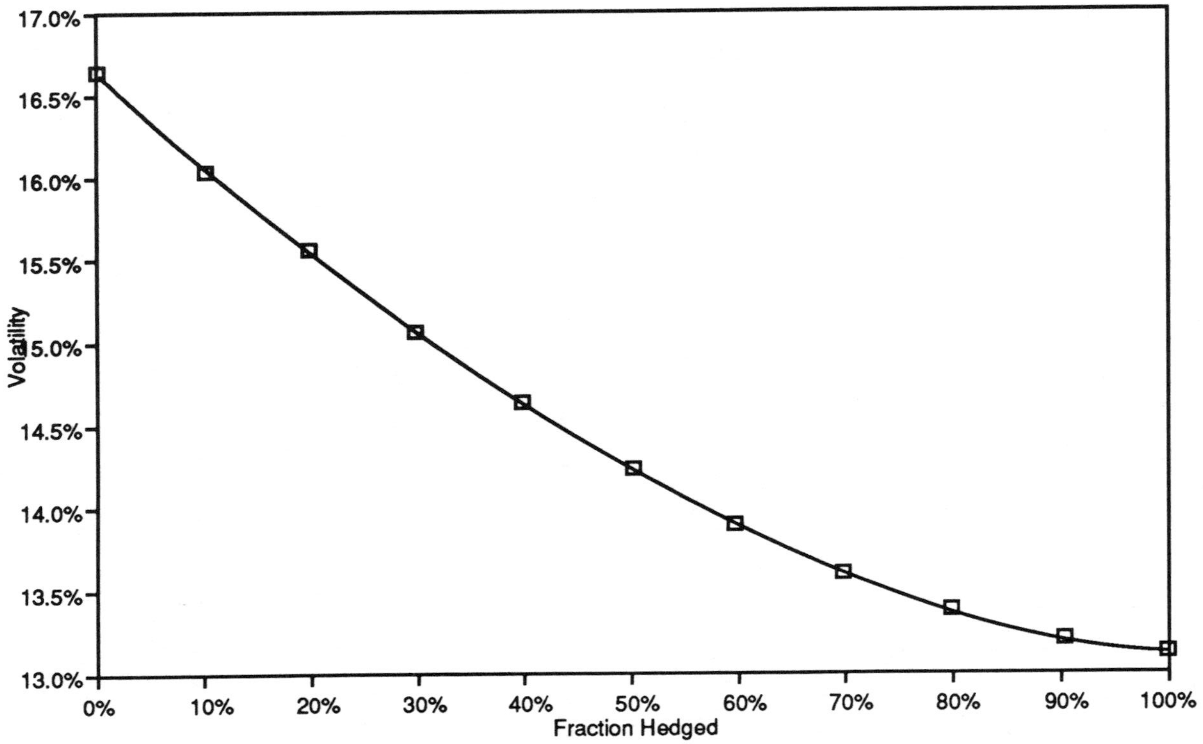

value of your foreign investments and roll the hedge forward at the end of each month. In every case, you sell foreign currency forward for U.S. dollars.

If you choose not to hedge, then your return approximately equaled the local currency return of your security (coupon income plus capital gain or loss, in the case of a bond, and dividend income plus capital gain or loss in the case of an equity investment) plus the percentage change in the exchange rate.[5] If you choose instead to currency hedge, then your return approximately equals the local currency return plus the forward discount or premium on the foreign exchange you sell forward to hedge your position.[6] More succinctly:

$$\text{Unhedged Return} = \text{Local Currency Return} + \text{Spot Exchange Rate Change;} \tag{1}$$

$$\text{Hedged Return} = \text{Local Currency Return} + \text{Forward Exchange Discount or Premium} \tag{2}$$

Comparing these returns, we see that the after-the-fact cost of hedging equals the difference between (1) the actual change in the spot exchange rate while you held your foreign investment and (2) the forward foreign exchange discount or premium that existed at the beginning of the period.

If the realized spot rate turns out to be higher than the forward rate at which you could have hedged your exposures at the beginning of the period, then the after-the-fact cost of hedging equals this difference, plus any transaction costs you paid to execute the hedge. If the realized spot rate turns out to be less than the forward rate at the beginning of the period, the realized cost of hedging is negative. In other words, after-the-fact currency hedging increased the return on your foreign investment. Notice that the investment's own local currency return does not matter. This means that the outcome of your decision to hedge or not to hedge is independent of your other decision regarding which foreign assets to hold. This reiterates a point we made in the introduction—that you can and should make these choices separately.

Before-the-Fact Hedging

Clearly if the realized (after-the-fact) cost of hedging equals the difference between the forward exchange rate and the realized ending spot exchange rate, then logically the expected (before-the-fact) cost of hedging equals the difference between the forward rate and the expected ending spot exchange rate. If the forward discount overestimates the rate of depreciation you expect or the forward premium underestimates the rate of appreciation you expect, then the difference represents your prospective cost of hedging. On the other hand, if the forward rate is higher than the spot rate you expect in the future, then the difference represents your expected profit from currency hedging. In either case, you must pay the transaction costs associated with a rolling forward hedge. Fortunately, for major currencies, the transaction costs are quite low—about 0.15% per year.

To decide whether to hedge, you must first compare the forward rate with your forecast of the future spot rate. The difference, plus transaction costs, is the expected cost of the hedge. You may compare the spot and forward rates on a case-by-case basis, hedge when you expect foreign currencies to perform poorly, and decline to hedge when you expect them to appreciate. We might call this approach a tactical hedging strategy. A tactical strategy is inherently speculative, in the sense that you are betting you can outforecast the forward foreign exchange markets. If you choose this approach, the ultimate cost of your hedging strategy will depend on how well you predict exchange rate changes.

As an alternative, however, you may wish to adopt a strategic hedging rule—one that is independent of particular exchange rate forecasts.

Strategic Hedging Rules: Alternative Theories

There are two simple theories of spot and forward exchange rates you will want to consider as the foundation of your hedging strategy: the uncovered parity hypothesis and the random walk hypothesis. Both are well regarded, and both produce specific estimates of the likely cost of hedging in a given situation. Normally, however, each theory's prediction of your cost of hedging is different. And thus each has different implications for your hedge/no hedge decision.

The Uncovered Parity Hypothesis

The uncovered parity hypothesis is the older theory. Until recently, it was accepted by virtually all international economists. Uncovered parity states that expected returns on similar interest-bearing securities will be equal, regardless of the currencies of denomination. Consequently, the current forward foreign exchange rate, for a contract maturing in one period, represents the best possible forecast of what the spot exchange rate will be one period from now.[7] That is:

$$\begin{matrix} \text{Forward Exchange} \\ \text{Discount or Premium} \end{matrix} = \begin{matrix} \text{Expected Depreciation or Appreciation} \\ \text{of the Spot Price} \end{matrix} \qquad (3)$$

You may be tempted to think this assertion is stronger than it really is. For example, uncovered parity does not mean that the spot rate will actually turn out to equal the current forward rate every time, most of the time, or even any time. The forward rate need not even be close to what the spot rate turns out to be, since it is likely that the "best possible" forecast will be a poor forecast. But uncovered parity does require the forward rate to reflect all known information about how the spot rate will evolve. Essentially, uncovered parity states that the forward rate takes into account everything that is knowable about the future exchange rate.

Roughly, uncovered parity implies that if you bet against the forward rate you will be right half of the time and wrong half of the time. This, in turn, means that: (a) the expected return to taking naked forward foreign exchange positions is zero; and (b) the cost of hedging a foreign exchange position with forward contracts is zero, ignoring transactions costs. Uncovered parity has a strong and obvious implication for formulating a currency hedging strategy.

Hedging Rule #1: If You Believe the Uncovered Parity Hypothesis

Since the forward rate will, on average, equal the future spot rate, currency hedging has a negligible cost; thus, hedging neither increases nor reduces a foreign investment's expected return. But hedging does reduce volatility. Consequently, if your objectives include reducing the volatility of your portfolio's return, you should routinely currency hedge.

Uncovered parity is probably the most studied relationship in all of international finance. It was once widely regarded as virtually an arbitrage relationship: If the forward rate and the expected future spot rate diverge, then speculators will react to the apparent profit opportunity by buying or selling forward foreign exchange until the forward rate is forced back into line. In recent years, however, both theoretical and empirical studies have cast doubt on the validity of the uncovered parity hypothesis.

Critics argue that uncovered parity ignores the substantial risks associated with taking uncovered "arbitrage" positions designed to exploit differences between the current forward exchange rate and the expected future spot rate. If taking currency positions is risky, then it may be that the forward rate can be expressed as:

$$\text{Forward Exchange Discount or Premium} = \text{Expected Depreciation or Appreciation of the Spot Price} + \text{A Risk Premium} \quad (4)$$

Compare this to equation (3). According to uncovered parity, there is no risk premium, and we can drop the second term on the right hand side of equation (4).

But are there reasons why a risk premium might exist? Some currencies may be riskier to hold than others. In such instances, investors must be "bribed" to bear exposures in these riskier currencies; the risk premium represents the required inducement. Identifying which currencies are riskier and thus command a risk premium is complicated, since a currency's perceived riskiness may depend on where the investor lives.[8]

In summary, the major determinants of the size and sign of the risk premiums in forward exchange rates—at least in theory—include the international distribution of wealth, the correlations between exchange rate changes and the returns to other assets, the denomination of the world's stock of outstanding government debts, and how much compensation the international investor will demand in order to take on exchange rate risk.[9] To the extent that these determinants change, we expect risk premiums to change too.

Of course, this only makes it more difficult for international investors to estimate the size and sign of the risk premium before the fact; historical data may be of limited use if the risk premium is constantly changing.

Theoreticians have established that risk premiums may exist, not that they must exist. The historical evidence, however, suggests that they do exist. Out of the extensive research done in this area, we consider some of the most significant findings to be: (1) that the forward rate is a biased predictor of the future spot rate; (2) that the current spot rate is a better predictor of the future spot rate than is the forward rate; (3) that risk premiums in forward rates vary through time; and (4) the average long-run risk premium probably is negligible for most currencies.[10]

In fact, the risk premium varies so much that most of the changes we observe in forward exchange discounts or premiums probably represent changes in risk premiums, not changes in exchange rate expectations.[11] So when the forward discount on a currency increases or the forward premium decreases, it does not necessarily mean that the market has become more pessimistic on that currency's future prospects.

The Random Walk Hypothesis

The empirical finding that the spot rate is a slightly better predictor of the future spot rate than the forward rate suggests using an alternative theory as the basis of your hedging strategy—the random walk hypothesis.[12] This hypothesis proposes that sometimes the exchange rate rises, and sometimes it falls. Each is equally likely. This hypothesis also proposes that on average, the current spot rate is your best prediction of the future spot rate.

To understand the relationship between the random walk and uncovered parity hypothesis, recall that we can represent the observed forward foreign exchange discount or premium in the following way:

$$\begin{matrix} \text{Forward Foreign} \\ \text{Exchange Rate} \\ \text{Discount or Premium} \end{matrix} = \begin{matrix} \text{Expected Change} \\ \text{in the Spot} \\ \text{Exchange Rate} \end{matrix} + \begin{matrix} \text{A Risk} \\ \text{Premium} \end{matrix} \quad (5)$$

The uncovered parity hypothesis asserts that there is no risk premium, so the forward foreign exchange premium or discount merely equals the expected change in the associated spot exchange rate. In contrast, the random walk hypothesis implies that the expected exchange rate change is zero, since the current spot exchange rate—not the current forward rate—is the best possible predictor of the future spot rate. So, under this theory, the forward foreign exchange discount or premium is entirely attributable to a risk premium.

This hypothesis also has important implications for the cost of currency hedging, and thus for the kinds of hedges you will want to use. Recall this approximate relationship:

$$
\begin{matrix}
\text{Expected Dollar Return} \\
\text{to an Unhedged} \\
\text{Foreign Asset Position}
\end{matrix}
=
\begin{matrix}
\text{Expected Return} \\
\text{to the Asset} \\
\text{in its Own Currency}
\end{matrix}
+
\begin{matrix}
\text{Expected Return} \\
\text{to the Currency}
\end{matrix}
\qquad (6)
$$

The random walk hypothesis sees the expected return to the currency as zero. So, under this theory, the expected dollar return to an unhedged foreign asset is approximately equal to the rate of return to that asset measured in its own currency. Further,

$$
\begin{matrix}
\text{Expected Dollar Return} \\
\text{to a Hedged} \\
\text{Foreign Asset Position}
\end{matrix}
=
\begin{matrix}
\text{Expected Return} \\
\text{to the Asset} \\
\text{in its Own Currency}
\end{matrix}
+
\begin{matrix}
\text{Forward Foreign} \\
\text{Exchange Premium} \\
\text{or Discount}
\end{matrix}
\qquad (7)
$$

Therefore,

$$
\begin{matrix}
\text{Expected Dollar Return} \\
\text{to a Hedged} \\
\text{Foreign Asset Position}
\end{matrix}
=
\begin{matrix}
\text{Expected Dollar Return} \\
\text{to an Unhedged} \\
\text{Foreign Asset Position}
\end{matrix}
+
\begin{matrix}
\text{Forward Foreign} \\
\text{Exchange Premium} \\
\text{or Discount}
\end{matrix}
\qquad (8)
$$

Equation (8) states that, according to the random walk hypothesis, hedging generally does affect a foreign position's expected, or average, return. If you hedge, the position's expected return rises by the forward foreign exchange premium you receive by selling foreign currency forward. Of course, if the forward currency sells at a discount, hedging reduces the position's expected return by the amount of the foreign discount. (As before, you must adjust for transaction costs.)

Hedging Rule #2: If You Believe the Random Walk Hypothesis

Thus, under the random walk hypothesis, the effect of currency hedging on the expected return to a foreign investment depends on whether the relevant foreign currency sells at a discount or a premium. For investments in countries where currency sells at a premium to the dollar (typically, Japan, Germany, and Switzerland), hedging generally increases a foreign security's expected return, as measured from a U.S. perspective. Since hedging also usually reduces volatility in these cases, you should always hedge. For other countries, where the local currency sells at a discount to the dollar (historically this has often been the case for Canada, the United Kingdom, and France), hedging reduces both expected return and volatility. In these cases, you must balance the risk reduction afforded by hedging against the reduction in your foreign investment's expected return—that is, against the forward foreign exchange discount.

In summary, both theories of exchange rate evolution—uncovered parity and random walk—agree that if the relevant currency sells at a premium for forward delivery, you should hedge. The two contending theories differ when the relevant currency sells at a discount. According to uncovered parity, you should hedge discount currencies too. The random walk hypothesis suggests that you will want to balance reduced expected return against reduced volatility.

A Common Sense Approach to Currency Hedging

Our discussion thus far makes choosing a general currency hedging strategy seem difficult. You must, it seems, choose between contending theories of exchange rate evolution that even on which professional economists cannot agree. Actually, there is a simple, common sense approach to evaluating the hedge/no hedge decision. Let's look at exchange rate risks more carefully via an example.

Imagine you are a U.S. dollar investor who owns U.K. securities denominated in pounds sterling.[13] If you choose not to hedge the pound exposures embedded in your U.K. investments by neglecting to sell pounds for dollars, you are betting that the return to pounds will exceed the return to dollars. You are making this currency bet independently of your expectations for the performance of U.K. equities or U.K. bonds.

Now consider a pound investor who owns dollar securities. If the U.K. investor simultaneously chooses not to currency hedge his U.S. investments, by failing to buy pounds for dollars, he is taking the opposite side of the bet that you are making. As a pair, the two of you are players in a zero sum game.[14] If you both decide not to hedge, you both cannot be right—one of you will win, the other will lose.

Is there any reason to believe that one of you will be right more often than the other? None whatsoever. In the long run, after making a series of these kinds of bets, the likelihood is that each of you will have won about as often as you have lost. That is, the expected cumulative profit of a long series of such bets would be about zero. (In the next section, we will look at the actual outcome of a long series of pound versus dollar currency bets.)

Ironically, if both of you had chosen to hedge, then each of you would have been better off, because each of you would have stabilized your portfolio's return. If, as we surmised, you lost your currency bets about as often as you won, then by hedging, your only real cost would have been the bid/ask spreads paid to establish and roll the hedges. And among all the financial markets, foreign exchange markets tend to have the lowest spreads.

In summary, currency hedging reduces the volatility of foreign securities for all investors. If it lowers the expected return for some, it simultaneously must be increasing the expected return for other investors. So, by definition currency hedging cannot lower or raise the expected return for the average international investor.

But what if forward foreign exchange rates contain risk premiums? After all, according to the previous discussion, the evidence is that they do. Shouldn't this influence your hedging decision? It should, but only if, when it is time to hedge, you can tell how large the risk premium is—or at the very least what its sign is. If forward rates do contain risk premiums, then sometimes, when the risk premium is positive for the currencies you sell, you pay to reduce your investment's return volatility. At other times, when the risk premium is negative, you are paid to reduce your risk. But if you cannot tell beforehand what the size and sign of the risk premium is, you cannot rationally determine when you are paying and when you are being paid. Nor can you tell whether the payment is significant in either case. Under these circumstances it is difficult to factor the risk premium into your hedging decisions.

Of course, you can try to estimate what the risk premium is on a case by case basis.[15] But then you don't have a general hedging rule, you're back to what we previously referred to as a tactical hedging strategy.

Hedging Rule #3: If You Believe in Common Sense

We recommend what we consider to be a more practical approach: Start with a portfolio in which all your foreign investments are currency hedged—at least conceptually. Then evaluate the strength of your currency views. If you have strong expectations that a particular currency will move in one direction or another relative to the forward rates, then you may wish to express those views by assuming active, open foreign exchange exposures. If not, stay completely hedged back into your home currency. Before the fact, consider foreign investments and foreign exchange exposures separately; after the fact, assess the outcome of your asset choices independently from that of your currency choices.

The Cost of Currency Hedging: Historical Evidence

In the hypothetical example above, we surmised that if, as a U.S. investor, you chose to take pound bets on top of your decision to invest in U.K. bond and stock markets—that is, if you decided not to currency hedge your sterling investments—you would have essentially broken even in the end. Exhibit 4 illustrates the actual results of making this series of pound bets, from 1975 to 1988. Spe-

Exhibit 4   Unhedged Less Hedged Return—Gilts 1975–1988 (Annualized and Cumulative)

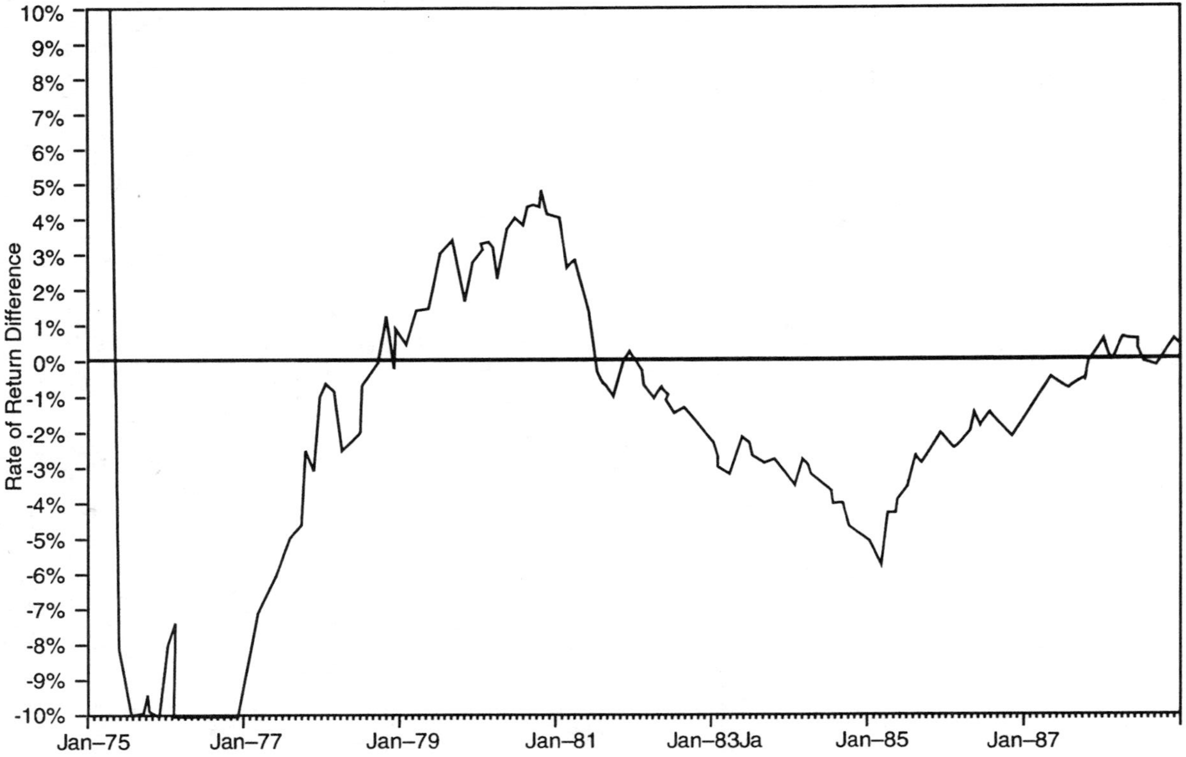

cifically, Exhibit 4 shows the cumulative average return difference (annualized) between a typical unhedged U.K. investment in stocks or bonds and the same investment currency hedged. The analysis is from a dollar investor's perspective.

You can see, for example, that after the first two years, the cumulative average difference was about –1.4%. This means that an investor, who chose not to currency hedge during those two years, earned 1.4% per year less than an otherwise identical investor who currency hedged. Thus, over that time period, taking pound bets turned out to be a bad idea for a U.S. investor in gilts. Currency hedging would have been a better choice.

According to Figure 3, after two years there appeared to be strong arguments that currency hedging increased the return from investing abroad—at least from your U.S. perspective. But remember from our example that this cannot be valid for all investors. If you earned 1.4% per year more by currency hedging pound investments, the U.K. investor who currency hedged U.S. investments during the same period must have earned 1.4% per year less than a U.K. counterpart who did not hedge. So from the perspective of the U.K. investor, the performance data over the 1975–77 period seem to suggest strongly that currency hedging reduced the return to foreign investing.

Who was right? The U.S. investor who decided that currency hedging increases return, or the U.K. investor who concluded it reduced return? Neither, as you will see. Let's look, for example, at the situation after five years rather than two years. As a U.S. investor, you would have earned about 4% per year less if you had currency hedged your U.K. investments than if you had not hedged (again based on a January 1975 starting date). The mirror image must be true for your U.K. counterpart. He would have earned about 4% per year more by covering his dollar exposures back into pounds. Based on these results you might now conclude that currency hedging reduces return, while the U.K. investor might contend the opposite.

With the benefit of hindsight—and more data—we find that neither conclusion stands the test of time. What we do learn is that our opinions of how currency hedging affects the returns to foreign investing will be strongly influenced by the time horizon and starting period we choose for our analysis.

By the end of our simulation period (1988), the difference between the cumulative average returns to hedged versus unhedged gilt portfolios shrinks to only 0.2% per year. This difference is not statistically significant, meaning that a difference of this size may well have arisen merely by chance. In other words if, starting in January 1975, you had taken a long series of pound/dollar bets by not currency hedging your U.K. security investments, then by the middle of 1988 your currency losses essentially would have offset your gains. Similarly, if a U.K. investor had taken a long series of pound/dollar bets by not currency hedging his U.S. security investments, he also would have essentially broken even on his currency bets. Either of you would have done about as well, in terms of cumulative total return, had you hedged instead. But, you each would have enjoyed a more stable pattern of returns.

How do these results compare with hedges in other currencies? Exhibits 5 through 9 illustrate similar analyses for a number of foreign markets, comparing the cumulative average return of unhedged and hedged investments over the same time period. We also look at the results for an internationally diversified portfolio of stocks or bonds. As you can see, for each individual market and for the diversified portfolio, there were large swings between the hedged and unhedged results.[16]

We are actually more interested in whether the cumulative average return differences tend to drift away from zero. This would indicate that currency hedging does affect the average long-run return to foreign investments.

Only in the case of the Japanese yen do the graphs suggest any persistent tendency for unhedged investments to outperform hedged ones. In none of the cases we looked at do hedged investments outperform unhedged investments. All the other single country results and the results for the portfolio stay around zero. The long-run difference between hedged and unhedged returns typically is insignificant.

Take, for example, the results for the internationally diversified portfolio (Exhibit 10). At times the average cumulative return to the unhedged portfolio substantially exceeded the return to its hedged counterpart. At other times the hedged portfolio's cumulative average return was greater. After thirteen and a half years (January 1975 to June 1988) the hedged and unhedged returns proved not to be significantly different, in a statistical sense. Although the results do vary—for the investments we chose, the unhedged portfolio outperformed the hedged portfolio by 1.4% per year—you can see that the maximum cumulative difference or the minimum cumulative difference registered in the past was much greater. In other words, in the long run the average difference is small relative to the short-run swings. Only an observer with a strong bias would conclude from these results that an unhedged portfolio systematically outperforms its hedged counterpart, or that a hedged portfolio systematically outperforms the unhedged portfolio.

Summing Up: Independent Decisions

International investors bear all of the risks domestic investors bear. But international investors who decide not to currency hedge also bear exchange rate risk. Your decision to bear foreign interest rate or equity market risks by investing abroad does not obligate you to bear exchange rate risks, too. In fact, shrewd investors choose the assets they hold independently of the currency risks those assets bear. They neither buy a particular foreign security just to get a currency

Exhibit 5   Unhedged Less Hedged Return—JGB
1975–1988 (Annualized and Cumulative)

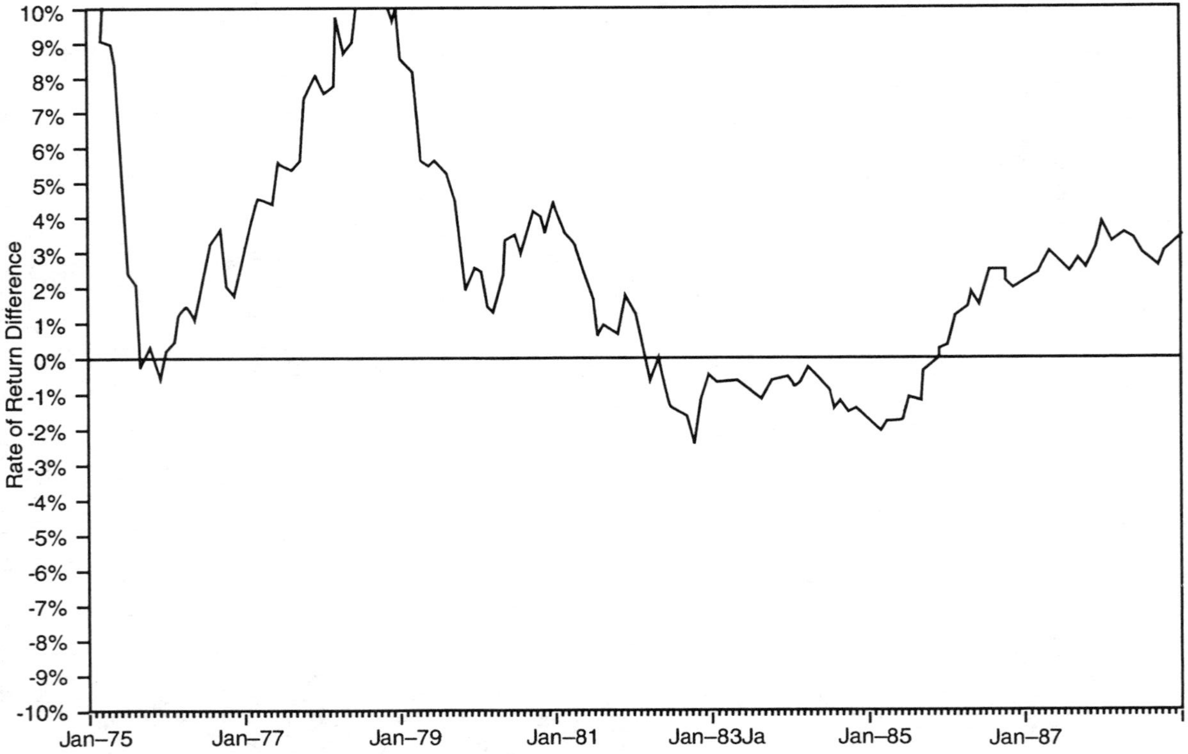

**Exhibit 6   Unhedged Less Hedged Return—Bunds
1975–1988 (Annualized and Cumulative)**

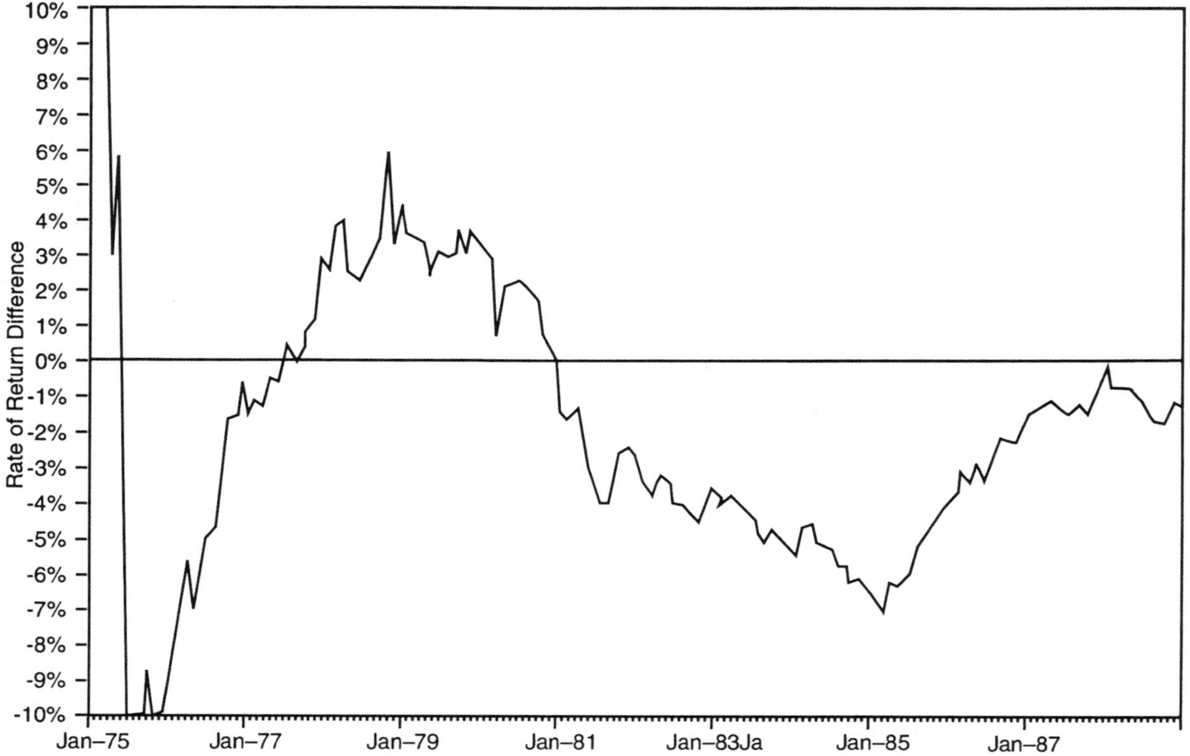

Exhibit 7   Unhedged Less Hedged Return—OATs 1975–1988 (Annualized and Cumulative)

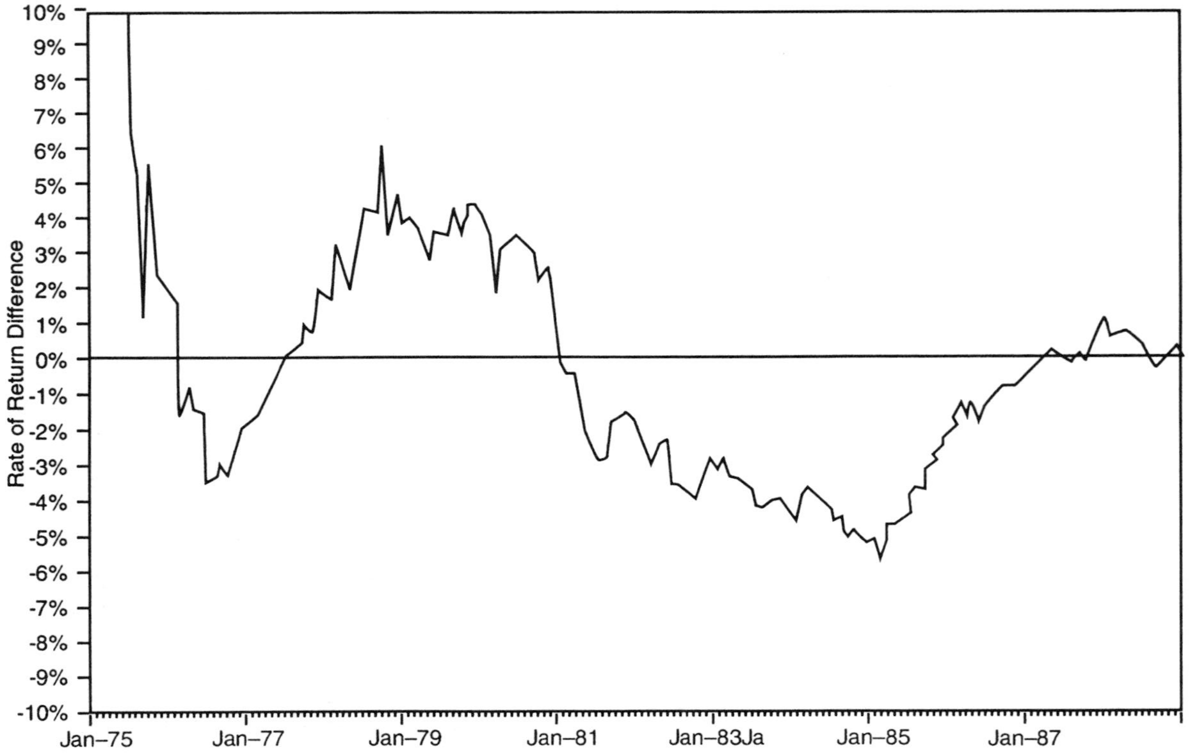

Exhibit 8   Unhedged Less Hedged Return—Canada 1975–1988 (Annualized and Cumulative)

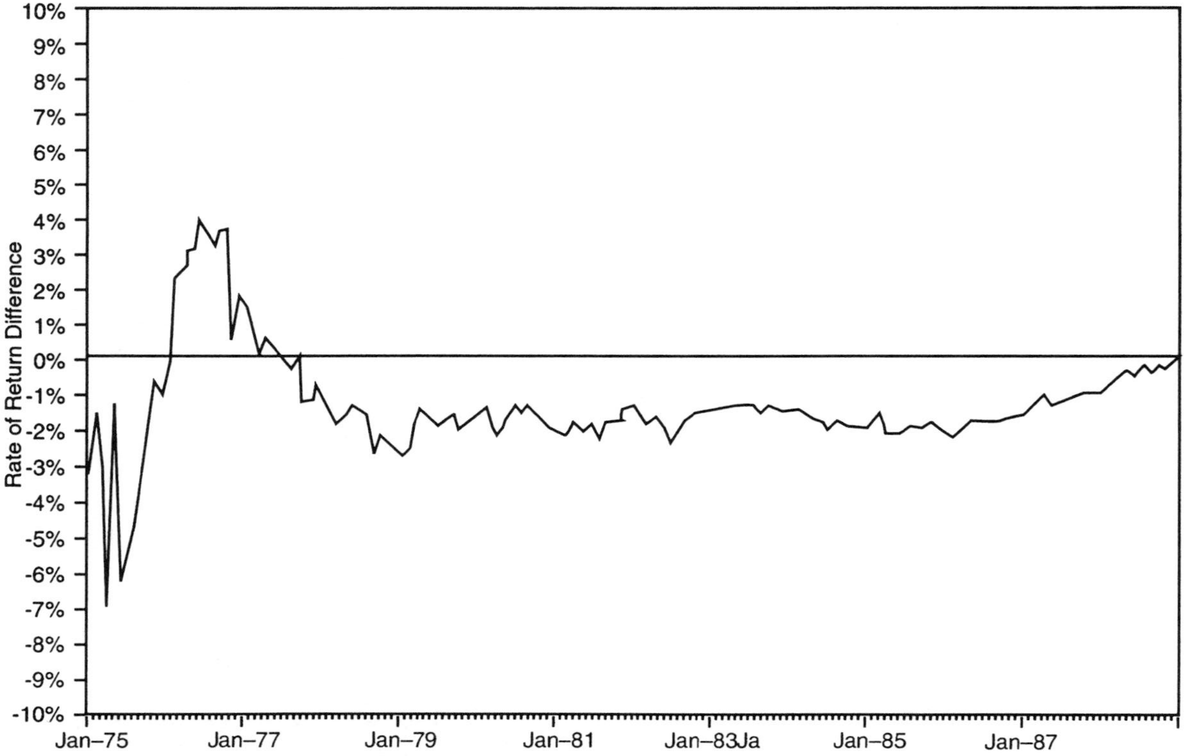

**Exhibit 9   Unhedged Less Hedged Return—DSL
1975–1988 (Annualized and Cumulative)**

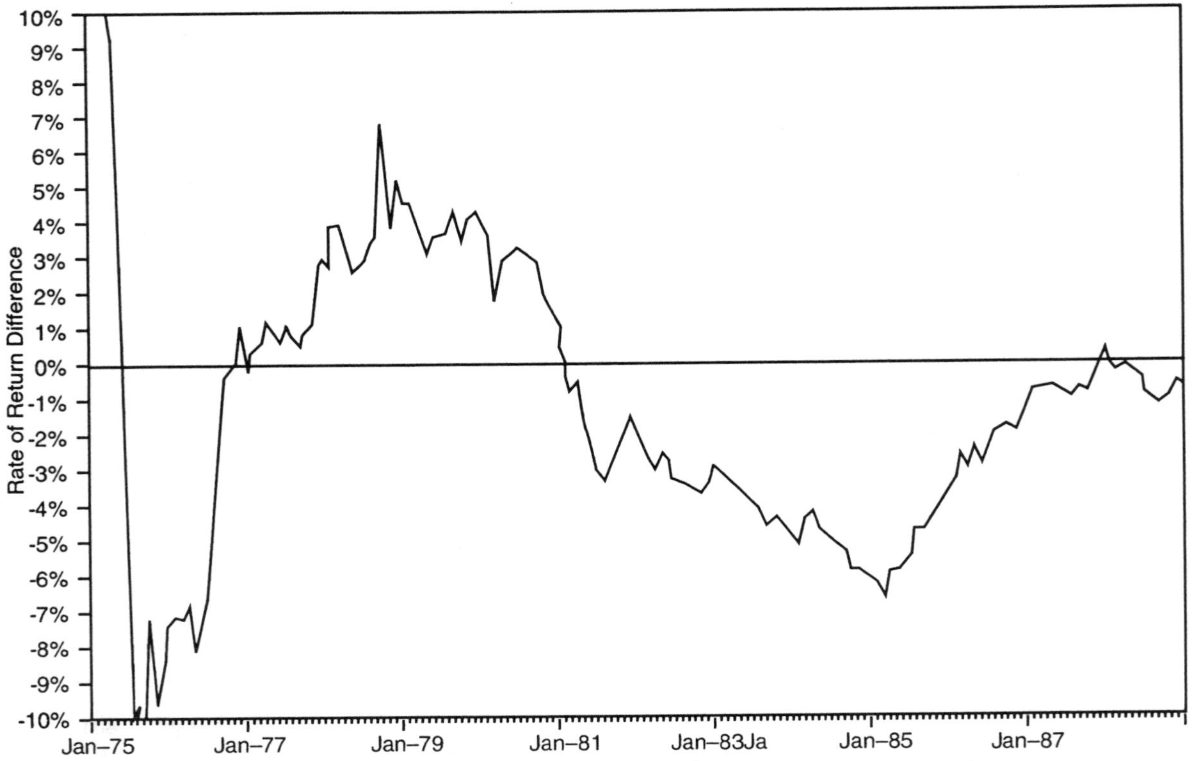

Exhibit 10   Unhedged Less Hedged Return—Portfolio 1975–1988 (Annualized and Cumulative)

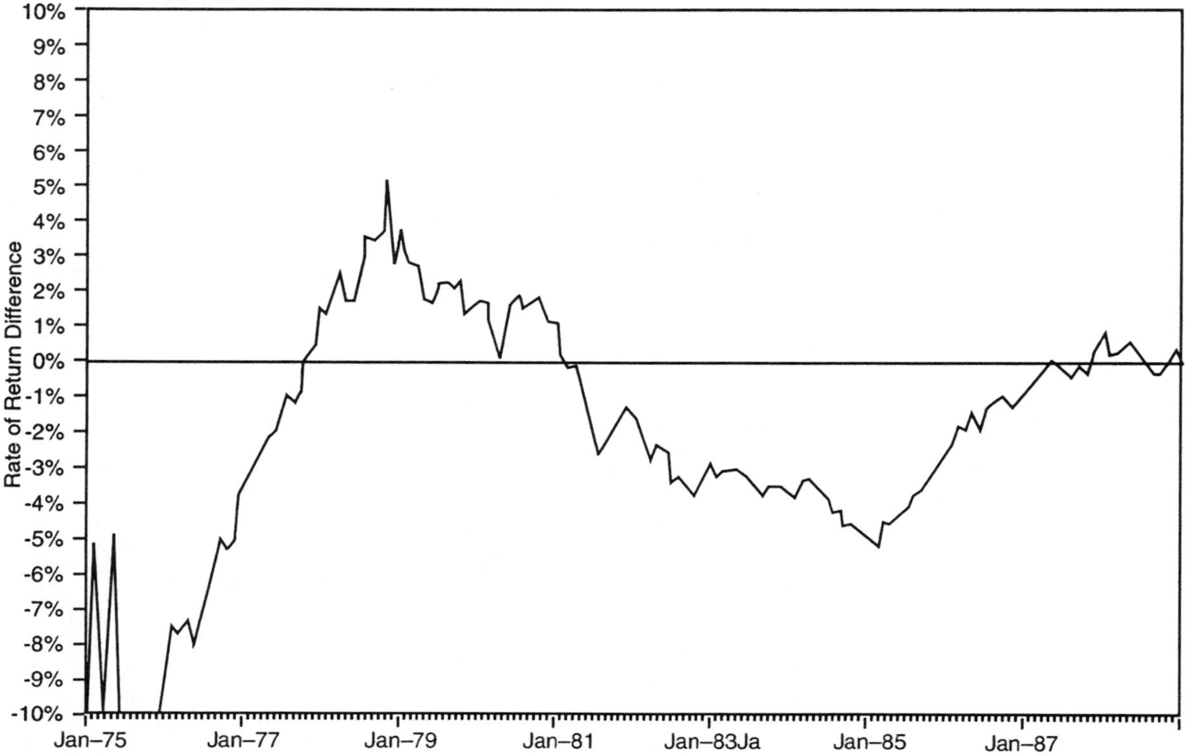

play nor do they avoid an otherwise attractive asset because they don't like the currency in which it is denominated.

In deciding whether your portfolio should bear unhedged foreign currency exposures, you will want to consider two key questions: First, how much does hedging reduce the risk of your overall portfolio in terms of volatility of returns? Second, how much does it cost you to currency hedge?

In the case of bond investments, currency hedging is very important in reducing risk. For a dollar-based investor, return volatility falls by roughly one half if you hedge. This applies particularly to investments in foreign bond markets or to well-diversified portfolios of foreign bonds. In the case of equity investments, exchange rate risk is relatively less important. But even a foreign stock investment's volatility falls significantly when you currency hedge.

Most of this report has focused on the second question—how currency hedging affects foreign investment returns. In essence, there are two costs associated with currency hedging. The first is the transaction cost, which will average about 0.15% per year for major foreign currency exposures. The second—potentially much more important for most investors—is the loss of potential gains from foreign currency appreciation against the U.S. dollar. Of course, if you expect the foreign currency in question to do worse than the forward rate, then this anticipated "cost" of hedging is negative. That is, currency hedging will increase your portfolio's expected return, while reducing its volatility.

There are two approaches you might take to estimating the cost of currency hedging in practice. The first involves forecasting—each period for each foreign currency—how you expect the spot exchange rate to evolve and comparing your forecast with the forward exchange rate. In this case, you hedge whenever you expect the currency in question to underperform the relevant forward exchange rate. You should choose not to hedge or only partially hedge when you expect the currency to outperform its forward. In the long run, your cost of hedging will depend on how accurate your exchange rate forecasts prove to be.

We considered at length another, more general, approach you may choose instead. Rather than forecasting exchange rates on a case-by-case basis using fundamental or technical analysis, you may choose a hedging strategy that does not rely on specific foreign exchange market conditions. Basically, this approach implicitly assumes that all the fundamental (or technical) information you would otherwise use to forecast currencies has been already discounted by the market and is reflected in observed exchange rates. We discussed two well-regarded theories you can use if you choose this non forecast-based approach to formulating a hedging plan—the uncovered parity hypothesis and the random walk hypothesis. Both of these theories conclude that you should always hedge when hedging involves selling premium currencies. For currencies selling at a forward discount, these theories disagree. According to uncovered parity, you should routinely hedge discount currencies, too. According to the random walk hypothesis, you should balance the risk reduction afforded by hedging against the forward discount, which represents an expected cost of hedging.

According to uncovered parity, hedging neither increases nor reduces your portfolio's expected return. The random walk hypothesis implies that hedging is costly for discount currencies, but increases expected return for premium currencies.

In conclusion, historically, foreign currency has not been a good buy-and-hold asset. In foreign currencies getting the timing right is everything. Foreign exchange is a tactical not a strategic asset class. So it is foolish to routinely neglect to currency hedge your foreign investments. The presumption should be to hedge, unless you choose to make a tactical decision to take an exchange rate bet. Then you may hedge, partially hedge, over hedge, or cross hedge, depending on what your exchange rate view is at the time. But choosing not to hedge represents an active decision to take a currency position. You should only make a currency bet after subjecting your exchange rate exposures to the same scrutiny that you insist upon when you make any other tactical investment decision.

Endnotes

[1] See Lee R. Thomas, III, "International Bonds: Stripping Away Currency Risk," Investment Management Review, Vol. 2, No. 2, March/April 1988.

[2] See, for example, Lee R. Thomas, III, "The Performance of Currency Hedged Foreign Equities," Goldman, Sachs & Co., July, 1988; "The Performance of Currency Hedged Foreign Bonds," November 1987.

[3] Andre Perold and Evan Schulman, "The "Free Lunch" in Currency Hedging," Financial Analysts Journal.

[4] The mechanics of currency hedging are described in detail in "International Bonds: Stripping Away Currency Risk," op cit. In our analysis here we assumed you hedged the initial foreign currency value of your position each month, not your capital gains or losses interest or dividends.

[5] To find the exact return, add to this sum the product of the local currency return and the percentage change in the exchange rate.

[6] With our simple hedge design, you remain currency-exposed on your monthly profit or loss on the underlying asset. In practice, with monthly hedge rebalancing this source of risk is insignificant. The exact return to the hedged position can be found by adding the product of the monthly local currency

gain or loss and the exchange rate change to the equation given in the text above.

[7] Actually there are technical, mathematical reasons for defining uncovered parity a little differently. Carefully stated, uncovered parity holds that the logarithm of the forward exchange rate represents the best possible forecast of the logarithm of the future spot rate. This almost, but not quite, means that the forward rate is equal to the expected future spot rate.

[8] For example, whenever the real (or price level adjusted) exchange rate fluctuates, each investor will typically see his own currency as being relatively low risk. So German marks may be a risky currency for a U.S. investor, but a low-risk currency for a German investor. Under these circumstances, whether or not marks command a risk premium may depend on who owns more of the world's wealth—German or U.S. investors.

[9] For a comprehensive and lucid survey of the literature on risk premiums in forward exchange rates, see Robert J. Hodrick, *The Empirical Evidence on the Efficiency of the Forward and Futures Foreign Exchange Markets,* Harwood Academic Publishers, Switzerland, 1987.

[10] On point (1) see Lars Hansen and Robert Hodrick, "Forward Exchange Rates as Optimal Predictors of Future Spot Rates: An Econometric Analysis," Journal of Political Economy 88, October 1980, pp. 829-53; and John F.O. Bilson, "The Speculative Efficiency Hypothesis," Journal of Business 54, July 1981, pp 435-52. Point (2) implies that the random walk hypothesis represents a potentially profitable trading strategy in the currency markets. On this point see Lee R. Thomas, III, "A Winning Strategy for Currency Futures Speculation," The Journal of Portfolio Management, 1985, pp. 65-69; Lee R. Thomas, III, "Random Walk Profits in Currency Futures Trading," The Journal of Futures Markets 6, 1986, pp. 109-24; and John F.O. Bilson, and David A. Hsieh, "The Profitability of Currency Speculation," International Journal of Forecasting 3, pp. 115-30.

[11] See Eugene Fama, "Forward and Spot Exchange Rates," Journal of Monetary Economics 14, 1984.

[12] We use the term "random walk hypothesis" rather loosely in this section, conforming to normal usage rather than to the formal definition in the finance literature. For example, we do not assume that the volatility of exchange rates remains constant through time.

[13] We have only selected pounds and dollars as a convenience. Our arguments apply to Japanese yen, German mark, French franc, and Canadian dollar investors, too—and, in fact, to any pair of currencies we might want to choose.

[14] There is one defect in the zero sum game argument: the central banks appear to be large net losers at the currency speculation game. That means that private speculators have, on net, been net winners. This fact—that the actions of central bankers may make exchange markets inefficient—may make currency markets easier to "beat" than other speculative markets.

[15] For example, when a currency sells at a forward discount the evidence suggests at least part of the discount represents a risk premium. Perhaps—if the random walk hypothesis is correct—all of it is.

[16] This was so even though the effect of using cumulative average returns is to smooth out year-to-year fluctuations in investment performance.

INTERNATIONAL GUIDE TO SECURITIES EXCHANGES

Thomas Carroll, Editor
Peat Marwick Main & Co., New York

Contents

Australia
The Australian Stock Exchange Limited

Belgium
Brussels Stock Exchange

Brazil
Bolsa de Valores de Sao Paulo
Bolsa Mercantile de Futuros

Canada
Toronto Stock Exchange
Toronto Futures Exchange
Bourse de Montreal
Vancouver Stock Exchange

Denmark
Copenhagen Stock Exchange

France
Bourse de Paris

Germany
Frankfurter Wertpapierborse

Hong Kong
The Stock Exchange of Hong Kong Limited
Hong Kong Futures Exchange Limited

Italy
Borsa Valori di Milano

Japan
Tokyo Stock Exchange
Osaka Stock Exchange

Korea
Korea Stock Exchange

Luxembourg
Societe de la Bourse de Luxembourg S.A.

Mexico
Bolsa Mexicana de Valores

Netherlands
Amsterdamse Effectenbeurs
European Options Exchange

New Zealand
New Zealand Stock Exchange
New Zealand Futures Exchange

Portugal
Bolsa de Valores de Lisboa
Bolsa de Valores do Porto

Singapore
The Stock Exchange of Singapore Limited

South Africa
Johannesburg Stock Exchange

Spain
Bolsa Oficial de Comercio

Sweden
Stockholm Stock Exchange
Sweden's Options & Futures Exchange
Stockholm Options Market

Switzerland
Zurich Stock Exchange
Geneva Stock Exchange

Taiwan (Republic of China)
Taiwan Securities and Exchange Corporation

United Kingdom
The International Stock Exchange of the United Kingdom
and the Republic of Ireland Limited
The London International Financial Futures Exchange

United States
New York Stock Exchange
American Stock Exchange
National Association of Securities Dealers Automated Quotations
Pacific Stock Exchange
Chicago Mercantile Exchange
Chicago Board Options Exchange
New York Futures Exchange

Australia

Australia has six stock exchanges/trading floors, located in Sydney, Melbourne, Perth, Hobart, Adelaide, and Brisbane. These exchanges were amalgamated on April 1, 1987, to form The Australian Stock Exchange Limited (ASX). It was incorporated by an act of the Commonwealth Parliament called the Australian Stock Exchange and National Guarantee Fund Act, 1987.

Main Board Market
The Australian Stock Exchange Limited (ASX)
Secretariat's Office
Level 9, Plaza Building
Australia Square
Sydney, NSW 2000
Australia
Telephone: (02) 227 0000

General Information

Types of Instruments Traded	Common and preferred stocks
	Rights
	Options on equities
	Convertible notes
	Fixed interest securities
	Treasury bonds
	Gold, silver, and U.S. dollar options
	Australian futures contracts
Trading Hours	1000–1215
	1400–1515
	Computerized trading continues up to 1700.
	(Sydney is ten hours ahead of Greenwich mean time.)
Market Capitalization	$A212.5 billion (June 1988)
Average Daily Turnover (equities)	$A170 million (January-June 1988)
Number of Listed Companies	Domestic: 1,406
	Foreign: 32
Number of Members	As of May 1988 there were 114 member organizations (76 corporations and 38 partnerships).

Market Indexes	All ordinaries
	All industrials
	Metals and minerals
	All resources
	Gold

Regulatory Authorities:
National Companies and Securities Commission operating through the Corporate Affairs Commission in each state
ASX listing rules

The statutory regulations that govern the securities industry are defined in the Securities Industry Act.

Membership Requirements
Citizenship/Residency and Other:
Nonmembers are permitted to hold up to 100 percent of the voting shares in a member corporation.

One quarter of the directors or two of the directors, whichever is greater, of a member corporation must be members of the exchange.

The majority of the directors of a member must be Australian residents.

Member organizations may be partnerships provided three quarters of the partners are members, or where there are three or fewer partners, at least two are members.

Cost of Membership:
Natural person—$A25,000
Member corporation—$A250,000

Minimum Capital Requirements:
Minimum liquid capital required is the greater of 5 percent of aggregate indebtedness or $A250,000 for corporations and $A50,000 for partnerships.

Insurance Coverage:
Indemnity insurance with minimum coverage of $A500,000

Periodic Financial Reporting:
Annual audited financial statements
Quarterly unaudited financial statements

Trading on the Exchange
Commissions:
Trading commissions are negotiable.

Settlement:
In practice there is no fixed settlement period, although settlement usually occurs within the same calendar month. Transactions are settled with cash against physical delivery.

Fails:
There are buying-in procedures to provide monetary penalties to selling brokers who fail to deliver sold securities within a specified period. Securities may be borrowed from other brokers to effect delivery.

Registration:
Securities are predominantly registered in the client's name. Most brokers provide nominee facilities enabling securities to be held on behalf of clients.

Safe Custody Depository:
There is no central safe custody depository. Brokers normally provide this service for clients.

Market Prices:
Information on current market prices is available through a variety of computerized systems.

Market Trading Systems:
Orders are placed through brokers in their capacity as agents for their clients. As a general rule, brokers deal directly with each other at trading posts on the floor of the exchange.

SEATS (Stock Exchange Automated Trading System)—This system was introduced on October 19, 1987. SEATS allows certain typical stocks to be traded via computer screens in the broker's office rather than on the trading floor.

DBCA (Distributed Broker Client Accounting System)—This system provides for a comprehensive management environment for processing in the back office.

BBS (Broker-to-Broker System)—A new BBS has recently been introduced for the Sydney and Melbourne exchanges, which operates on a trade-for-trade delivery basis. It will first evolve into a national system and then will incorporate a fixed period net settlement discipline, as envisaged with STARS (see the following paragraph). BBS complements STARS.

STARS (Settlement Transfer and Registration System)—STARS is currently under development. It is intended to improve the efficiency of Australian post-trade processing of stock exchange transactions and to ensure that Australian securities markets remain efficient and competitive with overseas markets. The proposed system is a "name-on-register" approach and is similar in concept to the book-entry transfer scheme called

TAURUS now being established for The International Stock Exchange in London. STARS consists of four parts:
- A national clearing system
- A national broker-to-broker settlement system
- A national institutional settlement system
- An uncertified securities registration system

Insider Trading:

Trading on insider information (information not available to the public) is prohibited by securities industry legislation.

Foreign Access
Foreign brokers are generally encouraged, but are subject to ASX approval.
Foreign companies may be listed on the exchange if the following conditions are met:
- Compliance with local listing requirements
- Maintenance of an Australian share register
- Distribution of 200,000 shares to 200 Australian residents
- Full disclosure of all relevant information to the Australian market

The Australian government places few restrictions on Australians who wish to purchase foreign securities. Foreign holdings of 15 percent or more in Australian listed stocks must be reported to the authorities.

Other Markets
Second Board Market
Each of the six state subsidiary stock exchanges has its own Second Board Market. These markets were established to provide a market for smaller industrial companies that would not otherwise be eligible for admission to the official lists of the ASX. The key features of the Second Board Markets are the following:
- The minimum number of shareholders is reduced from 300 persons (and $A300,000 paid-in capital), required for listing on the Main Board, to 100 persons (and $A200,000 paid-in capital) in Sydney and Melbourne and 50 persons (and $A100,000 paid-in capital) on other exchanges.
- Different classes of shares are permitted with differential voting.
- Listing fees are approximately half of the Main Board fees.
- Restrictions may be imposed on the payment of cash as vendor consideration and on the sale, assignment, or transfer of shares issued as vendor consideration.

Australian Options Market
The basic function of the options market is to permit the transfer of risks and opportunities between investors by providing a secondary market in listed options contracts. The Australian Options Market is conducted by the ASX in Sydney. It provides trading facilities in stock options, share price index options, and options over precious metals and currencies. The stock index options are cleared by Options Clearing House Pty.

(OCH), a wholly owned subsidiary of the ASX (Sydney). The precious metal and currency options are cleared by the International Options Clearing Corporation, B.V. (IOCC), a clearing corporation jointly owned by the ASX, the European Options Exchange (EOE) in the Netherlands, and the Montreal Exchange and the Vancouver Stock Exchange in Canada. As of June 30, 1987, there were 348 put and 348 call series being traded in 18 classes of stock options.

Australian Futures Market

In September 1985 the ASX established a new futures market in Melbourne—the Australian Financial Futures Market Pty. Limited. The unique aspect of this market is that the futures contracts (Australian futures contracts [AFCs]) are based on the specific individual listed shares, and all contracts are settled in cash. The AFCs are based on 10,000 ordinary shares and cover 10 major Australian companies. In September 1986 an Australian leaders portfolio contract based on 20 stocks was launched. A gold index contract was also introduced in March 1987 and is the only futures contract based on Australian gold-mining stocks.

Belgium

Belgium has four stock exchanges, located in Brussels, Antwerp, Ghent, and Liege. The Brussels Stock Exchange is the largest and will be the focus of this review.

Brussels Stock Exchange
Palais de la Bourse
1000 Brussels
Belgium
Telephone: (2) 509 12 11

General Information

Types of Instruments Traded	Common and preferred stocks
	Warrants and rights
	Options
	Bonds
	Investment fund certificates
Trading Hours	1130–1430
	(Brussels is one hour ahead of Greenwich mean time.)
Market Capitalization	$US137.5 billion
	(as of December 31, 1987)
Average Daily Turnover	Government bonds: $US16,645,000
	Industrial bonds: $US73,750
	Belgium shares: $US30,869,000
	Foreign shares: $US14,793,000
	(1987)
Number of Listed Securities Shares:	437 (representing 337 companies, 145 of which are foreign)
	Bonds: 151
Number of Members	741
Market Index	Brussels Cash Market Index (Total Return)
Regulatory Authority	Commission de la Bourse de Bruxelles
	Palais de la Bourse
	1000 Brussels

Membership Requirements
Citizenship/Residency and Other:
Members of the exchange must be citizens of a European Economic Community (EEC)

country. They may undertake the function of agents de change in partnership with other suitably qualified individuals. All transactions on the exchange must go through a broker. However, banks are permitted to carry out transactions of more than BF10 million off the floor of the exchange.

Minimum Capital Requirements:
There are no minimum capital requirements.

Insurance Coverage:
No specific insurance coverage is required.

Periodic Financial Reporting:
Annual audited financial statements

Trading on the Exchange
Commissions:
Trading commissions are a fixed percentage of the transaction value. The fixed rates vary by type of security and type of transaction (cash or forward).

Settlement:
Marche au Comptant (Cash Market)—one day after trade date
Marche a Terme (Forward Market)—two weeks after trade date

The Forward Market represents approximately two thirds of total activity.

Fails:
To cure a fail to deliver, the Stock Exchange Commission will intervene to try to settle the trade.

Clearing Organizations:
CIK—Interprofessional Organization for Deposits and Transfers of Securities
La Caisse de Compensation du Comptant
La Cooperative de Liquidation du Terme

Registration:
Securities may be registered in the customer's name or by book entry.

Market Prices:
Current market prices are immediately available.

Market Trading Systems:
Shares are currently traded through the open-outcry, or auction, system. The exchange plans to introduce shortly a computerized trading and retrieval system modeled on the Computer Assisted Trading System (CATS) employed by the Toronto Stock Exchange.

Insider Trading:
Trading on insider information (information not available to the public) is still allowed.

Foreign Access
There are currently no foreign members of the Brussels Stock Exchange. Foreign companies need the authorization of the Minister of Finance to list on the Brussels Stock Exchange. There are no restrictions on the acquisition of securities by foreign investors.

Brazil

Brazil's two securities exchanges are located in São Paulo and Rio de Janeiro. Both exchanges are subject to the same regulatory guidelines, share common listed companies, and follow similar trading practices. This review will focus on the São Paulo Exchange, since it is approximately three times larger than the Rio de Janeiro Exchange.

Due to recent economic reforms, the Brazilian stock market has become more popular as an investment alternative. Securities are generally held by institutional investors with very little participation by individual investors other than indirect investment through mutual funds.

Bolsa de Valores de São Paulo—São Paulo Exchange
Rua Alvares Penteado 151
01012 São Paulo SP
Brazil
Telephone: (5511) 258 7222

General Information

Types of Instruments Traded	Common and preferred stocks
	Options
Trading Hours	0930–1300
	(São Paulo is four hours behind Green-
	wich mean time.)
Market Capitalization	$US28 billion (March 1988)
Average Daily Turnover	$US125 million
Number of Listed Securities	590
Number of Members	83
Market Index	Bovespa index
Regulatory Authority	Comissao de Valores Mobiliarios
	Rua Sete de Septembro, 111–28
	Rio de Janeiro RJ
	Brazil

Membership Requirements
Citizenship/Residency:
Firms eligible for membership must be Brazilian majority-held companies.

Cost of Membership:
The price of a license is approximately $US1 million.

Minimum Capital Requirements:
The minimum capital requirement is approximately $US163,000.

Insurance Coverage:
The stock exchange maintains a liquidity fund for customer protection. Assessments are based on the volume of broker transactions.

Periodic Financial Reporting:
Traded financial institutions—semiannual audited financial statements

Trading on the Exchange

Commissions:
Trading commissions are fixed at rates that range from 0.5 percent for large transactions to 2 percent for small transactions. Additional charges are levied for special transactions such as options or margin transactions.

Settlement:
All trading is done on the floor of the exchange, with a three-business-day settlement for purchases and sales.

Fails:
Fails are subject to fines. The exchange cures fails in excess of seven days by purchasing the undelivered shares at market and charging the breaching broker. Securities may be borrowed from other brokers or clients to effect delivery.

Clearing Organization:
Transactions are cleared by the exchange.

Registration:
Nominal shares are registered by the transfer agent or issuing company in the purchaser's name. Bearer shares are registered only in the broker's name.

Safe Custody Depository:
The stock exchange acts as a depository, holding securities unless instructed to transfer. Banks also hold securities for customers or for their own accounts.

Market Prices:
Current market prices are available on-line by computer and are published in the daily financial news.

Insider Trading:
Trading on insider information (information not available to the public) is prohibited.

Foreign Access

Only Brazilian-controlled entities can be members of the exchange. A few older foreign majority-held brokers are permitted under "grandfather" provisions. Labor laws require that two thirds of the employees be Brazilian nationals. Registered foreigners can hold management positions.

Strict currency exchange controls require Brazilian Central Bank authorization of all remittances. Local investors cannot purchase foreign investments unless the remittance of foreign currency is authorized by the Central Bank.

Other Markets
Brazil has three main commodities and futures exchanges: two in São Paulo and one in Rio de Janeiro. All three exchanges are similar. The following information focuses on the São Paulo Mercantile and Futures Exchange, which began operations in 1986 and has recently been the most active of the three exchanges.

Bolsa Mercantile de Futuros—São Paulo Mercantile and Futures Exchange
Praca Antonio Prado 48
São Paulo SP
Brazil

General Information

Types of Instruments Traded	Stock index (Bovespa)
	Gold
	U.S. dollar
	Deutsche mark
	Japanese yen
	Brazilian Treasury bonds
	Certificates of deposit
Trading Hours	0930–1630
	(São Paulo is four hours behind Greenwich mean time.)
Average Daily Turnover	*Number of Contracts*
	Stock index: 33,000
	Gold: 4,000
	Treasury bonds: 200
Number of Members	225

Regulatory Authority:
The Brazilian Central Bank regulates the activities of the brokerage firms that make up the exchange.

All aspects of membership and trading are as discussed for the São Paulo Exchange.

Canada

Canada has six exchanges located in five cities: Toronto, Montreal, Vancouver, Winnipeg, and Calgary (Alberta). They operate independently of each other and compete for listings. This review will focus on the Toronto, Montreal, and Vancouver stock exchanges, and on the Toronto Futures Exchange.

Toronto Stock Exchange (TSE)
The Exchange Tower
2 First Canadian Place
Toronto, Ont.
Canada M5X 1J2
Telephone: 416–947–4700

The TSE is Canada's largest exchange.

General Information

Types of Instruments Traded	Common and preferred stocks Rights and warrants Options
Trading Hours	0930–1600 (Toronto is five hours behind Greenwich mean time.)
Market Capitalization	Can$738 billion (as of December 31, 1987)
Average Daily Turnover (equities)	Can$396.1 million (1987)
Number of Listed Securities	1,695 (representing 1,208 companies, 61 of which are foreign)
Number of Members	7
Market Index	TSE 300 Composite Index
Regulatory Authority	Ontario Securities Commission 20 Queen Street West, 18th Floor Toronto, Ont. Canada M5H 3S8

Membership Requirements
Cost of Membership:
The last bid price of a seat as of March 31, 1988, was Can$320,000.

Minimum Capital Requirements:
The required equity base varies depending on the size of the firm and the volume of activity. The firm's "net free capital" figure is calculated in accordance with the TSE's Joint Regulatory Financial Questionnaire and Report (JRFQ&R).

Insurance Coverage:
Fidelity bonds
Mail insurance
Brokers blanket bond covering
  • trading losses
  • on-premises
  • in-transit
  • forgery or alterations
  • securities
National contingency fund

Periodic Financial Reporting:
Annual audited financial statements
Annual audited and interim unaudited JRFQ&R
Monthly financial report

An annual audited statement of financial condition must be made available to customers upon request.

Trading on the Exchange
Commissions:
Trading commissions are negotiable.
Settlement:
Government of Canada Treasury bills—same clearing day as the transaction date
Other Government of Canada direct and guarantees maturing in less than one year—second clearing day following the transaction date
Government of Canada direct and guarantees with terms of one to three years—second clearing day following the transaction date
Other securities—fifth clearing day following the transaction date

Securities may be borrowed from other brokers or from the clearinghouse to effect delivery. A cash payment for the securities will also suffice.

Clearing Organizations:
Canadian Depository for Securities Ltd. (CDS)
Trans-Canada Options Inc. (TCO) (options only)

Transactions may occur directly between members without intermediary clearing organizations.

Registration:
Securities may be registered in the customer's name (power of attorney not required), in the dealer's name (in trust for the customer), or by book entry (not designating ownership on the security certificate).

Safe Custody Depositories:
CDS
Vancouver Stock Exchange Service Corporation (VSESC)

Market Prices:
Prices of securities exchanged are determined on a bid and offer basis on the exchange floor. Current market prices are immediately available to the public through on-line computer services provided by companies such as Reuters, Dataline, and Canadian Market Quotes (CMQ).

Market Trading Systems:
The TSE has developed the following five interrelated systems to handle a broad range of trading situations.

CATS (Computer Assisted Trading System)—This is an on-line trading and retrieval system, which at present handles nearly 800 stocks (excluding warrants and rights). There are approximately 300 CATS terminals in TSE members' offices across Canada. The system allows traders to enter orders, monitor their status, execute transactions, and receive printed confirmations of order fills. It also provides access to MOST and LOTS (see the following descriptions).

MOST (Market Order System of Traders)—This provides a fully automated system of handling small client orders for the 800 (excluding warrants and options) TSE floor-traded stocks. It instantly fills market orders for up to 1,099 shares on 86 mainly inter-listed stocks and for up to 599 shares on all other floor-traded stocks. Access to MOST is available through TSE members' order-routing system and CATS terminals. Confirmation of completed trades is received within seconds of the time of input.

LOTS (Limit Order System of Traders)—This system has automated booking and trading facilities designed to handle limit orders, including those that better the bid and offer market. Access to the system is available through TSE members' order-routing system and CATS terminals. When the market moves to the limit price, board lot orders are filled against matching orders from CATS and by traders with offsetting orders.

COATS (Canadian Over-the-Counter Automated Trading System)—This system is an electronic quotation and regulated trade reporting system for unlisted securities trading in Ontario. The COATS computer base and on-line system is provided by the TSE, and the Ontario Securities Commission is responsible for its operation and regulation.

Consolidated Canadian Data Feed Network—This network contains trade and quotation information listed on the Toronto, Montreal, Alberta, and Vancouver exchanges. The TSE acts as an agent on behalf of the other exchanges in capturing, consolidating, and broadcasting the data.

Exchange Links:
To establish cross-border trading the TSE has established two-way electron links with the American Stock Exchange (AMEX) in New York and the Midwest Stock Exchange (MSE) in Chicago. These links apply at present in a limited number of interlisted Canadian and U.S. issues, but are expected to eventually cover many other stocks listed on the three exchanges. The system is also supported by automated links between the CDS and the respective clearing corporations in New York and Chicago. Canadian and U.S. currency conversions are handled by a TSE-developed automatic foreign exchange facility. It allows Canadian and U.S. investors to settle completed trades in the currency of their choice.

Insider Trading:
Local and federal regulations require insiders of a public company or issue to file reports of their holdings of securities in the company. Trading on insider information (information not available to the public) is prohibited.

Foreign Access
On June 30, 1987, the Canadian government enacted Bill C-56, which changed the policy regarding foreign ownership and ownership by banks of member firms holding seats on any one of Canada's exchanges. A federally incorporated and regulated bank, loan company, trust company, insurance company, or cooperative credit association (FRFI) is now permitted to own more than 10 percent of the shares of any class of shares of a Canadian corporation, the activities of which are limited to dealing in securities (including portfolio management and investment counseling), provided that the Minister of Finance gives prior written approval. Other than a foreign-owned FRFI, an FRFI may own all or any number of shares of an investment dealer corporation.

Toronto Futures Exchange (TFE)
The Exchange Tower
2 First Canadian Place
Toronto, Ont.
Canada M5X 1J2
Telephone: 416–947–4700

The TFE began operating in 1984 as an independent exchange managed by the Toronto Stock Exchange (TSE).

General Information

Types of Instruments Traded (The TFE primarily trades futures	Actively traded contracts: Toronto 35 Index futures

and warrants.)	Toronto 35 Index options
	Silver options
	TSE 300 Spot Index contracts
Trading Hours	Toronto 35 Index futures: 0915–1615
	Toronto 35 Index options: 0915–1615
	Silver options: 0905–1600
	TSE 300 Spot Index contracts: 0920–1610
	(Toronto is five hours behind Greenwich mean time.)
Average Daily Turnover	504 contracts
Number of Members	From 1984 to 1988 the number of members has varied from 190 to 192.
Market Index	Toronto 35 Index
Regulatory Authority	Ontario Securities Commission
	20 Queen Street West, 18th Floor
	Toronto, Ont.
	Canada M5H 3S8

Membership Requirements
Citizenship/Residency:
The TFE has no citizenship or residency requirements for its members.

Cost of Membership:
The last bid price for a seat as of March 31, 1988, was Can$3,750.

Trading on the Exchange
Clearing Organizations:
Trans-Canada Options Inc. (TCO)
Intermarket Services Inc. (IMS)—used for silver options. IMS silver options are distinguishable from International Options Clearing Corporation, B (IOCC) silver options (Vancouver Stock Exchange [VSE]). Silver options purchased or written in one market may not be traded or exercised in other markets.

All other aspects of membership and trading are as discussed for the TSE.

Bourse de Montreal—Montreal Exchange (ME)
C.P. 61
800 Place Victoria
Montreal, Que.
Canada H4Z 1A9
Telephone: 514–871–2424

The ME is the only Canadian exchange with specialist traders. There are two different types of membership available: full or associate membership for various products trading. The province's stock saving plan (SSP) entitles an individual resident of Quebec to deduct up to Can$16,000 (in 1988) of the cost of certain stock of Quebec companies purchased in the year and included in an SSP under which the individual is the beneficiary.

General Information

Types of Instruments Traded	Common and preferred stocks Rights and warrants Options Financial Futures Commodity futures
Trading Hours	0930–1600 (Montreal is five hours behind Greenwich mean time.)
Market Capitalization	Can$430.8 billion (as of December 31, 1987)
Average Daily Turnover	8,087,604 shares Can$86,458,056 (1987)
Number of Listed Securities (equities)	1,196 (representing 738 companies, 24 of which are foreign)
Number of Members	83
Regulatory Authority	Quebec Securities Commission/ Commission des Valeurs Mobilieres du Quebec P.O. Box 246 Stock Exchange Tower Montreal, Que. Canada H4Z 1G3 Telephone: 514-873-5326

Membership Requirements
Citizenship/Residency:
The Canadian government now allows greater than 10 percent foreign ownership in member firms.

Cost of Membership:
The last bid price of a seat as of March 31, 1988, was Can$160,000.

Minimum Capital Requirements:
This is "net free capital" equal to a scaled percentage of the firm's adjusted liabilities (minimum of Can$75,000) adjusted by a percentage of futures contracts and a percentage of margin requirements.

Insurance Coverage:
Mail insurance
Brokers blanket insurance covering
  • fidelity
  • trading losses
  • on-premises
  • in-transit
  • forgery and alterations
  • securities

Periodic Financial Reporting:
Annual audited financial questionnaire
Annual audited financial statements
Interim unaudited financial questionnaire

Trading on the Exchange
Commissions:
Trading commissions are negotiable.

Settlement:
Stocks—five business days
Options—next business day after trade day
Precious metals certificates—two business days

Fails:
Brokers failing to deliver securities on the settlement date are charged interest. The ME may, upon request of the purchaser, cure a fail by purchasing the undelivered shares at market, charging the breaching broker. Securities may be borrowed from other brokers to effect delivery.

Clearing Organizations:
Trans-Canada Options Inc. (TCO)

International Options Clearing Corporation, B.V. (IOCC)
Canadian Depository for Securities Ltd. (CDS)

Registration:
Securities may be registered in the customer's name, in the dealer's name, by book entry (not designating ownership on the security certificate).

Safe Custody Depository:
CDS

Market Prices:
Current market prices are available immediately through Reuters, ADP, Starquote, and Canadian Market Quotes (CMQ).

Market Trading Systems:
Order Entry Systems
MORRE (Montreal Exchange Registered Representative Order Routing and Execution System)—The members' electronic order-routing systems are directly branched into the ME's front-end computer system so that small orders of 1,000 shares or less are automatically executed at the best Canadian market price and are reported back to the members' electronic network within 30 seconds.

FAST (Fully Automated Securities Trading System)—This system was implemented at the end of April 1988 to upgrade the present MORRE system. It is most comparable to the Toronto Stock Exchange's (TSE) MOST system. It contains automatic limit ordering for stocks that are relatively inactive or where there is no specialist for the stock. It is also used for active stocks.

On the ME, quotations and trades are sent by computer transmission to various data dissemination firms and to the ME's own ticket network. Data are then retransmitted to the financial communities in Canada and the United States. Reported data include the ME indexes, block trades, most active stocks, option quotations, and trading summaries.

Exchange Links:
The Montreal Exchange/Boston Stock Exchange (BSE) Trading Link enables ME members to direct retail or professional orders for virtually all U.S. stocks to the BSE floor for rapid execution at the best prevailing U.S. price. There is no maximum quantity on orders directed through the link. The BSE is an integral part of the U.S. Intermarket Trading System (ITS), a consolidated trading system that facilitates execution at the best available prices.

Access to the link via its order-routing cross-network features is open to any member of MORRE-Plus or to any ADP Financial Information Network user. For ME members without access to an order-match system, or for ME floor specialists, trading can be achieved via ME personnel on the exchange floor located at the MORRE Support Center. Communication between the ME and BSE trading floors is supported by computer and telephone facilities.

Insider Trading:
Trading on insider information (information not available to the public) is prohibited.

Foreign Access
See the discussion for the TSE.

Vancouver Stock Exchange (VSE)
Stock Exchange Tower
P.O. Box 10333
609 Granville Street
Vancouver, B.C.
Canada V7Y 1H1
Telephone: 604-689-3334

The VSE has a predominantly high-volume venture capital market.

General Information

Types of Instruments Traded	Common and preferred stocks Warrants and rights Options (The VSE trades two types of options: Trans-Canada Options Inc. (TCO) and International Options Clearing Corporation, B.V. (IOCC) TCO trades account for a majority of the options traded on the VSE.)

Trading Hours	Equities: 0630–1330
	Equity options: 0630–1330
	IOCC options:
	    Gold—1130–1600
	    Silver—0730–1600
	    Can$—1130–1600
	    Platinum—1130–1600
	TCO options: 0630–1300
	(Vancouver is eight hours behind Greenwich mean time.)

Market Capitalization (all listed securities)	Can$5.5 billion
Average Daily Turnover (equities)	19.2 million contracts Can$26.8 million

	(1987)
Number of Listed Securities	2,455
Total Number/Value of Contracts Traded (TCO options)	343,539 contracts Can$93.8 million
Number of Underlying Securities (TCO options)	14
Number of Members	49 (unchanged since 1984)
Regulatory Authority	British Columbia Securities Commission Room 1100 865 Hornby Street Vancouver, B.C. Canada V6Z 2H4 Telephone: 604-660-4800

Membership Requirements
Citizenship/Residency:
As of June 30, 1987, the Canadian government removed restrictions regarding foreign ownership in excess of 10 percent of the shares of brokerage firms as well as the ownership requirements of brokerage firms by Canadian financial institutions.

Cost of Membership:
The last bid price for a seat on the VSE as of March 31, 1988, was Can$275,000.

Minimum Capital Requirements:
The required equity base varies depending on the size of the firm and the volume of activity. The firm's "net free capital" figures is calculated in accordance with the Joint Regulatory Financial Questionnaire and Report (JRFQ&R).

Insurance Coverage:
Mail insurance
Brokers blanket bond
National contingency fund–investor protection insurance

Periodic Financial Reporting:
Annual audited financial statements
Monthly unaudited regulatory financial questionnaire
Yearly audited regulatory financial questionnaire

Trading on the Exchange
Commissions:

Trading commissions are not negotiable except where a security is listed on the Toronto, Alberta, or Montreal exchanges. Negotiable commissions apply to transactions in that listed security.

Settlement:
Five business days are required between trade and settlement dates.

Fails:
Securities may be borrowed from other brokers to effect delivery.

Clearing organizations:
TCO
IOCC
Vancouver Stock Exchange Service Corporation (VSESC)

The VSESC has an electronic interface with the Canadian Depository for Securities Ltd. (CDS), which allows book-based security movement between VSESC members and CDS participants.

Registration:
Securities may be registered in a VSE member's name, in a VSESC member's name, in the customer's name, or by book entry (not designated ownership on the security certificate).

Safe Custody Depository:
VSESC

Market Information Systems:
VSE quotations are available through the following systems:

MARS (Marketminding and Retrieval System)—MARS is designed as an interactive quotation service with personal computer user accessibility. The system offers real-time quotation information, a stock-monitoring system feature called Stockwatch, and two years of historical information.

VSE Ticker—This is a one-way raw data feed supplying last-sale trader bid/asked quotes, index levels, and end-of-day summaries. It was developed to be received by a printer/CRT for immediate viewing by the user.

HSVF (High-Speed Vendor Feed)—This is a one-way data feed supply last-sale trade data, bid/asked quotes, index levels, and end-of-day summaries. It was developed to be received, reformatted into a data base and then retransmitted to the user.

CCDF (Consolidated Canadian Data Feed)—This data feed is an amalgamation of the HSVF from the Vancouver, Alberta, Toronto, and Montreal exchanges into a single data flow. This is now available to 20 terminals in Canada, the United States, and parts of Europe.

Market Trading System:
VCT (Vancouver Computerized Trading System)—This is designed to handle 20,000 trades daily at start-up. It is currently targeted to handle trader workstations and can easily be expanded. The current technology permits workstations to be located in any VSE member's office worldwide. It will eventually incorporate 70 percent of the trading volume.

Exchange Links:
The VSE is a member of the IOCC, an international electronic clearing settlement network for commodity options. The VSE is connected with Montreal Exchange and the Amsterdam and Sydney trading markets. The exchange is also linked with U.S. and European markets by CCDF.

In addition the VSE is connected with a service called ACCESS (American and Canadian Connection for Efficient Securities Settlement). It was established by the VSESC and the Midwest Security Company/Midwest Clearing Company of Chicago (Midwest). With its link to Midwest, to the entire network of major U.S. clearing corporations and depositories, and to CDS, ACCESS can service virtually any broker anywhere in either Canada or the United States. Currently, 35 Canadian brokerage houses are members of the system, and daily ACCESS trades average 1,300, worth Can$9.7 million. To use ACCESS, Canadian firms must join the VSESC while American brokers must be official users of the U.S. OTC Comparison System. All North American—listed equity stocks, including those listed on the National Association of Securities Dealers Automated Quotations (NASDAQ) system, are eligible for settlement and deposit via ACCESS.

Insider Trading:
Trading on insider information (information not available to the public) is prohibited.

Solicitation:
It is prohibited for the purpose of trading securities to call on or telephone the residences of persons other than regular clients or those who have requested information regarding a security.

Foreign Access
See the discussion for the TSE.

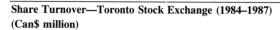

Share Turnover—Toronto Stock Exchange (1984–1987)
(Can$ million)

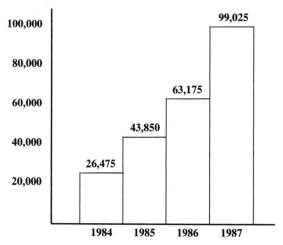

Denmark

Denmark has one stock exchange, located in Copenhagen.

Copenhagen Stock Exchange
2, Nikolaj Plads
DK-1067 Copenhagen K
Denmark
Telephone: 45 (1) 93 33 66

General Information

Types of Instruments Traded	Common and preferred stocks Bonds Options
Trading Hours	1030–1530 (Copenhagen is one hour ahead of Greenwich mean time.)
Market Capitalization	Equities: DKr124,015 million Bonds: DKr376 million (as of December 31, 1987)
Average Daily Turnover	DKr120 million (1987)
Number of Listed Securities	Shares: 433 (representing 280 companies) Bonds: 2,167
Regulatory Authority	Finanstilsyn Borstilsynet Norre Voldgade 94 DK-1358 Copenhagen K Denmark Telephone: 45 (1) 15 56 46

Membership Requirements
Citizenship/Residency and Other: Although the boards of directors and the general
managers of member firms are subject to Danish residency requirements, there is a general exemption for residents of other European Economic Community (EEC) countries.
The Ministry of Industry may grant exemptions to residents of other countries. The
management of member firms must possess industry experience and are prohibited from
managing other enterprises and making speculative personal investments.

Cost of Membership:
Firms with rights to trade in securities granted by the regulatory authority and the Danish Central Bank may obtain membership without charge.

Minimum Capital Requirements:
A member of the exchange must have capital of at least DKr5 million.

Insurance Coverage:
No specific insurance coverage is required.

Periodic Financial Reporting:
Annual audited financial statements are required and are available for inspection. A firm's fiscal year must follow the calendar year. In addition, annual audited statement must be submitted to the Stock Exchange Inspectorate stating that equity has not been reduced from the last fiscal year-end to June 30 of the following year.

Trading on the Exchange
Commissions:
Trading commissions are generally fixed according to a scaled schedule are negotiable for large transactions.
Settlement:
There are three days between trade and settlement dates.

Fails:
If securities are not delivered on the settlement date, trading companies issue a special document (godseddel), which must be exchanged by 1300 following day or the deal is canceled. Securities are not usually borrowed cure fails.

Clearing Organization:
Vaerdipapircentralen
Helgeshojalle 61
DK-2630 Tastrup
Copenhagen
Denmark

The Vaerdipapircentralen clears bonds only; it will begin clearing stock transactions in the near future.

Registration:
Shares may be registered in the customer's or the dealer's name on the share book maintained by the issuing company. Bonds may be registered in the owner's name via the on-line book-entry system of the Vaerdipapircentralen.

Market Prices:
Current market prices are immediately available through an on-line electronic data processing service.

Market Trading System:
During 1987 a computerized dealing system was launched on the exchange, replacing

the old floor-based system. It provides a fully automated on-screen price information and trading system that is interlinked with electronic book-entry settlement.

Insider Trading:
Trading on insider information (information not available to the public) is prohibited.

Solicitation:
Ethics rules of securities traders are restrictive and do not permit advertising as a means of increasing business.

Foreign Access
There are currently no foreign broker/dealers on the Copenhagen Stock Exchange.

Danish citizens may invest in foreign securities with repayment periods in excess of two years; in all other cases, permission must be granted by the Central Bank.

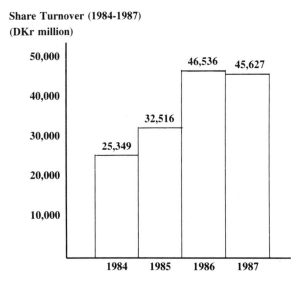

Share Turnover (1984-1987)
(DKr million)

France

The French bourses are located in Paris, Bordeaux, Lille, Marseille, Nancy, and Nantes. French securities with a national or international scale and foreign securities are traded on the Paris Bourse. Securities issued by regional companies are listed on the six regional bourses. No securities can be traded on more than one bourse. This review will focus on the Paris Bourse, which accounts for most securities transactions.

Bourse de Paris—Paris Bourse
Palais de la Bourse
75002 Paris
France
Telephone: 40 26 85 90

General Information

Types of Instruments Traded	Common and preferred stocks
	Bonds
	Warrants
	Options
Instruments Traded on Other Markets	Financial futures (traded on MATIF)
	Commercial paper
	Certificates of deposit
Trading Hours	Public and private bonds: 1130–1330
	French and foreign shares:
	morning session—0930–1100
	main session—1230–1430
	Equities and bonds traded on the
	continuous market: 1000–1700
	Stock options: 1000–1600
	Financial futures (MATIF): 1000–1600
	(Paris is one hour ahead of Greenwich
	mean time.)
Market Capitalization	Stocks: F934.7 billion
	Bonds: F1,954.1 billion
	Options: 364,000 call contracts
	342,000 put contracts
	(as of April 1988)
Average Daily Turnover	Stocks: F2.3 billion
	Bonds: F9.8 billion
	Options: 47,250 call contracts
	65,000 put contracts

Number of Listed Securities	Shares: 857 (207 of which represent foreign companies) Bonds: 2,363 Options: 10 classes
Number of Members	61
Market Index	Indice Generale CAC Actions Francaises
Regulatory Authorities	Conseil des Bourses de Valeurs 4, place de la Bourse 75080 Paris France Cedex 02 Commission des Operations de Bourse (COB) 39-43 quai Andre Citroen 75015 Paris France

Recent and Proposed Changes:
The Paris Bourse has recently undergone significant structural changes to position it to compete with the world's largest stock exchanges and to ready it for the creation of a single European market in 1992. The member brokerage firms have now been authorized to seek outside partners and to opt for a special banking status. Effective January 1, 1988, brokers can sell up to 30 percent of their capital to outsiders, increasing to 49 percent 12 months later and to 100 percent in 1990.

Other key reforms planned for the next few years are:
- The end of the brokers' monopoly on market transactions
- More widespread position taking by brokers on stocks
- Screen trading
- Negotiated commissions

Computer-assisted trading has steadily increased. By the end of 1987 there were 120 shares listed. It is expected that by the end of 1988 all stocks now listed on the Monthly Settlement Market will be traded continuously from 1000 to 1700, and eventually all bonds and stocks traded on the Cash Market will be covered by this system.

On September 10, 1987, the Marche des Options Negociables de Paris (MONEP), the stock options market, opened with trading in options in eight French shares.

The French government's privatization programs and the Second Market activity have shown considerable success. Privatization in 1987 increased the market value of French equities by 10 percent and increased the number of shareholders from 3.5 million to 9 million. The number of shares listed on the Second Market increased during 1987 from 181 to 258.

Membership Requirements

Citizenship/Residency and Other:

On January 22, 1988, reforms were enacted to open the bourse membership. In the past, membership was limited to French nationals with professional qualifications. They had to be appointed by the Ministry of Economy and Finance, be admitted by all the stockbrokers in the general assembly, and belong to the Compagnie des Agents de Change. The member firms were called *agents de change* and had an exclusive monopoly granted by law to engage in securities trading.

The *agents de change* have been renamed *societes de bourse* and are now authorized to seek outside partners and to opt for a special banking status. The *societes de bourse* must be authorized by the Conseil des Bourses de Valeurs. The number of *societes de bourse* will be limited to the existing agents de change as of January 22, 1988, and no new *societes de bourse* will be authorized before December 31, 1992. After that date access to the bourse will be open to other firms provided the Conseil des Bourses de Valeurs agrees to increase the number of seats.

Cost of Membership:

No fees are incurred on becoming a member of the bourse. However, a tax is levied on member firms based on annual revenue.

Minimum Capital Requirements:

No specific capital levels are required by the bourse.

Insurance Coverage:

Stockbrokers are secured by a guaranty fund backed by the Conseil des Bourses de Valeurs.

Periodic Financial Reporting:

While the bourse has no specific financial reporting requirements, general requirements for listed companies in France are:

- Annual consolidated financial statements, including inventory of securities holdings and proposed appropriation of results
- Semiannual financial statements
- Disclosure of investments acquired or controlling interest in excess of 10 percent, 33.3 percent, and 50 percent

Trading on the Exchange

Types of Markets:

The Marche Officiel (Official Market) is the market for the largest French and foreign companies. One listing requirement for this market is that at least 25 percent of the company's shares be available for distribution to the public.

The Marche Officiel is composed of the Marche au Comptant (Cash Market) and the Marche a Reglement Mensuel (Monthly Settlement Market). The Marche au Comptant requires immediate cash settlement and delivery of traded securities. The Marche a Reglement Mensuel requires settlement and delivery at the end of each month. A 20 percent cash security deposit is required. The major and most heavily traded securities are traded on the Marche a Reglement Mensuel.

The Second Marche (Second Market) was established for medium-sized companies with at least 10 percent of their capital available for distribution to the public. As of April 1, 1988, there were 258 companies listed on this market. Trading requires immediate cash settlement and delivery.

All other companies not listed on the Marche Officiel or on the Second Marche are traded on the Marche Hors-cote (Over-the-Counter Market).

The MONEP, the stock options market, opened in September 1987. As of June 1988 options were being traded on ten French securities; this will shortly be augmented by an index options contract. Trading requires immediate cash settlement.

The Marche a Terme d'Instruments Financiers (MATIF) (Financial Futures Market) was established in February 1986 and has witnessed rapid growth in trading volumes since then. Trading is located in the Palais de la Bourse, but the MATIF is an independent market and is not regulated by the Conseil des Bourses de Valeurs. It operates a market-maker system providing for the leading market makers to continuously display their option prices.

Commissions:
Trading commissions are fixed according to type of security, amount of transaction, and time to redemption. A stamp duty and value-added tax are levied correspondingly. It is generally envisaged that negotiated commissions will be introduced to the markets during 1989.

Clearing Organization:
Societe Interprofessionnelle de Compensation des Valeurs Mobilieres (SICOVAM) provides for the computerized delivery of most bearer stocks. Plans are being made to introduce a new computerized settlement system by the end of 1988.

Registration:
All securities are registered by book entry only.

Market Prices:
Transactions are executed at the prices determined under the auction system of trading. Information on current prices is available through the press and specialized publications.

Market Price Regulation:

The Conseil des Bourses de Valeurs is responsible for ensuring price controls. On the Cash Market, the Conseil des Bourses de Valeurs does not allow opening prices to differ from the previous day's closing prices by more than 2 to 3 percent for French bonds or by more than 4 to 5 percent for French equities. If market factors indicate that an opening price will exceed the limit, the Conseil will set a fixed price for that day, with a spread of about 2 percent for bonds and about 4 percent for shares. If less than 20 percent of the orders can be fulfilled at the set price, trading is suspended for the day. On the monthly market, the opening price of securities may vary from the prior day's closing price by a maximum of 8 percent. If the price movement exceeds this limit, trading is stopped. Trading is then resumed later in the same session.

Prices of foreign securities are not controlled by the Conseil des Bourses de Valeurs; they are free to move in accordance with the prices of their home market.

Market Trading Systems:

Computer-assisted continuous trading (CAC) has expanded steadily, displacing to a large extent the traditional floor-based system centered around the corbeille (ring). CAC is closely modeled on the Computer Assisted Trading System (CATS) used by the Toronto Stock Exchange. It allows traders to enter orders, monitor their status, execute transactions, and receive printed confirmations of order fills. Other developments include Chronoval and Topval, on-line data dissemination networks, which provide traders with essential price information.

Insider Trading:

Trading on insider information (information not available to the public) is prohibited and is a criminal offense. Solicitation: Business solicitation is allowed only if the COB gives the authorizing card.

Foreign Access

Foreign access is now allowed on the bourse through direct investment in a societe de bourse.

Nonresidents are free to purchase or sell securities. However, ownership of more than 20 percent of French companies is prohibited without prior authorization from the Ministry of Economy and Finance.

Share Turnover (1984-1987)

(F billion)

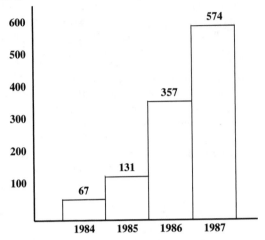

Germany

West Germany has eight stock exchanges, located in Frankfurt, Düsseldorf, Munich, Hamburg, Berlin, Stuttgart, Hannover, and Bremen. Effective July 1, 1986, the eight stock exchanges in Germany united to form the Federation of the German Stock Exchanges.

This review will focus primarily on Frankfurt, the leading stock exchange, which accounts for more than 70 percent of aggregate national turnover in bonds and shares.

Frankfurter Wertpapierborse—Frankfurt Stock Exchange
Borsenplatz 6
D-6000 Frankfurt am Main 1
Federal Republic of Germany
Telephone: 069–21971

General Information

Types of Instruments Traded	Common and preferred stocks
	Warrants
	Bonds
	Securities options
	Currencies (spot only)
	Gold (spot only)
Trading Hours	Securities: 1130–1330
	Currencies: 1300-about 1400
	Gold: 1200-about 1205
	(Frankfurt is one hour ahead of Greenwich mean time.)
Market Capitalization	Shares: DM303.6 billion
	Bonds: DM699.6 billion
	(as of December 31, 1987)
Average Daily Turnover	Shares: DM1.8 billion
	Bonds: DM3.7 billion
	(1987)
Number of Listed Securities	Shares:
	Domestic companies—410
	Foreign companies—310
	Bonds:
	Domestic—5,860
	Foreign—783

Number of Members	Banks: 116 *Kursmakler:** 34 *Freie Makler:** 53 Individuals: 2,288 Total: 2,491
Market Indexes	FAZ index, Commerzbank index, and DAX index, a real-time index of 30 leading shares launched in July 1988
Regulatory Authority	Der Hessische Minister fur Wirtschaft und Technik Kaiser-Friedrich-Ring 75 Landeshaus D-6200 Wiesbaden Federal Republic of Germany

Special Positions:
In addition to the regular members of the Frankfurt Stock Exchange there are members with special positions whose functions are as follows:

- *Kursmakler* are appointed to act as intermediaries between the members on the stock exchange floor and also to calculate and establish the official prices of individual securities.
- *Freie Makler* are appointed to act as intermediaries as well as to trade for their own accounts.

Kursmakler and *Freie Makler* may not have private customers.

Recent Changes:
During 1986 a second-tier market was established. The new market is called the Geregelter Markt (Regulated Market) and has less stringent listing and reporting requirements. At the end of 1987 the shares and profit participation certificates of 68 domestic companies and 2 foreign companies as well as 571 fixed interest rate securities were being traded on this market. A third type of market, the Free Market, operates on the German exchanges, encompassing all shares that do not belong to the Official Market or to the Regulated Market.

Futures trading had been terminated in 1931, but was permitted again to a limited extent in 1970 in the form of options trading in shares and bonds. A major objective of the Federation of the German Stock Exchanges is to set up a well-functioning futures market and futures exchange in Germany to enable institutional investors in particular to engage in selective risk management. A change in the Stock Exchange Act is required for a futures market to be set up. The deliberations regarding the legal form of the German futures market have not yet been finalized.

In addition the German stock markets have instituted fundamental changes to enhance their competitive position in the international arena. These changes include the reorganization of the Federation of the German Stock Exchanges; the merger of the Frankfurt and Dusseldorf computer centers for the settlement of stock market transactions; and an immediate technical linkup of all stock exchanges, giving all stock exchange members throughout the country real-time access to the quotations of the Frankfurt Stock Exchange. Significant construction is currently being undertaken to increase the size of both the trading section of the Frankfurt Stock Exchange and the trading floor.

The incorporation of the six securities clearing banks into one is also being discussed.

Membership Requirements
Citizenship/Residency and Other:
The Frankfurt Stock Exchange has no citizenship or residency requirements for membership. Firms eligible for membership must have an office in or near Frankfurt and be a bank as defined by German banking law.

Cost of Membership:
The admission fee is DM120,000, covering three employees, and DM15,000 for each additional employee registered in the first two years. An annual fee of DM8,000, covering three employees, and DM1,000 for each additional employee is also charged.

Minimum Capital Requirements:
Members (that is, banks) must maintain minimum capital positions of DM6 million.

Freie Makler must maintain a working capital position of at least DM200,000 and a net worth of DM400,000. They must also lodge a security deposit, usually in the form of a bank guarantee, with the exchange in the amount of DM200,000 (DM50,000 if they act as intermediaries only).

Kursmakler must maintain a minimum deposit of DM50,000 with the exchange.

Insurance Coverage:
No specific insurance coverage is required.

Periodic Financial Reporting:
Members that are stock corporations must comply with German commercial law, which requires that they publish annual audited financial statements. In addition banks are obliged to submit annual and monthly balance sheets to the Bundesaufsichtsamt fur das Kreditwesen (German Federal Banking Supervisory Authority) and to the Deutsche Bundesbank (German Central Bank).

Trading on the Exchange

Commissions:

Trading commissions charged by banks to customers have maximum limits and are negotiable. Kursmakler charge banks a fixed commission of 0.08 percent of the transaction value for share transactions.

Settlement:

There are two business days between trade and settlement.

Fails:

In the rare instance where delivery of a security is not made, forced settlement will be carried out by the Kursmakler. Borrowing securities to effect delivery occurs only rarely.

Clearing Organizations:

Frankfurter Kassenverein AG
Borsenplatz 7–11
D-6000 Frankfurt am Main 1
Federal Republic of Germany

Although the main clearing organization is Frankfurter Kassenverein AG, clearing functions are also provided by the regional offices of the Landeszentralbanken (Federal Central Bank) as well as by the Borsendatenzentrale (BDZ) (the data center of the Frankfurt Stock Exchange). Major aspects of the capital services system (KADI) of the security-clearing associations are currently being overhauled.

Although there is no requirement that all trades be reported on the exchange floor, they do have to be cleared at a clearing organization.

Registration:

Nearly all German officially listed stocks are "bearer" shares; therefore, registration is fairly uncommon. Registered shares are not yet integrated into the clearing system. However, most insurance stocks are registered and can only be transferred with the prior consent of the issuer.

Safe Custody Depository:

Banks may act as safe custody depositories. However, most securities are maintained in the custody of the clearing institutions (Kassenvereine).

Market Prices:

Current market prices and key exchange data are indicated by monitors (CRTs) linked with an electronic, real-time price information service system called Kurs Information und Service System (KISS) available to market participants. A list of prices (Kursblatt) is also available to the public at the end of each day.

Market Trading Systems:
Prices of securities exchanged are determined on a bid and offer basis on the exchange floor. For all shares with a narrow market, the price is fixed by the official Kursmakler once per day. Shares that are traded more frequently are subject to continuous trading throughout the session, using variable prices. Once the transaction price has been determined, the official broker enters the price into KISS through an input terminal.

The exchange is currently developing a new electronic order-routing system (BOSS), which would involve the electronic routing of orders from brokers to the trading floor to improve the order flow.

Insider Trading:
Trading on insider information (information not available to the public) is prohibited by a voluntary code of conduct. The Proposal for a Council Directive on Coordinating Regulations Concerning Insider Trading by the European Economic Community (EEC) Commission envisages minimal legislative regulations to prevent insider trading. The German government, the German Central Bank, and the Federation of the German Stock Exchanges have, however, voiced their considerable reservations. Their objections relate in particular to the obligations of the member states to create legislative norms to prevent insider trading.

Foreign Access
There are approximately 30 foreign banks that are members of the Frankfurt Stock Exchange. A foreign broker/dealer may become a member by establishing a branch or subsidiary in Frankfurt that is recognized by German banking authorities as a bank. There are no restrictions on foreign holdings in German companies, although stakes of more than 25 percent must be disclosed.

Share Turnover–All German Exchanges (1984–1987)
(DM billion)

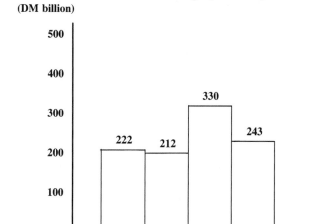

Hong Kong

In April 1986 Hong Kong's four stock exchanges (Hong Kong, Far East, Kam Ngan, and Kowloon) were consolidated into a single body. The Stock Exchange of Hong Kong Limited, commonly known as the Unified Stock Exchange.

The Stock Exchange of Hong Kong Limited (SEHK)
One Exchange Square, Central
Hong Kong
Telephone: (5) 221122

General Information

Types of Instruments Traded	Common and preferred stocks Warrants and rights Unit trusts Debt securities
Trading Hours	1000–1230 1430–1530 Monday-Friday (Hong Kong is eight hours ahead of Greenwich mean time.)
Market Capitalization	HK$519 billion (as of March 31, 1988)
Average Daily Turnover	HK$1.1 billion (based on trading during March 1988)
Number of Listed Securities	432
Number of Members	789
Market Indexes	Hang Seng Index (33 stocks) Hong Kong Index (49 stocks)
Regulatory Authority	Securities Commission Two Exchange Square, 38th Floor Central Hong Kong

Proposed Changes:
The Securities Review Committee, set up by the government shortly after the four-day closure of the exchange in October 1987, has proposed a number of reforms to restore investor confidence. These include creating a new regulatory authority under more professional management, introducing a computerized central clearing and settlement system, establishing new settlement procedures (settlement to be made within three days of

a deal), setting up basic minimum capital and liquidity rules for securities and futures intermediaries, reforming disclosure rules, and establishing new listing arrangements.

Membership Requirements

Citizenship/Residency and Other:
The Securities Ordinance requires all persons engaged in securities trading to be registered. To be accepted for registration, individuals must either have a minimum of three years' relevant work experience with a major exchange or pass a qualifying examination.

Corporate members must be incorporated in Hong Kong. Individual members must be born in Hong Kong or be residents of Hong Kong for five of the seven years preceding application, unless otherwise authorized by the Securities Commission.

Cost of Membership:
Membership is obtained by purchasing a seat, which costs HK$100,000 for the nominal value of an SEHK share plus a nonrefundable application fee of HK$5,000. The cost of transfer by private negotiation is currently around HK$600,000.

Minimum Capital Requirements:
Minimum net capital requirements vary by type of membership. Individuals must maintain a minimum net capital (defined as "approved assets" less "ranking liabilities") of HK$1 million for each share held.

Corporations must maintain a minimum net capital of HK$5 million or HK$1 million times the number of shares held if more than five. Dealing partnerships must maintain minimum net capital computed by aggregating calculations for individuals and corporations as previously described, according to their proportionate interests in the partnership.

All members are required to maintain a liquidity margin of at least 10 percent of their respective minimum capital requirements.

Fidelity Fund:
All members dealing in securities must participate in an exchange-established fidelity fund or alternatively furnish to the exchange a bank guarantee or similar guarantee for HK$2 million. This guarantee is to insure against pecuniary losses suffered as a result of the failure of any other member to honor obligations incurred as part of its business of dealing in securities. An initial deposit of HK$50,000 is required from each participating member, as well as pro rata (shareholdings) contributions to replenish the fund after any payments are made. Compensation payments from the fund are limited to HK$2 million in respect of each default.

The Securities Commission has also established the Unified Exchange Compensation Fund, which covers third parties other than stockbrokers for losses suffered as a result of a stockbroker's default. Initial deposits of HK$50,000 per membership, as well as any further deposits paid by the exchange to the Securities Commission to replenish payments made, are levied upon members in proportion to the number of shares held in the exchange. Compensation is limited to HK$2 million in respect of each stockbroker concerned.

Periodic Financial Reporting:
Annual audited financial statements
Quarterly schedules of approved and liquid assets, ranking liabilities, net capital, and liquidity margin

Trading on the Exchange
Commissions and Levies:
Trading commissions are negotiable, with a minimum level of 0.25 percent of transaction value. No rebates are allowed. Handling charges on registration of share certificates may be levied at a rate of HK$2 per board lot. A special transaction levy of 0.03 percent on the valuation of transactions, which is borne by the client, is payable to the SEHK.

Settlement:
Delivery and payment must be effected by 1545 on the business day following the trade. For transactions made on the day preceding the first date of ex-all quotation of the securities, delivery and payment must be effected by 1200 on the trading day following the transaction.

Fails:
In the event securities are not delivered as scheduled, the nondefaulting party must report the fail to the exchange. The SEHK may then instruct the broker in default to make delivery within a specified time period. Failure to comply will result in the defaulting broker's absorption of all price differentials and incidental expenses.

Securities may be borrowed from other brokers to effect delivery provided that the lending brokers have full title to the securities or possess the written authorization of the owner of the securities.

Clearing Organization:
There is no central clearing organization.

Registration:
Securities may be registered in the name of the customer, in the name of the dealer's nominee, or in street name. However, registration is generally in street name, thereby avoiding the long processing time required to register securities in the customer's name.

Safe Custody Depository:
There is no central safe custody depository. Securities registered in street name must be

deposited in safe custody in a designated account with the dealer's bankers or with any other institution approved by the Commissioner for Securities.

Market Prices:
Current market prices are available immediately through Viewdata Services, provided by Communication Services Ltd., a subsidiary of Hong Kong Telephone Company Limited. Information regarding each quoted stock includes the previous closing and current nominal prices, the day's highest and lowest prices, and the current turnover. In addition the Hang Seng Index and the trading data of the Future Hang Seng Contract are updated every minute and displayed on the system.

Market Trading System:
All securities trading is executed in the trading hall of the exchange through a computer-assisted auction system. Buy and sell orders placed with a broker are transmitted to a floor trader, who inputs the order using a computer terminal. The order is then displayed on all the terminals in the trading hall. Any negotiations over quantities to be transacted take place over the private internal telephone system.

Insider Trading:
Trading on insider information (information not available to the public) is prohibited.

Solicitation:
Members may not advertise without the prior written consent of the SEHK committee.

Foreign Access
Technically there are no foreign members of the SEHK. Foreign firms may trade on the SEHK, however, by establishing a Hong Kong subsidiary, by staffing a branch office with resident directors/employees who are members, by forming a partnership with a member, or by using intermediary brokers. There are generally no restrictions on foreign share ownership.

Hong Kong Futures Exchange Limited (HKFE)
Room 911, New World Tower
16–18 Queen's Road, Central
Hong Kong
Telephone: (5) 251005

The HKFE, originally called the Hong Kong Commodity Exchange Ltd., was incorporated in 1976.

General Information

Types of Instruments Traded	Stock index futures (Hang Seng Index)
	Commodities futures (sugar, soybeans, and gold)

Trading Hours	1000–1230
	1430–1530
	(Hong Kong is eight hours ahead of
	Greenwich mean time.)

Average Daily Turnover

Number of Contracts
Hang Seng Index: 626
Sugar: 668
Soybeans: 1,604
Gold: 8
(as of March 1988)

Number of Members

Full members: 71
Market members: 21
Floor members: 0
Trade-affiliated members: 32
Total: 124

Regulatory Authority

Commodities Trading Commission
Two Exchange Square, 38th Floor
Central
Hong Kong

Proposed Changes:
The board of the HKFE has resolved that a three-month Hong Kong dollar interest rate contract be introduced during 1988. The contract, on which preliminary work was begun in 1987, is to be the first in a series of new financial futures products to be offered by the HKFE in an effort to diversify its product range and to widen its member and investor base. The Securities Review Committee has also made a number of recommendations regarding the trading controls and surveillance of the exchange over the futures markets, including the creation of an improved risk management system and a guarantee backed by members of the exchange. In reaction to the October 1987 market crash, the exchange has introduced new capital requirements, tighter compliance rules, and more stringent margins and position limits.

Membership Requirements
Types of Membership:
Full members are companies or individuals who are entitled to trade free of commission on all commodity market divisions and who must hold one ordinary share (par value HK$100,000) of the HKFE.

Market members are companies or individuals who are entitled to trade free of commission in one commodity market division, unless granted approval for other divisions, and who hold one standard share (par value HK$25,000) of the HKFE.

Floor members are individuals who are entitled to trade on one or more commodity market divisions for their own accounts, who will not trade for any clients, and who must hold one ordinary share or one standard share of the HKFE.

Trade-affiliated members are companies that must place all trades through full or market members and that are not qualified to hold shares of the HKFE. No individuals qualify as trade-affiliated members.

Citizenship/Residency:
Full and market members must be companies incorporated in Hong Kong or individuals ordinarily resident in Hong Kong. Trade-affiliated members must be firms or corporations established outside Hong Kong that have a bona fide interest in the production, marketing, or processing of or trading in a commodity.

Minimum Capital Requirements:
Full and market members (both corporate and individual) who do not trade in Hang Seng Index futures must maintain at least HK$2 million in paid-up capital.

Effective March 31, 1988, full or market members who trade in the stock index market, or in any other financial futures market that may thereafter be introduced by the HKFE, must maintain at least HK$5 million in paid-up capital. The general manager of the futures exchange may extend the deadline to December 31, 1988, for individual members applying in writing. Individual members who fail to comply with the minimum capital requirements must cease all trading in Hang Seng Index futures contracts or make application to the HKFE to continue to trade as a floor member.

Every full or market member must maintain a maximum debt-to-equity ratio of 2:1.

Floor members must have capital of not less than HK$500,000 and maintain a maximum debt-to-equity ratio of 2:1.

Trade-affiliated members have no particular capital requirements.

Compensation Fund:
The Compensation Fund, or the Fund, has been established to cover defaults committed by members of the HKFE in connection with futures contracts business traded on the exchange. Any person suffering a pecuniary loss because of a default committed by a shareholder of the HKFE relating to business in futures contracts traded on the exchange can claim compensation. The maximum coverage provided by the Fund is HK$2 million per shareholder.

Immediately after the stock market crash in October 1987 the Hong Kong government announced a rescue package of HK$4 billion to support the futures market. It is a "drawing facility" that enables the Hong Kong Futures Guarantee Corporation Ltd. to finance the settlements of its obligations to members of the HKFE in respect of new and existing Hang Seng Index contracts.

Periodic Financial Reporting:
Every full, market, or floor member is required to submit to the HKFE annual audited financial statements and monthly financial returns, on prescribed forms.

Exchange members are required to report to the HKFE within 24 hours, in prescribed form, any client who acquires or accumulates 100 open positions in the Hang Seng Index Contract in any one contract month.

Trading on the Exchange (Hang Seng Index futures trading only)
Commissions:
Trading commissions are negotiable above a minimum set by the Indices Committee. The minimums are currently HK$60 for day trades and HK$100 for overnight trades.

Settlement:
Cash settlements must be made by 1000 on the second business day following the last trading day of the cash settlement month (cash settlement day).

Clearing Organizations:
International Commodities Clearing House (Hong Kong) Ltd. Hong Kong Commodities Guarantee Corp. Ltd.

Market Prices:
Market prices are available immediately through Reuters, UPI, and other media channels. The HKFE also issues daily and weekly market reports to the public.

Market Trading System:
The auction system is employed whereby transactions are executed on boards displaying bid and offer prices.

Solicitation:
Members may not advertise, publish, or circulate any material without the prior consent of the HKFE.

Foreign Access
The HKFE currently has 32 foreign trade-affiliated members. A trade-affiliated membership must be proposed and seconded by a full or market member. A foreign firm may become a full or market member by establishing a subsidiary incorporated in Hong Kong. It may become a trade-affiliated member by being incorporated outside of Hong Kong and having a business interest in trading commodities.

Share Turnover–The Stock Exchange of Hong Kong (1984—1987)
(HK$ million)

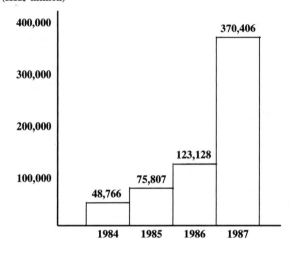

Italy

The ten securities exchanges in Italy are located in Milan, Rome, Turin, Genoa, Bologna, Florence, Naples, Palermo, Trieste, and Venice. This review will focus on Milan, the largest exchange.

Borsa Valori di Milano—Milan Exchange
Piazza Affari, 4 20100
Milan
Italy
Telephone: 02-85341

General Information

Types of Instruments Traded	Common and preferred stocks Warrants Bonds
Trading Hours	1000–1345 (Milan is one hour ahead of Greenwich mean time.)
Market Capitalization	Lit141,000 billion (May 1988)
Average Daily Turnover	Stock: Lit100 billion Bonds: Lit100 billion (May 1988)
Number of Listed Securities	346 (representing 229 companies)
Number of Members	Brokers (agenti di cambio): 124 Broker/dealers (commissionarie di borsa): 110
Market Indexes	BCI index MIB index
Regulatory Authority	Commissione Nazionale per la Societa e la Borsa (CONSOB) Via Isonzo, 16 00100 Rome Italy

Membership Requirements
Types of Membership:
Agenti di cambio—brokers or market makers who trade only with broker/dealers and not on behalf of customers

---

Commissionarie di borsa—broker/dealers who trade on their own behalf or on behalf of third parties

Citizenship/Residency:
Firms eligible for membership must be of Italian citizenship.

Cost of Membership:
Agenti di cambio are public officials. Seats are not transferable and are obtained by passing a public examination.

Commissionarie di borsa seats may be purchased from the Commissione di Borsa for an average cost of approximately Lit650 million. There are no auction sales for seats.

Minimum Capital Requirements:
Brokers—none
Broker/dealers—Lit500 million

Insurance Coverage:
No specific insurance coverage is required.

Periodic Financial Reporting:
Brokers—none
Broker/dealers—annual audited financial statements; semiannual unaudited financial statements (available for public inspection)

Trading on the Exchange
Commissions:
Trading commissions are fixed at 0.7 percent plus stamp duty for stocks, 0.3 percent plus stamp duty for bonds, and 0.15 percent plus stamp duty for Treasury bonds. Stamp duties vary according to the type of security and time, ranging from 0.06 percent to 0.1 percent.

Settlement:
Stocks and warrants are traded on an account system similar to that of The International Stock Exchange in London, with 15 to 45 days between trade and settlement. The settlement period currently averages about six weeks. Bonds have three days between trade and settlement.

Fails:
If securities are not delivered and if the seller is a bank, the clearing organization authorizes the issuance of a buono cassa (an instrument representing a valid claim to the securities at a bank branch). If the seller is not a bank, a similar instrument will be issued against the deposit of 130 percent of the securities' value.

Clearing Organization:
Stanza di Compensazione della Banca d'Italia

Transactions can take place between brokers without intermediary clearing organizations.

Registration:
Securities must be registered in the customer's name for stock transactions. Bonds may be registered in the customer's name or to the bearer.

A book-entry system is applied for certain stocks through Montetitoli, a limited company owned by many banks. Most bond transactions are recorded through book entry by Gestione Centralizzata, a company owned by the Bank of Italy.

Safe Custody Depository:
A safe custody depository service is provided by Montetitoli, if specifically required, to all members of the exchange and to shareholders.

Market Prices:
Current market prices are available immediately through the Reuters service.

Market Trading System:
At present most securities are traded at a fixed time each day, and daily prices are fixed at the end of each security trading period. This auction-based system is known as trading en corbeille, corbeille (ring) being the place where such trading takes place. A significant amount of trading also occurs off the exchange floor. This system is scheduled to be replaced in 1989 with a continuous trading system.

Insider Trading:
Trading on insider information (information not available to the public) is still legal, although the regulatory authorities have proposed that it be prohibited.

Solicitation:
There are no formal restrictions regarding advertising except for ethics rules. Solicitation of public savings is strictly regulated by CONSOB.

Foreign Access
There are no foreign members currently on any of the Italian stock exchanges because of the regulation restricting membership to Italian citizens. Foreign broker/dealers can establish subsidiaries but must use intermediary brokers to purchase securities. The commission for such trades would range from 0.8 percent to 1 percent inclusive of stamp duty.

No restrictions are placed on the purchase of foreign securities by local companies and individuals with the exception of options, futures, unlisted stocks, and non-OCSE bonds.

There are no restrictions on share ownership by foreigners, although holdings of more than 2 percent must be disclosed.

Share Turnover (1984–1987)
(lit billion)

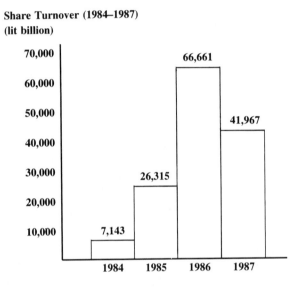

Japan

Japan has eight stock exchanges, located in Tokyo, Osaka, Nagoya, Kyoto, Hiroshima, Fukuoka, Niigata, and Sapporo. This review will focus on the Tokyo Stock Exchange, which accounts for over 80 percent of all the business conducted on Japan's stock exchanges. A brief outline is also given of the Osaka Stock Exchange, which is both Japan's second largest and the world's third largest stock market.

Tokyo Stock Exchange (TSE)
1-1, Nihonboshi Kayaba-cho 2-chome
Cho-ku, Tokyo 103
Japan
Telephone: 03-666-0141

General Information

Types of Instruments Traded	Common and preferred stocks Bonds Warrants Government bond futures
Trading Hours	Bonds of Foreign Issuers Monday—Friday: 1000–1030 1400–1430 Saturday: 1000–1030* All Other Instruments Monday—Friday: 0900–1100 1300–1500 Saturday: 0900–1100* (Tokyo is nine hours ahead of Greenwich mean time.)
Market Capitalization	Stocks: ¥447,319 billion Bonds: ¥125,485 billion (as of May 31, 1988)
Average Daily Turnover	Stocks: 962 million shares ¥1,000 billion Bonds: ¥396.7 billion Government bond futures: ¥3,370 billion (as of May 1988)
Number of Listed Securities	Stocks: 1,649 (90 of which represent foreign companies) Bonds: 973

*The exchange trades on Saturday morning except the second and third Saturdays of the month.

Number of Members	136 (regular and intermediary *saitori* members)
Market Index	Nikkei Average
Regulatory Authority	Securities Bureau, Ministry of Finance 1-1, 3-chome Kasumigaseki Chiyoda-ku, Tokyo Japan

Types of Listing:
The TSE assigns listed shares to different ""sections'' based on their turnover and number of shareholders. The first section consists of listed shares that are traded on the auction system through the saitori, who matches bids and offers according to specific rules. The second section consists of listed shares with less strict financial criteria that are traded electronically without the assistance of a saitori. The foreign section consists of non-Japanese stocks with financial criteria slightly different from those applicable to domestic shares.

Proposed Changes:
The TSE plans to introduce trading in stock index futures in September 1988. The contract will be based on the Tokyo Stock Exchange Price Index (Topix), a capitalization-weighted index of all 1,100 shares on the exchange's first section.

Membership Requirements
Types of Membership:
The TSE has regular members and saitori members. Regular members buy and sell securities on the TSE as either agents or principals. Saitori members are specialists, acting as intermediaries for securities transactions between regular members. Saitori members are not allowed to trade for their own accounts and are prohibited from having public customers.

Citizenship/Residency and Other:
TSE membership is available to companies licensed by the Minister of Finance. Applicants, which are limited to corporations, may request any of four licenses: to trade securities as a dealer, to trade as a broker, to underwrite new securities or secondary offerings, or to handle retail distribution of new or outstanding securities. While a firm may have more than one license, it is prohibited from acting as agent and principal in the same transaction. Most securities firms are licensed for dealing as principal, broker, and/or retail distributor.

Although foreign securities companies are permitted by law to obtain membership on the exchanges, the individual exchanges must determine whether membership will be granted.

Cost of Membership:
Membership requires the purchase of a seat, which costs about ¥1.13 billion. A non-member firm wishing to purchase a seat must negotiate with other member firms.

Minimum Capital Requirements: The minimum capital required varies from ¥200 million to ¥3 billion depending on the type of license held.

Insurance Coverage:
No specific insurance coverage is required.

Periodic Financial Reporting:
Annual
Audited financial statements
Schedule of tangible fixed assets
Schedule of rented property

Semiannual
Schedule of investment securities
Schedule of borrowings
Schedule of borrowed securities
Schedule of salaries

Monthly
Listing of significant accounts
Schedule of securities underwritten, purchased, and sold
Schedule of securities purchased and sold by prefecture
Schedule of merchandise securities

Annual audited financial statements and schedules of companies listed on Japanese stock exchanges are available for public inspection.

Trading on the Exchange
Commissions:
Trading commissions are at fixed scaled rates, which vary by type and value of the transaction as follows:
- Equities—0.15 percent to 1.20 percent plus a fixed charge of up to ¥712,500
- Nonconvertible bonds—0.05 percent to 0.85 percent
- Convertible bonds—0.15 percent to 1.0 percent
- Government bond futures—0.0025 percent to 0.015 percent plus a fixed charge of up to ¥200,000

Settlement:
Regular-way transactions—on or before the fourth business day
Cash transactions—on or before the next business day
Seller's option transactions—14 days following the contract day or day of seller's

choice

When-issued transactions—specified day after the share certificates are issued

Business days include Saturdays except the second and third Saturdays in each month, when the exchange is closed.

More than 99 percent of share trades are regular-way transactions.

Fails:

Securities may be borrowed from other brokers to effect delivery.

Clearing Organization:

Clearing on the TSE is by book entry rather than by physical delivery of securities. The Japan Securities Clearing Corporation (JSCC), a wholly owned subsidiary of the TSE, clears all transactions.

Transactions can take place between brokers without clearing through the JSCC. These transactions, which are called baikai transactions, are made between brokers off the floor of the exchange. Securities companies are required to report details of baikai transactions when they take place.

Registration:

The JSCC is in the process of registering share certificates in its nominee name. Most certificates are currently registered in the customer's name.

Safe Custody Depository:

The JSCC acts as a central depository for stocks. There is no central depository for bonds and other instruments.

Market Prices:

Current market prices are available immediately through the market information system of the TSE and Nikkei Quick.

Market Trading System:

The TSE market is a two-way, continuous, pure auction market where buy and sell orders interact directly with one another. As a general rule the members of the TSE buy or sell listed stocks on the trading floor only. Orders are centralized on the trading floor of the exchange, and transactions are carried out continuously during trading hours.

To maintain a stable market, the TSE will post a special bid/asked quote at a price slightly higher or lower than the last sale price in situations where there is a major order imbalance in a listed stock. The exchange also imposes a limit on the daily price fluctuation of a particular stock.

The TSE has developed the Computer-Assisted Order Routing and Execution System (CORES), which allows a regular member to enter orders and a saitori member to match them and provides both with a printed confirmation of the transaction. CORES will execute any orders automatically if such orders are to be executed within a specified narrow price range of the last sale price. When a transaction is completed the trade price is automatically transmitted from CORES to the Market Information System of the exchange. At present this system handles about 1,380 listed domestic stocks and all foreign stocks, with just the most active domestic stocks still traded on the exchange floor.

Insider Trading: Trading on insider information (information not available to the public) is prohibited.

Foreign Access
Overseas securities companies wishing to operate in Japan must obtain at least one of the four securities licenses and be organized as a branch office. The minimum number of staff to be employed by the branch depends on the number of licenses sought. The branch manager must be a resident of Japan.

Currently, 22 foreign brokerage companies are members of the exchange.

Securities companies that are not members of the exchange must use intermediary brokers to purchase and sell securities. Standard commissions are applied to share and bond transactions. Foreign securities companies earn approximately 80 percent of the total commission charged on a transaction.

Osaka Stock Exchange
2-1 Kitahama, Higashi-ku
Osaka-shi, Osaka 541
Japan
Telephone: 06-229-8610

General Information

Types of Instruments Traded	Stocks
	Government bonds
	Convertible bonds, bonds with warrants
	Foreign bonds in yen
	Other bonds
	Osaka 50 Stock Index futures
Market Capitalization (shares)	¥290,027 billion (as of December 31, 1987)
Average Daily Turnover (shares and bonds)	¥217 billion (1987)

Number of Listed Securities	Shares: 1,072
	Bonds: 892
Number of Members	82

The membership of the exchange is currently limited to 82 regular members and a na-kadachi member. The regular members' principal business is to execute customers' orders to buy or sell securities. They are also allowed to trade in securities on their own account and may underwrite new issues after obtaining a license. The nakadachi member's sole business is to act as broker for regular members on the exchange floor.

Of the 82 regular members, 62 are full members. The remaining firms, commonly known as out-of-town members, are restricted to trading in stock futures. The membership fee for out-of-town members is between Y200 million and Y300 million.

The exchange's stock index futures contract is unique because it is deliverable. All open positions not settled by a closing transaction before the last trading day of the delivery month are settled by physical delivery of the shares of underlying securities on the settlement day. In September 1988 the exchange plans to introduce an alternative stock index contract based on the Nikkei index of 225 leading stocks. Settlement of expired contracts will, in this case, be effected in cash.

Share Turnover—Tokyo Stock Exchange (1984–1987)
(¥ billion)

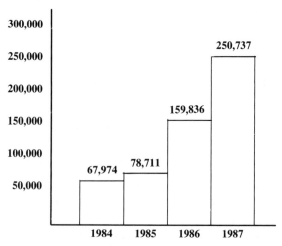

Korea

Korea Stock Exchange
33 Yeoido-dong
Yeongdeungpo-ku
Seoul
Korea
Telephone: (02) 783-3575

General Information

Types of Instruments Traded	Common and preferred stocks Bonds
Trading Hours	0940–1520 (Seoul is nine hours ahead of Greenwich mean time.)
Market Capitalization	W42,000 billion
Average Daily Turnover	Stocks: 20,353 shares* W70,185 million Bonds: W24,789 million
Number of Listed Securities	Stocks: 606 Bonds: 5,167
Number of Members	25
Market Index	Korea Composite Stock Price Index
Regulatory Authority	Securities and Exchange Commission 28-1 Yeoido-dong Yeongdeungpo-ku Seoul Korea

Proposed Changes:
The Korean government has announced its intention to extend direct investment privileges to foreign investors in the near future.

Membership Requirements
Citizenship/Residency:
Exchange membership is limited to Korean nationals.

*The par value of stock was changed to W5,000 from W500 following a change in the Korea Commercial Code in 1987.

Cost of Membership:
Seats are granted by the Korean government free of charge. However, members must hold a certain number of shares of the Korea Stock Exchange, as determined by the Minister of Finance.

Minimum Capital Requirements:
There are no specific minimum net capital requirements.

Insurance Coverage:
No specific insurance coverage is required.

Periodic Financial Reporting:
Semiannual audited financial statements

Trading on the Exchange
Commissions:
Trading commissions are fixed at scaled rates that vary with volume as follows:

Transaction Value (won)	Commission
below 1,000,000	0.8 percent
1,000,000 to 5,000,000	0.7 percent
above 5,000,000	0.6 percent

Settlement:
Trades are settled in two business days.

Fails:
Member firms may borrow securities from the Korea Securities Finance Corporation to effect delivery. Fails will result in loss of membership.

Clearing Organization:
Transactions are generally cleared by an electronic book-entry system through the Korea Securities Settlement Corporation, the sole transfer agent and central custodian. However, corporate bond and debenture transactions and stock transactions of less than ten shares can be traded directly between brokers without being cleared through the Korea Securities Settlement Corporation.

Registration:
Securities may be registered in the customer's name (requires power of attorney), in the dealer's name, or by book entry (not designating ownership on the security certificate).

Safe Custody Depository:
Korea Securities Settlement Corporation

Market Prices:
Current market prices are immediately available through Korea Securities Computer Corporation (KSCC), an on-line computer service.

Market Trading System:
A real-time computerized trading system has been installed for the 30 to 40 most actively traded stocks, and it is envisaged that its scope will be extended to trading in all listed stocks by 1990.

Insider Trading:
Trading on insider information (information not available to the public) is prohibited.

Solicitation:
Calling on local residents is allowed. However, calling on nonresidents and advertising to increase business are prohibited.

Foreign Access
At the present time nonresident foreigners are barred from owning South Korean stocks except indirectly through nine special trust funds. However, the government has expressed its commitment to open the domestic market to foreign investors by gradually lifting this restriction. No branch of a foreign securities firm is currently permitted to operate in South Korea, but 15 foreign securities firms have set up representative offices while their applications for branch status are being considered by the authorities. They are not able to deal with or give advice to South Korean clients.

Share Turnover (1984–1987)
(W billion)

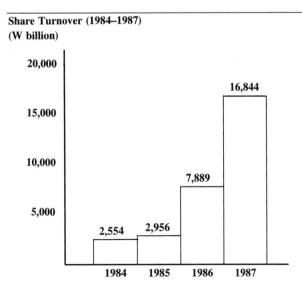

Luxembourg

The Grand Duchy of Luxembourg has one exchange, which transacts dealings in securities.

Societe de la Bourse de Luxembourg S.A.—Luxembourg Stock Exchange
11 avenue de la Porte-Neuve
L-2227 Luxembourg
Telephone: 47 79 36-1

General Information

Types of Instruments Traded	Domestic bonds of governments and corporations
	Bonds issued by supranational institutions
	International bonds (Eurobonds)
	Shares (domestic and foreign)
	Bearer certificates representing registered shares
	Collective investment undertakings
Trading Hours	Bond market: 1046–1315
	Stock market: 1145–1315
Market Capitalization	Lux F6,128 billion
	(as of December 31, 1987)
Annual Turnover	Luxembourg Francs (millions)
	Bonds: 19,392
	Shares: 4,020
	Collective investment undertakings: 2,338
Number of Listed Securities	Bonds: 4,893
	Shares: 236
	Collective investment undertakings: 495
	Warrants and others: 564
	(as of December 31, 1987)
Number of Members	Credit institutions: 52
	Brokerage firms: 18

Membership Requirements
Citizenship/Residency and Other:
Members can be either credit institutions, which are active locally, or firms of stockbrokers. Stockbroking firms may be either natural persons or legal entities. Each legal

entity admitted to membership must designate one or more natural persons duly authorized to represent it in relations with the exchange.

All members are obliged to provide a surety to cover their commitments to the stock exchange.

Cost of Membership:
An entry fee of Lux F250,000 is charged. There is also an annual membership fee of Lux F50,000.

Trading on the Exchange
Commissions:
Trading commissions are a fixed percentage of the transaction, varying by type of security.

Settlement:
The majority of transactions are settled through the international book-entry clearing systems recognized by the Luxembourg Stock Exchange: CEDEL and EUROCLEAR. Settlement occurs five business days after the trade date for shares and six business days after the trade date for bonds. Physical delivery of securities against payment can also take place via the Chambre de Liquidation (Liquidation Office).

Market Prices:
Current market prices are available to members during the course of the day.

Market Trading System:
Securities are traded on an open-outcry basis on three trading posts.

Insider Trading:
Trading on insider information (information not available to the public) is prohibited.

Foreign Access
There are no restrictions on the foreign ownership of brokerage firms. Special restrictions apply to the investment by foreigners in listed securities.

Mexico

The principal stock exchange in Mexico is located in Mexico City.

Bolsa Mexicana de Valores—Mexico Exchange
Uruguay 68
Colonia Centro
Mexico 06000, D.F.
Telephone: 510-46-20

General Information

Types of Instruments Traded	Common and preferred stocks
	Bonds, petrobonds
	Federal government securities (*cetes, pagares,* and so forth)
	Treasury and bank certificates of deposit
	Commercial notes (commercial paper, banker's acceptances, and so forth)
Trading Hours	Stocks: 1030–1400
	Bonds, petrobonds: 1030–1430
	Federal government securities: 1000–1400
	Commercial notes: 1000–1355
	Other securities: 1000–1340
	(Mexico City is six hours behind Greenwich mean time.)
Average Daily Turnover	<u>Mexican Pesos (millions)</u>
	Stocks: 63,958
	Bonds: 13,055
	Treasury certificates: 666,878
	Banker's acceptances: 71,868
	Commercial paper: 28,006
	Other: 13,360
Number of Listed Companies	213
Market Index	Bolsa index, based on the 50 most marketable shares
Regulatory Authority	Comisión Nacional de Valores (National Securities Commission) Barranca del Muerto 275 Colonia San Jose Insurgentes Mexico 03920, D.F.

Membership Requirements
Citizenship/Residency and Other:
The National Securities Commission restricts membership to Mexican citizens or foreign individuals with immigration status in Mexico. Moral behavior and economic solvency are also expected. All trades on the exchange must be handled by one of the 25 brokerage houses known as casas de bolsa.

Cost of Membership:
Seats are granted by the Mexican authorities. The cost is determined according to rates established periodically by the National Securities Commission.

Minimum Capital Requirements:
The minimum capital requirement is Mex$350 million.

Insurance Coverage:
Fidelity bond
Contingency fund—customer protection

Periodic Financial Reporting:
Annual audited financial statements, including investments, fixed assets, and insurance schedules, plus reports on foreign currency, contingent liabilities, and guarantees
Quarterly unaudited financial statements covering the preceding information
Trading on the Exchange
Commissions:
Trading commissions, which are fixed, are calculated according to the type of instrument and the volume of the transaction.
Settlement:
Settlement is required no later than two days after the trade date for cash transactions. Term transactions are settled on the maturity date, never exceeding 360 days. There is no physical delivery of securities, since they are deposited at the Institute for Deposit of Securities (INDEVAL). In the rare cases where fails occur, the brokerage houses absorb the losses.

Clearing Organization:
Bolsa Mexicana de Valores
Uruguay 68
Colonia Centro
Mexico 06000, D.F.

All transactions must be recorded through the clearing organization.

Registration:
All securities are registered in the name of the broker/dealer.

Market Prices:
Information on current market prices is immediately available through a computerized system.

Insider Trading:
Trading on insider information (information not available to the public) is prohibited.

Foreign Access
There are no foreign brokerage firms in Mexico because of the citizenship requirements. Foreign ownership of Mexican shares is limited to 49 percent.

Netherlands

There is one stock exchange in the Netherlands, located in Amsterdam. It ranks second worldwide, after London, in the number of foreign listings. Also located in Amsterdam are the European Options Exchange (EOE) and its subsidiary, the Financial Futures Market Amsterdam N.V. (FTA).

Amsterdamse Effectenbeurs—Amsterdam Stock Exchange (ASE)
Beursplein 5
1012 JW Amsterdam
Netherlands
Telephone: 020-239711

General Information

Types of Instruments Traded	Common and preferred stocks Warrants Bonds Claims and notes
Trading Hours	1000-1630 Trading in the more active securities continues for a further six hours. (Amsterdam is one hour ahead of Greenwich mean time.)
Market Capitalization (equities)	f.152 billion (as of May 31, 1988)
Average Daily Turnover	Stocks: f.438 million Bonds: f.924 million (as of May 1988)
Number of Listed Securities	Shares: 573 (representing 475 companies, 227 of which are foreign) Bonds: 1,325
Number of Members	160
Market Indexes	ANP-CBS general market index CBS trend index
Regulatory Authority	Vereniging voor de Effectenhandel Postbus 19163 1000 GD Amsterdam Netherlands

Membership Requirements
Types of Membership:
Corporate members
Personal members (representatives of corporate members of the floor)

Members may be banks/brokers or *hoekmannen*. *Hoekmannen* are market makers who act as intermediaries between banks/brokers. *Hoekmannen* may trade for their own accounts, but are not permitted to deal with the public. They are not obliged to trade in all market conditions. Banks/brokers must transact through *hoekmannen*. There are approximately 35 *hoekmannen* firms. Outside ownership of *hoekmannen* is currently limited to 5 percent.

Citizenship/Residency:
One member of the management staff must be a resident of the Netherlands.

Cost of Membership:
There is no seat system at the ASE. An entry fee of f.15,000 for a corporate membership and f.7,000 for a personal membership is charged. The annual membership fee is f.2,500.

Minimum Capital Requirements:
Banks–f.1 million
Nonbanks–f.200,000

Insurance Coverage:
Guarantee fund–customer protection insurance

Periodic Financial Reporting:
Annual audited financial statements
Interim unaudited financial statements

Trading on the Exchange
Types of Markets:
Official Market–first-tier market for listing of large domestic and foreign companies
Parallel Market–second-tier market for smaller companies with less stringent listing requirements than the Official Market
Unofficial Market–market for unofficially quoted companies

Commissions:
Trading commissions are fixed for stock transactions of up to f.1 million and bond transactions of up to f.2.5 million. Commissions on larger transactions are negotiable.

Settlement:
There is a maximum of ten business days between trade and settlement dates.

Fails:
Securities may not be borrowed from other brokers to effect delivery.

Clearing Organizations:
Dutch Central Organization for Securities Clearing (NECIGEF B.V.) Effectenclearing B.V.

Most securities are delivered by a computerized book-entry system, which is also used for financial settlement.

Registration:
Securities may be registered by book entry only.

Safe Custody Depository:
NECIGEF B.V.

Market Prices: Current market prices are available immediately.

Market Trading System:
The exchange maintains a floor-based trading system with hoekmannen acting as specialists in fixing prices in a range of stocks allotted to them.

A computerized system is currently being developed, which will automate floor trading, back-office processing, and the transfer of information between hoekmannen and the banks and brokers. This could also have a resultant effect on the traditional role and ownership of the hoekmannen. Trading in U.S., U.K., and Japanese shares outside local trading hours is effected via book entry under the Amsterdam Security Account System. The Amsterdam Interprofessional Market (AIM) provides for block trading by banks and institutions on a net basis on amounts over f.1 million in shares and f.2.5 million in bonds.

Insider Trading:
Trading on insider information (information not available to the public) is prohibited.

Foreign Access
There are currently ten foreign members of the ASE. Foreign firms may gain membership provided one member of the management staff is a resident of the Netherlands. Brokerage firms may operate either branches or subsidiaries. No restrictions are placed on the foreign ownership of stock or bonds.

European Options Exchange (EOE)
Rokin 65
1012 KK Amsterdam
Netherlands
Telephone: 020-5504550

The EOE is the only options exchange in the Netherlands. It cooperates with the Montreal Exchange, the Vancouver Stock Exchange, and The Australian Stock Exchange Limited in trading gold, silver, and platinum options around the world. In cooperation with the American Stock Exchange (AMEX) in New York, the EOE trades options on the Major Market Index (XMI), which are cleared by the Options Clearing Corporation (OCC) in Chicago.

General Information

Types of Options Traded	Stock options: 20 Bond options: 10 Currency options: 2 Precious metal options: 3 Index options: 2
Expiration Months	The expiration months run in three-, six-, and nine-month cycles.
Trading Hours	1000—1630 (Amsterdam is one hour ahead of Greenwich mean time.)
Average Daily Turnover	43,000 contracts (1987)
Number of Members	At the end of 1987, there were 387 capacities divided over 223 companies and individuals who were registered as members.
Market Index	EOE Dutch Stock Index
Regulatory Authority	The EOE is a self-regulatory exchange under the supervision of the Supervisory Commission of: Options Exchange c/o Ministry of Finance P.O. Box 20201 2500 EE's Gravenhage Netherlands

Membership Requirements

Types of Membership and Minimum Capital Requirements:
Public order member–f.250,000
Public order correspondent member–none
Floor broker–f.100,000/f.250,000
Off-floor trader–f.250,000

Market maker–f.100,000/f.250,000
Clearing member–f.1,000,000

Citizenship/Residency:
There are no specific citizenship or residency requirements except for clearing members, who are required to be an N.V. or a B.V., or a comparable legal entity registered outside the Netherlands under a foreign (non-Dutch) law, and to have an office in Amsterdam.

Cost of Membership:
The last sale of an exchange seat occurred in June 1988 for approximately f.540,000. In addition an annual membership fee of f.3,000 is charged.

Periodic Financial Reporting:
Annual audited financial statements must be submitted to the compliance department of the EOE within six months after the end of each annual accounting period.

Trading on the Exchange
Commissions:
Minimum commissions are fixed for the first ten contracts in an order. Above ten contracts, commissions are negotiable.

Settlement:
Settlement for stock and bond options occurs on the third business day following the exercise date. The settlement date for index options, which are settled in cash, is the next business day after the transaction date. Currency and precious metal options are settled on the fourth business day following the exercise date.

Fails:
The clearing organizations ensure the performance of each contract. To protect the clearing organizations from financial loss in event of defaults, clearing members with open positions on the exchange are required to deposit margins with the clearing organization.

Clearing Organizations:
All transactions must be recorded through the clearing organizations.

European Stock Options Clearing Corporation B.V. (ESCC)–The ESCC clears the stock, bond, and EOE Index options.

International Options Clearing Corporation, B.V. (IOCC)–The IOCC clears the currency and precious metal options.

Associate Clearing House Amsterdam B.V. (ACHA)–The ACHA clears the XMI options traded in Amsterdam in cooperation with the OCC in Chicago.

Market Prices:
Current market prices are available immediately through price information vendors such as Reuters, Telerate, Datastream, Telekurs, and Quotron.

Foreign Access
Foreign membership is unrestricted.

Financial Futures Market Amsterdam N.V. (FTA)
Nes 49
1012 KD Amsterdam
Netherlands
Telephone: 02-5504555

The European Options Exchange (EOE) initiated a financial futures market in Amsterdam. The FTA started on June 19, 1987, by listing a guilder bond future based on an index of Dutch government bonds. These are government bonds that are also traded in option form on the EOE. A main characteristic of the guilder bond future is that it is settled in cash.

On May 9, 1988, the FTA introduced the FTA Bullet Index. This index consists of government bonds, most of which are traded in option form on the EOE.

General Information

Type of Instrument Traded	Guilder bond future
Trading Hours	1030—1630 (Amsterdam is one hour ahead of Greenwich mean time.)
Average Daily Turnover	525 contracts (1987)
Number of Members	90
Regulatory Authority	The FTA is a self-regulatory ex-change under the supervision of the Ministry of Finance.
Contract Specifications/Contract Size	f.1,000 times the EOE-FTA Bond Index or FTA Bullet Index. If the index is quoted at 100, the value of the futures contract is f.100,000.
Settlement Months	The maximum term of a contract is one year. The settlement months are

New Zealand

There is one stock exchange in New Zealand. It is based in Wellington and has regional locations in Auckland, Christchurch/Invercargill, and Dunedin. There is also one futures exchange, not affiliated with the New Zealand Stock Exchange, which trades financial contracts.

New Zealand Stock Exchange (NZSE)
Executive Office
8th Floor, Caltex Tower
286-292 Lambton Quay
Wellington
New Zealand
Telephone: (04) 727 599

General Information

Types of Instruments Traded	Common and preferred stocks Fixed interest securities Warrants
Trading Hours	0930—1030 1430—1530 (Wellington is 12 hours ahead of Greenwich mean time.)
Market Capitalization	$NZ24.2 billion (May 1988)
Average Daily Turnover	Shares: $NZ21 million Fixed interest securities: $NZ31.9 million (1987)
Number of Listed Companies	Domestic: 361 Foreign: 178 (as of December 31, 1987)
Number of Members	235 (as of December 31, 1987)
Market Indexes	Barclays Index (top 40 stocks) NZSE Index (498 stocks)
Regulatory Authorities	Government Ministry Justice Department Bowen Street Wellington New Zealand

---

The Securities Commission
Greenock House
102-112 Lambton Quay
Wellington
New Zealand

Membership Requirements
Citizenship/Residency and Other:
A member is required to have worked with a sharebroker for at least three years.

Cost of Membership:
The cost of a seat is included in the membership fee, which is fixed by the regional exchange and varies between regions. For example, the Wellington region charges a membership fee of $NZ10,000 and an additional annual charge between $NZ3,000 and $NZ4,000.

Minimum Capital Requirements:
Minumum capital requirements are $NZ1 million per company, $NZ100,000 per individual member who does not have access to the trading floor, and $NZ200,000 per individual member who does have trading-floor access.

Insurance Coverage:
Fidelity bond–$NZ500,000 total for any failure; $NZ20,000 for any individual claim

Periodic Financial Reporting:
Monthly report to the stock exchange inspector Annual financial statements, subject to review by the stock exchange inspector

Trading on the Exchange
Commissions:
Trading commissions are negotiable

Settlement:
There is a maximum number of 30 business days between trade and settlement dates. Payment is made against delivery of the share certificate. At the beginning of 1988 the exchange introduced a fully computerized central system for settlements.

Fails:
In order to effect delivery in fail situations, the exchange settles trades and the dealing broker reimburses the exchange. Should the broker not do so within a certain period of time, the exchange will buy shares at market plus a premium, which the failing broker is then required to repay in full.

Clearing Organization:
There is no centralized clearing organization. However, five share registries handle approximately 80 percent of all trades.

Registration:
Securities may be registered in the customer's name or in the broker/dealer's name provided the other party to the transaction has been informed that the broker/dealer is acting as principal.

Safe Custody Depository:
No central safe custody depository exists. Banks currently provide this service.

Market Prices:
Current market prices are available immediately via on-line, computerized network facilities.

Market Trading System:
The NZSE is trying to improve the current settlement system by developing a computer-based trading and settlement process. The first phase of the computerization is complete with all quote and price information captured and disseminated on-line to brokers' offices and the media via the system. The completion of this system is the first stage of Kiwi Integrated Stock Market Electronic Trading (KISMET), which is a module-based integrated stock market trading system with a common data base.

The completion of the KISMET design, module by module, to enable screen trading and electronic settlement and registration, as well as to provide a publicly available data base, is anticipated to take place over the next three to four years. The first module of the six to be implemented is broker-to-broker accounting. It is to be installed in 1988 to undertake the accounting function for settlement between member firms.

Insider Trading:
Trading on insider information (information not available to the public) is prohibited. Legislation to codify this has been proposed and is expected to be passed in 1988.

Foreign Access
Foreign firms may be affiliated with a New Zealand brokerage firm provided that the outside shareholdings do not exceed 50 percent. The NZSE is currently considering allowing outside shareholders, whether they be New Zealand or offshore based, to take up to 100 percent of a brokerage firm's capital. If this were to occur, the companies involved would be required to contractually commit themselves to the disciplinary control of the stock exchange. For an offshore interest to take a holding in excess of 25 percent in any New Zealand company, the consent of the Minister of Finance is required under the Overseas Investments Regulations. Application should be made to the Overseas Investment Commission at the Reserve Bank of New Zealand if an overseas company intends to take an interest above 25 percent.

To be listed on the exchange, a foreign company must also be listed on its own country's stock exchange and is obligated to adhere to the reporting requirements of that country and of New Zealand.

Since deregulation in 1985 there are no longer any restrictions on New Zealand companies or individuals purchasing foreign securities or interests, nor are there restrictive foreign exchange controls.

Secondary Market
The exchange has implemented the Second Board for venture-type companies, which do not qualify for full listing on the exchange. These companies must fulfill all obligations as for listing on the stock exchange. There is little activity on this market, as it is still establishing itself. Trading volume for the six companies on the Second Board was 9.7 million shares during 1987 and is not anticipated to be significant over the next few years.

New Zealand Futures Exchange (NZFE)
191 Queen Street
Auckland
New Zealand

General Information

Types of Contracts Traded	Five-year government stock 90-day bank-accepted bills* U.S. dollars Barclays Share Price Index Wool
Trading Hours	0800—1700 Different contracts have different trading hours, the longest being government stock for the times noted here. (Auckland is 12 hours ahead of Greenwich mean time.)
Turnover	New Zealand Dollars (millions) U.S. dollars: 348.2 Prime commercial paper: 0.2 Bank-accepted bills: 5,767.1 Wool: 20.5 Government stock: 7,386.7 Barclays Share Price Index: 240.7 (as of March 31, 1988)

*The 90-day bank-accepted bills contract replaced the 90-day prime commercial paper contract in December 1986. There is still trade in the prime commercial paper contract, as it is necessary for institutions to close out their forward positions.

Average Daily Turnover	Lots
	Five-year government stock: 899
	Prime commercial paper: 1
	Bank-accepted bills: 239
	U.S. dollars: 80
	Wool: 21
	Barclays Share Price Index: 97
	(as of April 30, 1988)

Number of Members	17

Number of Affiliate Members	20

Regulatory Authority:
There is no independent regulatory authority. The board of the NZFE supervises activities and acts as a self-regulatory body. All conduct of members is enforced through the articles of association of the exchange.

Membership Requirements
Cost of Membership:
The cost of membership is set by market demand. The last recorded sale of seat in 1987 was for an amount in excess of $NZ300,000.

Minimum Capital Requirements:
The minimum capital requirement is $NZ350,000 in net tangible assets for trading members and $NZ150,000 for affiliate members.

Insurance Coverage:
No specific insurance coverage is required.

Periodic Financial Reporting:
Annual audited report
Quarterly financial statements
Monthly return of client funds

Trading on the Exchange
Commissions:
Trading commissions are negotiable.

Clearing Organization/Safe Custody Depository:
All trades are conducted through an intermediary clearinghouse called the International Commodities Clearing House Limited (ICCH)(Auckland), which guarantees the performance of every contract traded on the NZFE. It also acts as a safe custody depository, as required, for deliverable commercial paper. Other contracts involve only book entries.

Market Trading System:
The NZFE operates an interactive computer that links trading members from all around the country. The Automated Trading System (ATS) provides a clean audit trail of buy and sell orders, a complete accounting package for dealers, and international contacts through the ICCH.

Insider Trading:
Trading on insider information (information not available to the public) is possible, but the NZFE has promulgated certain rules to avoid this situation.

Foreign Access
Foreign broker/dealers must be affiliated with a local broker and must use an intermediary to conduct transactions. Commissions are negotiable.

There are no restrictions on domestic corporations or individuals engaging in foreign dealings.

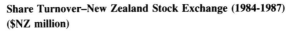

Share Turnover–New Zealand Stock Exchange (1984-1987)
($NZ million)

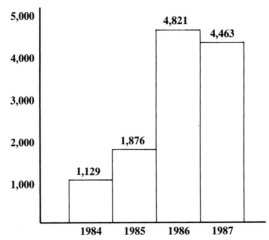

Portugal

Portugal has two exchanges, which deal in shares, bonds, and various other government and commercial securities. Both exchanges transact the same type of business.

Bolsa de Valores de Lisboa–Lisbon Stock Exchange
Praca do Comercio
1100 Lisboa
Portugal
Telephone: (01) 879416; 879417

Bolsa de Valores do Porto–Porto Stock Exchange
Edificio Bolsa
Rua Ferreira Borges
4000 Porto
Portugal
Telephone: (02) 22476; 322084

The Lisbon Stock Exchange is the larger of the two exchanges in terms of activity. The activity on both exchanges is governed by a central government decree, but each exchange has its own internal controlling regulations.

General Information

Types of Instruments Traded	Shares
	Bonds, subdivided into: Government of Portugal bonds Other public sector bonds Commercial bonds
	(There is an active unofficial market in these securities prior to the official listing on the stock exchange.)
Trading Hours	Bolsa de Valores de Lisboa: 1000—1230
	Bolsa de Valores do Porto: 0830—1230 1400—1630
	(Lisbon and Porto are one hour ahead of Greenwich mean time.)
Market Capitalization	Lisbon and Porto: Escl,337 billion (May 1988)
Average Daily Turnover	Lisbon: 123,156 contracts (shares and bonds)–Esc515,697,940
	Porto: 43,107 contracts(shares and bonds)—Esc 188,395,702
Number of Listed Securities	179(as of May 1988)

Number of Members	Lisbon: 9
	Porto: 3
Market Index	BTA General Index (30 stocks)
Regulatory Authority	Ministry of Finance
	Av. Infante D Henrique
	1200 Lisboa
	Portugal

Membership Requirements

Types of Membership: Currently, individuals act as members of the stock exchange. These individuals act as nominees for banks, investment companies, and so forth. Under legislation passed by the government, existing individual members have until December 31, 1990, to form brokerage companies.

Citizenship/Residency:
To qualify for membership, an individual must be:
• Portuguese
• Brazilian with Portuguese nationality
• Non-Portuguese with ten or more years of citizenship

The new rules referred to here will allow any individual or corporate body to hold up to a maximum of 49 percent in brokerage companies, but 51 percent must be held by one or more of the existing individual members.

Cost of Membership:
Under the present system, membership cannot be transferred from one individual to another. Membership can be obtained only by examination and with the approval of the administrative body of the respective exchange. Minimum Capital Requirements: There are no minimum capital requirements, but each individual member must provide a bail bond equivalent to Esc500,000. For brokerage companies this increases to Esc1,000,000.

Insurance Coverage:
This is not required at the present time.

Periodic Financial Reporting:
There are no special requirements at the present time.

Trading on the Exchange

Commissions:
These are generally fixed according to a scaled schedule, depending on the volume and whether the trades are done during official trading sessions.

The minimum value of any commission is Esc50.

Settlement:
The regulations allow for two types of settlement: contract operations and forward settlement transactions. In practice, only the first type applies. This means that in Lisbon five trading sessions are permitted between trade date and settlement. In Porto the number of sessions is reduced to three.

Clearing Organization:
Transactions on the exchanges in Portugal are recorded on a system called sistema Integrado de informacoes de Bolsa. At the end of each session it gives the net position of each broker in each stock. The broker's customer then settles directly with the broker. The underlying titles supporting the trades are normally held by safekeeping agents, such as banks, that will deal with the broker directly.

No separate clearing organization is currently established in Portugal.

Registration:
Securities are registered in the customer's name.

Safe Custody Depository:
Although agents, such as banks, do offer customers safe custody deposits, the Portuguese system still requires the physical movement of titles for registration of ownership. Therefore, it is not possible for separate safe depository trust companies to operate.

Market Prices:
Upon execution of a trade the transaction is recorded, processed, and displayed on an electronic board, which is also available to subscribers to the system.

Market Trading System:
A computerized system has recently been introduced, which records both offers to buy and sell and confirmed deals. The auction system of trading is still used by the exchange.

Insider Trading:
Trading on insider information (information not available to the public) is prohibited.

Foreign Access
Although there is no restriction on foreign-owned shareholdings in companies newly formed to conduct brokerage business, the existing individual brokers must retain some ownership. Furthermore, the maximum share any individual nonbroker can own is 25 percent of the total share capital. Foreign companies are required to obtain the foreign investment institute's approval for investments made in Portugal. It is generally easier for companies to obtain approval if they are residents of European Economic Community (EEC) countries.

Singapore

Investors in Singapore are able to participate in various securities markets.

The Stock Exchange of Singapore Limited (SES)	Main Board (closely linked with the stock exchange in neighboring Malaysia)
Stock Exchange of Singapore Dealing and Automated Quotation (SESDAQ) system	A second market for smaller companies not eligible for admission to the Main Board
National Association of Securities Dealer's (NASD) in the United States	SES link for trading in selected U.S. over-the-counter stocks
Singapore Government Securities (SGS) Market	Primary and secondary market for Singapore government bonds
Singapore International Monetary Exchange Ltd. (SIMEX)	Futures and options market linked to the Chicago Mercantile Exchange (CME)on the mutual offset system

The Stock Exchange of Singapore Limited (SES)
1 Raffles Place #04-07/09
OUB Centre
Singapore 0104
Telephone: 5353788

General Information

Types of Instruments Traded	Common and preferred stocks Warrants Convertible loan notes Loan stock Bonds Floating rate notes
Trading Hours	1000—1230 1430—1600 (Singapore is eight hours ahead of Greenwich mean time.)
Market Capitalization	S$270.9 billion (as of May 31, 1988)
Average Daily Turnover	19 million shares

Number of Listed Companies	319 (127 incorporated in Singapore, 181 incorporated in Malaysia, and 11 incorporated elsewhere)
Number of Members	25 (including one approved overseas representative office)
Market Index	Straits Times Industrial and Commercial Index: 30 stocks SES All-Share Price: all stocks
Regulatory Authority	Monetary Authority of Singapore (MAS) 10 Shenton Way MAS Building Singapore 0207

Recent Changes:
The exchange introduced a new delivery and settlement system in September 1987, which requires settlement of purchases and sales in seven days. This was followed by a revision of the commission structure, which allows for negotiation of rates for contract amounts exceeding S$1 million. The exchange is in the process of launching a new system of trading involving the electronic relaying of orders from brokerages to the trading floor, order routing, and ultimately automated execution of orders. Plans are also in hand for the phased introduction of scripless trading. Financial institutions are seeking approval from the authorities to engage in scrip-lending activities. A link with the Luxembourg Stock Exchange for the common listing of Asian and Eurodollar bonds is to be formed in late 1988.

Membership Requirements
Citizenship/Residency:
The SES has two categories of membership: individual and corporate. Individual members must be Singapore citizens or residents (of at least five years) who meet the professional requirements of the Committee of the Stock Exchange. Individual members are known as stockbroking members. Corporate members must be Singapore-incorporated stockbroking companies whose shareholders (or executive directors, in the case of subsidiaries of local banks) have been approved as stockbroking members by the Committee of the Stock Exchange.

Cost of Membership:
On the basis of the latest transaction, a seat is currently valued at S$3.8 million. The cost of membership to the clearinghouse is S$200,000.

Minimum Capital Requirements:
All member companies are required to have a paid-in capital of at least S$10 million. In addition their adjusted net capital must not fall below S$250,000, and their aggregate

indebtedness must not exceed 1,200 percent of their adjusted net capital. Adjusted net capital comprises shareholders' funds after adjustment for certain prescribed deductions, principally including deficits in clients' accounts and shortfalls in the value of securities held by the company. Furthermore, the member companies must maintain a statutory reserve fund out of their net profits, as prescribed by the Securities Industry Act.

Insurance Coverage:
There are no mandatory requirements, but the interests of investors are protected by provisions in the Securities Industry Act and by a fidelity fund.

Periodic Financial Reporting:
Annual audited financial statements must be filed at the Registry of Companies. The financial statements of member companies, other than exempt private companies, are open for public inspection. Exempt private companies submit financial statements on a voluntary basis.

Monthly and quarterly returns in the prescribed formats are required to be submitted to the exchange and the MAS in accordance with the requirements of the Securities Industry Act and the bylaws of the exchange.

An examination is conducted annually by members of the inspection department of the exchange and periodically by the MAS.

Trading on the Exchange
Commissions:
The revised commission structure, effective January 4, 1988, is as follows:

Contract Value	Rate
First S$250,000	1.0 percent
Next S$250,000	0.9 percent
Next S$250,000	0.8 percent
Next S$250,000	0.7 percent
Exceeding S$1 million	Negotiable, subject to a minimum of 0.5 percent

For contracts at prices below S$1 per share or stock unit, the common rates are:
• Under 50 cents–0.5 cents per share
• 5 to 99 cents–0.1 cents per share

A minimum brokerage fee of S$5 applies to all contracts traded.

Rebates on brokerage are allowed in the case of approved banks and merchant banks at a maximum of 25 percent of standard brokerage and in the case of foreign brokers, at a maximum of 50 percent of standard brokerage.

Government securities and Asian currency are transacted on a net contract basis. Corporate loan securities and debentures are charged fixed rates, ranging from 0.25 percent to 1 percent of transaction value. Minimum commission is S$5.

A stamp duty of S$1 per S$1,000 or part thereof is payable on securities transactions.

Settlement:
Immediate contracts–delivery on the same day; settlement on the next day
Ready contracts–delivery by 1230 seven days after transaction date; settlement the next day
Settlement contracts–suspended since 1986

Fails:
The exchange will institute compulsory buying-in procedures against selling brokers who fail to deliver on the due date. Member companies can similarly buy in against clients who fail to deliver. The rules of the exchange are silent as to borrowing securities to effect delivery.

Clearing Organization:
All transactions are cleared by Securities Clearing and Computer Services (Pte.) Ltd. (SCCS). Each member company holds one share in SCCS, while the exchange holds five shares.

Registration:
Securities may be registered in the customer's name or in a nominee company name for the benefit of the customer.

Safe Custody Depository:
There is currently no central depository system, although this is being considered by the exchange. Securities are generally held in safekeeping by banks, merchant banks, and other authorized depositories.

Market Prices:
Security prices are immediately available through the exchange's computer-based, real-time reporting systems SECOMS and STOCKWATCH.

Market Trading Systems:
In July 1988 the exchange moved to a new trading floor, and market orders and limit orders were introduced. Eight trading posts have been introduced, which display best buy and sell quotes.

On the Second Market, transactions are handled by SESDAQ, a computerized quotation system that is screen based and subject to competitive market making. Settlement of transactions is on a scripless basis through a central clearinghouse run by the Central Depository (Pte.) Ltd. (CDP). CDP maintains records and updates all SESDAQ securities accounts of investors and participants who are SES members or associates approved to deal in SESDAQ securities. CDP issues quarterly statements to investors.

Trading hours and transaction costs for the Second Market are the same as for the Main Board. Settlements are due on the fifth market day following the date of contract. Investors are protected from defaults by SESDAQ participants through the SES Fidelity Fund or the SESDAQ Compensation Fund (to a maximum of the lower of S$20,000 or 80 percent of net losses).

Exchange Links:
In March 1988 the SES established a trans-Pacific communication link with the NASD in the United States to enable trading of selected securities (link stocks) quoted on the National Association of Securities Dealers Automated Quotations (NASDAQ) system. The availability of link stocks will provide investors with a greater opportunity to diversify their investment portfolios. As of April 1988 there were 35 link stocks, 23 authorized participants, and 64 dealers.

Trading hours are similar to those of the Main Board and SESDAQ, but commission rates vary among participants. Transactions are effected in U.S. dollars, with settlement either in U.S. dollars or local currency at an agreed exchange rate. Transactions are on a scripless basis, with a minimum order of 100 shares or multiple thereof. The settlement day is the fifth market day following the deal date. Transactions are cleared through CDP, and quarterly statements are issued to investors.

Insider Trading:
Trading on insider information (information not available to the public) is prohibited.

Solicitation:
All forms of advertising must conform to guidelines issued by the exchange and approved by the board of directors of the member company.

Foreign Access
Foreign financial institutions are currently allowed to acquire up to 49 percent of the voting capital of member companies. This limit is being reviewed and may be raised in due course by the exchange.

Foreign brokers can apply to be approved overseas representatives of the SES, a status that carries certain privileges. However, all trades must be cleared through an exchange member. Commissions charged by intermediary brokers are generally at standard rates, but rebates for foreign brokers who are members of other recognized stock exchanges are permitted. Representative offices may be set up as branches or limited companies and may use foreign staff subject to normal immigration regulations.

No restrictions generally apply to the acquisition of securities by foreign investors, although limits are imposed on foreign investment in certain companies.

South Africa

The only stock exchange in South Africa is located in Johannesburg.

Johannesburg Stock Exchange (JSE)
Physical address:
17 Diagonal Street
2001 Johannesburg
South Africa
Telephone: (011) 833 6580

Postal address:
P.O. Box 1174
2000 Johannesburg
South Africa

General Information

Types of Instruments Traded	Shares (ordinary and preference) Gilts (loans to government, municipalities, and semi-government and statutory bodies) Krugerrands
Trading Hours	0930—1600 (Johannesburg is two hours ahead of Greenwich mean time.)
Market Capitalization	Nominal value: R109,376,132 Market value: R371,835,532
Average Daily Turnover	1.2 billion contracts
Number of Listed Companies	Companies with shares quoted: 668 Issuers of gilt and semi-gilt stock: 60
Number of Members	385 (85 of which are nonbroker) (as of February 29, 1988)
Market Indexes	JSE overall index JSE industrial index JSE gold index
Regulatory Authority	The JSE is controlled externally by the Stock Exchanges Control Act, 1985.

Membership Requirements
Types of Membership:
There are two types of members: natural persons and corporate bodies whose share-

holders are members of the JSE. There is no separation of function between member firms in trading. However, firms are prohibited from acting as principal and agent on the same transaction.

Citizenship/Residency:
Only South African citizens can become members of the JSE.

Cost of Membership:

Entrance fee–R5,000
Annual subscription–R2,000
Contribution to the Guarantee Fund–R800

Members must also purchase and retain during their membership three Stock Exchange Rights in the JSE. These are currently standing at R11,000 each.

Minimum Capital Requirements:
A member intending to trade as a sole proprietor must have R40,000 excess of liquid assets over liabilities in the stockbroking business, or R20,000 if joining a partnership or incorporated body.

Client Protection:
The JSE Committee established a company, JSE Trustees (Pty.) Limited, to accept all moneys held by brokers on behalf of their clients.

Insurance Coverage:
Client protection insurance—The JSE established a separate legal entity, the Guarantee Fund, to settle customer claims arising on the liquidation of a member of the JSE. The members are required to contribute to the fund.

Stockbrokers' indemnity—The JSE directives require all broker members to be covered by a Stockbrokers' Indemnity Policy of Insurance to a minimum of R350,000.

Periodic Financial Reporting:
The registers and mandates of safe custody, scrip, pledges, and managed accounts must be audited four times a year.

Audited annual financial statements must be sent to the Registrar of Financial Institutions and the JSE Committee by June 30 of each year.

Trading on the Exchange
Commissions:
Commission rates for equities are fixed, depending on the value of the transaction.

Settlement:
Seven business days between trade and settlement.

Clearing Organization:
The JSE operates a weekly computerized clearing system. The net balances owed to or by each broker firm are settled between them. For gilts, transactions are settled on each business day.

Market Trading System:
Trading takes the form of a two-way oral auction. When a sale is conducted, the price is recorded on the prices board in the market if it differs from the price of the previous sale.

Insider Trading:
The JSE is attempting to get an act passed in the next year making trading on insider information (information not available to the public) illegal.

Foreign Access
As stated previously, only South African citizens can become members of the JSE.

Spain

Spain has four official stock exchanges, or bolsas, located in Madrid, Barcelona, Bilbao, and Valencia. The Madrid Stock Exchange is dominant and is reviewed here. During 1987 the Madrid bolsa accounted for 77 percent of the total turnover of equity securities, compared with 16 percent for Barcelona, 5 percent for Bilbao, and 2 percent for Valencia.

Bolsa Oficial de Comercio—Madrid Stock Exchange
Plaza de la Lealtad, 2
28014 Madrid
Spain

General Information

Types of Instruments Traded	Common Stocks
	Bonds
	Treasury bills
	Promissory notes
	Notes of exchange
	Mutual fund participations
Trading Hours	1000—1300
	(Madrid is one hour ahead of Greenwich mean time.)
Market Capitalization	Pesetas (millions)
	Shares: 7,748,839
	Debentures: 2,232,000
	Bank bonds: 744,000
	Public securities: 3,900,000
	(as of December 31, 1987)
Average Daily Turnover	Pesetas (millions)
	Shares: 3,695,976
	Debentures: 39,133
	Bank bonds: 79,096
	Public securities: 105,750
	Treasury bills: 2,810,290
Number of Listed Securities	Stocks: 228
	Closed-end funds: 96
	Fixed interest bearing securities: 1,204
	(Of the equity stocks listed, about 50 percent are actively traded.)
Market Index	Madrid General Index

Regulatory Authority	Consejo Superior de Bolsas

Proposed Changes:
The government has introduced legislation to change the regulation of the exchanges providing for the incorporation of brokers, the removal of their monopoly on bond and share transactions, the end of fixed commissions, the formation of brokerage partnerships by banks and others, and the introduction of a new regulatory scheme involving greater participation by the Bank of Spain and the Ministry of Economy and Finance. The Madrid Stock Exchange also has proposed changes to improve settlement and trading procedures, including a computerized order system and continuous computer-linked trading on all four Spanish stock exchanges.

Membership Requirements
Citizenship/Residency and Other:
Membership is granted to registered public brokers who pass an official examination. Member firms are called agentes de cambio and currently have exclusive monopoly over executing share transactions. They act on a strictly single-capacity basis and are prohibited from taking positions on stocks, making markets, and holding a seat on the board of any company.

Trading on the Exchange
Commissions:
Trading commissions are fixed at 0.75 percent of the transaction value.

Settlement:
Seven days are required between trade and settlement, although settlement of securities transactions frequently takes longer.

Fails:
Brokers must balance their accounts daily; therefore, securities are not borrowed to effect delivery.

Clearing Organization:
Junta Sindical

Registration:
Securities must be registered in the customer's name.

Safe Custody Depository:
Junta Sindical

Market Prices:
Current market prices are available immediately.

Market Trading System:
A specific trading time confined to ten-minute operating sessions is allotted to each of nine industry groups. Trading is in the form of an open voice-auction system only during the time allotted (corro) to the industry group to which a company belongs. The quoted price for each stock is the closing price of that stock at the end of the corro for the relevant industry.

Trading in a particular security is not permitted if daily orders to buy (or sell) that security exceed by 20 percent or more the corresponding orders to sell (or buy) that security. When such a mismatch occurs, investors are unable to trade until supply and demand move closer to equilibrium.

The regulations prohibit upward and downward movements in the prices of securities in excess of a certain percentage of the previous day's quoted prices. This permitted range, which was set at 5 percent with changes of up to 10 percent in exceptional circumstances, is now set at 20 percent as a result of the substantial selling pressure during the last week of October 1987, when a significant number of securities did not trade. There is no indication that the new limit will be retained indefinitely.

Substantial trading in listed securities is transacted off the Madrid Stock Exchange. However, the rules require that such trading take place at a price within the range in which a transaction occurred during trading on the exchange. The prices of equity securities are currently quoted as a percentage of nominal value, although the Madrid Stock Exchange has proposed that trading prices be quoted in pesetas.

The reforms planned by the government include the computerization of trading on a continuous basis and the computerization of dealing and settlement.

Insider Trading:
Trading on insider information (information not available to the public) is currently permissible. The government's proposed reforms include a ban on insider trading.

Foreign Access
There are currently no foreign members of the Madrid Stock Exchange. Foreign companies must use Spanish brokers to transact all trading. No restrictions apply to the ownership of shares by foreign investors with the exception of investment in banks and companies connected with national security.

Share Turnover (1984–1987)
(Ptas million)

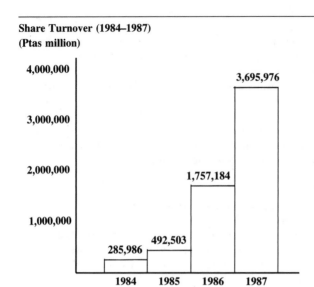

Sweden

Sweden's sole stock exchange is located in Stockholm.

Stockholm Stock Exchange
Kallargrand 2
Box 1256
S-111 82 Stockholm
Sweden
Telephone: 46-8-14 31 60

General Information

Types of Instruments Traded	Common and preferred stocks Convertible loans Promissory notes
Trading Hours	0930—1430 (Stockholm is one hour ahead of Green- wich mean time.)
Market Capitalization	Stocks: SKr520 billion (May 1988)
Average Daily Turnover	SKr500 million
Number of Listed Securities	Shares: 270 (representing 157 compa- nies, 7 of which are foreign) Bonds: 1,626
Number of Members	Banks: 14 Brokers: 16
Market Indexes	Veckans Affarer Affarvarlden
Regulatory Authority	The Swedish Bank Inspection Board Drottninggatan 50-52 Box 16096 S-103 22 Stockholm Sweden

Proposed Changes:
The exchange is set to replace the current auction system with computerized trading
having direct on-screen dealing of the current favorite. It is also taking measures to link
the computerized settlement system with the trading floor.

Membership Requirements

Citizenship/Residency:

Membership in the Stockholm Stock Exchange is normally restricted to Swedish citizens or Swedish companies with foreign ownership not exceeding 40 percent of total capital and voting rights not exceeding 20 percent of all the shares. In certain instances this prohibition may be waived by the authorities. As of April 1988 the Stockholm Stock Exchange did not have any foreign members.

Cost of Membership:

The cost of a seat is SKr100,000.

Minimum Capital Requirements:

The minimum capital requirement for a brokerage firm is SKr500,000.

Periodic Financial Reporting:

Annual audited financial statements
Semiannual unaudited financial statements
Monthly report to supervisory authority

Trading on the Exchange

Commissions:

Since July 1984 the commission rates have been negotiable. They usually approximate to the following:

- First list (A-1 list)–0.45 percent up to SKr500,000
  –0.30 percent for the portion above SKr500,000
- Second list (A-2 list)–0.65 percent

Turnover Tax:

A turnover tax based on the amounts traded is paid by both buyers (1 percent) and sellers (1 percent).

Settlement:

Five days between trade and settlement.

Market Prices:

Current market prices can be obtained through on-line computer services. International clients are informed through an international computerized line.

Market Trading System:

The exchange operates an auction system where issue prices are fixed daily. However, business transacted in this way accounts for only a small portion of the total trading volume. All other trading takes place outside the exchange, but has to be reported to it.

Foreign Access

Foreign brokers must use a Swedish broker as an intermediary to conduct transactions on the exchange. Foreign investments in Swedish shares purchased in Sweden must have the approval of the Swedish Central Bank. Once permission is granted there are no restrictions relating to foreign currency used to acquire the shares or to the repatriation of capital invested.

Sweden's Options & Futures Exchange (SOFE)
Regeringsgatan 38
Box 7267
S-103 89 Stockholm
Sweden
Telephone: 46-8-791 40 80

The SOFE market commenced trading in March 1987.

General Information

Types of Instruments Traded	Index options Index forwards
Trading Hours	October—April: 0945—2200 May—September: 0945—1900 (Stockholm is one hour ahead of Greenwich mean time.)
Average Daily Turnover	Index options: 25,000 contract (March 1988)
Ownership	SOFE's owners comprise banks and brokerage firms.
Regulatory Authority	The Swedish Bank Inspection Board Drottninggatan 50-52 Box 16096 S-103 22 Stockholm Sweden

Foreign Access
Options buyers and writers must conduct trading through a registered Swedish broker.

Stockholm Options Market (OM)
Brunkebergstorg 2
Box 16305
S-103 26 Stockholm
Sweden
Telephone: 46-8-11 4-70

The Stockholm OM commenced trading in June 1985.

General Information

Types of Instruments Traded	Stock options OMX (index) options OMX (index) forwards Interest rate options (Only stock options and OMX [index] options are currently available for international trading.)
Trading Hours	1000—1600 Interest rate options: 0930—1500 (Stockholm is one hour ahead of Greenwich mean time.)
Market Capitalization	SKr411.6 billion
Average Daily Turnover	Stock options: 8,200 contracts OMX options: 17,800 contracts OMX forwards: 2,000 contracts Interest rate options: 1,000 contracts (March 1988)
Ownership	OM's owners comprise Swedish banks, brokerage firms, and a number of additional companies and individuals. In all, OM has approximately 3,500 shareholders.
Regulatory Authority	The Swedish Bank Inspection Board Drottninggatan 50-52 Box 16096 S-103 22 Stockholm Sweden

Foreign Access

Options writers and buyers must conduct trading through registered Swedish brokers.

Share Turnover–Stockholm Stock Exchange (1984-1987)
(SKr billion)

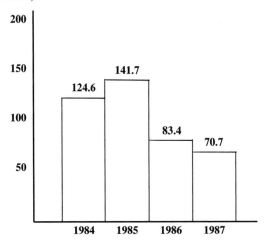

Switzerland

Switzerland has seven stock exchanges, located in Zurich, Geneva, Basel, Lausanne, Bern, Neuchâtel, and St. Gallen. This review will focus on the Zurich and Geneva stock exchanges, which together command 80 percent of the Swiss securities market.

Zurich Stock Exchange
Effektenboersverein, Bleicherweg 5
CH-8001 Zurich
Switzerland
Telephone: (41 1) 229 2111

General Information

Types of Instruments Traded	Common and preferred stocks Government and corporate bonds
Trading Hours	1000—1230 Zurich has no official fixed time for the end of the trading session, which continues as long as deals are being made. An official prebourse trading session for unlisted securities takes place before 1000. (Zurich is one hour ahead of Greenwich mean time.)
Market Capitalization (for the 300 quoted Swiss stocks only)	Swiss Frances (billions) Stocks: 165.8 Bonds: 106.6 (as of December 31, 1987)
Average Daily Turnover	Swiss Frances (billions) Stocks: 1.8 Bonds: 1.1 (1987)
Number of Listed Securities	Shares: 517 (representing 353 companies, 211 of which are foreign) Bonds: 2,355
Number of Members	28
Market Indexes	Swiss index Credit Suisse Global
Regulatory Authority	Kantonale Boersenkommission (Cantonal Advisory Commission on Se-

curities Trading)
Bleicherweg 5
CH-8001 Zurich
Switzerland

Recent Changes:
Zurich, Geneva, and Basel, the major stock exchanges, have recently installed computerized information-sharing and trade-matching systems on all three trading floors. An automatic settlement system will be installed during 1988 to handle settlement traffic between these exchanges.

In May 1988 a new market for options and financial futures called Soffex was launched by the three principal Swiss exchanges and the five largest Swiss banks. Participants interact with the market through computer terminals, entering orders or quotes and receiving market information electronically. Options on 11 major Swiss stocks are traded on the exchange, and the introduction of an options contract based on a new Swiss stock index is planned. Soffex option contracts can be traded in four maturity ranges, from one month to a maximum of six months. Exchange membership is limited to members of the Swiss stock exchanges and other professional securities dealers with offices in Switzerland.

Membership Requirements
Types of Membership:
A-concession holders–28 bank members authorized to trade directly on the exchange.

B-concession holders—221 individual members licensed to trade securities. B-concession holders may only buy and sell securities through an A-concession holder. B-concession holders are allowed to deal on the over-the-counter market.

No separation of functions exists between member firms in trading.

Citizenship/Residency and Other:
A-concession holders must be banking institutions domiciled in the canton of Zurich and incorporated in Switzerland.

B-concession holders must be professionally qualified and may be foreign companies.

Cost of Membership:
Membership is not sold by the seat. A-concession holder membership costs Sw F300,000 plus an additional annual fee based on trading volume. B-concession holders pay only an annual fee, which varies from Sw F50 to Sw F5,000

Minimum Capital Requirements:
There are no minimum capital requirements; however, members must maintain deposits with the canton of Zurich as follows:

- A-concession holders—Sw F30,000
- B-concession holders—varies from Sw F5,000 to Sw F20,000

Insurance Coverage:
No specific insurance coverage is required.

Periodic Financial Reporting:
Annual audited financial statements must be filed with the cantonal stock exchange authority.

Trading on the Exchange
Commissions:
Trading commissions are generally fixed according to volume. However, they are negotiable above the Sw F2 million level for stocks and Swiss franc bonds, and above the Sw F1 million level for foreign currency bonds.

Settlement:
There are generally three days between trade and settlement dates. However, the legal maximum is ten days.

Fails:
Securities may not be borrowed to effect delivery.

Clearing Organization:
Schweizerisch Effekten Giro AG (SEGA)

Registration:
Stocks are deposited in SEGA; therefore, registration is by book entry only.

Market Prices:
Information on current market prices is immediately available on-line via Telekurs AG, a company owned by several Swiss banks.

Market Trading Systems:
The exchange uses the open-outcry, or auction, system whereby transactions are executed at each of the ringside places operated by the ring traders. All transactions must be reported to the Stock Exchange Commission. A planned computer-assisted trading system for bonds was recently abandoned and will be replaced by a more advanced project directed toward a fully electronic securities market by the early 1990s.

Insider Trading:
No regulations forbid insider trading (trading on information not available to the public.) However, it is anticipated that legislation will be introduced in the near future.

Solicitation:
There are no official restrictions on promoting services; however, foreigners follow a gentleman's agreement to refrain from soliciting business.

Foreign Access
Zurich has approximately 120 foreign B-concession holders, and though they are not technically permitted, five foreign A-concession holders exist. Foreign firms may establish Swiss branches to trade securities. However, all transactions must be placed with Swiss exchange members (A-concession holders). Intermediaries charge discounted commissions to foreign firms.

At least one person working for a foreign branch must be a Swiss citizen and have a domicile in the canton of Zurich.

Swiss companies may choose to refuse registration of their registered shares by foreigners (residents or nonresidents). Foreign residents are, however, permitted to acquire bearer shares and participation certificates in those companies.

Geneva Stock Exchange
Rue de la Confederation 8
CH-1204 Geneva
Switzerland
Telephone: (002) 280 684

General Information

Types of Instruments Traded	Common and preferred stocks Government and corporate bonds
Trading Hours	0900—1400 The Geneva Stock Exchange, like the Zurich Stock Exchange, has no official fixed time for the end of trading; however, trading generally ceases at about 1400. (Geneva is one hour ahead of Greenwich mean time.)
Market Capitalization	Sw F165.2 billion
Average Daily Turnover	Swiss Francs (millions) Stocks: 409.9 Bonds: 227.2
Number of Members	17 full members

Regulatory Authorities	Commissioners of the State of Geneva
	The Arbitral Court of Geneva

Proposed Changes:
The exchange plans to introduce stock options and financial futures through a computer-aided trading system in 1988. Additionally, the exchange is expanding its membership from 17 to 22 full members.

Membership Requirements
Types of Membership:
Seventeen banks are full members, with access to the stock exchange ring, while 57 banks are ordinary members, without access to the ring.

Citizenship/Residency:
Only Swiss companies domiciled in the canton of Geneva are eligible for full membership.

Cost of Membership:
A membership fee of Sw F500,000 plus an annual fee of Sw F10,000 is required for both types of membership.

Minimum Capital Requirements:
There are no minimum capital requirements. However, members must maintain a deposit of Sw F400,000 in cash or Sw F420,000 in securities at the Swiss National Bank as a guarantee in favor of the Geneva Stock Exchange.

Insurance Coverage:
No specific insurance coverage is required.

Periodic Financial Reporting:
All banks, whether or not they are organized in the form of a limited company, must have their annual financial statements audited by independent auditors licensed by the federal banking commission.

Banks are required to publish financial statements and additional information within four months of year-end.

Trading on the Exchange
Commissions:
Trading commissions are generally fixed according to volume. However, they are negotiable above the Sw F2 million level for stock and Swiss franc bonds, and above the Sw F1 million level for foreign currency bonds for the entire amount.

Settlement:
There are generally three days between trade and settlement dates. However, the legal maximum is ten days.

Fails:
If securities are not delivered on the settlement date, the purchaser has 24 hours to obtain the securities at current market rates and charge the breaching counterparty.

Clearing Organization:
Schweizerisch Effekten Giro AG (SEGA)

Registration:
Securities may be registered in the customer's name (requiring power of attorney), the dealer's name, the portfolio manager's name, or the bank's name.

Market Prices:
Information on current market prices is immediately available on-line via Telekurs AG, a company owned by several Swiss banks.

Insider Trading:
The same policies apply as those for the Zurich Stock Exchange.

Foreign Access
There are no foreign broker/dealers on the Geneva Stock Exchange because of the Swiss citizenship and residency requirements. Foreign firms may operate either branch offices or subsidiaries, using Swiss broker/dealers as intermediaries to effect transactions.

Share Turnover–Zurich Stock Exchange (1984–1987)
(Sw F million)

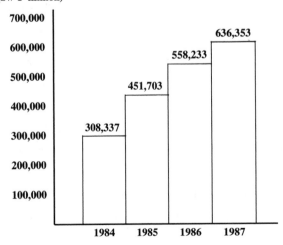

Taiwan (Republic of China)

Taiwan's sole stock exchange is located in Taipei.

Taiwan Securities and Exchange Corporation (TSE)
13th Floor
#3 Nan Hai Road
Taipei
Taiwan, Republic of China
Telephone: (02) 396-9270

General Information

Types of Instruments Traded	Common and preferred stocks are traded on the TSE; government and corporate bonds are mainly traded on the over-the-counter (OTC) market.
Trading Hours	Monday—Friday: 0900—1200 Saturday: 0900—1100 (Taipei is eight hours ahead of Greenwich mean time.)
Market Capitalization	NT$3,056 billion (as of July 1988)
Average Daily Turnover	NT$25 billion
Number of Listed Securities	141
Number of Members	Specialized brokers: 14 Concurrent brokers: 14 Securities traders: 10
Market Index	Taiwan Average Weighted Index (119 stocks)
Regulatory Authority	Securities Exchange Commission (SEC) 13th Floor #3 Nan Hai Road Taipei Taiwan, Republic of China

Recent Changes:
In March 1988 the OTC market was formally established and started accepting applications. Public companies not wishing to be listed on the TSE may apply to be placed on the OTC market.

In May 1988 a new governing regulation for security brokers, traders, and underwriters was enacted. It lifts the 15-year ban on new securities firms and allows foreigners to invest in local brokerage firms.

Membership Requirements
Citizenship/Residency:
There are no stated citizenship or residency requirements, but no foreign firms have as yet been admitted.

Cost of Membership:
There is no membership fee. However, members must make a deposit with the TSE as follows:
- Underwriters–NT$40 million
- Traders–NT$10 million
- Brokers–NT$50 million

In addition a settlement deposit is required in the amount of NT$20 million plus 0.015 percent of quarterly business volume, up to a maximum of NT$50 million.

Minimum Capital Requirements:
The minimum capital requirement for a specialized broker is NT$200 million; for a trader, NT$400 million; for an underwriter, NT$400 million; and for an integrated brokerage, NT$1,000 million.

Insurance Coverage:
No specific insurance coverage is required.

Periodic Financial Reporting:
Audited financial statements, comprising a balance sheet, an income statement, statements of changes in stockholders' equity, and a statement of changes in financial position, are required to be published annually and semiannually. Quarterly reports, including a balance sheet and an income statement, must be reviewed by CPAs.

Trading on the Exchange
Commissions:
Trading commissions are fixed at 0.15 percent of the transaction value for stocks traded in Taipei, 0.2 percent for those traded in other areas, and 0.1 percent of the transaction value for corporate/government bonds.

Settlement:
Third-day settlement

Fails:
Securities may not be borrowed from other brokers to effect delivery. Fails are reported to the SEC.

Clearing Organization:
Taiwan Securities and Exchange Clearing Department

Registration:
Securities can only be registered in the investor's name.

Safe Custody Depository:
A centralized custody depository system is available to investors, but is not compulsory.

Market Prices:
Current market prices are broadcast by radio stations and can be accessed by personal computer.

Daily Price Fluctuation Limits:
Currently, the daily price movements of stocks cannot exceed the closing price of the preceeding day by more than 3 percent.

Market Trading Systems:
In January 1987 the trading of all listed stocks was entered into the Computer-Assisted Trading System, including ordinary and block transactions and transactions that require advance delivery. In June 1987 odd-lot transactions were also carried out by the system.

Insider Trading:
Trading on insider information (information not available to the public) is prohibited.

Foreign Access
Foreign securities firms may have access to the Taiwan market only through joint ventures with local brokers. Total foreign investment in a local brokerage is restricted to 40 percent of that broker's issued capital, and no individual firm will be allowed to own more than 10 percent of a local brokerage firm.

At present, investors are not allowed to buy or sell shares on the exchange.

Share Turnover (1984–1987)
(NT$ million)

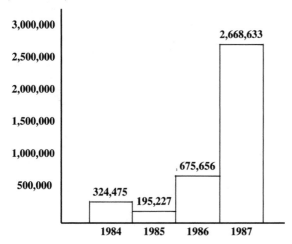

United Kingdom

The United Kingdom has one stock exchange. It is based in London and has operating units in Belfast, Birmingham, Bristol, Dublin, Edinburgh, Glasgow, Leeds, Liverpool, Manchester, and Newcastle. Birmingham, Dublin, and Glasgow have active trading floors where brokers meet to deal face to face. Dealing in this style has disappeared from the London trading floor except for the traded options market; a move to screen-based trading for U.K. company and government stock has replaced it. With the implementation of the powers of the Financial Services Act 1986, the regulatory structure of the U.K. securities market has also been radically changed. This review provides a current and prospective outline of The International Stock Exchange.

The International Stock Exchange of the United Kingdom and the Republic of Ireland Limited—The International Stock Exchange
The Stock Exchange
Old Broad Street
London
England EC2N 1HP

General Information

Types of Instruments Traded	Domestic equities International equities Gilts (U.K. government bonds) Company fixed interest securities Traded options
Trading Hours	U.K. equities: 0730–1800 International equities: 0700–2000 Gilts and fixed interest: 0900–1700 Options: U.K. equities, index, gilts—0905–1540 Currency—0900–1540 (Greenwich mean time)
Market Capitalization	Listed equities: £stg. 1,076 billion Unlisted Securities Market: £stg. 6,283 million Third Market: £stg. 240 million Gilts: £stg. 142,700 million Other fixed interest: £stg. 140,169 million (as of December 31, 1987)
Average Daily Turnover	Domestic equities: 53,586 bargains—£stg.2,059 million International equities: 4,477 bargains—£stg.433 million

	Gilts: 2,850 bargains—£stg. 2,271 million
	Other fixed interest: 1,503 bargains—£stg.90 million
	Options: 46,459 contracts—£stg. 13.9 million premium value
	(1987)
Number of Listed Securities	Domestic equities:
	Fully listed—1,964
	Unlisted securities market—375
	Third Market—37
	International equities: 613
	Gilts: 126
	Company fixed interest securities: 4,044
	Traded options: 59
	(as of December 31, 1987)
Number of Members	The International Stock Exchange has 5,242 individual members employed by 360 member firms.
	As of May 1988 The Securities Association had approximately 31,000 registered representatives and traders employed by 970 member firms.
Market Index	The Financial Times Stock Exchange (FT-SE) 100 Share Index, popularly known as the Footsie index

Regulatory Authority:

The Financial Services Act 1986 has required the regulatory structure of The International Stock Exchange to change significantly. The act put into law a structure of self-regulation within a statutory framework, combining the speed and flexibility of self-regulation with statutory protection for the investor.

The regulatory framework is overseen by a central agency, the Securities and Investments Board (SIB), which has certain powers under the act and is answerable to the Secretary of State for Trade and Industry.

The SIB has delegated its powers of regulating most authorized investment businesses to five self-regulating organizations (SROs). The SRO that regulates the members of The International Stock Exchange is principally The Securities Association (TSA). The rules of TSA as well as those of the other SROs and of the SIB basically comprise two elements: conduct-of-business rules, which place various requirements on how a firm can deal, and financial regulations, which place capital requirements on each firm.

The Financial Services Act 1986 as well as regulating members of The International Stock Exchange imposes regulations on the exchange. The International Stock Exchange has been classified as a Recognized Investment Exchange (RIE) and is authorized to regulate dealing in the following four markets:

* Domestic equities
* Foreign equities
* Gilt-edged and company fixed interest securities
* Options

For RIEs the rules that have been implemented under the act are designed to regulate the relationships between the users of a particular market and to ensure that an orderly and efficient market operates so as to provide adequate protection for investors.

Membership Requirements
Membership of The International Stock Exchange:
Citizenship/Residency and Other
There are no citizenship or residency requirements. Individual membership is granted based on professional experience and examinations.

Cost of Membership
The cost for firms has yet to be determined. The cost for individuals is £stg.75.

Membership of TSA:
Citizenship/Residency and Other
There are no citizenship or residency requirements. A firm's membership is granted when the association is satisfied that the firm is ""fit'' and ""proper'' to conduct investment business. In addition an individual's application to become either a registered representative or trader will only be accepted if that person has sufficient professional experience and has passed appropriate examinations.

Cost of Membership
The following subscriptions are levied on firms at the beginning of each financial year:

Number of Individual Registrations in Firm	Flat Firm Fee (pounds sterling)
1	1,100
2	1,870
3-6	3,300
7-10	5,500
11-20	11,000
21-50	16,500
51-100	22,000
101-250	33,000
251-500	55,000
501+	88,000

In addition £stg.110 is payable per registered person.

Minimum Capital Requirements:
A member firm shall not permit its total capital requirement to exceed its qualifying capital. The total capital requirement comprises the aggregate of the following three components:
- A base requirement, which is the highest of an absolute minimum requirement, 25 percent of annual audited expenditure, or a volume-of-business requirement (the volume of business rules still must be drafted)
- A position risk requirement, which quantifies the risks associated with holding securities positions
- A counterparty risk requirement, which quantifies the risk of default on overdue counterparty balances

The qualifying capital of a firm is determined as follows:
- Share capital, plus
- All reserves, less
- Noncurrent and nonmarketable assets, plus
- Qualifying subordinated loans (both long and short term), plus
- Permitted guarantees given by third parties, less
- Guarantees of other undertakings given, less
- Deficiencies in subsidiaries, plus
- Qualifying committed undrawn facilities

Insurance Coverage:
The International Stock Exchange stipulates that all members maintain insurance policies against losses caused by fraud, theft, and forgery. The minimum coverage is calculated by multiplying £stg.4,000 by the number of persons in the firm. There is an absolute minimum required cover of £stg.50,000, but it need not be more than £stg.500,000. TSA has no insurance requirements.

Compensation Fund:
The International Stock Exchange has a compensation fund available to compensate members of the public, up to a maximum of £stg.250,000 per claimant, in the event of the default of a member firm. TSA will also have compensation arrangements, although the exact scheme has yet to be finalized. It is currently thought that the SIB will control these arrangements and will compensate members of the public in the event of default as follows: 100 percent of the claim up to £stg.30,000 and 90 percent of the claim for the next £stg.20,000.

Periodic Financial Reporting:
Annual audited financial statements must be submitted to TSA's enforcement division within three months of the member firm's year-end.

Quarterly unaudited reporting statements comprising profit and loss account, balance sheet, capital calculation, and certain background information must be submitted to TSA's enforcement division within 20 business days of the end of the period.

A monthly unaudited reporting statement, comprising just a capital calculation, must be submitted to TSA's enforcement division within ten business days of the end of the period.

A monthly position risk reporting statement must be submitted to TSA's enforcement division within 10 or 20 business days, depending on whether it is a month- or quarter-end.

Biweekly position risk summary reporting statements must be submitted to TSA's enforcement division within two business days of the end of the period.

Transitional provisions have extended the period for the submission of the last three returns mentioned.

Trading on the Exchange
Types of Markets:
Domestic Equities
Three distinct domestic markets are in operation. Equities traded on the primary market are described as being fully listed. Full-listing requirements are stringent in terms of capital base and operating history. Fully listed securities are categorized as follows:

- Alpha stocks—the largest, most actively traded stocks for which market makers show firm, continuous two-way prices during the mandatory quote period. All trades are published within five minutes on TOPIC (see ""Market Information Systems"").
- Beta stocks—actively traded stocks for which market makers show firm, continuous two-way prices, but for which trades are not published immediately.
- Gamma stocks—less active stocks in which market makers are able to show continuous two-way quotes. The prices may be indicative rather than firm prices at which they are prepared to deal.
- Delta stocks—U.K. securities whose two-way prices do not appear on SEAQ (see ""Market Information Systems"").

This market has seen the greatest change since the restructuring and deregulation of the exchange's rules and practices occurred on October 27, 1986 (commonly referred to as Big Bang), with a move from single capacity to dual capacity (firms dealing as both agent and market maker). As a result the number of market makers has increased from 22 prior to Big Bang to 33 currently.

The secondary market, called the Unlisted Securities Market (USM), was established in 1980 as a market for smaller companies unable to meet the requirements of a full listing. The Third Market, launched in January 1987, was established to meet the need for access to the equity markets operated by the exchange of companies for which a listing or inclusion in the USM was not appropriate. The listing costs of these two markets are much lower than those of a full listing. The over-the-counter (OTC) market in the United Kingdom has declined because many companies have moved up to the Third Market.

Foreign Equities

The 1986 merger of The Stock Exchange with the International Securities Regulatory Organization (ISRO) has led to considerable development in this market. By the end of 1987 quotations were available in roughly 600 leading shares. Shares originating in 17 countries are now on SEAQ International (See ""Market Information Systems''), including those from the United States, France, West Germany, Hong Kong, and Japan.

Customers in this market are mainly professional or institutional clients who deal directly with market makers; there are no broker intermediaries. Bargain consideration is about five times greater than that in the domestic equity market.

U.K. Gilts

A dual-capacity trading system is now in operation. Since Big Bang the number of market makers has increased significantly and interdealer brokers have been established. As a result market liquidity has significantly increased. The Bank of England supervises the main participants, and the exchange maintains regulatory control of the market.

Gilt stock auctions have recently been introduced, and gilt warrant trading has also recently begun. However, to confine the trading of gilt warrants to professionals, the minimum denomination of an issue has been set at £stg.100,000 nominal of the underlying stock against which warrants are exercisable. Gilt-edged market makers largely issue these warrants. The general growth in the gilt market has occurred mainly through growth in the wholesale end of the business.

Company Fixed Interest Securities

Markets in other types of fixed interest securities are increasingly made on The International Stock Exchange. These include:
- Eurobonds
- Overseas public sector debt securities
- U.K. and overseas corporate loan and preference capital

Traded Options

The product range on the London Traded Options Market has been rapidly expanding. Much of the market's growth has come from increasing investor and professional use of traded options for hedging and investment purposes. There are currently 59 equity options based on alpha stocks, and two gilt options, two currency options, and the FT-SE 100 Index option.

Commissions:

Domestic Equities

Since Big Bang commissions have been negotiable. As a result the level of minimum commission has increased, particularly since the market crash in October 1987. In addition some transactions are now being dealt on a net basis (that is, at nil commission). These now account for more than 25 percent of turnover value and represent a more significant proportion in larger deal sizes.

Foreign Equities

About half the transactions are dealt on a net basis. Commissions charged are negotiable and are on average higher than those for domestic equities due to the greater complexity of international settlement procedures.

U.K. Gilts

Almost all trades of significant size are transacted on a net basis.

Commissions, which are negotiable, are normally charged on trades with lower values.

Company Fixed Interest Securities

All commissions are negotiable. Many trades are dealt on a net basis.

Traded Options

The average commission for a traded-option transaction is 1.25 percent, with approximately 20 percent of transactions being dealt net.

Settlement

Although there are certain exceptions, the normal rules for settlement are as follows:
- Gilts, new corporate issues, and options—next business day
- Equities—vary by type of client:
  —"Account day" clients (normally private clients). Settlement is the second Monday after the end of a trading period of ""account.'' Accounts are normally ten business days in duration. On the account day, or day of settlement, the client is required to tender payment or deliver shares whether or not the counterparty broker delivers.
  —"Cash against delivery" (CAD) client (normally institutions). Settlement is only upon delivery of stock, but, at the earliest, on account day.

Transaction Reporting:

All transactions entered into must be reported to the exchange. Where an intramarket transaction has been undertaken, the responsibility of reporting is assigned to one of the parties involved. If the transaction is carried out between 0900 and 1700, it should be reported within five minutes of the transaction's taking place. If carried out after 1700, it should be reported between 0730 and 0900 the following business day.

Fails:
In theory, buy-in and sell-out rules exist. In practice, if securities are not delivered on the settlement date nothing happens. However, a capital requirement is placed on unsettled trades when for account day clients they are overdue by more than 30 days, and for CAD clients they are overdue by 15 days for debt securities and 30 days for equity securities. The requirement is broadly the unsecured element of each trade.

Securities may be borrowed by market makers from money brokers to effect delivery. The number of money brokers as well as the level of stock borrowing has increased significantly since Big Bang. In April 1988 The International Stock Exchange authorized equity-only money brokers; previously, money brokers were restricted in their equity lending to a third of their gilt lending.

Clearing Organizations:
TALISMAN—the exchange's computerized settlement system. It is not a book-entry transfer system.

TAURUS (Transfer and Automatic Registration of Uncertificated Stock)—a book-entry transfer system for U.K. equities, to be implemented in 1989. This system will significantly reduce the paperwork in the settlement of U.K. equities.

CGO (Central Gilts Office)—a settlement service for the gilt-edged market. This system includes a facility allowing book-entry transfer of stock against a system of assured payments, which is provided through agreement with the clearing banks.

LOCH (London Options Clearing House)—the clearinhouse for the settlement of traded options. This is another book-entry system. It has recently introduced a facility for the automatic exercise of in-the-money equity options, removing the burden from the broker and client.

SEQUAL—an international equity trade confirmation system that the exchange is currently developing.

Other equities are mainly cleared through a system of tickets passed from seller to buyer after the transaction has been entered into.

Registration:
Securities may be registered in the customer's name, the broker/dealer's nominee name, the exchange's nominee name (that is, SEPON), or in any other nominee company owned by an RIE or a Designated Investment Exchange authorized by the SIB. Gilts and those Eurobonds dealt on the exchange are registered on a book-entry system.

Safe Custody Depository:
Allowable safe custody depositories are branches of a large number of banks that have the status of a recognized banking institution. Such banks must have share capital and

reserves of over £stg.5 million and be authorized by the Bank of England or another banking regulator deemed equivalent. A recognized custodian authorized by a client may also be used as a safe custody depository.

Market Information Systems:
SEAQ (Stock Exchange Automated Quotations system for U.K. securities)—a continuously updated computer data base containing quotations from competing market makers in each security and trade reports in U.K. securities. This system has changed the U.K. securities market from one that was exclusively conducted on the London trading floor to one that is screen based. Bid and offer prices are now available for over 3,500 securities. SEAQ is open from 0730 to 1800, with an 0900 to 1700 mandatory quote period.

SEAQ International—the exchange's electronic screen-based system for non-U.K. equities.

Both SEAQ and SEAQ International are available to a number of quote vendors worldwide.

TOPIC—The International Stock Exchange's own videotex terminal network used for disseminating information on SEAQ and SEAQ International. There are now well over 10,000 screens in operation. TOPIC Services Inc. is used to market TOPIC in the United States.

Company News Service—an electronic system that captures and distributes information to subscribers, giving market makers and brokers who use screen-based trading systems rapid access to the latest company news.

SAEF (SEAQ Automatic Execution Facility)—to be introduced early in 1989, it will allow automatic execution of trades in alpha and beta stocks. Initially it will handle orders of up to 1,000 shares from broker/dealers direct to market makers. The originator of the order will receive immediate confirmation of the trade, which will be reported simultaneously to the market makers and to the on-line supervision system.

MARKETEYE—a system that captures and distributes share prices for use by the retail end of the market, that is, branch banks.

RADIX—a dealing room system currently being developed. The objective of the system is to capture information from a number of sources and make it available on just one terminal.

BLOX—a block order exposure system currently being developed. The system will enable member firms to anonymously display block order information in deal sizes above the maximum currently permitted on SEAQ (1,000,000 shares). As proposed, the BLOX service will initially be available only for U.K. equities, and there will be set minimum order values for each category of stock. This system will be similar to the Autex System currently being used in the United States.

SEDOL (Stock Exchange Daily Official List)—places in printed form the closing price of each security quoted on the exchange together with the price range within which a security was traded on the previous day.

These systems have been or will be developed by the exchange. There are also a number of commercial information systems available, notably Reuters, Telerate, and Datastream.

Exchange Links:
Real-time prices are now being shared with the New York Stock Exchange (NYSE).

Certain National Association of Securities Dealers Automated Quotations (NASDAQ) prices on American OTC shares are now displayed in London.

Settlement links have been established with Midwest Securities Clearing Corporation (MSCC) in Chicago, which allows member firms to settle U.S. securities, and with the International Securities Clearing Corporation (ISCC) in New York, which permits U.S. firms to settle U.K. securities via TALISMAN. It is expected that reciprocal arrangements for both links will be established in the future. TALISMAN settlement of both Australian and South African securities can also be undertaken.

Safe custody links are available for U.K. securities with the following institutions:
- Japanese Securities Clearing Corporation (JSCC)—Tokyo
- Deutsche Auslandskassenverein (AKV)—Frankfurt
- Societe Interprofessionnelle de Compensation des Valeurs Mobilieres (SI-COVAM)—Paris
- Canadian Depository for Securities Ltd. (CDS)—Toronto
- Madrid Stock Exchange/Telefonica

Insider Trading:
Trading on insider information (information not available to the public) is prohibited according to the provisions of the Company Securities (Insider Dealing) Act 1985.

Solicitation:
A member firm must take reasonable care to ensure that any investment publication or publication in respect of investment business it issues or approves is both fair and not misleading and that no statement in a publication is either untrue or misleading. Certain risk warnings and other disclosure statements are often required; their exact nature depends on both the extend of any risks the investment carries and the persons likely to receive the publication.

Strict provisions exist for unsolicited calls. These provisions apply to both prospective and existing customers. The rules state that calls, whether by telephone or visit, must not be made other than at the express request of the customer. For existing customers the effect of this rule can be reduced by including the appropriate name in their customer agreement.

Foreign Access

Foreign membership is unrestricted. Many overseas banks have purchased significant stakes in stockbrokerages, while others have set up their own securities dealing operations.

The London International Financial Futures Exchange (LIFFE)

Royal Exchange
London
England EC3V 3PJ
Telephone: 01 623-0444

General Information

Types of Instruments Traded	Interest rate futures
	Currency rate futures
	Stock index futures (FT-SE 100)
	Options on interest rate futures
	Currency options
	Stock index options (FT-SE 100)
Trading Hours	Approximately 0830—1630
	The exact time varies according to the type of contract being transacted.
	(Greenwich mean time)
Average Daily Turnover	About 50,000 to 70,000 contracts
Number of Members	Approximately 375, including U.K. and overseas banks, U.K. and overseas investment brokers, U.K. and overseas commodity brokers, and members of The International Stock Exchange. Nearly half of the members are based outside the United Kingdom.

Regulatory Authority:
LIFFE was established with the approval of the Bank of England and the U.K. Department of Trade and Industry; regulation is overseen by the Bank of England. Under the Financial Services Act, LIFFE has been accepted as a Recognized Investment Exchange (RIE), and day-to-day supervision is carried out by the board of the exchange. The

board monitors the financial standing of the exchange's members and is authorized to inspect a member's accounting records.

Membership Requirements
Citizenship/Residency and Other:
There are no specific citizenship or residency requirements, but the potential member must enjoy ""a financial and business standing suitable for a member of the Exchange."

Cost of Membership:
The most recent price for a full seat was approximately £stg.80,000. Seats to trade in options only can be obtained, the most recent price being £stg.20,000.

Minimum Capital Requirements:
Members must maintain a net worth at or in excess of the amount prescribed by the board of directors based on the role the member intends to fulfill on the market.

Insurance Coverage:
No specific insurance coverage is required.

Periodic Financial Reporting:
An annual audited financial statement must be submitted to the market supervision department of LIFFE within six months of the end of each annual accounting period.

Quarterly balance sheets must be submitted to the market supervision department.

A member must also declare that it was, at the relevant date, in compliance with the financial requirements for members, with a report by the auditors of the member stating whether, in their opinion, the member had reasonable grounds for making such a declaration.

Trading on the Exchange
Commissions:
Commissions are negotiable.

Settlement:
Settlement for options is the second business day following the exercise date. Settlement for futures is based on delivery months, which in virtually all cases are March, June, September, and December. The actual delivery day in the month varies with each type of future.

Fails:
The clearinghouse ensures the performance of each contract. To protect the clearinghouse from financial loss in the event of defaults, members with open positions on the exchange are required to deposit margins with the clearinghouse in the form of cash.

Clearing Organization:

The principal clearinghouse is the International Commodities Clearing House Limited (ICCH), which is owned by the major U.K. clearing banks.

Market Prices:

Information on market prices is available through various information systems, notably Reuters and Telerate.

Solicitation:

All forms of advertising must conform to guidelines issued by the board of directors.

Foreign Access

Foreign membership is unrestricted. The various aspects of trading on LIFFE do not differ between foreign and domestic members.

Share Turnover—The International Stock Exchange (1984–1987)
(£stg. million)

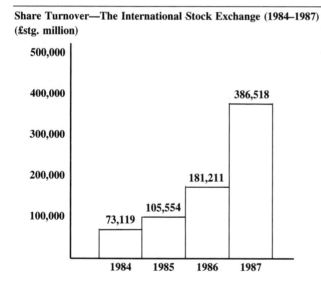

United States

The United States has a number of exchanges that transact dealings in securities and commodities. Each exchange competes for listings.

New York Stock Exchange (NYSE)
11 Wall Street
New York, NY 10005
Telephone: 212-623-3000

General Information

Types of Instruments Traded	Common and preferred stocks Warrants Bonds Rights Options
Trading Hours	0930–1600 (New York is five hours behind Greenwich mean time.)
Market Capitalization	$US2,216,311,000,000 (as of December 1987)
Average Daily Turnover	Stocks: 188,938,000 shares $US7,500 million Bonds: $US38,447,000 (1987)
Number of Listed Securities	Shares: 2,244 (representing 1,647 companies, 70 of which are controlled by a foreign parent) Bonds: 3,348 (as of May 31, 1988)
Number of Members	1,366 (as of December 31, 1987)
Market Indexes	Dow Jones Common Stock Index (which includes the Industrial Average and the Composite Index) NYSE Composite Stock Index Standard & Poor's 100 Stock Index Standard & Poor's 500 Stock Index

| Regulatory Authority | Securities and Exchange Commission (SEC) 26 Federal Plaza New York, NY 10007 Telephone: 212-264-1614 |

Membership Requirements

Types of Membership:

Membership on the NYSE is on an individual basis. Individuals may qualify for brokerage firms, allowing the firm to trade as a member of the exchange. Firms are permitted to trade as both agent and principal. Member firms can be divided into the following groups:

- Specialists—The stock specialists stand as the central figures on the exchange trading floor and have a twofold function: to maintain an orderly market in the stocks in which they are registered as a specialist by buying and selling for their own account when a temporary imbalance between supply and demand exists; and to act as a broker's broker, executing orders on behalf on another broker. Only one specialist is assigned to each security.
- Floor brokers—They, in turn, can be classified as follows:
  —Commission brokers, who are employed by individual member firms to represent the orders of the firm's customers
  —Individual floor brokers, who work for themselves and handle orders for their client firms
  —Registered competitive market makers, who are obliged when called upon by the exchange to trade for their own or their firm's account

Citizenship/Residency:

There are no citizenship or residency requirements for membership.

Cost of Membership:

Membership is sold by the seat. The last sale price as of December 31, 1987, was $US625,000. Memberships may be leased.

Minimum Capital Requirements:

Each member who executes orders on the floor of the NYSE is required to maintain net capital of $US100,000.

All U.S. stock exchanges are regulated by SEC Rule 15c3-1, which requires each broker/dealer to maintain capital in excess of either 6 2/3 percent of adjusted liabilities or 2 percent of aggregate debit items (primarily customer receivables and deposits with clearing organizations). Minimum requirements range from $US2,500 to $US100,000 depending on the volume and type of business conducted by the broker/dealer.

Client Protection:

The SEC limits a broker/dealer from using customer assets for proprietary financing.

Rule 15c3-3 requires broker/dealers to maintain funds equivalent to net customer-related liabilities in a special reserve bank account. The rule also requires broker/dealers to obtain possession or control of their customers' fully paid for and excess margin securities.

Insurance Coverage:
Fidelity bond
Misplacement and check forgery
Fraudulent trading
Security forgery
Consumer protection insurance—Broker/dealers are required to register with the Securities Investor Protection Corporation and remit annual assessments of $US100.

Periodic Financial Reporting:
Financial and Operational Combined Uniform Single (FOCUS) reports must be filed monthly or quarterly with regulatory authorities.

Annual audited financial statements must be filed with regulatory authorities within 60 days of the financial year-end.

An annual audited statement of financial condition must be filed with regulatory authorities and be open for public inspection.

Surprise examinations of the member's financial statements and operational activities may be made by the exchange's examiners.

Trading on the Exchange
Commissions:
Trading commissions are negotiable.

Settlement:
There are five business days between trade and settlement dates.

Fails:
Securities may be borrowed from other brokers to effect delivery.

Clearing Organizations:
Transactions on the NYSE are recorded by the Securities Industry Automation Corporation (SIAC) and are cleared by the National Securities Clearing Corporation (NSCC). The NSCC uses a continuous net settlement (CNS) process whereby members settle transactions directly with the clearing organization instead of with a counterparty broker/dealer.

Registration:
Securities can be registered in the customer's name or in the broker/dealer's name.

Safe Custody Depository:
Depository Trust Company

Market Prices:
Share prices are fixed using the auction system, with the specialist acting to ensure an
orderly market. Upon execution of a trade, the transaction is recorded and processed
into the exchange's market data system, which flashes it onto the electronic ticker tape
and to electronic displays and market information inquiry systems worldwide.

Market Trading Systems:
SuperDOT—the exchange's designated order turnaround system. It is the electronic order-routing system through which member firms transmit market and limit orders in
NYSE-listed securities directly to the specialist post where the securities are traded or
to the member firm's booth. After the order has been executed in the auction market, a
report of execution is returned directly to the member firm office over the same electronic circuit that brought the order to the floor and the execution is submitted directly
to the comparison systems. All SuperDOT service features apply to post opening market orders of up to 2,099 shares. However, SuperDOT's postopening market order system is designed to deliver member firms' postopening market orders of up to 30,099
shares. At the end of 1987, 183 member firms were SuperDOT subscribers.

OARS—the opening feature of the SuperDOT system. It is designed to accept member
firms' preopening market orders of up to 5,099 shares for rapid, systematic execution
and immediate reporting.

Limit Order System—has automated booking and trading facilities to execute orders
when and if the specific limit price is reached.

NYSE Display Book—a data base system available to specialists that facilitates the recording, reporting, and researching of limit and market orders.

NYSE Booth Program—allows member firms to route orders to either the specialist
post locations or their booths on the NYSE trading floor based on price or size parameters determined by the member.

Autex System—uses electronic screens to allow broker/dealers and other subscribers to
communicate about blocks of stock. Any transactions can then be executed on a securities exchange or on the over-the-counter (OTC) market.

Automated Bond System (ABS)—allows brokers around the country to transmit clients'
bond orders to the exchange for near-immediate execution. A significant amount of
bond trading on the NYSE takes place via ABS.

Exchange Links:
The Intermarket Trading System (ITS) is an electronic communications network that

links eight markets: the New York, American, Boston, Cincinnati, Midwest, Pacific, and Philadelphia stock exchanges, and the National Association of Securities Dealers (NASD). The system enables brokers, specialists, and market makers to interact with their counterparts in other markets whenever the nationwide Composite Quotation System shows a more favorable price. The 1,537 issues eligible for trading on ITS at the end of 1987 represented most of the stocks traded on more than one exchange.

Real-time prices are now shared with The International Stock Exchange in London.

Insider Trading:
Trading on insider information (information not available to the public) is prohibited.

Foreign Access
There are no significant impediments for foreign firms seeking membership on the NYSE. Currently there are 49 foreign members of the exchange.

American Stock Exchange (AMEX)
86 Trinity Place
New York, NY 10006
Telephone: 212-306-1000

The AMEX is a major market in U.S. options. Its most active index option is the Major Market Index (XMI), which historically has demonstrated a 97 percent correlation with the Dow Jones Industrial Average.

AMEX brokerage clubs are located in Montreal, Toronto, London, Edinburgh, Glasgow, Zurich, Geneva, Hong Kong, and Singapore. To further enhance its global presence the AMEX concluded an agreement with Instinet, giving institutional investors across Europe access to the AMEX options market through Reuters electronic terminals. The AMEX also established a two-way trading floor linkage with the Toronto Stock Exchange, the first such tie between primary equity markets in different countries.

General Information

Types of Instruments Traded	Common and preferred stocks
	Warrants
	Options
	Corporate bonds
	U.S. government and government agency securities
	Real estate investment trusts
	Currency exchange warrants
	Americus trusts
Trading Hours	Options: 0930–1610
	Equities: 0930–1610

	Other instruments: 0930–1600 (New York is five hours behind Greenwich mean time.)
Market Capitalization	$US99,171,058,732 (as of December 31, 1987)
Average Daily Turnover	Stock: 13,857,529 shares $US215 million Options: 280,433 (1987)
Number of Listed Securities	Shares: 1,078 (representing 869 companies, 51 of which are foreign) Bonds: 325
Number of Members	Regular members: 661 Options principal members: 203 Associate members: 163 Limited trading permit holders: 36
Regulatory Authority	Securities and Exchange Commission (SEC) 26 Federal Plaza New York, NY 10007 Telephone: 212-264-1614

Membership Requirements

Types of Membership:
Membership in the AMEX is on an individual basis according to the following categories:
- Regular member
- Options principal member
- Associate member
- Limited trading permit holder

Citizenship/Residency:
There are no citizenship or residency requirements for membership.

Cost of Membership:
Seats are sold on the auction market. The last sale in April 1988 was for $US250,000 for a regular membership and $US219,000 for an options principal membership.

Minimum Capital Requirements:
The minimum capital required by the AMEX is $US25,000 in liquid assets. Member

firms must also maintain minimum capital levels as prescribed by SEC Rule 15c3-1. See "Minimum Capital Requirements" for the New York Stock Exchange (NYSE).
Insurance Coverage:
Fidelity bond
Misplacement and check forgery
Fraudulent trading
Security forgery
Consumer protection insurance

Periodic Financial Reporting:
Periodic financial reporting requirements for members are as noted for the NYSE.

Trading on the Exchange
Commissions:
Trading commissions are negotiable.

Settlement:
There are five business days between trade and settlement dates.

Fails:
Securities may be borrowed from other brokers to effect delivery.

Clearing Organizations:
Transactions on the AMEX are recorded by the Securities Industry Automation Corporation (SIAC) and are cleared by the National Securities Clearing Corporation (NSCC). Option transactions are cleared through the Options Clearing Corporation (OCC).

Registration:

Securities may be registered in the customer's name or in the broker/dealer's name.

Safe Custody Depository:
Depository Trust Company

Market Prices:
Current market prices are available immediately.

Insider Trading:
Trading on insider information (information not available to the public) is prohibited.

Foreign Access
A foreign firm may become a member of the AMEX by establishing a U.S. subsidiary (partnership or corporation) and having a regular or options principal member of the exchange associated with the firm.

National Association of Securities Dealers Automated Quotations (NASDAQ)
1735 K Street, N.W.
Washington, D.C. 20006
Telephone: 202-728-8039

NASDAQ technically is not a stock exchange, but rather a computerized quotation system that supports the U.S. over-the-counter (OTC) market. Market makers of OTC securities use the NASDAQ network to trade with customers.

General Information

Types of Instruments Traded	Common and preferred stocks
Trading Hours	0930–1600 (Washington, D.C., is five hours behind Greenwich mean time.)
Market Capitalization	$US325,543,850,000 (as of December 31, 1987)
Average Daily Turnover	149,762,000 contracts $US2 million (1987)
Number of Listed Securities	Shares: 5,537 (representing 4,706 companies, 272 of which are foreign) Bonds: 301
Number of Market Makers	545
Number of Members	6,722
Regulatory Authority	National Association of Securities Dealers (NASD) 1735 K Street, N.W. Washington, D.C. 20006 Telephone: 202-728-8000

Proposed Changes:
The NASD has filed a proposal with the Securities and Exchange Commission (SEC) to operate its Portal system, which would facilitate the private placement of shares by both domestic and foreign issuers.

Membership Requirements
Citizenship/Residency and Other:

There are no citizenship or residency requirements for NASD membership. All securities firms with NASD membership may use the NASDAQ system. Nearly all securities firms in the United States are members of the NASD.

Minimum Capital Requirements:
All NASD broker/dealers must register with the SEC. As such, member firms must maintain minimum capital levels as prescribed by SEC Rule 15c3-1. See "Minimum Capital Requirements" for the New York Stock Exchange (NYSE).

Client Protection:
NASD broker/dealers are subject to SEC Rule 15c3-3. See "Client Protection" for the NYSE.

Insurance Coverage:
Insurance coverage requirements for members are as noted for the NYSE.

Periodic Financial Reporting:
Periodic financial reporting requirements for members are as noted for the NYSE. Members must also prepare and file NASD assessment forms.

Trading on the Exchange
Commissions:
Trading commissions are negotiable.

Settlement:
There are five business days between trade and settlement dates.

Fails:
Securities may be borrowed from other brokers to effect delivery.

Clearing Organizations:
National Securities Clearing Corporation (NSCC)
Facilities of various regional exchanges

In addition to trading through clearing organizations, members can engage in "ex-clearing" trades, which require physical delivery of the securities.

Registration:
Securities can be registered in the customer's name or in the broker/dealer's name.

Safe Custody Depository:
Depository Trust Company

Market Trading Systems:
NASDAQ trading does not occur on an auction floor. The NASDAQ system collects

price quotations from competing market makers through a computer network. Trades are consummated by telephone or telex.

NASDAQ also offers the Small Order Execution System (SOES), which provides for the automatic execution of customer orders of 1,000 shares or less, and the NASDAQ National Market System (NASDAQ/NMS), which provides detailed market information for larger, more actively traded NASDAQ issues. The Order Confirmation Transaction (OCT) service, in conjunction with SOES, lets securities firms initiate and confirm the execution of any size order through their NASDAQ terminals, without telephone contact.

Exchange Links:
NASDAQ's electronic link with The International Stock Exchange in London allows the exchange of real-time quotation and transaction information for 700 issues from the two markets. A similar link was developed with the quotation system of The Stock Exchange of Singapore.

In 1987 NASDAQ International opened in London, serving as a liaison to U.K. and European companies seeking to list securities on NASDAQ. Of the 139 companies whose shares trade as American Depository Receipts (ADRs) in the United States, 97 are NASDAQ companies.

Insider Trading:
Trading on insider information (information not available to the public) is prohibited.

Foreign Access
NASDAQ is available to foreign broker/dealers. There are currently more than 29,700 terminals located in 44 foreign countries that receive NASDAQ information. NASDAQ-traded securities are held by more than 600 foreign institutions worldwide.

Pacific Stock Exchange
301 Pine Street
San Francisco, CA 94104
Telephone: 415-393-4000

General Information

Types of Instruments Traded	Common and preferred stocks
	Bonds
	Warrants
	Options
Trading Hours	Options: 0630–1310
	Other securities: 0630–1330
	(San Francisco is eight hours behind Greenwich mean time.)

Market Capitalization	$US2,409,000,000 (as of December 1987)
Average Daily Turnover	6,524,000 shares (February 1988)
Number of Listed Securities	1,392
Number of Members	551
Regulatory Authority	Securities and Exchange Commission (SEC) 26 Federal Plaza New York, NY 10007 Telephone: 212-264-1614

Membership Requirements
Citizenship/Residency and Other:
There are no citizenship or residency requirements. Members must be of majority age.

Cost of Membership:
The cost of a seat at auction was $US65,000 on February 29, 1988.

Minimum Capital Requirements:
Member firms must maintain minimum capital levels as prescribed by SEC Rule 15c3-1. See "Minimum Capital Requirements" for the New York Stock Exchange (NYSE).

Insurance Coverage:
Fidelity bond
Misplacement and check forgery
Fraudulent trading
Security forgery
Consumer protection insurance

Periodic Financial Reporting:
Periodic financial reporting requirements for members are as noted for the NYSE.

Trading on the Exchange
Commissions:
Commissions are negotiable.

Settlement:
There are five business days between trade and settlement dates.

Fails:
Securities may be borrowed from other brokers to effect delivery.

Clearing Organizations:
Transactions are recorded by the Securities Industry Automation Corporation (SIAC) and are cleared by the National Securities Clearing Corporation (NSCC).

Registration:
Securities may be registered in the customer's name or in the broker/dealer's name.

Safe Custody Depository:
Depository Trust Company

Market Prices:
Current market prices are available immediately.

Insider Trading:
Trading on insider information (information not available to the public) is prohibited.

Foreign Access
A foreign firm may become a member of the Pacific Stock Exchange by establishing a U.S. subsidiary (partnership or corporation) and fulfilling minimum age requirements.

Futures Exchanges
Financial futures and options instruments are traded on most of the commodities exchanges in the United States. General information regarding the major exchanges is given here.

Chicago Mercantile Exchange (CME)
30 South Wacker Drive
Chicago, IL 60606-7499
Telephone: 312-930-1000

The CME contains the world's largest facilities for futures and options trading and is organized into three separate divisions: the CME, the International Monetary Market (IMM), and the Index and Options Market (IOM). The CME has branch offices in New York, Washington, D.C., London, and Tokyo.

The CME recently finalized plans with Reuters to develop an electronic trading network for futures contracts, through which deals can be transacted automatically outside the CME's regular trading hours.

General Information

Types of Instruments Traded	Standard & Poor's 100 Stock Index
	Standard & Poor's 500 Stock Index
	Foreign currency futures and options
	U.S. Treasury bill futures

	Three-month Eurodollar futures and options Options and futures contracts Gold futures Agricultural futures and options
Trading Hours	0720–1515 (Chicago is six hours behind Greenwich mean time.)
Average Daily Turnover	Number of Contracts Stock index contracts: 49,436 Foreign currencies: 114,712 U.S. Treasuries: 5,668 Three-month Eurodollars: 71,095 Agricultural futures: 44,746 (as of March 1988)
Number of Members	Full members (CME): 625 IMM: 812 IOM: 1,287 Total: 2,724
Regulatory Authority	Commodity Futures Trading Commission (CFTC) 1120 Connecticut Avenue, N.W. Washington, D.C. 20036 Telephone: 202-254-6387

The CFTC regulates commodity futures and options transactions, requiring the segregation of client funds and/or securities into special accounts and the daily reporting of trading activity when a customer's open positions reach a certain level. In addition the various exchanges and clearing organizations specify their own requirements, which include minimum margin deposits and the maintenance of minimum margin levels, as well as controls over the maximum price fluctuations permissible within a single day. The self-regulatory responsibilities of Futures Commission Merchants (FCMs) have been assigned by the CFTC to the National Futures Association (NFA).

Clearing Organization:
Chicago Mercantile Exchange Clearing House

Membership Requirements
Citizenship/Residency:
There are no citizenship or residency requirements.

Cost of Membership:
All memberships are sold by the seat; as of April 1988 seats were sold for the following:
- Full membership—$US420,000
- IMM—$US380,000
- IOM—$US91,000

Minimum Capital Requirements:
Each registered FCM is required to maintain adjusted net capital exceeding $US50,000 ($US100,000) where the firm is not a member of a designated self-regulatory organization) or, if greater, 4 percent of segregated customer funds. In practice, many FCMs are also registered securities broker/dealers and will have to comply with the net capital requirements of Rule 15c3-1 of the Securities and Exchange Commission (SEC) regulations.

Insurance Coverage:
There is no insurance coverage required.

Periodic Financial Reporting:
The periodic reporting requirements for an FCM are similar to those applied to a registered broker/dealer under the SEC regulations.

Chicago Board of Trade (CBOT)
141 West Jackson Blvd.
Chicago, IL 60604
Telephone: 312-435-3500

The CBOT is the world's largest futures exchange, accounting for 46 percent of U.S. trading volume in futures and options in futures during 1987.

General Information

Types of Instruments Traded	U.S. Treasury bond and note futures and options
	U.S. government agency (GNMA) issues futures and options
	Gold and silver futures and options
	Grain futures and options
Trading Hours	Day: 0720–1515
	Evening: 1800–2130
	Four contracts are traded during the evening sessions: futures and options on futures in Treasury bonds and notes.
	(Chicago is six hours behind Greenwich mean time.)

Average Daily Turnover	496,955 contracts (March 1988)
Number of Members	Full members: 1,402 Associate members: 713 Government instruments membership (GIM) interests: 263 Index, debt, and energy membership (IDEM) interests: 545 Commodity options membership (COM) interests: 566 Total members: 3,489
Regulatory Authority	Commodity Futures Trading Commission (CFTC) 1120 Connecticut Avenue, N.W. Washington, D.C. 20036 Telephone: 202-254-6387

Clearing Organization:
Chicago Board of Trade Clearing Corporation

All clearing members must submit a guarantee from their parent company covering all obligations to the clearing corporation relating to noncustomer trades.

Membership Requirements
Cost of Membership:
Full members—$US405,000
Associate members—$US222,000
IDEM—$US40,000
COM—$US79,000

All membership costs are as of April 1988.

All other aspects of membership and trading are as discussed for the Chicago Mercantile Exchange (CME).

Chicago Board Options Exchange (CBOE)
LaSalle at Van Buran
Chicago, IL 60605
Telephone: 312-786-5600

The CBOE is the world's largest options marketplace. In the last fiscal year trading activity represented approximately 60 percent of the total U.S. options market.

General Information

Types of Instruments Traded	Standard & Poor's 100 Stock Index
	Standard & Poor's 500 Stock Index
	U.S. Treasury bonds and notes
	Options on equities
Trading Hours	0830–1515
	(Chicago is six hours behind Greenwich mean time.)
Average Daily Turnover	719,821 contracts (1986–1987)
Number of Members	Full members: 911
	Special members: 431
	Exercisers: 700

Recent Changes:
The CBOE recently joined with the Chicago Board of Trade (CBOT) in a program to develop new trading products cooperatively under a joint venture. The first fruits of this relationship have been seen in the form of two new stock index futures products: the CBOE 50 and the CBOE 250. There are plans to list these sometime during 1988 and 1989. The exchange has also established a London office to serve as a liaison between the United Kingdom, Europe, and the United States.

Membership Requirements
Cost of Membership:
The cost of a full membership is approximately $US280,000.

All other aspects of membership and trading are as discussed for the Chicago Mercantile Exchange (CME).

Foreign Access
Currently there are approximately 25 foreign members of the exchange.

New York Futures Exchange
20 Broad Street
New York, NY 10005
Telephone: 212-656-4949

The New York Futures Exchange is a wholly owned subsidiary of the New York Stock Exchange (NYSE) and is also affiliated with the New York Cotton Exchange.

General Information

| Types of Instruments Traded | NYSE Composite Index futures and options |

	Commodity Research Bureau (CRB) Index futures Russell 2000 & 3000 Stock Index futures
Trading Hours	NYSE index: 0930–1615 CRB index: 0900–1515 Russell index: 0915–1610 (New York is five hours behind Greenwich mean time.)
Average Daily Turnover	13,000 contracts (11,525 of which represent trades in NYSE Composite Index futures)
Number of Members	1,421
Cost of Membership	$US100 (April 28, 1988)
Regulatory Authority	Commodity Futures Trading Commission (CFTC) 1120 Connecticut Avenue, N.W. Washington, D.C. 20036 Telephone: 202-254-6387
Clearing Organization	Intercompany Clearing Corporation (ICC)

Index

A

ADR's (American Depository Receipts),
69-95
  advantages, 85
  and Asian companies, 69-77
  benefits, 80, 85
  corporations, 74
  description, 79
  exemptions, 84
  large institutions, 71
  NASDAQ, 85-95
    cost of capital, 89
    listing an ADR, 89
    multiple market-maker system, 88
    notifications, 93
    preferences/advantages, 86
    tandards, 90
    trading, 90
  process, 75
  "pink sheet", 70, 72, 83
  regulation, 83
  trading, 83
  types, 83
Advance Corporation Tax (ACT), 111
American Council of Life Insurers, 28,
36-37
American Stock Exchange (ASE/AMEX)
  and ADR's, 70, 75
  comparison, 19
Asian-Pacific region
  see individual country
  see Salomon-Frank
  and ADR's, 69-77

Australia, 607
  cross-trading, 599
  EAFE (Europe, Australia, and Far East),
  9, 72, 536, 594
  and Europe, 473
  Futures and Options Market, 593
    dynamics, 606
    index battles, 600
    new choices, 603
  futures exchanges, 595
    cash-settled index futures, 598, 601
    comparison, 618
    Japan, 597
  Futures Trading Act, 614
  GLOBEX, 611, 617
  Hong Kong futures, 618
    regional niche, 624
  importance, 594
  Korea, 489
  Ministry of Posts and Tele-
    communication (MoPT), 607
  New Zealand, 624
    software, 625
  Newly Industrialized Countries
    (NICs), 496
  over-the-counter (OTC), 597
  performance, 492
  Singapore, 612
  T-bond futures, 600
  Tokyo, 598, 605
Association of South East Asian Nations
  (ASEAN), 497
Australia
  and ADR's, 74

Australian Stock Exchanges'
    All Ordinaries Index, 610
capitalization, 260
concentration, 262
Hong Kong market, 260
legislation, 278
NASDAQ market, 88
National Companies and Securities
    Commission (NCSC), 278
options market, 275
Semi-Government Contract, 610
SPI futures contract, 275
Stock Exchange Automated Trading
    System (SEATS), 276
stock market
    indices, 263
    performance, 264
    regulation, 277
    size, 260
    structure, 273
    trading, 276
    types of shares, 274
SYCOM, 612
Sydney Futures Exchange, 275, 595, 607
    Bank-Accepted Bills, 609
    structure, 608
    Futures Industry Code, 609
taxation, 279
Austria
    EEC, 476

B

Bank of England, 109
Bank of Japan, 236
Bank of Korea, 496, 504
BARRA model, 547
Bivariate regression, 6
Blue chips, 81, 118
Bonds versus equities, 579
Bourse valuation, 135, 207, 213
Brazil
    inflation, 468
Bretton Woods, 236

C

Canada
    Australian options market, 275
    equity market, 45-66
        characteristics, 45
        valuation, 46
    population, 45
    securities, 60
        transactions, 63
        types, 61
    stock market, 50
        brief history, 50
        exchanges, 50
        size, 55
        types of shares, 59
    taxation, 64
    U.S. Auto Pact, 46
    U.S. Free Trade Agreement, 46
    U.S. real estate, 29
Canadian Depository for Securities
    (CDS), 64
Capital asset pricing model (CAPM),
    4, 535, 537
The Cecchini Report, 474-475
Central Bank of China, 329
Chicago Board of Trade (CBOT), 600
Chicago Mercantile Exchange (CME),
    595, 612
    and GLOBEX, 617
CIFAR, 404
Closed-End Country funds, 499
    Alliance New Europe Fund (ANE), 341
    ASA Ltd. Fund (ASA), 340
    Asia Pacific Fund (APB), 342
    Austria Fund (OST), 343
    average premium/discount, 400
    Brazil Fund (BZF), 344
    Central Fund of Canada (CEF), 345
    Chile Fund (CH), 346
    Emerging Germany Fund (FRG), 347
    The Europe Fund (EF), 348
    European Warrant Fund (EWF), 349
    First Australia Fund (IAF), 350

First Australia Prime Income Fund
(FAX), 351
The First Iberian Fund (IBF), 352
First Philippine Fund (FPF), 353
France Growth Fund (FRF), 354
Future Germany Fund (FGF), 355
Germany Fund (GER), 356
Growth Fund of Spain (GSP), 357
GT Greater Europe Fund (GTF), 358
India Growth Fund (IGF), 359
The Indonesia Fund (IF), 360
The Irish Investment Fund (IRL), 361
Italy Fund (ITA), 362
The Jakarta Growth Fund (JGF), 363
Japan OTC Equity Fund (JOF), 364
Korea Fund (KF), 365
Latin America Investment Fund
(LAM), 366
Malaysia Fund (MF), 367
Mexico Fund (MXF), 368
Mexico Equity and Income Fund
(MXE), 369
New Germany Fund (GF), 370
Pacific-European Growth Fund
(PEF), 371
performance data, 384-400
price (local currency), 385
price (U.S. Dollars), 387
Portugal Fund (PGF), 372
regional funds, 389-391
Scudder New Asia Fund (SAF), 373
Scudder New Europe (NEF), 374
The Singapore Fund (SGF), 375
single-country funds, 392-396
Spain Fund (SNF), 376
specialized funds, 389-391
Swiss Helvetia Fund (SWZ), 377
The Taiwan Fund (TWN), 378
Templeton Emerging Markets Fund
(EMF), 380
Thai Capital Fund (TC), 381
Thai Fund (TTF), 379
Turkish Investment Fund (TKF), 382
United Kingdom Fund (UKM), 383

U.S.-listed funds, 398
Commodity Exchange in New York
(COMEX), 611
Commodity Futures Trading Commission
(CFTC), 609, 615
Communism, 473, 478
Correlation coefficient, 6
Cost of change, see risk
Currency hedging
after-the-fact, 632
before-the-fact, 634
common sense, 639
cost, 632, 640
decisions, 643
free lunch, 629
theories/hypotheses, 635
volatility, 630

D

DAP Account (Delivery against
payment), 63
Department of Commerce, 28, 37
Disinflation, see inflation
Dutch
pension fund, 29
stock exchange, see Netherlands

E

EAFE, see Asian-Pacific
Eastern Europe, 473, 478
Employee Stock Option Plan (ESOP), 71
Equities versus bonds, 579
Equity market
see individual country or global
see also inflation
see also European Economic
Community
ERISA (1974), 22
Euro-CBs, 503
Europe-Pacific (Euro-Pac) index, 564
European Currency Unit, 484
European Economic Community

Austria, 476
bonds, 483
the Cecchini Report, 474-475
EC norms, 197
EC regulations, 101
equity markets, 481
Gorbachev, 478
integration, 474
investment, 485
Italy, 211
LDC, 480
Netherlands, 147
risk, 480
Swiss market, 204, 477
Treaty of Rome, 474
VAT, 111, 475
the Werner Plan, 476
European Free Trade Association
(EFTA), 477
European investment opportunities,
473-487
European Monetary System, 117, 476
European Options Exchange, 147
EOE index, 565
European Stock Exchanges, 145
"Eurosclerosis", 135

F

FDI, *see* United States, FDI
The Federal Bank, 117
The Federal Reserve, 466
Financial Times indices, 100, 541
France
Bourse valuation, 135, 137-138, 140-141
capitalization, 136-139
earnings, 141
Eurosclerosis, 135
indices, 135
size, 136
stock market, 136
valuation, 140-143
Funds, *see* synthetic global
Futures
see synthetic global
see Asian-Pacific

cash-settled index futures, 598
comparison to stocks, 560
T-bond futures, 600
TIFFE, 605

G

Generally accepted accounting principles
(GAAP), 89
global equity markets, 435-436, 439-442
Germany
EEC, 478-479
inflation, 464, 469
the Stock Exchange Act (1896),
117, 120
Stock Exchange Admission Regulation,
131
Stock Index (DAX), 118, 123
stock market
exchanges, 121-122
operations, 126-128
segments, 120
size/volume, 123-125
structure, 119
types of shares, 126
taxation, 128-131
Tax Reform Act (1990), 129
U.S. real estate, 29
Global equity indexation
Capital asset pricing model (CAPM),
535, 537
indices, 536
passive investment, 535
trends, 537
Global equity markets
see Tactical Asset Allocation
accounting
format differences, 423-426
procedural matters, 413-423
standards differences, 423-444
company information, 405
correlation, 5
financial information, 407
GAAP, 435-436, 439-442
information
inconsistencies, 444

problems of merging, 444-457
types of stock, 450
investment analysis, 403-540
GLOBEX, 611
and CME, 617
Gorbachev, President Mikhail, 478
Gramm-Rudman-Hollings bill, 466
Grandfathering, 75

H

Hedge fund, 72
see currency hedging
Universal Hedging, 561
Hong Kong
and ADR's, 77
Australia market, 260
Hong Kong Interbank Offered Rate
(HIBOR), 622
Futures Exchange (HKFE), 595, 618
regional niche, 624
"Loco-London", 623
stock exchange, 77
House of Commons (Can.), 45

I

Indices
international
see individual country
alternatives, 556
BARRA model, 547
capitalization, 544
characteristics, 542
country, 544
investment potentials, 552
Relative Price Momentum, 549
United Kingdom, 550
Tokyo Stock Exchange, 548
synthetic, *see* synthetic global
Inflation, 459-472
Brazil, 468
comparisons, 466-469
direction, 465
equity returns, 459
the Federal Reserve, 466

Germany, 464, 469
Gramm-Rudman-Hollings bill, 466
Japan, 463, 469
Kondratieff long-wave, 468
model, 460
stock market, 462
International Monetary Fund (IMF), 107,
494
Investment Dealers' Association of
Canada, 63-64
Italy
Bourse, 213
EEC authorities, 211
exchanges, 211, 215
trading system, 224
ILOR, 229
IRPEG, 229
indices, 213
Main Market Index (MIB), 213
National Companies and Stock
Exchange Commission
CONSOB (1974), 212, 225, 229
performance, 213
settlement, 227
size, 217
Stockbrokers Managing Committee, 224
taxation, 228
types of shares, 223
value, 219
volume, 220

J

Japan
and ADR's, 71
American Securities Act (1933), 235
BARRA model, 547
capitalization, 238
cash-settled futures, 598, 601
exchanges, 253
foreign direct investment, 39
futures and options, 597
GAAP, 436
indices, 237
inflation, 463, 469
Middle East, 234

Ministry of Posts and Telecommunica-
tion (MoPT), 607
the Nixon shock, 236
oil shocks, 236
Osaka, 600
Securities Coordination Liquidation
Committee, 235
Securities and Exchange Act (1934), 235
Stock Exchange Ordinance (1878), 234
stock market
size/structure, 237
Swiss market, 205
Ten Year Government Bond futures
(JGB), 599
Tokyo, 233
Tokyo International Financial Futures
Exchange (TIFFE), 605
Tokyo Stock Exchange, 439, 548, 595
TOPIX, 564
U.S. real estate, 29
zaibatsu, 235

K

Kondratieff long-wave, 468
Korea
ASEAN, 497
chaebol, 498
equity market, 291, 492
correlations, 489
growth, 292
margin transactions, 300
operations, 296
rights/registration, 298
types of shares, 294
yield, 292
First Five-Year Plan, 282
Going Public Encouragement Act
(1972), 285
investment, 300-306, 498-499
issue price, 288
Investment Trust Companies (ITCs), 309
Korea Composite Stock Price Index
(KCSPI), 291, 492, 495, 504
Korea Development Bank, 494

Korea Europe Fund, 500, 504
Korea Securities Settlement Corporation (KSSC), 298
Korean Stock Exchange (KSE), 281
sections, 286
liberalization, 502
NYSE, 500
Over-The-Counter Market (OTC), 291
public offerings, 288
performance, 492, 495
problems/solutions, 495-497, 507-509
regulation, 313
Securities Exchange Commission, 285
Securities Supervisory Board, 285
stock market
indices, 281
investment, 306-311
performance, 282
Taiwan, 492
taxation, 311

L

Limited partner, 33
London International Financial Futures
Exchange
LIFFE and the ISE, 100
LIFFE and the SFE, 611
London Stock Exchange, *see* U.K.,
International Stock Exchange

M

Malaysia
and ADR's, 76
"Meech Lake" constitutional accord, 45
Morgan Stanley indices, 9, 72, 135, 140,
281, 536, 541, 594, 619

N

National Association of Securities and
Dealers (NASDAQ)
and ADR's, 70, 75, 85-95
notifications, 93

Australia, 88
Automated Quotation, 83
By-Laws, 93
Dutch Stock Exchange, 145
multiple market-maker system, 88
   rules, 94
National Market System
   (NASDAQ/NMS), 89
   Corporate Governance Standards, 90
Small Order Execution System, 94
National Contingency Fund, 64
National Council of Real Estate Invest-
   ment Fiduciaries
   (NCREIF), 37
Netherlands
   Dutch Insurance Chamber, 152
   Dutch Stock Exchange, 145
     Amsterdam Stock Exchange, 146
     indices, 146
     operations, 152
     performance, 146-148
     size, 150
     Trade Support System, 152, 154
     trading, 152-155
     types of shares, 150
   H.O.S., 152
   NECIGEF, 154-155
   taxation, 155
   U.S. real estate, 29
Netherlands Antilles
   U.S. real estate, 29
New York Stock Exchange
   and ADR's, 70, 75
   comparison, 19
   Dutch Stock Exchange, 145
   the Korea Fund, 500
   market participants, 21-23
   operations, 20
   real estate, 36
   share types, 24
   Toronto Stock Exchange, 59
New Zealand Futures Exchange (NZFE),
   595
New Zealand Futures and Options
   Exchange (NZFOE), 624

   software, 625
Non-U.S. corporation, 89

O

OECD, 46, 136, 495
OPEC, 105
Options, *see* Asian-Pacific
Over-the-counter (OTC) "pink sheet"
   market, 70, 72, 83
   and ADR's, 79
   derivatives, 597
   indexation, 537

P-Q

Passive arms length financing, 33
Philippines
   and ADR's, 74
Quantec, 576

R

Real estate
   United States, 27-43
     major players, 29
Risk
   see currency hedging
   definition, 3
   equities versus bonds, 579
   firm-specific, 4
   forecasts, 575
   premium, 463
   reduction, 3
     Quantec, 576
     software, 576
   risk-adverse portfolios, 589
   Tactical Asset Allocation, 529
   turnover, 583

S

Salomon Brothers, 489
Salomon-Frank Russell Europe-Asia
   index (SFR), 541

Salomon-Russell EPAC, 72
Securities and Exchange Act of 1934, 20
    Rules
        15d-17, 93
        10b-17, 93
        13a-17, 93
        Section 12(g), 89, 91
Securities Exchange Commission
    acquisitions, 86
    Forms
        F-6, 75
        6-K, 92
        10-C, 93
        10-K, 84, 88
        20-F, 75, 84, 89, 92
    grandfathering, 75
    Rules
        19c-4, 92
        144A, 76
        12g3-2(b), 84
Singapore
    see Asian-Pacific
    and ADR's, 74
    the Futures Trading Act, 614
    International Monetary Exchange
        (SIMEX), 595
        CME, 612
        membership, 614
        structure, 613
        threats, 615
    Monetary Authority of Singapore
        (MAS),
South Korea
    and ADR's, 70
Standard & Poor's Indices, 9, 23, 46,
513, 536
Stock
    splits, 93
Stock exchanges, see individual country
Stock market crash of October
    (1987), 103, 109, 118, 211, 233, 237,
        260, 264, 594, 611
SuperDOT, 21
Sweden
    GAAP, 436
Swiss National Bank (SNB), 200

Switzerland
    activity, 206
    banks, 165-169
    Bourse, 207
    certificates, 174
    currency, 198
    EEC, 477
    EC Single European Market, 204
    exchanges, 161
        rules and practices, 174
    International Federation of Stock
        Exchanges (FIBV), 164
    profits, 200
    rings, 182
    risk premium, 202-203
    securities, 169
    SEGA, 164, 169, 187
    stock market
        indices, 192
        liberalization, 195
        size/structure, 192
    Swiss Options and Financial Futures
        Exchange
        (SOFFEX AG), 187
    trading, 180
    transactions, 178
Synthetic global index fund
    comparison, 560, 565
    creation, 564
    drawbacks, 562
    futures, 560
        contracts, 566
    risk, 562
    selection, 564
    simulation, 571
    stockless fund, 559
    taxation, 561
    TOPIX, 564
    Universal Hedging, 561

T

Tactical Asset Allocation
    allocators, 515
    characteristics, 521
    comparisons, 531

Global (GTAA), 525
   assumptions, 526
International Tactical Country
   Allocation, 525
   methodology, 518
   models, 531
   philosophy, 513
   risk/return, 529
   structure, 515
Taiwan
   and ADR's, 70
   Central Bank of China, 329
   foreign exchange/investment, 329
   Korea, 492
   Land Reform (1953), 318
   performance, 492
   Securities and Exchange Commission
     (SEC), 318
   Stock Exchange (TSE), 315
     indices, 315
     investors, 322
     operations, 324
     rating, 315
     shares, 317
     size/volume, 319
     structure, 318
     taxation, 328
     types of shares, 322
   Stock Exchange's Weighted Price
     Index, 329
Taxation, *see* individual country
T-bill, 559
Thailand
   and ADR's, 74
Thatcher, Prime Minister Margaret, 107,
   476, 481
Tokyo, *see* Japan
TOPIC, 109
Treaty of Rome, 474

U

United Kingdom
   see also London
   BARRA model, 550
   EEC, 474
   equities
     classification, 104
     Daily Official List, 104
     indices, 105
     Personal Equity Plans, 112
   Faculty and Institute of Actuaries, 105
   GAAP, 436
   International Stock Exchange (ISE)
     Big Bang, 100-104
     development, 99
     Institutional Net Settlement System,
       112
     International Securities Regulatory
       Organization, 103
     London International Financial Futures
       Exchange (LIFFE), 611
     market makers, 104
     SAEF-SEAQ Automatic Execution
       Facility, 103
     size, 100
     Stock Exchange Automated Quota-
       tions (SEAQ), 103
     Take-over Code, 112
     TALISMAN, 112
     the Third Market, 100
     transactions, 109
     Transfer and Automated Registration
       of Uncertificated Stock
       (TAURUS), 112
   pension funds, 29
   regulatory organizations, 114
   Unlisted Securities Market, 100-101
   and U.S. real estate, 29
   VAT, 111
   utility authorities, 109
United States
   Australian options market, 275
   Canada-U.S. Auto Pact, 46
   Canada-U.S. Free Trade Agreement, 46
   Census, 36
   equity markets
     historical performance, 6-7
   foreign direct investment (FDI), 27-43
     developers, 34
     magnitude, 28
     organizational players, 34

ploys, 38
size, 36-37
stability, 36
strategies, 32
inflation, 463
pensions, 69

V

Value Added Tax (VAT)

EEC, 475
ISE, 111

W-Z

Wall Street, 19, 110, 149
The Werner Plan, 476
World equity markets, *see* global equity
market